MATHURA
A
DISTRICT MEMOIR;

WITH NUMEROUS ILLUSTRATIONS

MATHURA
A
DISTRICT MEMOIR;

WITH NUMEROUS ILLUSTRATIONS

BY

F. S. GROWSE, B.C.S.;

Magistrate and Collector of Bulandshahr;
Fellow of the Calcutta University

Though the groves of Brinda, in with Krishna disported with the Gopis, no longer resound to the echoes of his flute; though the waters of the Jamuna are daily polluted with the blood of the sacred kine; still it is the holy land of the pligrim, the sacred Jordan of his fancy, on whose banks he may sit and weep, as did the banished Israelite of old, for the glories of Mathura, his Jerusalem,—Tod.

THIRD EDITION.
Revised and Abridged.

GYAN

Published by

Gyan Publishing House
5, Ansari Road
Daryaganj, New Delhi-110002
Phone: 011-47034999, 9811692060
E-mail: books@gyanbooks.com

Distribution Network
gyanbooks.com
India, USA, Canada, UK, Australia, France

ISBN : 978-81-212-3765-9 (PB)
First Published, 1883

2nd Impression 2020

Printed at: Gyan Press, Delhi.

Mathura A District Memoir
Author: F. S. Growse

श्री काशी कान्ती च मायाख्या त्वयोध्या द्वारवत्यपि
मथुरावन्तिका चैता: सप्त पुर्य्याश्च मोक्षदा: । 卐

सर्वेषां देवतीर्थानां माथुरं परमं महत्

न केशवसमो देवो न माथुरसमो द्विजः ।

MATHURÁ:

A

DISTRICT MEMOIR;

WITH NUMEROUS ILLUSTRATIONS.

BY

F. S. GROWSE, B.C.S.;

M. A., OXON; C. I. E.;

Magistrate and Collector of Bulandshahr;

Fellow of the Calcutta University.

Though the groves of Brindá, in with Krishna disported with the Gopis, no longer resound to the echoes of his flute; though the waters of the Jamuna are daily polluted with the blood of the sacred kine; still it is the holy land of the pilgrim, the sacred Jordan of his fancy, on whose banks he may sit and weep, as did the banished Israelite of old, for the glories of Mathurá, his Jerusalem.—TOD.

THIRD EDITION.

Revised and Abridged.

1883.

PRINTED AT THE NORTH-WESTERN PROVINCES AND OUDH GOVERNMENT PRESS.

卐 मथुरायां कृतं पापं तत्रैवच विनश्यति श्री

SETH GOBIND DÁS, C.S.I.

PREFACE.

THIS Memoir was originally intended to form one of the uniform series of local histories compiled by order of the Government. Its main object was therefore to serve as a book of reference for the use of district officers; thus it touches upon many topics which the general reader will condemn as trivial and uninteresting, and in the earlier chapters the explanations are more detailed and minute than the professed student of history and archæology will probably deem at all necessary. But a local memoir can never be a severely artistic performance. On a small scale it resembles a dictionary or encyclopœdia and must, if complete, be composed of very heterogeneous materials, out of which those who have occasion to consult it must select what they require for their own purposes, without concluding that whatever is superfluous for them is equally familiar or distasteful to other people.

As good libraries of standard works of reference are scarcely to be found anywhere in India out of the presidency towns, I have invariably given in full the very words of my authorities, both ancient and modern. And if I have occasion to mention any historical character—though he may have achieved somewhat more than a mere local reputation—I still narrate succinctly all the material facts of his life rather than take them for granted as already known. Thus, before quoting the Chinese Pilgrims, I explain under what circumstances they wrote: and when describing the Mathurá Observatory, I introduce an account of the famous royal astronomer by whom it was constructed. Hence my pages are not unfrequently overcrowded with names and dates which must give them rather a repellent appearance; but I shall be compensated for this reproach if residents on the spot find in them an answer to all enquiries, without occasion to consult other authorities, which, though possibly far from obscure, may still under the circumstances be difficult to obtain.

I dwell at considerable length on the legends connected with the deified Krishna, the tutelary divinity of the district: because, however puerile and comparatively modern many of them may be, they have materially affected the whole course of local history and are still household words, to which allusion is constantly made in conversation, either to animate a description or enforce an argument.

The great years of famine and the mutiny of 1857, though the latter was a calamity much more lightly felt in this neighbourhood than in many other parts of India, yet form the eras, by which the date of all domestic occurrences is ordinarily calculated, and both subjects have therefore been duly noticed. But there has been no need to enter much into general history, for Mathurá has never been a political centre, except during the short period when it formed the theatre for the display of the ambitious projects of Súraj Mall and his immediate successors on the throne of Bharat-pur. All its special interest is derived from its religious associations in connection with the Vaishnava sects—far outnumbering all other Hindu divisions—of whom some took birth here, all regard it as their Holy Land. Thus, the space devoted to the consideration of the doctrines which they profess and the observances which they practise could scarcely be curtailed without impairing the fidelity of the sketch by suppression of the appropriate local colouring. It may also be desirable to explain that the long extracts of Hindi poetry from local writers of the last two centuries have been inserted not only as *à propos* of the subject to which they refer, but also as affording the most unmistakeable proofs of what the language of the country really is. No such specimens could be given of indigenous Urdu literature, simply because it is non-existent and is as foreign to the people at large as English.

So much irreparable damage has been done in past years from simple ignorance as to the value of ancient architectural remains, that I have been careful to describe in full every building in the district which possesses the slightest historical or artistic interest. I have also given a complete *resumé* of all the results hitherto obtained in archæological research among the relics of an earlier age, and have added a sketch of the development of the local style of architecture, as it exists at the present day.

Besides noting the characteristics of peculiar castes, I have given an account of the origin and present status of all the principal residents in the district, mentioning every particular of any interest connected with their family history or personal qualifications. Only a few such persons of special repute will be found included in the general narrative; the remainder have been relegated to the more strictly topographical sequel, where they are noticed in connection with their estates. Upon purely agricultural statistics I touch very briefly; all such matters have been most ably discussed by the officer in charge of the last settlement.

The village lists, which occupied a considerable space in the first and second editions, have now been omitted in consequence of my inability—here at Bulandshahr—to obtain the detailed results of the last census. I believe they had been found useful by district officials. No one who has not had experience in matters of the kind can form any idea of the labour and vexation involved in the preparation for the first time of such tables, when the materials on which they are based consist exclusively of manuscripts written in the Persian character. An attempt to secure accuracy induces a feeling of absolute despair; for the names of the places and people mentioned can only be verified on the spot, inasmuch as they are too obscure to be tested by reference to other authorities, and the words as written, if not absolutely illegible, can be read at least three or four different ways.

A remark, originally consisting of no more than three or four lines in my first edition, has been expanded into a thorough discussion on the etymology of local names, which occupies the whole of Chapter XII. It incidentally disposes of several crude theories on the subject, which have been advanced by scholars of more or less distinction under a misconception as to the historical growth of the modern vernacular of Upper India. The conclusions at which I arrive can scarcely be disputed, but they will probably be ignored as too fatal to whimsical speculation.

In the matter of transliteration I have been more consistent than was prescribed of necessity, in the belief that compromise is always an evil, and in this matter is exceptionally so; for with a definite orthography there is no reason whatever why in the course of two or three generations the immense diversity of Indian alphabets, which at present form such an obstacle to literary intercourse and intellectual progress, should not all be abolished and the Roman character substituted in their stead.

As to the word 'Mathurá' itself, the place has had an historical existence for more than 2,000 years, and may reasonably demur to appearing in its old age under such a vulgar and offensive form as 'Muttra,' which represents neither the correct pronunciation nor the etymology. Though it has been visited by Europeans of many different nationalities, it was never so mutilated till it fell into the hands of the English, now eighty years ago. Even the Chinese, with a language that renders transliteration all but impossible, represent it, more correctly than we have hitherto done, under the form Mothulo. Mathurá Dás, or some similar compound, is a name very frequently given by Hindus to a child who has been born after a pilgrimage to the holy city, and it is always so spelt. Hence results the egregious absurdity that in any official list 'Mathurá Dás of Mathurá' appears as 'Mathurá Dás of Muttra,' with two utterly different spellings for one and the same word.

BULANDSHAHR,
April 21*st*, 1882.

F. S. GROWSE.

RULES FOR PRONUNCIATION.

a unaccented is like	*a* in *India.*
á accented is like	*a* „ *bath.*
e is always long, like	*ê* „ *fête.*
i unaccented is like	*i* „ *India.*
í accented is like	*i* „ *élite.*
u unaccented is like	*u* „ *put.*
ú accented is like	*u* „ *rural.*
o is always long, like	*o* „ *oval.*
ai is like	*ai* „ *aisle.*
au is like	*ou* „ *cloud.*

The consonants are pronounced as in English: *th* as in *boot-hook,* never as in *father; g* is always hard, as in *gag; y* is always a consonant, and *c, q* and *x* are not used at all. The fixed sound of each letter never varies; and it is, therefore, impossible for any person of the most ordinary intelligence to hesitate for a moment as to the correct way of pronouncing a word the first time he sees it. Without the slightest knowledge of the language, he may read a page of a Romanized Sanskrit or Hindustani book to an Indian audience, and be perfectly intelligible, if he will only take the trouble to remember the few simple rules given above.

CONTENTS.

ILLUSTRATIONS.

MATHURÁ.

CHAPTER I.

THE MODERN DISTRICT; ITS CONFORMATION, EXTENT AND DIVISIONS AT DIFFERENT PERIODS. THE CHARACTER OF THE PEOPLE AND THEIR LANGUAGE. THE PREDOMINANT CASTES; THE JÁTS AND THEIR ORIGIN; THE CHAUBES; THE AHIVÁSIS; THE GAURUA THÁKURS. THE JAINIS AND THEIR TEMPLES. THE PRINCIPAL FAMILIES; THE SETH; THE RÁJA OF HÁTHRAS; THE RÁIS OF SA'DÁBÁD. AGRICULTURAL CLASSIFICATION OF LAND; CANALS; FAMINES; THE DELHI ROAD AND ITS SARÁES.

THE modern district of Mathurá is one of the five which together make up the Agra Division of the North West Provinces. It has an area of 1,453 square miles, with a population of 671,690, the vast majority of whom, *viz.*, 611,626, are Hindus.

In the year 1803, when its area was first included in British territory, part of it was administered from Agra and part from Sa'dábád. This arrangement continued till 1832, when the city of Mathurá was recognized as the most fitting centre of local government and, superseding the village of Sa'dábád, gave its name to a new district, comprising eight tahsílis, *viz.*, Aríng, Sahár, and Kosi, on the right bank of the Jamuná; and on the left, Mát, Noh-jhíl, Mahában, Sa'dábád, and Jalesar. In 1860, Mát and Noh-jhíl were united, with the former as the head-quarters of the Tahsíldár; and in 1868 the revenue offices at Aríng were transferred to Mathurá, but the general boundaries remained unchanged.

The district, however, as thus constituted, was of a most inconvenient shape. Its outline was that of a carpenter's square, of which the two parallelograms were nearly equal in extent; the upper one lying due north and south, while the other at right angles to it stretched due eastward below. The capital, situated at the interior angle of junction, was more accessible from the contiguous district of Aligarh and the independent State of Bharat-pur than from the greater part of its own territory. The Jalesar pargana was the most remote of all; its two chief towns, Awa and Jalesar, being respectively 55 and 43 miles from the local Courts, a greater distance than separated them from the capitals of four other districts.

This, under any conditions, would have been justly considered an inconvenience, and there were peculiar circumstances which rendered it exceptionally so. The transfer of a very large proportion of the land from the old proprietary village communities to wealthy strangers had created a wide-spread feeling of restlessness and impatience, which was certainly intensified by the remoteness of the Courts and the consequent unwillingness to have recourse to them for the settlement of a dispute in its incipient stages. Hence the frequent occurrence of serious outrages, such as burglaries and highway robberies, which were often carried out with more or less impunity, notwithstanding the number of people that must have been privy to their commission. However willing the authorities of the different districts were to act in concert, investigation on the part of the police was greatly hampered by the readiness with which the criminals could escape across the border and disperse themselves through the five districts of Mathurá, Agra, Mainpuri, Eta, and Aligarh. Thus, though a local administrator is naturally jealous of any change calculated to diminish the importance of his charge, and Jalesar was unquestionably the richest portion of the district, still it was generally admitted by each successive Magistrate and Collector that its exchange for a tract of country with much fewer natural advantages would be a most politic and beneficial measure.*

The matter, which had often before been under the consideration of Government, was at last settled towards the close of the year 1874, when Jalesar was finally struck off from Mathurá. At first it was attached to Agra ; but six years later it was again transferred and joined on to Eta, which was then raised to the rank of a full district. No other territory had been given in compensation till 1879, when 84 villages, constituting the pargana of Farrah, were taken from Agra and added on to the Mathurá tahsíli. The district has thus

* In the first edition of this work, written before the change had been effected, I thus summarized the points of difference between the Jalesar and the other parganas :—The Jalesar pargana affords a marked contrast to all the rest of the district, from which it differs no less in soil and scenery than in the character and social status of the population. In the other six parganas wheat, indigo, and rice are seldom or never to be seen, here they form the staple crops ; there the pasturage is abundant and every villager has his herd of cattle, here all the land is arable and no more cattle are kept than are barely enough to work the plough ; there the country is dotted with natural woods and groves, but has no enclosed orchards, here the mango and other fruit trees are freely planted and thrive well, but there is no jungle ; there the village communities still for the most part retain possession of their ancestral lands, here they have been ousted almost completely by modern capitalists ; there the Játs constitute the great mass of the population, here they occupy one solitary village ; there the Muhammadans have never gained any permanent footing and every spot is impregnated with Hindu traditions, here what local history there is is mainly associated with Muhammadan families.

been rendered much more manageable and compact. It is now in the shape of an imperfect crescent, with its convex side to the south-west and its horns and hollow centre on the left bank of the river looking upwards to the north-east. The eastern portion is a fair specimen of the land ordinarily found in the Doáb. It is abundantly watered, both by wells and rivers, and is carefully cultivated. Its luxuriant crops and fine orchards indicate the fertility of the soil and render the landscape not unpleasing to the eye; but though far the more valuable part of the district for the purposes of the farmer and the economist, it possesses few historical associations to detain the antiquary. On the other hand, the western side of the district, though comparatively poor in natural products, is rich in mythological legend, and contains in the towns of Mathurá and Brindá-ban a series of the master-pieces of modern Hindu architecture. Its still greater wealth in earlier times is attested by the extraordinary merit of the few specimens which have survived the torrent of Muhammadan barbarism and the more slowly corroding lapse of time.

Yet, widely as the two tracts of country differ in character, there is reason to believe that their first union dates from a very early period. Thus, Varáha Mihira, writing in the latter half of the fifth century of the Christian era, seems to speak of Mathurá as consisting at that time also of two very dissimilar portions. For, in the 16th section of the Brihat Sanhitá, he includes its eastern half, with all river lands (such as is the Doáb), under the protection of the planet Budha—that is, Mercury; and the western half, with the Bharatas and Purohits and other managers of religious ceremonies (classes which still to the present day form the mass of the population of western Mathurá, and more particularly so if the Bharatas are taken to mean the Bharat-pur Játs) under the tutelage of Jiva—that is, Jupiter. The Chinese pilgrim, Hwen Thsang, may also be adduced as a witness to the same effect. He visited India in the seventh century after Christ, and describes the circumference of the kingdom of Mathurá as 5,000 *li*, *i. e.*, 950 miles, taking the Chinese *li* as not quite one-fifth of an English mile. The people, he says, are of a soft and easy nature and delight to perform meritorious works with a view to a future life. The soil is rich and fertile and specially adapted to the cultivation of grain. Cotton stuffs of fine texture are also here obtainable and gold; while the mango trees* are so abundant that they form complete forests—the fruit being of two varieties, a smaller kind, which turns yellow as it ripens, and a larger, which remains always green. From this description it would appear that the then kingdom of Mathurá

*The fruit intended is *probably* the mango, *ámra*; but the word as given in Chinese is *an-mo-lo-ko*, which might also stand for *ámliká*, the tamarind, or *ámlá*, the Phyllanthus emblica.

extended east of the capital along the Doáb in the direction of Mainpuri; for there the mango flourishes most luxuriantly and almost every village boasts a fine grove; whereas in Western Mathurá it will scarcely grow at all except under the most careful treatment. In support of this inference it may be observed that, notwithstanding the number of monasteries and stúpas mentioned by the Buddhist pilgrims as existing in the kingdom of Mathurá, comparatively few traces of any such buildings have been discovered in the modern district, except in the immediate neighbourhood of the capital. In Mainpuri, on the contrary, and more especially on the side where it is nearest to Mathurá, fragments of Buddhist sculpture may be seen lying in almost every village. In all probability the territory of Mathurá, at the time of Hwen Thsang's visit, included not only the eastern half of the modern district, but also some small part of Agra and the whole of the Shikohábád and Mustafábád parganas of Mainpuri; while the remainder of the present Mainpuri district formed a portion of the kingdom of Sankasya, which extended to the borders of Kanauj. But all local recollection of this exceptional period has absolutely perished, and the mutilated effigies of Buddha and Maya are replaced on their pedestals and adored as Brahma and Devi by the ignorant villagers, whose forefathers, after long struggles, had triumphed in their overthrow.

In the time of the Emperor Akbar the land now included in the Mathurá district formed parts of three different Sarkárs, or Divisions—*viz.*, Agra, Kol, and Sahár.

The Agra Sarkár comprised 33 mahále, four of which were Mathurá, Maholi, Mangotla, and Mahá-ban. Of these, the second, Maholi, (the Madhupuri of Sanskrit literature) is now quite an insignificant village and is so close to the city as almost to form one of its suburbs. The third, Mangotla or Magora, has disappeared altogether from the revenue-roll, having been divided into four *pattis*, or shares, which are now accounted so many distinct villages. The fourth, Mahá-ban, in addition to its present area, included some ten villages of what is now the Sa'dábád pargana and the whole of Mát; while Noh-jhíl, lately united with Mát, was at that time the centre of pargana Noh,* which was included in the Kol Sarkár. The Sa'dábád† pargana had no independent existence till the reign of Shahjahán, when his famous minister, Sa'dullah Khán,

* There is another large town, bearing the same strange name of Noh, at no great distance, but west of the Jamuná, in the district of Gurgánw. It is specially noted for its extensive salt works.

† Dr. Hunter, in his Imperial Gazetteer, has thought proper to represent the name of this pargana as Saidabad, which he *corrects* to Sayyidabad!

founded the town which still bears his name, and subordinated to it all the surrounding country, including part of Khandauli, which is now in the Agra district.

The Sahár Sarkár consisted of seven mahâls, or parganas, and included the territory of Bharat-pur. Its home pargana comprised a large portion of the modern Mathurá district, extending from Kosi and Shergarh on the north to Aríng on the south. It was not till after the dissolution of the Muhammadan power that Kosi was formed by the Játs into a separate pargana; as also was the case with Sháhpur, near the Gurgánw border, which is now merged again in Kosi. About the same unsettled period a separate pargana was formed of Gobardhan. Subsequently, Sahár dropped out of the list of Sarkárs altogether; great part of it, including its principal town, was subject to Bharatpur, while the remainder came under the head of Mathurá, then called Islámpur or Islámábád. Since the mutiny, Sahár has ceased to give a name even to a pargana; as the head-quarters of the Tahsíldár were at that time removed, for greater safety, to the large fort-like saráe at Chhátá.

As might be expected from the almost total absence of the Muhammadan element in the population, the language of the people, as distinct from that of the official classes, is purely Hindi. In ordinary speech 'water' is *jal;* 'land' is *dharti;* 'a father,' *pitá;* 'grandson,' *náti* (from the Sanskrit *naptri*), and 'time' is often *samay*. Generally speaking, the conventional Persian phrases of compliment are represented by Hindi equivalents, as for instance, *ikbál* by *pratáp* and *tashríf láná* by *kripá karná*. The number of words absolutely peculiar to the district is probably very small; for Braj Bháshá (and Western Mathurá is coterminous with Braj), is the typical form of Hindi, to which other local varieties are assimilated as far as possible. A short list of some expressions that might strike a stranger as unusual has been prepared and will be found in the Appendix. In village reckonings, the Hindustani numerals, which are of singularly irregular formation and therefore difficult to remember, are seldom employed in their integrity, and any sum above 20, except round numbers, is expressed by a periphrasis—thus, 75 is not *pachhattar*, but *pánch ghat assi, i.e.,* 80—5; and 97 is not *suttánawe*, but *tin ghat sau, i.e.,* 100—3. In pronunciation there are some noticeable deviations from established usage; thus—1*st*, *s* is substituted for *sh*, as in *sámil* for *shámil; sumár* for *shumár: 2nd, ch* takes the place of *s* as in *Chita* for *Sítá*, and occasionally *vice versâ;* as in *charsa* for *charcha*: and 3*rd*, in the vowels there is little or no distinction between *a* and *i*, thus we have *Lakshmin* for *Lakshman*. The prevalence of this latter

2

vulgarism explains the fact of the word *Bráhman* being ordinarily spelt in English as *Brahmin.* It is still more noticeable in the adjoining district of Mainpuri ; where, too, *á* generally becomes *ó*, as *chalo gayo*, "he went," for *chalá gaya*—a provincialism equally common in the mouths of the Mathurá peasants. It may also, as a grammatical peculiarity, be remarked that *kari*, the older form of the past participle of the verb *karná*, 'to do,' is much more popular than its modern abbreviation, *kí* ; *ne*, which is now generally recognized as the sign of the agent, is sometimes used in a very perplexing way, for what it originally was, *viz.*, the sign of the dative ; and the demonstrative pronouns with the open vowel terminations, *yá* and *wá*, are always preferred to the sibilant Urdu forms *is* and *us*. As for Muhammadan proper names, they have as foreign a sound and are as much corrupted as English ; for example, *Wazír-ud-dín*, *Hidáyat-ullah* and *Táj Muhammad* would be known in their own village only as *Waju*, *Hatu* and *Taju*, and would themselves be rather shy about claiming the longer title ; while *Mauja*, which stands for the Arabic Mauj-ud-dín, is transformed so completely that it is no longer recognized as a specially Muhammadan name and is often given to Hindus.

The merest glance at the map is sufficient proof of the almost exclusively Hindi character of the district. In the two typical parganas of Kosi and Chhátá there are in all 172 villages, not one of which bears a name with the elsewhere familiar Persian termination of *-ábád*. Less than a score of names altogether betray any admixture of a Muhammadan element, and even these are formed with some Hindi ending, as *pur*, *nagar*, or *garh* ; for instance, Akbar-pur, Sher-nagar, and Sher-garh. All the remainder, to any one but a philological student, denote simply such and such a village, but have no connotation whatever, and are at once set down as utterly barbarous and unmeaning. An entire chapter further on will be devoted to their special elucidation. The Muhammadans in their time made several attempts to remodel the local nomenclature, the most conspicuous illustrations of the vain endeavour being the substitution of Islámpur for the venerable name of Mathurá and of Muminábád for Brindá-ban. The former is still occasionally heard in the law Courts when documents of the last generation have to be recited ; and several others, though almost unknown in the places to which they refer, are regularly recorded in the register of the revenue officials. Thus, a village near Gobardhan is Parsoli to its inhabitants, but Muhammad-pur in the office ; and it would be possible to live many years in Mathurá before discovering that the extensive gardens on the opposite side of the river were not properly described as being at Hans-ganj, but belonged to a place called Isa-pur. A yet more curious fact, and one which would scarcely be possible in any country but India, is this, that a name has sometimes been changed simply through the mistake of a copying clerk. Thus, a village in the Kosi pargana had always been known as Chacholi till the name was inadvertently copied in the settlement papers as Piloli and has remained so ever since. Similarly with two populous villages, now called Great and Little Bharna, in the Chhátá pargana : the Bharna Khurd of the record-room is Lohra Marna on the spot; *lohra* being the Hindi equivalent for the more common *chhotá*, 'little,' and Marna being the original name, which from the close resemblance in Nágari writing of *m* to *bh* has been corrupted by a clerical error into Bharna.

As in almost every part of the country where Hindus are predominant, the population consists mainly of Bráhmans, Thákurs, and Baniyas; but to these three classes a fourth of equal extent, the Játs, must be added as the specially distinctive element. During part of last century the ancestors of the Ját Rájá, who still governs the border State of Bharat-pur, exercised sovereign power over nearly all the western half of the district; and their influence on the country has been so great and so permanent in its results that they are justly entitled to first mention. Nothing more clearly indicated the alien character of the Jalesar pargana than the fact that in all its 203 villages the Játs occupied only one; in Kosi and Mahá-ban they hold more than half the entire number and in Chhátá at least one-third.

It is said that the local traditions of Bayána and Bharat-pur point to Kandahár as the parent country of the Játs, and attempts have been made* to prove their ancient power and renown by identifying them with certain tribes mentioned by the later classical authors—the Xanthii of Strabo, the Xuthii of Dionysius of Samos, the Jatii of Pliny and Ptolemy—and at a more recent period with the Jats or Zaths, whom the Muhammadans found in Sindh when they first invaded that country.† These are the speculations of European scholars, which, it is needless to say, have never reached the ears of the persons most interested in the discussion. But lately the subject has attracted the attention of Native enquirers also, and a novel theory was propounded in a little Sanskrit pamphlet, entitled Játharotpati, compiled by Sástri Angad Sarmma for the gratification of Pandit Giri Prasád, himself an accomplished

* Cunningham's Archæological Survey, Vol. II., page 55.

† Tod, however, considered the last-mentioned tribe quite distinct. He writes: "The Jats or Jits, far more numerous than perhaps all the Rájput tribes put together, still retain their ancient appellation throughout the whole of Sindh. They are amongst the oldest converts to Islam."

Sanskrit scholar,* and a Ját by caste, who resided at Beswa on the Aligarh border. It is a catena of all the ancient texts mentioning the obscure tribe of the Játharas, with whom the writer wishes to identify the modern Játs and so bring them into the ranks of the Kshatriyas. The origin of the Játharas is related in very similar terms by all the authorities ; we select the passage from the Padma Purána as being the shortest. It runs as follows :—" Of old, when the world had been bereft, by the son of Bhrigu, of all the Kshatriya race, their daughters, seeing the land thus solitary and being desirous of conceiving sons, laid hold of the Bráhmans, and carefully cherishing the seed sown in their womb (*jathara*) brought forth Kshatriya sons called Játharas."† Now, there is no great intrinsic improbability in the hypothesis that the word Játhara has been shortened into Ját ; but if the one race is really descended from the other, it is exceedingly strange that the fact should never have been so stated before. This difficulty might be met by replying that the Játs have always been, with very few exceptions, an illiterate class, who were not likely to trouble themselves about mythological pedigrees ; while the story of their parentage would not be of sufficient interest to induce outsiders to investigate it. But a more unanswerable objection is found in a passage which the Sástri himself quotes from the Brihat Sanhitá (XIV., 8). This‡ places the home of the Játharas in the south-eastern quarter, whereas it is certain that the Játs have come from the west. Probably the leaders of Ját society would refuse to accept as their progenitors either the Játharas of the Beswa Pandit or the Sindhian Zaths of General Cunningham ; for the Bharat-pur princes affect to consider themselves as the same race with the Jádavas, and the Court bards in their panegyrics are always careful to style them Jadu-vansi.

However, all these speculations and assumptions have little basis beyond a mere similarity of name, which is often a very delusive test ; and it is certain

---

* He is the author of a Hindi commentary on the White Yajur Veda.

† क्षत्रशून्ये पुरा लोके भार्गवेण यदा कृते ॥
विलोक्यक्षत्रियां धात्रीं कन्यास्तेषां सहस्रशः ॥
ब्राह्मणान् जगृहुस्तस्मिन् पुत्रोत्पादनलिप्सया ॥
जठरे धारितं गर्भं संरक्ष्य विधिवत्पुरा ॥
पुत्रान् सुषुविरे कन्या जाठरान् क्षत्रवंशजान् ॥

‡ आग्नेय्यां दिशि कोशलकलिङ्गवङ्गोपवङ्गजठराङ्गा ॥

that whatever may have been the status of the Játs in remote antiquity, in historic times they were no way distinguished from other agricultural tribes, such as the Kurmis and Lodhas, till so recent a period as the beginning of last century.

Many of the largest Ját communities in the district distinctly recognize the social inferiority of the caste, by representing themselves as having been *degraded* from the rank of Thákurs on account of certain irregularities in their marriage customs or similar reasons. Thus, the Játs of the Godha sub-division, who occupy the 18 villages of the Ayra-khera circle in the Mahá-ban pargana, trace their pedigree from a certain Thákur of the very ancient Pramár clan, who emigrated into these parts from Dhár in the Dakhin. They say that his sons, for want of more suitable alliances, married into Ját families in the neighbourhood and thus came to be reckoned as Játs themselves. Similarly the Dangri Játs of the five Madem villages in the same pargana have a tradition, the accuracy of which there seems no reason to dispute, that their ancestor, by name Kapúr, was a Sissodíya Thákur from Chítor. These facts are both curious in themselves and also conclusive as showing that the Játs have no claim to pure Kshatriya descent ; but they throw no light at all upon the origin of the tribe which the new immigrants found already settled in the country and with which they amalgamated : and as the name, in its present form, does not occur in any literary record whatever till quite recent days, there must always remain some doubt about the matter. The sub-divisions are exceedingly numerous : one of the largest of them all being the Nohwár, who derive their name from the town of Noh and form the bulk of the population throughout the whole of the Noh-jhíl pargana.

Of Bráhmans the most numerous class is the Sanádh, frequently called Sanaurhiya, and next the Gaur ; but these will be found in every part of India, and claim no special investigation. The Chaubes of Mathurá however, numbering in all some 6,000 persons, are a peculiar race and must not be passed over so summarily. They are still very celebrated as wrestlers and, in the Mathurá Máhátmya, their learning and other virtues also are extolled in the most extravagant terms ; but either the writer was prejudiced or time has had a sadly deteriorating effect. They are now ordinarily described by their own countrymen as a low and ignorant horde of rapacious mendicants. Like the Prágwálás at Allahabad, they are the recognized local cicerones ; and they may always be seen with their portly forms lolling about near the most popular gháts and temples, ready to bear down upon the first pilgrim that approaches. One of their most noticeable peculiarities is that they are very reluctant to make a

3

match with an outsider, and if by any possibility it can be managed, will always find bridegrooms for their daughters among the residents of the town.* Hence the popular saying—

मथुरा की बेटी गोकुल की गाय
कर्म्म फूटे तेा अनत जाय

which may be thus roughly rendered—

Mathurá girls and Gokul cows
Will never move while fate allows:

because, as is implied, there is no other place where they are likely to be so well off. This custom results in two other exceptional usages : *first,* that marriage contracts are often made while one, or even both, of the parties most concerned are still unborn ; and *secondly,* that little or no regard is paid to relative age ; thus a Chaube, if his friend has no available daughter to bestow upon him, will agree to wait for the first grand-daughter. Many years ago, a considerable migration was made to Mainpuri, where the Mathuríya Chaubes now form a large and wealthy section of the community and are in every way of better repute than the parent stock.

Another Bráhmanical, or rather pseudo-Bráhmanical, tribe almost peculiar to the district, though found also at the town of Háthras and in Mewát, is that of the Ahivásis, a name which scarcely any one beyond the borders of Mathurá is likely to have heard, unless he has had dealings with them in the way of business.† They are largely employed as general carriers and have almost a complete monopoly of the trade in salt, and some of them have thus acquired

* Tieffenthaller mentions this as a peculiarity of the women of Gokul. He says : "Vis a vis d'Aurengabád est un village nommé Gokul, où l'on dit que demeuraient sixe mille femmes avec les quelles Krishna était marié. Les femmes de ce village se distinguent in ce quelles n'en sortent pas et ne se marient pas ailleurs." The writer, Father Joseph Tieffenthaller, a native of Bolzano, in the Austrian Tyrol, came out to India as a Jesuit missionary in 1743 and remained in the country all the rest of his life, nearly 42 years. As he never resided long in any one place, his travels eventually extended over nearly the whole continent and supplied him with matter for several treatises which he composed in Latin. None of them have been published in that language ; but a French translation of his Indian Geography, from which the above extract is taken, appeared in 1786 at Berlin as the first volume of Bernoulli's Description de l'Inde. He died at Lucknow in July, 1785, but was buried at Agra, where on the stone that covers his grave may still be read the words : "*Pater Joseph Tieffenthaller, obiit Lacnoi 5 Julii, 1785.*" This is at the back of the old Catholic Church (built by Walter Reinhard), which stands in the same enclosure as the modern Cathedral, but has been long disused. I quote from him on several occasions rather on account of the rarity than the intrinsic value of the book.

† They are not mentioned either by Wilson or Elliot in their Glossaries. They have as many as seventy-two sub-divisions, two of the principal of which are called Dighiya and Bajrávat.

considerable substance. They are also the hereditary proprietors of several villages on the west of the Jamuná, chiefly in the pargana of Chhátá, where they rather affect large brick-built houses, two or more stories in height and covering a considerable area of ground, but so faultily constructed that an uncracked wall is a noticeable phenomenon. Without exception they are utterly ignorant and illiterate, and it is popularly believed that the mother of the race was a Chamár woman, who has influenced the character of her offspring more than the Bráhman father. The name is derived from *ahi*, the great 'serpent' Káliya, whom Krishna defeated; and their first home is stated to have been the village of Sunrakh, which adjoins the Káli-mardan ghát at Brindá-ban. The Pándes of the great temple of Baladeva are all Ahivásis, and it is matter for regret that the revenues of so wealthy a shrine should be at the absolute disposal of a community so extremely unlikely ever to make a good use of them.

The main divisions of Thákurs in Mathurá are the Jádon and the Gaurua The former, however, are not recognized as equal in rank to the Jádons of Ráj-putána, though their prinicipal representative, the Rájá of Awa,* is one of the wealthiest landed proprietors in the whole of Upper India. The origin of the latter name is obscure, but it implies impure descent and is merely the generic

*Now that Jalesar, the Rájá's residence, has been included in the Eta district, he can no longer be reckoned among the gentry of Mathurá: but as part of his estate still lies here, it may be convenient to give, in the form of a note, a brief sketch of the family history. The pedigree begins only in the reign of Muhammad Sháh (1720—1748 A.D.), when Thákur Chaturbhuj, a zamindár of Nari in the Chhátá pargana, came and settled at Jalesar, and was employed by the local governor in the professional capacity of a physician. His son, Bijay Sinh, for a short time also followed the vocation of his father, but was afterwards appointed to a small military command. The Jádon zamindárs of some adjacent villages, having become involved in pecuniary difficulties, were assisted by Chaturbhuj, now become a wealthy man, and his son, themselves also members of the Jádon clan. They thus acquired considerable local influence, which was further extended by Bijay Sinh's eldest son, Bhakt Sinh. He was for a time in the service of Jawáhir Sinh, the Mahárája of Bharat-pur, and also lent some support to Thákur Bahádur Sinh of Umargarh, from whom he received a grant of the village of Misa. A number of other villages, belonging to different Thákur clans, also passed into his hands; and this accession of revenue enabled him to enlist under his standard a troop of marauding Mewátis, with whose aid he established himself, according to the custom of the time, as an independent free-booting chief. Finally he obtained a *sanad* from the Mahrattas authorizing him to build a fort at Awa. This was simply a *garhi* with a circuit of mud walls. The present formidable stronghold was built by his successor, Híra Sinh. In the Mahratta war the latter was able to render some good service to the English; and in 1838 it is said that his son, Pitambar Sinh, was recognised as Rájá by the then Governor-General, Lord Auckland. He died in 1845, leaving no issue of his own save one daughter, who was married to a Rájput chief in the Gwáliar territory. His son by adoption, Rájá Prithi Sinh, a descendant of Thákur Bijay Sinh, the second of the family, died in July, 1876, leaving an infant heir, the present Rájá, Chitra Pál Sinh, born 12th August, 1874; his mother being a member of the branch of the Nepal royal family residing at Banarás. The estate pays a Government revenue of Rs. 3,67,515. The sanad conferring the title is not forthcoming, nor is it known when it was conferred. It is said to have been given by a Rána of Udaipur.

title which has as many subordinate branches as the original Thákur stock. Thus we have Gauruas, who call themselves—some Kachhwáhas, some Jasáwats, some Sissodiyas, and so on, throughout the whole series of Thákur clans. The last named are more commonly known as Báchhals from the Bachh-ban at Sehi, where their Guru always resides. According to their own traditions they emigrated from Chitor some 700 or 800 years ago, but probably at rather a later period, after Alá-ud-din's famous siege of 1303. As they gave the name of Ránera to one of their original settlements in the Mathurá district, there can be little doubt that the emigration took place after the year 1202, when the Sovereign of Chitor first assumed the title of *Rána* instead of the older *Rával*. They now occupy as many as 24 villages in the Chhátá pargana, and a few of the same clan—872 souls in all—are also to be found in the Bhaugánw and Bewar parganas of the Mainpuri district.

The great majority of Baniyas in the district are Agarwálas. Of the Saráugis, whose ranks are recruited exclusively from the Baniya class, some few belong to that sub-division, but most of them, including Seth Raghunáth Dás, are of the Khandel *gachchha* or *got*. They number in all 1593 only and are not making such rapid progress here as notably in the adjoining district of Mainpuri and in some other parts of India. In this centre of orthodoxy 'the naked gods' are held in unaffected horror by the great mass of Hindus, and the submission of any well-to-do convert is generally productive of local disturbance, as has been the case more than once at Kosi. The temples of the sect are therefore few and far between, and only to be found in the neighbourhood of the large trading marts.

The principal one is that belonging to the Seth, which stands in the suburb of Kesopur. After ascending a flight of steps and entering the gate, the visitor finds himself in a square paved and cloistered court-yard with the temple opposite to him. It is a very plain solid building, arranged in three aisles, with the altar under a small dome in the centre aisle, one bay short of the end, so as to allow of a processional at the back. There are no windows, and the interior is lighted only by the three small doors in the front, one in each aisle, which is a traditional feature in Jaini architecture. What with the want of light, the lowness of the vault, and the extreme heaviness of the piers, the general effect is more that of a crypt than of a building so well raised above the ground as this really is. It is said that Jambu Swámi here practised penance, and that his name is recorded in an old and almost effaced inscription on a stone slab that is still preserved under the altar. He is reputed the last of the Kevalis, or divinely inspired teachers, being the pupil of Sudharma, who

AUTOTYPE

SETH RAGHUNÁTH DÁS.

was the only surviving disciple of Mahávíra, the great apostle of the Digambaras, as Parsva Náth was of the Svetámbara sect. When the temple was built by Mani Rám, he enshrined in it a figure of Chandra Prabhu, the second of the Tirthankaras ; but a few years ago Seth Raghunáth Dás brought, from a ruined temple at Gwáliar, a large marble statue of Ajít Náth, which now occupies the place of honour. It is a seated figure of the conventional type, and beyond it there is nothing whatever of beauty or interest in the temple, which is as bare and unimpressive a place of worship as any Methodist meeting-house. The site, for some unexplained reason, is called the Chaurási, and the temple itself is most popularly known by that name. An annual fair is held here, lasting for a week, from Kártik 5 to 12 : it was instituted in 1870 by Nain-Sukh, a Saráugi of Bharat-pur. In the city are two other Jain temples, both small and both dedicated to Padma Prabhu—the one in the Ghiya mandi, the other in the Chaubes' quarter. There are other temples out in the district at Kosi and Sahpau.

The Muhammadans, who number only 58,088 in a total population of 671,690, are not only numerically few but are also insignificant from their social position. A large proportion of them are the descendants of converts made by force of the sword in early days and are called Malakánas. They are almost exclusively of the Sunni persuasion, and the Shias have not a single mosque of their own, either in the city or elsewhere. In Western Mathurá they nowhere form a considerable community, except at Sháhpur, where they are the zamindárs and constitute nearly half of the inhabitants of the town, and at Kosi, where they have been attracted by the large cattle-market, which they attend as butchers and dealers. To the east of the Jamuná they are rather more numerous and of somewhat higher stamp ; the head of the Muhammadan family seated at Sa'dábád ranking among the leading gentry of the district. There is also, at Mahá-ban, a Saiyid clan, who have been settled there for several centuries, being the descendants of Sufi Yahya of Mashhad, who recovered the fort from the Hindus in the reign of Alá-ud-dín ; but they are not in very affluent circumstances and, beyond their respectable pedigree, have no other claim to distinction. The head of the family, Sardár Ali, officiated for a time as a tahsíldar in the Mainpuri district. The ancestral estate consists, in addition to part of the township of Mahá-ban, of the village of Goharpur and Nagara Bháru ; while some of his kinsmen are the proprietors of Sháhpur Ghosna, where they have resided for several generations.

Though more than half the population of the district is engaged in agricultural pursuits, the number of resident country gentlemen is exceptionally small.

Two of the largest estates are religious endowments ; the one belonging to the Seth's temple at Brindá-ban, the other to the Gosáin of Gokul. A third is enjoyed by absentees, the heirs of the Lála Babu, who are residents of Calcutta ; while several others of considerable value have been recently acquired by rich city merchants and traders.

For many years past the most influential person in the district has been the head of the great banking firm of Mani Rám and Lakhmî Chand. The house has not only a wider and more substantial reputation than any other in the North-Western Provinces, but has few rivals in the whole of India. With branch establishments in Delhi, Calcutta, Bombay, and all the other great centres of commerce, it is known everywhere, and from the Himalayas to Cape Comorin a security for any amount endorsed by the Mathurá Seth is as readily convertible into cash as a Bank of England Note in London or Paris. The founder of the firm was a Gujarátí Brahman of the Vallabhácharya persuasion. As he held the important post of 'Treasurer' to the Gwáliar State, he is thence always known as Párikh Jí, though, strictly speaking, that was only his official designation, and his real name was Gokul Dás. Being childless and on bad terms with his only brother, he, at his death in 1826, bequeathed the whole of his immense wealth to Mani Rám, one of his office subordinates, for whom he had conceived a great affection ; notwithstanding that the latter was a Jaini, and thus the difference of religion between them so great, that it was impossible to adopt him formally as a son. As was to be expected, the will was fiercely disputed by the surviving brother ; but after a litigation which extended over several years, its validity was finally declared by the highest Court of appeal, and the property confirmed in Mani Rám's possession. On his death, in 1836, it devolved in great part upon the eldest of his three sons, the famous millionaire, Seth Lakhmi Chand, who died in 1866, leaving an only son, by name Raghunáth Dás. As the latter seemed scarcely to have inherited his father's talent for business, the management of affairs passed into the hands of his two uncles, Rádhá Krishan and Gobind Dás. They became converts to Vaishnavism, under the influence of the learned scholar, Swámi Rangácharya, whom they afterwards placed at the head of the great temple of Rang Jí, which they founded at Brindá-ban ; the only large establishment in all Upper India that is owned by the followers of Rámánuja.

On the death of Rádhá Krishan in 1859, the sole surviving brother, Gobind Dás, became the recognized head of the family. In acknowledgment of his many distinguished public services, he was made a Companion of the

AUTOTYPE.

SETH LACHHMAN DÁS.

Star of India on the 1st of January, 1877, when Her Majesty assumed the Imperial title. Unfortunately he did not live long to enjoy the well-merited honour, but died only twelve months afterwards, leaving as his joint heirs his two nephews, Raghunáth Dás, the son of Lakhmi Chand, and Lachhman Dás, the son of Rádhá Krishan. For many years past the business has been mainly conducted by the head manager, Seth Mangi Lál, who is now also largely assisted by his two sons, Náráyan Dás and Srínivása Dás. The latter, who has charge of the Delhi branch, is an author as well as a man of business, and has published a Hindi drama of some merit entitled 'Randhír and Prem-mohiní.' Náráyan Dás is the manager of the Brindá-ban Temple estate, and a very active member of the Municipal Committee, both there and at Mathurá. For his personal exertions in superintending the relief operations during the late severe famine he received a khilat of honour from the Lieutenant-Governor in a public Darbár held at Agra in the year 1880.

At the time of the mutiny, when all the three brothers were still living, with Seth Lakhmi Chand as the senior partner, their loyalty was most conspicuous. They warned the Collector, Mr. Thornhill, of the impending outbreak a day before it actually took place ; and after it had occurred they sent such immediate information to the authorities at Agra as enabled them to disarm and thus anticipate the mutiny of the other companies of the same Native Regiments, the 44th and the 67th, which were quartered there. After the houses in the station had been burnt down, they sheltered the Collector and the other European residents in their house in the city till the 5th of July, when, on the approach of the Nimach force, they took boat and dropped down the river to Agra. After their departure the Seths took charge of the Government treasure and maintained public order. They also advanced large sums of money for Government purposes on different occasions, when other wealthy firms had positively refused to give any assistance ; and, so long as the disturbances lasted, they kept up at great expense, for which they never made any claim to reimbursement, a very large establishment for the purpose of procuring information and maintaining communication between Delhi and Agra. In acknowledgment of these services, the title of Ráo Bahádur was conferred upon Seth Lakhmi Chand, with a *khilat* of Rs. 3,000. A grant was also made him of certain confiscated estates, yielding an annual revenue of Rs. 16,125, rent-free for his own life and at half rates for another life.

During the more than 20 years of peace which have now elapsed since those eventful days, the Seths, whenever occasion required, have shown themselves equally liberal and public spirited. Thus, when Sir William Muir started his scheme for a Central College at Allahabad, they supported him with a subscription of Rs. 2,500 ; and in the famine of 1874, before the Government had put forth any appeal to the public, they spontaneously called a relief meeting and headed the list with a donation of Rs. 7,100. Again, when the construction of the Mathurá and Háthras Light Railway was made conditional on its receiving a certain amount of local support, they at once took shares to the extent of a lakh and-a-half of rupees, simply with the view of furthering the wishes of Government and promoting the prosperity of their native town : profit was certainly not their object, as the money had to be withdrawn from other investments, where it was yielding a much higher rate of interest. In short, it has always been the practice of the family to devote a large proportion of their ample means to works of charity and general utility. Thus their great temple at Brindá-ban, built at a cost of 45 lakhs of rupees, is not only a place for religious worship, but includes also an alms-house for the relief of the indigent and a college where students are trained in Sanskrit literature and philosophy. Again, the city of Mathurá, which has now become one of the handsomest in all Upper India, owes much of its striking appearance to the buildings erected in it by the Seths. It is also approached on either side, both from Delhi and from Agra, by a fine bridge constructed at the sole cost of Lakhmi Chand. To other works, which do not so conspicuously bear their names, they have been among the largest contributors, and it would be scarcely possible to find a single deserving institution in the neighbourhood, to which they have not given a helping hand. Even the Catholic Church received from them a donation of Rs. 1,100, a fact that deserves mention as a signal illustration of their unsectarian benevolence.

The Ját family of highest ancestral rank in the district is the one represented by the titular Rájá of Háthras, who comes of the same stock as the Rájá of Mursán. His two immediate predecessors were both men of mark in local history, and his pedigree, as will be seen from the accompanying sketch, is one of respectable antiquity.

Makhañ Sinh, the founder of the family, was an immigrant from Rájputána, who settled in the neighbourhood of Mursán about the year 1860 A.D. His great-grandson, Thákur Nand Rám, who bore also the title of Faujdár, died in 1696, leaving 14 sons, of whom it is necessary to mention two only, *viz.*, Jalkaran Sinh and Jai Sinh. The great-grandson of the former was Rájá Bhagavant Sinh of Mursán, and of the latter Thákur Daya Rám of Háthras,

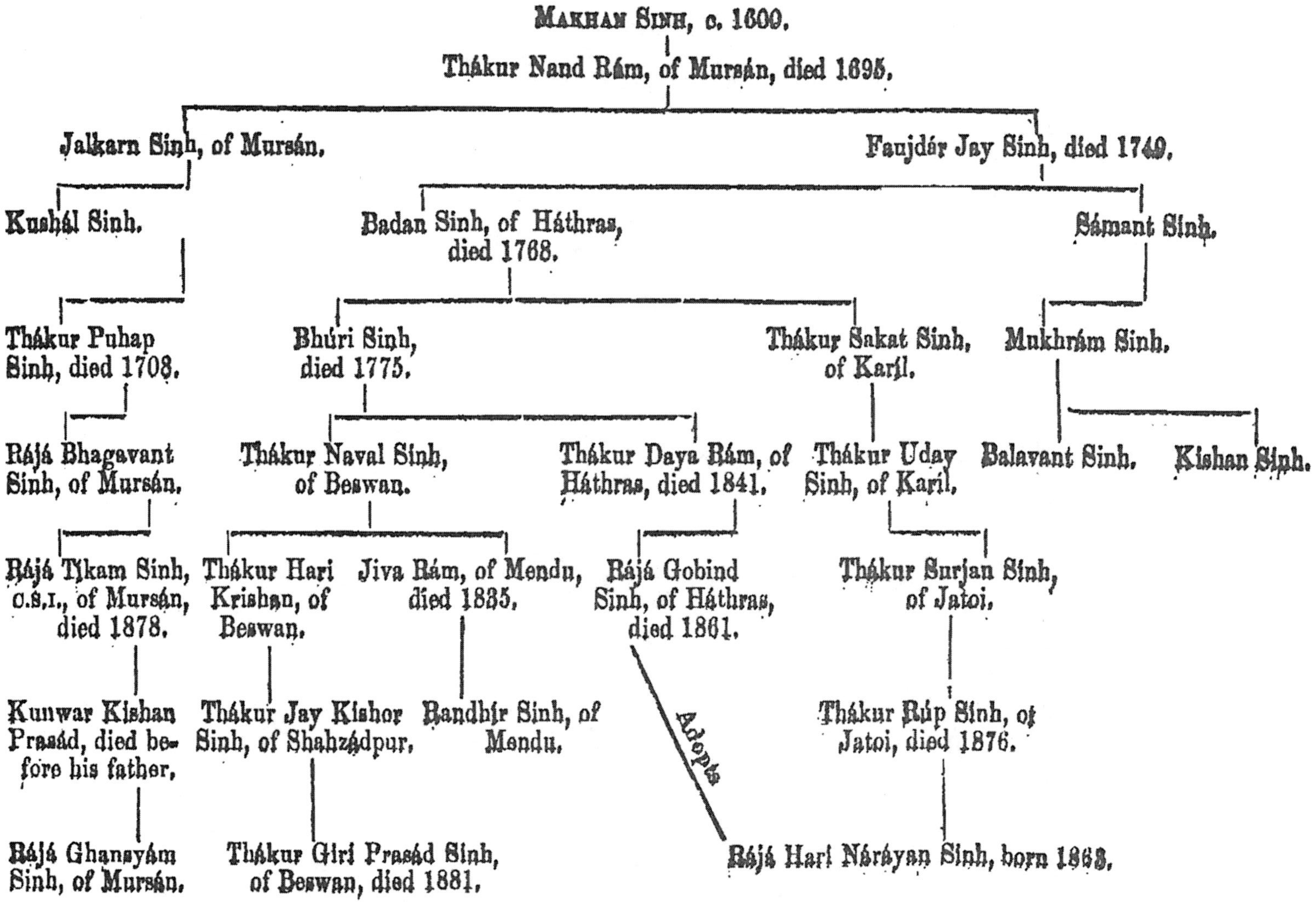
MAKHAN SINH, c. 1600.
Thákur Nand Rám, of Mursán, died 1695.
Jalkarn Sinh, of Mursán.
Faujdár Jay Sinh, died 1749.
Kushál Sinh.
Badan Sinh, of Háthras, died 1768.
Sámant Sinh.
Thákur Puhap Sinh, died 1708.
Bhúri Sinh, died 1775.
Thákur Sakat Sinh, of Karil.
Mukhrám Sinh.
Rájá Bhagavant Sinh, of Mursán.
Thákur Naval Sinh, of Beswan.
Thákur Daya Rám, of Háthras, died 1841.
Thákur Uday Sinh, of Karil.
Balavant Sinh.
Kishan Sinh.
Rájá Tikam Sinh, C.S.I., of Mursán, died 1878.
Thákur Hari Krishan, of Beswan.
Jiva Rám, of Mendu, died 1835.
Rájá Gobind Sinh, of Háthras, died 1861.
Thákur Surjan Sinh, of Jatoi.
Kunwar Kishan Prasád, died before his father.
Thákur Jay Kishor Sinh, of Shahzádpur.
Bandhir Sinh, of Mendu.
Adopts
Thákur Rúp Sinh, of Jatoi, died 1876.
Rájá Ghansyám Sinh, of Mursán.
Thákur Giri Prasád Sinh, of Beswan, died 1881.
Rájá Hari Náráyan Sinh, born 1863.

who, during the early years of British administration, were the two most powerful chiefs in this part of the country. From a report made by the Acting Collector of Aligarh in 1808, we learn that the Mursán Rájá's power extended at that time over the whole of Sa'dábád and Sonkh, while Mát, Mahá-ban, Sonai, Raya Hasangarh, Sahpau and Khandauli, were all held by his kinsman at Háthras. Their title, however, does not appear to have been altogether unquestioned, for the writer goes on to say:—"The valuable and extensive parganas which they farmed were placed under their authority by Lord Lake, immediately after the conquest of these Provinces; and they have since continued in their possession, as the resumption of them was considered to be calculated to excite dissatisfaction and as it was an object of temporary policy to conciliate their confidence."

This unwise reluctance on the part of the paramount power to enquire into the validity of the title, by which its vassals held their estates, was naturally construed as a confession of weakness and hastened the very evils which it was intended to avert. Both chieftains claimed to be independent and assumed so menacing an attitude that it became necessary to dislodge them from their strongholds; the climax of Daya Rám's recusancy being his refusal to surrender four men charged with murder. A force was despatched against them under Major-General Marshall, and Mursán was reduced without difficulty. But Háthras, which was said to be one of the strongest forts in the country, its defences having been improved on the model of those carried out by British Engineers in the neighbouring fort of Aligarh, had to be subjected to a regular siege. It was invested on the 21st of February, 1817. Daya Rám, it is said, was anxious to negotiate, but was prevented from carrying out his intention by Nek Rám Sinh (his son by an *ahiri* concubine), who even made an attempt to have his father assassinated as he was returning in a litter from the English camp. Hostilities, at all events, were continued, and on the 1st of March fire was opened on the fort from forty-five mortars and three breaching batteries of heavy guns. On the evening of the same day a magazine exploded and caused such general devastation that Daya Rám gave up all for lost and fled away by night on a little hunting pony, which took him the whole way to Bharat-pur. There Rájá Randhír Sinh declined to run the risk of affording him protection, and he continued his flight to Jaypur. His fort was dismantled and his estates all confiscated, but he was allowed a pension of Rs. 1,000 a month for his personal maintenance.

On his death in 1841, he was succeeded by his son, Thákur Gobind Sinh, who at the time of the mutiny in 1857 held only a portion of one village,

Sháhgarh, and that merely in mortgage. "With his antecedents," writes Mr. Bramley, the Magistrate of Aligarh, in his report to the Special Commissioner, dated the 4th of May, 1858, "it would, perhaps, have been no matter for surprise had he, like others in his situation, taken part against the Government. However, his conduct has been eminently loyal. I am not aware that he at any time wavered. On the first call of the Magistrate and Collector of Mathurá, he came with his personal followers and servants to the assistance of that gentleman, and was shortly afterwards summoned to Aligarh; there he remained throughout the disturbed period, ready to perform any services within his power; and it was in a great measure due to him that the important town of Háthras was saved from plunder by the surrounding population. He accompanied the force under Major Montgomery to Kol, and was present with his men in the action fought with the rebel followers of Muhammad Ghos Khán at Mán Sinh's Bágh on the 24th of August. On the flight of the rebel Governor of Kol, he was put in charge of the town and was allowed to raise a body of men for this service. He held the town of Kol and assisted in collecting revenue and recovering plundered property till September 25th, when he was surprised by a Muhammadan rabble under Nasím-ullah and forced to leave the town with some loss of men. This service was one, I presume, of very considerable danger, for he was surrounded by a low and incensed Muhammadan population and on the high road of retreat of the Delhi rebels, while the support of Major Montgomery's force at Háthras was distant and liable itself to be called away on any exigency occurring at Agra.

"On the re-occupation of the Aligarh district Gobind Sinh resumed his post in the city, and by his good example rendered most important aid in the work of restoring order. His followers have at all times been ready for any service and have been extremely useful in police duties and in escorting treasure to Agra and Bulandshahr; in guarding gháts and watching the advance of rebels; in performing, indeed, the duties of regular troops. His loyalty has exposed him to considerable pecuniary loss; his losses on September 25th being estimated at upwards of Rs. 30,000, while his house at Brindá-ban was also plundered, by rebels returning from Delhi, to a much larger amount of ancestral property that cannot be replaced."

In compensation for these losses and in acknowledgment of the very valuable services which he had rendered to Government by his family influence and personal energy, he received a grant of Rs. 50,000 in cash, together with a

AUTOTYPE.

RÁJÁ HARI NÁRÁYAN SINH, OF HÁTHRAS.

landed estate* lying in the districts of Mathurá and Bulandshahr, and was also honoured with the title of Rájá; the sanad, signed by Lord Canning, being dated the 25th of June, 1858.

Rájá Gobind Sinh was connected by marriage with the head of the Ját clan; his wife, a daughter of Chaudhari Charan Sinh, being sister to Chaudhari Ratan Sinh, the maternal uncle of Mahárája Jasvant Sinh of Bharat-pur. This lady, the Ráni Sahib Kunvar, is still living and manages her estate with much ability and discretion through the agency of Pandit Chítar Sinh, a very old friend of the family. At the time of her husband's decease in 1861, there was an infant son, but he died very soon after the father. As this event had been anticipated, the Rájá had authorized his widow to adopt a son, and she selected for the purpose Hari Náráyan Sinh, born in 1863, the son of Thákur Rúp Sinh of Jatoi, a descendant, as was also Rájá Gobind Sinh himself, of Thákur Nand Rám's younger son, Jai Sinh. This adoption was opposed by Kesri Sinh, the son of Nek Rám, who was the illegitimate offspring of Thákur Daya Rám. But the claim that he advanced on behalf of his own sons, Sher Sinh and Balavant Sinh, was rejected by the Judge of Agra in his order dated November, 1872, and his view of the case was afterwards upheld by the High Court on appeal. At the Delhi Assemblage of the 1st of January, 1877, in honour of Her Majesty's assumption of the Imperial title, Rájá Gobind Sinh's title was formally continued to Hari Náráyan Sinh for life. He resides with his mother, the Ráni Sáhib Kunvar, at Brindá-ban, where he has a handsome house on the bank of the Jamuná, opposite the Kesi ghát, and here, on the occasion of his marriage in February, 1877, he gave a grand entertainment to all the European residents of the station, including the officers of the Xth Royal Hussars. Though only 14 years of age, he played his part of host with perfect propriety and good breeding—taking a lady into dinner, sitting at the head of his table—though, of course, not eating anything—and making a little speech to return thanks after his health had been proposed.

The only Muhammadan family of any importance is the one seated at Sa'dábád. This is a branch of the Lál-Kháni stock, which musters strongest in the Bulandshahr district, where several of its members are persons of high distinction and own very large estates.

* The estate consists—1st, of the zamindári of the township of Kol and some shops and gardens at Háthras, valued at Rs. 3,000; 2ndly, of eight confiscated Gújar villages in the Chhátá and Kosi parganas of the Mathurá district, now assessed at over Rs. 10,000; and 3rdly, of five villages in the Bulandshahr district, assessed at Rs. 7,000.

They claim descent from Kunvar Pratáp Sinh, a Bargujar Thákur of Rajaur, in Rájputána, who joined Prithi Ráj of Delhi in his expedition against Mahoba. On his way thither he assisted the Dor Rájá of Kol in reducing a rebellion of the Mínas, and was rewarded by receiving in marriage the Rájá's daughter, with a dowry of 150 villages in the neighbourhood of Pahásu. The eleventh in descent from Pratáp Sinh was Lál Sinh, who, though a Hindu, received from the Emperor Akbar the title of Khán ; whence the name Lál-Kháni, by which the family is ordinarily designated. It was his grandson, Itimád Ráe, in the reign of Aurangzeb, who first embraced Muhammadanism. The seventh in descent from Itimád Ráe was Náhar Ali Khán, who, with his nephew, Dunde Khán, held the fort of Kumona, in Bulandshahr, against the English, and thus forfeited his estate, which was conferred upon his relative, Mardán Ali Khán.

The latter, who resided at Chhatári, which is still regarded as the chief seat of the family, was the purchaser of the Sa'dábád estate, which on his death passed to his eldest son, Husain Ali Khán, and is now held by the widow, the Thákuráni Hakim-un-nissa. It yields an annual income of Rs. 48,569, derived from as many as 26 different villages. The Thakuráni being childless, the property was long managed on her behalf by her husband's nephew, the late Kunvar Irshád Ali Khán. He died in 1876 and was succeeded by his son, Itimád Ali Khán, who is the present head of the family in this district. Several of his relatives have other lands here. Thus his uncle, Nawáb Sir Faiz Ali Khán, K.C.S.I., owns the village of Nánau ; and the villages of Chháva and Dauhai, yielding a net income of Rs. 1,993, belong to Thakuráni Zeb-un-nissa, the widow of Kamr Ali Khán, Sir Faiz's uncle. Two other villages, Bahardoi and Náráyanpur, are the property of a minor, Ghulám Muhammad Khán, the son of Hidáyat Ali Khán, who was adopted by Zuhur Ali Khán of Dharmpur on the failure of issue by his first wife ; they yield an income of Rs. 3,555. The relationship existing between all these persons will be best understood by a glance at the accompanying genealogical table.

The family, in commemoration of their descent, retain the Hindu titles of Kunvar and Thakuráni and have hitherto, in their marriage and other social customs, observed many old Hindu usages. The tendency of the present generation is, however, rather to affect an ultra-rigid Muhammadanism ; and the head of the house, the Nawáb of Chhatári, is an adherent of the Wahábis.

Of the smaller estates in the district, some few belong to respectable old families of the yeoman type ; others have been recently acquired by speculating money-lenders ; but the far greater number are split up into infinitesimal fractions among the whole village community. Owing to this prevalence of the Bhaiyáchári system, as it is called, the small farmers who cultivate their own lands constitute a very large class, while the total of the non-proprietary classes is proportionately reduced. A decided majority of the latter have no assured status, but are merely tenants-at-will. Throughout the district, all the land brought under the plough is classified under two heads,—*first*, according to its productiveness ; *secondly*, according to its accessibility. The fields capable of artificial irrigation—and it is the supply of water which most influences the amount of produce—are styled *cháhi*, all others *kháki ;* those nearest the village are known as *bárá*, those rather more remote as *manjhá*, and the furthest away *barhá*.* The combination of the two classes gives six varieties, and ordinarily no others are recognized, though along the course of the Jamuná the tracts of alluvial land are, as elsewhere, called *khádar*—the high sterile banks are *bángar*, and where broken into ravines *behar ;* a soil exceptionally sandy is *bhúr*, sand-hills are *púth*, and the levels between the hills *púlaj*.

The completion of the Agra Canal has been a great boon to the district. It traverses the entire length of Western Mathurá, passing close to the towns of Kosí, Sahár, and Aríng, and having as its extreme points Hathána to the north and Little Kosí to the south. It was officially opened by Sir William Muir on the 5th of March, 1874, and became available for irrigation purposes about the end of 1875, by which time its distributaries also had been constructed. Its total length from Okhla to the Utangan river at Bihári below Fatihabád is 140 miles, and it commands an area of three-quarters of a million acres, of which probably one-third—that is 250,000 acres—will be annually irrigated. The cost has been above £710,000, while the net income will be about £58,000, being a return of 8 per cent. It will be practicable for boats and barges, both in its main line and its distributaries, and thus, instead of the shallow uncertain course of the Jamuná, there will be sure and easy navigation between the three great cities of Delhi, Mathurá, and Agra. One of the most immediate effects of the canal will probably be a large diminution of the area under bájra and joár, which, by reason of their requiring no artificial irrigation, have hitherto been almost the only crops grown on much of the land. For,

* It is exactly the same in Russia. "All the arable land of the commune is divided into three concentric zones, which extend round the village: and these three zones are again divided into three fields according to the triennial arrangement of crops. More regard is paid to proximity than to fertility, as this varies very little in the same district in Russia. The zones nearest the village are alone manured."—*Laveleye's Primitive Property,*

with water ordinarily from 40 to 60 feet below the surface and a sandy subsoil, the construction of a well is a costly and difficult undertaking. In future, wheat and barley, for which the soil when irrigated is well adapted, will be the staple produce; indigo and opium, now almost unknown, will be gradually introduced; vegetables will be more largely cultivated and double-cropping will become the ordinary rule. Thus, not only will the yield per acre be increased by the facilities for irrigation, but the produce will be of an entirely different and much more valuable character.

A scheme for extending the irrigation of the Ganges Canal through the parganas on the opposite—that is to say, the left—side of the Jamuná has long been held in view. The branch which takes off from the main canal at Dehra in the Merath district has by anticipation been termed the Mát branch, though its irrigation stops short in the Tappal pargana of Aligarh, one distributary only irrigating a few villages north of Noh-jhíl. The water-supply in the Ganges Canal is limited, and would not have sufficed for any further extension; but now that the Kánhpur branch is supplied from the new Lower Ganges Canal, a certain volume of water has become available, a portion of which has been allotted for the Mát branch extension. If the project be sanctioned in its entirety, the existing sub-branch will be widened to carry the additional supply and extended through the Tappal pargana, entering Noh-jhíl in the village of Bhure-ká. The course of the main supply line will pass along the watershed of the Karwan and Jamuná Doáb to the east of Bhure-ká, and then by the villages of Dandísara, Harnaul, Nasíthi, and Arua till it crosses the Mát and Ráya road and the Light Railway. Thence it will extend to Kárab, Sonkh, and Pachawar, where at its 40th mile it will end in three distributaries, which will carry the water as far as the Agra and Aligarh road. The scheme thus provides for the irrigation of the parganas of Noh-jhíl, Mát, Mahá-ban, and that portion of Sa'dábád which lies to the west of the Karwan nadi. About five miles of the main line were excavated as a famine relief work in 1878; but operations were stopped in consequence of financial difficulties, and it is doubtful whether they will be resumed. There is also a considerable amount of well-irrigation in Mahá-ban and Sa'dábád, which renders the extension into those parganas a less pressing necessity.

The district is one which has often suffered severely from drought. In 1813-14 the neighbourhood of Sahár was one of the localities where the distress was most intense. Many died from hunger, and others were glad to sell their wives and children for a few rupees or even for a single meal. In 1825-26 the whole of the territories known at that time as the Western Provinces were afflicted with a terrible drought. The rabi crops of the then Sa'dádád district were estimated by Mr. Boddam, the Collector, as below the average by more than 200,000 *mans;* Mahá-ban and Jalesar being the two parganas which suffered most. But the famine of 1837-38 was á far greater calamity, and still forms an epoch in native chronology under the name of 'the *chauránawe,*' or 'the 94'; 1894 being its date according to the Hindu era. Though Mathurá was not one of the districts most grievously afflicted, distress was still extreme, as appears from the report submitted by the Commissioner, Mr. Hamilton, after personal investigation. About Ráya, Mát, and Mahá-ban he found the crops scanty, and the soil dry, and cultivated only in the immediate vicinity of masonry wells. About Mathurá, the people were almost in despair from the wells fast turning so brackish and salt as to destroy rather than refresh vegetation. "All of the Aríng and Gobardhan parganas (he writes) which came under my observation was an extensive arid waste, and for miles I rode over ground which had been both ploughed and sown, but in which the seed had not germinated and where there seemed no prospect of a harvest. The cattle in Aríng were scarcely able to crawl, and they were collected in the village and suffered to pull at the thatch, the people declaring it useless to drive them forth to seek for pasture. Emigration had already commenced, and people of all classes appeared to be suffering."

Of the famine of 1860-61 (commonly called the *áth-sera,* from the prevalent bazar rate of eight sers only for the rupee) the following narrative was recorded by Mr. Robertson, Officiating Collector :—" Among prosperous agriculturists," he says, "about half the land usually brought under cultivation is irrigated, and irrigated lands alone produce crops this year. But though only half the crop procured in ordinary years was obtained by this class of cultivators, the high price of corn enabled them, while realizing considerable profits, to meet the Government demand without much difficulty. The poorer class of cultivators were, however, ruined, and with the poorest in the cities, taking advantage of the position of Mathurá as one of the border famine tracts, they abandoned the district in large numbers, chiefly towards the close of 1860. Rather more than one-fourth of the agricultural emigrants have returned, and the quiet, unmurmuring industry with which they have recommenced life is not a less pleasing feature than the total absence of agrarian outrage during the famine. The greatest number of deaths from starvation occurred during the first three months of 1861, when the average per mensem was 497. During the succeeding three months this average was reduced to 85, while the deaths in July and August were only five and six respectively. The total number of deaths during the eight months has been 1,758. Viewing the universality of the famine, these results sufficiently evidence the active co-operation in measures of relief rendered by the native officials assisted by the police, and the people everywhere most pointedly express their obligation to the Government and English liberality. No return of the number of deaths caused by starvation seems to have been kept from October, 1860, to January, 1861, but judging by the subsequent returns, 250 per mensem might be considered as the highest average. Thus, the mortality caused by the famine in this district in the year 1860-61 may approximately be estimated at 2,500."* If such a large number of persons really died simply from starvation—and there seems no reason to doubt the fact—the arrangements for dispensing relief can scarcely have merited all the praise bestowed upon them. There was certainly no lack of funds towards the end, but possibly they came when it was almost too late. In the month of April some 8,000 men were employed daily on the Delhi road; the local donations amounted to Rs. 16,227, and this sum was increased by a contribution of Rs. 8,000 from the Agra Central Committee, and Rs. 5,300 from Government, making a total of Rs. 29,528. An allotment of Rs. 5,000 was also made from the Central Committee for distribution among the indigent agriculturists, that they might have wherewithal to purchase seed and cattle.

At the present time the district has scarcely recovered from a series of disastrous seasons, resulting in a famine of exceptional severity and duration, which will leave melancholy traces behind it for many years yet to come. Both in 1875 and 1876 the rainfall was much below the average, and the crops on all unirrigated land proportionately small. In 1877 the entire period of the ordinary monsoon passed with scarcely a single shower, and it was not till the beginning of October, when almost all hope was over, that a heavy fall of rain was vouchsafed, which allowed the ground to be ploughed and seed to be sown for the ensuing year. The autumn crops, upon which the poorer classes mainly subsist, failed absolutely, and for the most part had never even been sown. As early as July, 1877, the prices of every kind of grain were at famine rates, which continued steadily on the increase, while the commoner sorts were before long entirely exhausted. The distress in the villages was

* Mr. Robertson's narrative has been copied from the original paper in the District Office. The other particulars have been extracted from Mr. Girdlestone's Report on Past Famines, published by Government in 1868.

naturally greatest among the agricultural labourers, who were thown out of all employ by the cessation of work in the fields, while even in the towns the petty handicraftsmen were unable to purchase sufficient food for their daily subsistence on account of the high prices that prevailed in the bazar. In addition to its normal population the city was further thronged by crowds of refugees from outside, from the adjoining native states, more especially Bharat-pur, who were attracted by the fame of the many charitable institutions that exist both in the city itself and at Brindá-ban. No relief works on the part of the Government were started till October, when they were commenced in different places all over the district under the supervision of the resident Engineer. They consisted chiefly of the ordinary repairs and improvements to the roads, which are annually carried out after the cessation of the rains. The expense incurred under this head was Rs. 17,762, the average daily attendance being 5,519. On the 25th of November in the same year (1877) it was found necessary to open a poorhouse in the city for the relief of those who were too feeble to work. Here the daily average attendance was 890 ; but, on the 30th July, 1878, the number of inmates amounted to 2,139, and this was unquestionably the time when the distress was at its highest. The maximum attendance at the relief works, however, was not reached till a little later, *viz.*, the 19th of August, when it was 20,483, but it would seem to have been artificially increased by the unnecessarily high rates which the Government was then paying.

The *rabi* crops, sown after the fall of rain in October, 1877, had been further benefited by unusually heavy winter rains, and it was hoped that there would be a magnificent outturn. In the end, however, it proved to be even below the average, great damage having been done by the high winds which blew in February. Thus, though the spring harvest of 1878 gave some relief, it was but slight, and necessarily it could not affect at all the prices of the common autumn grains. The long-continued privation had also had its effect upon the people both physically and mentally, and they were less able to struggle against their misfortunes. The rains for 1878 were, moreover, very slight and partial and so long delayed that they had scarcely set in by the end of July, and thus it was, as already stated, that this month was the time when the famine was at its climax. In August and September matters steadily improved, and henceforth continued to do so ; but the poorhouse was not closed till the end of June, 1879. The total number of inmates had then been 395,824, who had been relieved at a total cost of Rs. 43,070, of which sum Rs. 2,990 had been raised by private subscription and Rs. 3,500 was a grant from the Municipality.

Beside the repairs of the roads the other relief works undertaken and their cost were as follows: the excavation of the Jait tank, Rs. 6,787 ; the deepening of the Balbhadra tank, Rs. 5,770 ; and the levelling of the Jamálpur mounds, Rs. 7,238 : these adjoined the Magistrate's Court-house, and will be frequently mentioned hereafter as the site of a large Buddhist monastery. On the 11th of May, 1878, the earthwork of the Mathurá and Achnera Railway was taken in hand and continued till the beginning of September, during which time it gave employment to 713,315 persons, at an expenditure of Rs. 56,639. An extension of the Mát branch of the Ganges Canal was also commenced on the 30th July, and employed 579,351 persons, at a cost of Rs. 43,142, till its close on the 16th of October. There should also be added Rs. 6,379, which were spent by the Municipality through the District Engineer, in levelling some broken ground opposite the City Police Station. The total cost on all these relief works thus amounted to Rs. 1,80,630. No remission of revenue was granted by the Government, but advances for the purchase of bullocks and seed were distributed to the extent of Rs. 35,000.*

The following tabular statement shows the mortality that prevailed during the worst months of this calamitous period : the total population of the district being 778,839 :—

	July.	August.	September.	October.	November.	December.	January.	February.	March.	April.	May.	June.
1877-78 ..	973	1,126	932	1,337	1,579	1,973	1,869	1,725	2,018	2,511	2,189	3,672
1878-79...	2,562	2,970	6,579	10,414	8,643	4,710	2,491	1,474	1,148	1,511	1,891	1,661

The metalling of the Delhi road, which has been incidentally mentioned as the principal relief work in 1860, was not only a boon at the time, but still continues a source of the greatest advantage to the district. The old imperial thoroughfare, which connected the two capitals of Agra and Lahor, kept closely to the same line, as is shown by the ponderous kos minars, which are found still standing at intervals of about three miles, and nowhere at any great

* I saw nothing of the famine myself, as I left the district in April, 1877, before it had begun. Selfishly, I am glad to have escaped the sight of so much misery; though, possibly, if I had been on the spot, my local experience might have proved useful both to the Government and the people.

distance from the wayside. Here was the "delectable alley of trees, the most incomparable ever beheld," which the Emperor Jahángír enjoys the credit of having planted. That it was really a fine avenue is attested by the language of the sober Dutch topographer, John de Laet, who, in his India Vera, written in 1631, that is, early in the reign of Sháhjahán, speaks of it in the following terms :—"The whole of the country between Agra and Lahor is well-watered and by far the most fertile part of India. It abounds in all kinds of produce, especially sugar. The highway is bordered on either side by trees which bear a fruit not unlike the mulberry,* and," as he adds in another place, "form a beautiful avenue." "At intervals of five or six coss," he continues, "there are saráes built either by the king or by some of the nobles. In these travellers can find bed and lodging ; when a person has once taken possession he cannot be turned out by any one." The glory of the road, however, seems to have been of short duration, for Bernier, writing only thirty years later, that is, in 1663, says :—"Between Delhi and Agra, a distance of fifty or sixty leagues, the whole road is cheerless and uninteresting ;" and even so late as 1825, Bishop Heber, on his way down to Calcutta, was apparently much struck with what he calls "the wildness of the country," but mentions no avenue, as he certainly would have done had one then existed. Thus it is clear that the more recent administrators of the district, since its incorporation into British territory, are the only persons entitled to the traveller's blessing for the magnificent and almost unbroken canopy of over-arching boughs, which now extends for more than thirty miles from the city of Mathurá to the border of the Gurgánw district, and forms a sufficient protection from even the mid-day glare of an Indian summer's sun.

Though the country is now generally brought under cultivation, and can scarcely be described as even well wooded, there are still here and there many patches of waste land covered with low trees and jungle, which might be considered to justify the Bishop's epithet of wild-looking. The herds of deer are so numerous that the traveller will seldom go many miles in any direction along a bye-road without seeing a black-buck, followed by his harem, bound across the path. The number has probably increased rather than diminished in late years,

* In the original Latin text the word is *morus*, which Mr. Lethbridge, in his scholarly English edition, translates by 'fig;' but I think 'mulberry' a more accurate rendering, and that to be the tree intended. It is to this day largely used for roadside planting at Lahor, and still more so in the Peshâwar valley and in Kábul and on the Oxus. De Laet says it was only *like* the mulberry, and not that it positively was the mulberry, on account of the difference of the two varieties of the fruit, the Indian and the European, which is very considerable. In the Kashmír valley both are to be seen.

as the roving and vagabond portion of the population, who used to keep them in check, were all disarmed after the mutiny. Complaints are now frequent of the damage done to the crops; and in some parts of the district yet more serious injury is occasioned by the increase in the number of wolves.

The old Customs hedge, now happily abolished, used to run along the whole length of this road from Jait, seven miles out of Mathurá, to the Gurgánw border. Though in every other respect a source of much annoyance to the people living in its neighbourhood, the watchmen, who patrolled it night and day, were a great protection to travellers, and a highway robbery was never known to take place; while on the corresponding road between Mathurá and Agra they were at one time of frequent occurrence.*

The quantity of sugarcane now grown in this part of the district is very inconsiderable. The case may have been different in De Laet's time; but on other grounds there seems reason for believing that his descriptions are not drawn from actual observation, and are therefore not thoroughly trustworthy. For example, he gives the marches from Agra to Delhi as follows:—"From Agra, the residence of the king, to Rownoctan, twelve coss; to Bady, a saráe, ten; to Achbarpore, twelve (this was formerly a considerable town, now it is only visited by pilgrims, who come on account of many holy Muhammadans buried here); to Hondle, thirteen coss; to Pulwool, twelve; to Fareedabad, twelve; to Delhi, ten." Now, this passage requires much manipulation before it can be reconciled with established facts. Rownoctan, it may be presumed, would, if correctly spelt, appear in the form Raunak-thán, meaning "a royal halting-place," and was probably merely the fashionable appellation, for the time, of the Hindu village of Rankatá, which is still the first stage out of Agra. Bády or Bád, is a small village on the narrow strip of Bharat-pur territory which so inconveniently intersects the Agra and Mathurá road. There has never been any saráe there; the one intended is the Jamál-pur saráe, some three coss further on, at the entrance to the civil station. The fact that Mathurá has dropt out of the Itinerary altogether, in favour of such an insignificant little hamlet as Bád,

* This Inland Customs Line, which had no parallel in the world except the great wall of China, was about 1,200 miles in length, from the Tápti to the Indus, and was manned by an establishment of between 8,000 and 9,000 officers and men. It consisted of a barrier, chiefly in the form of a thick, thorny hedge, along which were placed at short intervals more than 1,300 guard posts. The cost was about £100,000 per annum, and the revenue realized about a million sterling; the yearly import of salt from Rájputána being about 80,000 tons, of which on an average one-half came from the Bharat-pur State.

is a striking illustration of the low estate to which the great Hindu city had been reduced at the time in question.* Again, the place with the Muhammadan tombs is not Akbar-pur, but the next village, Dotáná; and the large saráes at Kosi and Chhátá are both omitted.

These saráes are fine fort-like buildings, with massive battlemented walls and bastions and high-arched gateways. They are five in number: one at the entrance to the civil station; the second at 'Azamabád, two miles beyond the city on the Delhi road; another at Chaumuhá; the fourth at Chhátá, and the fifth at Kosi. The first, which is smaller than the others and has been much modernized,† has for many years past been occupied by the police reserve, and is ordinarily called 'the Damdama.' The three latter are generally ascribed by local tradition to Sher Sháh, whose reign extended from 1540 to 1545, though it is also said that Itibár Khán was the name of the founder of the two at Mathurá and Kosi, and A'saf Khán of the one at Chhátá. It is probable that both traditions are based on facts: for at Chhátá it is obvious at a glance that both the gateways are double buildings, half dating from one period and half from another. The inner front, which is plain and heavy, may be referred to Sher Sháh, while the lighter and more elaborate stone front, looking towards the town, is a subsequent addition. As A'saf Khán is simply a title of honour (the 'Asaph the Recorder' of the Old Testament) which was borne by several persons in succession, a little doubt arises at first as to the precise individual intended. The presumption, however, is strongly in favour of Abd-ul-majíd, who was first Humáyun's Díwán, and on Akbar's accession was appointed Governor of Delhi. The same post was held later on by Khwájá Itibár Khán, the reputed founder of the Kosi saráe. The general style of architecture is in exact conformity with that of similar buildings known to have been erected in Akbar's reign, such, for example, as the fort of Agra. The Chaumuhá saráe‡

---

* Similarly, it will be seen that Tavernier, writing about 1650, recognizes Mathurá as the name of a temple only, not of a town at all.

† A range of vaulted chambers flanking the central gateway were pulled down by the Public Works Department in 1876, to make way for some modern buildings intended to answer the same purpose, but necessarily of much less substantial construction. The old cells had been rendered unsightly by the mud walls with which the arches had been closed; but these excrescences could all have been cleared away at very slight expense.

‡ Chaumuhá is distorted by Tieffenthaler into Tschaomao. He speaks of its saráe as "hotellerie belle et commode."

8

is, moreover, always described in the old topographies as at Akbarpur.* This latter name is now restricted in application to a village some three miles distant; but in the 16th century local divisions were few in number and wide in extent, and beyond a doubt the foundation of the imperial saráe was the origin of the village name which has now deserted the spot that suggested it. The separate existence of Chaumuhá is known to date from a very recent period, when the name was bestowed in consequence of the discovery of an ancient Jain sculpture, supposed by the ignorant rustics to represent the four-headed (*chaumuha*) god, Brahma.

Though these saráes were primarily built mainly from selfish motives on the line of road traversed by the imperial camp, they were at the same time enormous boons to the general public; for the highway was then beset with gangs of robbers, with whose vocation the law either dared not or cared not to interfere. On one occasion, in the reign of Jahángír, we read of a caravan having to stay six weeks at Mathurá before it was thought strong enough to proceed to Delhi; no smaller number than 500 or 600 men being deemed adequate to encounter the dangers of the road. Now, the solitary traveller is so confident of protection that, rather than drive his cart up the steep ascent that conducts to the portals of the fortified enclosure, he prefers to spend the night unguarded on the open plain. Hence it comes that not one of the saráes is now applied to the precise purpose for which it was erected. At Chhátá, one corner is occupied by the school, another by the offices of the tahsíldar and local police, and a street with a double row of shops has recently been constructed in the centre; at Chaumuhá the solid walls have in past years been undermined and carted away piecemeal for building materials; and at Kosi, the principal bazar lies between the two gateways and forms the nucleus of the town.

Still more complete destruction has overtaken the 'Azamabád saráe, which seems to have been the largest of the series, as it certainly was the plainest and the most modern. Its erection is ordinarily ascribed by the people on the spot to Prince 'Azam, the son of Aurangzeb, being the only historical personage of

* At Akbarpur, by the roadside is a large and very deep báuli approached by a flight of 76 steps, once cased with stone, which has now been almost all stripped off and applied by the villagers to other purposes. Immediately adjoining are the ruins of a mosque and tomb, and masonry tank 12 bíghas in extent. The boundary walls of the latter are now for the most part broken down, and of the eight kiosques that crowned the extremities of the ghâts only one remains. These extensive works are said to have been constructed some two centuries ago by a converted Thákur named Dhakmal. A rájbaha of the Agra Canal passes through the village lands, and a rest-house is being built at the point where it crosses the high road.

the name with whom they are acquainted. But, as with the other buildings of the same character, its real founder was a local governor, 'Azam Khán Mír Muhammad Bákir, also called Irádat Khán, who was faujdár of Mathurá from 1642 to 1645. In the latter year he was superseded in office, as his age had rendered him unequal to the task of suppressing the constant outbreaks against the Government, and in 1648 he died.* As the new road does not pass immediately under the walls of the saráe, it had ceased to be of any use to travellers; and a few years ago, it was to a great extent demolished and the materials used in paving the streets of the adjoining city. Though there was little or no architectural embellishment, the foundations were most securely laid, reaching down below the ground as many feet as the superstructure which they supported stood above it. Of this ocular demonstration was recently afforded, for one of the villagers in digging came upon what he hoped would prove the entrance to a subterranean treasure chamber; but deeper excavations showed it to be only one of the line of arches forming the foundation of the saráe wall. The original mosque is still standing, but is little used for religious purposes, as the village numbers only nine Muhammadans in a population of 343. They all live within the old ruinous enclosure.

* For this and several other facts gathered from the Persian chronicles, I was indebted to the late Mr. Blochmann, the Secretary of the Calcutta Asiatic Society, a gentleman whose knowledge of Muhammadan history and literature was as unlimited as was the courtesy with which he communicated it.

CHAPTER II.

MATHURÁ SACKED BY MAHMÚD OF GHAZNI, 1017 A.D. ITS TREATMENT BY THE DELHI EMPERORS. RISE AND PROGRESS OF THE JÁT POWER. MASSACRE AT MATHURÁ, 1757. BATTLE OF BARSÁNA, 1775. EXECUTION OF GHULÁM KÁDIR, 1788. BRITISH OCCUPATION, 1803. BATTLE OF DÍG, 1804. MUTINY, 1857.

APART from inscriptions and other fragmentary archæological vestiges of its ancient glory, the first authentic contemporary record of Mathurá that we find in existing literature is dated the year 1017 A.D., when it was sacked by Mahmúd of Ghazni in his ninth invasion of India. The original source of information respecting Mahmúd's campaigns is the Táríkh Yamíni of Al Utbi, who was himself secretary to the Sultán, though he did not accompany him in his expeditions. He mentions by name neither Mathurá nor Mahá-ban, but only describes certain localities, which have been so identified by Firishta and later historians. The place supposed to be Mahá-ban he calls "the Fort of Kulchand," a Rájá, who (he writes) "was, not without good reason, confident in his strength, for no one had fought against him and not been defeated. He had vast territories, enormous wealth, a numerous and brave army, huge elephants, and strong forts that no enemy had been able to reduce. When he saw that the Sultán advanced against him, he drew up his army and elephants in a 'deep forest'* ready for action. But finding every attempt to repulse the invaders fail, the beleaguered infidels at last quitted the fort and tried to cross the broad river which flowed in its rear. When some 50,000 men had been killed or drowned, Kulchand took a dagger, with which he first slew his wife and then drove it into his own body. The Sultán obtained by this victory 185 fine elephants besides other booty." In the neighbouring holy city, identified as Mathurá, "he saw a building of exquisite structure, which the inhabitants declared to be the handiwork not of men but of Genii.† The town wall was constructed of solid stone, and had opening on to the river two gates, raised on high and massive basements to protect them from the floods. On the two sides of the city were thousands of houses with idol temples attached, all of masonry and strengthened with bars of iron; and opposite them were other buildings supported on stout wooden pillars. In the middle of the city was a temple, larger and finer than the rest, to which neither painting nor description could

* These words may be intended as a literal translation of the name "Mahá-ban."

† Possibly "Jina," the name both of the Buddhist and Jaini deity, was the word actually used, which was mistaken for the Arabic "Jinn."

do justice. The Sultán thus wrote respecting it:—'If any one wished to construct a building equal to it, he would not be able to do so without expending a hundred million dinars, and the work would occupy two hundred years, even though the most able and experienced workmen were employed.' Orders were given that all the temples should be burnt with naphtha and fire and levelled with the ground." The city was given up to plunder for twenty days. Among the spoil are said to have been five great idols of pure gold with eyes of rubies and adornments of other precious stones, together with a vast number of smaller silver images, which, when broken up, formed a load for more than a hundred camels. The total value of the spoil has been estimated at three millions of rupees; while the number of Hindus carried away into captivity exceeded 5,000.

Nizám-ud-din, Firishta, and the other late Muhammadan historians take for granted that Mathurá was at that time an exclusively Bráhmanical city. It is possible that such was really the case: but the original authorities leave the point open, and speak only in general terms of idolaters, a name equally applicable to Buddhists. Many of the temples, after being gutted of all their valuable contents, were left standing, probably because they were too massive to admit of easy destruction. Some writers allege that the conqueror spared them on account of their exceeding beauty, founding this opinion on the eulogistic expressions employed by Mahmúd in his letter to the Governor of Ghazni quoted above. It is also stated that, on his return home, he introduced the Indian style of architecture at his own capital, where he erected a splendid mosque, upon which he bestowed the name of 'the Celestial Bride.' But, however much he may have admired the magnificence of Mathurá, it is clear that he was influenced by other motives than admiration in sparing the fabric of the temples; for the gold and silver images, which he did not hesitate to demolish, must have been of still more excellent workmanship.

During the period of Muhammadan supremacy, the history of Mathurá is almost a total blank. The natural dislike of the ruling power to be brought into close personal connection with such a centre of superstition divested the town of all political importance; while the Hindu pilgrims, who still continued to frequent its impoverished shrines, were not invited to present, as the priests were not anxious to receive, any lavish donation which would only excite the jealousy of the rival faith. Thus, while there are abundant remains of the earlier Buddhist period, there is not a single building, nor fragment of a building, which can be assigned to any year in the long interval between the

9

invasion of Mahmúd in 1017 A.D. and the reign of Akbar in the latter half of the sixteenth century; and it is only from the day when the Játs and Mahrattas began to be the virtual sovereigns of the country that any continuous series of monumental records exists.

Nor can this be wondered at, since whenever the unfortunate city did attract the Emperor's notice, it became at once a mark for pillage and desecration : and the more religious the sovereign, the more thorough the persecution. Take for example the following passage from the Táríkh-i-Dáúdi of Abdullah (a writer in the reign of Jahángír), who is speaking of Sultán Sikandar Lodi (1488—1516 A.D.), one of the most able and accomplished of all the occupants of the Delhi throne : " He was so zealous a Musalmán that he utterly destroyed many places of worship of the infidels, and left not a single vestige remaining of them. He entirely ruined the shrines of Mathurá, that mine of heathenism, and turned their principal temples into *saráes* and colleges. Their stone images were given to the butchers to serve them as meat-weights, and all the Hindus in Mathurá were strictly prohibited from shaving their heads and beards and performing their ablutions. He thus put an end to all the idolatrous rites of the infidels there ; and no Hindu, if he wished to have his head or beard shaved, could get a barber to do it." In confirmation of the truth of this narrative, it may be observed that when the Muhammadan Governor Abd-un-Nabi, in 1661, built his great mosque as a first step towards the construction of the new city, of which he is virtually the founder, the ground which he selected for the purpose, and which was unquestionably an old temple site, had to be purchased from the butchers.

During the glorious reign of Akbar, the one bright era in the dreary annals of Imperial misrule, there was full toleration at Mathurá as in all other parts of his dominions. Of this an illustration is afforded by the following incident, which is narrated by Badauni : Among the persons held in high favour at the Court was a Shaikh, by name Abd-un-Nabi, who occupied the distinguished position of Sadr-us-Sadúr. A complaint was made to him by Kázi Abd-ur-Rahím of Mathurá that a wealthy Bráhman had appropriated some materials that had been collected for the building of a mosque, and not only used them in the construction of a temple, but, when remonstrated with, had, in the presence of a crowd of people, foully abused the Prophet and all his followers. The Bráhman, when summoned to answer the charge, refused to come ; whereupon Ab-ul-Fazl was sent to fetch him, and on his return reported that all the people of Mathurá agreed in declaring that the Bráhman had used abusive language. The doctors of the law accordingly gave it as their opinion—some that he should be put to death, others that he should be publicly disgraced and fined. The Shaikh was in favour of the capital punishment, and applied to the Emperor to have the sentence confirmed ; but the latter would give no definite reply, and remarked that the Shaikh was responsible for the execution of the law and need not apply to him. The Bráhman meanwhile was kept in prison, the Hindu ladies of the royal household using every endeavour to get him released, while the Emperor, out of regard for the Shaikh, hesitated about yielding to them. At last Abd-un-Nabi, after failing to elicit any definite instructions, returned home and issued orders for the Bráhman's execution. When the news reached the Emperor, he was very angry, and though he allowed Abd-un-Nabi to retain his post till his death, which occurred in 1583, he never took him into favour again.

Jahángír, on his accession to the throne, continued to some extent his father's policy of religious tolerance ; but in the following reign of Sháhjahán, we find Murshid Ali Khán, in the year 1636, made a commander of 2,000 horse, and appointed by the Emperor Governor of Mathurá and Mahá-ban, with express instructions to be zealous in stamping out all rebellion and idolatry. The climax of wanton destruction was, however, attained by Aurangzeb, the Oliver Cromwell of India, who, not content with demolishing the most sacred of its shrines, thought also to destroy even the ancient name of the city by substituting for it Islámpur or Islámabád.

Mathurá was casually connected with two important events in this Emperor's life. Here was born, in 1639, his eldest son, Muhammad Sultán, who expiated the sin of primogeniture in the Oriental fashion by ending his days in a dungeon, as one of the first acts of his father, on his accession to the throne, was to confine him in the fortress of Gwáliar, where he died in 1665. In the last year of the reign of Sháhjahán, Aurangzeb was again at Mathurá, and here established his pretensions to the crown by compassing the death of his brother Murád. This was in 1658, á few days after the momentous battle of Samogarh,* in which the combined forces of the two princes had routed the army of the rightful heir, Dárá. The conquerors encamped together, being apparently on the most cordial and affectionate terms ; and Aurangzeb, protesting that for himself he desired only some sequestered spot where, unharrassed by the toils of government, he might pass his time in prayer and

* Samogarh is a village, one march from Agra, since named, in honour of the event, Fatihábád, 'the place of victory.'

religious meditation, persistently addressed Murád by the royal title as the recognized successor of Sháhjahán. The evening was spent at the banquet; and when the wine cup had begun to circulate freely, the pious Aurangzeb, feigning religious scruples, begged permission to retire. It would have been well for Murád had he also regarded the prohibition of the *Kurán.* The stupor of intoxication soon overpowered him, and he was only restored to consciousness by a contemptuous kick from the foot of the brother who had just declared himself his faithful vassal. That same night the unfortunate Murád, heavily fettered, was sent a prisoner to Delhi and thrown into the fortress of Salím-garh.* He, too, was subsequently removed to Gwáliar and there murdered.

In spite of the agreeable reminiscences which a man of Aurangzeb's temperament must have cherished in connection with a place where an act of such unnatural perfidy had been successfully accomplished, his fanaticism was not a whit mitigated in favour of the city of Mathurá. In 1668, a local rebellion afforded him a fit pretext for a crusade against Hinduism. The insurgents had mustered at Sahora,† a village in the Mahá-ban pargana, where (as we learn from the Maásiri-i-Alamgíri) the Governor Abd-un-Nabi advanced to meet them. "He was at first victorious, and succeeded in killing the ring-leaders; but in the middle of the fight he was struck by a bullet, and died the death of a martyr." It was he who, in the year 1661, had founded the Jama Masjid, which still remains, and is the most conspicuous building in the city which has grown up around it. He was followed in office by Sáff-Shikan Khán; but as he was not able to suppress the revolt, which began to assume formidable dimensions, he was removed at the end of the year 1669, and Hasan Alí Khán appointed Faujdar in his place. The ringleader of the disturbances, a Ját, by name Kokila, who had plundered the Sa'dábád pargana, and was regarded as the instrument of Abd-un-Nabi's death, fell into the hands of the new Governor's Deputy, Shaikh Rázi-ud-dín, and was sent to Agra and there

* Bernier, on whose narrative the above paragraph is founded, calls Salím-garh by the very English-looking name 'Slinger;' a fine illustration of the absurdity of the phonetic system. By phonetic spelling I mean any arbitrary attempt to represent by written characters the sound of a word as pronounced by the voice without reference to its etymology. This would seem to be the most natural use of the term; but as critics have objected, I add this explanation.

† As is always the case when an attempt is made to identify the local names mentioned by any historian who writes in the Persian character, it is extremely uncertain whether Sahora is really the village intended. The word as given in the manuscript begins with *s* and ends with *a*, and has an *r* in the middle; but beyond that much it is impossible to predicate anything with certainty about it.

executed.* A few months earlier, in February of the same year, during the fast of Ramazán, the time when religious bigotry would be most inflamed, Aurangzeb had descended in person on Mathurá. The temple specially marked out for destruction was one built so recently as the reign of Jahángír, at a cost of thirty-three lakhs, by Bir Sinh Deva, Bundela, of Urcha. Beyond all doubt this was the last of the famous shrines of Kesava Deva, of which further mention will be made hereafter. To judge from the language of the author of the Maásir, its demolition was regarded as a death-blow to Hinduism. He writes in the following triumphant strain :—"In a short time, with the help of numerous workmen, this seat of error was utterly broken down. Glory be to God that so difficult an undertaking has been successfully accomplished in the present auspicious reign, wherein so many dens of heathenism and idolatry have been destroyed! Seeing the power of Islam and the efficacy of true religion, the proud Rájás felt their breath burning in their throats and became as dumb as a picture on a wall. The idols, large and small alike, all adorned with costly jewels, were carried away from the heathen shrine and taken to Agra, where they were buried under the steps of Nawáb Kudsia Begam's mosque, so that people might trample upon them for ever." It was from this event that Mathúra was called Islámabád.

In 1707 Aurangzeb died, and shortly after began the rule of the Játs of Bharat-pur.

The founder of this royal house was a robber chief, by name Chúrá-mani, who built two petty forts in the villages of Thún and Sinsini,† a little south of Díg, from which he organized marauding expeditions, and even ventured to harass the rear of the imperial army on the occasion of Aurangzeb's expedition to the Dakhin. This statement is contradicted by Thornton in his Gazetteer, under the word Bharat-pur ; but his reasons for doing so are not very conclusive. He writes :—"Chúrá-mani did not become the leader of the Játs until after the death of Aurangzeb. Besides, the scene of the operations of the Játs was widely remote from that of the disasters of Aurangzeb, which occurred near Ahmad-nagar. According to the Sair-i-Mutá-akhkhirin, during the struggle between Aurangzeb's sons, 'Azam and Muazzim, Chúrá-mani beset the camp of the latter for the purpose of plunder." This correction, if it really is one, is so slight as to be absolutely immaterial ; the army, which was led into the Dakhin

* His son and daughter were both brought up as Muhammadans, and eventually the girl married Shah Kuli, and the boy, who had received the name of Fázil, became famous for his skill in reciting the Kurán.

† From this place the Bharat-pur Rájá's family derives its name of Sinsinwar.

10

by Aurangzeb, was brought back by 'Azam after the Emperor's decease, and both father and son died within four months of each other.

A little later, Jay Sinh of Amber was commissioned by the two Saiyids, then in power at Delhi, to reduce the Ját freebooters. He invested their two strongholds, but could not succeed in making any impression upon them, and accordingly retired : only, however, to return almost immediately ; this time bringing with him a larger army, and also a local informant in the person of Badan Sinh, a younger brother of Chúrá-mani's, who, in consequence of some family feud, had been placed in confinement, from which he had contrived to escape and make his way to Jaypur. Thún was then (1712 A.D.) again invested, and after a siege of six months taken and its fortifications demolished. Chúrá-mani and his son Muhkam fled the country, and Badan Sinh was formally proclaimed at Díg as leader of the Játs, with the title of Thákur.

He is chiefly commemorated in the Mathurá district by the handsome mansion he built for himself at Sahár. This appears to have been his favourite residence in the latter years of his life. Adjoining it is a very large tank, of which one side is faced with stone and the rest left unfinished, the work having probably been interrupted by his death. The house was occupied as a tahsíli under the English Government till the mutiny, when all the records were transferred for greater safety to Chhátá, which has ever since continued the head of the pargana, and the house at Sahár is now unoccupied and falling into ruin. He married into a family seated at Kámar, near Kosi, where also is a large masonry tank, and in connection with it a walled garden containing three Chhattris in memory of Chaudhri Mahá Rám, Ját, and his wife and child. The Chaudhri was the Thákuráni's brother, and it appears that her kinsmen were people of some wealth and importance, as the Castle Hill at Kámar is still crowned with several considerable edifices of brick and stone where they once resided.

For some years before his death, Thákur Badan Sinh had retired altogether from public life. To one of his younger sons, by name Pratáp Sinh,* he had especially assigned the newly erected fort at Wayar, south-west of Bharat-pur, with the adjoining district, while the remainder of the Ját principality was administered by the eldest son, Súraj Mall. On his father's death, Súraj Mall assumed the title of Rája and fixed his capital at Bharat-pur, from which place he had ejected the previous governor, a kinsman,

* Two other sons were named Sobhá Rám and Bír Náráyan.

by name Khema. The matrimonial alliances which he contracted indicate his inferiority to the Rájput princes of the adjoining territories, for one of his wives was a Kurmin, another a Málin, and the remainder of his own caste, Játnis. Yet, even at the commencement of his rule, he had achieved a conspicuous position, since, in 1748, we find him accepting the invitation of the Emperor Ahmad Sháh to join with Holkar, under the general command of the Vazir, Safdar Jang, in suppressing the revolt of the Rohillas. In the subsequent dispute that arose between Safdar Jang and Ghází-ud-din, the grandson of the old Nizám, the former fell into open rebellion and called in the assistance of the Játs, while his rival had recourse to the Mahrattas. Safdar, seeing the coalition against him too strong, withdrew to his vice-royalty of Audh, leaving Súraj Mall to bear alone the brunt of the battle. Bharat-pur was besieged, but had not been invested many days when Ghází-ud-din, suspecting a secret understanding between his nominal allies, the Mahrattas and the Emperor, discontinued his operations against the Játs and returned hastily to Delhi, where he deposed Ahmad Sháh and raised Alamgír II. to the throne in his stead. This was in 1754.

Three years later, when the army of Ahmad Sháh Duráni from Kandahár appeared before Delhi, Ghází-ud-din, by whose indiscretion the invasion had been provoked, was admitted to pardon, in consideration of the heavy tribute which he undertook to collect from the Doáb. Sardár Jahán Khán was despatched on a like errand into the Ját territory; but finding little to be gained there, as the entire populace had withdrawn into their numerous petty fortresses and his foraging parties were cut off by their sudden sallies, he fell back upon the city of Mathurá, which he not only plundered of all its wealth, but further visited with a wholesale massacre of the inhabitants.

In the second invasion of the Duráni, consequent upon the assassination of the Emperor Alamgír II. in 1759, the infamous Ghází-ud-din again appeared at the gates of Bharat-pur; this time not with a hostile army, but as a suppliant for protection. By his unnatural persuasions a powerful Hindu confederacy was formed to oppose the progress of the Muhammadan, but was scattered for ever in the great battle of Pánipat, in January, 1761, when the dreams of Mahratta supremacy were finally dissolved. Súraj Mall, foreseeing the inevitable result, withdrew his forces before the battle, and falling unexpectedly upon Agra, ejected from it the garrison of his late allies and adopted it as his own favourite residence. Meanwhile, Sháh Alam was recognized by the Duráni as the rightful heir to the throne, but continued to hold his poor semblance of a Court at Allahabad ; and, at Delhi, his son Mirza Jawán Bakht was placed in nominal charge of the Government under the active protectorate of the Rohilla, Najíb-ud-daula. With this administrator of imperial power, Súraj Mall, emboldened by past success, now essayed to try his strength. He put forth a claim to the Faujdárship of Farrukh-nagar ; and when the envoy, sent from Delhi to confer with him on the subject, demurred to the transfer, he dismissed him most unceremoniously and at once advanced with an army to Shahdara on the Hindan, only six miles from the capital. Here, in bravado, he was amusing himself in the chase, accompanied by only his personal retinue, when he was surprised by a flying squadron of the enemy and put to death. His army coming leisurely up behind, under the command of his son Jawáhir Sinh, was charged by the Mughals, bearing the head of Súraj Mall on a horseman's lance as their standard, the first indication to the son of his father's death. The shock was too much for the Játs, who were put to flight, but still continued for three months hovering about Delhi in concert with Holkar. This was in 1764.*

In spite of this temporary discomfiture, the Játs were now at the zenith of their power ; and Jawáhir had not been a year on the throne when he resolved to provoke a quarrel with the Rája of Jaypur. Accordingly, without any previous intimation, he marched his troops through Jaypur territory with the ostensible design of visiting the holy lake of Pushkara. There his vanity was gratified by the sovereign of Marwár, Rájá Bijay Sinh, who met him on terms of brotherly equality ; but he received warning from Jaypur that if he passed through Amber territory on his return, it would be considered a hostile aggression. As this was no more than he expected, he paid no regard to the caution. A desperate conflict ensued on his homeward route (1765 A.D.), which resulted in the victory of the Kachhwáhas, but a victory accompanied with the death of almost every chieftain of note. Soon after, Jawáhir Sinh was murdered at Agra, at the instigation, as is supposed, of the Jaypur Rájá.

Súraj Mall had left five sons, *viz.*, Jawáhir Sinh, Ratn Sinh, Naval Sinh, and Ranjit Sinh, and also an adopted son, Hardeva Bakhsh, whom he is said to have picked up in the woods one day when hunting. On the death of Jawáhir, Ratn succeeded, but his rule was of very short duration. A pretended

* A magnificent cenotaph was erected by Jawáhir Sinh in honour of his father on the margin of the Kusam Sarovar, an artificial lake a short distance from Gobardhan, and will be described in connection with that town.

alchemist from Brindá-ban had obtained large sums of money from the credulous prince to prepare a process for the transmutation of the meaner metals into gold. When the day for the crucial experiment arrived and detection had become inevitable, he assassinated his victim and fled.*

His brother, Naval Sinh, succeeded, nominally as guardian for his infant nephew, Kesari, but virtually as Rájá. The Mahrattas had now (1768) recovered from the disastrous battle of Pánipat, and, re-asserting their old claim to tribute, invaded first Jaypur and then Bharat-pur, and mulcted both territories in a very considerable sum. They then entered into an understanding with the Delhi Government which resulted in the restoration of Sháh Alam to his ancestral capital. But as the only line of policy which they consistently maintained was the fomentation of perpetual quarrels, by which the strength of all parties in the State might be exhausted, they never remained long faithful to one side; and, in the year 1772, we find them fighting with the Játs against the Imperialists. Naval Sinh, or, according to some accounts, his brother and successor, Ranjit Sinh, laid claim to the fort of Ballabhgarh held by another Ját chieftain. The latter applied to Delhi for help and a force was despatched for his relief; but it was too weak to resist the combined armies of Sindhia and Bharat-pur, and was driven back in disorder. The Mahrattas then pushed on to Delhi; but finding the Commander-in-Chief, Niyáz Khán, ready to receive them, they, with incomparable versatility, at once made terms with him and even joined him in an expedition to Rohilkhand.

Meanwhile, the Játs, thus lightly deserted, espoused the cause of Najaf's unsuccessful rival, Zábita Khán. But this was a most ill-judged move on their part: their troops were not only repulsed before Delhi, but their garrison was also ejected from Agra,† which they had held for the last 13 years since its occupation by Suraj Mall after the battle of Pánipat in 1761. From Agra the Vazir Najaf Khán hastily returned in the direction of the capital, and found Ranjit Sinh and the Játs encamped near Hodal. Dislodged from this position, they fell back upon Kot-ban and Kosi, which they occupied for nearly a fort-

* It was probably this Ratn Sinh, for whom was commenced the large chhattrí near the Madan Mohan temple at Brindá-ban, where it is still to be seen in its unfinished state, as left at the time of his sudden death.

† The commander of the Ját garrison in Agra was Dán Sahay, brother-in-law (sála) of Naval Sinh.

night, and then finally withdrew towards Díg ; but at Barsána were overtaken by the Vazir and a pitched battle ensued. The Ját infantry, 5,000 strong, were commanded by Sumroo, or, to give him his proper name, Walter Reinhard, an adventurer who had first taken service under Ranjit's father, Suraj Mall.* The ranks of the Imperialists were broken by his impetuous attack, and the Játs, feeling assured of victory, were following in reckless disorder, when the enemy rallied from their sudden panic, turned upon their pursuers, who were too scattered to offer any solid resistance, and effectually routed them. They contrived, however, to secure a retreat to Díg,† while the town of Barsána, which was then a very wealthy place, was given over to plunder, and several of the stately mansions recently erected almost destroyed in the search for hidden treasure.

---

* He was a native of the Electorate of Treves and came out to India as a carpenter in the French navy. After serving under several native chiefs, but staying with none of them long, he joined one Gregory, an Armenian, who was high in the favour of Mir Kásim, the Nawáb of Bengal. It was after the fall of Mongir that he did his employer the base service of putting to death all the English prisoners who had been collected at Patna ; a deed for which his name will ever be held in abhorrence. He next joined the Bharat-pur chief, and from him finally went over to Najaf Khán, from whom he received a grant of the pargana of Sardhana, then valued at six lakhs a year, and to whom he remained faithful for the rest of his life. He died in 1778, and was buried in the cemetery at Agra, where is also a church that he built, now disused, adjoining the new cathedral. The Begam, who had lived with him (she is said to have been originally a Kasmírí dancing girl) was recognized as his widow and succeeded to all his estate. In 1781 she was received into the Catholic Church, and in 1792 married a French adventurer, a M. Le Vaisseau. He, however, made himself so unpopular that her people revolted, under the leadership of a son of Reinhard's, Zafar-yáb Khán. By an artifice, that she practised upon her husband, the latter was induced to commit suicide, and the disturbance was soon after quelled by the intervention of one of her old servants, the famous George Thomas. In 1802 Zafar-yáb died, leaving a daughter, whom the Begam gave in marriage to a Mr. Dyce, an officer in her army. The issue was a son and two daughters, of whom the one married Captain Rose Troup, the other the Marquis of Briona. The son, David Ochterlony Dyce Sombre, was adopted by the Begam, and on her death in 1836, succeeded to the estate. He married Mary Anne, the daughter of Viscount St. Vincent, and died at Paris, in 1851. His widow, in 1862, married the Hon'ble George C. Weld Forester, who has now succeeded his brother as third Baron Forester. The Begam by her will left to the Catholic Cathedrals of Calcutta, Bombay, Madras, and Agra, Rs. 32,000 Rs. 31 800, Rs. 31,000, and Rs. 28,700, respectively ; to the Sardhana Cathedral which she herself had built, Rs. 95,600 ; to the school or seminary there, called St. John's College, Rs. 95,600. to the poor of the place Rs. 47,800, and to the Merath Chapel, also of her foundation, Rs. 12,500 ; The administration of the Sardhana endowments has for several years past formed the subject of a dispute between the Roman Catholic Bishop of Agra, who had for some time acted as sole trustee, and Lady Forester, who, as the Begam's legal representative, claims to act as a trustee also : until it is settled the interest on the money cannot be drawn.

† According to local tradition, Naval Sinh died some 20 days after the battle of Barsána

Díg was not reduced till March of the following year, 1776; the garrison escaping to the neighbouring castle of Kumbhír. The value of the spoil taken is said to have amounted to six lakhs of rupees. The whole of the country also was reduced to subjection, and it was only at the intercession of the Ráni Kishori, the widow of Súraj Mall, that the conqueror allowed Ranjít Sinh to retain the fort of Bharat-pur with an extent of territory yielding an annual income of nine lakhs.

In 1782, the great minister, Najaf Khán, died; and in 1786 Sindhia, who had been recognized as his successor in the administration of the empire, proceeded to demand arrears of tribute from the Rájputs of Jaypur. His claim was partly satisfied; but finding that he persisted in exacting the full amount, the Rájás of Jaypur, Jodh-pur, and Uday-pur, joined by other minor chiefs, organized a formidable combination against him. The armies met at Lalsot, and a battle ensued which extended over three days, but without any decisive result, till some 14,000 of Sindhia's infantry, who were in arrears of pay, went over to the enemy. In consequence of this defection, the Mahrattas fell back upon the Játs and secured the alliance of Ranjit Sinh by the restoration of Díg, which had been held by the Emperor since its capture by Najaf Khán in 1776, and by the cession of eleven parganas yielding a revenue of ten lakhs of rupees. The main object of the new allies was to raise the siege of Agra, which was then being invested by Ismail Beg, the Imperial captain, in concert with Zábita Khán's son, the infamous Ghulám Kádir. In a battle that took place near Fatihpur Síkri, the Játs and Mahrattas met a repulse, and were driven back upon Bharat-pur; but later in the same year 1788, being reinforced by troops from the Dakkhin under Ráná Khán, a brother of the officer in command of the besieged garrison, they finally raised the blockade, and the province of Agra again acknowledged Sindhia as its master.

Ghulám Kádir had previously removed to Delhi and was endeavouring to persuade the Emperor to break off intercourse with the Mahrattas. Failing in this, he dropped all disguise and commenced firing upon the palace, and having in a few days taken possession of the city, he indulged in the most brutal excesses, and after insulting and torturing his miserable and defenceless sovereign in every conceivable way, completed the tragedy by, at last, with his own dagger, robbing him of his eye-sight. Sindhia, who had before been urgently summoned from Mathurá, one of his favourite residences, on hearing of these horrors, sent a force to the relief of the city. Ghulám Kádir, whose atrocities had disgusted all his adherents, fled to Merath, and endeavouring to escape from there at night alone on horseback, fell into a well from which he was unable to extricate himself. There he was found on the following morning by a Bráhman peasant by name Bhikha, who had him seized and taken to the Mahratta camp. Thence he was despatched to Sindhia at Mathurá, who first sent him through the bazar on an ass with his head to the tail, and then had him mutilated of all his members one by one, his tongue being first torn out, and then his eyes, and subsequently his nose, ears and hands cut off. In this horrible condition he was despatched to Delhi; but to anticipate his death from exhaustion, which seemed imminent, he was hanged on a tree by the roadside. It is said that his barbarous treatment of the Emperor, for which he suffered such a condign penalty, was in revenge for an injury inflicted upon him when a handsome child by Shah Alam, who converted him into a haram page.

It was in 1803 that Mathurá passed under British rule and became a military station on the line of frontier, which was then definitely extended to the Jamuna. This was at the termination of the successful war with Daulat Ráo Sindhia; when the independent French State, that had been established by Perron, and was beginning to assume formidable dimensions, had been extinguished by the fall of Aligarh; while the protectorate of the nominal sovereign of Delhi, transferred by the submission of the capital, invested the administration of the Company with the prestige of Imperial sanction. At the same time a treaty was concluded with Ranjít Sinh, who with 5,000 horse had joined General Lake at Agra and thereby contributed to Sindhia's defeat. In return for this service he received a part of the districts of Kishangarh, Katháwar, Rewári, Gokul and Sahár.

In September of the following year Mathurá was held for a few days by the troops of Holkar Jasavant Ráo; but on the arrival of reinforcements from Agra, was re-occupied by the British finally and permanently. Meanwhile, Holkar had advanced upon Delhi, but the defence was so gallantly conducted by Ochterlony that the assault was a signal failure. His army broke up into two divisions, one of which was pursued to the neighbourhood of Farrukhábád, and there totally dispersed by General Lake; while the other was overtaken by General Fraser between Díg and Gobardhan and defeated with great slaughter. In this latter engagement the brilliant victory was purchased by the death of the officer in command, who was brought into Mathurá fatally wounded, and survived only a few days. He was buried in the Cantonment Cemetery, where a monument* is erected to his memory with the following inscription :—

"Sacred to the memory of Major-General Henry Fraser, of His Majesty's 11th Regiment of Foot, who commanded the British Army at the battle of Deig on the 13th of November, 1804, and by his judgment and valour achieved an important and glorious victory. He died in consequence of a wound he received when leading on the troops, and was interred here on the 25th of November, 1804, in the 40th year of his age. The army lament his loss with the deepest sorrow ; his country regards his heroic conduct with grateful admiration ; history will record his fame and perpetuate the glory of his illustrious deeds."

Holkar, who had fled for refuge to the fort of Bharat-pur, was pursued by General Lake and his surrender demanded ; but Ranjít refused to give him up. The fort was thereupon besieged ; Ranjít made a memorable defence, and repelled four assaults with a loss to the besiegers of 3,000 men, but finally made overtures for peace, which were accepted on the 4th of May, 1805. A new treaty was concluded, by which he agreed to pay an indemnity of twenty lakhs of rupees, seven of which were subsequently remitted, and was guaranteed in the territories which he held previously to the accession of the British Government. The parganas granted to him in 1803 were resumed.

Ranjít died that same year, leaving four sons,—Randhír, Baladeva, Harideva, and Lachhman. He was succeeded by the eldest, Randhír, who died in 1822, leaving the throne to his brother, Baladeva.† After a rule of about 18 months he died, leaving a son, Balavant, then six years of age. He was recognized by the British Government, but his cousin, Durjan Sál, who had also advanced claims to the succession on Randhír's death, rose up against him and had him cast into prison. Sir David Ochterlony, the Resident at Delhi, promptly moved out a force in support of the rightful heir, but their march was stopped by a peremptory order from Lord Amherst, who, in accordance with the disastrous policy of non-interference which was then in vogue, considered that the recognition of the heir-apparent during the life of his father did not impose on the Government any obligation to maintain him in opposition to the presumed wishes of the chiefs and people. Vast preparations were made, with the secret support of the neighbouring Rájput and Mahratta States, and at last, when the excitement threatened a protracted war, the Governor-General reluctantly confirmed the eloquent representations of

* To judge from the extreme clumsiness both of the design and execution, the irregular spacing of the inscription, and the quaint shape of some of the letters, this must have been one of the very first attempts of a native mason to work on European instructions.

† Randhir Sinh and Baladeva Sinh are commemorated by two handsome chhattries on the margin of the Mánasi Ganga at Gobardhan.

Sir Charles Metcalfe and consented to the deposition of the usurper. After a siege that extended over nearly six weeks, Bharat-pur was stormed by Lord Combermere on the 18th of January, 1826. Durjan Sál was taken prisoner to Allahabad, and the young Mahárája established on the throne under the regency of his mother and the superintendence of a political agent.* He died in 1853 and was succeeded by his only son, Jasavant Singh, the present sovereign, who enjoys a revenue of about Rs. 21,00,000 derived from a territory of 1,974 square miles in extent, with a population of 650,000.

With 1804 began a period of undisturbed peace and rapid growth of prosperity for the city of Mathurá, which in 1832 was made the capital of a new district, then formed out of parts of the old districts of Agra and Sa'dábád; nor does any event claim notice till we come down to the year 1857. It was on the 14th of May in that eventful year that news arrived of the mutiny at Merath. Mr. Mark Thornhill, who was then Magistrate and Collector of the district, with Ghulám Husain as Deputy Collector, sent an immediate requisition for aid to Bharat-pur. Captain Nixon, the political agent, accompanied by Chaudhari Ratn Sinh, chief of the five Sardárs, and Gobardhan Sinh, the Faujdár, came with a small force to Kosi on the northern border of the district and there stayed for a time in readiness to check the approach of the Mewáris of Gurgáon and the other rebels from Delhi. Mr. Thornhill had meanwhile removed to Chhátá, a small town on the high-road some eight miles short of Kosi, as being a place which was at once a centre of disaffection, and at the same time possessed in its fortified *saráe* a stronghold capable of long resistance against it. The first outbreak, however, was at Mathurá itself. The sum of money then in the district treasury amounted to rather more than 5½ lakhs, and arrangements had been made for its despatch to Agra, with the exception of one lakh kept in reserve for local requirements. The escort consisted of a company of soldiers from the cantonments, supported by another company which had come over from Agra for the purpose.† The chests were being put

* The Ráni of Balavant Sinh was a native of Dhádhu in the Sa'dábád pargana, where is a garden with a double chhatri erected by her in memory of two of her relatives.

† There were present at the time Mr. Elliot Colvin, the son of the Lieutenant-Governor, who had been sent from Agra to supersede Mr. Clifford, laid up by severe fever; Lieutenant Graham, one of the officers of the Treasury Guard; Mr. Joyce, the head clerk, and two of his subordinates, by name Hashman. As they were cut off from the civil station by the rebels, who occupied the intermediate ground, they made their way into the city to the Seth, by whom they were helped on to Mr. Thornhill's camp at Chhátá. Mr. Nicholls, the Chaplain, with his wife and child and a Native Christian nurse, took refuge in the Collector's house, and waited there for some time in hopes of being joined by the others; but on hearing that the jail was broken open, they fled to Agra.

on the carts, when one of the súbadárs suddenly called out '*hoshiyár, sipáhi,*' 'look alive, my man,' which was evidently a preconcerted signal; and at once a shot was fired, which killed Lieutenant Burlton, commandant of the escort, dead on the spot.* The rebels than seized the treasure, together with the private effects of the residents in the station, which were also ready to be transported to Agra, and went off in a body to the Magistrate's Court-house, which they set on fire, destroying all the records, and then took the road to Delhi. But first they broke open the jail and carried all the prisoners with them as far as the city, where they got smiths to strike off their fetters. Besides Lieutenant Burlton, one of the treasury officials also was killed. An attempt was made to check the rebel body as it marched through Chhátá, but it was quite ineffectual, and on the 31st of May they entered the town of Kosi. There, after burning down the Customs bungalow and pillaging the police-station, they proceeded to plunder the tahsíli. But some Rs. 150 was all they could find in the treasury, and most of the records also escaped them. The townspeople and most of the adjoining villages remained well-affected to the Government; and subsequently, as a reward, one year's revenue demand was remitted and a grant of Rs. 50 made to each headman. Mr. Thornhill and the other Europeans with him now determined to abandon their position at Chhátá and return to Mathurá, where they took refuge in the city in the house of Seth Lakhmi Chand. While there a report came that the Játs had set up a Rája, one Devi Sinh, at Rayá, on the other side of the Jamuná. His reign was of no long continuance, for the Kota Contingent, which happened to be on the spot at the time, seized and hanged him with little ceremony. But as soon as this was accomplished, they themselves mutinied; and Mr. Thornhill, who had accompanied them to Rayá, had to make a hasty flight back to Mathurá, bringing some small treasure in the buggy with him.

On the 6th of July, the mutineers of Morár and Nimach, on their retreat from Agra, entered the city. In anticipation of their arrival, Mr. Thornhill, disguised as a native and accompanied by a trusty jamadár, Diláwar Khán, started to flee to Agra. When they reached Aurangabad, only some four miles on the way, they found the whole country on both sides of the road in

* The site of the old Court-house is now utterly out of the beaten track and is all overgrown with dense vegetation, among which may be seen a plain but very substantial stone table tomb, with the following inscription: "Sacred to the memory of Lieutenant P. H. C. Burlton, 67th Native Infantry, who was shot by a detachment of his regiment and of the 11th Native Infantry near this spot on the 30th of May, 1857. This tomb is erected by his brother officers."

the possession of the rebels. The men whom the Seth had despatched as an escort took fright and decamped ; but the jamadár, by his adroit answers to all enquiries, was enabled to divert suspicion and bring Mr. Thornhill safely through to Agra. On the suppression of the disturbances, he received, as a reward for his loyalty, a small piece of land on the Brindá-ban road, just outside Mathurá, called after the name of a Bairági who had once lived there, Dudhádhári.

Though the rebels stayed two days in Mathurá before they passed on to Delhi, the city was not given up to general plunder, partly in consequence of the prudent management of Seth Mangi Lál, who levied a contribution, according to their means, on all the principal inhabitants. At this time Seth Lakhmi Chand was at Díg, but the greater part of his establishment remained behind and rendered Government the most valuable assistance by the despatch of intelligence. Order in the city was chiefly maintained by Mír Imdád Ali Khán, tahsíldár of Kosi, who had been specially appointed Deputy Collector.

On the 26th of September, the rebels, in their retreat from Delhi, again passed through Mathurá. Their stay on this occasion lasted for a week, and great oppression was practised on the inhabitants, both here and in the neighbouring town of Brindá-ban. They were only diverted from general pillage by the influence of one of their own leaders, a súbadár from Nimach, by name Híra Sinh, who prevailed upon them to spare the Holy City. For a few days there was a show of regular government ; some of the chief officers in the Collector's court, such as the Sadr Kánungo, Rahmat-ullah, the Sarishtadár, Manohar Lál, and Wazír Ali, one of the muharrirs, were taken by force and compelled to issue the orders of the new administrators ; while Maulvi Karámat Ali was proclaimed in the Jama Masjid as the Viceroy of the Delhi Emperor. It would seem that he also was an involuntary tool in their hands, as he was subsequently put on his trial, but acquitted. He is since dead. It is said that during their stay in the city the rebels found their most obliging friends among the Mathuriya Chaubés, who, perhaps, more than any others, have grown rich and fat under the tolerance of British rule. After threatening Brindá-ban with their cannon and levying a contribution on the inhabitants, they moved away to Háthras and Bareli. Mir Imdád Ali and the Seth returned from Bharat-pur ; and in October Mr. Thornhill arrived from Agra with a company of troops, which in the following month he marched up to Chhátá. There the rebel zamindárs had taken possession of the fortified *sarác*, and one of its bastions had to be blown up before an entry could be effected: at the same time the town was set on fire and partially destroyed, and twenty-two of the leading men were shot. A few days previously, Mir Imdád Ali with Nathu Lál, tahsíldár of Sahár, had gone up into the Kosi pargana and restored order among the Gújars there, who alone of all the natives of the district had been active promoters of disaffection. While engaged in their suppression, Imdád Ali received a gun-shot wound in the chest, but fortunately it had no fatal result. He is now Deputy Collector of Murádabad, with a special additional allowance of Rs. 150 per mensem, and has been made a C.S.I. By the end of November general tranquillity was restored; but it was not till July, 1858, that the treasury was transferred from the Seth's house in the city to the Police lines in the civil station.* In Christmas week of the following year, 1859, the Viceroy held a Darbár, in which many honours were conferred upon different individuals, and in particular the ten villages, which the Gújars had forfeited by their open rebellion, were bestowed upon Rájá Gobind Sinh of Háthras, in acknowledgment of his distinguished loyalty and good services. The value of this grant has been largely diminished by the persistent lawlessness of the ejected Gújars, who have always sullenly resented the loss of their estates.

* Here it remained till after the completion, in 1861, of the new Court-house and district offices, which, with important results to archæological research, as will hereafter be shown, were rebuilt on a new site.

CHAPTER III.

THE STORY OF KRISHNA, THE TUTELARY DIVINITY OF MATHURÁ.

Of all the sacred places in India, none enjoys a greater popularity than the capital of Braj, the holy city of Mathurá. For nine months in the year festival follows upon festival in rapid succession, and the gháts and temples are daily thronged with new troops of way-worn pilgrims. So great is the sanctity of the spot that its panegyrists do not hesitate to declare that a single day spent at Mathurá is more meritorious than a lifetime passed at Banáras. All this celebrity is due to the fact of its being the reputed birth-place of the demi-god Krishna; hence it must be a matter of some interest to ascertain who this famous hero was, and what were the acts by which he achieved immortality.

The attempt to extract a grain of historical truth from an accumulation of mythological legend is an interesting, but not very satisfactory, undertaking: there is always a risk that the theorist's kernel of fact may be itself as imaginary as the accretions which envelop it. However, reduced to its simplest elements, the story of Krishna runs as follows :—At a very remote period, a branch of the great Jádav clan settled on the banks of the Jamuná and made Mathurá their capital city. Here Krishna was born. At the time of his birth, Ugrasen, the rightful occupant of the throne, had been deposed by his own son, Kansa, who, relying on the support of Jarásandha, King of Magadha, whose daughter he had married, ruled the country with a rod of iron, outraging alike both gods and men. Krishna, who was a cousin of the usurper, but had been brought up in obscurity and employed in the tending of cattle, raised the standard of revolt, defeated and slew Kansa, and restored Ugrasen to the throne of his ancestors.

All authorities lay great stress on the religious persecution that had prevailed under the tyranny of Kansa, from which fact it has been surmised that he was a convert to Buddhism, zealous in the propagation of his adopted faith; and that Krishna owes much of his renown to the gratitude of the Bráhmans, who, under his championship, recovered their ancient influence. If, however, 1000 B. C. is accepted as the approximate date of the Great War in which Krishna took part, it is clear that his contemporary, Kansa, cannot have been a Buddhist, since the founder of that religion, according to the now most generally accepted chronology, died in the year 477 B. C., being then about 80 years of age.

Possibly he may have been a Jaini, for the antiquity of that religion* is now thoroughly established; it has even been conjectured that Buddha himself was a disciple of Mahavíra, the last of the Jaini Tirthankaras.† Or the struggle may have been between the votaries of Siva and Vishnu; in which case Krishna, the apostle of the latter faction, would find a natural enemy in the King of Kashmír, a country where Saivism has always predominated. On this hypothesis, Kansa was the conservative monarch, and Krishna the innovator: a position which has been inverted by the poets, influenced by the political events of their own times.

To avenge the death of his son-in-law, Jarásandha marched an army against Mathurá, and was supported by the powerful king of some western country, who is thence styled Kála-Yavana: for *Yavana* in Sanskrit, while it corresponds originally to the Arabic *Yúnán* (Ionia) denotes secondarily—like *Viláyat* in the modern vernacular—any foreign, and specially any western, country. The actual personage was probably the King of Kashmír, Gonanda I., who is known to have accompanied Jarásandha; though the description would be more applicable to one of the Bactrian sovereigns of the Panjáb. It is true they had not penetrated into India till some hundreds of years after Krishna; but their power was well established at the time when the Mahábhárat was written to record his achievements: hence the anachronism. Similarly, in the Bhágavat Purána, which was written after the Muhammadan invasion, the description of the Yavana king is largely coloured by the author's feelings towards the only western power with which he was acquainted. Originally, as above stated, the word denoted the Greeks, and the Greeks only.‡ But the Greeks were the foremost, the most dreaded of all the Mlechhas (*i. e.*, Barbarians) and thus Yavana came to be applied to the most prominent Mlechha power for the time being, whatever it might happen to be. When the Muhammadans trod in the steps of the Greeks, they became the chief Mlechhas, and they also were consequently styled Yavanas.

* The oldest Jain *inscription* that has as yet been discovered is one from the hill Indragiri at Srávana Belgola in the South of India. It records an emigration of Jainis from Ujayin under the leadership of Swámi Bhadra Bahu, accounted the last of the Sruta Kevalis, who was accompanied by Chandragupta, King of Pataliputra. As the inscription gives a list of Bhadra Bahu's successors, it is clearly not contemporary with the events which it records; but it may be inferred from the archaic form of the letters that it dates from the third century B. C.

† More recent research, however, has revealed the fact that the Gotama Swámi, who was Mahávira's pupil, was not a Kshatriya by caste, as was Sakya Muni, the Buddha, but a Brahman of the well-known Gautama family, whose personal name was Indra-bhúti.

‡ This, however, is stoutly denied by Dr. Rajendra Lal Mittra. See his *Indo-Aryans.*

Krishna eventually found it desirable to abandon Mathurá, and with the whole clan of Yádavs retired to the Bay of Kachh. There he founded the flourishing city of Dwáraká, which at some later period was totally submerged in the sea. While he was reigning at Dwáraká, the great war for the throne of Indraprastha (Delhi) arose between the five sons of Pándu and Durjodhan, the son of Dhritaráshtra. Krishna allied himself with the Pándav princes, who were his cousins on the mother's side, and was the main cause of their ultimate triumph. Before its commencement Krishna had invaded Magadha, marching by a circuitous route through Tirhút and so taking Jarásandha by surprise: his capital was forced to surrender, and he himself slain in battle. Still, after his death, Karna, a cousin of Krishna's of illegitimate birth, was placed on the throne of Mathurá and maintained there by the influence of the Kauravas, Krishna's enemies: a clear proof that the latter's retirement to Dwáraká was involuntary.

Whether the above narrative has or has not any historical foundation, it is certain that Krishna was celebrated as a gallant warrior prince for many ages before he was metamorphosed into the amatory swain who now, under the title of Kanhaiya, is worshipped throughout India. He is first mentioned in the Mahábhárat, the most voluminous of all Sanskrit poems, consisting in the printed edition of 91,000 couplets. There he figures simply as the King of Dwáraká and ally of the Pándavs; nor in the whole length of the poem, of which he is to a great extent the hero, is any allusion whatever made to his early life, except in one disputed passage. Hence it may be presumed that his boyish frolics at Mathurá and Brindá-ban, which now alone dwell in popular memory, are all subsequent inventions. They are related at length in the Harivansa, which is a comparatively modern sequel to the Mahábhárat,* and with still greater circumstantiality in some of the later Puránas, which probably in their present form date no further back than the tenth century after Christ. So rapid has been the development of the original idea when once planted in the congenial soil of the sensuous East, that while in none of the more genuine Puránas, even those specially devoted to the inculcation of Vaishnava doctrines, is so much as the name mentioned of his favourite mistress, Rádhá: she now is jointly enthroned with him in every shrine and claims a full half of popular devotion. Among ordinary Hindus the recognized authority for his life and exploits is

* Though many episodes of later date have been interpolated, the composition of the main body of the Mahábhárat may with some confidence be referred to the second or third century before Christ.

Descent of Krishna through his father, Vasudeva, from the Súrajvansí Kshatriyas.

From the patriarch Ikshváku, generated by a *sneeze* of the Supreme Being, descended at a long interval

Madhu, giant king of Madhu-vana.

Haryasva, banished king of Ajodhya, founder of Gobardhan. = Madhumati.

Lavana, slain by Satrughna.

Mádhava.

Bhíma (annexes Mathurá).

Andhaka.

Revati.

Visvagarbha.

Vasu, or Súra.

Vasudeva = Devaki.

The Sun-God = Prithá or Kunti. = Pándu.

Suprabhá or Sruta-srava. = Dama-Ghosha, Rájá of Chedí.

Krishna.

Karna.

Yudhisthir.

Bhíma.

Arjuna.

Sisupál.

Descent of Krishna through his mother, Devaki, from the Yádava clan of Soma-vansi Kshatriyas.

Soma, the Moon-God, by Tárá, 'the bright star,' whom he stole away from Vrihaspati, had a son Budha. married to Ilá. From this union sprang Pururavas = Urvasi, 'the dawn.'

Ayus.

Nahusha.

Yayáti.

Yadu.

Vidarbha.

Andhaka.

Abhijit.

Ahuka.

Devaka.

Devaki = Vasudeva = Rohiní.

Krishna = Rukmini, daughter of Bhíshmaka, King of Vidardha.

Pradyumna = a daughter of Rukmin, the brother of Rukmini.

Aniruddha = Ushá.

Vajra, who is generally said to have been crowned King of Mathurá on Kríshna's death. But this belief rests on a verse in the Vishnu Purána, where for Mathurá other MSS.—preferably as it would seem from the context—read Indra-prastha, or Hastinapura. The more unscientific native philologers are disposed to derive from Vajra the name of the country, Vraja (Braj).

Balaráma = Revatí.

Ugrasen, King of Mathurá.

Kansa = Rájivalochana, daughter of Jarásandha, King of Magadha.

the Bhágavat Purána,* or rather its tenth Book, which has been translated into every form of the modern vernacular. The Hindi version, entitled the Prem Ságar, is the one held in most repute. In constructing the following legend of Krishna, in his popular character as the tutelary divinity of Mathurá, the Vishnu Purána has been adopted as the basis of the narrative, while many supplementary incidents have been extracted from the Bhágavat, and occasional references made to the Harivansa.

In the days when Ráma was king of Ajodhyá, there stood near the bank of the Jamuná a dense forest, once the stronghold of the terrible giant Madhu, who called it after his own name, Madhu-ban. On his death it passed into the hand of his son, Lavana, who in the pride of his superhuman strength sent an insolent challenge to Ráma, provoking him to single combat. The god-like hero disdained the easy victory for himself, but, to relieve the world of such an oppressor, sent his youngest brother, Satrughna, who vanquished and slew the giant, hewed down the wood in which he had entrenched himself, and on its site† founded the city of Mathurá. The family of Bhoja, a remote descendant of the great Jadu, the common father of all the Jádav race, occupied the throne for many generations. The last of the line was King Ugrasen. In his house Kansa was born, and was nurtured by the king as his own son, though in truth he had no earthly father, but was the great demon Kálanemi incarnate. As soon as he came to man's estate he deposed the aged monarch, seated himself on the throne, and filled the city with carnage and desolation. The priests and sacred cattle were ruthlessly massacred and the temples of the gods defiled with blood. Heaven was besieged with prayers for deliverance from such a monster, nor were the prayers unheared. A supernatural voice declared to Kansa that an avenger would be born in the person of the eighth son of his kinsman, Vasudeva. Now, Vasudeva had married Devaki, a niece of King Ugrasen, and was living away from the court in retirement at the hill of Gobardhan. In the hope of defeating the prediction, Kansa immediately summoned them to Mathurá and there kept them closely watched.‡ From

* The Bhágavat is written in a more elegant style than any of the other Puránas, and is traditionally ascribed to the grammarian Bopadeva, who flourished at the Court of Hemádri, Rájá of Devagiri or Daulatabad, in the twelfth or thirteenth century after Christ.

† The present Madhu-ban is near the village of Maholi, some five miles from Mathurá and from the bank of the Jamuná. The site, however, as now recognized, must be very ancient, since it is the *ban* which has given its name to the village ; Maholi being a corruption of the original form, Madhupuri.

‡ The site of their prison-house, called the Kárá-grah, or more commonly Janm-bhúmi, *i. e.*, 'birth-place,' is still marked by a small temple in Mathurá near the Potara-kund.

year to year, as each successive child was born, it was taken and delivered to the tyrant, and by him consigned to death. When Devaki became pregnant for the seventh time, the embryo was miraculously transferred to the womb of Rohini, another wife of Vasudeva, living at Gokul, on the opposite bank of the Jamuná, and a report was circulated that the mother had miscarried from the effects of her long imprisonment and constant anxiety. The child thus marvellously preserved was first called Sankarshana,* but afterwards received the name of Balarám or Baladeva, under which he has become famous to all posterity.

Another year elapsed, and on the eighth of the dark fortnight of the month of Bhádon† Devaki was delivered of her eighth son, the immortal Krishna. Vasudeva took the babe in his arms and, favoured by the darkness of the night and the direct interposition of heaven, passed through the prison guards, who were charmed to sleep, and fled with his precious burden to the Jamuná. It was then the season of the rains, and the mighty river was pouring down a wild and resistless flood of waters. But he fearlessly stepped into the eddying torrent: at the first step that he advanced the wave reached the foot of the child slumbering in his arms; then, marvellous to relate, the waters were stilled at the touch of the divine infant and could rise no higher,‡ and in a moment of time the wayfarer had traversed the torrent's broad expanse and emerged in safety on the opposite shore.§ Here, he met Nanda, the chief herdsman of Gokul, whose wife, Jasodá, at that very time had given birth to a daughter, no earthly child, however, save in semblance, but the delusive power Joganidrá. Vasudeva dexterously exchanged the two infants and, returning, placed the female child in the bed of Devaki. At once it began to cry. The guards rushed in and carried it off to the tyrant. He, assured that it was the very child of fate, snatched it furiously from their hands and dashed it to the

* Signifying 'extraction,' *i. e.*, from his mother's womb. The word is also explained to mean 'drawing furrows with the plough,' and would thus be paralleled by Balaráma's other names of Haláyudha, Haladhara, and Halabhrit.

† On this day is celebrated the annual festival in honour of Krishna's birth, called Janm Ashtami.

‡ This incident is popularly commemorated by a native toy called 'Vásudeva Katora' of which great numbers are manufactured at Mathurá. It is a brass cup with the figure of a man in it carrying a child at his side, and is so contrived that when water is poured into it it cannot rise above the child's foot, but is then carried off by a hidden duct and runs out at the bottom till the cup is empty.

§ The landing-place is still shown at Gokul and called 'Uttaresvar Ghat.'

ground: but how great his terror when he sees it rise resplendent in celestial beauty and ascend to heaven, there to be adored as the great goddess Durgá.* Kansa started from his momentary stupor, frantic with rage, and cursing the gods as his enemies, issued savage orders that every one should be put to death who dared to offer them sacrifice, and that diligent search should be made for all young children, that the infant son of Devaki, wherever concealed, might perish amongst the number. Judging these precautions to be sufficient, and that nothing further was to be dreaded from the parents, he set Vasudeva and Devaki at liberty. The former at once hastened to see Nanda, who had come over to Mathurá to pay his yearly tribute to the king, and after congratulating him on Jasoda's having presented him with a son, begged him to take back to Gokul Rohini's boy, Balarám, and let the two children be brought up together. To this Nanda gladly assented, and so it came to pass that the two brothers, Krishna and Balarám, spent the days of their childhood together at Gokul, under the care of their foster-mother Jasodá.

They had not been there long, when one night the witch Pútaná, hovering about for some mischief to do in the service of Kansa, saw the babe Krishna lying asleep, and took him up in her arms and began to suckle him with her own devil's milk. A mortal child would have been poisoned at the first drop, but Krishna drew the breast with such strength that her life's blood was drained with the milk, and the hideous fiend, terrifying the whole country of Braj with her groans of agony, fell lifeless to the ground. Another day Jasodá had gone down to the river-bank to wash some clothes, and had left the child asleep under one of the waggons. He all at once woke up hungry, and kicking out with his baby foot upset the big cart, full as it was of pans and pails of milk. When Jasoda came running back to see what all the noise was about, she found him in the midst of the broken fragments quietly asleep again, as if nothing had happened. Again, one of Kansa's attendant demons, by name Trinávart, hoping to destroy the child, came and swept him off in a whirlwind, but the child was too much for him and made that his last journey to Braj.†

The older the boy grew, the more troublesome did Jasodá find him; he would crawl about everywhere on his hands and knees, getting into the cattle-sheds and pulling the calves by their tails, upsetting the pans of milk and whey, sticking his fingers into the curds and butter, and daubing his face and clothes

* The scene of this transformation is laid at the Jog Ghát in Mathurá, so called from the child Joganidrá.

† The event is commemorated by a small cell at Mahában, in which the demon whirlwind is represented by a pair of enormous wings overshadowing the infant Krishna.

all over; and one day she got so angry with him that she put a cord round his waist and tied him to the great wooden mortar* while she went to look after her household affairs. No sooner was her back turned than the child, in his efforts to get loose, dragged away with him the heavy wooden block till it got fixed between two immense Arjun trees that were growing in the court-yard. It was wedged tight only for a minute, one more pull and down came the two enormous trunks with a thundering crash. Up ran the neighbours, expecting an earthquake at least, and found the village half buried under the branches of the fallen trees, with the child between the two shattered stems laughing at the mischief he had caused.†

Alarmed at these successive portents, Nanda determined upon removing to some other locality and selected the neighbourhood of Brindá-ban as affording the best pasturage for the cattle. Here the boys lived till they were seven years old, not so much in Brindá-ban itself as in the copses on the opposite bank of the river, near the town of Mát; there they wandered about, merrily disporting themselves, decking their heads with plumes of peacocks' feathers, stringing long wreaths of wild flowers round their necks and making sweet music with their rustic pipes.‡ At evening-tide they drove the cows home to the pens, and joined in frolicsome sports with the herdsmen's children under the shade of the great Bhàndír tree.§

But even in their new home they were not secure from demoniacal aggression. When they had come to five years of age, and were grazing their

* From this incident Krishna derives his popular name of Dámodar, from *dám* a cord, and *udar*, the body. The mortar, or *ulúkhala*, is generally a solid block of wood, three or four feet high, hollowed out at the top into the shape of a basin.

† The traditionary scene of all these adventures is laid, not at Gokul, as might have been anticipated, but at Mahabán, which is now a distinct town further inland. There are shown the *jugal arjun ki thaur*, 'or site of the two Arjun trees,' and the spots where Pútaná, Trinávart, and Sakatásur, or the cart-demon (for in the Bhágavat the cart is said to have been upset by the intervention of an evil spirit), met their fate. The village of Koila, on the opposite bank, is said to derive its name from the fact that the 'ashes' from Pútaná's funeral pile floated down there; or that Vasudeva, when crossing the river and thinking he was about to sink, called out for some one to take the child, saying 'Koi le, koi le.'

‡ From these childish sports, Krishna derives his popular names of *Ban-máli*, 'the wearer of a chaplet of wild flowers,' and *Bansi-dhar* and *Murli-dhar*, 'the flute-player.' Hence, too, the strolling singers, who frequent the fairs held on Krishna's féte days, attire themselves in high-crowned caps decked with peacocks' feathers.

§ The Bhándír-ban is a dense thicket of *ber* and other low prickly shrubs in the hamlet of Chháhiri, a little above Mát. In the centre is an open space with a small modern temple and well. The Bhándír *bat* is an old tree a few hundred yards outside the grove.

cattle on the bank of the Jamuná the demon Bachhásur made an open onset against them.* When he had received the reward of his temerity, the demon Bakásur tried the efficacy of stratagem. Transforming himself into a crane of gigantic proportions he perched on the hill-side, and when the cowherd's children came to gaze at the monstrous apparition, snapped them all up one after the other. But Krishna made such a hot mouthful that he was only too glad to drop him; and as soon as the boy set his feet on the ground again, he seized the monster by his long bill and rent him in twain.

On another day, as their playmate Tosh† and some of the other children were rambling about, they spied what they took to be the mouth of a great chasm in the rock. It was in truth the expanded jaws of the serpent-king Aghásur, and as the boys were peeping in he drew a deep breath and sucked them all down. But Krishna bid them be of good cheer, and swelled his body to such a size that the serpent burst, and the children stept out upon the plain uninjured.

Again, as they lay lazily one sultry noon under a Kadamb tree enjoying their lunch, the calves strayed away quite out of sight.‡ In fact, the jealous god Brahma had stolen them. When the loss was detected, all ran off in different directions to look for them; but Krishna took a shorter plan, and as soon as he found himself alone, created other cattle exactly like them to take their place. He then waited a little for his companions' return; but when no signs of them appeared, he guessed, as was really the case, that they too had been stolen by Brahma; so without more ado he continued the work of creation, and called into existence another group of children identical in appearance with the absentees. Meanwhile, Brahma had dropped off into one of his periodical dozes, and waking up after the lapse of a year, chuckled to himself over the forlorn condition of Braj, without either cattle or children. But when he got there and began to look about him, he found everything just the same as before: then he made his submission to Krishna, and acknowledged him to be his lord and master.

One day, as Krishna was strolling by himself along the bank of the Jamuná, he came to a creek by the side of which grew a tall Kadamb tree. He

* This adventure gives its name to the Bachh-ban near Sehi.

† Hence the name of the village Tosh in the Mathurá pargana.

‡ The scene of this adventure is laid at Khadira-ban, near Khaira. The *khadira* is a species of acacia. The Sanskrit word assumes in Prákrit the form *khaira*.

15

climbed the tree and took a plunge into the water. Now, this recess was the haunt of a savage dragon, by name Káliya, who at one started from the depth, coiled himself round the intruder, and fastened upon him with his poisonous fangs. The alarm spread, and Nanda, Jasoda and Balarám, and all the neighbours came running, frightened out of their senses, and found Krishna still and motionless, enveloped in the dragon's coils. The sight was so terrible that all stood as if spell-bound ; but Krishna with a smile gently shook off the serpent's folds, and seizing the hooded monster by one of his many heads, pressed it down upon the margin of the stream and danced upon it, till the poor wretch was so torn and lacerated that his wives all came from their watery cells and threw themselves at Krishna's feet and begged for mercy. The dragon himself in a feeble voice sued for pardon ; then the beneficent divinity not only spared his life and allowed him to depart with all his family to the island of Ramanak, but further assured him that he would ever thereafter bear upon his brow the impress of the divine feet, seeing which no enemy would dare to molest him.*

After this, as the two boys were straying with their herds from wood to wood, they came to a large palm-grove (tál-ban), where they began shaking the trees to bring down the fruit. Now, in this grove there dwelt a demon, by name Dhenuk, who, hearing the fruit fall, rushed past in the form of an ass and gave Balarám a flying kick full on the breast with both his hind legs. But before his legs could again reach the ground, Balarám seized them in his powerful grasp, and whirling the demon round his head hurled the carcase on to the top of one of the tallest trees, causing the fruit to drop like rain. The boys then returned to their station at the Bhándír fig-tree, and that very night, while they were in Bhadra-ban† close by, there came on a violent storm. The tall dry grass was kindled by the lightning and the whole forest was in a blaze. Off scampered the cattle, and the herdsmen too, but Krishna called to the cowards to stop and close their eyes for a minute.

---

* One of the ghâts at Brindá-ban is named, in commemoration of this event, Káli-mardan, or Káli-dah, and *the*, or rather *a*, Kadamb tree is still shown there.

† *Bhadra-ban* occupies a high point on the left bank of the Jamuná, some three miles above Mát. With the usual fate of Hindi words, it is transformed in the official map of the district into the Persian *Bahádur-ban*. Between it and Bhándír-ban is a large straggling wood called *mekh-ban*. This, it is said, was open ground, till one day, many years ago, some great man encamped there, and all the stakes to which his horses had been tethered took root and grew up.

When they opened them again, the cows were all standing in their pens, and the moon shone calmly down on the waving forest trees and rustling reeds.

Another day Krishna and Balarám were running a race up to the Bhándír tree with their playmate Sridáma, when the demon Pralamba came and asked to make a fourth. In the race Pralamba was beaten by Balarám, and so, according to the rules of the game, had to carry him on his back from the goal to the starting-point. No sooner was Balarám on his shoulders than Pralamba ran off with him at the top of his speed, and recovering his proper diabolical form made sure of destroying him. But Balarám soon taught him differently, and squeezed him so tightly with his knees, and dealt him such cruel blows on the head with his fists, that his skull and ribs were broken, and no life left in the monster. Seeing this feat of strength, his comrades loudly greeted him with the name of Balarám, 'Ráma the strong,'* which title he ever after retained.

But who so frolicsome as the boy Krishna? Seeing the fair maids of Braj performing their ablutions in the Jamuná, he stole along the bank, and picking up the clothes of which they had divested themselves, climbed up with them into a Kadamb tree. There he mocked the frightened girls as they came shivering out of the water; nor would he yield a particle of vestment till all had ranged before him in a row, and with clasped and uplifted hands most piteously entreated him. Thus the boy-god taught his votaries that submission to the divine will was a more excellent virtue even than modesty.†

At the end of the rains all the herdsmen began to busy themselves in preparing a great sacrifice in honour of Indra, as a token of their gratitude for the refreshing showers he had bestowed upon the earth. But Krishna, who had already made sport of Brahma, thought lightly enough of Indra's claims

---

* Balarám, under the name of Belus, is described by Latin writers as the Indian Hercules and said to be one of the tutelary divinities of Mathurá. Patanjali also, the celebrated Grammarian, a native of Gonda in Oudh, whose most probable date is 150 B. C., clearly refers to Krishna as a divinity and to Kansa's death at his hands as a current tradition, both popular and ancient; the events in the hero's life forming the subject of different poems, from which he quotes lines or parts of lines as examples of grammatical rules. Thus, whatever the date of the eighteen Puránas, as we now have them, Pauránik mythology and the local cultus of Krishna and Balarám at Mathurá must be of higher antiquity than has been represented by some European scholars.

† This popular incident is commemorated by the Chír Ghát at Siyára; *chír* meaning clothes. The same name is frequently given to the Chain Ghát at Brinda-ban, which is also so called in the Vraja-bhakti-vilása, written 1553 A.D.

and said to Nanda :—"The forests where we tend our cattle cluster round the foot of the hills, and it is the spirits of the hills that we ought rather to worship. They can assume any shapes they please, and if we slight them, will surely transform themselves into lions and wolves and destroy both us and our herds." The people of Braj were convinced by these arguments, and taking all the rich gifts they had prepared, set out for Gobardhan, where they solemnly circumambulated the mountain and presented their offerings to the new divitity. Krishna himself, in the character of the mountain gods, stood forth on the highest peak and accepted the adoration of the assembled crowd, while a fictitious image in his own proper person joined humbly in the ranks of the devotees.

When Indra saw himself thus defrauded of the promised sacrifice, he was very wrath, and summoning the clouds from every quarter of heaven, bid them all descend upon Braj in one fearful and unbroken torrent. In an instant the sky was overhung with impenetrable gloom, and it was only by the vivid flashes of lightning that the terrified herdsmen could see their houses and cattle beaten down and swept away by the irresistible deluge. The ruin was but for a moment ; with one hand Krishna uprooted the mountain from its base, and balancing it on the tip of his finger called all the people under its cover. There they remained secure for seven days and nights and the storms of Indra beat harmlessly on the summit of the uplifted range : while Krishna stood erect and smiling, nor once did his finger tremble beneath the weight. When Indra found his passion fruitless, the heavens again became clear ; the people of Braj stepped forth from under Gobardhan, and Krishna quietly restored it to its original site. Then Indra, moved with desire to behold and worship the incarnate god, mounted his elephant Airávata and descended upon the plains of Braj. There he adored Krishna in his humble pastoral guise, and saluting him by the new titles of Upendra* and Gobind placed under his special protection his own son the hero Arjun, who had then taken birth at Indraprastha in the family of Pandu.

---

* The title Upendra was evidently conferred upon Krishna before the full development of the Vaishnava School ; for however Paurának writers may attempt to explain it, the only grammatical meaning of the compound is 'a lesser Indra.' As Krishna has long been considered much the greater god of the two, the title has fallen into disrepute and is now seldom used. Similarly with 'Gobind'; its true meaning is not, as implied in the text, 'the Indra of cows,' but simply 'a finder, or 'tender of cows,' from the root '*vid*.' The Hindus themselves prefer to explain Upendra as meaning simply Indra's younger brother,' Vishnu, in the dwarf incarnation, having been born as the son of Kasyapa, who was also Indra's father.

When Krishna had completed his twelfth year, Nanda, in accordance with a vow that he had made, went with all his family to perform a special devotion at the temple of Devi. At night, when they were asleep, a huge boa-constrictor laid hold of Nanda by the toe and would speedily have devoured him; but Krishna, hearing his foster-father's cries, ran to his side and lightly set his foot on the great serpent's head. At the very touch the monster was transformed and assumed the figure of a lovely youth; for ages ago a Ganymede of heaven's court by name Sudarsan, in the pride of beauty and exalted birth, had vexed the holy sage Angiras, when deep in divine contemplation, by dancing backwards and forwards before him, and by his curse had been metamorphosed into a snake, in that vile shape to expiate his offence until the advent of the gracious Krishna.

Beholding all the glorious deeds that he had performed, the maids of Braj could not restrain their admiration. Drawn from their lonely homes by the low sweet notes of his seductive pipe, they floated around him in rapturous love, and through the moonlight autumn nights joined with him in the circling dance, passing from glade to glade in ever increasing ecstasy of devotion. To whatever theme his voice was attuned, their song had but one burden—his perfect beauty; and as they mingled in the mystic maze, with eyes closed in the intensity of voluptuous passion, each nymph as she grasped the hand of her partner thrilled at the touch, as though the hand were Krishna's, and dreamed herself alone supremely blest in the enjoyment of his undivided affection. Rádhá, fairest of the fair, reigned queen of the revels, and so languished in the heavenly delights of his embraces, that all consciousness of earth and self was obliterated.*

One night, as the choir of attendant damsels followed through the woods the notes of his wayward pipe, a lustful giant, by name Sankhchúr, attempted to intercept them. Then Krishna showed himself no timorous gallant, but casting crown and flute to the ground pursued the ravisher, and seizing him from behind by his shaggy hair, cut off his head, and taking the precious jewel which he had worn on his front presented it to Balarám.

---

* Any sketch of Krishna's adventures would be greatly defective which contained no allusion to his celebrated amours with the Gopís, or milkmaids of Braj. It is the one incident in his life upon which modern Hindu writers love to lavish all the resources of their eloquence. Yet in the original authorities it occupies a no more prominent place in the narrative than that which has been assigned it above. In pictorial representations of the 'circular dance' or Rásmandal, whatever the number of the Gopis introduced, so often is the figure of Krishna repeated. Thus each Gopí can claim him as a partner, while again, in the centre of the circle, he stands in larger form with his favourite Rádhá.

Yet once again was the dance of love rudely interrupted. The demon Arishta, disguised as a gigantic bull, dashed upon the scene and made straight for Krishna. The intrepid youth, smiling, awaited the attack, and seizing him by the horns forced down his head to the ground; then twisting the monster's neck as it had been a wet rag, he wrenched one of the horns from the socket and with it so belaboured the brute that no life was left in his body. Then all the herdsmen rejoiced; but the crime of violating even the semblance of a bull could not remain unexpiated. So all the sacred streams and places of pilgrimage, obedient to Krishna's summons, came in bodily shape to Gobardhan and poured from their holy urns into two deep reservoirs prepared for the occasion.* There Krishna bathed, and by the efficacy of this concentrated essence of sanctity was washed clean of the pollution he had incurred.

When Kansa heard of the marvellous acts performed by the two boys at Brindá-ban he trembled with fear and recognized the fated avengers, who had eluded all his cruel vigilance and would yet wreak his doom. After pondering for a while what stratagem to adopt, he proclaimed a great tournay of arms, making sure that if they were induced to come to Mathurá and enter the lists as combatants, they would be inevitably destroyed by his two champions Chánur and Mushtika. Of all the Jádav tribe Akrúr was the only chieftain in whose integrity the tyrant could confide: he accordingly was despatched with an invitation to Nanda and all his family to attend the coming festival. But though Akrúr started at once on his mission, Kansa was too restless to wait the result: the demon Kesin, terror of the woods of Brindá-ban, was ordered to try his strength against them or ever they left their home. Disguised as a wild horse, the monster rushed amongst the herds, scattering them in all directions. Krishna alone stood calmly in his way, and when the demoniacal steed bearing down upon him with wide-extended jaws made as though it would devour him, he thrust his arm down the gaping throat and, with a mighty heave, burst the huge body asunder, splitting it into two equal portions right down the back from nose to tail.†

---

* These are the famous tanks of Rádhá-kund, which is the next village to Gobardhan; while Aring, a contraction for Arishta-gánw, is the scene of the combat with the bull.

† There are two gháts at Brindá-ban named after this adventure: the first Kesi Ghát, where the monster was slain; the second Chain Ghát, where Krishna 'rested' and bathed. It is from this exploit, according to Pauránik etymology, that Krishna derives his popular name of Kesava. The name, however, is more ancient than the legend, and signifies simply the long-haired, 'crinitus,' or radiant, an appropriate epithet if Krishna be taken for the Indian Apollo.

All unconcerned at this stupendous encounter, Krishna returned to his childish sports and was enjoying a game of blind-man's buff, when the demon Byomásur came up in guise as a cowherd and asked to join the party. After a little, he proposed to vary the amusement by a turn at wolf-and-goats, and then lying in ambush and transforming himself into a real wolf he fell upon the children, one by one, and tore them in pieces, till Krishna, detecting his wiles, dragged him from his cover and, seizing him by the throat, beat him to death.

At this juncture, Akrúr* arrived with his treacherous invitation: it was at once accepted, and the boys in high glee started for Mathurá, Nanda also and all the village encampment accompanying them. Just outside the city they met the king's washerman and his train of donkeys laden with bundles of clothes, which he was taking back fresh washed from the river-side to the palace. What better opportunity could be desired for country boys, who had never before left the woods and had no clothes fit to wear. They at once made a rush at the bundles and, tearing them open, arrayed themselves in the finery just as it came to hand, without any regard for fit or colour; then on they went again, laughing heartily at their own mountebank appearance, till a good tailor called them into his shop, and there cut and snipped and stitched away till he turned them out in the very height of fashion : and to complete their costume, the *máli* Sudáma gave them each a nosegay of flowers. So going through the streets like young princes, there met them the poor hump-backed woman Kubja, and Krishna, as he passed, putting one foot on her feet and one hand under her chin, stretched out her body straight as a dart.†

In the court-yard before the palace was displayed the monstrous bow, the test of skill and strength in the coming encounter of arms. None but a giant could bend it; but Krishna took it up in sport, and it snapped in his fingers like a twig. Out ran the king's guards, hearing the crash of the broken beam, but all perished at the touch of the invincible child : not one survived to tell how death was dealt.

When they had seen all the sights of the city, they returned to Nanda, who had been much disquieted by their long absence, and on the morrow repaired to the arena, where Kansa was enthroned in state on a high dais overlooking

---

* Akrúr is the name of a hamlet between Mathurá and Brindá-ban.

† "Kubja's well" in Mathurá commemorates this event. It is on the Delhi road, a little beyond the Katra. Nearly opposite, a carved pillar from a Buddhist railing has been set up and is worshipped as Párvati.

the lists. At the entrance they were confronted by the savage elephant Kuvala-yapída, upon whom Kansa relied to trample them to death. But Krishna, after sporting with it for a while, seized it at last by the tail, and whirling it round his head dashed it lifeless to the ground. Then, each bearing one of its tusks, the two boys stepped into the ring and challenged all comers. Chánur was matched against Krishna, Mushtika against Balarám. The struggle was no sooner begun than ended: both the king's champions were thrown and rose no more. Then Kansa started from his throne, and cried aloud to his guards to seize and put to death the two rash boys with their father Vasudeva—for his sons he knew they were—and the old King Ugrasen. But Krishna with one bound sprung upon the dais, seized the tyrant by the hair as he vainly sought to fly, and hurled him down the giddy height into the ravine below.* Then they dragged the lifeless body to the bank of the Jamuná, and there by the water's edge at last sat down to 'rest,' whence the place is known to this day as the 'Visránt' Ghát.† Now that justice had been satisfied, Krishna was too righteous to insult the dead; he comforted the widows of the fallen monarch, and bid them celebrate the funeral rites with all due form, and himself applied the torch to the pyre. Then Ugrasen was reseated on his ancient throne, and Mathurá once more knew peace and security.

As Krishna was determined on a lengthened-stay, he persuaded Nanda to return alone to Brindá-ban and console his foster-mother Jasodá with tidings of his welfare. He and Balarám then underwent the ceremonies of caste-initiation, which had been neglected during their sojourn with the herdsmen; and, after a few days, proceeded to Ujjayin, there to pursue the prescribed course of study under the Kásya sage Sandípani. The rapidity with which they mastered every science soon betrayed their divinity; and as they prepared to leave, their instructor fell at their feet and begged of them a boon—namely, the restoration of his son, who had been engulfed by the waves of the sea when on a pilgrimage to Prabhása. Ocean was summoned to answer the charge, and taxed the demon Panchajana with the crime. Krishna at once plunged into the unfathomable depth and dragged the monster lifeless to the surface. Then

---

* Kansa's Hill and the Rang-Bhúmi, or 'arena,' with an image of Rangesvar Mahádeva, where the bow was broken, the elephant killed and the champion wrestlers defeated, are still sacred sites immediately outside the city of Mathurá, opposite the new dispensary.

† The Visránt Ghát, or *Resting* Ghát, is the most sacred spot in all Mathurá. It occupies the centre of the river front, and is thus made a prominent object, though it has no special architectural beauty.

with Balarám he invaded the city of the dead and claimed from Jama the Bráhman's son, whom they took back with them to the light of day and restored to his enraptured parents. The shell in which the demon had dwelt (whence his title Sankhásur) was ever thereafter borne by the hero as his special emblem* under the name of Pánchajanya.

Meanwhile, the widows of King Kansa had fled to Magadha, their native land, and implored their father, Jarásandha, to take up arms and avenge their murdered lord. Scarcely had Krishna returned to Mathurá when the assembled hosts invested the city. The gallant prince did not wait the attack; but, accompanied by Balarám, sallied forth, routed the enemy and took Jarásandha prisoner. Compassionating the utterness of his defeat, they allowed him to return to his own country, where, unmoved by the generosity of his victors, he immediately began to raise a new army on a still larger scale than the preceding, and again invaded the dominions of Ugrasen. Seventeen times did Jarásandha renew the attack, seventeen times was he repulsed by Krishna. Finding it vain to continue the struggle alone, he at last called to his aid King Kála-yavana,† who with his barbarous hordes from the far west bore down upon the devoted city of Mathurá. That very night Krishna bade arise on the remote shore of the Bay of Kachh the stately Fort of Dwáraká, and thither, in a moment of time, transferred the whole of his faithful people: the first intimation that reached them of their changed abode was the sound of the roaring waves when they woke on the following morning. He then returned to do battle against the allied invaders; but being hard pressed by the barbarian king, he fled and took refuge in a cave, where the holy Muchkunda was sleeping, and there concealed himself. When the Yavana arrived, he took the sleeper to be Krishna and spurned him with his foot, whereupon Muchkunda awoke and with a glance reduced him to ashes.‡ But meanwhile Mathura had

---

* The legend has been invented to explain why the *sankha*, or conch-shell, is employed as a religious emblem: the simpler reason is to be found in the fact of its constant use as an auxiliary to temple worship. In consequence of a slight similarity in the name, this incident is popularly connected with the village of Sonsa in the Mathurá pargana, without much regard to the exigencies of the narrative, since Prabhása, where Panchajana was slain, is far away on the shore of the Western Ocean in Gujarát.

† The soul of Kála-yavana is supposed in a second birth to have animated the body of the tyrannical Aurangzeb.

‡ The traditional scene of this event is laid at Muchkund, a lake three miles to the west of Dholpur, where two bathing fairs are annually held: the one in May, the other at the beginning of September. The lake has as many as 114 temples on its banks, though none are of great antiquity. It covers an area of 41 acres and lies in a natural hollow of great depth,

17

fallen into the hands of Jarásandha, who forthwith destroyed all the palaces and temples and every memento of the former dynasty, and erected new buildings in their place as monuments of his own conquest.*

Thenceforth Krishna reigned with great glory at Dwáraká ; and not many days had elapsed when, fired with the report of the matchless beauty of the princess Rukmini, daughter of Bhíshmak, king of Kundina in the country of Vidarbha, he broke in upon the marriage feast, and carried her off before the very eyes of her betrothed, the Chanderi king Sisupál.† After this he contracted many other splendid alliances, even to the number of sixteen thousand and one hundred, and became the father of a hundred and eighty thousand sons.‡ In the Great War he took up arms with his five cousins, the Pándav princes, to terminate the tyranny of Duryodhan ; and accompanied by Bhíma and Arjuna, invaded Magadhá, and taking Jarásandha by surprise, put him to death and burnt his capital : and many other noble achievements did he perform, which are written in the chronicles of Dwáraka ; but Mathurá saw him no more, and the legends of Mathurá are ended.

To many persons it will appear profane to institute a comparison between the inspired oracles of Christianity and the fictions of Hinduism. But if we

filled in the rains by the drainage of the neighbourhood and fed throughout the year by a number of springs, which have their source in the surrounding sand-stone hills. The local legend is that Rájá Muchkund, after a long and holy life, desired to find rest in death. The gods denied his prayer, but allowed him to repose for centuries in sleep and decreed that any one who disturbed him should be consumed by fire. Krishna, in his flight from Kála-yavana, chanced to pass the place where the Rájá slept and, without disturbing him, threw a cloth over his face and concealed himself close by. Soon after arrived Kála-yavana, who, concluding that the sleeper was the enemy he sought, rudely awoke him and was instantly consumed. After this Krishna remained with the Rájá for some days and finding that no water was to be had nearer than the Chambal, he stamped his foot and so caused a depression in the rock, which immediately filled with water and now forms the lake.

* As Magadha became the great centre of Buddhism, and indeed derives its latter name of Bihár from the numerous Viháras, or Buddhist monasteries, which it contained, its king Jarásandha and his son-in-law Kansa have been described by the orthodox writers of the Mahábhárat and Sri Bhágavat with all the animus they felt against the professors of that religion, though in reality it had not come into existence till some 400 years after Jarásandha's death. Thus the narrative of Krishna's retreat to Dwáraká and the subsequent demolition of Hindu Mathurá, besides its primary signification, represents also in mythological language the great historical fact, attested by the notices of contemporary travellers and the results of recent antiquarian research, that for a time Brahmanism was almost eradicated from Central India and Buddhism established as the national religion.

† Sisupál was first cousin to Krishna ; his mother, Srutadevá, being Vasudeva's sister.

‡ These extravagant numbers are merely intended to indicate the wide diffusion and power of the great Jádava (vulgarly Jádon) clan.

fairly consider the legend as above sketched, and allow for a slight element of the grotesque and that tendency to exaggerate which is inalienable from Oriental imagination, we shall find nothing incongruous with the primary idea of a beneficent divinity manifested in the flesh in order to deliver the world from oppression and restore the practice of true religion. Even as regards the greatest stumbling-block, *viz.*, the 'Panchádyáya,' or five chapters of the Bhágavat, which describe Krishna's amours with the Gopís, the language is scarcely, if at all, more glowing and impassioned than that employed in 'the song of songs, which is Solomon's;' and if theologians maintain that the latter must be mystical because inspired, how can a similar defence be denied to the Hindu philosopher? As to those wayward caprices of the child-god, for which no adequate explanation can be assigned, the Bráhman, without any derogation from his intellect, may regard them as the sport of the Almighty, the mysterious dealings of an inscrutable Providence, styled in Sanskrit terminology *máyá*, and in the language of Holy Church *sapientia—sapientia ludens omni tempore, ludens in orbe terrarum.*

Attempts have also been made to establish a definite and immediate connection between the Hindu narrative and at least the earlier chapters of S. Matthew's Gospel. But I think without success. There is an obvious similarity of sound between the names Christ and Krishna; Herod's massacre of the innocents may be compared with the massacre of the children of Mathurá by Kansa; the flight into Egypt with the flight to Gokul; as Christ had a forerunner of supernatural birth in the person of S. John the Baptist, so had Krishna in Balarám; and as the infant Saviour was cradled in a manger and first worshipped by shepherds, though descended from the royal house of Judah, so Krishna, though a near kinsman of the reigning prince, was brought up amongst cattle and first manifested his divinity to herdsmen.* The inference drawn from these coincidences is corroborated by an ecclesiastical tradition that the Gospel which S. Thomas the Apostle brought with him to India

* Hindu pictures of the infant Krishna in the arms of his foster-mother Jasodá, with a glory encircling the heads both of mother and child and a background of Oriental scenery, might often pass for Indian representations of Christ and the Madonna. Professor Weber has written at great length to argue a connection between them. But few scenes (as remarked by Dr. Rájendralála Mitra) could be more natural or indigenous in any country than that of a woman nursing a child, and in delineating it in one country it is all but utterly impossible to design something which would not occur to other artists in other parts of the world. The relation of original and copy in such case can be inferred only from the details, the technical treatment, general arrangement and style of execution; and in these respects there is no similarity between the Hindu painting and the Byzantine Madonna quoted by Professor Weber.

was that of S. Matthew, and that when his relics were discovered, a copy of it was found to have been buried with him. It is further to be noted that the special Vaishnava tenets of the unity of the Godhead and of salvation by faith are said to have been introduced by Nárada from the Sweta-dwipa, an unknown region, which if the word be interpreted to mean 'White-man's land,' might well be identified with Christian Europe. It is, on the other hand, absolutely certain that the *name* of Krishna, however late the full development of the legendary cycle, was celebrated throughout India long before the Christian era; thus the only possible hypothesis is that some pandit, struck by the marvellous circumstances of our Lord's infancy as related in the Gospel, transferred them to his own indigenous mythology, and on account of the similarity of name selected Krishna as their hero. It is quite possible that a new life of Krishna may in this way have been constructed out of incidents borrowed from Christian records, since we know as a fact of literary history that the converse process has been actually performed. Thus Fr. Beschi, who was in India from 1700 to 1742, in the hope of supplanting the Rámáyana, composed, on the model of that famous Hindu epic, a poem of 3,615 stanzas divided into 30 cantos, called the Tembávaní, or Unfading Garland, in which every adventure, miracle and achievement recorded of the national hero, Ráma, was elaborately paralleled by events in the life of Christ. It may be added that the Harivansa, which possibly is as old* as any of the Vaishnava Puránas, was certainly written by a stranger to the country of Braj;† and not only so, but it further shows distinct traces of a southern origin, as in its description of the exclusively Dakhini festival, the Punjal: and it is only in the south of India that

---

* It is quoted by Bírúni (born 970, died 1038 A. D.) as a standard authority in his time.

† The proof of this statement is that all his topographical descriptions are utterly irreconcilable with facts. Thus he mentions that Krishna and Balaráma were brought up at a spot selected by Nanda on the bank of the Jamuná near the hill of Gobardhan (Canto 61). Now, Gobardhan is some fifteen miles from the river; and the neighbourhood of Gokula and Mahában, which all other written authorities and also ancient tradition agree in declaring to have been the scene of Krishna's infancy, is several miles further distant from the ridge and on the other side of the Jamuná. Again, Tál-ban is described (Canto 79) as lying north of Gobardhan—

गोवर्द्धनस्योत्तरतो यमुनातीरमाश्रितम्
ददृशाते ततो वीरौ रम्यं तालवनं महत्

It is south-east of Gobardhan and with the city of Mathurá between it and Brindá-ban, though in the Bhágavat it is said to be close to the latter town. So also Bhándír-ban is represented in the Harivansa as being on the same side of the river as the Káli-Mardan Ghát, being in reality nearly opposite to it.

a Bráhman would be likely to meet with Christian traditions. There the Church has had a continuous, though a feeble and struggling existence, from the very earliest Apostolic times* down to the present; and it must be admitted that there is no intrinsic improbability in supposing that the narrative of the Gospel may have exercised on some Hindu sectarian a similar influence to that which the Pentateuch and the Talmud had on the founder of Islam. Nor are the differences between the authentic legends of Judaism and the perversions of them that appear in the Kurán very much greater than those which distinguish the life of Christ from the life of Krishna. But after all that can be urged there is no historical basis for the supposed connection between the two narratives, which probably would never have been suggested but for the similarity of name. Now, that is certainly a purely accidental coincidence; for Christos is as obviously a Greek as Krishna is a Sanskrit formation, and the roots from which the two words are severally derived are entirely different.

The similarity of doctrine is perhaps a yet more curious phenomenon, and Dr. Lorinser, in his German version of the Bhagavad Gíta, which is the most

* According to Eusebius, the Apostle who visited India was not Thomas, but Bartholomew There is, however, no earlier tradition to confirm the latter name; while the 'Acts of S. Thomas'—though apocryphal—are mentioned by Epiphanius, who was consecrated Bishop of Salamis about 368 A.D., and are attributed by Photius to Lucius Charinas, by later scholars to Bardesanes at the end of the second century. Anyhow, they are ancient, and as it would have been against the writer's interest to contradict established facts, the probability is that his historical groundwork—S. Thomas' visit to India—is correct. That Christianity still continued to exist there, after the time of the Apostles, is proved by the statement of Eusebius that Pantanus, the teacher of Clemens Alexandrinus, visited the country in the second century and brought back with him to Alexandria a copy of the Hebrew Gospel of S. Matthew. S. Chrysostom also speaks of a translation into the Indian tongue of a Gospel or Catechism; a Metropolitan of Persia and India attended the Council of Nice; and the heresiarch Mani, put to death about 272 A.D., wrote an Epistle to the Indians. Much stress, however, must not be laid on these latter facts, since India in early times was a term of very wide extent. According to tradition S. Thomas founded seven Churches in Malabar, the names of which are given and are certainly old; and in the sixth century, Cosmas Indico-pleustes, a Byzantine monk, speaks of a Church at Male (Malabar) with a Bishop in the town of Kalliena (Kalyán) who had been consecrated in Persia. The sculptured crosses which S. Francis Xavier and other Catholic Missionaries supposed to be relics of S. Thomas have Pahlavi inscriptions, from the character of which it is surmised that they are not of earlier date than the seventh or eighth century. The old connection between Malabar and Edessa is probably to be explained by the fact that S. Thomas was, as Eusebius and other ecclesiastical historians describe him, the Apostle of Edessa, while Pahlavi, which is an Aramean dialect of Assyria, may well have been known and used as far north as that city, since it was the language of the Persian Court. From Antioch, which is not many miles distant from ancient Edessa, and to which the Edessa Church was made subject, the Malabar Christians have from a very early period received their Bishops.

authoritative exponent of Vaishnava tenets, has attempted to point out that it contains many coincidences with and references to the New Testament. As Dr. Muir has very justly observed, there is no doubt a general resemblance between the manner in which Krishna asserts his own divine nature, enjoins devotion to his person and sets forth the blessing which will result to his votaries from such worship on the one hand, and the language of the fourth Gospel on the other. But the immediate introduction of the Bible into the explanation of the Bhagavad Gíta is at least premature. For though some of the parallels are curious, the ethics and the religion of different peoples are not so different from one another that here and there coincidence should not be expected to be found. Most of the verses cited exhibit no very close resemblance to Biblical texts and are only such as might naturally have occurred spontaneously to an Indian writer. And more particularly with regard to the doctrine of 'faith' *bhakti* may be a modern term, but *sraddhá*, in much the same sense, is found even in the hymns of the Rig Veda.

A striking example of the insufficiency of mere coincidence in name and event, to establish a material connection between the legends of any two reigions, is afforded by the narrative of Buddha's temptation as given in the Lalita Vistara. In all such cases the metaphysical resemblance tends to prove the identity of the religious idea in all ages of the world and among all races of mankind ; but any historical connection, in the absence of historical proof, is purely hypothetical. The story of the Temptation in the fourth Chapter of S. Matthew's Gospel, which was undergone after a long fast and before the commencement of our Lord's active ministry, is exactly paralleled by the circumstances of Buddha's victory over the assaults of the Evil One, after he had completed his six years of penance and before he began his public career as a national Reformer. But the Lalita Vistara is anterior in date to the Christian revelation, and therefore cannot have borrowed from it ; while it is also certain that the Buddhist legend can never have reached S. Matthew's ears, and therefore any connection between the two narratives is absolutely impossible. My belief is that *all* the supposed connection between Christ and Krishna is equally imaginary.

CHAPTER IV.

THE BRAJ-MANDAL, THE BAN-JÁTRA, AND THE HOLI.

NOT only the city of Mathurá, but with it the whole of the western half of the district, has a special interest of its own as the birth-place and abiding home of Vaishnava Hinduism. It is about 42 miles in length, with an average breadth of 30 miles, and is intersected throughout by the river Jamuná. On the right bank of the stream are the parganas of Kosi and Chhátá—so named after their principal towns—with the home pargana below them to the south ; and on the left bank the united parganas of Mát and Noh-jhíl, with half the pargana of Mahá-ban as far east as the town of Baladeva. This extent of country is almost absolutely identical with the Braj-mandal of Hindu topography ; the circuit of 84 kos in the neighbourhood of Gokul and Brindá-ban, where the divine brothers Krishna and Balarám grazed their herds.

The first aspect of the country is a little disappointing to the student of Sanskrit literature, who has been led by the glowing eulogiums of the poets to anticipate a second vale of Tempe. A similarly unfavourable impression is generally produced upon the mind of any chance traveller, who is carried rapidly along the dusty high-road, and can scarcely see beyond the hideous strip of broken ground which the engineers reserve on either side, in order to supply the soil required for annual repairs. As this strip is never systematically levelled, but is dug up into irregular pits and hollows, the size and depth of which are determined solely by the requirements of the moment, the effect is unsightly enough to spoil any landscape. The following unflattering description is that given by Mons. Victor Jacquemont, who came out to India on a scientific mission on behalf of the Paris Museum of Natural History, and passed through Agra and Mathurá on his way to the Himalayas in the cold weather of 1829-30. "Nothing," he writes, "can be less picturesque than the Jamuná. The soil is sandy and the cultivated fields are intermingled with waste tracts, where scarcely anything will grow but the *Capparis aphylla* and one or two kinds of *zyzyphus*. There is little wheat ; barley is the prevailing cereal, with peas, sesamum, and cotton. In the immediate neighbourhood of the villages the *Tamarix articulata* gives a little shade with its delicate foliage, which is superlatively graceful no doubt, but as melancholy as that of the pine, which it strangely resembles. The villages are far apart from one another and present every appearance of decay. Most of them are surrounded by strong walls flanked with towers, but their circuit often encloses only a few miserable cottages." After a lapse of 50 years the above description is still fairly applicable. The villages are now more populous and the mud walls by which they were protected, being no longer required, have been gradully levelled with the ground. But the general features remain unchanged. The soil, being poor and thin, is unfavourable to the growth of most large forest trees; the mango and *shísham*, the glory of the lower Doáb, are conspicuously absent, and their place is most inadequately supplied by the *ním*, *farás*, and various species of the fig tribe. For the same reason the dust in any ordinary weather is deep on all the thoroughfares and, if the slightest air is stirring, rises in a dense cloud and veils the whole landscape in an impenetrable haze. The Jamuná, the one great river of Bráj, during eight months of the year meanders sullenly, a mere rivulet, between wide expanses of sand, bounded by monotonous flats of arable land, or high banks, which the rapidly expended force of contributory torrents has cracked and broken into ugly chasms and stony ravines, naked of all vegetation.

As the limits of Braj from north to south on one side are defined by the high lands to the east of the Jamuná, so are they on the other side by the hill ranges of Bharat-pur; but there are few peaks of conspicuous height and the general outline is tame and unimpressive. The villages, though large, are meanly built, and betray the untidiness characteristic of Játs and Gújars, who form the bulk of the population. From a distance they are often picturesque, being built on the slope of natural or artificial mounds, and thus gaining dignity by elevation. But on nearer approach they are found to consist of labyrinths of the narrowest lanes winding between the mud walls of large enclosures, which are rather cattle-yards than houses. At the base of the hill is ordinarily a broad circle of meadow land, studded with low trees, which afford grateful shade and pasturage for the cattle; while the large pond, from which the earth was dug to construct the village site, supplies them throughout the year with water. These natural woods commonly consist of *pílu*, *chhonkar*, and *kadamb* trees, among which are always interspersed clumps of *karíl* with its leafless evergreen twigs and bright-coloured flower and fruit. The *pasendu*, *pápri*, *arni*, *hingot*, *gondi*, *barna*, and *dho* also occur, but less frequently; though the last-named, the Sanskrit *dhava*, at Barsána clothes the whole of the hill-side. At sun-rise and sun-set the thoroughfares are all but impassable, as the straggling herds of oxen and buffaloes leave and return to the homestead: for in the straitened precincts of an ordinary village are stalled every night from 500 or 600 to 1,000 head of cattle, at least equalling, often outnumbering, the human population.

The general poverty of the district forms the *motif* of the following popular Hindi couplet, in which Krishna's neglect to enrich the land of his birth with any choicer product than the *karíl*, or wild caper, is cited as an illustration of his wilfulness:

कहा कहैं रघुनाथ को गई सतलो नाहि ॥
काबुल में मेवा करी टेंटी ब्रज की माहि ॥

which may be thus done into English :

Krishna, you see, will never lose his wayward whims and vapours ;
For Kábul teems with luscious fruit, while Braj boasts only capers.

In the rains however, at which season of the year all pilgrimages are made, the Jamuná is a mighty stream, a mile or more broad; its many contributory torrents and all the ponds and lakes, with which the district abounds, are filled to overflowing; the rocks and hills are clothed with foliage, the dusty plain is transformed into a green sward, and the smiling prospect goes far to justify the warmest panegyrics of the Hindu poets, whose appreciation of the scenery, it must be remembered, has been further intensified by religious enthusiasm. Even at all seasons of the year the landscape has a quiet charm of its own ; a sudden turn in the winding lane reveals a grassy knoll with stone-built well and overhanging *pípal;* or some sacred grove, where gleaming tufts of *karíl* and the white-blossomed *arúsa* weed are dotted about between the groups of weird *pílu* trees with their clusters of tiny berries and strangely gnarled and twisted trunks, all entangled in a dense undergrowth of prickly *ber* and *hins* and *chhonkar:* while in the centre, bordered with flowering oleander and *nivára*, a still cool lake reflects the modest shrine and well-fenced bush of *tulsi* that surmount the raised terrace, from which a broad flight of steps, gift of some thankful pilgrim from afar, leads down to the water's edge. The most pleasing architectural works in the district are the large masonry tanks, which are very numerous and often display excellent taste in design and skill in execution. The temples, though in some instances of considerable size, are all, excepting those in the three towns of Mathurá, Brindá-ban and Gobardhan, utterly devoid of artistic merit.

To a very recent period almost the whole of this large area was pasture and woodland and, as we have already remarked, many of the villages are still environed with belts of trees. These are variously designated as *ghaná, jhári, rakhyá, ban*, or *khandi,** and are often of considerable extent. Thus, the Koki-

* When the last term is used, the name of the most prevalent kind of tree is always added, as for instance *kadamb-khandi.*

la-ban at Great Bathan covers 723 acres ; the *rakhya* at Kámar more than 1,000; and in the contiguous villages of Pisáya and Karahla the *rakhya* and *kadamb-khandi* together amount to nearly as much. The year of the great famine, 1838 A. D., is invariably given as the date when the land began to be largely reclaimed ; the immediate cause being the number of new roads which were then opened out for the purpose of affording employment to the starving population.

Almost every spot is traditionally connected with some event in the life of Krishna or of his mythical mistress Rádhá, sometimes to the prejudice of an earlier divinity. Thus, two prominent peaks in the Bharat-pur range are crowned with the villages of Nand-gánw and Barsána : of which the former is venerated as the home of Krishna's foster-father Nanda, and the latter as the residence of Rádhá's parents, Vrisha-bhánu and Kírat.* Both legends are now as implicitly credited as the fact that Krishna was born at Mathurá ; while in reality, the name Nand-gánw, the sole foundation for the belief, is an ingenious substitution for Nandísvar, a title of Mahá-deva, and Barsána is a corruption of Brahma-sánu, the hill of Brahma. Only the Giri-ráj at Gobardhan was, according to the original distribution, dedicated to Vishnu, the second person of the *tri-murti*, or Hindu trinity ; though now he is recognized as the tutelary divinity at all three hill-places. Similarly, Bhau-gánw, on the right bank of the Jamuná, was clearly so called from Bhava, one of the eight manifestations of Siva ; but the name is now generally modified to Bhay-gánw, and is supposed to commemorate the alarm (*bhay*) felt in the neighbourhood at the time when Nanda, bathing in the river, was carried off by the god Varuna. A masonry landing-place on the water's edge called Nand-Ghát, with a small temple, dating only from last century, are the foundation and support of the local legend. Of a still more obsolete cultus, *viz.*, snake-worship, faint indications may be detected in a few local names and customs. Thus, at Jait, on the highroad to Delhi, there is an ancient five-headed Nága, carved in stone, by the side of a small tank† which occupies the centre of a low plain adjoining the village. It stands some four feet above the surface of the ground, while its tail was supposed to reach away to the Káli-mardan Ghát at Brindá-ban, a distance of seven miles. A slight excavation at the base of the figure has, for a few years at

---

* Kirat is the only name popularly known in the locality ; in the Padma Purána it appears in its more correct form as Kirttida: in the Brahma Vaivarta she is called Kalávati. It may also be mentioned that Vrisha-bhánu is always pronounced Brikh-bhán.

† This tank was re-excavated as a famine relief work in the year 1878 at a cost of Rs. 6,787.

least, dispelled the local superstition. So again, at the village of Paigánw, a grove and lake called respectively Pai-ban and Pai-ban-kund are the scene of an annual fair known as the *Barasi Nágá ji mela*. This is now regarded more as the anniversary of the death of a certain Mahant; but in all probability it dates from a much earlier period, and the village name would seem to be derived from the large offerings of milk (*payas*) with which it is usual to propitiate the Nága, or serpent-god.

Till the close of the 16th century, except in the neighbourhood of the one great thoroughfare, there was only here and there a scattered hamlet in the midst of unreclaimed woodland. The Vaishnava cultus then first developed into its present form under the influence of Rupa and Sanátana, the celebrated Bengáli Gosáins of Brindá-ban; and it is not improbable that they were the authors of the Brahma Vaivarta Purána,* the recognized Sanskrit authority for all the modern local legends. It wás their disciple, Náráyan Bhatt, who first established the Ban-játra and Rás-lílá, and it was from him that every lake and grove in the circuit of Braj received a distinctive name, in addition to the some seven or eight spots which alone are mentioned in the earlier Puránas. In the course of time, small villages sprung up in the neighbourhood of the differentshrines bearing the same name with them, though perhaps in a slightly modified form. Thus the *khadira-ban*, or 'acacia grove,' gives its name to the village of Khaira; and the *anjan pokhar*, on whose green bánk Krishna pencilled his lady's eyebrows with *anjan*, gives its name to the village of Ajnokh, occasionally written at greater length Ajnokhari. Similarly, when Krishna's home was fixed at Nand-gánw and Rádhá's at Barsána, a grove half-way between the two hills was fancifully selected as the spot where the youthful couple used to meet to enjoy the delights of love. There a temple was built with the title of Rádhá-Raman, and the village that grew up under its walls was called Sanket, that is,

---

* The Brahma Vaivarta Purána is, as all critics admit, an essentially modern composition, and Professor Wilson has stated his belief that it emanated from the sect of the Vallabhácháris, or Gosáins of Gokul. Their great ancestor settled there about the year 1489 A. D. The popular Hindi authority for Rádhá's Life and Loves is the Braj Bilás of Braj-vási Dás. The precise date of the poem, *sambat* 1800, corresponding to 1743 A. D., is given in the following line—

सम्वत सुभ पुराण शत जानेा

Another work of high repute is the Súr Ságar of Súr Dás Jí (one of the disciples of the great religious teacher Rámánand) as edited and expanded by Krishnánand Vyása.

'place of assignation.* Thus we may readily fall in with Hindu prejudices, and admit that many of the names on the map are etymologically connected with events in Krishna's life, and yet deny that those events have any real connection with the spot, inasmuch as neither the village nor the local name had any existence till centuries after the incidents occurred which they are supposed to commemorate.

The really old local names are almost all derived from the physical character of the country, which has always been celebrated for its wide extent of pasture land and many herds of cattle. Thus Gokul means originally a herd of kine ; Gobardhan a rearer of kine ; Mát is so called from *mát*, a milk-pail ; and Dadhigánw (contracted into Dah-gánw) in the Kosi pargana, from *dadhi*, 'curds.' Thus, too, 'Braj' in the first instance means 'a herd,' from the root *vraj*, 'to go,' in allusion to the constant moves of nomadic tribes. And hence it arises that in the earliest authorities for Krishna's adventures, both Vraja and Gokula are used to denote, not the definite localities now bearing those names, but any chance spot temporarily used for stalling cattle ; inattention to this archaism has led to much confusion in assigning sites to the various legends. The word 'Mathurá' also is probably connected with the Sanskrit root *math*, 'to churn ;'

* The temple dedicated to Rádha Raman, which was built by Rúp Rám, of Barsána, is in precisely the same style as the one at Nand-gánw, though on rather a smaller scale. The exterior has an imposing appearance, and is visible from a considerable distance, but there is nothing worth seeing inside, the workmanship being of a clumsy description, and the whole of the cloistered court-yard crowded with the meanest hovels. There is, however, a pretty view from the top of the walls. The original shrine, which Rúp Rám restored, is ascribed to Todar Mall, Akbar's famous minister. The little temple of Bihári (otherwise called Sija Mahal), built by a Rája of Bardwán, seems to be accounted much more sacred. It stands in a walled garden, all overgrown with *hins* jungle, in which is a high *Jhúlá* with several *baithaks* and other holy spots marked by inscribed commemorative tablets set up by one of Sindhia's Generals (as at Paitha and other places in the neighbourhood) in *sambat* 1885. It is here, on the occasion of any *játra*, that the spectacles of Krishna's marriage is represented as a scene in the Rás Lílá. The Krishna-kund is a large sheet of water, fifty yards square, with masonry steps on one of its sides. In the village are three large and handsome dwelling-houses, built in the reign of Súraj Mall, by one of his officials, Jauhari Mall of Fatihabad, and said to have been reduced to their present ruinous condition by the succeeding occupant of the Bharat-pur throne, the Rájá Jawáhir Sinh. The Vihvala-kund is a few hundred yards from the village on the road to Karahla. It is of stone, and has on its margin a temple of Devi, built by a Mahárája of Gwalior. The Doman-ban is within the boundaries of Nand-gánw, but is about the same distance from that town as it is from Bijwári and Sanket. It is a very pretty spot, of the same character as Pisáya, and of considerable extent; the name being always explained to mean 'the double wood,' as if a corruption of *do van*. At either extremity is a large pond embosomed in the trees, the one called Púran-mási, 'the full moon,' the other Rundki jhundki, 'jingle jingle.' A few fields beyond is the Kamál-pur grove.

the churn forming a prominent feature in all poetical descriptions of the local scenery. Take, for example, the following lines from the Harivansa, 3395 :—

क्षेम्यं प्रचारवहुलं हृष्टपुष्टजनावृतं ।
दामनीप्रायवहुलं गर्गरोद्गारनिस्वनं ॥
तक्रनिस्रावबहुलं दधिमण्डार्द्रमृत्तिकं ।
मन्थानवलयोद्गारै गोपीनां जनितस्वनं ॥

"A fine country of many pasture-lands and well-nurtured people, full of ropes for tethering cattle, resonant with the voice of the sputtering churn, and flowing with butter-milk; where the soil is ever moist with milky froth, and the stick with its circling cord sputters merrily in the pail as the girls spin it round."

And, again, in section 73 of the same poem—

व्रजेषु च विशेषेण गर्गरोद्गारहासिषु ॥

"In homesteads gladdened by the sputtering churn."

In many cases a false analogy has suggested a mythological derivation. Thus, all native scholars see in Mathurá an allusion to Madhu-mathan, a title of Krishna. Again, the word Bathan is still current in some parts of India to designate a pasture ground, and in that sense has given a name to two extensive parishes in Kosi; but as the term is not a familiar one thereabouts, a legend was invented in explanation, and it was said that here Balaráma 'sat down' (*baithen*) to wait for Krishna. The myth was accepted; a lake immediately outside the village was styled Bal-bhadra kund, was furnished with a handsome masonry ghát by Rúp Rám, the Katára of Barsána, and is now regarded as positive proof of the popular etymology which connects the place with Balaráma. Of Rúp Rám, the Katára, further mention will be made in connection with his birth-place, Barsána. There is scarcely a sacred site in the whole of Braj which does not exhibit some ruinous record, in the shape of temple or tank, of his unbounded wealth and liberality. His descendant in the fourth degree, a worthy man, by name Lakshman Dás, lives in a corner of one of his ancestor's palaces and is dependent on charity for his daily bread. The present owners of many of the villages which Rúp Rám so munificently endowed are the heirs of the Lálá Bábu, of whom also an account will be given further on.

In the Váráhá Purána, or rather in the interpolated section of that work known as the Mathurá Máhátmya, the Mathurá Mandal is described as twenty *yojanas* in extent.

विंशतिर्योजनानां च माथुरं मम मंडलं ॥
यत्र यत्र नरः स्नातो मुच्यते सर्वपातकैः ॥

"My Mathurá circle is one of twenty *yojanas;* by bathing at any place therein a man is redeemed from all his sins."

And taking the yojana as 7 miles and the kos as 1⅔ mile, 20 yojanas would be nearly equal to 84 kos, the popular estimate of the distance travelled by the pilgrims in performing the Pari-krama, or 'perambulation' of Braj. It is probable that if an accurate measurement were made, this would be found a very rough approximation to the actual length of the way; though liberal allowance must be made for the constant ins and outs, turns and returns, which ultimately result in the circuit of a not very wide-spread area. There can be no doubt that the number 84, which in ancient Indian territorial divisions occurs as frequently as a hundred in English counties, and which enters largely into every cycle of Hindu legend and cosmogony, was originally selected for such general adoption as being the multiple of the number of months in the year with the number of days in the week. It is therefore peculiarly appropriate in connection with the Braj Mandal; if Krishna, in whose honour the perambulation is performed, be regarded as the Indian Apollo, or Sun-God. Thus, the magnificent temple in Kashmír, dedicated to the sun under the title of Mártand, has a colonnade of exactly 84 pillars.*

It is sometimes said that the circle originally must have been of wider extent than now, since the city of Mathurá, which is described as its centre, is more than 30 miles distant from the most northern point, Kotban, and only six from Társi to the south; and Elliot in his glossary quotes the following couplet as fixing its limits :—

इत बरहद इत सोनहद उत सूरसेन का गांव ॥
ब्रज चौरासी कोस में मथुरा मंडल मांह ॥

"On one side Bar, on another Sona, on the third the town of Súrasen; these are the limits of the Braj Chaurási, the Mathurá circle."

* Mr. Fergusson, in his *Indian Architecture*, doubts whether this temple was ever really dedicated to the sun. In so doing he only betrays his wonted linguistic ignorance. Mártand is not, as he supposes, simply a place-name, without any known connotation, but is the actual dedication title of the temple itself.

According to this authority the area has been diminished by one half; as Bar is in the Aligarh district, Sona, famous for its hot sulphur springs, is in Gur-gánw; while the 'Súrasen ka gánw' is supposed to be Batesar,* a place of some note on the Jamuná and the scene of a large horse fair held on the full moon of Kártik. It might equally mean any town in the kingdom of Mathurá, or even the capital itself, as King Ugrasen, whom Krishna restored to the throne, is sometimes styled Súrasen. Thus, too, Arrian mentions Mathurá as a chief town of the Súraseni, a people specially devoted to the worship of Hercules, who may be identified with Balaráma: and Manu (II., 19) clearly intends Mathurá by Súrasena† when he includes that country with Kuru-kshetra, Panchála and Matsya, in the region of Brahmarshi, as distinguished from Brahmávarta. But though it must be admitted that the circle is sometimes drawn with a wider circumference, as will be seen in the sequel to this chapter, still it is not certain which of the two rests upon the better authority. In any case, the lines above quoted cannot be of great antiquity, seeing that they contain the Persian word *hadd*;‡ and, as regards the unequal distances between the city of Mathurá and different points on the circumference, it has only to be remembered that the circle is an ideal one, and any point within its outer verge may be roughly regarded as its centre.

As the anniversary of Krishna's birth is kept in the month of Bhádon, it is then that the perambulation takes place, and a series of *melas* is held at the different woods, where the *rás-lilá* is celebrated. This is an unwritten religious drama, which represents the most popular incidents in the life of Krishna, and thus corresponds very closely with the miracle plays of mediæval Christendom. The arrangement of the performances forms the recognized occupation of a class of Bráhmans residing chiefly in the villages of Karahla and Pisaya who are called Rásdháris and have no other profession or means of livelihood. The complete series of representations extends over a month or more, each scene

* Father Tieffenthaler, in his Geography of India, makes the following mention of Batesar:—"Lieu célèbre et bien bâti sur le Djemna, 28 milles d'Agra. Une multitude de peuple s'y rassemble pour se laver dans ce fleuve et pour célèbrer une foire en Octobre. On rend un culte ici dans beaucoup de temples bâtis sur le Djemna, à Mahadeo tant revèrè de tout l'univers adonné à la luxure; car Mahadeo est le Priape des anciens qu'encensent, ah quelle honte! toutes les nations."

† कुरुक्षेत्रं च मत्स्याश्च पञ्चालः शूरसेनकाः ॥
एष ब्रह्मर्षिदेशो वै ब्रह्मावर्त्तादनन्तरः ॥

‡ It is however possible, though I think improbable, that *had* may here stand for the Sanskrit *hruda*, a lake.

being acted on the very spot with which the original event is traditionally connected. The marriage scene, as performed at Sanket, is the only one that I have had the fortune to witness : with a garden-terrace for a stage, a grey stone temple for back-ground, the bright moon over head, and an occasional flambeau that shot a flickering gleam over the central tableau framed in its deep border of intent and sympathizing faces, the spectacle was a pretty one and was marked by a total absence of anything even verging upon indecorum. The cost of the whole perambulation with the performances at the different stations on the route is provided by some one wealthy individual, often a trader from Bombay or other distant part of India ; and as he is always accompanied by a large gathering of friends and retainers, numbering at least 200 or 300 persons, the outlay is seldom less than Rs. 5,000 or Rs. 6,000. The local Gosain, whom he acknowledges as his spiritual director, organizes all the arrangements through one of the Rásdháris, who collects the troupe (or *mandali* as it is called) of singers and musicians, and himself takes the chief part in the performance, declaiming in set recitative with the *mandali* for chorus, while the children who personate Rádhá and Krishna act only in dumb show.

The number of sacred places, woods, groves, ponds, wells, hills, and temples—all to be visited in fixed order—is very considerable ; there are generally reckoned five hills, eleven rocks, four lakes, eighty-four ponds, and twelve wells ; but the twelve bans or woods, and the twenty-four upabans or groves, are the characteristic feature of the pilgrimage, which is thence called the Ban-Játra. The numbers 12 and 24 have been arbitrarily selected on account of their mystic significance ; and few of the local pandits, if required to enumerate either group offhand, would be able to complete the total without some recourse to guesswork. A little Hindi manual for the guidance of pilgrims has been published at Mathurá and is the popular authority on the subject. The compiler, however great his local knowledge and priestly reputation, has certainly no pretensions to accuracy of scholarship. His attempts at etymology are, as a rule, absolutely grotesque, as in the two sufficiently obvious names of Khaira (for Khadira) and Sher-garh (from the Emperor Sher Sháh), the one of which he derives from *khedna*, 'to drive cattle,' and the other, still more preposterously, from *sihara*, 'a marriage crown.' The iist which he gives is as follows, his faulty orthography in some of the words being corrected :—

The 12 Bans : Madhu-ban, Tál-ban, Kumud-ban, Bahulá-ban, Kám-ban, Khadira-ban, Brindá-ban, Bhadra-ban, Bhándír-ban, Bel-ban, Loha-ban and Mahá-ban.

The 24 Upabans : Gokul, Gobardhan, Barsáná, Nand-gánw, Sanket, Paramadra, Aríng, Sessái, Mát, Uncha-gánw, Khel-ban, Srí-kund, Gandharv-ban, Parsoli, Bilchhu, Bachh-ban, Adi-badri, Karahla, Ajnokh, Pisáya, Kokila-ban, Dadhi-gánw, Kot-ban, and Rával.

This list bears internal evidence of some antiquity in its want of close correspondence with existing facts ; since several of the places, though retaining their traditionary repute, have now nothing that can be dignified with the name either of wood or grove ; while others are known only by the villagers in the immediate neighbourhood and have been supplanted in popular estimation by rival sites of more easy access or greater natural attractions.

Starting from Mathurá, the pilgrims made their first halt at Madhu-ban, in the village of Maholi, some four or five miles to the south-west of the city. Here, according to the Puránas, Ráma's brother, Satrughna, after hewing down the forest stronghold of the giant Madhu, founded on its site the town of Madhu-puri. All native scholars regard this as merely another name for Mathurá, regardless of the fact that the locality is several miles from the river, while Mathurá has always, from the earliest period, been described as situate on its immediate bank. The confusion between the two places runs apparently through the whole of classical Sanskrit literature ; as, for example, in the Harivansa (Canto 95) we find the city founded by Satrughna distinctly called, not Madhu-puri, but Mathurá, which Bhima, the king of Gobardhan, is represented as annexing :—

शत्रुघ्नो लवणं हत्वा चिच्छेद स मधोर्वनं ॥
तस्मिन्मधुवने स्थाने पुरीञ्च मथुरामिमां ॥
निवेशयामास विभुः सुमित्रानन्दवर्द्धनः ॥
पर्य्याये चैव रामस्य भरतस्य तथैव च ॥
सुमित्रासुतयोश्चैव प्राप्तयोर्वैष्णवं पदं ॥
भीमेनेयं पुरी तेन राज्यसम्बन्धकारणात् ॥
स्ववंशे स्थापिता पूर्व्वं स्वयमध्यासिता तथा ॥

"When Sumitrá's delight, prince Satrughna, had killed Lavana, he cut down the forest of Madhu, and in the place of that Madhu-ban founded the present city of Mathurá. Then, after Ráma and Bharata had left the world, and the two sons of Sumitrá had taken their place in heaven, Bhíma, in order to consolidate his dominions, brought the city, which had formerly been independent, under the sway of his own family."

Some reminiscence of the ancient importance of Maholi would seem to have long survived; for though so close to Mathurá, it was, in Akbar's time and for many years subsequently, the head of a local division. By the sacred wood is a pond called Madhu-kund and a temple dedicated to Krishna under his title of Chatur-bhuj, where an annual mela is held on the 11th of the dark fortnight of Bhádon.

From Maholi, the pilgrims turn south to Tál-ban, 'the palm grove,' where Balaráma was attacked by the demon Dhenuk. The village in which it is situated is called Társi, probably in allusion to the legend; though locally the name is referred only to the founder, one Tárá Chand, a Kachhwáhá Thákur, who in quite modern time moved to it from Satoha, a place a few miles off on the road to Gobardhan. They then visit Kumud-ban, 'of the many water-lilies,' in Uncha-gánw, and Bahulá-ban in Báthi, where the cow Bahulá, being seized by a tiger, begged the savage beast to spare her life for a few minutes, while she went away and gave suck to her little one. On her return, bringing the calf with her, the tiger vanished and Krishna appeared in his stead; for it was the god himself who had made this test of her truthfulness. The event is commemorated by the little shrine of Bahulá Gáe, still standing on the margin of the Krishna-kund.* They next pass through the villages of Tos, Jakhin-gánw, and Mukharái, and arrive at Rádhá-kund, where are the two famous tanks

* The village of Báthi, has long been held muáfi, by the Gurus of the Rájá of Bharatpur, for the use of the temple of Sítá Rám, of which they are the hereditary mahants. The shrine stands within the walls of the village fort, built by Mahant Rám Kishan Dás in the time of Súraj Mall. The first zamindárs were Kaláls, but more recently Bráhmans and Kachhwáhás. They have sold 8 biswás of their estate to the muáfidár, which have now been made a separate mahál. The sacred grove of Bahulá-ban, from which the place derives its name (originally Bahulavati) is separated from the village by a large pond, which has three broad flights of masonry steps in front of the little cell called the Go Mandir. In this is a bas-relief of the famous cow and its calf with their divine protector. Close by is a modern temple of Rádhá Krishan or Bihári Ji. On the other side of the water is a ruinous temple in the old style of architecture, dedicated to Murli Manohar, with a *sikhara* of curvilinear outline over the god, and a *mandap* with three open arches on either side to serve as the nave. The buildings in the fort are of substantial character and comprise, besides the temple and ordinary domestic offices, a court-room with stone arcades, the roof of which commands a very extensive view of the country round as far as Mathurá, Brindabán, and Nandgánw. The front of the temple of Sita Rám is an interesting and successful specimen of architectural eclecticism; the pillars being thoroughly Hindu in their proportions, but with capitals of semi-Corinthian design; not unlike some early adaptations of Greek models found in the ruined cities of the Euzufzai. The Gosáin belongs to the Sri Sampradáya. The *ban* is one of the stations of the Ban-játra, and the mela is held in it on Bhádon badí 12.

prepared for Krishna's expiatory ablution after he had slain the bull Arishta.* Thence they pass on to Gobardhan, scene of many a marvellous incident, and visit all the sacred sites in its neighbourhood; the village of Basái, where the two divine children with their foster-parents once came and dwelt (*basáé*); the Kallol-kund by the grove of Aríng; Mádhuri-kund; Mor-ban, the haunt of the peacock, and Chandra-sarovar, 'the moon lake;' where Brahma, joining with the Gopís in the mystic dance, was so enraptured with delight that, all unconscious of the fleeting hours, he allowed the single night to extend over a period of six months. This is at a village called Parsoli by the people, but which appears on the maps and in the revenue-roll only as Muhammad-pur. The tank is a fine octagonal basin with stone ghâts, the work of Rájá Náhar Sinh of Bharat-pur. After a visit to Paitha,† where the people of Braj 'came in' (*paithá*) to take shelter from the storms of Indra under the uplifted range, they pass along the heights of the Giri-ráj to Anyor,‡ 'the other side,' and so by many sacred rocks, as Sugandhi-sila, Sindúri-sila, and Sundar-sila, with its temple of Gobardhan-náth, to Gopál-pur, Bilchhu, and Gánthauli, where the marriage 'knot' (*gánth*) was tied, that confirmed the union of Rádhá and Krishna.

* Aríng, which is on the road from Mathurá to Gobardhan, and only a few miles distant from Rádhá-kund, is supposed to have been the place where the bull was slain, and to have derived its name, originally Aríshta-gánw, from the event.

† At Paitha the original temple of Chatur-bhuj is said to have been destroyed by Aurangzeb. Its successor, which also is now in ruins, was probably built on the old foundations, as it comprised a nave, choir, and sacrarium, each of the two latter cells being surmounted by a *sikhara*. It thus bore a general resemblance to the temples of Akbar's reign at Brindá-ban. The nave is unroofed, and both the towers partly demolished; what remains perfect is only of brick and quite plain and unornamented. It stands in the *kadamb-khandi* (107 bighas), which spreads over the low ground at the foot of the village *Khera*; its deepest hollows forming the Náráyan Sarovar, which is only a succession of ponds with here and there a flight of masonry steps. A cave is shown, which is believed to reach the whole way to Gobardhan, and to be the one that the people of Braj went into (*paitha*) to save themselves from the wrath of Indra. On the road to Gobardhan near Parsoli is the Moha-ban, and in it a lingam called Mohesvar Mahádeva, that is said to be sunk an immense depth in the ground, and will never allow itself to be covered over. Several attempts have been made to build a temple over it; but whenever the roof began to be put on, the walls were sure to fall in. This and several other of the sacred sites in the neighbourhood are marked by inscribed tablets set up last century by an officer under Sindhia.

‡ Here are two ancient temples dedicated to Gobind Deva and Baladeva, and a sacred tank, called Gobind kund, ascribed to Ráni Padmavati, the waters of which are supposed to be very efficacious in the cure of leprosy. The Pind-dán, or offerings to the dead, in the ceremonials of the Sráddh, have as much virtue here as even at Gaya. There are 40 acres of woodland. The original occupants are said to have been Kirárs. After the mutiny the village was conferred for a time on Chaudhari Daulat Sinh, but eventually restored to the existing zamindár.

Then, following the line of frontier, the pilgrims arrive at Kám-ban, now the head-quarters of a tahsíli in Bharat-pur territory, 39 miles from Mathurá, with the Luk-luk cave, where the boys played blind-man's buff ; and Aghásur's cave, where the demon of that name was destroyed ; and leaving Kanwáro-gánw, enter again upon British ground near the village of Uncha-gánw, with its ancient temple of Baladeva. High on the peak above is Barsána, with its series of temples dedicated to Lárlijí, where Rádhá was brought up by her parents, Brikhhbhán and Kírat ; and in the glade below, Dohani-kund near Chaksauli, where as Jasodá was cleansing her milk-pail (*dohani*) she first saw the youthful pair together, and vowed that one day they should be husband and wife. There too is Prem Sarovar, or love lake, where first the amorous tale was told ; and Sánkari Khor, 'the narrow opening' between the hills, where Krishna lay in ambush and levied his toll of milk on the Gopís as they came in from Gahvarban, the 'thick forest' beyond. Next are visited Sanket, the place of assignation : Rithora, home of Chandrávali, Rádhá's faithful attendant ; and Nand-gánw, long the residence of Nanda and Jasodá, with the great lake Pán-Sarovar at the foot of the hill, where Krishna morning and evening drove his foster-father's cattle to water (*pán*). Next in order come Karahla,* with its fine *kadamb* trees ; Kamai, where one of Rádhá's humble friends was honoured by a visit from her lord and mistress in the course of their rambles : Ajnokh,† where Krishna pencilled his lady's eyebrows with *anjan* as she reclined in careless mood on the green sward : and Pisáya,‡ where she found

* Karahla, or, as it is often spelt, Karhela, is locally derived from *kar hilna*, the movements of the hands in the *rás-lílá*. At the village or Little Marna, a pond bears the same name—karhelá-kund—which is there explained as *karm hilna*, equivalent to *páp mochan*. But in the Mainpuri district is a large town called Karhal—the same word in a slightly modified form—where neither of the above etymologies could hold. The name is more probably connected with a simple natural feature, *viz.*, the abundance of the *karíl* plant at each place.

† Ajnokh, or, in its fuller form, Ajnokhari, is a contraction for *Anjan Pokhar*, 'the anjan lake.'

‡ *Bhúkho pisáyo* is, in the language of the country, a common expression for 'hungry and thirsty.' But most of these derivations are quoted, not for their philological value, but as showing how thoroughly the whole country side is impregnated with the legends of Krishna, when some allusion to him is detected in every village name. In the Vraja-bhakti-vilása Pisáyo is called Pipása-vana ; but it would seem really to be a corruption of *pasavya*. It is one of the most picturesque spots in the whole district, being of very great extent, and in the centre consisting of a series of open glades leading one into the other, each encircled with a deep belt of magnificent *kadamb* trees, interspersed with a few specimens of the *pápri*, *pasendu*, *dhák* and *sahora*, of lower growth. These glades, which are often of such regular outline that they scarcely seem to be of natural formation, are popularly known as the *bávan chauk* or '52 courts,' though they are not

him fainting with 'thirst,' and revived him with a draught of water. Then still bearing due north the pilgrims come to Khadira-ban, 'the acacia grove,' in Khaira; Kumar-ban and Jávak-ban in Jáu, where Krishna tinged his lady's feet with the red Jávak dye, and Kokila-ban, ever musical with the voice of 'the cuckoo'; and so arrive at the base of Charan Pahár in Little Bathan, the favoured spot, where the minstrel god delighted most to stop and play his flute, and where Indra descended from heaven on his elephant Airávata, to do him homage, as is to this day attested by the prints of the divine 'feet' *charan*, impressed upon the rock.

They then pass on through Dadhi-gánw, where Krishna stayed behind to divert himself with the milk-maids, having sent Baladeva on ahead with the cows to wait for him at Bathan: and so reach Kot-ban, the northernmost point of the perambulation. The first village on the homeward route is Sessai (a hamlet of Hathána), where Krishna revealed his divinity by assuming the emblems of Náráyan and reclining under the canopying heads of the great serpent Sesha, of whom Baladeva was an incarnation; but the vision was all too high a mystery for the herdsmen's simple daughters, who begged the two boys to doff such fantastic guise and once more, as they were wont, join them in the sprightly dance.* Then, reaching the Jamuná at Khel-ban by Shergarh,† where Krishna's temples were, decked with 'the marriage weath' (*sihara*), they follow the course of the river through Bihár-ban in Pír-pur, and by Chírghát in the village of Siyára, where the frolicsome god stole‡ the bathers' 'clothes' (*chír*), and arrive at Nand-ghát. Here Nanda, bathing one night, was carried off by the myrmidons of the sea-god Varuna, who had long been lying in wait for this very purpose, since

---

really so many. They all swarm with troops of monkeys. On the eastern border the jungle is of more ordinary character, with ragged *pilu* and *renja* trees and *karil* bushes; but to the west, where a pretty view is obtained of the temple-crowned heights of Barsána in the distance, almost every tree is accompanied by a stem of the *arni*, which here grows to a considerable height and scents the whole air with its masses of flower, which both in perfume and appearance much resemble the English honeysuckle. Adjoining the village is a pond called Kishori-kund and two temples, visited by the Ba[illegible]ra pilgrims, Bhádon sudi 9.

* According to the [illegible] Purána, this transformation was not effected for the benefit of the Gopís, but was a [illegible] vouchsafed to Akrúr on the bank of the Jamuná the day he fetched the boys from Brind[illegible] attend the tourney at Mathurá.

† This is a c[illegible] men of perverted etymology, illustrating the persistency with which Hindus and Muha[illegible] each go their own way and ignore the other's existence. The town unqestionably derives [illegible] me from a large fort, of which the ruins still remain, built by the Emperor Sher Sháh.

‡ In the Vishnu Purána this famous incident is not mentioned at all.

their master knew that Krishna would at once follow to recover his foster-father, and thus, the depths of ocean, too, no less than earth, would be gladdened with the vision of the incarnate deity. The adjoining village of Bhay-gánw derives its name from the 'terror' (*bhay*) that ensued on the news of Nanda's disappearance. The pilgrims next pass through Bachh-ban, where the demon Bachhásur was slain; the two villages of Basái, where the Gopís were first 'subdued' (*bas-ái*) by the power of love ; Atas, Nari-semri,* Chhatíkra, and Akrúr, where Kansa's perfidious invitation to the contest of arms was received; and wend their way beneath the temple of Bhatrond, where one day, when the boys' stock of provisions had run short, some Brahmans' wives supplied their wants, though the husbands, to whom application was first made, had churlishly refused.† So

* A large fair, called the Nau Durgá, is held at the village of Nari-Semri during the dark fortnight of Chait, the commencement of the Hindu year. The same festival is also celebrated at Sánchauli in the Kosi pargana and at Nagar-Kot in Gur-gánw, though not on precisely the same days. The word Semri is a corruption of Syámalá-ki, with reference to the ancient shrine of Devi, who has Syámalá for one of her names (compare *simika*, 'an ant-hill,' for *syamika*). The present temple is a small modern building, with nothing at all noteworthy about it. It stands on the margin of a fine large piece of water, and in connection with it are two small *dharmsalas*, lately built by pilgrims from Agra. A much larger building for the same purpose was commenced by a baniya before the mutiny, but the work was stopt by his death. The offerings ordinarily amount to at least Rs. 2,000 a year, and are enjoyed in turn by three groups of shareholders, *viz.*, the zamindárs of Semri old village, of Birja-ka-nagara and of Devi Sinh-ka-nagara, to each of whom a turn comes every third year. They had always spent the whole of the money on their own private uses, but at my suggestion they all agreed to give an annual sum of Rs. 150 to expend on conservancy during the fair time and on local improvements. The first work to have been taken in hand was the completion of the baniya's rest-house. I estimated the cost at Rs. 1,050 and had begun to collect bricks and stone and mortar, when my transfer from the district took place, and the project immediately fell through. If the work had once been started, the pilgrims would have gladly contributed to it ; and in addition to the *dharmsála*, which was of very substantial construction, so far as it had gone, there would soon have been a masonry ghát to the pond and a plantation of trees round about the temple. But *Diis aliter visum est.* The principal fair begins on the new moon of Chait and lasts for nine days. On the sixth there is a very large gathering at the rival shrine of the same goddess at Sanchauli ; but during all the remainder of the time the Agra and Delhi road is crowded day and night with foot passengers and vehicles of every description. Fortunately none of the visitors for religious purposes stay more than a few hours ; and thus, though it is the most popular melá in the whole district, there is never any very great crowd at any one particular time, for as one set of people comes, another goes. Special days are even assigned to particular castes and localities : thus the Agra people have one day, the Jádons of the neighbourhood another, the Gauruas a third, and so on. The second fair is held on the Akh-tij, the third day of the bright fortnight of Baisákh.

† To commemorate the event, a fair called the Bhatmela is held on the spot on the full moon of Kartik. Compare the story of David repulsed by the churlish Nabal, but afterwards succoured by his wife Abigail.

they arrive at Brindá-ban, where many a sacred ghát and venerable shrine claim devout attention.

The pilgrims then cross the river and visit the tangled thickets of Bel-ban in Jahángír-pur; the town of Mát with the adjoining woods of Bhadra-ban, scene of the great conflagration, and Bhándír-ban, where the son of Rohini first received his distinctive title of Bala-ráma, *i.e.*, Ramá the strong, in consequence of the prowess he had displayed in vanquishing the demon Pralamba; Dángoli, where Krishna dropt his 'staff (*dang*)* and the fair lake of Mán-sarovar,† scene of a fit of lover's 'pettishness' (*mán*). Then follow the villages of Piparauli, with its broad spreading *pípal* trees; Loha-ban, perpetuating the defeat of the demon Lohásur‡; Gopálpur, favourite station of the herdsmen, and Rával, where Rádhá's mother, Kírat, lived with her father, Surbhán, till she went to join her husband at Barsána. Next comes Burhiya-ká-kherá, home of the

* The name Dángoli is really derived from the position of the village on the 'high river bank,' which is also called *dang*.

† The name is probably derived from the tree *lodha* or *lodhra*. The demon slain by Krishna is styled Loha-jangha in late local Sanskrit literature, but apparently is not mentioned at all in any ancient work. Here is a pond called Krishna-kund, and a temple of Gopináth, built in the old style with a shrine and porch, each surmounted by a *sikhara*, the one over the god being much the higher of the two. The doorways have square lintels and jambs of stone with a band of carving. The date assigned to the building is 1712, which is probably not far from correct. Outside is the lower part of a red sandstone figure set in the ground, called Lohásur Daitya, the upper part much worn by the knives and mattocks that are sharpened upon it. Here are made offerings of iron (*loha*) which become the perquisite of a family of Mahá Brahmans living in Mathurá. The Sanádh Bráhman at the temple has only the offerings that are made specially there. About the Krishna-kund is a Kadamb-khandi of rather stunted growth, and some very fine pipal trees. Immediately under the roots of one of them is a small well, called Gop kúa, which always has water in it, though the pond dries up in the month of Jeth. Over it is a stone rudely carved with two figures said to represent Gopis. A small shrine on the opposite side of the *kund* has been erected over some sculptures of no great antiquity, which were found in the pond. I arranged with the Gokul Gosáins to have the *ban* planted with trees, which when grown up would be a great boon to the pilgrims. They were getting on well when I left, but probably no further care will now be taken for their maintenance.

‡ The Mán-sarovar on the borders of Páni-gánw is a lake of no great depth or extent and in the hot weather most of it dries up. Lakhmi Dás, a Gosáin of the Rádhá Ballabh persuasion, owns the whole of the village and has a little hermitage on the bank, prettily situated in the midst of some venerable jáman trees, the remains of an old garden, said to have been planted by a Rája of Ballabh-garh, to whom is also ascribed a *chhattri*, with a ribbed stone roof. There are two small and plain modern shrines, one of which was built by Mohani, the Ráni of Súraj Mall, who is commemorated by the Gangá Mohan *Kunj* at Brindá-ban. The adjoining *ghana*, or wood, spreads over several hundreds of acres and is quite different in character from any other in Braj, the trees being all, with scarcely an exception, *babúl*,

old dame whose son had taken in marriage Rádhá's companion, Mánvati. The fickle Krishna saw and loved, and in order to gratify his passion undisturbed, assumed the husband's form. The unsuspecting bride received him fondly to her arms; while the good mother was enjoined to keep close watch below and, if any one came to the door pretending to be her son by no means to open to him, but rather, if he persisted, pelt him with brick-bats till he ran away. So the honest man lost his wife and got his head broken into the bargain.

After leaving the scene of this merry jest, the pilgrims pass on to Bandigánw, a name commemorative of Jasodá's two faithful domestics, Bandi and Anandi, and arrive at Baladeva, with its wealthy temple dedicated in honour of that divinity and his spouse, Revatí. Then, beyond the village of Hathaura, are the two river landing-places, Chintá-haran, 'the end of doubt,' and Brahmánda, 'creation,' ghát. Here Krishna's playmates came running to tell Jasodá that the naughty boy had filled his mouth with mud. She took up a stick to punish him, but he, to prove the story false, unclosed his lips and showed her there, within the compass of his baby cheeks, the whole 'created' universe with all its worlds and circling seas distinct. Close by is the town of Mahá-ban, famous for many incidents in Krishna's infancy, where he was rocked in the cradle, and received his name from the great pandit Garg, and where he put to death Pútaná and the other evil spirits whom Kansa had commissioned to destroy him. At Gokul, on the river-bank, are innumerable shrines and temples dedicated to the god under some one or other of his favourite titles, Madan Mohan, Mádhava Ráe, Brajesvara, Gokul-náth, Navanít-priya, and Dwáraká-náth: and when all have been duly honoured with a visit, the weary pilgrims finally recross the stream and sit down to rest at the point from which they started, the Visránt Ghát, the holiest place in the holy city of Mathurá.

---

remja, or *chhonkar*, three kindred species of acacia. Part of it lies within the borders of Arua and Piparauli; but by far the greater part is in Páni-gánw and is the property of the Mahárája of Bharatpur, who has frequently been tempted to sell the timber and convert it into firewood. It is much to be hoped that he will always withhold his consent from an act which would destroy all the beauty of the scene and be so offensive to the religious sentiments of his fellow Hindús. There are no relics of antiquity, nor indeed could there be; for both lake and wood are all in the *khádar*, or alluvial land, which at no very distant period must have been the bed of the Jamuná; it is still flooded by it in the rains. Though a legend has been invented to connect the place with Rádha and Krishna, the name as originally bestowed probably bore reference to the Mánasa lake on Mount Kailás in the Himalayas, sacred to Mahadeva.

As may be gathered from the above narrative, it is only the twelve *bans* that, as a rule, are connected with the Pauránik legends of Krishna and Bala-ráma, and these are all specified by name in the Mathurá Máhátmya. On the other hand, the twenty-four *upabans* refer mainly to Rádhá's adventures, and have no ancient authority whatever. Of the entire number, only three were, till quite recent times, places of any note, *viz.*, Gokul, Gobardhan, and Rádhá-kund, and their exceptional character admits of easy explanation: Gokul, in all classical Sanskrit literature, is the same as Mahá-ban, which is included among the *bans*; Gobardhan is as much a centre of sanctity as Mathurá itself, and is only for the sake of uniformity inserted in either list; while Rádhá-kund, as the name denotes, is the one primary source from which the goddess derives her modern reputation. It is now insisted that the parallelism is in all respects complete; for, as Krishna has four special dwelling-places, Mathurá, Mahá-ban, Gobardhan, and Nand-gánw, so has Rádhá four also in exact correspondence, *viz.*, Brindá-ban, Rával,* Rádhá-kund, and Barsána.

The perambulation, as traced in the foregoing sketch, is the one ordinarily performed, and includes all the most popular shrines; but a far more elaborate enumeration of the holy places of Braj is given in a Sanskrit work, existing only in manuscript, entitled Vraja-bhakti-vilása. It is of no great antiquity, having been compiled, in the year 1553 A.D., by the Náráyan Bhatt, who has been already mentioned.† He is said to have been a resident of Unchá-gánw near Barsána, but he describes himself as writing at Srí-kund, *i. e.*, Rádhá-kund. It is divided into 13 sections extending over 108 leaves, and is professedly based on the Paramahansa Sanhita. It specifies as many as 133 *bans* or woods, 91 on

* Rával is still included in the perambulation of Gokul, and till the foundation of the new temple of Lárli Jí at Barsána was a much more popular place of pilgrimage than it is now. Probably the whole of old Rával has been washed away by the Jamuná, and a similar fate threatens before long to overtake the present temple of Lárli Jí, built by Kushál, Seth, in the early part of this century. The river wall, by which it was protected, has already in great measure fallen. The Pujári, Chhote Lál, has a *sanad* dated the 20th year of Muhammad Shah (1739 A.D.) in which the Vazir Karm-ud-din Khán assigns Rúp Chand, the then Pujári, one rupee a day for his support from the revenues of the Mahá-ban tahsil. There is a garden surrounded by a substantial wall, from the top of which there is a good view of the City and Cantonments of Mathurá. In its centre is a pavilion with stone arcades in the same style as the temple and built by the same Seth. About one-half of the village land is cut up by ravines and unculturable. Some years ago there used to be a ferry here and a large colony of boatmen, who were all thrown out of employ when the ferry was closed and a pontoon bridge substituted for the old bridge of boats between Mathurá and Hansganj.

† The colophon of the Vraja-bhakti-vilása runs as follows :—Srímad Bháskar-átmaja-Náráyana-Bhatta-virachite Vraja-bhakti-vilase Paramahansa-sanhitodáharane Vraja-Máhátmya-nirúpane Vana-yátra-prasange Vraja-yátra-prasangike trayodaso' dhyáyah.

23

the right bank of the Jamnná and 42 on the left, and groups them under different heads as follows:—

I.—The 12 Bans: 1, Mahá-ban; 2, Kámya-ban; 3, Kokila-ban; 4, Tál-ban; 5, Kumud-ban; 6, Bhándír-ban; 7, Chhatra-ban;* 8, Khadira-ban; 9, Loha-ban, 10, Bhadra-ban; 11, Bahulá-ban; 12, Vilva-ban, *i. e.*, Bel-ban.

II.—The 12 Upabans: 1, Brahma-ban; 2, Apsará-ban; 3, Vihvala-ban; 4, Kadamb-ban; 5, Svarna-ban; 6, Surabhi-ban; 7, Prem-ban;† 8, Mayúra, *i. e.*, Mor-ban; 9, Manengiti-ban; 10, Sesha-saiyí-ban; 11, Nárada-ban; 12, Paramánanda-ban.

III.—The 12 Prati-bans: 1, Ranka-ban; 2, Vártá-ban; 3, Karahla; 4, Kámya-ban; 5, Anjana-ban; 6, Káma-ban; 7, Krishna-kshipanaka; 8, Nanda-prekshana; 9, Indra-ban; 10, Siksha-ban; 11, Chandrávati-ban; 12, Lohaban.‡

IV.—The 12 Adhi-bans: 1, Mathurá; 2, Rádhá-kund; 3, Nanda-gráma; 4, Gata-sthána; 5, Lalita-gráma; 6, Brisha-bhánu-pur;§ 7, Gokul; 8, Baladeva; 9, Gobardhan; 10, Jáva-ban; 11, Brindá-ban; 12, Sanket.

V.—The 5 Sevya-bans; VI. the 12 Tapo-bans; VII. the 12 Moksha-bans; VIII. the 12 Káma-bans; IX. the 12 Artha-bans; X. the 12 Dharma-bans; XI. the 12 Siddhi-bans—all of which the reader will probably think it unnecessary to enumerate in detail.

To every ban is assigned its own tutelary divinity; thus Haláyudha (Báladeva) is the patron of Mahá-ban; Gopínáth of Kám-ban; Nata-vara of Kokila-ban; Dámodar of Tál-ban; Kesava of Kumud-ban; Sridhara of Bhándír-ban; Hari of Chhatra-ban; Náráyan of Khadira-ban; Hayagríva of Bhadra-ban; Padma-nábha of Bahulá-ban; Janardana of Bel-ban; Adi-vadrisvara of Paramánanda; Paramesvara of Kam-ban (prati-ban); Jasodá-nandan of Nand-gánw; Gokulchandrama of Gokul; Murlidhar of Karahla; Líla-kamala-lochana of Hásya-ban; Lokesvara of Upahára-ban; Lankadhipa-kula-dhvansi of Jahnu-ban; and Sríshatsilankshyana of Bhuvana-ban.

---

* Chhatra-ban represents the town of Chhátá. The only spot mentioned in connection with it is the Súraj-kund, a pond which still exists and bears the same name, but is not now held in much regard.

† Surabhi-ban adjoins Gobardhan. Near Prem-ban is the Prem-sarovar.

‡ The one Loha-ban on the right bank of the river is described as the scene of the destruction of Jarásandha's armies; the other, on the left bank, is more correctly styled Loha-jangha-ban.

§ Brisha-bhánu-pur is intended as the Sanskrit original of Barsána, but incorrectly so.

The four last-named woods are given as the limits of the Braj Mandal in the following sloka, and it is distinctly noted that the city of Mathurá is at the same distance, *viz.*, 21 kos, from each one of them :—

पूर्वे हास्यवनं नीय पश्चिमस्यापहारिकं ॥
दक्षिणे जन्हुसंज्ञाकं भुवनाख्यं तथोत्तरे ॥

The Pandits, who were asked to reconcile these limits with those mentioned in the Hindi couplet previously quoted, declared Hásya-ban in the east to be the same as Barhadd in Aligarh: Upahára-ban in the west as Sona in Gurgánw; Jahnu-ban to the south the same as Súrasen-ká-gánw, or Batesar; and Bhuvana-ban to the north, Bhúkhan-ban near Shergarh. The identification is probably little more than conjectural; but a superstition, which is at once both comparatively modern and also practically obsolete, scarcely deserves a more protracted investigation than has already been bestowed upon it.

Next to the Ban-játra, the most popular local festvity is the Holi, which is observed for several days in succession at different localities. Several of the usages are, I believe, entirely unknown beyond the limits of Braj, even to the people of the country ; and, so far as I could ascertain by enquiries, they had never been witnessed by any European. Accordingly, as the festival fell unusually early in 1877, while the weather was still cool enough to allow of a mid-day ride without serious inconvenience, I took advantage of the opportunity thus afforded me and made the round of all the principal villages in the Chhátá and Kosi parganas where the rejoicings of the Phúl Dol, for so these Hindu Saturnalia are popularly termed, are celebrated with any peculiarities, visiting each place on its special fête-day. The following is an account of what I saw:—

Feb. 22nd, Barsána, the Rangíla Holi.—In the middle of the town is a small open square, about which are grouped the stately mansions and temples built by the great families who resided here during the first half of the 18th century. A seat in the balcony over the gateway of the house still occupied by the impoverished descendants of the famous Katára, Rúp Rám, the founder of Barsána's short-lived magnificence, commands a full view of the humours of the crowd below. The cheeriness of the holiday-makers as they throng the narrow winding streets on their way to and from the central square, where they break up into groups of bright and ever-varying combinations of colour ; with the buffooneries of the village clowns and the grotesque dances of the lusty swains, who with castanets in hand caricature in their movements the conventional graces of the Indian ballet-girl,

Crispum sub crotalo docta movere latus,

all make up a sufficiently amusing spectacle; but these are only interludes and accessories to the great event of the day. This is a sham fight between the men from the neighbouring village of Nand-gánw and the Barsána ladies, the wives of the Gosáins of the temple of Lárli Ji, which stands high on the crest of the rock that overlooks the arena. The women have their mantles drawn down over their faces and are armed with long heavy bambus, with which they deal their opponents many shrewd blows on the head and shoulders. The latter defend themselves as best they can with round leather shields and stags' horns. As they dodge in and out amongst the crowd and now and again have their flight cut off and are driven back upon the band of excited viragoes, many laughable incidents occur. Not unfrequently blood is drawn, but an accident of the kind is regarded rather as an omen of good fortune and has never been known to give rise to any ill-feeling. Whenever the fury of their female assailants appears to be subsiding, it is again excited by the men shouting at them snatches of the following ribald rhymes. They are not worth translation, since they consist of nothing but the repetition of the abusive word *sálá*, applied to every person and thing in Barsána. That town being the reputed home of Rádhá, the bride, its people are styled her brothers; while the Nand-gánw men account themselves the brothers of Krishna, the bridegroom:—

श्रीभांडबधाई बरसांने की ।

सब सारे बरसांनेबारे रावलबारे सारे ।
जगन्नाथके नाती सारे वे बरसांनेबारे ॥
लवानियां श्रोर कटारे सारे जे बरसांनेबारे ।
डोंम ढढ़ेरे सबही सारे श्रोर पत्तराबारे ॥
बाग बगीचा सबही सारे सारे सींचनबारे ।
बिरकत श्रोर गुदरिया सारे लंबे सुतनाबारे ॥
बाबाजी भानोंखरि सारे प्रेंमसरोवरबारे ।
खाट खटोला सबही सारे चोका चूल्हे सारे ॥
महलायत महलायत सारे सारे खंभ तिहारे ।
अगवारे पिछवारे सारे गेल गिरारे सारे ॥

Feb. 23rd, Nand-gánw.—Another sham fight, as on the preceding day, only with the characters reversed; the women on this occasion being the wives of the Gosáins of the Nand-gánw temple, and their antagonists the men of Barsána. The combatants are drawn up more in battle-array, instead of skirmishing by twos and threes, and rally round a small yellow pennon that is carried in their midst; but the show is less picturesque in its accessories, being held on a very dusty spot outside the town, and was more of a Phallic orgie.

Feb. 27th, the Holi. Phálen.—Here is a sacred pond called Prahlád-kund, and the fact of its having preserved its original name gives a clue, as in so many parallel cases, to the older form of the name now borne by the village. Local pandits would derive the word *phálen* from the verb *phárna*, "to tear in pieces," with a reference to the fate of Prahlád's impious father, Hiranya-Kasipu: but such a formation would be contrary both to rule and to experience, and the word is, beyond a doubt, a corruption of Prahláda-gráma.

Arriving at the village about an hour before sunset, I found a crowd of some 5,000 people closely packed in the narrow spaces on the margin of the pond and swarming over the tops of the houses and the branches of all the trees in the neighbourhood. A large bonfire had been stacked half-way between the pond and a little shrine dedicated to Prahlád, inside which the Khera-pat, or Panda, who was to take the chief part in the performance of the day, was sitting telling his beads. At 6 P. M. the pile was lit, and, being composed of the most inflammable materials, at once burst into such a tremendous blaze that I felt myself scorching, though the little hillock where I was seated was a good many yards away. However, the lads of the village kept on running close round it, jumping and dancing and brandishing their *láthis*, while the Pánda went down and dipped in the pond and then, with his dripping *pagri* and *dhoti* on, ran back and made a feint of passing through the fire. In reality he only jumped over the outermost verge of the smouldering ashes and then dashed into his cell again, much to the dissatisfaction of the spectators, who say that the former incumbent used to do it much more thoroughly. If on the next recurrence of the festival the Pánda shows himself equally timid, the village proprietors threaten to eject him, as an impostor, from the land which he holds rent-free simply on the score of his being fire-proof.

Feb. 28th, Kosi.—After sitting a little while at a *nach* of the ordinary character, given by one of the principal traders in the town, I went on to see the *chaupáis*, or more special Holi performances, got up by the different bodies of Ját zamindárs, each in their own quarter of the town. The dancers, exclusively men and boys, are all members of the proprietory clan, and are all dressed alike in a very high-waisted full-skirted white robe, reaching to the ankles, called a *jhagá*, with a red *pagri*, in which is set at the back of the head a long tinsel plume, *kalangi*, to represent the peacock feathers with which Krishna was wont to adorn himself as he rambled through the woods. The women stand at one end of the court-yard with their mantle drawn over their faces and holding long *láthis*, with which, at a later period of the proceedings, they join in the Holi sports. Opposite them are the bandsmen with drums, cymbals and timbrels, and at their back other men with sticks and green twigs, which they brandish about over their heads. The space in the middle is circled by torch-bearers and kept clear for the dancers, who are generally six in number, only one pair dancing at a time. Each performer, in the dress as above described, has a knife or dagger in his right hand and its scabbard in his left. At first, darting forward, they make a feint of thrusting at the women or other spectators, and then pointing the knife to their own breast they whirl round and round, generally backwards, the pace growing faster and more furious and the clash of the band louder and louder, till at last they sink down, with their flowing robe spread out all round them, in a sort of curtsey, and retire into the back ground, to be succeeded by another pair of performers. After a pair of men comes a pair of boys, and so on alternately with very little variation in the action. Between the dances a verse or two of a song is sung, and at the end comes the *Holi khelna*. This is a very monotonous performance. The women stand in a line, their faces veiled, and each with a *láthi* ornamented with bands of metal and gaudy pendents, like the Bacchantes of old with the thyrsus, and an equal number of men oppose them at a few yards' interval. The latter advance slowly with a defiant air and continue shouting snatches of scurrilous song till they are close upon the women, who then thrust out their *láthis*, and without uttering a word follow them as they turn their back and retreat to their original standing-place. Arrived there, they let the women form again in line as they were at first and then again advance upon them precisely as before, and so it goes on till their repertory of songs is exhausted, or they have no voice left to sing them. To complete my description I here give some specimens of these *sákhis* or verses, and have added notes to all the words that seemed likely to require explanation. They are many of them too coarse and at the same time too stupid to make it desirable for me to translate them in full.

होली खेलने के समय की साखी ।

बूझो याहि संग चलेगी ।
सई सांझ से धरी कढ़ैया आधीरात नसेगी ॥ १ ॥
हरलेगे चीर मुरारी ।
लेके चीर कदम पे बैठे हम जल मांझ उघारी ॥
तुम्हरो चीर जबै हम दें हैं जल ते होजाउ न्यारी ।
जो हम जल ते न्यारी होंगी जायगी लाज तिहारी ॥
चीर हमारो देहु सांवरे तुम जीते हम हारी ॥ २ ॥
राधे क्यों दलगीरी मन में ।
के कहूं स्याम सेज न आए के परगई चूक भजन में ॥ ३ ॥
बिंदाबन से बन नहीं नंदगांव से गांव ।
बंसीबट से बट नहीं कृष्ण नाम से नांव ॥ ४
ब्रज चौरासी कोसमें चार गांव निज धाम ।
बृंदाबन अरु मधपुरी बरसानो नंदगांम ॥ ५ ॥
राधे दीजे बंसी मेरी ।
के दीजे के नाहीं कीजे देख गरीबी मेरी ॥ ६ ॥
मन मोहन खेले होरी ।
घर घर तें बनता बन आईं अपनी अपनी जोरी ॥
इत ते निकसे कुंवर कन्हैया इत ब्रषभान किशोरी ।
ताल मृदंग झांझ डप बाजे मोंह चंगन की जोरी ॥
उड़त गुलाल लाल भए बादर केसर गागर घोरी ॥ ७ ॥
होरी खेलें श्रीगिरिधारी ।
कोनस पे केसरिया बानो कोन पे चीर हजारी ॥

---

1. Krishna says to Udho: Ask her if she will come. She set the *karáhi* on the fire the first thing in the evening and will slip out at midnight.
2. *Jabi*, then: *jayegi láj tihári*. you will be put to shame.
3. *Dilgiri*, sadness.
6. Whether you give or whether you refuse
7. *Apni apni jori*, in pairs, two and two: *morchang*, or *mohchang*, a Jew's-harp. *Gágar*, ajar: *Ghori* for *ghóli*, mixed.

कान्हा पै केसरिया बानो राधे चीर हजारी ॥
कौन के हाथ गड़ुरा सोहै कौनस पै पिचकारी ॥
राधे हाथ गड़ुरा सोहै कान्हा पै पिचकारी ॥ ८ ॥
दधि पीजा स्याम सलोना ।
काहे की तेरी बनी मथनिया काहे के तेरे दौना ॥
ब्रजरज की मेरी बनी मथनिया कदम पात के दौना ॥ ९ ॥
मेरी स्याम बिना कल काते ।
झुर झुर पिंजर ह्वै गई राधे सूखलगी पलकाते ॥ १० ॥
दधि को तू चोर कन्हैया ।
दधि मेरी खाय मथनिया फोरी और मरोरी बैंया ॥ ११ ॥
दधि लूट लई दगरे में ।
दधि मेरी खाय मथनिया फोरी ग्वाल बाल सगरेन्ने ॥
उंगरी में की मुंदरी लूटी नौलखहार गरेमें ॥
बाजूबंद खमला लूटे नथ राखी झगरे में ॥ १२ ॥
ऐसो कब करहे मन मेरो ।
ब्रजबासिन के टूक भूक में घर घर छांछ महेरो ॥
भूक लगे जल मांग खातहूं सांझ गिनू न सवेरो ॥ १३ ॥
कान्हा धरे रे मुकट खेले होरी ।
एक ओर खेले कुंवर कन्हैया एक ओर राधा गोरी ॥ १४ ॥
इन गलियन काम कहा तेरो ।

---

8. *Kaunas* for *kaun sá*; *bána*, clothes; *garúr á*, a pot.
9. *Píja*, for *pijiye ákar*.
10. *Kal*, happiness.
11. *Baiyán*, for *bánh*, arm.
12. *Khaela*, an ornament that hangs pendent from the elbow.
13. *Mahero*, a mess of rice and sour milk.

इन गलियन मेरो स्यालू फार्‌यो में तो फाडूंगी यार झगा तेरो ॥ १५ ॥
खिसली तोहि देख घटा ते ।
तू जु कहेहो तोहि अध्‌बर लूंगो अब मेरी टूटी हे बांह बरा ते ॥ १६ ॥
कब निकसेगो सूक चले चालो ।
गोरीने डोला सजवायो रसियाने बिकल कर्‌यो भालो ॥ १७ ॥
जोरी मत करे मान राख देंउगी ।
रंग महल मेरो पलंग बिछ्‌यो हे ह्वां तेरो जोम डाट लेंउगी ॥ १८ ॥
संग सोयवेकी द्योस कहो होती ।
माटी खोदन गई खदाने ह्वां मेरी बांह गही होती ॥ १९ ॥

March 1*st*, *Kosi*.—Spend an hour or two in the afternoon as a spectator of the Holi sports at the Gomati-Kund. Each of the six Ját villages of the Denda Pál* has two or more *chaupáis*, which come up one after the other in a long procession, stopping at short intervals on the way to dance in the manner above described, but several at a time instead of in single pairs. One of the performers executed a *pas de seul* mounted on a *daf*, or large timbrel, which was supported on the shoulders of four other men of his troupe. Bands of mummers (or *swángs*) were also to be seen, one set attired as Muhammadan fakirs; another (*ghάyalon ká swáng*) as wounded warriors, painted with streaks, as it were of blood, and with sword-blades and daggers so bound on to their neck and arms

15. *Syálu*, a woman's *dopatta*.
Jhagá, a man's dress.
16. *Adhbar*, in the middle.
Bará, an ornament worn by women on the elbow.
17. *Suk*, the planet Venus, which is regarded as auspicious.
Chalan, the same as the more common *gauna*.
18. *Jori*, for *zori*. *zabrdasti*.
Jom, lust, passion.
19. *Dyaus*, the day-time.
Khaddna, a clay pit.

* Any subdivision of a *Ját* clan is called a *Pál*, and the town of Kosi is the centre of one such sub-division, which is known as the Denda Pál.

and other parts of the body that they seemed to be transfixed by them. Some long iron rods were actually thrust through their protruded tongue and their cheeks, and in this ghastly guise and with drawn swords in their hands, with which they kept on dealing and parrying blows, the pair of combatants perambulated the crowd.

March 2nd.—At 2 P. M. ride over to Bathen for the Holanga mela, and find a place reserved for me on a raised terrace at the junction of fourstreets in the centre of the village. Every avenue was closely packed with the densest throng, and the house-tops seemed like gardens of flowers with the bright dresses of the women. Most of them were Játs by caste and wore their distinctive costume, a petticoat of coarse country stuff worked by their own hands with figures of birds, beasts, and men, of most grotesque design, and a mantle thickly sewn all over with discs of talc, which flash like mirrors in the sun and quite dazzle the sight. The performers in the *chaupái* could scarcely force their way through the crowd, much less dance, but the noise of the band that followed close at their heels made up for all shortcomings. There was a great deal of singing, of a very vociferous and probably also a very licentious character; but my ears were not offended, for in the general din it was impossible to distinguish a single word. Handfuls of red powder (*abír*) mixed with tiny particles of glistening talc were thrown about, up to the balconies above and down on the heads of the people below, and seen through this atmosphere of coloured cloud, the frantic gestures of the throng, their white clothes and faces all stained with red and yellow patches, and the great timbrels with bunches of peacocks' feathers, artifical flowers and tinsel stars stuck in their rim, borne above the players' heads and now and again tossed up high in the air, combined to form a curious and picturesque spectacle. After the music came a *posse* of rustics each bearing a rough jagged branch of the prickly acacia, stript of its leaves, and in their centre one man with a small yellow pennon on a long staff, yellow being the colour appropriate to the Spring season and the God of Love. The whole party slowly made its way through the village to an open plain outside, where the crowd assembled cannot have numbered less than 15,000. Here a circular arena was cleared and about a hundred of the Bathen Játnis were drawn up in a line, each with a long bambu in her hands, and confronting them an equal number of the bough-men who are all from the neighbouring village of Jau. A sham fight ensued, the women trying to beat down the thorny bushes and force their way to the flag. A man or two got a cut in the face, but the most perfect good humour prevailed, except when an outsider from some other village attempted to join in the play ; he was at once hustled out with kicks and blows that meant mischief. The women were backed up by their own husbands, who stood behind and encouraged them by word, but did not move a hand to strike. When it was all over, many of the spectators ran into the arena and rolled over and over in the dust, or streaked themselves with it on the forehead, taking it as the dust hallowed by the feet of Krishna and the Gopís.

The forenoon had been devoted to the recitation of Hindi poems appropriate to the occasion. I was not on the spot in time enough to hear any of this, but with some difficulty I obtained for a few days the loan of the volume that was used, and have copied from it three short pieces. The actual M.S. is of no greater antiquity than 1776A. D., the colophon at the end, in the curious mixture of Sanskrit and Hindi affected by village pandits, standing thus :

Sambat 1852 *Bhadrapad sudi* 2 *dwitiya, rabibár, likhitam idam pustakam, Sri Gopál Dás Charan-Pahari**-*madhye parhan árthi Sri Seva Dás Bari Bathain vási* :

but probably many successive copies have been made since the original was thumbed to pieces. The first stanzas, which are rather prettily worded, are, or at least profess to be, the composition of the famous blind poet Súr Dás.

॥ पद ॥

तेरी गति जानी न परै करुणामे हो
आगम अगम अगाधि अगोचर केहवुधिविधिसचरै ॥
अति प्रचंड बल पौरिषतामें केहरि भूष मरै ।
अनाआस बिन उद्दिम कियें अजगर पेट भरै ॥
कबहुक पंन डूबत पानीमें कबहुक सिला तिरै ।
बागरमें सागर करिडारै चहुंदिस नीर भरै ॥
रीते भरै भरे फिर डारै मेहरि करै तो फेरि भरै ।
पाहन बीच कमल परगासै जलमें अगिन जरै ॥

* Charan-Pahári is the name of a small detached rock, of the same character as the Bharat-pur range, that crops up above the ground in the village of Little Bathen.

राजा रंक रंकते राजा ले सिरछत्र धरै ।
सूर पतित तिरिजाय छिनकमें जो प्रभु नेंक करै ॥

Translation.

"Thy ways are past knowing, full of compassion, Supreme Intelligence, unapproachable, unfathomable beyond the cognizance of the senses, moving in fashion mysterious.

"A lion, most mighty in strength and courage, dies of hunger; a snake fills his belly without labour and without exertion.

"Now a straw sinks in the water, now a stone floats: he plants an ocean in the desert, a flood fills it all round.

"The empty is filled, the full is upset, by his grace it is filled again; the lotus blossoms from the rock and fire burns in the water.

"A king becomes a beggar and again a beggar a king with umbrella over his head: even the guiltiest (says Súr Dás) in an instant is saved, if the Lord helps him the least."

The second piece, in a somewhat similar strain, is by Dámodar Dás:

॥ पद ॥

अरे मन भजिले नंदलला ।
गृह बाननमें रह्यो किन कोऊ पकरत्त नाहि पला ॥
वेद पुरान संमृत यों भाषी याते नाहि भला ।
दिन दिन बढ़त प्रताप चोगुनो जैसें चंद्रकला ॥
काको धन काको गृह संपति काके सुत अबला ।
दामोदर कछु थिर न रहेगो जगमें चलोचला ॥

Translation.

"Come, my soul, adore Nand-lala (*i. e.*, Krishna), whether living in the house or in the woods (*i. e.*, whether a man of the world or a hermit), there is no other help to lay hold of.

"The Veda, the Puránas, and the Law declare that nothing is better than this; every day honour increases four-fold, like the moon in its degrees.

"Who has wealth? who has house and fortune? who has son and wife? says Dámodar, nought will remain secure in the world: it is gone in a moment."

The third piece, an encomium of the blooming Spring, is too simple to require any translation:

राग बसंत ॥

नवल बसंत नवल बृंदाबन नवले फूले फूल ।
नवले कान्ह नवल सब गोपी निर्तत एकेतूल ॥
नवले साष जवादि कुमकुमा नवले बसन अमूल ।
नवले छीट बनी केसरिकी मेटत मनमथ सूल ॥
नवल गुलाल उड़े रंगबूका नवल पवनके झूल ।
नवलहीं बाजे बाजें श्रीभट कालिंदी के कूल ॥

The only divinities who are now popularly commemorated at the Holi Festival are Rádhá, Krishna, and Balaráma; but its connection with them can only be of modern date. The institution of the Ban-játra and the Rás-líla, and all the local legends that they involve is (as has been already stated) traceable to one of the Brindá-ban Gosáins at the beginning of the 17th century A. D. The fact, though studiously ignored by the Hindus of Mathurá, is distinctly stated in the Bhakt-málá, the work which they admit to be of paramount authority on such matters. But the scenes that I have described carry back the mind of the European spectator to a far earlier period and are clearly relics, perhaps the most unchanged that exist in any part of the world, of the primitive worship of the powers of nature on the return of Spring. Such were the old English merry-makings on May Day and, still more closely parallel, the Phallic orgies of Imperial Rome as described by Juvenal. When I was listening to the din of the village band at Bathen, it appeared to be the very scene depicted in the lines—

Plangebant aliæ proceris tympana palmis,
Aut tereti tenuis tinnitus ære ciebant;
Multis raucisonos efflabant cornua bombos,
Barbaraque horribili stridebat tibia cantu.

26

Or, again, in the words of Catullus—

> Leve tympanum remugit, cava cymbala recrepant,
> Ubi sacra sancta acutis ululatibus agitant,
> Quatiuntque terga tauri teneris cava digitis:

while the actors in the *chaupái* with dagger in hand recalled the pictures of the Corybantes or Phrygian priests of Cybele, the very persons to whom the poet refers. In Greece the Indian Holi found its equivalent in the Dionysia, when the phallus, the symbol of the fertility of nature, was borne in procession, as it now is here, and when it was thought a disgrace to remain sober. In like manner the Gosáins and other actors in the Indian show are quite as much inspired in their frenzied action by their copious preliminary libations as by the excitement of the scene and the barbarous music of the drums, cymbals, and timbrels that accompany them.

CHAPTER V

THE BUDDHIST CITY OF MATHURÁ AND ITS ANTIQUITIES.

APART from its connection with the deified Krishna, the city of Mathurá has been a place of note from the most distant antiquity. In Buddhist times it was one of the centres of that religion, and its sacred shrines and relics attracted pilgrims even from China, two of whom have left records of their travels. The first, by name Fa Hian, spent, as he informs us, three years in Western Asia, visiting all the places connected with events in the life of the great teacher or of his immediate successors ; his main object being to collect authentic copies of the oldest theological texts and commentaries, to take back with him to his own country. Commencing his journey from Tibet, he passed successively through Kashmír, Kábul, Kandahár, and the Panjáb, and so arrived in Central India, the *madhya-des* of Hindu geographers. Here the first kingdom that he entered was Mathurá, with its capital of the same name situate on the bank of the Jamuná. All the people from the highest to the lowest were staunch Buddhists, and maintained that they had been so ever since the time of Sákya Muni's translation. This statement must be accepted with considerable reserve, since other evidence tends to show that Hinduism was the prevalent religion during part of the interval between Buddha's death and Fa Hian's visit, which was made about the year 400 A. D. He assures us, however, that many of the ecclesiastical establishments possessed copper plates engraved with the original deeds of endowment in attestation of their antiquity. In the capital—where he rested a whole month—and its vicinity, on the opposite banks of the river, were twenty monasteries, containing in all some 3,000 monks. There were, moreover, six relic-towers, or *stúpas*, of which the most famous was the one erected in honour of the great apostle Sári-putra. The five other *stúpas* are also mentioned by name ; two of them commemorated respectively Ananda, the special patron of religious women, and Mudgala-putra, the great doctor of *Samádhi* or contemplative devotion. The remaining three were dedicated to the cultus of the Abhi-dharma, the Sutra, and the Vináya divisions of the sacred books, treating respectively of Metaphysics, Religion, and Morality, and known in Buddhist literature by the collective name of the Tri-pitaka or 'three baskets.'

Some 200 years later, Hwen Thsang, another pilgrim from the Flowery Land, was impelled by like religious zeal to spend sixteen years, from 629 to 645 A.D., travelling throughout India. On his return to China, he compiled, by special command of the Emperor, a work in twelve Books entitled 'Memoirs of Western Countries,' giving succinct geographical descriptions of all the kingdoms, amounting in number to 128, that he had either personally visited, or of which he had been able to acquire authentic information. After his death, two of his disciples, wishing to individualize the record of their master's adventures, compiled in ten Books a special narrative of his life and Indian travels. This has been translated into French by the great Orientalist, Mons. S. Julien. Mathurá is described as being 20 *li*, or four miles in circumference, and as containing still, as in the days of Fa Hian, 20 monasteries. But the number of resident monks had been reduced to 2,000, and five temples had been erected to Bráhmanical divinities ; both facts indicating the gradual decline of Buddhism. There were three *stupas*, built by King Asoka, and many spots were shown where the four former Buddhas had left the marks of their feet. Several other *stupas* were reverenced as containing relics of the holy disciples of Sákya Muni, *viz.*, Sári-putra, Mudgaláyana, Purna-maitráyani-putra, Upali, Ananda, Ráhula, Manjusri, and other Bodhi-satwas. Every year (he writes) in the months of the three long fasts (the first, fifth, and ninth) and on the six monthly fasts the religious assemble in crowds at these *stupas*, and make their several offerings at the one which is the object of their devotion. The followers of Abhi-dharma offer to Sári-putra, and those who practise contemplation (*dhyána*) to Mudgaláyana. Those who adhere to the Sútras pay their homage to Púrna-maitráyani-putra ; those who study the Vináya honour Upali ; religious women honour Ananda ; those who have not yet been fully instructed (catechumens) honour Ráhula ; those who study the Mahá-yána honour all the Bodhi-satwas.* Banners enriched with pearls float in the air, and gorgeous umbrellas are grouped in procession. Clouds of incense and constant showers of flowers obscure the sight of the sun and moon. The king and his ministers apply themselves with zeal to the practice of meritorious works. Five or six *li*—*i.e.*, about a mile and a quarter—to the east of the town is a monastery on a hill, the sides of which have been excavated to allow of the construction of cells. The approach is by a ravine. It is said to have been built by the venerable Upagupta. In its centre may be seen a *stupa* which encloses some nail-parings

* A Bodhi-satwa is defined as a being who has arrived at supreme wisdom (*bodhi*), and yet consents to remain as a creature (*satwa*) for the good of men.

of the Tathágata. At a hill to the north of this monastery is a cave in the rock, twenty feet high and thirty feet broad, where had been collected an immense number of little bambu spikes, each only four inches long. When a married couple, whom the venerable Upagupta had converted and instructed, obtained the rank of Arhat, * he added a spike. But he took no note of other persons, even though they had attained the same degree of sanctity. Twenty-four or 25 *li* to the south-east of this cave was a large dry tank with a stúpa by its side, where it was said that one day as Buddha was pacing up and down, he was offered some honey by a monkey, which he graciously told him to mix with water and divide among the monks. The monkey was so charmed at the condescension that he forgot where he was, and in his ecstasy fell over into the tank and was drowned: as a reward for his meritorious conduct, when he next took birth, it was in human form. A little to the north of this tank was a wood with several *stúpas* to mark the spots that had been hallowed by the presence of the four earlier Buddhas, and where 1,250 famous teachers of the law, such as Sáriputra and Mudgala-putra, had given themselves up to meditation. When the Tathágata (he adds) lived in the world, he often travelled in this kingdom, and monuments have been erected in every place where he expounded the law.

The Lalita Vistara, which is the oldest and most authentic record that the Buddhists possess, gives a most elaborate account of Sákya Muni's early adventures, and of the six years of preliminary penance and seclusion that he spent in the woods of Uruvilva (now Buddh Gaya) before he commenced his public ministry; but the narrative terminates abruptly with his departure for Banáras, which was the first place to which he betook himself after he had attained to the fulness of perfect knowledge. There is no equally trustworthy and consecutive record of the second and more important half of his life—the 40 years which he spent in the promulgation of his new creed—and it is therefore impossible to say at what period he paid those frequent visits to Mathurá of which Hwen Thsang speaks. There is, however, no reason to doubt that they were paid; for the place was one of much importance in his time and, like every other new teacher, it was the great centres of population that he laboured most to influence. In Beal's translation of the Chinese version of the Abhinishkramana Sútra we find Mathurá styled the capital of all Jambu-dwípa, and on that account it was one of the first suggested as a fit place for Buddha to take birth in. He rejected it, however, on the ground that the king by whom it was ruled, a powerful monarch, Subáhu by name, was a

* An Arhat is a saint who has attained to the fourth grade in the scale of perfection.

heretic. The objections to other large cities were, either that the king's pedigree had some flaw; or that he was a Bráhman, not a Kshatriya by caste; or that he had already a large family; or that the people were insubordinate and self-willed. Banáras and Ujaiyin were considered unworthy for a similar reason as Mathurá, *viz.*, that at the former there were four heretical schools of philosophy, and that the king of the latter did not believe in a future state. The use of the word 'heretical' is to be noted, for it clearly indicates that Buddha did not intend to break entirely with Hinduism; or rather, like the English 'Reformers' of the 16th century, and Dr. Dollinger and his "old Catholics" on the continent of Europe at the present day, or Bábu Kesav Chandra Sen in Calcutta, or, in short, like *all* subverters of established systems, he found it politic to disguise the novelty of his theories by retaining the old terminology, and thus investing them with the prestige of a spurious antiquity.

In consequence of the changes in religion and the long lapse of time, the whole of the ancient Buddhist buildings described by the Chinese pilgrims had been overthrown, buried, and forgotten, till quite recently, when some fragments of them have been again brought to light. The first discovery was made by General Cunningham, in 1853, who noticed some capitals and pillars lying about within the enclosure of the Katra, the site of the Hindu temple of Kesava Deva. A subsequent search revealed the architrave of a gateway and other sculptures, including in particular a standing figure of Buddha, three and-a-half feet high, which was found at the bottom of a well, with an inscription at its base recording the gift of the statue to the 'Yasa Vihára,' or 'Convent of Glory,' which may be taken as the name of one of the Buddhist establishments that had existed on the spot. The date of the presentation was recorded in figures which could not be certainly deciphered.*

A far more important discovery was made in 1860, in digging the foundation of the Magistrate and Collector's new court-house. The site selected for this building was an extensive mound overhanging the Agra road at the entrance to the civil station. It had always been regarded as merely the remains of a series of brick-kilns, and had been further protected against exploration by the fact that it was crowned by a small mosque. This was, for military reasons, blown down during the mutiny; and afterwards, on clearing away the rubbish and excavating for the new foundations, it was found to have been erected, in accordance with the common usage of the Muhammadan conquerors, upon the ruins of a destroyed temple. A number of Buddhist statues, pillars,

* This statue was one of those removed by Dr. Playfair to the Museum at Agra.

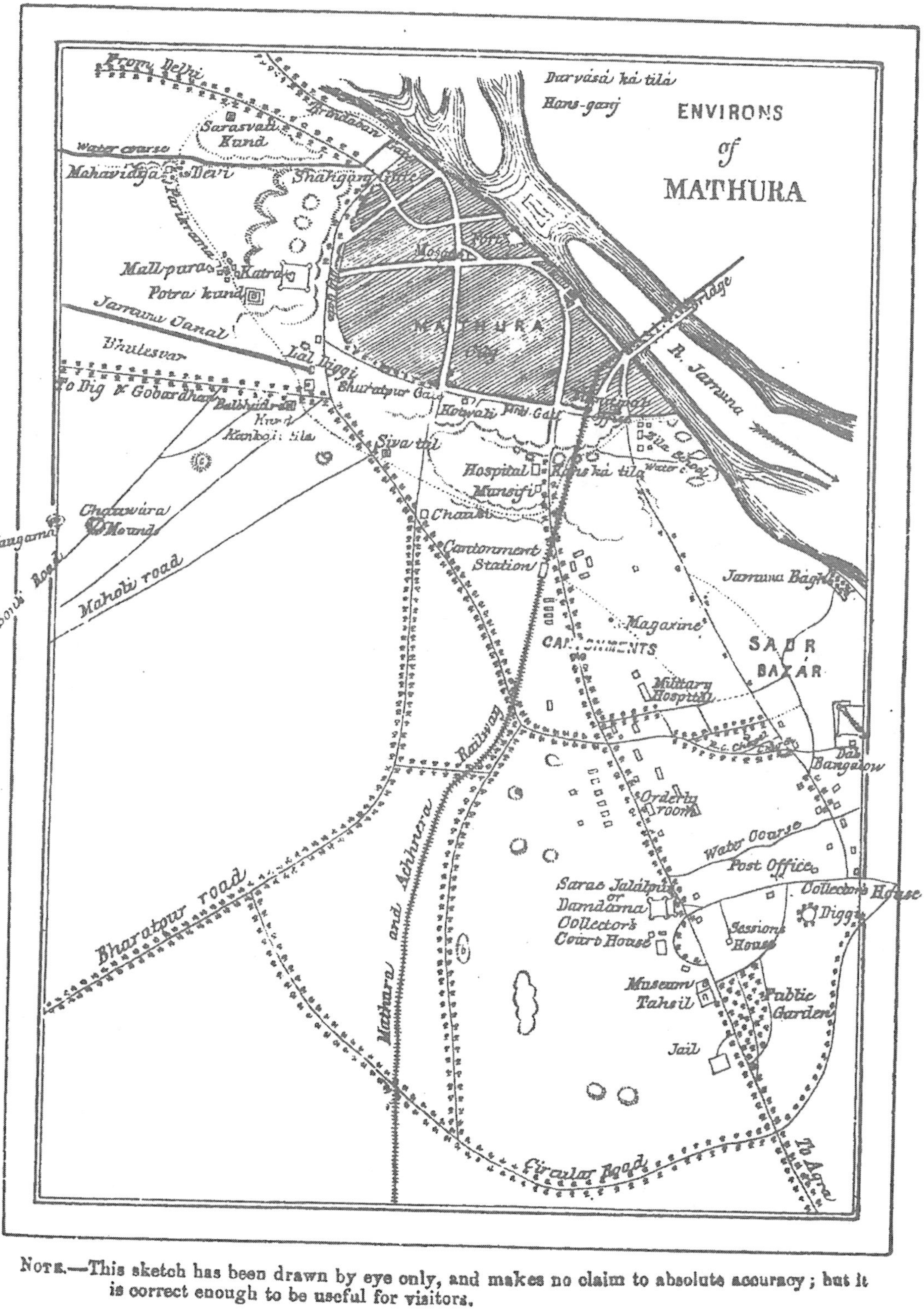

NOTE.—This sketch has been drawn by eye only, and makes no claim to absolute accuracy; but it is correct enough to be useful for visitors.

and basso-relievos, were disinterred; and the inscriptions, as partially deciphered, would seem to indicate that the mound was occupied by several different monasteries; three of which, according to General Cunningham, bore the names of Sanghamittra-sada Vihára, Huvishka Vihára, and Kundokhara,* or as it may be read, Kunda-Suka Vihára. On the pedestal of a seated figure was found recorded the first half of a king's name, Vasu; the latter part was broken away, but the lacuna should probably be supplied with the word 'deva,' as a group of figures inscribed with the name of King Vasudeva and date 87 was discovered in 1871 at a neighbouring mound called the 'Kankálí tíla.' The most numerous remains were portions of stone railing of the particular type used to enclose Buddhist shrines and monuments. The whole were made over to the Agra museum, where the railings were roughly put together in such a way as to indicate the original arrangement. The entire collection has since been again removed elsewhere, I believe to Allahabad; but as there is no proper building for their reception there, nobody appears to know anything about them, and it is very much to be regretted that they were ever allowed to be taken from Mathurá. Many of the pillars were marked with figures as a guide to the builder; and thus we learn that one set, for they were of various sizes, consisted of at least as many as 129 pieces. There were also found three large seated figures of Buddha, of which two were full, the third a little less than life-size; and the bases of some 30 large columns. It was chiefly round these bases that the inscriptions were engraved. One of the most noticeable fragments was a stone hand, measuring a foot across the palm, which must have belonged to a statue not less than from 20 to 24 feet in height.

Most of the sculptures were executed in common red sandstone and were of indifferent workmanship, in every way inferior to the specimens more recently discovered at other mounds in the neighbourhood. The most artistic was the figure of a dancing-girl, rather more than half life-size, in a tolerably natural and graceful attitude.† Like the so-called figure of Silenus, discovered by James Prinsep in 1836, of which a detailed description will be given further on, it was thought that it might have been the work of a Greek artist. This conjecture, though I do not accept it myself, involves no historical difficulty, since in the Yuga-Purána of the Gárgi-Sanhitá, written about the year

* It must be admitted that Kundokhara, *i.e.*, Kunda-pushkara, is a very questionable compound, since the two members of which it is composed would bear each precisely the same meaning.

† Two representations of this figure are given in Cunningham's Archæological Survey, Vol. I., page 240.

50 B. C., it is explicitly stated that Mathurá was reduced by the Greeks, and that their victorious armies advanced into the very heart of Hindustan, even as far as Pátali-putra. The text is as follows:—

ततः साकेतमाक्रम्य पञ्चालान् मथुरां तथा ।
यवना दुष्टविक्रान्ताः प्राप्स्यन्ति कुसुमध्वजम् ।
ततः पुष्पपुरे प्राप्ते कर्दमे प्रथिते हिते ।
आकुला विषयाः सर्वे भविष्यन्ति न संशयः ।

"Then those hateful conquerors, the Greeks, after reducing Sáketa,* the country of Panchála and Mathurá, will take Kusuma-dhvaja (Pátali-putra); and when Pushpa-pura (*i. e.*, Pátali-putra) is taken, every province will assuredly become disordered."

In close proximity to the mound where the antiquities, which we have described above were discovered is a large walled enclosure, called the Damdama, for some years past occupied by the reserves of the district police, but originally one of a series of *saráes* erected in the time of the Delhi Emperors along the road between the two royal residences of Agra and Delhi. Hence the adjoining hamlet derives its name of Saráe Jamálpur; and for the sake of convenience, when future reference is made to the mound, it will be by that title. As it is at some distance to the south-east of the katra, the traditional site of ancient Mathurá, and so far agrees with the position assigned by Hwen Thsang to the stúpa erected to commemorate Buddha's interview with the monkey, there is plausible ground for identifying the two places. The identification is confirmed by the discovery of the inscription with the name Kundo-khara or Kundasuka; for, whichever way the word is read, it would seem to contain a reference to a tank (*kunda*), and a tank was the characteristic feature of Hwen Thsang's monkey stúpa. It at first appears a little strange that there should be, as the inscriptions lead us to infer, four separate monasteries on one hill, but General Cunningham states that in Barma, where Buddhism is still the national religion, such juxtaposition is by no means uncommon.

* The siege of Sáketa is ascertained to have taken place early in the reign of Menander, who ascended the throne in the year 144 B. C., Pushpa-mitra being at that time King of Pátali-putra. The Gárgi Sanhitá is an ancient and extremely rare work, of which only five MSS.—all apparently imperfect—are as yet known to be in existence. Three are in European libraries; one belongs to Dr. Kern, who was the first to call attention to the work in the Preface to his edition of Varáha Mihira's Brihat Sanhita, in which it is frequently quoted; and the fifth has been recently discovered by Dr. Buhler.

Transcripts and translations of many of these inscriptions have been since made by different scholars and have been published by General Cunningham in Volume III. of his Archæological Survey; but they are for the most part of a very tentative character and leave much room for uncertainty, both as regards reading and interpretation.* They are all brief votive records, giving only the name of the obscure donor, accompanied by some stereotyped religious formula. The dates, which it would be specially interesting to ascertain, are indicated by figures, the value of which has been definitely determined; but the era to which they refer is still matter of dispute. Dr. Rajendra-lála Mitra has consistently maintained from the first that it is the Sáka era, beginning from 76 A. D.; and if so, the series ranges between 120 and 206 A. D. But the era intended might also be that of Vikramáditya, or of the Seleucidæ, or of Buddha's Nirvána, or of the particular monarch whose name is specified.

Before the discovery of these and similar inscriptions, the history of India, from the invasion of Alexander the Great to that by Mahmúd of Ghazni, was almost an absolute blank, in which however the name of Vikramáditya, the reputed founder of the era still most in vogue among Hindus, enjoyed such universal celebrity that it seemed impossible for any question to be raised regarding him. This solitary stand-point has completely given way under the weight of modern researches, and not only Vikramáditya's paramount sovereignty, but even his existence, is now denied, and that by disputants who will scarcely find a single other matter on which to agree. Mr. Fergusson writes: "No authentic traces exist of any king bearing the name or title of Vikramáditya having lived in the first century before Christ; nor"—though here his assertion will be disputed—"has it been possible to point to any event as occurring B. C. 56, which was of sufficient importance to give rise to the institution of an era for its commemoration." Similarly, Professor Bhau Daji, of Bombay, declared that he knew of no inscription, dated in this *Sambat*, before the eleventh century of the Christian era; and, though this appears to be carrying incredulity a little too far, General Cunningham, upon whose accuracy every reliance can be placed, says that the earliest inscription of the Vikramáditya era, that he has seen, bears date 811, that is A. D. 754. Now, if the era was really

* It may be hoped that Dr. Hoernlé of the Calcutta Madrasa will at some time find leisure to revise and translate the whole series of these early inscriptions. There is no one in India, or even among European scholars, who is equally qualified for the task by his knowledge of Sanskrit, of literary Prákrit and of the modern vernacular, which last is often of the greatest service in supplying parallel examples of colloquial usage. His corrected readings of the inscriptions from the Bharhat stupa, as published in the *Indian Antiquary*, are a triumph of scholarly ingenuity.

established before the birth of Christ, it is difficult to understand why it should have lain so long dormant and then have become so curiously revived and so generally adopted.

Various solutions of the difficulty have been attempted. It has been definitely ascertained that the title Vikramáditya was borne by a king Sri Harsha, who reigned at Ujaiyin, in the first half of the sixth century A. D., and General Cunningham conjectures with some probability that it was he who restored the general use of the old era (which had been to a great extent superseded by the introduction of the Sáka era in 79 A. D.) and made it his own, simply by changing its name to that which it now bears. The king by whom it was really established about the year 57 B. C. he conceives to have been the Indo-Scythian Kanishka.

This is a personage who as yet scarcely figures at all in histories intended for the general reader ; but it is certain that he was one of the greatest sovereigns that ever held sway in Upper India and, if not the first to introduce Buddhism, was at least the one who definitely established it as the state religion. The Sanskrit Chronicle, entitled the Raja-Taranginí, mentions among the successors of the great Asoka, in the latter half of the century immediately preceding the birth of Christ, three kings of foreign descent named Hushka (or Huvishka), Jushka, and Kanishka. The later Muhammadan writers represent them as brothers : but it is not so stated in the original text, the words of which are simply as follows :—

हुष्कजुष्ककनिष्काख्यास्त्रयस्तत्रैव पार्थिवाः ।
ते तुरुष्कान्वयोद्भूता अपि पुण्याश्रया नृपाः ।
प्राज्ये राज्यक्षणे तेषां प्रायः काश्मीरमण्डलं ।
भोज्यमास्ते च बौद्धानां प्रव्रज्योर्जिततेजसां ।

"There, too, the three kings, Hushka, Jushka, and Kanishka, born of Turushka descent, monarchs of eminent virtue. In their exalted reign a great part of the region of Kashmír was occupied by peripatetic Buddhist ascetics."

Their dominions are known to have included Kábul, Kashmír, and the Panjáb ; and recently discovered inscriptions imply that their sway extended thence as far south as Mathurá. It is true that many of the religious buildings in holy places have been founded by foreign princes, who had no territorial connection with the neighbourhood ; but there seems to have been some special bond of union between Mathurá and Kashmír. Incredible as it has been deemed by most geographers, it is yet within the range of possibility, as pointed out by Professor Wilson, that Ptolemy intended, by the close similarity of names, to indicate a connection between *Κασπηρία ὑπὸ τὰς τοῦ Βιδάσπου καὶ τοῦ Σανδόβαλ καὶ τοῦ Ροαδίος πηγάς*—that is, Kasperia, or Kashmír, at the sources of the Vitasta, the Chandra-bhága, and the Rávi—and the Kashpeiræi, dwelling lower down on the Vindhya range and the banks of the Jamuná, one of whose chief towns was Mathurá. For, further, Ptolemy represents *ἡ πανδώου Χώρα* 'the country of Pándu,' as lying in the neigbourhood of the Vitasta, or Jhelam ; while Arrian, quoting from Megasthenes, says it derived its name from Pandœa, the daughter of Hercules, the divinity specially venerated by the Suraseni on the Jamuná. Thus, as it would seem, he identifies Mathurá, the chief town of the Suraseni, with Pandœa. Balaráma, one of its two tutelary divinities, may be certainly recognized as Belus, the Indian Hercules ; while, if we allow for a little distortion of the original legend, Prithá, another name of Kuntí, the mother of the Pándavas and sister of Krishna and Balaráma's father, Vasudeva, may be considered the native form which was corrupted into Pandœa.

In historical illustration of the same line of argument, it may be remarked that Gonanda I., the king of Kashmír contemporary with Krishna, is related (Rája-Tarangini, I., 59) to have been a kinsman of Jarásandha and to have assisted him in the siege of Mathurá.* He was slain there on the bank of the Kálindi, *i.e.*, the Jamuná, by Balaráma. His son and successor, Dámodara, a few years later, thinking to avenge his father's death, made an attack on a party of Krishna's friends, as they were returning from a wedding at Gandhára near the Indus, but himself met his death at that hero's hands. The next occupant of the throne of Mathurá in succession to Jarásandha was Karna, the faithful ally of the Kauravas, against whom the great war was waged by Krishna and the Pándavas. Gonanda II., the son of Dámodara, was too young to take any

---

* काश्मीरेन्द्रः स गोनंदः .. .. .. ।
साहायकार्थमाहूतो जरासन्धेन बन्धुना ।
समं रुरोध कंसारेर्मथुरां पृथुभिर्व्बलैः ।

"Gonanda, the king of Kashmír, having been summoned by his relation, Jarásandha, to his assistance, besieged with a mighty army Krishna's city of Mathurá."

part in the protracted struggle; but the reigning houses of Mathurá and Kashmír acknowledged a common enemy in Krishna, and the fact appears to have conduced to a friendly feeling between the two families, which lasted for many generations. Thus we read in the Rájá-Tarangini (IV., 512)* that when Jayapída, who reigned over Kashmír at the end of the eighth century after Christ, built his new capital of Jayapura, a stately temple was founded there and dedicated to Mahádeva under the title of Achesvara, by Acha, the son-in-law of Pramoda, the king of Mathurá.†

Three inscriptions have been found bearing the name of Kanishka.‡ Of these one is dated 9, another 28; in the third the year has unfortunately been broken away. The memorials of his successor, the Maharaja Huvishka,§ are more numerous, and the dates range from 33 to 50. In one instance, however, the gift is distinctly made to the king's Vihára, which does not necessarily imply that the king was still living at the time; and the same may have been the intention of the other inscriptions; since the grammatical construction of the words, which give the king's name and titles in the genitive case, is a little doubtful, the word upon which they depend not being clearly expressed. Huvishka was succeeded by Vasudeva, who, notwithstanding his purely Indian name, must be referred to the same dynasty, since ordinarily he is honoured with the same distinctive titles, *Mahárája Rájatirája Devaputra*; and for *Devaputra* is in one legend substituted *Sháhi*, by which the Indo-Scythian Princes were specially distinguished. On gold coins, moreover, his name is given in Greek characters, Bazodeo.

---

* तस्मिन् जयपुरे कोट्टे जयदत्तोव्यधान्मठं ।
राजचक्षुः प्रमोदस्य जामाता मथुरापतेः ।
आचाभिधोव्यचरयच्छुचिराचेश्वरं हरं ।

† I have not been able to trace king Pramoda's name elsewhere. He may have been one of the seven Nága (or, according to another MS., Mauna) princes, whom the Vayu Purána mentions as destined to reign over Mathurá—

मथुरां च पुरीं रम्यां नागा भोक्ष्यन्ति सप्त वै ।

"The seven Nágas will possess the pleasant city of Mathurá."

‡ On his coins his name appears in the form Kanerki.

§ On coins the name Huvishka is given as Ooerki.

In an article contributed to the *Indian Antiquary* for 1881 Dr. Oldenberg of Berlin seeks to identify the great Kanishka, not, as General Cunningham has done, with the mythical Vikramáditya, but with the founder of the Saka era in 78 A.D., thus supporting the same chronological theory as Dr. Mitra. The Kushana dynasty, to which Kanishka belonged, seems to have first established itself about 24 B.C. in the person of Hermaens. The coins of this Prince, in which he is styled Basilevs Soter, are well known to numismatists, as also are those of his three successors, who bear the barbarous names of Kozulokadphises, Kozolakadaphes and Ooemakadphises. The Chinese speak of this dynasty as of great power in India in 159 A.D., but after the death of Vasudeva *c.* 178 A.D. it rapidly declined and was altogether extinguished about the year of our era 220. After a century of darkness, regarding which nothing is known, the Guptas rose to power in 319 A.D. and held the throne, for five generations, till about 480 A.D., when they were deposed by the Vallabhis, who, however, continued to date events by the same era as their predecessors. The Satrapas or Kshatrapas, who are commemorated by an inscription at Mathura, dated in the reign of the Satrap Saudasa, probably employed a local era of their own dynasty. This appears to have been founded in Gujarat about 100 A.D. and to have continued in power for three centuries, when it was overthrown by the Guptas.

Mr. Thomas, the celebrated numismatist, has broached a theory that the era intended is that of the Seleucidæ, which commenced on the last of October, 310 B. C. The long interval of time between this date and either the Vikramáditya or the Sáka initial year would seem to render his hypothesis altogether untenable, as being utterly subversive of accepted chronology. But from such an inscription as that of Kanishka with the date *Sambat* 9 he does not deduce the year 303 B. C. (that is 312-9), but rather supposes that as we ourselves ordinarily write 75 for 1875, so the Indo-Scythians wrote 9 for 309 ; and thus *Sambat* 9 might correspond with the year 3 B.C. A curious confirmation of this view may be observed in the fact that the inscriptions, in which the dates range from 9 to 98, employ a division of the year into the three seasons, Grishma, Varsha, and Hemanta—that is to say, the hot weather, the rains and the winter ; and the day is specified as (for example) the 11th of the 4th month of the particular season. In only one of the Mathurá inscriptions is the date above a hundred, *viz.*, 135 ; and here the division of time is according to the Hindu Calendar still in use, the particular month named being Púshya. Hence it may be inferred that this inscription

29

belongs to an entirely different series and may very probably refer to the Sáka era.

The Seleucidan era is obiously one that might have recommended itself to a dynasty of mixed Greek descent; but another that might with equal or even greater probability have been employed is the Kashmírian era used by Kalhana in the last three books of his Rájá-Taranginí, and which is still familiar to the Bráhmans of that country. It is otherwise called the era of the Saptarshis and dates from the secular procession of Ursa Major, Chaitra sudi 1 of the 26th year of the Kali-yuga, 3076 B.C. It is known to be a fact and is not a mere hypothesis that when this era is used, the hundreds are generally omitted. The chronologieal difficulties involved in these inscriptions seem therefore almost to defy solution; for the era may commence either in March, 3076 B.C., or in October, 312 B.C., or in 57 B.C., or in 78 A.D. There is further a difficulty in considering that *any* one era can be intended; for one inscription has been found, dated 47, mentioning Huvishka as king, while two others bearing Vasudeva's name are dated respectively 44 and 83, which would thus make Vasudeva at once the predecessor and the successor of Huvishka. The simplest way of meeting this difficulty would be to refer the figures to the year of the king's reign, and a small fragment of an inscription that I found in the Jamálpur mound bears the words...*shkasya rájya-samvatsare* 28 *Hemant* 3 *div.*, of which the most obious translation would be 'On the day of the third winter month of the 28th year of the reign of Kanishka' (as the name it would seem must have been). Nor need any difficulty be occasioned by the use of the word *Sambat* to denote the year of a monarch's reign. For though modern practice restricts the term exclusively to the Vikramáditya era, such was not always the case: witness the inscription on the temple of Gobind Deva at Brindá-ban—*Sambat 34 Sri Sakabandh Akbar Sháh ráj*—' in the 34th year of the reign of the Emperor Akbar.' But the height to which the figures run is fatal to this theory, and a final solution to the mystery has yet to be sought.

About half-a-mile due west of the Jamálpur mound is a small one on the edge of the Circular Road, where I found the lower extremities of two large seated figures, in red sandstone: the one a Buddha, with an inscription at the base, of which the only words legible are: *varsha máse* 2 *divas* 6, ' on the 6th day of the 2nd month of the rains.' The other is almost a facsimile of a sculpture figured at page 36 of Mr. Oldham's Memoir of Gházipur, among the antiquities found at a place called Aonrihár. It is well executed and represents a woman with her left hand clasping an infant in her lap. One foot rests on an elaborately ornamented stool, the other is doubled under her body. There are five small accessory figures, one in front and two on either side at the back.

Between this mound and Jamálpur is an extensive ridge, which I spent some days in exploring, but found nothing of interest. The most likely place in this immediate neighbourhood that yet remains to be examined is a mound at the back of the jail and within its outer precincts. I brought away one figure from it. Close by is an enormous pit out of which earth was taken to construct the mud walls of the enclosure. As this is objectionable from a sanitary point of view as well as unsightly, prison labour might with advantage be employed in levelling the mound and using the earth to fill up the pit; by which means two objects would be obtained.

After my transfer from the district, the Jamálpur mound, which had so often been explored before with valuable results, was completely levelled, at a cost of Rs. 7,236, the work having been sanctioned by Government as a famine relief operation. A large number of miscellaneous sculptures was discovered, of which I have received no definite description. But the more prominent object is a life-size statue of Buddha, which is very finely executed and, when found, was in excellent preservation, though unfortunately broken in two pieces by a fracture just above the ankles.* On the base is an inscription in Páli characters, of which a transcript has been sent me by a clever native draughtsman. I decipher it as follows :—

"Deyadharmáyam Sákya-bhikshu Yasa-dittasya. Yad atra punyam, tad bhavatu mátá-pitroh sukhá *rya páddhya yatám* cha sarvva-satv-ánuttarajnána-váptaye."

I have probably misread some of the letters printed in italics, for as they stand they yield no sense. The remainder I translate as follows :

"This is the votive offering of the Buddhist monk Yasa-ditta. If there is any merit in it, may it work for the good of his father and mother and for the propagation of perfect knowlege throughout the world."

---

* The face of this statue was a really beautiful piece of sculpture, of far more artistic character than in any other figure that has yet been discovered. However, not the slightest care was taken to preserve it from injury; and the nose was soon broken off, either by some bigoted iconoclastic Muhammadan, or by some child in the mere spirit of mischief. The disfigurement is irreparable, and that it should have been allowed to occur is not very creditable to the local authorities.

In Sanskrit the primary meaning of *deya-dharma* is 'the duty of giving;' but in Páli it ordinarily stands for 'the gift' itself. The literal signification of the monks' name, Yasa-ditta is 'Resplendent with glory'; *ditta* being the Páli, Prákrit, or Hindi form of the Sanskrit *dípta*, by a rule of Vararuchi's, under which the example given is *sutta* (the modern *sotá*) for *supta*. *Vápti*, 'the propagation,' is from the root *vap*, to sow; from which also comes the Hindi word *báp*, a father,' like the Latin *sator* from *sero*.

A second inscription of some length commences with the words *Mahárájasya Devaputrasya Huvishkasya Samvatsare* 51 *Hemunta mása* 1 *div.* .... but I have not been able to read further, as the only transcript that I have received is a very imperfect one. A great number of fragmentary sculptures of different kinds were also discovered, as I understand, and some of them have been photographed for General Cunningham, who spent several days at Mathurá for the purpose of exmamining them. An account may possibly appear in some future volume of his Archæological Survey; but already four years have elapsed and not a sign has been made.

After General Cunningham's visit a third inscribed slab was found of which a transcript was made and sent. It begins with the word *siddham;* then apparently followed the date, but unfortunately there is here a flaw in the stone. After the flaw is the word *etasya.** The second line begins with *Bhagavat.* In the third line is the name *Mathurá*; at the end of the sixth line *mátapitroh*; in the middle of the seventh line *bhavatu sarvva.*

Incidental allusion has already been made to the Kankáli, or, as it is occasionally called, the Jaini Tíla.† This is an extensive mound on the side of the Agra and Delhi road, between the Bharat-pur and Díg gates of the city. A frag-

* The word following *etasya* begins with the letters *pu*—the remainder being defaced—and was probably *purvaye*. This phrase *etasya purvaye* is of frequent ocsurrence in these inscriptions and is translated by General Cunning ham 'on this very date'. I do not think it can bear such a meaning. It might be literally rendered 'after this;' but it is really an expletive like the Hindi *áge*, or occasionally the Sanskrit *tad-anantaram*, with which an Indian correspondent generally begins a letter—after the stereotyped complimentary exordium—and which, in the absence of full stops and capital letters, serves to indicate a transition to a new subject.

† By the roadside, between the Kankáli Tíla and the Siva Tál, there is a handsome chhatri built in 1873, in memory of Chaubé Genda, Purohit to the Rájá of Jhálrá-pattan. It was intended to add a rest-house; but, in consequence of a complaint made by the District Engineer, the design was abandoned and the chhatri itself has never been thoroughly completed. The building is so ornamental that I hoped an encroachment of a few inches on to the side of the road might have been pardoned, but my suggestion to that effect was summarily scouted.

ment of a carved Buddhist pillar is set up in a mean little shed on its summit and does duty for the goddess Kankáli, to whom it is dedicated. A few years ago, the hill was partially trenched, when two colossal statues of Buddha in his character of teacher were discovered. They are each seven and-a-half feet in height, and are probably now in the Allahabad museum. Whatever else was found was collected on the same spot as the remains from the Jamálpur mound, and it is therefore possible (as no accurate note was made at the time) that some of the specimens referred to the latter locality were not really found there; but there is no doubt as to the inscriptions, and this is the only point of any importance. Further excavations resulted in the discovery of several mutilated statues of finer stone and superior execution, and it was thought that many more might still remain buried; as the adjoining fields for a considerable distance were strewn with fragments applied to all sorts of vile purposes. A large figure of an elephant—unfortunately without its trunk—standing on the capital of a pillar and in all respects similar to the well-known example at Sankisa, but of much coarser work, was found in 1871 in a neigbouring garden. On the front of the abacus is engraved an inscription with the name of King Huvishka and date 'Sambat 39.' Another inscription, containing the name of King Kanishka, with date 'Sambat 9,' was discovered the same day on the mound itself below a square pillar carved with four nude figures, one on each face. This is of special interest, inasmuch as nude figures are always considered a distinctive mark of the Jain sect, which was supposed to be a late perversion of Buddhism; an opinion, however, which most scholars have now abandoned. Mahávira the 24th and *last* of the great Jinas died in 526 B.C., while the Nirvána, or death, of Buddha, the *founder* of the rival faith, has finally been determined as having taken place in 477 B.C. Indeed, it was suggested by Colebrooke, though further research would seem to have disproved the theory, that Buddha was actually a disciple of Mahávira's.

Among other sculptures found here while I was in the district may be mentioned the flollowing :—

1*st.*—A life-size seated figure with an elaborately carved nimbus and long hair flowing over the shoulders and down the back. The head is lost. 2*nd.*—A teacher of the law standing between two tiers of small figures seated in the attitude of contemplation, with a Caliban-like monster sprawling over the top of the canopy above his head. The arms and feet of the principal figure are missing: but with this exception the group is in good preservation and is well executed. 3*rd.*—A spandril of a doorway carved with the representation of a triumphal column with a bell capital surmounted by winged lions supporting the figure of an elephant. The reverse has an ornamental border enclosing a short inscription in which the name of the donor is given as Mugali-putra. *4th.*—A *chaumukhi*, or pillar of four (headless) Buddhas, seated back to back, well executed in fine white stone. *5th.*—A *chaumukhi* of four standing nude figures, roughly carved in coarse red sandstone. *6th.*—A pair of columns, 3½ feet high, characteristically carved with three horizontal bands of conventional foliage and festoons, which are slightly suggestive of a classic model. *7th.*—A cross-bar of a Buddhist railing with a sculptured medallion on either side. *8th.*—A small seated figure with six persons standing in a line below, three on each side of a chakra which they are adoring. There is an inscription in one line as follows :—

Siddham. Jivikasya datta Bhikshusya viharasya ;

Which I would translate thus : 'May it prosper ; the gift of Jivika, a mendicant, for the monastery."

It is worthy of remark that no definite line of foundation has ever been brought to light nor any large remains of plain masonry superstructure ; but only a confused medley of broken statues without even the pedestals on which they must have been originally erected. This suggests a suspicion that possibly there never was a temple on the site, but that the sculptures were brought from different places in the neighbourhood and here thrown into a pit by the Muhammadans to be buried. They clearly belong to two very different periods. The more ancient are roughly carved in coarse red sandstone and, whenever there is any lettering, it is in Páli ; the more modern display much higher artistic skill, are executed in much finer material, and all the inscriptions are in the Nágari character, one being apparently dated in the twelfth century after Christ. But upon the whole I conclude that the discovery of no foundations in situ is rather to be explained by the fact that the mound has long served as a quarry, and that bricks and small blocks of stone, being more useful for ordinary building purposes, would all be removed, when cumbrous and at the same time broken statues might be left undisturbed.

It is possible that here may have stood the Upagupta monastery, mentioned by Hwen Thsang. As there is no trace of any large tank in its immediate proximity, it was more probably the site of a monastery than of a stúpa. For a tank was almost a necessary concomitant of the latter ; its excavation supplying the earth for the construction of the mound, in the centre of which the relics were deposited. Hence a different procedure has to be adopted in exploring a mound believed to have been a stupa from what would be followed in other cases. Unless the object be to discover the relics, it is ordinarily a waste of labour to cut deep into its centre; for the images which surmounted it must have fallen down outside its base, where they have been gradually buried by the crumbling away of the stúpa over them and will be found at no great depth below the surface. But, in the case of a temple or monastery, the mound is itself the ruined building; if Muhammadans were the destroyers, it was generally utilized as the substructure of a mosque. The Upagupta monastery, it is true, is said to have comprised a stúpa also, but it would appear from the way in which it is mentioned to have been comparatively a small one: it may well have formed the raised centre of the Kankáli Tíla, into which I dug and found nothing.

But whatever the purpose of the original buildings, it is clear that the hill was frequented as a religious site for upwards of a thousand years. Some of the statues are unmistakeably Buddhist and about coeval with the institution of Christianity; while others are as clearly Jain and one of these is dated *Sambat* 1134. Either the Jains succeeded the Buddhists in the same way as Protestants have taken the place of Catholics in our English Cathedrals; or the two rival sects may have existed together, like Greek and Latin Christians in the holy places of Jerusalem.

Hwen Thsang describes the Upagupta monastery as lying to the east of the town and the Kankali Tilá is a little to the east of the katra, which was certainly the centre of the old Buddhist city, the local tradition to that effect having been confirmed by the large number of antiquities recently found in its neighbourhood. The only difficulty in so considering it arises from the fact that Mathurá has at all times been represented as standing on the bank of the Jamuná, while the katra is nearly a mile away from it. Popularly, this objection is removed by an appeal to the appearance of the ground, which has evidently been affected by fluvial action, and also by the present habits of the river, which is persistent in endeavouring to desert its present channel in favour of one still more to the east. The stream, it is said, may have so worked its way between the natural hills and artificial mounds that the temples, which once stood on its east bank, found themselves on the west, while those that were originally on the western verge of the river were eventually left far inland. This was the view taken by Tavernier more than two centuries ago,* who was so far influenced by the popular tradition and the appearance of the

* The edition from which I translate was published at Paris in 1677.

country as to assert positively, not only that the course of the river had changed, but that the change had taken place quite recently. His words are as follows:—"At Cheka Sera" (by which he must intend the Shahganj saráe, then recently built) "may be seen one of the largest pagodas in all India. Connected with it is a hospital for monkeys, not only for those that are ordinarily on the spot, but also for any that may come from the surrounding country, and Hindus are employed to feed them. This pagoda is called Maturá, and was once held in much greater veneration by the heathen than it is now; the reason being that the Jamuná used to flow at its foot, and so the Hindus, whether natives, or strangers who had come from a distance on a pilgrimage for purposes of devotion, had facilities for bathing in the river both before they entered the pagoda and also before eating when they went away. For they must not eat without bathing, and they believe that their sins are best effaced by a dip in flowing water. But for some years past the river has taken a turn to the north, and now flows at the distance of a *kos* or more; whence it comes about that the shrine is less frequented by pilgrims than it used to be."

The third of the principal Buddhist sites is the vicinity of the katra. Here, at the back of the temple of Bhútesvar Mahádeva, is rather a high hill of very limited area, on the top of which stood, till removed by the writer, a Buddhist pillar of unusually large dimensions. It is carved in front with a female figure, nearly life-size, bearing an umbrella, and above her head is a grotesque bas-relief representing two monkeys, a bird, and a misshapen human dwarf. Immediately opposite the temple is a large ruinous tank, called Balbhadra Kund, with a skirting wall, into which had been built up some good specimens of the cross-bars of a Buddhist railing. From an adjoining well was recovered a plain pillar neasuring four feet seven inches in height by eleven inches in breadth, carved in front merely with two roses. The elliptical holes in the sides of the pillar were too large for the cross-bars, which must have belonged to a smaller range. They measure only one foot three inches in length, and are enriched with various devices, such as a rose, a lotus, some winged monster, &c. These were eleven in number: four of the most perfect were taken away by General Cunningham, the rest are still *in situ*. Built into the verandah of a *chaupál* close by were five other Buddhist pillars of elaborate design and almost perfect preservation. It is said that there was originally a sixth, which some years ago was sent down to Calcutta; there it has been followed by two more; the remaining three were left, by the writer, for the local museum, where possibly they may now have been placed. They are each four feet four inches in height and eleven inches broad ; the front is carved with a standing female figure, whose feet rest upon a crouching monster. In an upper compartment, divided off by a band of Buddhist railing, are two demi-figures, male and female, in amorous attitudes, of very superior execution. On one pillar the principal figure is represented as gathering up her drapery, in another as painting her face with the aid of a mirror, and in the third as supporting with one hand a wine-jar and in the other, which hangs down by her side, holding a bunch of grapes. Each of these figures is entirely devoid of clothing : the drapery mentioned as belonging to one of them is simply being gathered up from behind. They have, however, a profusion of ornaments—*karas* on the ankles, a belt round the waist, a *mohan málá* on the neck, *karn-phúls* in the ears, and *báju-band*, *chúri*, and *pahunchi* on the arms and wrists. There are also three bas-reliefs at the back of each pillar ; the subject of one is most grossly indecent ; another represents Buddha's mother, Máyá Devi, with the sál tree under which she gave birth to her son. A fragment of a pillar from one of the smaller concentric circles of this same set was at some time sent to Lahor, and is now to be seen in the museum there.

General Cunningham, in his Archæological Report, has identified the Upagupta monastery with the Yasa Vihára inside the katra ; but in all probability he would not now adhere to this theory. At the time when he advanced it, he had never visited the Kankáli Tilá, and was also under the impression that the Fort had always been, as it now is, the centre of the city. Even then, to maintain his theory, he was obliged to have recourse to a very violent expedient and in the text of the Chinese pilgrim alter the word 'east' to 'west,' because, he writes, "a mile to the east would take us to the low ground on the opposite bank of the Jamuná, where no ruins exist ;" forgetting apparently Fa Hian's distinct statement that in his time there were monasteries on both sides of the river, and being also unaware that there are heights on the left bank, at Isapur* and Mahában, where Buddhist remains have been found. The topographical descriptions of the two pilgrims may be reconciled with existing facts without any tampering with the text of their narrative. Taking the katra, or the adjoining shrine of

* At Isapur, almost facing the Visránt Ghát is the Duvása tila, a high mound of artificial formation, with some modern buildings on its summit, enclosed within a bastioned wall, part of which has been lately restored. A small nude statue of a female figure has been found here, and there are also the remains of a *báuli* constructed of large blocks of red sandstone fitted together without cement and therefore probably of early date.

Bhútesvar, as the omphalos of the ancient city and the probable site of the great stúpa of Sáriputra, a short distance to the east will bring us to the Kankáli Tílá, *i. e.,* the monastery of Upagupta ; the Jamálpur mound has already been identified with the monkey stúpa ; while some mounds to the north, that will shortly be mentioned, may have been "the stúpas of the four earlier Buddhas and other great teachers of the law."

Close at the back of the Balbhadra Kund and the katra is a range of hills of considerable elevation, commonly called *dhúl kot,* literally 'dust-heaps,' the name given to the accumulation of refuse that collects outside a city, and so corresponding precisely to the Monte Testaccio at Rome. Some of these are, however, clearly of natural formation and probably indicate the old course of the Jamuná or its tributaries. Others are the walls of the old city, which in places are still of great height. They can be traced in a continuous line from the Rangesvar Mahádeo on the Kans ká tílá outside the Holi gate of new Mathurá, across the Agra road, to the temple of Bhútesvar, and thence round by an orchard called the Uthaigira ká bágh, where the highest point is crowned by a small Bairágí's cell, at the back of Kesav Dev and between it and the Seth's Chaurási temple, to the shrine of Gartesvar, 'the God of the Moat,' and so on to the Mahávidya hill and the temple of Gokarnesvar near the Sarasvati Sangam.

At the distance of about a mile to the south-west of these ancient ramparts, at the junction of the boundaries of the township of Mathurá and the villages of Bákirpur and Giridharpur, is a group of some twelve or fourteen circular mounds, commonly known as the Chauwára mounds, from a rest-house that once stood there ; *Chauwára* and *Chaupál* being different forms of the same word, like *gopála* and *gwála.* They are strewn with fragments of brick and stone and would seem all to have been stúpas. As they are to the north of the Jamálpur mound, they may with great probability be identified with the stupas described by Hwen Thsang as lying to the north of the monkey tank and marking the spots that had been hallowed by the presence of the 1,250 famous teachers of the law.

In the year 1868, the new road to Sonkh was carried through one of these mounds, and in the centre was disclosed a masonry cell containing a small gold reliquary, the size and shape of a pill-box. Inside was a tooth, the safe-guard of which was the sole object of box, cell, and hill ; but it was thrown away as of no value. The box was preserved on account of the material and has been given to the writer by Mr. Hind the district engineer, whose workmen had discovered it.

Another mound was, as I am informed, examined, by General Cunningham in 1872, when, on sinking a well through its centre, he found, at a depth of 13½ feet from the summit, a small steatite relic casket imbedded in a mass of unburnt bricks. Here I found subsequently the head of a colossal figure of very Egyptian cast of features with a round hole in its forehead, in which was once set a ruby or other precious stone. The lower part of a large seated Buddha was also unearthed with an inscription in the Páli character on the ledge beneath, of which the first three words read *Mahárájasya Devaputrasya Huvishkasya, i. e.*, 'of the great king, the heaven-born Huvishka,' followed by the date *sam* 33, *gri* 1, *di* 8, 'the 8th day of the 1st summer month of the 33rd year.' The remainder has not been deciphered with any certainty. I found also several cross-bars and uprights of Buddhist rails of different sizes and a great number of small fragments of male and female figures, animals, grotesques, and decorative patterns, showing that the sculptures here must have been far more varied in design than at most of the other sites. One of the uprights has a well-executed and decently draped figure of a dancing-girl, with the right hand raised and two fingers placed upon her chin. The lower part of the post has been broken away, carrying with it her feet and the third of the three groups at the back. Of the two groups that remain, the upper one represents two seated figures, apparently a teacher and his disciple, with two attendants standing in the back-ground, and has a single line of inscription below, recording the donor's name. The second group shows a sacred tree, enclosed with the conventional rails, and a pilgrim on either side approaching in an attitude of veneration. The only other sculpture deserving special notice is a small bas-relief that represents a capacious throne resembling a garden chair of rustic wood-work, with a foot-stool in front of it and some drapery spread over the seat, on which is placed a relic casket. In the back-ground are two figures leaning over the high back of the chair. Their peculiarly furtive attitude is characteristic of the style; almost every group includes one or more figures peeping over a balcony, or a curtain, or from behind a tree. On this stone was found a copper coin so much corroded that no legend was visible, but bearing in its centre a running figure, which was the device employed both by Kanishka and Huvishka. I had great hopes of discovering another inscription here, as I had picked up a small fragment with the letters , that is, 'Budhánam,' cut very clear and deep; but my search was unsuccessful. Digging in the field some twenty paces from the base of the mound, I came upon the original pavement only two or three feet below the surface, with three large square graduated pedestals, ranged in close line, one overthrown, the other two erect. A capital, found by General

Cunningham in 1872, measuring 3ft. ×2×2, and carved with four winged lions and bulls conjoined, probably belonged to one of the pillars that had surmounted these pedestals. Thay have been put in the local museum, together with the antiquities above described and the knee of a colossal statue found by General Cunningham in sinking the well through the centre of the mound. A large dry tank, adjoining the mound, is proved to be also of Buddhist construction, as I had anticipated ; for I found in one of the mounds on its margin a broken stone inscribed with the letters 𑀤𑀸𑀦𑀁𑀙 that is, 'Dánam Chh.'

Between the Kankáli Tila and these Chauwára mounds, all the fields are dotted with others, so close together and so much worn by time that they can scarcely be distinguished from the natural level of the ground. One that I searched, after an exploration extending over several days, yielded nothing beyond a few arabesque fragments and, at a depth of six feet below the surface, a small pediment containing in a niche, flanked by fabulous monsters and surmounted by the mystic wheel, a figure of Buddha, canopied by a many-headed serpent and seated on a lion throne. A mound immediately adjoining the pillar that marks the boundary of the township of Mathurá and the villages of Maholi and Páli-kherá, lying due south of the Kankali *Tíla* and east of the Girdharpur mound, has yielded a strange squat figure of a dwarf, three feet nine inches high and two feet broad, of uncertain antiquity ; and at another mound, just outside the Páli-kherá village site, I came upon the counter-part of Colonel Stacey's so-called Silenus, which he found in 1836 and placed in the Asiatic Society's Museum in Calcutta, where it still is. A full description of this curious sculpture will be given in another chapter. On further excavating the mound, in which I found it, I discovered *in situ* three bell-shaped bases of large columns at 13 feet distance from one another, at the three corners of a square ; the fourth had completely disappeared. In clearing the space between them I came upon some small figures of baked clay, glazed, of a bluish colour, similar in character to the toys still sold at Hindu fairs ; also a few small fragments of carved stone and some corroded pieces of metal bangles. According to village tradition this khera was the fort of a demon, Nonásur ; the exploration proves it to have been a Buddhist site ; it adjoins a temple court, of the early part of the 17th century, now occupied by a married Bairági as an ordinary dwelling-house. Close by, on the border of the hamlet of Dhan Sinh, is a small Buddhist rail (now reverenced as the village Devi) with the usual figure of Buddha's mother under the sál tree on its front, and three roses at the back. A few paces further on is the central portion of a very large Buddhist pillar, with a head on either side, the exact counter-part of one that I extracted from the Chhatthi Pálna at Mahában.

The hill known as the Kans ká Tílá just outside the south, or, as it is called, the Holi Gate of the city, is supposed to be the one from the summit of which the tyrant of that name was tumbled down by Krishna. General Cunningham suggests that this might be one of the seven great stúpas mentioned by the Chinese pilgrims, and adds that on the north of the city there are two hills still bearing the names of Anand and Vináyaka, titles which they specify. But in this it appears that he was misinformed, as no such localities can be traced. Of the hills to the north of Mathurá, the most conspicuous are the Kailás and Mahal* or Jaysinhpura *khera*, sometimes called the Ganes from the Ghat of that name which is immediately below it. An Anant tirtha, easily to be confounded with Anand, is noted in the Mathurá Máhátmya ; and the fact that Vináyaka, besides its Buddhist meaning, is also an epithet of Ganes, may have given rise to an error in the other name. The Kans ká Tílá certainly appears to be primarily of natural formation and hence to have been selected as the river boundary of the old city wall. The whole country, indeed, has been broken up into heights and hollows of indefinite number and extent: but most ancient Buddhist sites must be looked for at a greater distance from the river and outside the modern city, in what is now open country at the back of the katra, and in the direction of Maholi, the ancient Madhu-puri, where the aboriginal Madhu held his court. Subsequently to his defeat, the Aryan city was built in the neighbourhood of the present Katra and the temple of Bhútesvar ; and, being the seat of the new Government, it appropriated in a special way the name which formerly had denoted, not the capital, but the whole extent of territory. This view is confirmed by observing that, philologically, 'Mathurá' appears a more fitting name for a country than for a city, and one that could be applied to the latter only inferentially. The present city is the third in order and has for its centre the Fort ; as the second had the temple of Bhútesvar, and the first the grove of Madhu-ban. Thus, speaking generally, the further we move back from the city in the direction of Maholi, the older will probably be the date of any antiquities that may be discovered.

* So called from a dwelling-house that was built there by Sawáe Jay Sinh.

CHAPTER VI.

THE HINDU CITY OF MATHURÁ.

On the decline of Buddhism, Mathurá acquired that character for sanctity which it still retains, as the reputed birth-place of the deified Krishna. Or, more probably, the triumph of Buddhism was a mere episode, on the conclusion of which the city recovered a character which it had before enjoyed at a much earlier period ; for it may be inferred from the language of the Greek geographers that Bráhmanism was in their time the religion of the country, while Hindu tradition is uniform in maintaining its claims both to holiness and antiquity. Thus it is represented as the second of the capitals of the Lunar race, which were in succession Prayág, Mathurá, Kusasthali, and Dwáraká ; and in the following well-known couplet it is ranked among the seven sanctuaries of Hindustán :—

Kási Kántí cha Máyákhyá twayodhyá Dwáravatyapi
Mathurávantiká chaitá sapta puryo tra mokshadáh.

"Kási (*i. e.*, Banáras), Kánti (probably Kanchi), Mayá (*i. e.*, Haridwár), with Ayodhyá, Dwáravati, Mathurá, and Avantiká, are the seven cities of salvation."

At the present day it has no lack of stately edifices, with which, as described of old in the Harivansa, " it rises beautiful as the cresent moon over the dark stream of the Jamuná ;* but they are all modern. The neighbourhood is crowded with sacred sites, which for many generations have been reverenced as the traditionary scenes of Krishna's adventures ; but, thanks to Muhammadan intolerance, there is not a single building of any antiquity either in the city itself or its environs. Its most famous temple—that dedicated to Kesava Deva—was destroyed, as already mentioned, in 1669, the eleventh year of the reign of the icnoclastic Aurangzeb. The mosque erected on its ruins is a building of little architectural value, but the natural advantages of its lofty and isolated position render it a striking feature in the landscape. The so-called katra, in which it stands, a place to which frequent allusion has been made in the previous chapter, is an oblong enclosure, like a *sarác*, 104 feet in length by 653 feet in breadth. In its centre is a raised terrace, 172 feet long and 86 feet broad, upon which

---

* अर्द्धचन्द्रप्रतीकाशा यमुनातीरशोभिता ॥ Harivansa, 3,100.

now stands the mosque, occupying its entire length, but only 60 feet of its breadth. About five feet lower is another terrace, measuring 286 feet by 268. There may still be observed, let into the Muhammadan pavement, some votive tablets with Nágari inscriptions, dated *Sambat* 1713 and 1720, corresponding to 1656 and 1663 A. D. In the latter year the temple attracted the notice of the traveller Bernier, who writes :—" Between Delhi and Agra, a distance of fifty or sixty leagues, there are no fine towns ; the whole road is cheerless and uninteresting ; nothing is worthy of observation but Mathurá, where an ancient and magnificent pagan temple is still to be seen." The plinth of the temple-wall may be traced to this day at the back of the mosque and at right angles to it for a distance of 163 feet ; but not a vestige of the superstructure has been allowed to remain.

The following description of this famous building is given by Tavernier, who visited it about the year 1650. He writes :—" After the temples of Jagrenath and Banárous, the most important is that of Matura, about 18 *kos** from Agra on the road to Delhi. It is one of the most sumptuous edifices in all India, and the place where there used to be formerly the greatest concourse of pilgrims ; but now they are not so many, the Hindus having gradually lost their previous veneration for the temple, on account of the Jamuná, which used to pass close by, now having changed its bed and formed a new channel half a league away. For, after bathing in the river, they lose too much time in returning to the temple, and on the way might come across something to render them unclean.

" The temple is of such a vast size that, though in a hollow, one can see it five or six *kos* off, the building being very lofty and very magnificent. The stone used in it is of a reddish tint, brought from a large quarry near Agra. It splits like our slate, and you can have slabs 15 feet long and nine or ten broad and only some six inches thick ; in fact, you can split them just as you like and according to your requirements, while you can also have fine columns. The whole of the fort at Agra, the walls of Jehánábád, the king's palace, and some of the houses of the nobles are built of this stone. To return to the temple.—It is set on a large octagonal platform, which is all faced with cut stone, and has round about it two bands of many kinds of animals, but particularly monkeys, in relief ;

* Here he states the distance correctly ; but in another place he gives the stages from Delhi to Agra as follows :—" From Delhi to Badelpoura, 8 *kos* ; from Badelpoura to Pelwel ki sera, 18 ; from Pelwel ki sera to Cot ki sera (Kosi) 15 ; from Cot ki sera to Cheki sera (Mathurá, 'Cheki' standing for 'Sháhki') 16 ; from Cheki sera to Goodki sera, 5 ; from Gooki sera to Agra, 6." One stage must have been omitted at the end.

the one band being only two feet off the ground level, the other two feet from the top. The ascent is by two staircases of 15 or 16 steps each; the steps being only two feet in length, so that two people cannot mount abreast. One of these staircases leads to the grand entrance of the temple, the other to the back of the choir. The temple, however, occupies only half the platform, the other half making a grand square in front. Like other temples, it is in the form of a cross, and has a great dome in the middle with two rather smaller at the end. Outside, the building is covered from top to bottom with figures of animals, such as rams, monkeys, and elephants, carved in stone: and all round there are nothing but niches occupied by different monsters. In each of the three towers there are, at every stage from the base to the pinnacle, windows five or six feet high, each provided with a kind of balcony where four persons can sit. Each balcony is covered with a little vault, supported some by four, others by eight columns arranged in pairs and all touching. Round these towers there are yet more niches full of figures representing demons; one has four arms, another four legs; some, human heads on bodies of horned beasts with long tails twining round their thighs. There are also many figures of monkeys, and it is quite shocking to have before one's eyes such a host of monstrosities.

"The pagoda has only one entrance, which is very lofty, with many columns and images of men and beasts on either side. The choir is enclosed by a screen composed of stone pillars, five or 6 inches in diameter, and no one is allowed inside but the chief Bráhmans, who make use of a little secret door which I could not discover. When in the temple, I asked some of the Bráhmans if I could see the great Rám Rám, meaning the great idol. They replied that if I would give them something, they would go and ask permission of their superior:* which they did as soon as I had put in their hands a couple of rupees After waiting about half an hour, the Bráhmans opened a door on the inside in the middle of the screen—outside, the screen is entirely closed—and, at about 15 or 16 feet from the door, I saw, as it were, a square altar, covered with old gold

* Regarding the veneration paid to the head of the temple. Tavernier, in another place, relates the following anecdote:—"While I was at Agra, in the year 1642, a very odd thing happened. A Hindu broker in Dutch employ, by name Voldas, some 80 or so years of age, received tidings of the death of the chief Bráhman, that is to say, the high priest of the temple of Mathurá. He at once went to the head of the office and begged him to take his accounts and finish them off, for as his high priest was dead he wished to die too, that he might serve the holy man in the other world. Directly his accounts had been inspected, he got into his carriage together with some relations who followed him, and as he had taken nothing either to eat or drink since the news had reached him, he died on the road, without ever expressing a wish for any food."

and silver brocade, and on it the great idol that they call Rám Rám. The head only is visible and is of very black marble, with what seemed to be two rubies for eyes. The whole body from the neck to the feet was covered with an embroidered robe of red velvet and no arms could be seen. There were two other idols, one on either side, two feet high, or thereabouts, and got up in the same style, only with white faces ; these they called Becchor. I also noticed in the temple a structure 15 or 16 feet square, and from 12 to 15 feet high, covered with coloured clothes representing all sorts of demons. This structure was raised on four little wheels, and they told me it was the moveable altar on which they set the great god on high feast days, when he goes to visit the other gods, and when they take him to the river with all the people on their chief holiday."

From the above description, the temple would seem to have been crowded with coarse figure-sculptures, and not in such pure taste as the somewhat older temple of Govind Deva at Brindá-ban ; but it must still have been a most sumptuous and imposing edifice, and we cannot but detest the bigotry of the barbarian who destroyed it. At the time of its demolition it had been in existence only some fifty years, but it is certain that an earlier shrine, or series of shrines, on the same site and under the same dedication, had been famous for many ages. Thus it is said in the Varáha Purana—

Na Kesava samo deva na Mathurá samo dvija,

" No god like Kesava, and no Bráhman like a Mathuriya Chaube. "

In still earlier times the site now wrested by the Muhammadans from the Hindus had been seized by the Hindus themselves to the prejudice of another religion, as is attested by the Buddhist remains which we have already described as found there.

With regard to the change in the course of the stream, all engineers whom I have consulted are unanimous in declaring that the main channel of the Jamuná can never in historic time have been at the foot of the temple, as Tavernier imagined. The traces of fluvial action, which he observed, are unmistakeable, but they date from the most remote antiquity. This, however, need not occasion any difficulty : for, as Madhu-puri, the first capital, was established at a point which clearly the Jamuná could never have reached, there is no improbability in supposing that the second capital also, though much nearer the stream, was not actually on its bank. The temples which Fa Hian mentions as being on the other side of the river were probably situate at Isapur and Mahá-ban. It is also to be noted that a *tributary* stream, the bed of which is now partly occupied by the Delhi road, did certainly flow past the katra. This being joined, at the point still called the Sangam, or 'confluence,' by another considerable water-course from the opposite direction, fell into the channel now crossed by the Seth's bridge, and so reached the Jamuná.

In anticipation of Aurangzeb's raid, the ancient image of Kesava Deva was removed by Ráná Ráj Sinh of Mewár, and was set up on the spot where, as they journeyed, the wheels of the chariot sank in the deep sand and refused to be extricated. It happened to be an obscure little village, then called Siarh, on the Banás, 22 miles north-east of Udaypur. But the old name is now lost in the celebrity of the temple of Náth Ji, 'the Lord,' which gives its designation to the town of Náth-dwára, which has grown up round it.* This is the most highly venerated of all the statues of Krishna. There are seven others of great repute, which also deserve mention here, as a large proportion of them came from the neighbourhood of Mathurá, *viz.*, Nava-níta, which is also at Náth-dwára; Mathura-náth at Kota; Dwáraká-náth at Kankarauli, brought from Kanauj; Bál Kishan at Surat, from Mahá-ban; Bitthal-náth or Pándu-rang at Kota, from Banáras; Madan Mohan from Brindá-ban; and Gokul-náth and Gokul chandramá, both from Gokul. These two last were at Jaypur till a few years ago, when, in consequence of the Mahárája's dislike to all the votaries of Vishnu, they were removed to Kám-ban in Bharat-pur territory. In all probability before very long they will be brought back to their original homes.

At the back of the katra is the modern temple of Kesava Deva, a cloistered quadrangle of no particular archtectural merit and, except on special occasions,

* It is described, in the lately published report of the Indian Survey Department, as "a large walled city on the right bank of the Banás river. On the north-east and south it is surrounded by hills, but to the west, across the river, which here takes a very sharp bend, it is fairly open. It has the reputation of being an enormously wealthy city, which I have no doubt is true, as it is a great place of pilgrimage; every pilgrim giving what he can as an offering at the shrine of Srináth. Amongst the more valuable presents given to the Bráhmans, are elephants and cattle; large herds of the latter graze on the hills to the east of the city, where there is a regular cattle farm surrounded by a high wall and guarded by sepoys; the cows in milk receive a daily ration of grain, all sorts mixed, which is boiled in an immense iron caldron. About two years ago the Mahant, or head Gosáin, of Náth-dwára, became troublesome, ignoring all orders of the Darbár, and otherwise misconducted himself to such an extent that it was found necessary to send a force against him. It was supposed that he would resist, but on seeing some guns commanding his city, he gave in; he was banished to Mathurá and his son allowed to take his place; but at the same time 300 sepoys, under the orders of a Kámdár, appointed by the Darbár, were stationed there to ensure his good behaviour. Even now it is a place rather to be avoided, as the Bráhmans are a very independent set and apt to be insolent on very small provocation. All fishing and shooting is strictly prohibited within the ground belonging to this city.

little frequented, in consequence of its distance from the main town. It is supported by an annual endowment of Rs. 1,027, the rents of the village of Undí in the Chhátá pargana. Close by is a very large quadrangular tank of solid masonry, called the Potara-kund, in which, as the name denotes, Krishna's 'baby linen' was washed. There is little or no architectural decoration, but the great size and massiveness of the work render it imposing, while the effect is much enhanced by the venerable trees which overhang the enclosing wall. Unfortunately, the soil is so porous that the supply of water is rapidly absorbed, and in every season but the rains the long flights of steps are dry to their very base. Its last restoration was made, at considerable cost, in 1850, by the Kámdár of the Gwáliar Ráj. It might now be easily filled from the canal. A small cell on the margin of the tank, called indifferently Kárá-grah, 'the prison-house,' or Janm-bhúmi, 'the birth-place,' marks the spot where Vasudeva and Devakí were kept in confinement, and where their son Krishna was born. The adjoining suburb, in its name Mallpura, commemorates, it is said, Kansa's two famous *mallas, i. e.*, 'wrestlers,' Chánura and Mushtika. At the back of the Potara-kund and within the circuit of the Dhúl-kot, or old ramparts of the city, is a very large mound (where a railway engineer had a house before the Mutiny) which would seem to have been the site of some large Buddhist establishment. It is strewn with broken bits of stone and fragments of sculpture, and I found in particular two large but headless and armless and otherwise mutilated figures of Buddha seated and fully clothed. In this respect they agreed with all the figures found in this particular neighbourhood, as also in the position of the hands, which are not crossed on the feet, but the right is raised in admonition, while the left rests on the thigh. At the Kankáli tíla the statues are mostly nude ; and at the Jamálpur mound they are more commonly standing than seated.

In connection with the discovery of Buddhist antiquities, allusion has already been made to the temple of Bhútesvar Mahádeva, which overlooks the old and ruinous Balbhadra-kund. In its present form it is a quadrangle of ordinary character with pyramidal tower and cloister built by the Mahrattas towards the end of last century. The site has probably been occupied by successive religious buildings from most remote antiquity, and was at one time the centre of the town of Mathurá, which has now moved away from it more than a mile to the east. In the earlier days of Bráhmanism, before the development of the Krishna cultus, it may be surmised that Bhútesvar was the special local divinity. There are in Braj three other shrines of Mahádeva, which are also of high traditional repute in spite of the meanness of their modern accessories, *viz.*, Kámesvar at Káma, Chakresvar at Gobardhan, and Gopesvar at Brindában. A mela is held by the Balbhadra-kund on the full moon of Srávan, the feast of the Salúno. The pond was partially cleaned out and repaired as a relief work during the late famine, and, as the Aríng navigation channel terminates in a reservoir close by, there will now be no difficulty in keeping it always filled with water. This branch of the canal has a length of eight or nine miles, with two locks, one at Ganesra, the other immediately opposite the Chaurási temple. For some little distance it runs directly under the Dhúl-kot, or old city wall.

Of the many little shrines that cluster about the Balbhadra-kund, one is dedicated to Balaráma under his title of Dau-jí, 'the elder brother;' another to Ganes, and a third to Nar-Sinha, 'the man-lion,' the fourth incarnation of Vishnu. According to the legend, there was an impious king, by name Hiranya Kasipu, who claimed universal sovereignty over all powers on earth, in heaven, and hell. No one had the hardihood to oppose him, save his own son, the pious prince Prahlád, who was for ever singing the praises of the great god Vishnu. "If," said the king, "your god is everywhere present, let him now show himself in this pillar which I strike." At the word the pillar parted in twain and revealed the god in terrible form, half lion half man, who seized the boastful monarch and tore him in pieces and devoured him.

In an adjoining orchard called the Kází's Bágh is a small modern mosque, and in connection with it a curious square building of red sand-stone. It now encloses a Muhammadan tomb, and in all probability was originally constructed for that purpose, though it has nothing Saracenic about it and is a good specimen of the pure Hindu style of architecture, with characteristic columns and square architraves supported on brackets instead of arches. Similarly, almost all the oldest buildings that now remain in and about the city are houses or tombs, that were constructed for Muhammadans by Hindus and in purely Hindu style. At the present day all the new buildings are intended for Hindu use, but their architectural forms have been greatly modified by Muhammadan influences.

After leaving the great entrance to the katra, the Dehli road passes a masonry well* called 'Kubjá's' in commemoration of the miracle which Krishna wrought in straightening the hump-backed maiden who met him there. The

* Immediately opposite the well a fragment of a sculptured Buddhist pillar has been set up, and receives religious honours as representing the Hindu goddess Devi.

turn to the right leads into the city by the Brindá-ban gate, under the Ambarisha hill, and past the Sháhganj saráe, which has a once handsome, but now sadly ruinous, stone front. In the Muhammadan burial-ground, on the opposite side of the street, is a fine large stone Chhattri, similar to the one near the Idgah at Mahá-ban, which commemorates Ali Khan, the local Governor of that town. It is probably of the reign of Akbar, and is said to cover the ashes of a certain Khwája. Nearer the roadside is an unfinished square stone building with very elegant tracery, which is said to have been commenced as the monument of some grandee of Darbhanga. The handsome bridge which here crosses the natural water-course known as the Sarasvati Sangam, or 'confluence of the Sarasvati,' was built by Seth Lakhmi Chand in 1849.

To the right of it is a temple of Mahádeva, which forms a very conspicuous object. It was built in the year 1850 by Ajudhyá Prasád of Lucknow, and the court-yard is in the debased style of architecture for which that city is notorious. Close by is a walled garden with another temple to the same divinity and a much frequented stone ghát on the river-bank, all constructed at the cost of Srí Gopál, the head of the money-changers in the city, who is now represented by his son Rádhá Krishan. Round the garden wall on the inner side are rooms for the accommodation of pilgrims, the arches being filled in with doors and panels of reticulated tracery, in wood. A daily distribution of grain is here made to the poor. The adjoining hill is called Kailás, and on its slope is the shrine of Gokarnesvar, who is represented as a giant seated figure, with enormous eyes and long hair and beard and moustaches. In one hand is what appears to be a wine cup, in the other some flowers or grapes. The stone is much worn. The figure is certainly of great antiquity and might have been originally intended to represent some Indo-Scythian king. In a niche in the wall are two small statues, about 1½ foot high, called by the Bráhmans Sati and Párvati. They really are both well executed and early figures of Buddha, seated and preaching. One has lost the right hand. In the same set of buildings is the tomb of Gautama Rishi. Now, Gokarna is the name of a place near the Malabar coast where Bhagirath practised austerities before he brought down the Ganges from heaven, and Gotama (not Gautama) is the author of some of the hymns in the Rig Veda; so that both names might be connected with Hinduism; but both are also Buddhist, and this fact, combined with the existence of unmistakeably Buddhist sculptures on the spot, may be taken as proof that this is one of the old Buddhist sites. Gautama, it need scarcely be said, is one of the commonest names of Buddha himself, and Gokarnesvar is one of the eight great Vita-rágas, or passionless deified saints.

34

Immediately under the bridge is a shrine bearing the singular name of Gárgi Sárgi, or as it is sometimes called the Great and Little Pathawári. They are said to have been the two wives of Gokarn, who when translated to heaven became the equal of Mahádeva. The *mantra* to be repeated in honour of the younger lady runs as follows :—

शार्गीदेवि नमस्तुभ्यमृषिपत्नि मनोरमे ।
शुभगे वरदे गौरि सर्वदा सिद्धिदायिनी ॥

" Honour to thee, O divine Sárgi, the Rishi's beautiful wife, happy mother, beneficent incarnation of Gauri, ever bestowing success."

Here are several other groups of rude vermilion-stained stones, some in the open, some housed in shrines of their own, which do duty for Bháirav, Sítala Devi, and Masáni. Two fragments are of Buddhist type : one a rail, the other a sculpture of Maya Devi standing under a pillar with bell-shaped capital. Opposite the Kailás hill, across the road, is an open plain, where the sports of the Rám Lilá are celebrated on the festival of the Dasahara. Close by is a tank called the Sarasvati-kund, measuring 125 feet square. Owing to some fault in the construction, it is almost always dry, and the adjoining buildings have also rather a ruinous and deserted appearance. We learn, however, from the following inscription, which is on a tablet over the entrance to the temple, that the last restoration was completed so recently as the year 1846 :—

श्रीमत् परमहंस परिव्राजकाचार्य्य श्री० स्वामी परमहंसजी तच्चरण सेवापरायण बलदेव देव गोस्वामी बासी मथुराजी दशावतार की गली के नें सरस्वती कुण्ड को जीर्णोद्धार सर्व ओर तें तथा नवीन सरस्वती को मन्दिर श्रीमूर्त्ति प्रतिष्ठा सुद्धां बनवायो मार्फ़त छोटेलाल मन्नूलाल सनाढ्य की उस्तां चुन्नी में लागत रुपया २०३५) मिती कार्त्तिक शु० १३ सं० १९०३ ॥

The above, which exhibits several peculiarities, both in style and phraseology, may be rendered as follows :—" Baladeva Gosáin, resident of the Dasávatár Gali of Mathurá, the devoted servant of the venerable contemplative ascetic the right reverend Swámi Paramhans, thoroughly restored from ruin the Sarasvati-kund, and built this new temple and in due form set up a god in it. His agents were Chhote Lál and Mannú Lál, Sanádhs; the head of the works Chunni: the cost Rs. 2,735. Kártik sudi 13th, Sambat 1903." The Swámi's actual name was Náráyan, and his disciple, Baladeva, was a foundling whom he picked up in the street. Both were Pandits of high local repute.

At no great distance is the temple of Mahá Vidyá Devi. The original image with that dedication is said to have been set up by the Pándavas; the present shrine, a *Sikhara* of ordinary character in a small quadrangle, was built by the Peshwá towards the end of last century. The hill upon which it stands is ascended by flights of masonry steps between 30 and 40 in number. At the foot is a small dry tank, completely overgown with a dense jungle of *ber*, *pílu*, and *híns*. In the court-yard, which occupies the entire plateau, is a *karíl* tree said to be of enormous age, under which were to be seen, among other fragments, a Buddhist pillar carved with the figure of Máyá Devi under the sál-tree, and a square stone box with a seated Buddha on each of its four sides. Two melas are held here on the 8th of the light fortnight of Chait and Kuwár. This again, like Gokarnesvar, is unquestionably one of the old Buddhist sites, with its name still unchanged; for Mahávidyá or Vidyá Devi is, strictly speaking, a Buddhist goddess.

The Jaysinh-pura *Khera*, which overlooks the Sarasvati Sangam and is separated by a deep ravine from the Mahávidyá hill, is of great extent and has been tunnelled all over in search for bricks. Several Buddhist sculptures have been found at different times and collected at a shrine of Chámund Devi, which is immediately under the khera at the back of Seth Mangi Lál's new garden, whence I brought away some of the best for the museum. Across the road, under Jay Sinh's old palace, I found, in the bed of the river, near the ghát erected by one of Sindhia's generals and hence called the Senapati's, a draped Buddhist figure of the earliest period, with a Páli inscription at the base, so much obliterated by the washermen, who had used it for beating linen upon, that only a few letters here and there were legible. The figure had lost both head and hands, but was otherwise in good preservation.

At several of the holy places, as we have had occasion to remark, a large tank forms one of the principal features; but the only one that can be called a success is the Siva tál, not far from the Kankáli tíla. This is a spacious quadrangular basin of great depth and always well supplied with water. It is enclosed in high boundary wall with corner kiosques and a small arched doorway in the centre of three of its sides. On the fourth side is the slope for watering cattle or 'go-ghát,' with two memorial inscriptions facing each other, the one in

Sanskrit, the other in Persian ; from which we learn that the tank was constructed by order of Rájá Patni Mall (of Banáras) in the year 1807 A.D. :—

श्रीमन्माथुरमण्डले सुरनते शैवस्थले निर्मले
वाराहोक्तपुराणवर्णितगुणं प्राक्पुण्यलभ्यं जनैः
तीर्थं तीर्थवरं विशेष सुखदं श्रीनिर्मलोदाह्वयं
दुर्ज्ञेयं बहुकालतस्तदधुना श्रुत्वा महत्त्वाधिकम् ॥ १ ॥
कृत्वा नेत्रपथं सुशिल्परचितं नानागवाक्षैर्युतं
तस्योत्सर्गविधिः कृतो हि पटनी मल्लेन राज्ञाद्विजैः
विष्णोः पादसमुद्भवोत्सव इव चैविष्टपानन्ददो
वर्षे ब्ध्यङ्गगजेन्दुके सितदले ज्येष्ठे दशम्यां भृगौ ॥ २ ॥

"In the holy circuit of Mathurá, reverenced by the gods, pure home of the votaries of Siva, is a sacred place, whose virtues are told in the Varáha Purána, inaccessible by men save through the efficacy of virtuous deeds performed in a previous state of existence ; chief of all sacred places, giver of special graces : a pellucid lake, whose praises no length of time would suffice fully to tell. After a careful survey and employing the best of architects, who adorned it with tracery of varied design, the ceremony of its donation was performed by Rájá Patni Mall through the Bráhmans, causing gladness like that which arises from the touch of the foot of Vishnu, rejoicing even the gods. In the year of the (4) oceans, the (6) members, the (8) elephants, and the (solitary) moon (that is, *Sambat* 1864) on Friday, the 10th of the light fortnight of the month Jeth."

هو المستعان العباد

شد جدید آثار نام نیک این دیر قدم * در سواد شهر متهرا تیرتهه هر شش جهات
چون بنا فرمود معبد کهنهٔ شوتال نام * بانی جود و عنایت منتهائی محسنات
فیض بخش اهل عالم مرجع اِحسان عام * راجه پتنی مل بهادر منبع عالی صفات
یکهزار و دو صد و بست و دو آمد در شمار * سال تعمیرش برائی یادگار کائنات
در حساب ابجدی هم سال تاریخ از ذکا * می شود این بیگمان هر شهار (?) آب حیات
سنه ۱۲۲۲ هجری

" He is the one who is asked for help and who is constantly worshipped. The famous remains of this ancient shrine in the neighbourhood of Mathurá, the place of pilgrimage from all six quarters, have now been renewed. When the

AUTOTYPE

THE SIVA TÁL, MATHURÁ.

old buildings of the Siva tál were restored by that generous and benevolent founder, the goal of good deeds, the bestower of benefits on all the people of the world, the centre of public gratitude, Rájá Patnì Mall, Bahádur, fountain of excellent virtue; then the year of its construction—for the remembrance of all the world—was found to be 1222. Thought (or the poet Zaká) suggested the following *tarikh* according to the *abjad* reckoning [illegible] water of life."

The design and execution are both of singular excellence and reflect the highest credit on the architect whom he employed; the sculptured arcades, which project far into the centre of the basin and break up the long flights of steps into three compartments on each side, being especially graceful. The place is visited by a large number of bathers from the neigbourhood every morning and is the scene of an annual *mela* held on the 11th of the dark fortnight of the month Bhádon. Outside the enclosure is a small temple in the same style of architecture dedicated to Mahádeva under the title of Achalesvar. In the Manoharpur quarter of the city is a large temple of this Rájá's foundation, bearing the title of Dírgha Vishnu. The name is unusual and refers to the 'gigantic' stature which the boy Krishna assumed when he entered the arena to fight with Kansa's champions, Chánura and Mushtika. The Rájâ's dwelling-house is still standing, on the Nakárchi tíla, and was recently occupied for a time as a normal school for the training of female teachers. He is further commemorated by another small shrine near the Holi gate of the city, which he rebuilt in honour of Víra-bhadra, the terrible being created by Siva and Devi in their wrath, to disturb the sacrifice of Daksha, a ceremony to which they had not been invited. His great ambition was to rebuild the ancient temple of Kesava Deva, and with this view he had gradually acquired a considerable part of the site. But as some of the Muhammadans, who had occupied the ground for nearly two centuries, refused to be bought out and the law upheld them in their refusal, he was at last, and after great expense had been incurred, reluctantly obliged to abandon the idea. Should a stranger visit the tank early in the morning and enquire of any Hindu he meets there by whom it was constructed, he will find considerable difficulty in eliciting a straightforward answer. The Rájá, it is said, was a man of such delicate constitution that he never could take at one time more than a very few morsels even of the simplest food; hence arises a belief that any one, who mentions him by name the first thing in the morning, will, like him, have to pass the day fasting.

From the katra, the centre of all the localities which we have hitherto been describing, a fine broad road has been carried through the high ridge, which appears to have been at one time part of the mediæval city wall, down to the edge of the river. On the right-hand side is the stone-cutters' quarter with the small old temple of Bankhandi Mahádeva, near which is a high mound, lying back from the main streets between the dispensary and the kotwali, and now crowned by a ruinous little shrine dedicated to Bihári; from this I brought a Buddhist pillar, bearing the figure of a dancing-girl, with a leonine monster at her feet and over her head a group representing a teacher of the law seated under an umbrella addressing an audience of ten persons. To the left of the road is the suburb of Manoharpur, with a mosque which, as we learn from the following inscription over the centre arch, was erected in the year 1158 Hijri, *i. e.* 1745 A.D., during the reign of Muhammad Sháh :—

در زمان شه محمدشاه   مسجد عبدالرشید کرد بنا
سال تاریخ او خرد فرمود   داد ترتیب مسجدے زیبا

" In the reign of Sháh Muhammad Sháh, Abdurrashíd built this mosque: thought suggested the *tárikh*, ' He built a beautiful mosque.' " [A. H. 1158; or A.D. 1745].

From an adjoining street, where it had been built up into a mud wall, I removed to the museum a stone fragment of exceptional interest. It is only a small headless seated nude figure and, to judge from the style of the sculpture and the ill-formed letters in the Páli inscription at the base, is of no very great antiquity. Under it is a row of six standing figures, three on either side of a central *chakra*. The inscription records nothing whatever beyond the date, but this is given both in words and figures as follows : *Samvatsare sapta panyáse* 57 *hemanta tritiye divase trayadase asya purvayam*, that is to say ' in the year fifty-seven (57) on the thirteenth day of the third winter month.' It is curious in two ways : *first*, because it definitely fixes, beyond any possibility of doubt, the value of the symbol representing 50 ; and *secondly*, because if the date is really the year 57 of the same era as that employed in the inscriptions of Kanishka and Huvishka, it is the earliest unmistakeable Jaina figure yet found in the neighbourhood. The computation by seasons certainly favours the idea of antiquity and the argument for its modern date, derived from the character of the sculpture and of the lettering, may be deceptive ; for at any period different styles both of carving and writing may exist simultaneously ; yet probably the solution of the difficulty is to be found in Mr. Thomas's theory already mentioned, according to which the date is not given in full, but specifies only the year of the century, omitting the century itself, as being at the time well known.

In the streets are many broken Buddhist pillars and other sculptures. The road was constructed in the collectorate of Mr. Best, and in the progress of the work a column was found bearing an inscription in some ancient character; to reduce the size of the stone, the inscribed face was ruthlessly cut away, and it was then converted into a buttress for a bridge. As it approaches the river, the road opens out into a fine square, with graceful arcades of carved stone. These are the property of the Mahárája of Bharat-pur and Gosáin Purushottam Lál, and, though ordinarily they have rather a deserted appearance, on the ocasion of any great local festival they let for as much as Rs. 2 to 3 each a day. On the other side of the square opposite the road is a pontoon bridge, which was opened for traffic in 1870. The tolls were farmed for the large sum of Rs. 40,500 a year: whence it is obvious that any reasonable outlay incurred in its construction would soon have been repaid. But, unfortunately, everything was sacrificed to a false economy; it was made so narrow that it could not allow of two carts passing, and so weak that it could not bear even a single cart if heavily laden. Thus it was no sooner opened than it broke down; and repairs were in constant progress, till the night of the 13th of August, 1871, when it was completely swept away by a heavy flood. It was immediately reconstructed; but it is impossible that it should ever present a satisfactory appearance, while at the same time its cost has been excessive. It may be hoped that it will, before many years are over, be superseded by a masonry bridge in connection with the railway, which at present pays for its use a fixed annual sum of Rs. 4,044: its original value having been put at Rs. 1,15,566.

The city stretches for about a mile and-a-half along the right bank of the Jamuná, and from the opposite side has a very striking and picturesque appearance, which is owing not a little to the broken character of the ground on which it is built. Were it not for this peculiarity of site, the almost total absence of towers and spires would be felt as a great drawback; for all the large modern temples have no *sikharas*, as are usually seen in similar edifices, but are simple cloistered quadrangles of uniform height. The only exceptions are the lofty minarets of the Jama Masjid on the one side, and the campanile of the English Church seen through the trees in the distance below.

Looking up the stream, the most prominent object is the old Fort, or rather its massive sub-structure, for that is all that now remains, called by the people Kans-ká-kila. Whatever its legendary antiquity, it was rebuilt in historical times by Rájá Mán Sinh of Jaypur, the chief of the Hindu princes at Akbar's Court. At a later period it was the occasional residence of Mán Sinh's still more famous successor on the throne of Amber, the great astronomer Sawái Jay

Sinh, who commenced his long reign of 44 years in 1699 A.D. Till the day of his death he was engaged in almost constant warfare, but is less known to posterity by his military successes, brilliant though they were, than by his enlightened civil administration and still more exceptional literary achievements. At the outset he made a false move; for in the war of succession that ensued upon the death of Aurangzeb, he attached himself to prince Bedár Bakht and fought by his side in the fatal battle of Dhol-pur. One of the first acts of Sháh Alam, on his consequent elevation to the throne, was to sequester the principality of Amber. An Imperial Governor was sent to take possession, but Jay Sinh drove him out sword in hand, and then formed a league with Ajít Sinh of Márwár for mutual protection. From that day forward he was prominently concerned in all the troubles and warfare of that anarchic period, but never again on the losing side. In 1721, he was appointed Governor of the Province of Agra and later of Málwa; but he gradually loosened his connection with the Court of Delhi, from a conviction that the dissolution of the Muhammadan empire was inevitable, and concluded terms with the Mahrattas. At his accession, Amber consisted only of the three parganas of Amber, Deosa, and Barsao, as the Shaikháwats had made themselves independent and the western tracts had been attached to Ajmer. He not only recovered all that his ancestors had lost, but further extended his frontiers by the reduction of the Bargújars of Deoti and Rájáur and made his State worthy to be called the dominious of a Rájá—a title which he was the first of his line to assume. The new capital, which he founded, he called after his own name Jaypur, and it is still to the present day the only native city in India built upon a regular plan; the only one also, it must unfortunately be added, in which the street architecture is absolutely bad and systematically false and pretentious; though it is the fashion for Anglo-Indians to admire it. He is said to have been assisted in the execution of his design by an architect from Bengal.

In consequence of his profound knowledge of astronomy, he was entrusted by Muhammad Sháh with the reformation of the calendar. To ensure that amount of accuracy which he considered the small instruments in ordinary use must always fail to command, he constructed observatories with instruments of his own invention on a gigantic scale. One of these was on the top of the Mathurá Fort, the others at Delhi, Jaypur, Ujaiyin, and Banáras. His success was so signal that he was able to detect errors in the tables of De la Hire, which had been communicated to him by the King of Portugal. His own tables were completed in 1728 and are those still used by native astronomers. He died in 1743. His voluminous correspondence is said by Tod* still to exist and his acts to be recorded in a miscellaneous diary entitled Kalpadruma and a collection of anecdotes called the *Éksau nau gun Jay Sinh ká.*

The whole of the Mathurá observatory has now disappeared. A little before the mutiny the buildings were sold to the great Government contractor, Joti Prasád, who destroyed them for the sake of the materials. Certainly, they had ceased to be of any practical use ; but they were of interest, both in the history of science and as a memorial of one of the most remarkable men in the long line of Indian sovereigns and their inconsiderate demolition is a matter for regret. The old hall of audience, which is outside the actual Fort, is a handsome and substantial building divided into three aisles by ranges of red sand-stone pillars. Soon after the mutiny it was converted into a school and, in order to render it as unsightly as such Government buildings ordinarily are, the front arches were all blocked up with a mud wall which concealed every trace of them. Quite by an accident I discovered their existence and, after opening them out again, filled in their heads with iron bars set in a wooden frame and the lower part with a slight masonry wall, thus preserving all the architectural effect without any sacrifice of convenience.

About the centre of the river front is the most sacred of all the ghats, marking the spot where Krishna sat down to take 'rest' after he had slain the tyrant Kansa and hence called the 'Visránt' Ghát. The small open court has a series of marble arches facing the water, which distinguishes it from all the other landing-places ; and on the other three sides are various buildings erected at intervals during the last century and-a-half by several princely families ; but none of them possesses any architectural beauty. The river here swarms with turtles of an enormous size, which are considered in a way sacred, and generally receive a handful or two of grain from every visitor. Close by is a natural water-course, said to have been caused by the passage of Kansa's giant body, as it was dragged down to the river to be burnt, and hence called the 'Kans Khár.' The following lines in the Vishnu Purána are alleged in support of the tradition :—

गोरवेगातिमहता परिखा तेन कृष्यता ।
कृता कंसस्य देहेन वेगेनेव महाम्भसः ॥

" By the trailing body of Kansa, with its prodigious weight, a channel was made as by the rush of a mighty stream. "

* From whom all the facts in the above narrative of Jay Sinh's life are borrowed.

It is now arched over, like the Fleet river in London, and for many years formed one of the main sewers of the town ; a circumstance which possibly did not affect the sanctity, but certainly detracted somewhat from the material purity of this favourite bathing place. It is now being closed, as it was throught to have contributed not a little to the abnormal sickness which has lately prevailed in the city.

Wite reference to this spot a story is told in the Bhakt Mála, of Kesav Bhatt, one of the most celebrated of the Vaishnava teachers. After spreading his doctrines through all the chief cities of India and demolishing every argument that the most learned Pandits could bring against him, he was himself unable to reply to the questions put him by Chaitanya, though at the time a child only seven years of age. Thereupon he abandoned the career of a controversialist and retired to his native country Kashmír, where he remained in solitude, absorbed in humble and devout meditation, till roused to action by news of the tyranny that prevailed at Mathurá. For the Muhammadans had set up a diabolical engine at the Visránt Ghát, which perforce circumcised every Hindu who went there to bathe. Hearing this, he gathered together a thousand of his disciples and on arriving at Mathurá, went straight to the spot, where the Governor's myrmidons set upon him and thought to bring him too under the yoke of Islam. But he broke the engine in pieces and threw it into the river. An army was then sent against him, but not a man of it escaped ; for he slew the greater number with the sword and the rest were driven into the Jamuná and drowned.

For this legend it is possible there may be some slight historical foundation ; the next to be told can at the best be regarded as only a pious fiction. It is given in the Mathurá Mahátmya, or Religious Chronicle of Mathurá, which is an interpolation on the Váraha Purána, though of sufficient extent to be itself divided into 29 sections. After expatiating in the most extravagant terms on the learning, piety and other virtues of the Mathuriya Chaubes, and the incomparable sanctity of the city in which they dwell, it briefly enumerates the twelve Vanas, or woods, that are included in the perambulation of the land of Braj, and then at greater length describes the principal shrines which the pilgrim is bound to visit in the capital itself. As a rule, no attempt is made to explain either the names borne by the different holy places, or the origin of their reputed sanctity ; but their virtue is attested by the recital of some of the miracles, which have been worked through their supernatural influence, such as the following :—

THE VISRÁNT GHÁT, MATHURÁ

"Once upon a time there was a Bráhman living at Ujjaiyin, who neglected all his religious duties, never bathed, never said a prayer, never went near a temple. One night, when out with a gang of thieves, he was surprised by the city watchmen, and in running away from them fell down a dry well and broke his neck. His ghost was doomed to haunt the place, and was so fierce that it would tear to pieces and devour every one who came near it. This went on for many years, till at last one day a band of travellers happened to pitch their tents by the well, and among their number was a very holy and learned Bráhman. So soon as he knew how the neighbourhood was afflicted, he had recourse to his spells and compelled the evil spirit to appear before him. Discovering, in the course of his examination, that the wretched creature had in his lifetime been a Bráhman, he was moved with pity for him and promised to do all in his power to alleviate his sentence. Whereupon the ghost begged him to go straight to Mathurá, and bathe on his behalf at the Visránt Ghát, 'for,' said he, 'I once in my life went into a temple of Vishnu, and heard the priest repeat this holy name and tell its wondrous saving power.' The Bráhman had often bathed there and readily agreed to transfer the merit of one such ablution. The words of consent had no sooner passed his lips than the guilty soul was absolved from all further suffering."*

* To a devout Hindu, who believes that Krishna was an incarnation of the Deity, and that he hallowed with his presence the place now called the Visránt Ghát, there is no intrinsic absurdity in the legend as above quoted. It can be paralleled in all its particulars by many that have been recorded for the edification of the faithful by canonized saints of the Church. That the merit of good deeds can be transferred—the point upon which the story mainly turns is a cardinal Catholic doctrine; and as to the dying in sin and yet being saved through the efficacy of a formal act of devotion, take the following example from the pages of S. Alphonsus Liguori:—"A certain Canon was reciting some prayers in honour of the Divine Mother, and, whilst doing so, fell into the river Seine and was drowned. Being in mortal sin, the devils came to take him to hell. In the same moment Mary appeared and said, 'How do you dare to take possession of one who died in the act of praising me?' Then addressing herself to the sinner, she said, 'Now change thy life and nourish devotion to my Conception.' He returned to life and became a Religious." Here the concluding words correspond precisely with the finale of the story of the barber Tinduk, as told on the next page. In short, the Hindu in his ideas of divine worship, of the religious life, of the efficacy of faith and good works, of the earnest sympathy of the Divine Being with human distress, and His occasional miraculous intervention for its relief, falls little, if at all, short of Catholic truth. Unhappily he has no clear perception of the true God to whom the devotion, which he understands so well, should alone be paid: yet for all this drawback, Hinduism remains in one aspect divine, which is more than can be said either of Islam or of Protestantism. They are both essentially human inventions in direct antagonism to the truth, while Hinduism is a genuine natural religion, which only needs to be sustained and completed by Revelation. Thus S. Augustine says of the heathen of old: "Res ipsa quæ nunc

On the other side of this sacred spot, a number of minor gháts stretch up and down the river, those to the north being called the *uttar kot* and those to the south the *dakshin kot*. They are invariably represented as twenty-four in all, twelve in either set; but there is a considerable discrepancy as to the particular names. The following list was supplied by a Pandit of high local repute, Mákhan Misr, a Gaur Bráhman, from whose extensive library of manuscripts I was able to procure almost every Sanskrit work that I had occasion to consult.

To the north: Ganes Ghát; Mánasa Ghát; Dasasvamedha Ghát, under the hill of Ambarísha; Chakra-tirtha Ghát; Krishna-Gangá Ghát, with the shrine of Kálinjaresvar Mahádeva; Som-tirtha Ghát, more commonly called Vasudeva Ghát or Shaikh Ghát; Brahmalok Ghát; Ghantábharan Ghát: Dhárá-patan Ghát; Sangaman-tirtha Ghát, otherwise called Vaikunth Ghát; Nava-tirtha Ghát; and Asikunda Ghàt.

To the south: Avimukta Ghát; Visránti Ghát; Prág Ghát; Kankhal Ghát; Tinduk Ghát; Súrya Ghát; Chintá-mani Ghát; Dhruva Ghát; Rishi Ghát; Moksha Ghát; Koti Ghát; and Buddh Ghát.

The more common division is to include the Avimukta Ghát in the first set, from which the Mánasa is then omitted; to except the Visránt Ghát altogether from the number of the twenty-four; and to begin the second series with the Balabhadra and the Jog Ghát. By the former of these two are the Satghara or 'seven chapels,' commemorating Krishna's seven favourite titles, and the shrine of Gata Sram or 'ended toil.' The Jog Ghát is supposed to mark the spot where Joga-Nidra, the infant daughter of Nanda and Jasodá, whom Vasudeva had substituted for his own child Krishna, was dashed to the ground by Kansa and thence in new form ascended to heaven as the goddess Durgá. Between it and the Prág Ghát (where is the shrine of Beni Mádho) is one of more modern date called Sringár Ghát, with two temples dedicated respectively to Pipalesvar Mahádeva and Batuk-náth: by Prág Ghát is also the shrine of Rámesvar Mahádeva. Two other gháts occupy far more conspicuous sites than any of the above, but are included in no list, as being devoid of any legendary reputation. The first bears the name of Sámi Ghát,

christiana religio nuncupatur, erat apud antiquos, nec defuit ab initio generis humani quousque Christus veniret in carne, unde vera religio, quæ jam erat, cœpit appellari christiana." It is upon this principle that the Church has admitted into the calendar, among her canonized saints, certain worthies of the old dispensation, such as the Machabees, with reference to whom S. Gregory Nazianzen, in a sermon preached on their feast day, declares it to be a pious opinion "neminem eorum, qui ante christi adventum martyrio consummati sunt, id sine fide in Christum consequi potuisse."

not, as might be supposed, a corruption of *swámi*, but of *Sámhne*, 'opposite,' as it faces the main street of the city, where is a mansion of carved stone built by the famous Rúp Rám, Katára, of Barsána. The second is the Bengáli Ghát, at the foot of the pontoon bridge and close to a large house, the property of the Rája of Jhálra-pattan. It is so called from having been built by the Gosáin of the temple of Gobind Deva at Brindá-ban, the head of the Bengáli Vaishnavas, who has a residence on the opposite side of the street. The end of the ghát adjoining the Rája of Jhálra-pattan's house has been left unfinished, as the right to the ground forms the subject of a dispute between the Rája and the Gosáin.

Most of the gháts refer in their names to well-known legends and are of no special historical or architectural interest. The list is appropriately headed by one dedicated to Ganes, the god invoked at the commencement of every undertaking ; the second and third are both sacred to Siva—the one commemorating the Mánasa lake, a famous place of pilgrimage on mount Kailás in the Himalayas ; the other the Dasasvamedh Ghát, the holiest spot in Siva's city of Banáras. The fourth or Chakra-tirtha, with the hill of Ambarisha, refers to Vishnu's magic discus, *chakra*, with which he defended his votary Ambarisha against the assaults of the Sivite Durvásas. The hill is between 60 and 70 feet high, and according to popular rumour there is in the centre of it a cave containing an enormous treasure. I did not expect to discover this, but as General Cunningham had told me of a gold coin of Apollodotus that had been found there, I got some men to dig, thinking it not unlikely something might turn up. The only reward for my trouble was a small fragment of Buddhist sculpture representing a devotee under a niche with the rail pattern below and the capitals of the pillars of Indo-Ionic type. This however was sufficient proof of the great antiquity and also of the Buddhist occupation of the mound.

The temple of Mahádeva at the Ganga Krishan Ghát has some very rich and delicate reticulated stone tracery, and all the work about this ghát is exceptionally good, both in design and execution. It was done, a little before the mutiny, under the immediate superientendence of the Bráhman then in charge of the shrine, Baladeva Byás by name. The title Kalinjaresvar would seem to be a mistake for Kálindisvár : Kálindi being a name of the Jamuná, which takes its rise in the Kalinda range. A little above the ghát is an old red stone chhattri, which has a singularly graceful finial.

A little below the Sámi Ghát is a small mosque and group of tombs commemorating a Muhammadan saint, Makhdúm Sháh Wilayat, of Hirát. The tombs date apparently from the sixteenth century and the architecture is in all its details so essentially of Hindu design that, were it not for the word 'Allah' introduced here and there into the sculptured decorations, there would be nothing to distinguish them from Hindu chhattris. The Muhammadans call this the Shaikh Ghát, while the Hindus maintain that the word is not Shaikh, but Shesh, the name of the thousand-headed serpent that forms Vishnu's couch and canopy. This is probable enough, for the final cerebral sibilant is vulgarly pronounced and indeed often written as the guttural *kh*. After long dispute between the two parties as to who should have the privilege of rebuilding the ghát, the work was taken in hand in 1875 by Viláyat Husain, the Seth's house agent, who also added a mosque and gave no little offence thereby. He died in 1879, leaving one minaret of the mosque still unfinished.

The word Ghantábharan (which would be derived from *ghanta*, 'a bell,' and *bharan*, 'bearing,') is in the Vraj-bhakti-vilás perhaps more correctly written Ghantábhan, *bhan* meaning 'sound.' The allusion is to the bell, by the ringing of which Vishnu is roused from his four months' slumber on the 11th of the month Kártik.

The name Dhárápatan (from *dhárá*, 'a stream,' and *patan*, 'falling,') probably referred primarily to the position of the ghát, which is on a projecting point where it bears the full force of the 'fall of the stream.' But in the Máhátmya it is explained by the following legend :—" Once upon a time, a woman, whose home was on the bank of the Ganges, came on a pilgrimage to Mathurá and arrived there on the 12th of Kártik. As she was stepping into a boat near the place where now is the Dhárá-patan Ghát, she fell over and was drowned. By virtue of this immersion in the sacred flood, she was born again in an exalted position as the daughter of the king of Banáras, and, under the name of the Ráni Pivari, was married to Kshatra-dhanu, the king of Suráshtra, by whom she had seven sons and five daughters. Upon one occasion when the royal pair were comparing notes, it came to light that he too had undergone a very similar experience : for, originally he had been a wild savage who had come over to Mathurá from the Naimisha forest and was crossing the Jamuná with his shoes balanced on the top of his head, when they fell off into the water. He dipped down to recover them and was swept away by the torrent and drowned. Every stain of sin being thus washed out of his body, when he again took birth it was no longer as a barbarous Nishádha, or wild man of the woods, but as a noble Kshatriya king."

Dhruva who gives a name to one of the most southern of the ghâts was, according to the legend, the son of a king by name Uttána-páda. Indignant at the slights put upon him by his stepmother, he left his father's palace to make a name for himself in the world. By the advice of the seven great Rishis, Maríchi, Atri, Angiras, Pulastya, Kratu, Pulaha, and Vasishta, he repaired to Madhu-ban near Mathurá, and there, absorbed in the contemplation of Vishnu, continued for seven years a course of the severest penance. At last the god appeared to him in person and promised to grant him any boon he might desire. His request was for a station exalted above every station and which should endure for ever; whereupon he was translated to heaven as the polar star together with his mother Suníti.

On the Dhruva *tila*, or hill at the back of the ghát, is a small temple, built *Sambat* 1894, in place of an older shrine, of which the ruins remain close by, dedicated to Dhruva Jí. Here I found a set of Buddhist posts, with the cross rails and top bar all complete, cut out of a single slab of stone, measuring two feet two inches square. The *Pujáris*, or priests in charge, by name Dámodar Dás and Chhote Lál, belong to the Sanákadi or Nimbárak Sampradáya of Vaishnavas, and produce a manuscript pedigree in Sanskrit in proof of their direct spiritual descent from Kesava Bhatt, one of Nimbárak's successors, who is regarded as the head of the secular, or *Grihastha*, sub-division of the sect, as his brother-in-law, Hari Vyása, was of the celibate, or *Virakta*, order. In the temple are figures of Rádhá Krishan, whom the Nimbáraks have adopted as their special patrons. The list of superiors, or Guru-parampará, as it is called, runs as follows :—

I.—1 Hansávatár ; 2 Sanakádi ; 3 Nárada; 4 Nimbárak Swámi: all deified characters.

II.—1 Sríniváságchárya ; 2 Biswáchárya ; 3 Purushottam ; 4 Bilása ; 5 Sarúpa ; 6 Madhava ; 7 Balbhadra ; 8 Padma ; 9 Syáma ; 10 Gopála ; 11 Kripála ; 12 Deva : all distingushed by the title of Achárya.

III.—1 Sundar Bhatt ; 2 Padma-nábha ; 3 Srí Ráma-chandra ; 4 Baman ; 5 Srí Krishna ; 6 Padmákara ; 7 Sravan ; 8 Bhúri ; 9 Mádhava ; 10 Syáma ; 11 Gopála ; 12 Sri-bal, or Balbhadra ; 13 Gopináth ; 14 Kesava ; 15 Gangal ; 16 Kesava Kashmíri ; 17 Srí Bhatt ; 18 Kesava Bimáni : all bearing the title of Bhatt.

IV.—1 Giridhar Gosáin ; 2 Ballabh Lál ; 3 Mukund Lál ; 4 Nand Lál ; 5 Mohan Lál ; 6 Rám Jí Lál ; 7 Manu Lál ; 8 Rádhá Lál ; 9 Kanhaiya Lál ; and 10 Dámodar Dás : all bearing the title of Gosáin.

The Nimbáraks have also a temple at Brindában, dedicated to Rasak Bihári, and some account of their tenets will be given in connection with that town. Their distinguishing sectarial mark consists of two white perpendicular streaks on the forehead with a black spot in the centre. The natural parents of their founder are said to have been named Aruna Rishi and Jayanti.

The Tinduk Ghát, according to the Máhátmya, is so called after a barber who lived at Kámpilya, the capital of Pánchála, in the reign of King Devadatta. After losing all his family, he came to live at Mathurá and there practised such rigorous austerities and bathed so constantly in the sanctifying stream of the Jamuná, that after death he took birth once more as a high-caste Brahman.

The legend of the Asikunda Ghát is told on this wise:—A pious king, by name Sumati, had started on a pilgrimage, but died before he was able to complete it. His son, Vimati, on succeeding to the throne, was visited by the sage Nárad, who, at the time of taking his departure, uttered this oracular sentence : 'A pious son settles his father's debts.' After consulting with his ministers, the prince concluded that the debt was a debt of vengeance, which he was bound to exact from the places of pilgrimages, which had tempted his father to undertake the fatal journey. Accordingly, having ascertained that every holy place paid an annual visit in the season of the rains to the city of Mathurá, he assembled an army and marched thither with full intent to destroy them all. They fled in terror to Kalpa-gráma to implore the aid of Vishnu, who at last yielded to their entreaties, and assuming the form of a boar joined in combat with King Vimati on the bank of the Jamuna and slew him. In the fray, the point of the divine sword, '*asi*,' snapped off and fell to the ground ; whence the ghát to this day is called Asi-kunda Ghát, and the plain adjoining it Váráha Kshetra, or 'the field of the boar.'

Before finally leaving the river-side, one other building claims a few words *viz.*, 'the Sati Burj.' This is a slender quadrangular tower of red sand-stone commemorating the self-sacrifice of some faithful wife. According to the best authenticated tradition, she is said to have been the queen of Raja Bihár Mal of Jaypur and the mother of the famous Raja Bhagaván Dás, by whom the monument was erected in the year 1570 A.D. It has, as it now stands, a total height of 55 feet and is in four stories: the lowest forms a solid basement ; the second and third are lighted by square windows and are supplied with an internal staircase. The exterior is ornamented with rude bas-reliefs of elephants and other devices, but is in a very ruinous condition. The tower was originally

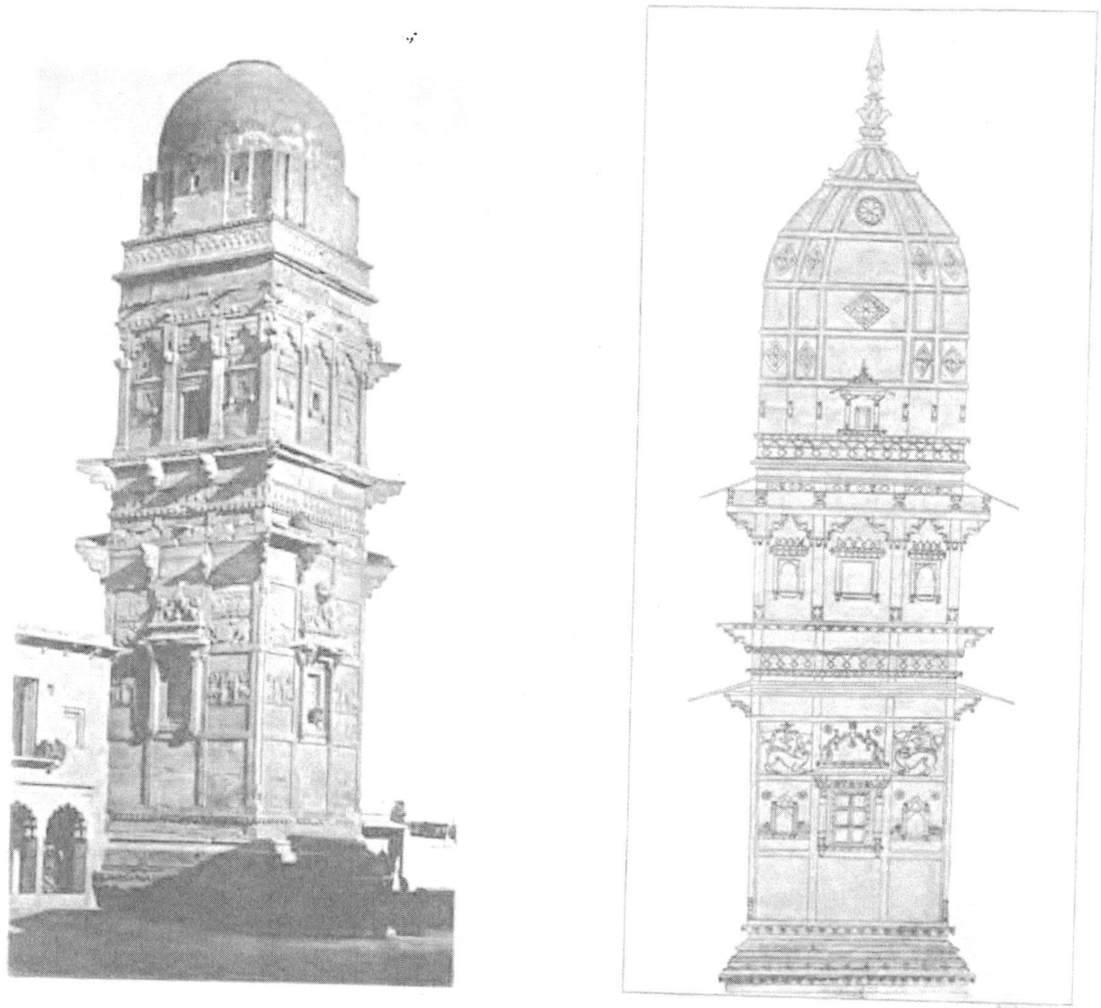

THE SATÍ BURJ, MATHURÁ.

of much greater height; but all the upper part was destroyed, it is said, by Aurangzeb. The exceedingly ugly and incongruous plaster dome, which now surmounts the building, was apparently added about the beginning of the present century. It no doubt helps to preserve what yet remains of the original work, but it sadly detracts from its architectural effect. I had hoped that the reigning Maharaja might be induced to undertake the complete restoration of this interesting family monument, and if the matter had been properly represented to him, he would in all probability have consented to do so. It is not at all likely that anything will be done now; but the design that I had prepared may be thought worthy of preservation. No small amount of time and thought was bestowed upon it; and I hope that architects will consider it both a pleasing object in itself and also a faithful reproduction of the destroyed original.

At the time when it was built, that is, at the end of the 16th century, it may be presumed that the city of Mathurá occupied its old position in the neighbourhood of the katra, and that the river-bank was used as the ordinary place for the cremation of the dead. Several cenotaphs of about the same period still remain, being mostly in old Hindu style, with brackets of good and varied design. The two largest bear the dates 1638 and 1715 *Sambat*, coresponding to 1581 and 1638 A.D. They had all been taken possession of by the Chaubes, who blocked up the arches with mud or rough brick-work and converted them into lodging-houses, which they rented to pilgrims. In 1875 I had them all opened out when widening and paving the street along the river-bank. This work was left unfinished, but enough had been done to render the street, though still narrow, the most picturesque in the city. Many of the ghâts had been repaired, while the removal of a number of obstructions had opened out a view not only of the river but also of the houses and temples on the land site. Some of these are very graceful specimens of architecture, in particular the house of Purushottam Lál, the Gokul Gosáin, close to the Bengali ghát, which has a most elaborate façade and a balcony displaying a great variety of patterns of reticulated tracery.

Immediately below the last of the gháts and opposite the Sadr Bazar, which has a population of some 6,000 souls and forms a small town by itself, entirely distinct both from the city and the European quarter, are two large walled gardens on the river-bank. One of these, called the Jamuná bágh, is the property of the Seth. It is well kept up and contains two very handsome chhattris, or cenotaphs, in memory of Párikh Jí, the founder of the family, and

Mani Rám, his successor. The latter, built in the year of the chaurásnawe famine, 1837 A.D., is of exceedingly beautiful and elaborate design : perhaps the most perfect specimen ever executed of the reticulated stone tracery, for which Mathurá is famous. It has been purposely made a little lower and smaller then the earlier monument, the eaves of which at one corner completely overhang it. The adjoining garden, which may be of even greater extent, has a small house and enclosed court-yard, in the native style, on the bank of the river, and, in the centre, an obelisk of white stone raised on a very high and substantial plinth of the same material with the following inscription : " Erected to the memory of Robert Sutherland, Colonel in Maháráj Daulat Rao Scindia's service, who departed this life on the 20th July, 1804, aged 36 years. Also in rememberance of his son, C. P. Sutherland (a very promising youth), who died at Hindia on the 14th October, 1801, aged 3 years. " The monument is kept in repair by the grandson, Captain S. S. Sutherland, of the Police Department. Colonel Sutherland was the officer whom De Boigne, on his retirement in 1795, left in command of the brigade stationed at Mathurá, one of three that he had raised in the service of Mádho Jí Sindhia. The Mahratta Commander-in-Chief, who also had his head-quarters at Mathurá, was at that time one Jagu Bapu, who was probably the Senapat of whom local tradition still speaks. In 1797 he was superseded by Perron, to whom Daulat Rao had given the supreme command of all his forces and who thereupon established himself at Kol, as virtual sovereign of the country. In the following year he discharged Sutherland for intriguing with the other Mahratta chiefs, but not long after he recovered his post through the interest of his father-in-law, Colonel John Hessing, to whose memory is erected the very fine monnument in the Catholic cemetry at Agra, which Jacquemont considered superior to the Taj. In 1813 Sutherland, like the other British officers in Sindhia's service, received a pension from the Government, but he lived only one year to enjoy it.

On a rising ground in the very heart of the city stands the Jáma Masjid, erected in the year 1661 A.D., by Abd-un-Nabi Khán, the local Governor. The following inscription seems very clearly to indicate that it was erected on the ruins of a Hindu temple :—

بعهد شاه عالمگیر محی الدین والمله * شهنشاه جهان اورنگ زیب معدلت پیرا
بحمدالله تابان است انوار مسلمانی * که از عبدالنبی خان شد بنا این مسجد زیبا
بتان را درسجود آورد این بیت الله ثانی * بهاین معنی جاءالحق که باطل گشت ناپیدا
چو جستم سال تاریخش زفیض حق ندا آمد * بگو عبدالنبی خان بانی این مسجد زیبا

AUTOTYPE.

CENOTAPH IN THE SETH'S GARDEN

1. In the reign of Sháh Alamgír Muhíuddin Walmillah, the king of the world, Aurangzeb, who is adorned with justice,

2. The lustre of Islám shone forth to the glory of God; for Abd-un-Nabi Khán built this beautiful mosque.

3. This second 'Holy Temple' caused the idols to bow down in worship. You will now see the true meaning of the text; 'Truth came and error vanished. ['Korán, XVII. 83'.]

4. Whilst I searched for a *tárikh*, a voice came from blissful Truth, ordering me to say 'Abd-un-Nàbi Khán is the builder of this beautiful mosque.' A.H. 1071, or 1660-61.

این مسجد جامع همایون بنیاد * بادا چو دل خدا پرستان آباد

بامے دارد چو همت عشق بلند * صحنے دارد چو عرصهٔ فکر کشاد

1. May this Jáma Masjid of majestic structure shine forth for ever like the hearts of the pious!

2. Its roof is high like aspirations of love; its court-yard is wide like the arena of thought.*

The founder is first mentioned by the Muhammadan historians as fighting on the side of Dárá Shikoh at the battle of Samogarh in 1658. About a week after the defeat, he joined Aurangzeb and was immediately appointed faujdár of Itáwa. This office he retained only till the following year, when he was transfered to Sirhind and thence, after a few months, to Mathurá. Here he remained from August, 1660, to May, 1668, when, as we have already mentioned, he met his death at Sahora, a village in the Mahá-ban pargana on the opposite side of the Jamuná, while engaged in quelling a popular *émeute*. The author of the Maasir-i-Alamgíri says of him:—"He was an excellent and pious man, and as courageous in war as successful in his administration. He has left a mosque in Mathurá as a monument, which, for a long time to come, will remind people of him. Muhammad Anwar, his nephew, received from His Majesty a mourning dress of honour; but the property of the deceased lapsed (according to custom) to the State, and the Imperial Mutasaddis reported it to be 93,000 gold muhrs, 13,00,000 rupees, and

* For this and other translations from the Persian I am indebted to the kindness of the late Mr. Blochmann, whose immense fund of information was always at the service of all enquirers, and whose untimely death is an irreparable loss to the Calcutta Branch of the Asiatic Society, of which he was for many years the Secretary.

14,50,000 rupees' worth of property." The architecture of his mosque is not of particularly graceful character, but there are four lofty minarets, and as these and other parts of the building were originally veneered with bright-coloured plaster mosaics, of which a few panels still remain, it must at one time have presented a brilliant appearance.*

It was greatly injured by an earthquake which took place, strange to say, in 1803, the very year in which the country was first brought under British rule. The following account of this most exceptional event is copied from pages 57 and 58 of 'The Asiatic Annual Register' for 1804:—

DREADFUL EARTHQUAKE.

Mathurá, September 24, 1803.

"On the night between the 31st August and the 1st of September, at half-an-hour after midnight, a severe shock of an earthquake was felt at this place, which lasted for many minutes and was violent beyond the memory of man. Probably not a living creature in the place but was roused from his slumbers by the alarm and felt its effects. Many of the pucka buildings were cast down and zanánas, hitherto unassailed by violence, were deserted, and their fair inhabitants took refuge in the streets and in the fields, seeking protection with men, whose visages it would otherwise have disgraced them to behold. The night was calm and enjoyed the full influence of a bright moon.

"In the morning very extensive fissures were observed in the fields, which had been caused by the percussion of the night before, through which water rose with great violence and continues to run to the present date, though its violence has gradually abated. This has been a great benefit to the neighbouring ryots, as they were thence enabled to draw the water over their parched fields.

* Father Tieffenthaller, who visited Mathurá in 1745, after mentioning the two mosques, says that Abd-un-Nabi was a convert from Hinduism, a statement for which there seems to be no authority. He describes the mosaics as "un ouvrage plombé en diverses couleurs et incrusté á la maniére dont sont vernis les poeles in Allemagne." "La ville," he says, "est entouré d'une levée de terre, et obeit aujourdhui au Dját. Auparavant elle etait sous les ordres du Raja de Djepour á qui l'empereur Mogol en avait confié le gouvernement:" *i. e.*, Raja Jay Sinh, who died 1743. He goes on to describe the streets as narrow and dirty and most of the buildings as in ruins; the fort very large and massive, like a mountain of hewn stone, with an observatory, which was only a feeble imitation of the one at Jaypur, but with the advantage of being much better raised. The only other spot that he particularises is the Visránt ghát. Jacquemont's description is in very similar terms: he says: "The streets are the narrowest, the crookedest, the steepest and dirtiest that I have ever seen."

"The principal mosque of the place, erected on an eminence by the famous Ghází Khan, as a token of his triumph over the infidelity of the Hindus, has been shattered to pieces, and a considerable part of the dome was swallowed up during the opening of the earth.

"Several slighter shocks have since occurred, but I do not hear they have occasioned any further damage."*

The above description certainly exaggerates and also to some extent misrepresents the effects of the shock upon the mosque. The gateway was cracked from top to bottom, the upper part of one of the great minarets was thrown down and one of the little corner kiosques of the mosque itself was also destroyed, but the dome was uninjured. In 1875 the Sa'dábad family started a subscription for the repairs of the building and over Rs. 5,000 were collected. This sum I expended on the restoration of the fallen minaret and kiosque and of the two *hujras* or alcoves at the sides of the court-yard. Several of the shops that disfigured the approaches were also bought up and demolished. As soon as I left, the work came to a standstill.

The mosque now appears out of place as the largest and most conspicuous edifice in what is otherwise a purely Hindu city, and there is also every reason to suppose that it was founded on the ruins of a pagan temple. But at the same time it should be observed that all the buildings by which it is now surrounded are of more modern date than itself. It was not planted in the midst of a Hindu population; but the city, as we now see it, has grown up under its shadow. Old Mathurá had been so often looted and harried by the Muhammadans that, as has been noted in other parts of this work, it had actually ceased to exist as a city at all. It was a place of pilgrimage, as it had ever been; there were saráes for the accommodation of travellers and ruins of temples and a few resident families of Bráhmans to act as cicerones, living for the most part in the precincts of the great temple of Kesava Deva, or still further away towards Madhuban; but it was as much a scene of desolation as Goa with its churches and convents now is, and on the spot where the present Mathurá stands there was no town till Abd-un-Nabi founded it. The whole of the land was in the possession of Muhammadans. The ground, which he selected as the site of his mosque, he purchased from some butchers, and the remainder he obtained from a family of Kázis, whose descendants still occupy what is called the Kushk Mahalla, one of the very few quarters

* For the knowledge of this curious letter I am indebted to the courtesy of Mr. A. Constable, of the Oudh and Rohilkhand Railway, who sent me a copy of it.

of the city that are known by a Persian name. They continued to be regarded as the zamindars of the township till the time of the Játs, when Saiyid Bákir, their then head, quarrelled with the local governor, and being afraid of the consequences made over all his rights to some Chaubes and others. When the English Government took possession, the Chaubes' title was alone recognized and the first settlement was made with one of their number, Shio Lál, as mukaddam. A claim was brought forward by Imám Bakhsh, a son of the Sáiyid abovenamed, but he died before it could be heard, and the suit thus falling through has never since been revived. In 1812, the then Chaube landholders, Bishna, Ajita, Shio Lál, Ghisa and Jwála, styling themselves mukaddams, made over their rights to the Lála Bábu, who engaged to pay them Rs. 150 a year and 5 per cent. on his collections. The area so transferred, according to the settlement of 1841, was only 568 bíghas 11 biswas ; but in the revision of records the Lála Bábu's widow had herself entered as owner of every rood of land, excepting only such as was or had been rent-free, and the agreement was with her as sole zamindar of the township of Mathurá. On the strength of this she claimed to exercise over the whole city the same rights that a zamindar can claim in any petty village ; but, after oft-renewed litigation, these extravagant claims have been set aside, and by the new settlement the property of her heirs is shown as a separate thok, the muáfi and resumed muáfi grants forming another, while the Jamuná sands, used for melon cultivation, all nazúl lands and the streets and city generally are shown as Government property.*

From the mosque as a central point diverge the main thoroughfares, leading respectively towards Brindá-ban, Díg, Bharat-pur,† and the civil station. They are somewhat broader than is usual in Indian cities, having an average breadth of 24 feet, and were first opened out at the instance of Mr. E. F. Taylor in 1843. A number of houses were demolished for the purpose, but, in every instance, all claim to compensation was waived. Seth Lakhmi Chand's loss, thus voluntarily sustained for the public good, was estimated at a lakh of rupees, as he had recently completed some handsome premises, which had to be taken down and rebuilt.

---

* *Vide* a report on the Proprietory Rights claimed by the heirs of the Lala Bábu, drawn up by Mr. Whiteway, Settlement Officer, in 1875.

† Close to the mosque on the left-hand side of the Bharat-pur gate bazár is a high hill with very steep ascent, all built over. On the summit, which is called Sítalá ghát, may be seen many fragments of Buddhist pillars and bas-reliefs, and an armless seated figure, the size of life.

These streets have now, throughout their entire length and breadth, been paved by the municipality with substantial stone flags brought from the Bharatpúr quaries.* The total cost has been Rs. 1,38,663. Many of the towns-people and more particularly the pilgrims, who go about barefooted, are by no means pleased with the result ; for in the winter the stone is too cold to be pleasant to tread upon, while in the summer again, even at sunset, the streets do not cool down as they used to do aforetime, but retain their heat through the greater part of the night. As is the custom in the East, many mean tumble down hovels† are allowed here and there to obtrude themselves upon the view ; but the majority of the buildings that face the principal thoroughfares are of handsome and imposing character. With only two exceptions all have been erected during the seventy years of British rule. The first of the two exceptional buildings is a large red sandstone house, called Chaube Jí ká Burj, which may be as old as the time of Akbar. The walls are divided into square panels, in each of which, boldly carved in low relief, is a vase filled with flowers, executed in a manner which is highly effective, but which has quite gone out of fashion at the present day, when pierced tracery is more appreciated. The second is a temple near the turn to the Sati Burj. This is remarkable for a long balcony supported on brackets quaintly carved to represent elephants. Many of these had been built up with masonry, either by the Hindus to protect the animal form from iconoclastic bigotry, or else by the Muhammadans themselves to conceal it from view. This unsightly casing was at last removed in 1875.

In all the modern buildings, whether secular or religious, the design is of very similar character. The front is of carved stone with a grand central archway and arcades on both sides let out as shops on the ground floor. Storey upon storey above are projecting balconies supported on quaint corbels, the arches being filled in with the most minute reticulated tracery of an infinite variety of pattern, and protected from the weather by broad eaves, the under-surface of which is brightly painted. One of the most noticeable buildings in point of size, though the decorations perhaps are scarcely so elegant as in some of the latter examples, is the temple of Dwárakadhis, founded by the Gwaliar treasurer, Parikh Jí, and visited in 1825 by Bishop Heber, who in his journal describes it as follows :—" In the centre, or nearly so, of the town, Colonel

* This important work was commenced in November, 1857.

† As an indication that many of the houses are not of the most substantial construction, it may be observed that, after three days of exceptionally heavy rain in the month of August, 1873, as many as 6000 were officially reported to have come down ; 14 persons, chiefly children, having been crushed to death under the ruins.

Penny took us into the court of a beautiful temple or dwelling-house, for it seemed to be designed for both in one, lately built and not yet quite finished, by Gokul Pati Sinh, Sindhia's treasurer, and who has also a principal share in a great native banking-house, one branch of which is fixed at Mathurá. The building is enclosed by a small but richly carved gateway with a flight of steps which leads from the street to a square court, cloistered round, and containing in the centre a building, also square, supported by a triple row of pillars, all which, as well as the ceiling, are richly carved, painted, and gilt. The effect internally is much like that of the Egyptian tomb, of which the model was exhibited in London by Belzoni; externally, the carving is very beautiful. The cloisters round were represented to me as the intended habitations of the Brahmans attached to the fane; and in front, towards the street, were to be apartments for the founder on his occasional visits to Mathurá." To show how differently the same building sometimes impresses different people, it may be mentioned that Jacquemont, only four years later, describes the temple as like nothing but a barrack or cotton factory: but possibly he may have seen it soon after the festival of the Diwáli, when, according to barbarous Hindu custom, the whole of the stone front is beautified with a thick coat of whitewash. This gentleman's architectural ideas were, however, a little peculiar. Thus he says, of the Jáma Masjid at Agra, that the bad taste of the design and the coarseness of the materials are good reason for leaving it to the ravages of time; that the tomb of Itimád-ud-daula is in the most execrable taste; that the Taj, though pretty, cannot be called elegant; and that the only building in Agra which is really a pure specimen of oriental architecture is the tomb of Colonel Hessing in the Catholic cemetery, the work of 'a poor devil' called Latif. His theological views would seem to have been equally warped, for in another place he thus expresses himself:—"Of all the follies and misfortunes of humanity, religion is the one which is the most wearisome and the least profitable to study."

The Dwárakádhis temple has always been in the hands of the Vallabhácháryas, the sect to which the founder belonged. It is now administered by the Gosáin who is the hereditary lord of the much older and yet wealthier shrine with the same name at Kankarauli in Udaypur (see page 130). Hitherto the expenses of the Mathurá establishments have been defrayed by annual grants from the Seth's estate; but the firm has lately made an absolute transfer to the Gosáin of landed property yielding an income of Rs. 25,000; thus religiously carrying out the intention of their ancestor, though in so doing they further the interests of a sect not a little antagonistic to the one of which they themselves are members.

AUTOTYPE.

THE CITY GATE, MATHURA.

On the opposite side of the street is the palace of the princes of Bharat-pur. The lofty and highly enriched entrance gateway was added by Rájá Balavant Sinh, and the magnificent brass doors by the present Rájá. Close by is the mansion of Seth Lakhmi Chand, built at a cost of Rs. 1,00,000. The latest of the architectural works with which the city is decorated, and one of the most admirable for elegance and elaboration, is a temple near the Chhata Bazar built by Deva Chand Bohra, and completed only at the end of the year 1871. Whatever other buildings there are of any note will be found enumerated in the list at the end of the next chapter. In most cases the greatest amount of finish has been bestowed upon the street front, while the interior court is small and confined; and the practice of having only a single gate both for entrance and exit occasions great, and sometimes dangerous, crowding on high feast days. It is, as before remarked, a peculiarity of the Mathurá temple architecture to have no tower over the seat of the god.

If the new city was ever surrounded by walls, not a vestige of them now remains, though the four principal entrances are still called the Brinda-ban, Díg, Bharat-pur, and Holi gates. The last-named is the approach from the Civil Station, and here a lofty and elaborately sculptured stone arch has been erected over the roadway, in accordance with an elegant design in the local style, supplied by Yúsuf, the municipal architect, a man of very exceptional taste and ability. As the work was commenced at the instance of the late Mr. Bradford Hardinge, who was for several years Collector of the district, and took a most lively interest in all the city improvements, it is named in his honour* 'the Hardinge arch,' though it is not very often so called. Since his death, it has been surmounted by a cupola, which was intended at some future time to receive a clock, with four corner kiosques, the cost of these additions being Rs. 3,493. Two shops in uniform style were also built in 1875, one on either side, at a farther cost of Rs. 1,621, in order to receive and conceal the ponderous staged buttresses, which the engineers in the Public Works Department had thought it necessary to add. The expenditure on the gate itself was Rs. 8,617, making a total of Rs. 13,731.

As may be inferred from the above remarks stone-carving, the only indigenous art of which Mathurá can boast, is carried to great perfection. All the temples afford specimens of elegant design in panels of reticulated tracery (*jáli*), as also do the *chhatris* of the Seth's family in the Jamuná bágh. The

* The little marble tablet, on which the name has been inscribed in the straightest and most uncompromising Roman capitals, is a conspicuous disfigurement and looks exactly like an auction ticket. The Engineer who inserted it cannot have had much of an eye for harmony of effect.

only other specialities are of very minor importance. One is the manufacture of little brass images, which, though of exceedingly coarse execution, command a large sale among pilgrims and visitors, especially the religious toy called Vásudeva Katorá (described at page 54); the other the manufacture of paper. This is made in three sizes. The smallest, which is chiefly in demand, is called Mán-Sinhi and varies in price, according to quality, from Rs. 1-8 to Rs. 2-6 a *gaddi* or bundle; the medium size, called Bichanda, sells for Rs. 4 a *gaddi;* and the larger size, called Syálkoti, for Rs. 10. The factories are some 100 in number and can turn out in the course of the day 150 *gaddis,* every *gaddi* containing 10 *dastas* of 24 *takhtas,* or sheets, each. There is also a kind of string made which is much appreciated by natives. It is chiefly used for lowering *lotas,* the ordinary brass drinking cups of the country, into wells to draw water with. The price is about three or four anas for 40 yards. A coloured variety is made for temple use.

CHAPTER VII.

The City of Mathurá (*concluded*): its European Institutions and Museum.

A light railway, on the metre gauge, 29½ miles in length, which was opened for traffic on the 19th of October, 1875, now connects the city with the East India Line, which it joins at the Háthras Road station. The cost was Rs. 9,55,868, being about Rs. 30,000 a mile, including rolling stock and everything else. Of this amount Rs. 3,24,100 were contributed by local shareholders, and the balance, Rs. 6,31,763, came from Provincial Funds. Interest is guaranteed at the rate of 4 per cent. per annum, with a moiety of the surplus earnings that may at any time be realized. The line has proved an unquestionable success and its yearly earnings continue to show a steady increase. But the principal shareholders—including the Seth, who invested as much as a lakh and-a-half in it—were certainly not attracted by the largeness of the pecuniary profit; for 12 per cent. is the lowest return which Indian capitalists ordinarily receive for their money. They were entirely influenced by a highly commendable public spirit and a desire to support the local European authorities, who had shown themselves personally interested in the matter.* The ultimate success of the line has now been secured by its junction with the Rajputana State Railway. The distance being only some 25 miles, the earthwork was carried out during the late famine, and the scheme is now completed but for the bridge over the Jamuná. In the design that has been supplied there are 12 spans of 98 feet each, with passage both for road and railway traffic and two foot-paths, at an estimated cost of Rs. 3,00,000. As the receipts from tolls on the existing pontoon bridge are about Rs. 45,000 per annum, even a larger expenditure might safely be incurred. Cross sections of the river have been obtained, and a series of borings taken, which show a flood channel of 1,000 feet and clay foundations underlying the sand at 33 feet. The site is in every way well suited for the purpose and presents no special engineering difficulties; but the construction of so large a bridge must necessarily be a work of time, and before it is completed it is probable that the line will have been extended from its other end, the Háthras terminus, to Farukhabad and so on to Cawnpur, the

* Next to the Seth—*longo intervallo*—the largest number of shares were taken up by myself; for at that time I never expected to be moved from the district.

great centre of the commerce of Upper India. As yet, the line labours under very serious disadvantages from being so very short and from the necessity of breaking bulk at the little wayside station of Mendu, the Háthras Road junction. Consequently, traders who have goods to despatch to Háthras find it cheaper and more expeditious to send them all the way by road, rather than to hire carts to take them over the pontoon bridge and then unlade them at the station and wait hours, or it may be days, before a truck is available to carry them on. Thus the goods traffic is very small, and it is only the passengers who make the line pay. These are mostly pilgrims, who rather prefer to loiter on the way and do not object to spending two hours and fifty minutes in travelling a distance of 29½ miles. As the train runs along the side of the road, there are daily opportunities for challenging it to a race, and it must be a very indifferent country pony which does not succeed in beating it.

The Municipality has a population of 55,763, of whom 10,006 are Muhammadans. The annual income is a little under Rs. 50,000; derived, in the absence of any special trade, almost exclusively from an octroi tax on articles of food, the consumption of which is naturally very large and out of all proportion to the resident population, in consequence of the frequent influx of huge troops of pilgrims. The celebrity among natives of the Mathurá *perá*, a particular kind of sweetment, also contributes to the same result. Besides the permanent maintenance of a large police and conservancy establishment, the entire cost of paving the city streets has been defrayed out of municipal funds, and a fixed proportion is anually allotted for the support of different educational establishments.

The High School, a large hall in a very un-Oriental style of architecture, was opened by Sir William Muir on the 21st January, 1870. It was erected at a cost of Rs. 13,000, of which sum Rs. 2,000 were collected by voluntary subscription, Rs. 3,000 were voted by the municipality, and the balence of Rs. 8,000 granted by Government.* The City Dispensary, immediately opposite the Kans-ká-tílá and adjoining the Munsif's Court, has accommodation for 20 in-door patients; there is an ordinary attendance *per*

* The School, Court-house, and Protestant Church are—fortunately, as I think—the only local buildings of any importance, in the construction of which the Public Works Department has had any hand. I have never been able to understand why a large and costly staff of European engineers should be kept up at all, except for such Imperial undertakings as Railways, Military Roads and Canals. The finest buildings in the country date from before our arrival in it, and the descendants of the men who designed and executed them are still employed by the natives themselves for their temples. tanks, palaces, and mosques. If the Government utilized the same agency, there would be a great saving in cost and an equal gain in artistic result.

AUTOTYPE

CATHOLIC CHURCH OF THE SACRED HEART, MATHURÁ

diem of 50 applicants for out-door relief, and it is in every respect a well-managed and useful institution.

The Cantonments, which are of considerable extent, occupy some broken and undulating ground along the river-side between the city and the civil lines. In consequence of the facilities for obtaining an abundant supply of grass in the neighbourhood, they are always occupied by an English cavalry regiment. The barracks are very widely scattered, an arrangement which doubtless is attended with some inconveniences, but is apparently conducive to the health of the troops, for there is no station in India where there is less sickness*—a happy result, which is also due in part to the dryness of the climate during the greater part of the year and the excellence of the natural drainage in the rains.

The English Church, consecrated by Bishop Dealtry in December, 1856, is in a nondescript style of architecture, but has a not inelegant Italian campanile, which is visible from a long distance. The interior has been lately enriched by a stained-glass window in memory of a young officer of the 10th Hussars, who met his death by an accident while out pig-sticking near Shergarh.

The adjoining compound was for many years occupied by a miserably mean and dilapidated shed, which was most appropriately dedicated to St. Francis, the Apostle of Poverty, and served as a Catholic Chapel. This was taken down in January, 1874, and on the 18th of the same month, being the feast of the Holy Name, the first stone was laid of the new building, which bears the title of the Sacred Heart. The ground-plan and general proportions are in accordance with ordinary Gothic precedent, but all the sculptured details, whether in wood or stone, are purely Oriental in design. The carving in the tympanum of the three doorways, the tracery in the windows, both of the aisles and the clerestory, and the highly decorated altar in the Lady Chapel, may all be noted as favourable specimens of native art. The dome which surmounts the choir is the only feature which I hesitate to pronounce a success, as seen from the outside; its interior effect is very good. I originally intended it to be a copy of a Hindu *sikhara*, such as that of the temple of Madan Mohan at Brindában; but fearing that this might prove an offence to clerical prejudices, I eventually altered it into a dome of the Russian type, which also is distinctly of Eastern origin and therefore so far in keeping with the rest of the building. As every compromise must, it fails of being entirely satisfactory.

The eastern half of the Church, consisting of the apse, choir, and two transepts, was roofed in and roughly fitted up for the celebration of Mass by

* Occasionally it has so happened that every single ward in the hospital has been empty.

All Saints' Day, 1874, only nine months after the work had been commenced. The nave and aisles were then taken in hand, and on the recurrence of the same feast, two years later, in 1876, the entire edifice was solemnly blessed by the Bishop of Agra. On that occasion the interior presented a very striking appearance, the floor being spread with handsome Persian carpets, and a profusion of large crystal chandeliers suspended in all the inter-columniations; while the Bishop's throne of white marble was surmounted by a canopy of silk and cloth of gold; magnificent baldachinos, also of gold embroidery, were suspended above the three altars, and the entire sanctuary was draped from top to bottom with costly Indian tapestry. These beautiful accessories, several thousands of rupees in value, were kindly lent by the Seths, the Rája of Háthras and other leading members of the Hindu community, many of whom had also assisted with handsome pecuniary donations. As a further indication of their liberal sentiments, they themselves attended the function in the evening—the first public act of Christian worship at which they had ever been present—and expressed themselves as being much impressed by the elaborate ceremonial and the Gregorian tones, which latter they identified with their own immemorial Vedic chants. In consequence of my transfer from the district, the building, though complete in essentials, will ever remain architecturally unfinished. The western façade is flanked by two stone stair-turrets (one built at the cost of Lála Syám Sundar Dás) which have only been brought up to the level of the aisle roof, though it was intended to raise them much higher and put bells in them. There were also to have been four kiosques at the corners of the dome, for the reception of statues, but two only have been executed; the roof of the transepts was to have been raised to a level with that of the nave, and the plain parapet of the aisles would have been replaced by one of carved stone. The High Altar, moreover, is only a temporary erection of brick and plaster. I was at work upon the Tabernacle for it, when I received Sir George Couper's orders to go; and naturally enough they were a great blow to me. The total cost had been Rs. 18,100.

In the civil station most of the houses are large and commodious and, being the property of the Seth, the most liberal of landlords, are never allowed to offend the eye by falling out of repair. One built immediately after the mutiny for the use of the Collector of the district is an exceptionally handsome and substantial edifice. The Court-house, as already mentioned on page 106, was completed in the year 1861, and has a long and rather imposing façade; but though it stands at a distance of not more than 100 yards from the high road, the ground in front of it has been so carelessly planted that a person, who had no

THE MUSEUM

professional business to take him there, might live within a stone's throw for years and never be aware of its existence. In immediate proximity are the offices of the Tahsíldar, a singularly mean and insignificant range of buildings, as if purposely made so to serve for a foil to another building which stands in the same enclosure.

This is now used, or (as perhaps it would be more correct to say) at the time of my leaving the district was intended to be used, as a Museum. It was commenced by Mr. Thornhill, the Magistrate and Collector of the district, who raised the money for the purpose by public subscription, intending to make of it a rest-house for the reception of native gentlemen of rank, whenever they had occasion to visit head-quarters. Though close to the Courts, which would be a convenience, it is too far from the bazár to suit native tastes, and even if it had been completed according to the original design, it is not probable that it would ever have been occupied. After an expenditure of Rs. 30,000, the work was interrupted by the mutiny. When order had been restored, the new Collector, Mr. Best, with a perversity by no means uncommon in the records of Indian local administration, set himself at once, not to complete, but to mutilate, his predecessor's handiwork. It was intended that the building should stand in extensive grounds of its own, where it would certainly have had a very pleasing architectural effect; but instead of this the high road was brought immediately in front of it, so as to cut it off entirely from the new public garden; the offices of the Tahsíldar were built on one side, and on the other was run up, at a most awkward angle, a high masonry wall; a rough thatched roof was thrown over its centre court; doorways were introduced in different places where they were not wanted and only served as disfigurements, and the unfortunate building was then nick-named "Thornhill's Folly" and abandoned to utter neglect.

It remained thus till 1874, when the idea of converting it into a Museum received the support of Sir John Strachey, who sanctioned from provincial funds a grant-in-aid of Rs. 3,500. The first step taken was to raise the centre court by the addition of a clerestory, with windows of reticulated stone tracery, and to cover it with a stone vault, in which (so far as constructional peculiarities are concerned) I reproduced the roof of the now ruined temple of Harideva at Gobardhan. The cost amounted to Rs. 5,336. A porch was afterwards added at a further outlay of Rs. 8,494; but for this I am not responsible. It is a beautiful design, well executed, and so far it reflects great credit on Yúsuf, the Municipal architect; but it is too delicate for an exterior façade on the side of a dusty road. Something plainer would have answered the purpose as well, besides having a more harmonious effect. After my transfer, operations at once came to a stand-still and the valuable collection of antiquities I had left behind me remained utterly uncared for, till I took upon myself to represent the matter to the local Government. I was thereupon allowed to submit plans and estimates for the completion of the lower story by filling in the doors and windows, without which the building could not possibly be used, and my proposals were sanctioned. When I last visited Mathurá, the work had made good progress, and I believe has now been finished for some time; but many of the most interesting sculptures are still lying about in the compound of my old bungalow.

Though the cost of the building has been so very considerable, nearly Rs. 44,000, it is only of small dimensions; but the whole wall surface in the central court is a mass of geometric and flowered decorations of the most artistic character. The bands of natural foliage—a feature introduced by Mr. Thornhill's own fancy—are very boldly cut and in themselves decidedly handsome, but they are not altogether in accord with the conventional designs of native style by which they are surrounded.

The following inscription is worked into the cornice of the central hall :—

جو بس سرکار کو منظور آرام خلائق تھا * کیا با صاحب کیلکٹر و مجسٹریٹ ایما
اُنھوں نے تب رئیسوں کی مددگاری سے متھرامیں * منبت کام کا نادر مسافرخانہ بنوایا
صفائی میں در و دیوار ھی مانند آئینہ * بگلکاری ھر ایک درجہ نظر آتا ھی گلشن کا
بحد اعتدال اب اِسنے پائی رفعت و وسعت * بہت خوش قطع اور موزون ھی یہہ تعمیر سر تا پا
روا ھی گر بتاویں گنبد افراسیاب اِسکو * بجا ھی جو کہیں اِسکو کہ ھی یہہ قصر قیصر کا
جو دیکھا اِسکو شوکت نے یہہ تاریخ بنا لکھی * مسافر خانۂ موزون بھی بس رشک چمن زیبا

سنہ ۱۸۵۶ عیسوی — سنہ ۱۲۶۴ فصلی

"The State having thought good to promote the ease of its subjects, gave intimation to the Magistrate and Collector, ; who then, by the co-operation of the chief men of Mathurá, had this house for travellers built with the choicest carved work.* Its doors and walls are polished like a mirror; in its sculpture every kind of flower-bed appears in view; its width and height were assigned in harmonious proportion; from top to bottom it is well shaped and well balanced. It may very properly be compared to the dome of Afrasyáb, or it may

* Upon the word *munabbat*, which is used here to denote arabesque carving, the late Mr. Blochmann communicated the following note:—"The Arabic *nabata* means 'to plant,' and the intensive form of the verb has either the same signification or that of 'causing to appear like plants': hence *munabbat* comes to mean 'traced with flowers,' and may be compared with *mushajjar*, 'caused to appear like trees,' which is the word applied to silk with tree-patterns on it," like the more common '*búta-dár*.'

justly be styled the palace of an emperor. One who saw its magnificence (*or* the poet Shaukat on seeing it) composed this *tarikh,* so elegant a rest-house makes even the flower garden envious."

As the building afforded such very scant accommodation, I proposed to make it not a general, but simply an architectural and antiquarian museum, arranging in it, in chronological series, specimens of all the different styles that have prevailed in the neighbourhood from the reign of the Indo-Scythian Kanishka, in the century immediately before Christ, down to the Victorian period which would be illustrated in perfection by the building itself.

It cannot be denied that it is high time for some such institution to be established; for in an ancient city like Mathurá interesting relics of the past, even when no definite search is being made for them, are constantly cropping up; and unless there is some easily accessible place to which they can be consigned for custody, they run an imminent risk of being no sooner found than destroyed. Inscriptions in particular, despite their exceptional value in the eyes of the antiquary, are more likely to perish than anything else, since they have no beauty to recommend them to the ordinary observer. Thus, as already mentioned, a pillar, the whole surface of which is said to have been covered with writing, was found in 1860 in making a road on the site of the old city wall. There was no one on the spot at the time who took any interest in such matters, and the thrifty engineer, thinking such a fine large block of stone ought not to be wasted, had it neatly squared and made into a buttress for a bridge. Another inscribed fragment, which had formed the base of a large seated statue, had been set up by a subordinate in the Public Works Department to protect a culvert on the high road through cantonments, from which position I rescued it. It bears the words *Mahárajasya Deva-putrasya Huvishkasya rájya sam.* 50 *he* 3 *di* 2, and is of value as an unquestionably early example of the same symbol, which in the inscription of doubtful age given at page 138 is explained in words as denoting 'fifty.' A third illustration of official indifference to archæological interests, though here the culprit was not an engineer, but the Collector himself, is afforded by the base of a pillar, which, after it had been accidentally dug up, was plastered and whitewashed and imbedded in one of the side pillars of the Tahsíli gateway, where I re-discovered it, when the gateway was pulled down to improve the approach. The words are cut in bold clear letters, which for the most part admit of being deciphered with certainty, as follows: *Ayam kumbhaka dánam bhikshunam Suriyasya Buddha-rakshitasya cha prahitakánam. Anantyam* (?) *deya dharmma pa............nam. Sarvasa prahitakánam arya dakshitaye bhavatu.* The purport of this would be:

"This base is the gift of the mendicants Surya and Buddha-rakshita, *prahitakas*. A religious donation in perpetuity. May it be in every way a blessing to the *prahitakas*." A question has been raised by Professor Kern, with reference to another inscription, in which also a *bhikshu* was mentioned as a donor, on the score that a mendicant was a very unlikely person to contribute towards the expenses of any building, since, as he says, 'monks have nothing to give away, all to receive.' But in this particular instance the reading and meaning are both unmistakeably clear, nor is the fact really at all inconsistent with Hindu usage. In this very district I can point to two large masonry tanks, costing each some thousands of rupees, which have been constructed by mendicants, *bairágis*, out of alms that they had in a long course of years begged for the purpose. The word *prahitaka*, if I am right in so reading it, is of doubtful signification. It might mean either 'messenger' or 'committee-man ;' a commissioner or a commissionaire.

The other inscriptions have for the most part been already noticed in the preceding chapters, when describing the places where they were found.

As a work of art, the most pleasing specimen of sculpture is the Yasa-ditta statue of Buddha, noticed at page 115 ; but archæologically the most curious object in the collection is certainly the large carved block which I discovered at Pálikhera in the cold weather of 1873-74. On one side is represented a group of six persons, the principal figure being a man of much abdominal development, who is seated in complete nudity on a rock, or low stool, with a large cup in in his hand. At his knee is a little child ; two attendants stand at the back ; and in the front two women are seen approaching, of whom the foremost bears a cup and the second a bunch of grapes. Their dress is a long skirt with a shorter jacket over it ; shoes on the feet and a turban on the head. The two cups are curiously made ; the lower end of the curved handle being attached to the bottom of the stem instead of the bowl. On the opposite side of the block the same male figure is seen in a state of helpless intoxication, supported on his seat from behind by two attendants, the one male, the other female. By his right knee stands the child as before, and opposite him to the left was apparently another boy, of somewhat larger growth, but this figure has been much mutilated. The male attendant wears a mantle, fastened at the neck by a fibula and hanging from the shoulder in vandyked folds, which are very suggestive of late Greek design.

The stone on which these two groups are carved measures three feet ten inches in height, three feet in breadth and one foot four inches in thickness, and the top has been scooped out so as to form as it were a shallow circular basin. A block, of precisely the same dimensions and carved with two similar groups, was discovered somewhere near Mathurá, the precise locality not having been placed on record, by Colonel Stacy in the year 1836, who deposited it in the Calcutta museum, where it still is. His idea was that the principal figure represented Silenus, that the sculptors were Bactrian Greeks, and that their work was meant to be a tazza, or rather a pedestal for the support of a tazza or large sacrificial vase. These opinions were endorsed by James Prinsep, and have prevailed to the present day. I believe them however to be erroneous, though not unnaturally suggested by a general resemblance to some such a picture as is given in Woolner's Pygmalion of—

> "Weak-kneed Silenus puffing, on both sides
> Upheld by grinning slaves, who plied the cup
> Wherein two nymphs squeezed juice of dusky grapes."

Of the two groups on the Stacy stone one represents the drunkard after he has drained the cup, and is almost identical with that above described. The other exhibits an entirely different scene in the story, though some of the characters appear to be the same. There are four figures—two male and two female—standing under the shade of a tree with long clusters of drooping flowers. The first figure to the right is a female dressed in a long skirt and upper jacket, with a narrow scarf thrown over her arms. Her right hand is grasped by her male companion, who has his left arm round her neck. He is entirely naked, save for a very short pair of drawers barely reaching to the middle of the thigh, and a shawl which may be supposed to hang loosely at his back, but in front shows only the ends tied loosely in a knot under his chin. Behind him and with her back to his back is another female dressed as the first, but with elaborate bangles covering nearly half the fore-arm. Her male companion seems to be turning away as if on the point of taking his leave. He wears light drawers reaching to the ankles and a thin muslin tunic, fitting close to the body and terminating a little below the knees. On the ground at the feet of each of the male figures is a covered cup.

As to the names of the personages concerned and the particular story which the sculptor intended to represent, I am not able to offer any suggestion. Probably, when Buddhist literature has been more largely studied, the legend thus illustrated will be brought to light. The general purport of the three scenes appear to me unmistakeable. In the first the two male conspirators are persuading their female companions to take part in the plot, the nature of the plot being indicated by the two cups at their feet. In the second the venerable ascetic has been seduced by their wiles into tasting the dangerous draught; one of the two cups is in his hand, the other is ready to follow. In the third one, of which there are two representations, the cups have been quaffed, and he is reeling from their effects.

Obviously all this has nothing to do with Silenus; the discovery of the second block, which supplies the missing scene in the drama, makes it quite clear that some entirely different personage is intended. The tazza theory may also be dismissed; for the shallow bason at the top of the stone seems to be nothing more than the bed for the reception of a round pillar. A sacrificial vase was a not uncommon offering among the Greeks; and if the carving had been shown to represent a Greek legend, there would have been no great improbability in supposing that the work had been executed for a foreigner who employed it in accordance with his own national usage. But in dedicating a cup to one of his own divinities, he would not decorate it with scenes from Hindu mythology; while, on the other hand, the offering of a cup of such dimensions to any monastery or shrine on the part of a Buddhist is both unprecedented and intrinsically improbable.

Finally, as to the nationality of the artist. The foliage, it must be observed, is identical in character with what is seen on many Buddhist pillars found in the immediate neighbourhood and generally in connection with figures of Maya Devi; whence it may be presumed that it is intended to represent the sál tree, under which Buddha was born, though it is by no means a correct representation of that tree. The other minor accessories are also, with one exception, either clearly Indian, or at least not strikingly un-Indian: such as the earrings and bangles worn by the female figures and the feet either bare or certainly not shod with sandals: the one exception being the mantle of the male attendant in the drunken scene. Considering the local character of all the other accessories, I find it impossible to agree with General Cunningham in ascribing the work to a foreign artist, "one of a small body of Bactrian sculptors, who found employment among the wealthy Buddhists at Mathurá, as in later days Europeans were employed under the Mughal emperors." The thoroughly Indian character of the details seems to me, as to Dr. Mitra, decisive proof that the sculptor was a native of the country; nor do I think it very strange that he should represent one of the less important characters as clothed in a modified Greek costume, since it is an established historical fact that Mathurá was included in the Bactrian Empire, and the Greek style of dress cannot have been altogether unfamiliar to him. The artificial folds of the drapery were probably borrowed from what he sawon coins.

AUTOTYPE

1. BACCHANALIAN SCULPTURE FROM PÁLI-KHERA.

2. BACCHANALIAN SCULPTURE FROM PÁLI-KHERA.

In the Hindu Pantheon the only personage said to have been of wine-bibbing propensities is Balaráma himself, one of the tutelary divinities of Mathurá ; and it is probably he who was intended to be represented by a second Bacchanalian figure included in the museum collection. This is a mutilated statue brought from the village of Kukargama, in the Sa'dábád pargana.* He stands under the conventional canopy of serpents' heads, with a garland of wild-flowers (*ban-mála*) thrown across his body ; his right hand is raised above his head in wild gesticulation and in his left hand he holds a cup very similar to the one shown in the Páli-kherá sculpture. His head-dress closely resembles Krishna's distinctive ornament, the *mukut* ; but it may be only the spiral coil of hair observable in the Sanchi and Amaravati sculptures. In any case, the inference must not be presed too far ; for, *first*, the hooded snake is as constant an accompaniment of Sákya Muni as of Balaráma ; and *secondly*, a third sculpture of an equally Bacchanalian character is unmistakeably Buddhist. This is a rudely executed figure of a fat little fellow, who has both his hands raised above his hand, and holds in one a cup, in the other a bunch of grapes. The head with its close curling hair leaves no doubt that Buddha is the person intended ; though possibly in the days of his youth, when " he dwelt still in his palace and indulged himself in all carnal pleasures." Or it might be a caricature of Buddhism as regarded from the point of view of a Bráhmanical ascetic.

---

*At Kukargama is an ancient shrine of Kukar Deví, where a melá is held on the festival of the Phul-dol, Chait badi 7. Though in a dilapidated condition, the building is quite a modern one, a small dome supported on plain brick arches ; but on the floor, which is raised several feet above the level of the ground, is a plinth, 4 feet 8 inches square, formed of massive blocks of a hard and closely grained grey stone. The mouldings are bold and simple, like what may be seen in the oldest Kashmír temples. One side of the plinth is imperfect and the stone has also been removed from the centre, leaving a circular hollow, which the villagers think was a well. But more probably the shrine was originally one of Mahádeva, and this was the bed in which a round lingam had been set. In a corner of the building were two mutilated sculptures of similar design, and it was the more perfect of these two that I removed to Mathurá. A sketch of it may be seen in Volume XLIV. of the Journal of the Calcutta Asiatic Society's Journal for 1875. A few paces from the shrine is a small brick platform, level with the ground, which is said to cover the grave of the dog (*Kukura*) from whom the village is supposed to derive its name ; and persons bitten by a dog are brought here to be cured. The adjoining pond called Kúrha (for *Kukura-ká*) is said to have been constructed by a Banjára. Very large bricks are occasionally dug up out of it, as also from the village Khera ; one measured 1 foot 5 inches in length by 10 inches in breadth and 3 in thickness, another 1 foot 7 inches × 9 inches × 2½ inches. It is of interest to observe that on the west coast of the Gulf of Cambay, 20 miles south of Bhaunagar, is another place now called Kúkar, the ancient name of which, as appears from an inscription found there, was Kukata ; but the derivation is uncertain. The old Ját zamindárs are Gahlot, or Sisodiya, Thákurs from Sabpau.

However, Buddhism itself, though originally a system of abstractions and negations, was not long before it assumed a concrete development. In one of its schools, which from the indecency of many of the figures that have been discovered would seem to have been very popular at Mathurá, debauchery of the most degrading description was positively inculcated as the surest means for attaining perfection. The authority for these abominable doctrines, which, in the absence of literary proof might have been considered an impossible outcome of such teaching as that of Sákya Muni, is a Sanskrit composition called *Tathágata Guhyaka*, or *Guhya samagha*, 'the collection of secrets,' of which the first published notice is that given by Dr. Rajendra Lála Mittra in the introduction to his edition of the Lalita Vistara. He describes it as having all the characteristics of the worst specimens of the Hindu Tantras. The professed object, in either case, is devotion of the highest kind—absolute and unconditional—at the sacrifice of all worldly attachments, wishes, and aspirations ; but in working it out theories are indulged in and practices enjoined, which are at once the most revolting and horrible that human depravity could imagine. A shroud of mystery alone seems to prevent their true character from being seen ; but divested of it, works of this description would deserve to be burnt by the common hangman. Looking at them philosophically, the great wonder is that a system of religion, so pure and so lofty in its aspirations as Buddhism, could be made to ally itself with such pestilent dogmas and practices. Perfection is described as attainable not by austerity, privations and painful rigorous observances, but by the enjoyment of all the pleasures of the world, some of which are described with a minuteness of detail which is simply revolting. The figures of nude dancing-girls in lascivious attitudes with other obscene representations, that occur on many of the Buddhist pillars in the museum, are clear indications of the popularity which this corrupt system had acquired in the neighbourhood. The two figures of female monsters, each with a child in its lap, which it is preparing to tear in pieces and devour, are in all probability to be referred to the same school : though they appear also in the Hindu Tantras and under the same name, that of Dákini. In the oldest sculptures the figures are all decently draped, and it has been the custom to regard them only as Buddhist, and all the nude or otherwise objectionable representations as Jaini. But this is an error arising out of the popular Hindu prejudice against what they call in reproach 'the worship of the naked gods.' The out cry is simply an interested one and has no foundation in fact : for though many Hindu temples, especially in Bengal, are disfigured by horrible obscenities,

I know of no Jaini temple in which there is anything to shock the most sensitive delicacy; while the length to which some of the recognized followers of Buddha could go in the deification of lust has been sufficiently shown by Dr. Mitra's description of the *Guhya samagha.* And this, it should be added, though hitherto almost unknown to European students, is no obscure treatise, but is one of the nine most important works to which divine worship is constantly offered by the Buddhists of Nepál.

Of the different styles of architecture that have prevailed in the district, the memory of the earliest, the Indo-Greek, is preserved by a single small fragment found in the Ambarisha hill, where a niche is supported by columns with Ionic capitals. Of the succeeding style, the Indo-Scythian, there are a few actual architectural remains and a considerable number of sculptured representations. No complete column has been recovered; but the plain square bases, cut into four steps, found at the Chauwára mounds, belong to this period, as also the bell-shaped capital, surmounted by an inscribed abacus with an elephant standing upon it, brought from a garden near the Kankáli tíla. It is dated the year 39, in the reign of Huvishka. In the sculptures, where an arcade is shown, the abacus usually supports a pair of winged lions, crouching back to back; but in a fragment from the Kankáli tíla, where the column is meant for an isolated one, it bears an elephant. In this last example the shaft appears to be round, but it is more commonly shown as octagonal. The round bases, of which such a large number were unearthed from the Jamálpur mounds, many of them inscribed with the names of the donors, would seem to have been used for the support of statues. The name by which they are designated in the inscriptions is *Kumbhaka.* The miniature pediments, carved as a diaper or wall decoration, show that the temple fronts presented the same appearance as in the Násik caves. This was peculiarly the Buddhist style and died with the religion to whose service it had been dedicated. After it came the mediæval Bráhmanic style, which was prevalent all over Upper India in the time of Prithi Ráj and the Muhammadan conquest. In this the bell-shaped capital appears as a vase with masses of dependent foliage at its four corners. These have not only a very graceful effect, but are also of much constructional significance, since they counteract the weakness which would otherwise have resulted from the attenuation of the vase at its base and neck. The shaft itself frequently springs from a similar vase set upon a moulded base. In early examples, as in a pair of columns from the Kankáli tíla and a fragment from Shergarh, the shaft has a central band of drooping lily-like flowers, with festoons dependent from them. Later on, instead of the band a grotesque face is introduced, with the moustaches prolonged into fanciful arabesque continuations, and strings of pearls substituted for the festoons, or a knotted scarf is grasped in the teeth and hangs half down to the base with a bell attached to its end. Occasionally the entire shaft or some one of its faces is enriched with bands of foliage. Probably for the sake of securing greater height, a second capital was added at the top, either in plain cushion shape, or carved into the semblance of two squat monsters supporting the architrave on their head and upraised hands. For still loftier buildings it was the practice to set two columns of similar character one on the other, crowning the uppermost with the detached capital as above described; and afterwards it became the fashion to make even short columns with a notch in the middle, so as to give them the appearance of being in two pieces. Examples of this peculiarity may be seen in the Chhatthi Pálna at Mahá-ban and the Dargáh at Noh-jhíl. The custom, which prevailed to a very late period, of varying the shape of a shaft by making it square at bottom, then an octagon, and then polygonal, is probably of different origin and was only a device for securing an appearance of lightness.

From about the year 1200 A.D. the architectural history of Mathurá is an absolute blank till the middle of the 16th century, when, under the beneficent sway of the Emperor Akbar, the eclectic style, so characteristic of his own religious views, produced the magnificent series of temples, which even in their ruin are still to be admired at Brindá-ban. The temple of Rádhá Ballabh, in that town, built in the next reign, that of Jahángir, is the last example of the style. Its characteristic note can scarcely be defined as the fusion, but rather as the parallel exhibition of the Hindu and Muhammadan method. Thus in a façade one story, or one compartment, shows a succession of multifoil saracenic arches, while above and below, or on either side, every opening is square-headed with the architrave supported on projecting brackets. The one is purely Muhammadan, the other is as distinctly Hindu; yet, without any attempt made to disguise the fact beyond the judicious avoidance of all exaggerated peculiarities in either style, the juxta position of the two causes no sentiment of incongruity. If in any art it were possible to revive the dead, or if it were in human nature ever to return absolutely upon the past, this style would seem to be the one for our architects to copy. But simple retrogression is impossible. Every period has an environment of its own, which, however studiously ignored in artificial imitations, must have its effect in any spontaneous development of the artistic faculty. The principle, however, is as applicable as ever, though it will deal with altered materials and be manifested in novel phenomena. Indian architecture, as

AUTOTYPE

GROUP OF ANTIQUITIES, MATHURÁ MUSEUM.

now in vogue at Mathurá, is the result of Muhammadan influences working upon a Hindu basis. The extraordinary power that resulted from the first introduction of the new element is all but exhausted ; the system requires once more to be invigorated from without. A single touch of genius might restore it to more than all its pristine activity by wedding it to the European Gothic, to which it has a strong natural affinity. The product would be a style that would satisfy all the practical requirements of modern civilization, and at the same time display the union of oriental and western idea, in a concrete form, which both nationalities could appreciate. The combination of dome and spire, the dream of our last great Gothic architect, but which he died without accomplishing, would follow spontaneously ; and Anglo-Indian architecture, no longer a bye-word for Philistinism and vulgarity, might spread through the length and breadth of the empire with as much success as Indo-Greek art in the days of Alexander, or Hindu-Saracenic art in the reign of Akbar.

The eclecticism of the last-named period, which has suggested the above remarks, was followed by the Ját style, of which the best examples are the tombs and palaces erected by Súraj Mall, the founder of the Bharatpur dynasty, and his immediate successors. In these the arch is thoroughly naturalized ; the details are also in the main dictated by Muhammadan precedent, but they are carried out with much of the old Hindu solidity and exuberance of fanciful decoration. The arcade of the Ganga Mohan Kunj at Brindá-ban is a very fine specimen of this style at its best. In later buildings, as in those on the bank of the Mánasi Ganga at Gobardhan, the mouldings are shallower and the wall-ornamentation consists of nothing but an endless succession of niches and vases repeated with wearisome uniformity. The Bangala, or oblong alcove, with a vaulted roof of curvilinear outline, is always a prominent feature in this style and is introduced into some part of every façade. From the name it may be inferred that it was borrowed from Bengal and was probably intended as a copy of the ordinary cottage roof made of bent bambus. It does not appear in Upper India till the reign of Aurangzeb ; the earliest example in Mathurá being the alcoves of the mosque built by Abd-un-Nabi in 1661 A.D.

The style in vogue at the present day is the legitimate descendant of the above, and differs from it in precisely the same way as Perpendicular differs from Decorated Gothic. It has greater lightness, but less freedom : more elaboration in details, but less vigour in conception. The panelling of the walls and piers is often filled in with extremely delicate arabesques of intricate design ;

but the effect is scarcely in proportion to the labour expended upon them; for the work is too slightly raised and too minute to catch the eye at any distance. Thus, the first impression is one of flatness and a want of accentuation; artistic defects for which no refinement of detail can adequately compensate. The pierced tracery, however, of the screens and balconies is as good in character as in execution. The geometrical patterns are old traditions and can be classified under a few well-defined heads, but they admit of almost infinite modifications under skilful treatment. They are cut with great mathematical nicety, the pattern being drawn on both sides of the slab, which is half chiselled through from one side and then turned over and completed from the other. The temples that line both sides of the High Street in the city, the monument to Seth Mani Rám in the Jamuná bágh and the porch of the museum itself are fine specimens of the style, and are conclusive proofs that, in Mathurá at all events, architecture is, to this day, no mere galvanized revival of the past, but is still a living and progressive art. If a model of some one of the best and most typical buildings in each of the late styles were added to the museum collection of antiquities, as was my intention, the series would give a complete view of the architectural history of the district, from which a student would be able to gather much instruction. A specimen of modern official architecture (?), as conceived by our Engineers in the Public Works Department, should further be placed in juxtaposition with them, as a model also, but a model of everything to be avoided.

Immediately opposite the museum is the Public Garden, in which the museum itself ought to have been placed. It contains a considerable variety of choice trees and shrubs, but unfortunately it has not been laid out with much taste, and its area is too large to be kept in good order out of the funds that are allowed for its maintenance. It was extended a few years ago, so as to include the site of a large mound and tank. The former was levelled and the latter filled up. During the progress of the work a number of copper coins were discovered, which may very possibly have been of the same date as the adjoining Buddhist monastery; but being of no intrinsic value, there was no one on the spot who cared to preserve them. A little further on is the Jail, constructed on the approved radiating principle, and sufficiently strong under ordinary circumstances to ensure the safe-guard of native prisoners, though an European would probably find its walls not very difficult either to scale or break through. This exhausts the list of public institutions and objects of interest; whence it may be rightly inferred that the English quarter of Mathurá is as dull and common-place as most other Indian stations. Still, in the rains it has a pleasant park-like appearance with its wide expanse of green sward, reserved for military uses from the encroachments of the plough ; its well-kept roads with substantial bridges to span the frequent ravines ; and the long avenues of trees that half conceal the thatched and verandahed bungalows that lie behind, each in its own enclosure of garden and pasture land ; while in the distant back-ground an occasional glimpse is caught of the broad stream of the Jamuná.

NOTES ON CHAPTER VII.

I.—LIST OF GOVERNORS OF MATHURÁ IN THE 17TH CENTURY.

1629. Mirza Isa Tarkhán ; who gave his name to the suburb of Isa-pur (now more commonly called Hans-ganj), on the opposite bank of the river.

1636. Murshid Kuli Khan, promoted, at the time of his appointment, to be commander of 2,000 horse, as an incentive to be zealous in stamping out idolatry and rebellion. From him the suburb of Murshid-pur derives its name.

1639. Allah Virdi Khán. After holding office for three years, some disloyal expressions to which he had given utterance were reported to the emperor, who thereupon confiscated his estates and removed him to Delhi.

1642. Azam Khán Mír Muhammad Bákir, also called Irádat Khán. He is commemorated by the Azam-abad Saráe, which he founded (see page 31), and by the two villages of Azam-pur and Bákir-pur. He came of a noble family seated at Sáwa in Persia, and having attached himself to the service of Asaf Khán Mirza Jafar, the distinguished poet and courtier, soon after became his son-in-law and was introduced to the notice of the Emperor Jahángír. He thus gained his first appointment under the Crown ; but his subsequent promotion was due to the influence of Yamín-ud-daula, Asaf Khán IV., the father of Mumtáz Mahall, the favourite wife of Sháhjahán. On the accession of that monarch he was appointed commander of 5,000, and served with distinction in the Dakhin in the war against the rebel Khán Jahán Lodi and in the operations against the Nizám Sháhi's troops. In the fifth year of the reign, he was made Governor of Bengal in succession to Kásim Khán Juwaini. Three years later he was transferred to Allahabad, but did not remain there long, being moved in the very next year to Gujarát, as Subadar. In the twelfth year of Sháhjahán his daughter was married to prince Shuja, who had by her a son named Zain-ul-abidin. From 1642 to 1645 he was Governor of Mathurá, but in the latter year, as he did not act with sufficient vigour against the Hindu malcontents, his advanced age was made the pretext for transferring him to Bihar. Three years later he received orders for Kashmír; but as he objected to the cold climate of that country he was allowed to exchange it for Jaun-pur, where he died in 1648, at the age of 76. He is described in the Naasir-ul-Umará as a man of most estimable character, but very harsh in his mode of collecting the State revenue. Azamgarh, the capital of the district of that name in the Banáras Division, was also founded by him.

1645. Makramat Khán, formerly Governor of Delhi.

1658. Jafar, son of Allah Virdi Khán.

1659. Kásim Khán, transferred from Murádábád, but murdered on his way down.

1660. Abd-un-Nabi, founder of the Jama Masjid (see page 150).

1668. Saff-Shikan Khán. Fails in quelling the rebellion.

1669. Hasan Ali Khán. During his incumbency the great temple of Kesava Deva was destroyed.

1676. Sultan Kuli Khán.

II.—Names of the City Quarters, or Mahallas.

1 Mandavi Ráni.
2 Bairág-pura.
3 Khirki Bisáti.
4 Naya-bás.
5 Arjun-pura.
6 Tek-narnaul.
7 Gali Seru Kasera.
8 Gali Ravaliya.
9 Gali Rám-pál.
10 Tek Raná Kháti.
11 Gali Mathurá Megha.
12 Bázár Chauk.
13 Gali Bhairon.
14 Gali Thatherá.
15 Lál Darwázá.
16 Gali Lohiya.
17 Gali Nanda.
18 Teli-párá.
19 Tila Chaube.
20 Brindában Darwázá.
21 Gher Gobindi.
22 Gali Gopa Sháh.
23 Shah-ganj Darwázá.
24 Halan-ganj.
25 Chakra Tírath.
26 Krishan Gangá.
27 Go-ghát.
28 Kans ká kila.
29 Hanumán tila.
30 Zer masjid.
31 Kushk.
32 Sámi Ghát.
33 Makhdúm Sháh.
34 Asi-kunda Ghát.
35 Visránt Ghát.
36 Kans-khár.
37 Gali Dasávatár.
38 Gor-pára.
39 Gosáin Ghát.
40 Kil-math.
41 Syám Ghát.
42 Rám Ghát.
43 Rámjí-dwára.
44 Bihári-pura.
45 Ballabh Ghát.
46 Máru Gali.
47 Bengáli Ghát.
48 Kálá Mahal.
49 Chúna kankar.
50 Chamarháná.
51 Gopál-pura.
52 Sarái Rájá Bhadauria.
53 Sengal-pura.
54 Chhonkar-pára.
55 Mir-ganj.
56 Holi Darwáza.
57 Sítala Gali.
58 Kampu Ghát.

II.—Names of the City Quarters or Mahallas—(*concluded*).

59 Dharmsálá Rájá Awa (built by Rájá Pitambar Sinh).
60 Dhruva Ghát.
61 Dhruva tíla.
62 Bal tila.
63 Bárá Jay Rám Dás.
64 General-ganj.
65 Anta-párá
66 Gobind-ganj.
67 Chhagan-pura.
68 Santokh-pura.
69 Chháh kathauti.
70 Kotwáli.
71 BharatpurDarwáza.
72 Lálá-ganj.
73 Sitala Paesa.
74 Maholi Pol.
75 Nagra Paesa.
76 Gujarhána.
77 Roshan-ganj.
78 Bhár-ki gali.
79 Khirki Dalpat Rae.
80 Táj-pura.
81 Chaubachcha.
82 Sat Ghará.
83 Chhattá Bazár.
84 Gali Páthakán.
85 Mandar Párikh Jí.
86 Kázi-pára.
87 Naya Bazár (from Mr. Thornton's time).
88 Gháti chikne patharon ki.
89 Gali Gotawálá.
90 Gata sram.
91 Ratn kund.
92 Chhonká-párá.
93 Mánik chauk.
94 Gaja Paesa.
95 Gháti Bitthal Rae.
96 Sitalá Gháti.
97 Nakárchi tila.
98 Gujar Gháti.
99 Gali Kalál.
100 Kaserat.
101 Gali Durgá Chand.
102 Bazázá.
103 Mandavi Ghiya.
104 Gali Dhúsaron ki.
105 Manohar-pura.
106 Kasái-pára.
107 Kesopura.
108 Mandavi Rám Dás.
109 Matiya Darwáza.
110 Díg Darwáza.
111 Mahalla khákrobán.

III.—Principal Buildings in the City of Mathurá.

1. Hardinge Arch, or Holi Darwáza, forming the Agra gate of the city, erected by the municipality at a cost of Rs. 13,731.

2. Temple of Radhá Kishan, founded by Deva Chand, Bohra, of Tenda-Khera near Jabalpur, in 1870-71. Cost Rs. 40,000. In the Chhata Bazár.

3. Temple of Bijay Gobind, in the Satghara Mahalla, built in 1867 by Bijay Rám, Bohra, of Dattia, at a cost of Rs. 65,000.

4. Temple of Bala Deva, in the Khans-khár Bazár, built in 1865 by Kushali Rám, Bohra, of Sher-garh, at a cost of Rs. 25,000.

5. Temple of Bhairav Náth, in the Lohárs' quarter, built by Bishan Lal, Khattri, at a cost of Rs. 10,000. It is better known by the name of Sarvar Sultán, as it contains a chapel dedicated in honor of that famous Muhammadan saint, regarding whom it may be of interest to subjoin a few particulars. The parent shrine, situate in desert country at the mouth of a pass leading into Kandahár, is served by a company of some 1,650 priests besides women and children; who, with the exception of a small grant from Government yielding an annual income of only Rs. 350, are entirely dependent for subsistence on the charity of pilgrims. The shrine is equally reverenced by Hindus, Sikhs, and Muhammadans, and it is said to be visited in the course of a year by as many

as 200,000 people of all castes and denominations, who come chiefly from the Panjáb and Sindh. The saint in his lifetime was so eminent for his universal benevolence and liberality (whence his title of *sakhi*) that he is believed still to retain after death the power and will to grant every petition that is presented to him. At the large fair held in February, March and April, the shrine is crowded with applicants, many of whom beg for aid in money. As the shrine is poor and supported by charity, this cannot be given on the spot ; but the petitioner is told to name some liberal-minded person, upon whom an order is then written and sealed with the great seal of the temple and handed to the applicant. When presented by him to the person, on whom it was drawn, it is not unfrequently honoured. Such a parwána, drawn on one Muhammad Khán Afghan, was found on the fakír Nawáb Sháh, who in 1871 made a murderous attack on the Secretary of the Lahor Municipality. A report on the peculiar circumstances of the case was submitted to Government, and it is from it that the above sketch has been extracted in explanation of the singular fact that a Muhammadan saint has been enthroned as a deity in a Hindu temple in the most exclusive of all Hindu cities.

6. Temple of Gata-sram, near the Visránt Ghát, built by Prán-náth Sástri, at a cost of Rs. 25,000, about the year 1800.

7. Temple of Dwárakádhís commonly called the Seth's temple, in the Asikunda Bazár, built by Párikh Ji, in 1815, at a cost of Rs. 20,000.

8. House of the Bharat-pur Rájás, with gateway added by the late Rájá Balavant Sinh.

9. House of Seth Lakhmi Chand, built in 1845 at a cost of Rs. 1,00,000.

10. Temple of Madan Mohan, by the Sámi Ghát, built by Seth Anant Rám of Chúri by Ram-gárh, in 1859, at a cost of Rs. 20,000.

11. Temple of Gobardhan Náth, built by Seth Kushál, commonly called Seth Bábú, kámdár of the Barodara Rájá, in 1830.

12. Temple of Bihári Ji, built by Chhakki Lál and Kanhaiya Lál, bankers of Mhow near Nímach, in 1850, at at a cost of Rs. 25,000, by the Sámi Ghát : has a handsome court-yard as well as external façade.

13. Temple of Gobind Deva, near the Nakárchi tila, built by Gaur Sahay Mall and Ghan-Syám Dás, his son, Seths of Chúri, in 1848, with their residences and that of Ghan-Syám's uncle, Rámchandra, adjoining.

14. Temple of Gopi-nath, by the Sámi Ghát, built by Gulráj and Jagannath, Seths of Chúri, in 1866, at a cost of Rs. 30,000.

15. Temple of Baladeva, near the Hardinge Arch, built by Balá, Ahír, a servant of Seth Lakhmi Chand, as a dwelling-house, about the year 1820, at a cost of Rs. 50,000, and sold to Ráe Báí, a baniya's wife, who converted it into a temple.

16. Temple of Mohan Jíin the Satghara Mahalla, built about 70 years ago by Kripá Rám, Bohra; more commonly known as Daukala Kunj, after the Chaube who was the founder's purohit.

17. Temple of Madan Mohan, in the Asikunda Mahalla, built by Dhanráj, Bohra, of Aligarh.

18. Temple of Gobardhan Náth, in the Kans-khár, built by Devi Dás, Bohra, of Urai.

19. Temple of Dírgha Vishnu, by the street leading to the Bharat-pur gate, built by Rájá Patni Mall of Banáras.

20. The Sati Burj, or 'faithful widow's tower,' built by Rájá Bhagaván Dás in 1570.

21. The mosque of Abd-un-Nabi Khán, built 1662.

22. The mosque of Aurangzeb, built 1669, on the site of the temple of Kesava Deva.

IV.—Calendar of Festivals observed in the City of Mathurá.

Chait Sudi (*April* 1-15).

1. *Chait Sudi* 8.—Durgá Ashtami. Held at the temple of Mahávidya Devi.

2. *Chait Sudi* 9.—Rám Navami. Held at the Rám Jí Dwára.

Baisákh (*April—May*).

3. *Baisákh Sudi* 14.—Nar Sinh lílá. Held at Gor-pará, Mánik Chauk, and the temple of Dwárakádhís.

4. *Baisákh full moon.*—Perambulation of Mathurá, called Ban-bihár, starting from the Visránt Ghát; the only one made in the night.

5. *Jeth Sudi* 10.—The Jeth Dasahara. In the middle of the day, bathing at the Dasasvamedh Ghát; in the evening kite-flying from the Gokarnesvar hill.

6. *Jeth full moon.*—Jal-játra. All the principal people bring the water for the ablution of the god into the temples on their own shoulders in little silver urns.

Asárh (June—July).

7. *Asárh Sudi* 2.—Rath-játra.

8. *Asárh Sudi* 11.—Principal perambulation of Mathurá and Brindá-ban before the god takes his four months' sleep; called *jugal jori ki parikramá*. The people start early in the morning either from the Visránt, or some other Ghát nearer their home, and after passing by the Sarasvati kund continue their way for about a mile along the Delhi road. The majority then make a straight cut across to Brindá-ban, while the others go on first to the Garur Gobind shrine at Chhatíkra. This is the longest perambulation made and is said to be of 20 kos. All return to Mathurá the same day; any one who fails to do so being thought to lose the whole benefit of his pilgrimage.

9. *Asárh full moon.*—Byás-púno. In the morning the Guru is formally reverenced; in the evening there are wrestling matches, and the Pandits assemble on the hills or house-tops for the 'pavan pariksha,' or watching of the wind; from which they predict when the rains will commence and what sort of a season there will be. When the wind is from the north, as it was in 1879, it is thought to be a good sign; and certainly the rain that year was superabundant.

Srávan (July—August).

10. *Srávan Sudi* 3.—Commonly called *Tij ka mela.* Wrestling matches near the temple of Bhútesvar Mahádeva.

11. *Srávan Sudi* 5.—The Pánch Tirath mela begins. A pilgrimage starts from the Visránt Ghát for Madhu-ban; proceeds on the next day to Santanu kund at Satoha and the Gyán-bauli near the Katra; on the third day to Gokarnesvar; on the fourth to the shrine of Garur Gobind at Chhatíkra* and on the fifth to the Brahm kund at Brindá-ban.

12. *Srávan Sudi* 11.—Perambulation of Mathurá and Pavitra-dháran, or offering of Bráhmanical threads to the Thákur.

13. *Srávan full moon.*—The Salúno or Raksha-bandhan. Wrestling matches in different orchards near the temple of Bhútesvar.

Bhádon (August—September).

14. *Bhádon Badi* 8.—Janm Ashtami; Krishna's birthday. A fast till midnight.

---

* *Chhatíkra*, on the Dehli road, was founded by Manu, Jama, and Ror, three Kachwáhás, who are said to have come from Rál fourteen generations, *i.e.*, about 300 years ago. Their

15. *Bhádon Sudi* 11.—A special pilgrimage to Madhu-ban, Tál-ban, and Kumud-ban. The general Ban-játra also commences and lasts for 15 days.

16. *Bhádon Sudi* 14.—The Anant Chaudas. The Pairáki, or swimming festival, is held every Thursday in Srávan and Bhádon, but the principal day is the last Thursday before the Anant Chaudas, when there is a very great concourse of people, occupying the walls of the old fort and all the river-side ghâts. There is no racing : but the swimmers, almost all of whom have with them large hollow gourds, or inflated skins for occasional support, perform a variety of strange antics in the water; while some are mounted upon grotesque structures in the shape of horses, or peacocks, or different kinds of carriages. The scene, which is an amusing one, is best witnessed from a barge towed up the stream to the highest ghát near Jaysinghpura, where the swimmers start, and allowed to drop down with the current to the pontoon bridge. About sunset there is a rude display of fireworks accompanied with much smoke and noise; but the swimmers remain in the water some two or three hours longer, when the proceedings terminate with music and dancing in the streets of the city.

Kuvár (*September—October*).

17. *Kuvár Badi* 8.—Perambulation of the city followed by five days' festivities, during which it is customary to make a great number of little pewter

---

descendants now retain only 1½ biswa, the rest having been sold to the mahant of the temple of Syám Sundar at Brindá-ban, who is also muáfidár. They say that the name of the place, when their ancestors first occupied it, was the same as now, and that it refers to the six (*chha*) sakhis, or companions of Rádhá, whose *gupt bhavan*, or unseen abode, is one of the sites visited by pilgrims. Another local explanation of the name is that it refers to the six villages, each of which had to cede part of its land to form the Kachhwáhás' new settlement. There is a *rakhya*, wherein the trees are chiefly kadambs of small growth, though old, mixed with dhák, ním, karil, and híns, and in it is a highly venerated shrine, dedicated to Garúr Gobind. The present building, which is small and perfectly plain, enshrines a black stone image of the god Gobind mounted on Garúr. Close by is a cave with a longish flight of winding steps simply dug in the soil, but no one can penetrate to the end on account of the fleas with which the place swarms. On Sávan Sudi 8, during the *panch tirath ka mela*, the temple is visited by the largest number of pilgrims. There is a second fair on the day after the Holi, and a third on the full moon of Jeth. The revenue of the village all goes to the temple of Syám Sundar at Brindá-ban. The local shrine has no endowment. In a field immediately adjoining the homestead are some fragments of Buddhist rails. These were probably brought from the Gobind-kund, about a mile away, where some ancient building must once have stood. For digging the foundations of the small masonry ghát there, 20 years or so ago, it is said that some large sculptures were discovered ; but as they were mutilated, no one took the trouble to remove them. I told Kúrha—the Pujári—to let me know when the tank was dry enough to allow of excavations being made, but I left the district before any such opportunity occurred.

figures called *sánjhi,* representing Krishna and the Gopís, in whose honour also there are performances, all through the night, of the Rás dance.

18. *Kuvár Sudi* 8.—Meghnád Líla, or representation of the death of Rávan's son Megh-nád. This is the first of the three great days of the Rám Líla, which is held on the open plain near the temple of Mahávidyá. The entire series of performances, which commences from the new moon, includes most of the leading events in the Rámáyana, such as the tournament, the defeat of Táraká, the departure into exile, Bharat's expedition to Chitra-kút, the mutilation of Surpa-nakhá, the rape of Síta, the meeting with Sugriv, and the building of the bridge. A separate day is assigned to each incident, but the first six or seven acts of the drama are not invariably the same, and it is only on the 8th, 9th, and 10th days that many people assemble to see the show.

19. *Kuvár Sudi* 9.—Kumbhakaran Líla, with representation of the death of Rávan's brother, Kumbhakaran.

20. *Kuvár Sudi* 10.—Last day of the Dasahara, with representation of Ráma's final victory over Rávan. Though this fète attracts a large concourse of people, the show is a very poor one and the display of fireworks much inferior to what may be seen in many second-rate Hindu cities.

21. *Kuvár Sudi* 11.—Bharat Miláp. A platform is erected in the street under the Jama Masjid, on which is enacted a respresentation of the meeting at Ajudhyá between Prince Bharat and Ráma, Sitá and Lakshman, on their return from their wanderings. For the whole distance from that central spot to the Holi Gate not only the thoroughfare itself, but all the balconies and tops of the houses are crowded with people in gay holiday attire ; and as the fronts of all the principal buildings are also draped with party-coloured hangings, and the shops dressed up to look their best, the result is a very picturesque spectacle, which is more pleasing to the European eye than any other feast in the Hindu calendar ; the throng, however, is so dense that it is rather a hazardous matter to drive a carriage through it.

22. *Kuvár full moon*—Sarad-púno. Throughout the night visits are paid to the different temples.

Kártik (October—November).

23. *Kártik new moon*—Diwáli, or Dip-dán—feast of lamps.

24. *Kártik Sudi* 1.—Anna-kut. The same observances as at Gobardhan, but on a smaller scale.

25. *Kártik Sudi.*—Dhobi-maran Líla. Held near the Brindá-ban gate to commemorate Krishna's spoliation of Kansa's washerman.

26. *Kártik Sudi* 8.—Gocháran, or pasturing the cattle. Held in the evening at the Gopál Bágh on the Agra Road.

27. *Kártik Sudi* 9.—Akhay-Navami. The second great perambulation of the city, beginning immediately after midnight.

28. *Kártik Sudi* 10.—Kans badh ka mela, at the Rangesvar Mahádeva. Towards evening, a large wicker figure of Kans is brought out on to the road, when two boys, dressed to represent Krishna and Baladeva, and mounted either on horses or an elephant, give the signal, with the staves all wreathed with flowers that they have in their hands, for an assault upon the monster. In a few minutes it is torn to shreds and tatters by the Chaubes and a procession is then made to the Visránt Ghát.

22. *Kártik Sudi* 11.—Deotthán. The awakening of the god from his four months' slumber. A similar perambulation as on Asárh Sudi 11.

Mágh (January—February).

30. *Magh Sudi* 5.—Basant Panchami. The return of spring; corresponding to the English May-day.

Phálgun (February—March).

31 *Phálgun full moon.*—The Holi, or Indian saturnalia.

Chait badi (March 15—30).

32. *Chait Badi* 1.—Gathering at the temple of Kesava Deva.

33. *Chait Badi* 5.—Phúl-dol. Processions with flowers and music and dancing.

CHAPTER VIII.

BRINDÁ-BAN AND THE VAISHNAVA REFORMERS.

SOME six miles above Mathurá is a point where the right bank of the Jamuná assumes the appearance of a peninsula, owing to the eccentricity of the stream, which first makes an abrupt turn to the north and then as sudden a return upon its accustomed southern course. Here, washed on three of its sides by the sacred flood, stands the town of Brindá-ban, at the present day a rich and prosperous municipality, and for several centuries past one of the most holy places of the Hindus. A little higher up the stream a similar promontory occurs, and in both cases the curious formation is traditionally ascribed to the resentment of Baladeva. He, it is said, forgetful one day of his habitual reserve, and emulous of his younger brother's popular graces, led out the Gopís for a dance upon the sands. But he performed his part so badly, that the Jamuná could not forbear from taunting him with his failure and recommending him never again to exhibit so clumsy an imitation of Krishna's agile movements. The stalwart god was much vexed at this criticism and, taking up the heavy plough which he had but that moment laid aside, he drew with it so deep a furrow from the shore that the unfortunate river, perforce, fell into it, was drawn helplessly away and has never since been able to recover its original channel.

Such is the local rendering of the legend ; but in the Puránas and other early Sanskrit authorities the story is differently told, in this wise ; that as Balaráma was roaming through the woods of Brindá-ban, he found concealed in the cleft of a *kadamb* tree some spirituous liquor, which he at once consumed with his usual avidity. Heated by intoxication he longed, above all things, for a bathe in the river, and seeing the Jamuná at some little distance, he shouted for it to come near. The stream, however, remained deaf to his summons ; whereupon the infuriated god took up his ploughshare and breaking down the bank drew the water into a new channel and forced it to follow wherever he led. In the Bhágavata it is added that the Jamuná is still to be seen following the course along which she was thus dragged. Professor Wilson, in his edition of the Vishnu Purána, says, "The legend probably alludes to the construction of canals from the Jamuná for the purpose of irrigation ; and the works of the Muhammadans in this way, which are well known, were no doubt proceded by similar canals dug by the order of Hindu princes." Upon this suggestion it may be remarked, first, that in Upper India, with the sole exception of the canal constructed by Firoz Sháh (1351-1388 A.D.) for the supply of the city of Hisár, no irrigation works of any extent are known ever to have been executed either by Hindus or Muhammadans : certainly there are no traces of any such operations in the neighbourhood of Brindá-ban ; and secondly, both legends represent the Jamuná itself as diverted from its straight course into a single winding channel, not as divided into a multiplicity of streams. Hence it may more reasonably be inferred that the still existing involution of the river is the sole foundation for the myth.

The high road from Mathurá to Brindá-ban passes through two villages, Jay-sinh-pur and Ahalya-ganj, and about half way crosses a deep ravine by a bridge that bears the following inscription :—*Sri. Pul banwáyá Mahárój Des mukh Bálá-bai Sáhib beti Mahárój Mádho Jí Saindhiya Bahádur Ki ne marfat Khazánchi Mánik Chand ki, Jisukh kárkun, gumáshta Mahtáb Ráe ne sambat* 1890, *mahina asárh badi* 10 *guruvásare.* Close by is a masonry tank, quite recently completed, which also has a commemorative inscription as follows : *Taláb banwáyá Lálá Kishan Lál beta Fakir Chand Sahukár, ját Dhúsar, Rahnewala Dilli ke ne, sambat* 1929 *mutabik san* 1872 *Isvi.* That the bridge should have been built by a daughter of the Maháraja of Gwáliar and the tank constructed by a banker of Delhi, both strangers to the locality, is an example of the benefits which the district enjoys from its reputation for sanctity. As the road between the two towns is always thronged with pilgrims, the number of these costly votive offerings is sure to be largely increased in course of time ; but at present the country on either side has rather a waste and desolate appearance, with fewer gardens and houses than would be expected on a thoroughfare connecting two places of such popular resort. An explanation is afforded by the fact that the present road is of quite recent construction. Its predecessor kept much closer to the Jamuná, lying just along the *khádar* lands—which in the rains form part of the river bed—and then among the ravines, where it was periodically destroyed by the rush of water from the land. This is now almost entirely disused ; but for the first two miles out of Brindában its course is marked by lines of trees and several works of considerable magnitude. The first is a large garden more than 40 bighas in extent, surrounded by a masonry wall and supplied with water from a distance by long aqueducts.* In its centre is a stone temple of some size, and among the trees, with which the grounds are ever-

* By some extraordinary misconception Dr. Hunter in his Imperial Gazetteer speaks of this garden aqueduct as if it were an elaborate system of works for supplying the whole town with drinking-water.

crowded, some venerable specimens of the *khirni* form an imposing avenue. The garden bears the name of Kushál, a wealthy Seth from Gujarát, at whose expense it was constructed, and who also founded one of the largest temples in the city of Mathurá. A little beyond, on the opposite side of the way, in a piece of waste ground, which was once an orchard, is a large and handsome *báuli* of red sand-stone, with a flight of 57 steps leading down to the level of the water. This was the gift of Ahalya Bái, the celebrated Mahratta Queen of Indor, who died in 1795. It is still in perfect preservation, but quite unused. Further on, in the hamlet of Akrúr, on the verge of a cliff overlooking a wide expanse of alluvial land, is the temple of Bhat-rond, a solitary tower containing an image of Bihári Jí. In front of it is a forlorn little court-yard with walls and entrance gateway all crumbling into ruin. Opposite is a large garden of the Seth's, and on the roadway that runs between, a fair, called the Bhat-mela, is held on the full moon of Kártik ; when sweetmeats are scrambled among the crowd by the visitors of higher rank, seated on the top of the gate. The word Bhat-rond is always popularly connected with the incident in Krishna's life which the mela commemorates—how that he and his brother Balarám one day, having forgotten to supply themselves with provisions before leaving home, had to borrow a meal of rice (*bhát*) from some Bráhmans' wives—but the true etymology (though an orthodox Hindu would regard the suggestion as heretical) refers, like most of the local names in the neighbourhood, merely to physical phenomena, and Bhat-rond may be translated 'tide-wall,' or 'break-water.'

Similarly, the word Brindá-ban is derived from an obvious physical feature, and when first attached to the spot signified no more than the 'tulsi grove ;' *brindá* and *tulsi* being synonymous terms, used indifferently to denote the sacred aromatic herb known to botanists as *Ocymum sanctum*. But this explanation is far too simple to find favour with the more modern and extravagant school of Vaishnava sectaries ; and in the Brahma Vaivarta Purána, a mythical personage has been invented bearing the name of Vrindá. According to that spurious composition (Brah. Vai, v. iv. 2) the deified Rádhá, though inhabiting the Paradise of Goloka, was not exempt from human passions, and in a fit of jealousy condemned a Gopa by name Sridáma to descend upon earth in the form of the demon Sankháchura. He, in retaliation, sentenced her to become a nymph of Brindá-ban and there accordingly she was born, being, as was supposed, the daughter of Kedára, but in reality the divine mistress of Krishna : and it was simply his love for her which induced the god to leave his solitary throne in heaven and become incarnate. Hence in the following list of Rádhá's titles, as given by the same authority (Brah. Vai., v. iv. 17), there are three which refer to her predilection for Brindá-ban :—

Rádhá, Rásesvari, Rásavásini, Rásikesvari,
Krishna-pranádhiká, Krishna-priyá, Krishna-swarúpini,
Krishná, Vrindávani, Vrindá, Vrindávana-vinodini,
Chandávati, Chándra-kántá, Sata-chandra-nibhánaná,
*Krishna-vámánga-sambhútá, Paramánanda-rúpini.**

In the Padma Purána, Rádha's incarnation is explained in somewhat different fashion; that Vishnu being enamoured of Vrindá, the wife of Jalandhara, the gods, in their desire to cure him of his guilty passion, begged of Lakshmi the gift of certain seeds. These, when sown, came up as the *tulsi, málati* and *dhátri* plants, which assumed female forms of such beauty that Vishnu on seeing them lost all regard for the former object of his affections.

There is no reason to suppose that Brindá-ban was ever the seat of any large Buddhist establishment; and though from the very earliest period of Brahmanical history it has enjoyed high repute as a sacred place of pilgrimage, it is probable that for many centuries it was merely a wild uninhabited jungle, a description still applicable to Bhándir-ban, on the opposite side of the river, a spot of equal celebrity in Sanskrit literature. Its most ancient temples, four in number, take us back only to the reign of our own Queen Elizabeth; the stately courts that adorn the river bank and attest the wealth and magnificence of the Bharat-pur Rájás, date only from the middle of last century; while the space now occupied by a series of the largest and most magnificent shrines ever erected in Upper India was, fifty years ago, an unclaimed belt of wood-land and pasture-ground for cattle. Now that communication has been established with the remotest parts of India, every year sees some splendid addition made to the artistic treasures of the town; as wealthy devotees recognize in the stability and tolerance of British rule an assurance that their pious donations will be completed in peace and remain undisturbed in perpetuity.

When Father Tieffenthaler visited Brindá-ban, in 1754, he noticed only one long street, but states that this was adorned with handsome, not to say magnificent, buildings of beautifully carved stone, which had been erected by different Hindu Rájas and nobles, either for mere display, or as occasional residences, or as embellishments that would be acceptable to the local divinity. The absurdity

* "Rádhá, queen of the dance, constant at the dance, queen of the dancer; dearer than Krishna's life, Krishna's delight, Krishna's counter-part; Krishná, Brinda, Brinda-ban born, sporting at Brinda-ban; moon-like spouse of the moon-like god, with face bright as a hundred moons; created as the left half of Krishna's body, incarnation of heavenly bliss."

of people coming from long distances merely for the sake of dying on holy ground, all among the monkeys—which he describes as a most intolerable nuisance—together with the frantic idolatry that he saw rampant all around, and the grotesque resemblance of the Bairágis to the hermits and ascetics of the earlier ages of Christianity, seem to have given the worthy missionary such a shock that his remarks on the buildings are singularly vague and indiscriminating.

Mons. Victor Jacquemont' who passed through Brindá-ban in the cold weather of 1829-30, has left rather a fuller description. He says, "This is a very ancient city, and I should say of more importance even than Mathurá. It is considered one of the most sacred of all among the Hindus, an advantage which Mathurá also possesses, but in a less degree. Its temples are visited by multitudes of pilgrims, who perform their ablutions in the river at the different ghâts, which are very fine. All the buildings are constructed of red sandstone, of a closer grain and of a lighter and less disagreeable colour than that used at Agra : it comes from the neighbourhood of Jaypur, a distance of 200 miles. Two of these temples have the pyramidal form peculiar to the early Hindu style, but without the little turrets which in the similar buildings at Benares seem to spring out of the main tower that determines the shape of the edifice. They have a better effect, from being more simple, but are half in ruins." (The temples that he means are Madan Mohan and Jugal Kishor). "A larger and more ancient ruin is that of a temple of unusual form. The interior of the nave is like that of a Gothic church ; though a village church only, so far as size goes. A quantity of grotesque sculpture is pendent from the dome, and might be taken for pieces of turned wood.* An immense number of bells, large and small, are carved in relief on the supporting pillars and on the walls, worked in the same stiff and ungainly style. Many of the independent Rájás of the west, and some of their ministers (who have robbed them well no doubt) are now building at Brindá-ban in a different style, which, though less original, is in better taste, and are indulging in the costly ornamentation of pierced stone tracery. Next to Benares, Brindá-ban is the largest purely Hindu city that I have seen. I could not discover in it a single mosque. Its suburbs are thickly planted with fine trees, which appear from a distance like an island of verdure in the sandy plain." (These are the large gardens beyond the temple of Madan Mohan, on the old Delhi road.) "The Doáb, which can be seen

* The description of the temple of Gobind Deva in Thornton's Gazetteer contains the following sentence, which had often puzzled me. He says :—"From the vaulted roof depend numerous idols rudely carved in wood." He has evidently misunderstood Mons. Jacquemont's meaning, who refers not to any idols, but to the curious quasi-pendentives, like fir-cones, that ornament the dome.

from the top of ths temples, stretching away on the opposite side of the Jamuná, is still barer than the country on the right bank."

At the present time there are within the limits of the municipality about a thousand temples, including, of course, many which, strictly speaking, are merely private chapels, and thirty-two ghâts constructed by different princely benefactors. The tanks of reputed sanctity are only two in number. The first is the Brahm Kund at the back of the Seth's temple ; it is now in a very ruinous condition, and the stone kiosques at its four corners have in part fallen, in part been occupied by vagrants, who have closed up the arches with mud walls and converted them into dwelling-places. I had begun to effect a clearance and make arrangements for their complete repair when my transfer took place and put an immediate stop to this and all similar improvements. The other, called Govind Kund, is in an out-of-the-way spot near the Mathurá road. Hitherto it had been little more than a natural pond, but has lately been enclosed on all four sides with masonry walls and flights of steps, at a cost of Rs. 30,000, by Chaudharáni Káli Sundari from Rajshahi in Bengal. To these may be added, as a third, a masonry tank in what is called the Kewar-ban. This is a grove of pípal, gúlar, and kadamb trees which stands a little off the Mathurá road near the turn to the Madan Mohan temple. It is a halting-place in the Banjátra, and the name is popularly said to be a corruption of *kin várí*, 'who lit it?' with reference to the forest conflagration, or *davánal*, of which the traditional scene is more commonly laid at Bhadra-ban, on the opposite bank of the river. There is a small temple of Davánal Bihári, with a cloistered court-yard for the reception of pilgrims. The Gosáin is a Nimbárak. A more likely derivation for the name would be the Sanskrit word *kaivalya*, meaning final beatitude. Adjoining the ban is a large walled garden, belonging to the Tehri Rájá, which has long been abandoned on account of the badness of the water. The peacocks and monkeys, with which the town abounds, enjoy the benefit of special endowments bequeathed by deceased Rájás of Kotá and Bharat-pur. There are also some fifty *chhattras*, or dole-houses, for the distribution of alms to indigent humanity, and extraordinary donations are not unfrequently made by royal and distinguished visitors. Thus the Rájá of Dátiá, a few years ago, made an offering to every single shrine and every single Brahman that was found in the city. The whole population amounts to 21,000, of which the Bráhmans, Bairágis and Vaishnavas together make up about one half. In the time of the emperors, the Muhammadans made a futile attempt to abolish the ancient name, Brindá-ban, and in its stead substitute that of Múminábád ; but now, more wisely, they leave the place to its own Hindu name and devices and keep themselves as clear of it as possible. Thus, besides an occasional official, there are in Brindá-ban no followers of the prophet beyond only some fifty families, who live close together in its outskirts and are all of the humblest order, such as oilmen, lime-burners and the like. They have not a single public mosque nor even a karbala in which to deposit the tombs of Hasan and Husain on the feast of the Muharram, but have to bring them into Mathurá to be interred.

It is still customary to consider the religion of the Hindus as a compact system, which has existed continuously and without any material change ever since the remote and almost pre-historic period when it finally abandoned the comparatively simple form of worship inculcated by the ritual of the Vedas. The real facts, however, are far different. So far as it is possible to compare natural with revealed religion, the course of Hinduism and Christianity has been identical in character; both were subjected to a violent disruption, which occurred in the two quarters of the globe nearly simultaneously, and which is still attested by the multitude of uncouth fragments into which the ancient edifice was disintegrated as it fell. In the west, the revival of ancient literature and the study of forgotten systems of philosophy stimulated enquiry into the validity of those theological conclusions which previously had been unhesitatingly accepted—from ignorance that any counter-theory could be honestly maintained by thinking men. Similarly, in the east, the Muhammadan invasion and the consequent contact with new races and new modes of thought brought home to the Indian moralist that his old basis of faith was too narrow; that the division of the human species into the four Manava castes and an outer world of barbarians was too much at variance with facts to be accepted as satisfactory, and that the ancient inspired oracles, if rightly interpreted, must disclose some means of salvation applicable to all men alike, without respect to colour or nationality. The professed object of the Reformers was the same in Asia as in Europe—to discover the real purpose for which the second Person of the Trinity became incarnate; to disencumber the truth, as He had revealed it, from the accretions of later superstition; to abolish the extravagant pretensions of a dominant class and to restore a simpler and more severely intellectual form of public worship.* In Upper India the tyranny of the Muhammadans was too tangible a fact to allow of the hope, or even the wish, that the conquerors and conquered could ever coalesce in one common faith: but in the

* Thus, as it may be interesting to note, the Bráhma Samáj of the present day is no isolated movement, but only the most modern of a long series of similar reactions against current superstitions.

Dakhin and the remote regions of Eastern Bengal, to which the sword of Islam had scarcely extended, and where no inveterate antipathy had been created, the contingency appeared less improbable. Accordingly, it was in those parts of India that the great teachers of the reformed Vaishnava creed first meditated and reduced to system those doctrines, which it was the one object of all their later life to promulgate throughout Hindustan. It was their ambition to elaborate a scheme so broad and yet so orthodox that it might satisfy the requirements of the Hindu and yet not exclude the Muhammadan, who was to be admitted on equal terms into the new fraternity ; all mankind becoming one great family and every caste distinction being utterly abolished.

Hence it is by no means correct to assert of modern Hinduism that it is essentially a non-proselytizing religion; accidentally it has become so, but only from concession to the prejudices of the outside world and in direct opposition to the tenets of its founders. Their initial success was necessarily due to their intense zeal in proselytizing; and was marvellously rapid. At the present day their followers constitute the more influential, and it may be even numerically the larger half of the Hindu population: but precisely as in Europe so in India no two men of the reformed sects, however immaterial their doctrinal differences, can be induced to amalgamate ; each forms a new caste more bigoted and exclusive than any of those which it was intended to supersede, while the founder has become a deified character, for whom it is necessary to erect a new niche in the very Pantheon he had laboured to destroy. The only point upon which all the Vaishnavas sects theoretically agree is the reverence with which they profess to regard the Bhagavad Gíta as the authoritative exposition of their creed. In practice their studies—if they study at all—are directed exclusively to much more modern compositions, couched in their own vernacular, the Braj Bháshá. Of these the work held in highest repute by all the Brindá-ban sects is the Bhakt-málá, or Legends of the Saints, written by Nábhá Ji in the reign of Akbar or Jahángir. Its very first couplet is a compendium of the theory upon which the whole Vaishnava reform was based :

Bkakt-bhakti-Bhagavant-guru, chatura nám, vapu ek :

which declares that there is a divinity in every true believer, whether learned or unlearned, and irrespective of all caste distinctions. Thus the religious teachers that it celebrates are represented, not as rival disputants—which their descendants have become—but as all animated by one faith, which varied only in expression ; and as all fellow-workers in a common cause, *viz.*, the moral and spiritual elevation of their countrymen. Nor can it be denied that the writing of many of the actual leaders of the movement are instinct with a spirit of asceticism and detachment from the world and a sincere piety, which are very different from the ordinary outcome of Hinduism. But in no case did this catholic simplicity last for more than a single generation. The great teacher had no sooner passed away than his very first successor hedged round his little band of followers with new caste restrictions, formulated a series of narrow dogmas out of what had been intended as comprehensive exhortations to holiness and good works ; and substituted for an interior devotion and mystical love—which were at least pure in intent, though perhaps scarcely attainable in practice by ordinary humanity—an extravagant system of outward worship with all the sensual accompaniments of gross and material passion.

The Bhakt-málá, though an infallible oracle, is an exceedingly obscure one, and requires a practised hierophant for its interpretation. It gives no legend at length, but consists throughout of a series of the briefest allusions to legends, which are supposed to be already well-known. Without some such previous knowledge the poem is absolutely unintelligible. Its concise notices have therefore been expanded into more complete lives by different modern writers, both in Hindí and Sanskrit. One of these paraphrases is entitled the Bhakt Sindhu, and the author, by name Lakshman, is said to have taken great pains to verify his facts. But though his success may satisfy the Hindu mind, which is constitutionally tolerant of chronological inaccuracy, he falls very far below the requirements of European criticism. His work is however useful, since it gives a number of floating traditions, which could otherwise be gathered only from oral communications with the Gosáins of the different sects, who, as a rule, are very averse to speak on such matters with outsiders.

The four main divisions, or Sampradáyas, as they are called, of the reformed Vaishnavas are the Srí Vaishnava, the Nimbárak Vaishnava, the Madhva Vaishnava, and the Vishnu Swámi. The last sect is now virtually extinct ; for though the name is occasionally retained, their doctrines were entirely remodelled in the sixteenth century by the famous Gokul Gosáin Vallabhácharya, after whom his adherents are ordinarily styled either Vallabhácháryas or Gokulastha Gosáins. Their history and tenets will find more appropriate place in connection with the town of Gokul, which is still their head-quarters.

The Srí Sampradáya was altogether unknown at Brindá-ban till quite recently, when the two brothers of Seth Lakhmi Chand, after abjuring the Jaini faith, were enlisted in its ranks, and by the advice of the Guru, who had received their submission, founded at enormous cost the great temple of Rang Jí.

AUTOTYPE.

THE SETH'S TEMPLE, BRINDÁ-BAN.

It is the most ancient and the most respectable of the four reformed Vaishnava communities, and is based on the teaching of Rámánuja, who flourished in the 11th or 12th century of the Christian era. The whole of his life was spent in the Dakhin, where he is said to have established no less than 700 monasteries, of which the chief were at Kánchi and Srí Ranga. The standard authorities for his theological system are certain Sanskrit treatises of his own composition entitled the Srí Bháshya, Gítá Bháshya, Vedártha Sangraha, Vedánta Pradípa and Vedánta Sára. All the more popular works are composed in the dialects of the south, and the establishment at Brindá-ban is attended exclusively by foreigners, the rites and ceremonies there observed exciting little interest among the Hindus of the neighbourhood, who are quite ignorant of their meaning. The sectarial mark by which the Srí Vaishnavas may be distinguished consists of two white perpendicular streaks down the forehead, joined by a cross line at the root of the nose, with a streak of red between. Their chief dogma, called Visishthádwaita, is the assertion that Vishnu, the one Supreme God, though invisible as cause, is, as effect, visible in a secondary form in material creation.

They differ in one marked respect from the mass of the people at Brindá-ban, in that they refuse to recognise Rádhá as an object of religious adoration. In this they are in complete accord with all the older authorities, which either totally ignore her existence, or regard her simply as Krishna's mistress and Rukmini as his wife. Their *mantra* or formula of initiation, corresponding to the *In nomine Patris*, &c., of Christian Baptism, is said to be *Om Rámáya namah*, that is, 'Om, reverence to Ráma.' This Sampradáya is divided into two sects, the Tenkalai and the Vadakalai. They differ on two points of doctrine, which however are considered of much less importance than what seems to outsiders a very trivial matter, *viz.*, a slight variation in the mode of making the sectarial mark on the forehead. The followers of the Tenkalai extend its middle line a little way down the nose itself, while the Vadakalai terminate it exactly at the bridge. The doctrinal points of difference are as follows : the Tenkalai maintain that the female energy of the god-head, though divine, is still a finite creature that serves only as a mediator or minister (*purusha-kára*) to introduce the soul into the presence of the Deity ; while the Vadakalai regard it as infinite and uncreated, and in itself a means (*upaya*) by which salvation can be secured. The second point of difference is a parallel to the controversy between the Calvinists and Arminians in the Christian Church. The Vadakalai, with the latter, insist on the concomitancy of the human will in the work of salvation, and represent the soul that lays hold of God as a young monkey which grasps its mother in order to be conveyed to a place of safety. The

Tenkalai, on the contrary, maintain the irresistibility of divine grace and the utter helplessness of the soul, till it is seized and carried off like a kitten by its mother from the danger that threatens it. From these two curious but apt illustrations the one doctrine is known as the *markata kishora-nyáya*, the other as the *márjála-kishora-nyáya*; that is to say 'the young monkey theory,' or 'the kitten theory.' The habitués of the Seth's temple are all of the Tenkalai persuasion.

The Nimbárak Vaishnavas, as mentioned in a previous chapter, have one of their oldest shrines on the Dhruva hill at Mathurá. Literally interpreted, the word Nimbárak means 'the sun in a *ním* tree;' a curious designation, which is explained as follows. The founder of the sect, an ascetic by name Bháskárá-chárya, had invited a Bairági to dine with him and had prepared everything for his reception, but unfortunately delayed to go and fetch his guest till after sun-set. Now, the holy man was forbidden by the rules of his order to eat except in the day-time and was greatly afraid that he would be compelled to practise an unwilling abstinence: but at the solicitation of his host, the sun-god, Súraj Náráyan, descended upon the *nim* tree, under which the repast was spread, and continued beaming upon them till the claims of hunger were fully satisfied. Thenceforth the saint was known by the name of Nimbárka or Nimbáditya. His special tenets are little known; for, unlike the other Sampradáyas, his followers (so far as can be ascertained) have no special literature of their own, either in Sanskrit or Hindi; a fact which they ordinarily explain by saying that all their books were burnt by Aurangzeb, the conventional *bête noire* of Indian history, who is made responsible for every act of destruction. Most of the solitary ascetics who have their little hermitages in the different sacred groves, with which the district abounds, belong to the Nimbárak persuasion. Many of them are pious, simple-minded men, leading such a chaste and studious life, that it may charitably be hoped of them that in the eye of God they are Christians by the baptism of desire, *i. e.*, according to S. Thomas Aquinas, by the grace of having the will to obtain salvation by fulfilling the commands of God, even though from invincible ignorance they know not the true Church. The one who has a cell in the Kokila-ban assured me that the distinctive doctrines of his sect were not absolutely unwritten (as is ordinarily supposed), but are comprised in ten Sanskrit couplets that form the basis of a commentary in as many thousands. One of his disciples, a very intelligent and argumentative theological student, gave me a sketch of his belief which may be here quoted as a proof that the esoteric doctrines of the Vaishnavas generally have little in common with the gross idolatry which the Christian Missionary is too often content to demolish as the equivalent of Hinduism. So far is this from being the case, that many of their dogmas are not only of an eminently philosophical character, but are also much less repugnant to Catholic truth than either the colourless abstractions of the Brahma Samáj, or the defiant materialism into which the greater part of Europe is rapidly lapsing.

Thus their doctrine of salvation by faith is thought by many scholars to have been directly borrowed from the Gospel; while another article in their creed, which is less known, but is equally striking in its divergence from ordinary Hindu sentiment, is the continuance of conscious individual existence in a future world, when the highest reward of the good will be, not extinction, but the enjoyment of the visible presence of the divinity, whom they have faithfully served while on earth; a state therefore absolutely identical with heaven, as our theologians define it. The one infinite and invisible God, who is the only real existence, is, they maintain, the only proper object of man's devout contemplation. But as the incomprehensible is utterly beyond the reach of human faculties, He is partially manifested for our behoof in the book of creation, in which natural objects are the letters of the universal alphabet and express the sentiments of the Divine Author. A printed page, however, conveys no meaning to anyone but a scholar, and is liable to be misunderstood even by him; so, too, with the book of the world. Whether the traditional scenes of Krishna's adventures have been rightly determined is a matter of little consequence, if only a visit to them excites the believer's religious enthusiasm. The places are mere symbols of no value in themselves; the idea they convey is the direct emanation from the spirit of the author. But it may be equally well expressed by different types; in the same way as two copies of a book may be word for word the same in sound and sense, though entirely different in appearance, one being written in Nágari, the other in English characters. To enquire into the cause of the diversity between the religious symbols adopted by different nationalities may be an interesting study, but is not one that can affect the basis of faith. And thus it matters little whether Rádhá and Krishna were ever real personages; the mysteries of divine love, which they symbolize, remain, though the symbols disappear; in the same way as a poem may have existed long before it was committed to writing, and may be remembered long after the writing has been destroyed. The transcription is a relief to the mind; but though obviously advantageous on the whole, still in minor points it may rather have the effect of stereotyping error: for no material form, however perfect and semi-divine, can ever be created without containing in itself an element of deception; its appearance varies according to the point of view and the distance from which it is regarded. It is to convictions of this kind that must be attributed the utter indifference of the Hindu to chronological accuracy and historical research. The annals of Hindustan date only from its conquest by the Muhammadans—a people whose faith is based on the misconception of a fact, as the Hindus' is on the corrupt embodiment of a conception. Thus the literature of the former deals exclusively with events ; of the latter with ideas.

At Báthi another Bairági of the same Sampradáya, by name Gobardhan Dás, who knew most of the Bhagavad Gíta by heart, told me that their chief seat was at Salimabad in Jodhpur territory, where the Gosáin had a complete library of the literature of the sect. He quoted some of the books by name, the Siddhánta Ratnanjali, the Girivajra, the Ratna-málá, the Setuká, the Jahnavi, and the Ratna-manjushá ; but he could not specify the authors, or give any definite information as to their contents. Neither could he give a clear explanation of any difference of doctrine between his own sect and the Srí Vaishnavas. Like Rám Dás, the Pandit at Kokila-ban, the great point on which he insisted was that all visible creation is a shadow of the Creator and is therefore true in a measure, though void of all substantial and independent existence. A view which is aptly represented by the lines :—

" The sun, the moon, the stars, the seas, the hills and the plains?
Are not these, O soul, the vision of him who reigns ?
Is not the vision He? tho' He be not that which He seems ?
Dreams are true while they last, and do we not live in dreams ?
All we have power to see is a straight staff bent in a pool :"

the illustration given in the last line being the very one which these Hindu dreamers most frequently bring forward.

The Madhva Vaishnavas form a scattered and not very numerous community, and none of their temples, either at Brindá-ban or elsewhere in the district, are of any note. Their founder, Madhváchárya, was a native of Southern India, born in the year 1199 A. D. The temple where he ordinarily resided is still in existence at a place called Udipi. Here he had set up a miraculous image of Krishna, made with the hero Arjun's own hands, which had been casually thrown as ballast into a ship from Dwáraká, which was wrecked on the Malabar coast. He is said to have been only nine years of age when he composed the Bhásha or commentary on the Gíta, which his disciples accept as of divine authority. Their distinctive doctrine is the assertion of an essential Duality (Dwaita) between the Jívatma, or principle of life, and the Paramátma, or Supreme Being. Their sectarial mark consists of two perpendicular white lines down the forehead, joined at the root of the nose and with a straight black streak between, terminating in a round mark made with turmeric.

In addition to these four original Sampradáyas, there are three schools of more modern origin, called respectively Bengali, or Gauriya Vaishnavas, Rádhá Vallabhis and the disciples of Swámi Hari Dás.

The first-named community has had a more marked influence on Brindá-ban than any of the others, since it was Chaitanya, the founder of the sect, whose immediate disciples were its first temple builders. He was born at Nadiya in Bengal, in 1485 A. D., and in his youth is said to have married a daughter of Vallabhácharya. However that may be, when he had arrived at the age of 24 he formally resigned all connection with secular and domestic affairs and commenced his career as a religious teacher. After spending six years in pilgrimages between Mathurá and Jagannáth, he finally settled down at the latter place, where, in 1527 A.D., being then only 42 years old, he disappeared from the world. There is reason to believe that he was drowned in the sea, into which he had walked in an ecstasy, mistaking it for the shallow waters of the Jamuná, where he saw, in a vision, Krishna sporting with the Gopís. His life and doctrines are recorded in a most voluminous Bengáli work entitled Chaitanya Charitámrita, composed in 1590 by one of his disciples, Krishna Dás. Two of his colleagues, Adwaitanand and Nityánand, who, like himself, are styled Mahá Prabhus, presided over his establishments in Bengal; while other six Gosáins settled at Brindá-ban. Apart from metaphysical subtleties, which naturally have but little hold on the minds of the populace, the special tenet of the Bengáli Vaishnavas is the all-sufficiency of faith in the divine Krishna; such faith being adequately expressed by the mere repetition of his name without any added prayer or concomitant feeling of genuine devotion. Thus roughly stated, the doctrine appears absurd; and possibly its true bearing is as little regarded by many of the more ignorant among the Vaishnavas themselves as it is by the majority of superficial outside observers. It is, however, a legitimate deduction from sound principles: for it may be presumed that the formal act of devotion would never have been commenced had it not been prompted at the outset by a devotional intention, which intention is virtually continued so long as the act is in performance. And to quote from a manual of a purer faith, "it is not necessary that the intention should be actual throughout; it is sufficient if we pray in a human manner; and for this only a virtual intention is required; that is to say, an intention which has been actual and is supposed to continue, although, through inadvertence or distraction, we may have lost sight of it."

The sectarial mark consists of two white perpendicular streaks down the forehead, united at the root of the nose and continued to near the tip. Another characteristic is the use of a rosary of 108 beads made of the wood of the *tulsi*.

The recognized leaders of the Brindá-ban community were by name Rúpa and Sanátana, the authors of several doctrinal commentaries and also, as is said, of the Mathurá Máhátmya. With them were associated a nephew, named Jíva, who founded the temple of Rádhá Dámodar, and Gopál Bhatt, founder of the temple of Rádhá Raman, together with some others of less note, whose names vary in different lists.* In the Bhakta Málá they are enumerated as follows :—

श्रीरूपसनातन भक्तिजल श्रीजीवगुसांई सर गंभीर ॥
वेला भजन सुपक्क कषायन कबहु न लागी ।
बृन्दाबन दृढ़वास जुगल चरनन अनुरागी ।
पोथी लेखनि पांनि अघट अचर चित दीनेा ।
सद ग्रंथन को सार सबे हस्तामल † कीनेा ।
संदेह ग्रंथ छेदन समर्थ रस राशि उपासिक परम धीर ।
श्रीरूपसनातन भक्तिजल श्रीजीवगुसांई सर गंभीर ॥ १ ॥

२

श्रीबृन्दाबन की माधुरी इनि मिलि आस्वादन कियेा ।
सरवस राधारमन भट्टगोपाल उजागर ।
हृषीकेश भगवान विपुलबीठल रस सागर ।
थानेश्वरी जगन्नाथ लोकनाथ महामुनि मधु श्रीरंग ।
कृष्णदास पण्डित उभै अधिकारी हरि अंग ।

* The Tuzúk mentions another famous Gosáin of somewhat later date, 1619 A. D., by name Jadu-Rúp, who came from Ujjaiyin to Mathurá, and who had been visited both by Akbar and Jahángir.

† *Hastámal* would be literally 'a plum in the palm of the hand,' that is to say, a little thing completely in one's grasp. A similar phrase occurs in the Rámáyana of Tulsi Das, Book I, 36. *Kartál-gat ámalak samán*.

घमण्डी जुगलकिशोर भृत्य भूगर्भ दृढ़ व्रत लियो ।
बृन्दाबन की माधुरी इनि मिलि आस्वादन कियो ॥ २ * ॥

Translation.

"Srí Rúpa and Sanátan and Srí Jíva Gosáin were as a deep lake filled with water of devotion. With them prayer was ever ripe and in season and never bitter to the taste. Firmly fixed at Brindá-ban, full of devotion to the feet of the dual god, with their hands writing books and with their soul fixed on the formless idea, they held in their grasp all the essence of divine love, able to resolve the mysteries of the scriptures, worshippers of the all-blissful, ever staunch in faith. Srí Rúpa and Sanátan and Srí Jíva Gosáin were as a deep lake filled with water of devotion.

"These are they who met together at Brindá-ban and tasted all its sweetness. Gopál Bhatt, who beautified the temple of Rádhá Raman with all that he possessed; Hrishikes and Bhagaván Dás and Bíthal-vipul, that ocean of grace: Jagannáth of Thanesar; the great sage Loknáth; Madhu and Srí Rang; the two Pandits named Krishan Dás, who had mastered Hari in all his parts; Ghamandi, servant of Jugal Kishor, and Bhúgarbha, the rigid ascetic. These are they who met together at Brindá-ban and tasted all its sweetness."

The founder of the Rádhá Vallabhis was by name Hari Vans. His father, Vyása, was a Gaur Bráhman of Deva-ban in the Saháranpur district, who had long been childless. He was in the service of the Emperor and on one occasion was attending him on the march from Agra, when at last his wife, Tára, gave birth to a son at the little village of Bád, near Mathurá, in the *Sambat* year 1559. In grateful recognition of their answered prayers, the parents named the child after the god they had invoked, and called him Hari Vans, *i.e.*, Hari's issue. When he had grown up, he took to himself a wife, by name Rukmini, and had by her two sons and one daughter. Of the sons, the elder, Mohan Chand, died childless; the descendants of the younger, Gopináth, are still at Devaban. After settling the daughter in marriage, he determined to abandon the world and lead the life of an ascetic. With this resolution he set out alone on the road to Brindá-ban and had reached Charthával, near Hodal, when there met him a Bráhman, who presented him with his two daughters and insisted upon his marrying them, on the strength of a divine command, which he said he had received in a vision. He further gave him an image of Krishna

* In the above passage the words underlined are proper names.

with the title of Rádhá Vallabh, which on his arrival at Brindá-ban was set up by Hari Vans in a temple that he had founded between the Jugal and the Koliya gháts on the bank of the Jamuná. Originally he had belonged to the Madhvácharya Sampradáya and from them and the Nimbáraks, who also claim him, his doctrine and ritual were professedly derived. But in consequence of the mysterious incident, by which he had been induced to forego his intention of leading a celibate life and take to himself two now wives ; or rather in consequence of his strong natural passions, which he was unable to suppress and therefore invented a fiction to excuse, his devotion was all directed not to Krishna himself, except in a very secondary degree, but to his fabled mistress Rádhá, whom he deified as the goddess of lust. So abominable a system was naturally viewed at first with no little amazement, as is clear from the language of the Bhakt Málá, which is as follows :—

॥ मूल ॥

श्रीहरिवंसगुसांई भजन की रीति सकृत कोउ जानि है ॥
श्रीराधाचरणप्रधान हृदे अति सदृढ़ उपासी ।
कुंजकेलि दंपति तहांकी करत षवासी ॥
सर्वसुमहाप्रसाद प्रसिधिता के अधिकारी ।
विधि निषेध नहि दास अनन्य उत्कंठ ब्रतधारी ॥
श्रीव्याससुवन पथ अनुसरै सोई भलें पहिचानि है ।
श्रीहरिवंसगुसांईं भजन की रीति सकृत कोउ जानि है ॥

TRANSLATION OF THE TEXT OF NÁBHA JÍ.

"The Gosáin Srí Hari Vans : who can understand all at once his method of devotion? with whom the feet of blessed Rádhá were the highest object of worship ; a most staunch-souled devotee ; who made himself the page in waiting on the divine pair in their bower of love ; who gloried in the enjoyment of the remnants of all that was offered at their shrine ; a servant who never pleaded obligation or dispensation ; a votary of incomparable zeal. Account him blessed who follows in the path of Vyása's great son, the Gosáin Srí Hari Vans ; who can understand all at once his method of devotion ?"

In the gloss, or supplement of Priya Dás, composed in the year *Sambat* 1769, the same sentiment is expanded and a reference made to the legend of the Bráhman and his two daughters.

॥ टीका ॥

श्रीजूकी रीति कोऊ लाषनिमें एक जानें
राधाई प्रधान मानें पाछें कृष्ण ध्याइये ।
निपट विकट भात होत न सुभाव ऐसो
उनही की कृपादृष्टि नेंकु किहूं पाईये ।
विधि औ निषेध छेद डारे प्रानप्यारे हियें
जियें निज दास निस दिन वहे गाईये ।
सुषद चरित्र सब रसिक विचित्र नीकें
जानत प्रसिद्ध कहा कहिके सुनाईये ।
आये ग्रह त्यागि राग बढ्यो प्रिय प्रीतम सों
विप्र बड़भाग हरिआज्ञा दई जानियें ।
तेरी उभय सुता व्याह देवो नाम मेरो
उनको जो वंस प्रसंस जग मांनियें ।
ताही द्वार सेवा विस्तार निज भगतनि को
भगतनिकी गति सो प्रसिद्ध पहिचांनियें ।
मांनि प्रिय बात ग्रह गह्यो सुष लह्यो सब
कह्यो कैसें जात यह मनमें न आंनियें ।
राधिकावल्लभलाल आज्ञा सो रसाल दई
सेवा मो प्रकास औ विलास कुंजधाम को ।
सोई विस्तार सुषसार दृगरूप पियो
दियो रसिक जिन लियो पछि वाम को ।
निसि दिन गांन रस माधुरी को पान उर
अंतर सिहांन एक काम स्यामास्याम को ।
गुन सो अनूप कहि कैसेंके सरूप कहैं
लहे मन मोद जैसें और नहीं नाम को ॥

TRANSLATION.

"Would you know the one point in a thousand of Sri Hit Ji's ways? he adored Rádhá first and after her Krishna. A most strange and unnatural fashion, that none could even faintly comprehend save by his favour. He obliterated all distinction between obligation and dispensation; his beloved was in his heart: he lived only as her servant, singing the praises of the divinity night and day. All the faithful know his many edifying and holy actions; why tell and repeat them, since they are famous already.

"He left his home and came; his passion for Rádhá and Krishna had so grown: but you must know Hari had given an order to a wealthy Bráhman: 'Bestow your two daughters in marriage, taking my name, and know that their issue shall be famous throughout the world. By their means my worship shall spread among my faithful people, a path for the pathless, of high renown.' Obedient to the loving order he went home; the delight of all was past telling, for it was more than the mind could even conceive. Rádhá's dear spouse gave the gracious command: 'Publish abroad my worship and the delights of my sylvan abode.' He drank in with his very eyes the essence of bliss and gave it to every client who supported the cause of the female divinity. Night and day imbibing the honeyed draught of sweet song and cherishing it in his soul, with no thought but for Syámá and Syám. How is it possible to declare such incomparable merit? the soul is enraptured at the sound more than at that of any other name."

By his later wives he had two sons, Braj Chand and Krishan Chand, of whom the latter built a temple to Rádhá Mohan, which is still in the possession of his descendants. The former was the ancestor of the present Gosáins of the temple of Rádhá Vallabh, the chief shrine of the sect. This was built by one of his disciples, a Káyath named Sundar Das, who held the appointment of treasurer at Delhi. One of the pillars in the front gives the date as *Sambat* 1683. An earlier inscription, of 1641, was noticed by Professor Wilson, but this would seem to have been over the gateway leading into the outer court, which since then has fallen down and been removed. On the opposite side of the street is a monument to the founder, which however the present generation of Gosáins are too ungrateful to keep in repair. They are the descendants of Braj Chand's four sons, Sundar-Bar, Rádhá Ballabh Dás, Braj-Bhúkhan and Nagar Bar Jí; and the heads of the four families so derived are now Daya Lál, Manohar Ballabh, Sundar Lál and the infant son of Kanhaiya Lál.

Hari Vans was himself the author of two poems; the one, the *Chaurási Pada*, or '84 Stanzas,' in Hindi; the other the *Rádhá Sudhá Nidhi*, or 'Treasury of Rádhá's Delights,' in 170 Sanskrit couplets. The latter, though not much read, is held in great esteem and, regarded solely as a piece of highly impassioned erotic verse, it is a spirited and poetic composition. There is a good Hindi commentary upon it by one Bansidhar, dated *Sambat* 1820. As MSS. are scarce and Sanskritists may like to see a specimen of the text, I subjoin the first 25 and the last couplet in the original, followed by a translation:—

॥ अथ राधासुधानिधिर्लिख्यते ॥

॥ श्लोक ॥

यस्याः कदापि वसनाञ्चलखेलनोत्थधन्यातिधन्यपवनेन कृतार्थमानी ।
योगीन्द्रदुर्गमगतिर्मधुसूदनोऽपि तस्या नमोऽस्तु वृषभानुभुवो दिशेऽपि ॥ १ ॥
ब्रह्मेश्वरादिसुदुरूहपदारविन्दश्रीमत्परागपरमाद्भुतवैभवायाः ।
सर्वार्थसाररसवर्षिकृपार्द्रदृष्टेस्तस्या नमोऽस्तु वृषभानुभुवो महिम्ने ॥ २ ॥
यो ब्रह्मरुद्रशुकनारदभीष्ममुख्यैरालक्षितो न सहसा पुरुषस्य तस्य ।
सद्योवशीकरणचूर्णमनन्तशक्तिं तं राधिकाचरणरेणुमहं स्मरामि ॥ ३ ॥
आधाय मूर्द्धनि यदापुरुदारगोप्यः काम्यं पदं प्रियगुणैरपि पिच्छमौलेः ।
भावोत्सवेन भजतां रसकामधेनु तं राधिकाचरणरेणुमहं स्मरामि ॥ ४ ॥
दिव्यप्रमोदरससारनिजाङ्गसङ्गपीयूषवीचिनिचयैरभिषेचयन्ती ।
कन्दर्पकोटिसरमूर्च्छितनन्दसूनुसञ्जीविनी जयति कापि निकुञ्जदेवी ॥ ५ ॥
तन्नः प्रतिक्षणचमत्कृतचारुलीलालावण्यमोहनमहामधुराङ्गभङ्गि ।
राधाननं हि मधुराङ्गकलानिधानमाविर्भविष्यति कदा रससिन्धुसारम् ॥ ६ ॥
यत्किङ्करीषु बहुशः खलु काकुवाणी नित्यं परस्य पुरुषस्य शिखण्डमौलेः ।
तस्याः कदा रसनिधेर्वृषभानुजायास्तत्केलिकुञ्जभवनाङ्गनमार्जनी स्याम् ॥ ७ ॥
वृन्दानि सर्वमहतामपहाय दूराद्वृन्दाटवीमनुसर प्रणयेन चेतः ।
सत्तारणीकृतसुभावसुधारसौघं राधाभिधानमिह दिव्यनिधानमस्ति ॥ ८ ॥

केनापि नागरवरेण पदे निपत्य सम्प्रार्थितैकपरिरम्भरसोत्सवायाः ।
सभ्रूविभङ्गमतिरङ्गनिधेः कदा ते श्रीराधिके नहि नहीति गिरः शृणोमि ॥ ९ ॥
यत्पादपद्मनखचन्द्रमणिच्छटाया विस्फूर्ज्जितं किमपि गोपवधूष्वदर्शि ।
पूर्णानुरागरससागरसारमूर्त्तिः सा राधिका मयि कदापि कृपां करोतु ॥ १० ॥
उज्जृम्भमानरसवारिनिधेस्तरङ्गैरङ्गैरिव प्रणयलोलविलोचनायाः ।
तस्याः कदानु भविता मयि पुण्यदृष्टिर्वृन्दाटवीनवनिकुञ्जगृहाधिदेव्याः ॥ ११ ॥
वृन्दावनेश्वरि तवैव पदारविन्दं प्रेमामृतैकमकरन्दरसौघपूर्णं ।
हृद्यर्पितं मधुपतेः स्मरतापमुग्रं निर्वापयत्परमशीतलमाश्रयामि ॥ १२ ॥
राधाकरावचितपल्लववल्लरीके राधापदाङ्कविलसन्मधुरस्थलीके ।
राधायशोमुखरमत्तखगावलीके राधाविहारविपिने रमतां मनो मे ॥ १३ ॥
कृष्णामृतं चल विगाढुमितीरिताहं तावत्सहस्व रजनी सखि यावदेति ।
इत्थं विहस्य वृषभानुसुते हि लप्स्येमानं कदा रसदकेलिकदम्बजातं ॥ १४ ॥
पादाङ्गुलीनिहितदृष्टिमपत्रपिष्णुं दूरादुदीक्ष्य रसिकेन्द्रमुखेन्दुबिम्बं ।
वीक्षे चलत्पदगतिं चरिताभिरामां झङ्कारनूपुरवतीं वत कर्हि राधाम् ॥ १५ ॥
उज्जागरं रसिकनागरसङ्गरङ्गे कुञ्जोदरे कृतवती नु मुदार जन्याम् ।
सुस्वापिताहि मधुनैव सुभोजिता त्वं राधे कदा स्वपिषि मत्करलालिताङ्घ्रिः ॥ १६ ॥
वैदग्ध्यसिन्धुरनुरागरसैकसिन्धुर्वात्सल्यसिन्धुरतिसान्द्रकृपैकसिन्धुः ।
लावण्यसिन्धुरमृतच्छविरूपसिन्धुः श्रीराधिका स्फुरतु मे हृदि केलिसिन्धुः ॥ १७ ॥
दृष्ट्वैव चम्पकलतेव चमत्कृताङ्गी वेणुध्वनिं क्व च निशम्य च विह्वलाङ्गी ।
सा श्यामसुन्दरगुणैरनुगीयमानैः प्रीता परिष्वजतु मां वृषभानुपुत्री ॥ १८ ॥
श्रीराधिके सुरतरङ्गिनितम्बभागे काञ्चीकलापकलहंसकलानुलापैः ।
मञ्जीरसिञ्जितमधुव्रतगुञ्जिताङ्घ्रिःपङ्केरुहैः शिशिरयस्व रसच्छटाभिः ॥ १९ ॥
श्रीराधिके सुरतरङ्गिणिदिव्यकेलिकल्लोलमालिनि लसद्वदनारविन्दे ।
श्यामामृताम्बुनिधिसङ्गमतीव्रवेगिन्यावर्त्तनाभिरुचिरे मम सन्निधेहि ॥ २० ॥

सत्प्रेमसिन्धुमकरन्दरसौघधारासारानजस्रमभितः स्रवदाश्रितेषु ।
श्रीराधिके तव कदा चरणारविन्दगोविन्दजीवनधनं शिरसा वहामि ॥ २१ ॥
सङ्केतकुञ्जमनु कुञ्जरमन्दगामिन्यादाय दिव्यमृदुचन्दनगन्धमाल्यम् ।
त्वां कामकेलिरभसेन कदा चलन्तीं राधे नु यामि पदवीमुपदर्शयन्ती ॥ २२ ॥
गत्वा कलिन्दतनयाविजनावतारमुद्वर्त्तयन्त्यमृतमङ्गमनङ्गजीवम् ।
श्रीराधिके तव कदा नवनागरेन्द्रं पश्यामि मग्ननयनं स्थितमुच्चनीपे ॥ २३ ॥
सत्प्रेमराशिसरसो विकसत्सरोजं स्वानन्दसिन्धुरससिन्धुविवर्द्धनेन्दुम् ।
तच्छ्रीमुखं कुटिलकुन्तलभृङ्गजुष्ट श्रीराधिके तव कदा नु विलोकयिष्ये ॥ २४ ॥
लावण्यसाररससारसुखैकसारे कारुण्यसारमधुरच्छविरूपसारे ।
वैदग्ध्यसाररतिकेलिविलाससारे राधाभिधे मम मनोऽखिलसारसारे ॥ २५ ॥
अद्भुतानन्दलोभश्चेन्नाम्ना रससुधानिधिः ।
स्तवोऽयं कर्णकलशैर्गृहीत्वा पीयतां बुधाः ॥ १०० ॥
इति श्रीवृन्दावनेश्वरीचरणकृपामात्रविजृम्भितश्रीहितहरिवंशगोस्वामिना
विरचिता श्रीराधारससुधानिधिः संपूर्णम् ॥ ० ॥

TRANSLATION.

1. "Hail to the home of Vrisha-bhánu's daughter, by whom once and again even Madhu-sudan—whose ways are scarce intelligible to the greatest sages—was made happy, as she playfully raised the border of her robe and fanned him with its delicious breeze.

2. "Hail to the majesty of Vrisha-bhánu's daughter, the holy dust of whose lotus feet, beyond the conception of Brahma, Siva and the other gods, is altogether supernaturally glorious, and whose glance moistened with compassion is like a shower of the refined essence of all good things.

3. "I call to mind the dust of the feet of Rádhiká, a powder of infinite virtue, that incontinently and at once reduces to subjection the great power, that was beyond the ken even of Brahma, Rudra, Sukadeva, Nárada, Bhíshma and the other divine personages.

4. "I call to mind the dust of the feet of Rádhiká, which the noble milk-maids placed upon their head and so attained an honour much desired by the

votaries of the god with the peacock crest, dust that like the cow of heaven yields the fullness of enjoyment to all who worship with rapturous emotion.

5. "Glory to the goddess of the bower, who with an embrace the quintessence of heavenly bliss, like a bountiful wave of ambrosia, sprinkled and restored to life the son of Nanda, swooning under the stroke of Love's thousand arrows.

6. "When will there visit us that essence of the ocean of delight, the face of Rádhá with sweet coy glances, bewildering us with the brilliance of ever twinkling sportive play, a store-house of every element of embodied sweetness?

7. "When shall I become the handmaid to sweep the court-yard of the bower of love for the all-blissful daughter of Vrisha-bhánu, among whose servants oft and again every day are heard the soft tones of the peacock-crested god?

8. "O my soul, leave at a distance all the host of the great, and affectionately hie to the woods of Brindá-ban: here Rádhá's name is as a flood of nectar on the soul for the beatification of the pious, a store-house of all that is divine.

9. "When shall I hear the voice of blessed Rádhá, that fountain of delights crying 'Nay, Nay,' with knitted brows, as some gallant suitor, fallen at her feet, begs for the rapturous joy of her embrace?

10. "When, oh when, will Rádhiká show me favour, that incarnation of the fullness of the ocean of perfect love, the marvellous glory of the glistening splendour of whose lotus feet was seen among the herdsmen's wives?

11. "When shall I attain to the blissful vision of the golddess of the blooming bowers of the woods of Brindá-ban, her eyes all tremulous with love, and the different members of her body like the waves of an overflowing ocean of delight?

12. "O queen of Brindá-ban, I betake me to thy lotus feet, fraught with the honeyed flood of love's ambrosia, which planted in Madhu-pati's heart, assuaged by their grateful coolness the fierce fever of desire.

13. "Fain would my soul loiter in the woods sacred to Rádhá's loves, where the sprays of the creepers have been plucked by Rádhá's hands, where the fragrant soil blossoms with Rádhá's footprints, and where the frequent birds are madly garrulous with Rádhá's praises.

14. "When, O daughter of Vrisha-bhánu, shall I experience the conceit induced by excess of voluptuous dalliance, I your handmaid, charged with the message, 'Come and enjoy Krishna's dainties,' and answered with the smile, 'Only stay, friend, till night comes.'

15. "Ah! when shall I behold Rádhá, with downcast eyes, bashfully stealing a distant glance at the moon-like orb of the face of the lord of lovers, as she trips with twinkling feet, all graceful in her movements, to the music of her own bangles?

16. "When, O Rádhá, will you fall asleep, while my hands caress your feet, after I have tenderly bathed you and fed you with sweet things, wearied with your vigil through a night of dalliance in the inmost bower, in the delicious embrace of your paragon of lovers?

17. "O that the ocean of wit, the singular ocean of love's delights, the ocean of tenderness, the ocean of exuberant pitifulness, the ocean of loveliness, the ocean of ambrosial beauty and grace, the ocean of wantonness, blessed Rádhiká, would manifest herself in my soul!

18. "O that the daughter of Vrisha-bhánu, looking up all tremulous and glistening in every limb like the flowering *champa*, would clasp me in her arms, charmed by my chanted praises of Syám-sundar, as she listens for the sound of his pipe!

19. "Blessed Rádhiká, cool me with the multiplicity of love that breathes in the swan-like melody of the girdle that binds your loins reddened with dalliance, and in the tinkling of the bangles, like the buzzing of bees, clustered round your sweet lotus feet.

20. "Blessed Rádhiká, wreathed with the surge of a Ganges wave of heavenly dalliance, with lovely lotus face and navel as a whirl in the stream, hastening on to the confluence with Krishna, that ocean of sweetness, draw near to me.

21. "When, O blessed Rádhiká, shall I rest upon my head your lotus feet, Govind's life and all, that ever rain down upon the faithful abundant torrents of the honeyed flood of the ocean of perfect love?

22. "When, O Rádhá, stately as an elephant in gait, shall I accompany you to the bower of assignation to show the way, bearing divinely sweet sandal wood and perfumes and spices, as you march in the excitement of love's rapture?

23. "O blessed Rádhá, having gone to some secluded slope of the Jamuná and there rubbing with fragrant unguents your ambrosial limbs, the very life of Love, when shall I see your prince of lusty swains, with longing eyes, mounted on some high *kadamb* tree?

24. "When, O blessed Rádhiká, shall I behold your heavenly face, clustered—as if with bees—with wanton curls, like some lotus blossoming in a lake of purest love, or a moon swelling an ocean of enjoyment, an ocean of delight.

25. "Ah! the name of Rádhá, perfection of loveliness, perfection of delight, sole perfection of happiness, perfection of pity, perfection of honeyed beauty and grace, perfection of wit, perfection of the rapturous joys of love, perfection of all the most perfect that my soul can conceive!

170. "O ye wise, if there be any one desirous of transcendental happiness, let him fill the pitcher of his ears and drink in this panegyric, called the *Rasa-sudhá-nidhi*, or 'Treasury of Love's delights."

The Hindu poem, the *Chaurási Pada*, is much more popular, and most of the Gosáins know at least some of its stanzas by heart. There is a commentary upon it by Lok-náth, dated *Sambat* 1855, and another in verse, called the *Rahasya artha-nirúpana* by Rasik Lal, written in *Sambat* 1734. Neither of the two, however, is of much assistance to the student; all the simple passages being paraphrased with wearisome prolixity, while real difficulties are generally skipped. I subjoin the text and translation of the first 12 stanzas:—

अथ श्रीहितहरिवंशकृतवाणी लिख्यते ॥

राग बिभास ॥

॥ १ ॥

जोई जोई प्यारौ करै सोई मोहि भावै
भावै मोहि जोई सोई सोई करैं प्यारे ।
मोकौं तौ भावती ठौर प्यारेके नैंननि मैं
प्यारौ भयौ चाहै मेरे नैंननिके तारे ।
मेरैं तौ तन मन प्राणहूं तैं प्रीतम प्रिय
अपने कोटिक प्राण प्रीतम मोसौं हारे ।
जै श्रीहित हरिवंश हंसहंसिनी सांवल गौर
कहौ कौंन करै जलतरंगनि न्यारे ॥

॥ २ ॥

प्यारे बोली भामिनी आजु नीकी जामिनी भेट नवी मेघमों दामिनी ॥
मोहन रसिकराइ री माई तासों जु मानु करै ऐसी कौन कामनी ॥
जै श्रीहितहरिवंश श्रवन सुनत प्यारी राधिकारवनसों मिली गजगामिनी ॥

॥ ३ ॥

प्रात समे दोऊ रस लंपट सुरत जुद्ध जेजुत अतिफूल ।
श्रमवारिज घन विंदु वदनपर भूषन अंगहि अंग विकूल ॥
कछु रह्यो तिलक सिथल अलकावलि वदनकमल मानों अलिभूल ।
जै श्रीहितहरिवंश मदनरंग रंगि रहे नैंन बैन कटि सिथल दुकूल ॥

॥ ४ ॥

आजु तो जुवती तेरो वदन आनंद भर्यो पियके संगमके सूचत सुषचैंन ।
आलस वलित बोल सुरंगरंगे कपोल विथकित अरुण उनींदे दोऊ नैंन ॥
रुचिर तिलक लेस किरत कुसुम केस सिर सीमंत भूषित मानों तैं न
करुणा करि उदार राषत कछू न सार दसन वसन लागत जब दैंन ॥
काहेकों दुरति भीर पलटे प्रीतम चीर बस किये स्यांम सिषे सत मैंन ।
गलित उरसि माल सिथल किंकिनीजाल जैश्रीहितहरिवंश लतागृह सैंन ॥

॥ ५ ॥

आजु प्रभात लतामंदिर में सुष वरषत अति हरष जुगल वर ।
गौरस्यांम अभिराम रंगरंगभरे लटकि लटकि पग धरत अवनि पर ॥
कुच कुमकुम रंजित मालावलि सुरतनाथ श्रीस्याम धामधर ।
प्रिया प्रेम के अंक अलंकृत चितृत चतुर सिरोमणि निजु कर ॥
दंपति अति अनुराग मुदित कल गान करत मन हरत परस्पर ।
जै श्रीहितहरिवंश प्रसंस परायन गाइन अलि सुर देत मधुरतर ॥

॥ ६ ॥

कौंन चतुर जुवती प्रिया जाहि मिलत लाल चोरह्वै रैंन ।
दुरवति क्यौंच दुरै सुनि प्यारे रंगमे गहले चैंनमैं नैंन ॥
उर नषचंद बिराने पट अटपट से बैंन ।
जै श्रीहितहरिवंश रसिक राधापति प्रमथित मैंन ॥

॥ ७ ॥

॥ राग विलावल ॥

आजु निकुंजमंजुमैं षेलत नवलकिशोर नवीन किशोरी ।
अति अनुपम अनुराग परस्पर सुनि अभूत भूतल पर जोरी ॥
विद्रुम फटिक बिविध निर्मित धर नवकर्पूरपराग न थोरी ।
कोमल किशलय सैंन सुपेसल तापर स्याम निवेसित गोरी ॥
मिथुन हासि परिहासि परायन पीक कपोल कमल पर झोरी ।
गौर स्याम भुज कलह मनोहर नीवी बंधन मोचत डोरी ॥
हरिउर मुकर बिलोकि अपुनपो बिभ्रम बिकल मानजुत भोरी ।
चिबुक सुचारु प्रलोइ प्रबोधित प्रिय प्रतिबिंब जनाइ निहोरी ॥
नेति नेति वचनामृत सुनि सुनि ललितादिक देषत दुरिचोरी ।
जै श्रीहितहरिवंश करत करधूनन प्रनय कोप मालावलि तोरी ॥

॥ ८ ॥

अतिहीं अरुण तेरे नैंन नलिन री ।
आलसजुत इतरात रगमगे भए निशिजागर मषिन मलिन री ॥
सिथल पलकमैं उठत गोलकगति बिधयो मोहन मृग सकत चलि न री ॥
जै श्रीहितहरिवंश हंसकलगामिनि संभम देत भंवरिनी अलीन री ॥

॥ ९ ॥

बनी राधा मोहनकी जोरी ।
इंद्रनीलमणि स्याम मनोहर सातकुंभ तन गोरी ॥
भाल विसाल तिलक हरि कामिनि चिकुरचंद विच रोरी ।
गज नाइक प्रभु चाल गयंदनि गति वृषभानु किसोरी ॥
नील निचोल जुवति मोहन पटपीती अरुण सिर खोरी ।
जै श्रीहितहरिवंश रसिक राधापति सु रत रंग में बोरी ॥

॥ १० ॥

आजु नागरीकिशोर भांवती विचित्र जोर
कहा कहौं अंग अंग परममाधुरी ॥
करत केलि कंठ मेलि बाहुदंड गंड गंड
परस सरस रासलास मंडली जुरी ।
स्यांम सुंदरी बिहार बांसुरी मृदंग तार
मधुर घोस नूपुरादि किंकिनी चुरी ।
जै श्री देषति हरिवंश आलि निर्तनी सुगंध चालि
वारि फेरिदेति प्राण देह सों दुरी ॥

॥ ११ ॥

मंजुल कल कुंजदेस राधाहरि विशदवेश
राकानभ कुमुदबंधु शरद जामिनी ।
स्यामलदुति कनकअंग विहरत मिलि एकसंग
नीरद मनी नील मध्य लसत दामिनी ।
अरुन पीत नव दुकूल अनुरागमूल
सौरभजुत सीत अनिल मंदगामिनी ।

किशलयदलरचित सैंन बोलत पिय चाटु बैंन
मान सहित प्रतिपद प्रतिकूल कामिनी ।
मोहनमन मथत मार परसत कुच नीवी हार
वेपथजुत नेति नेति वदत भामिनी ।
नरवाहन प्रभुसुकेल बहु बिधि भर भरत झेलि
सौरतरसरूपनदी जगतपावनी ॥

॥ १२ ॥

चलहि राधिके सुजान तेरे हित सुषनिधान
रासु रच्यो स्याम तट कलिंदनंदिनी ।
निर्तत जुगवतीसमूह रागरंग अतिकतूह
बाजत रसमूल मुरलिका अनंदिनी ।
बंसीबट निकट जंहां परमरमणभूमि तंहां
सकलसुषद मलय बहे वायु मंदिनी ।
जाति ईषदविकास कानन अतिसय सुवास
राकानिस सरदमास विमल चांदिनी ।
नरवाहन प्रभु निहार लोचन भरि घोषनारि
नषसिष सौंदर्य काम दुषनिकंदनी ।
विलसहु भुज ग्रीव मेल भामिनि सुषसिंधु झेलि
नव निकुंज स्याम केलि जगतबंदनी ॥

Translation of the first twelve Stanzas of the Chaurási pada.

I. "Whatever my Beloved doeth is pleasing to me; and whatever is pleasing to me, that my Beloved doeth. The place where I would be is in my Beloved's eyes; and my Beloved would fain be the apple of my eyes. My Love is dearer to me than body, soul, or life; and my Love would lose a thousand lives for me. Rejoice, Srí Hit Hari Vans! the loving pair, one dark, one fair, are like two cygnets ; tell me who can separate wave from water ?*

II. "O my Beloved, has the fair spoken ? this is surely a beautiful night ; the lightning is folded in the lusty cloud's embrace. O friend, where is the woman who would quarrel with so exquisite a prince of gallants ? Rejoice, Srí Hari Vans! dear Rádhiká hearkened with her ears and with voluptuous emotion joined in love's delights.†

III. "At day-break the wanton pair, crowned with victory in love's conflict, were all-exuberant. On her face are frequent beads of labour's dew, and all the adornments of her person are in disarray, the paint-spot on her brow is all but effaced by heat, and the straggling curls upon her lotus face resemble roaming bees. (Rejoice, Srí Hit Hari Vans!) her eyes are red with love's colours and her voice and loins feeble and relaxed.

IV. "Your face, fair dame, to-day is full of joy, betokening your happiness and delight in the intercourse with your Beloved. Your voice is languid and tremulous, your cheeks aflame, and both your weary eyes are red with sleeplessness ; your pretty *tilak* half effaced, the flowers on your head faded, and the parting of your hair as if you had never made it at all. The Bountiful one of his grace refused you no boon, as you coyly took the hem of your robe between your teeth. Why shrink away so demurely ? you have changed clothes with your Beloved, and the dark-hued swain has subdued you as completely as though he had been tutored by a hundred Loves. The garland on his breast is faded, the clasp of his waist-belt loose (Rejoice, Srí Hit Hari Vans!) as he comes from his couch in the bower.

V. "To-day at dawn there was a shower of rapture in the bower, where the happy pair were delighting themselves, one dark, one fair, bright with all gay colours, as she tripped with dainty foot upon the floor. Great Syám, the glorious lord of love, had his flower wreath stained with the saffron dye of her breasts, and was embellished with the scratches of his darling's nails ; she too was marked by the hands of her jewel of lovers. The happy pair in an ecstasy

---

* That is to say, it is nothing strange that Rádhá and Krishna should take such mutual delight in one another, since they are in fact one and are as inseparable as a wave and the water of which the wave is composed.

† The first line is a question put to Krishna by one of Rádhá's maids, asking him if her mistress had promised him an interview. The second line is a remark which she turns and makes to one of her own companions.

of affection make sweet song, stealing each other's heart (Rejoice, Sri Hit Hari Vans !) the bard is fain to praise, but the drone of a bee is as good as his ineffectual rhyme.

VI. "Who so clever, pretty damsel, whom her lover comes to meet, stealing through the night ? Why shrink so coyly at my words ? Your eyes are suffused and red with love's excitement, your bosom is marked with his nails, you are dressed in his clothes, and your voice is tremulous. (Rejoice, Srí Hit Hari Vans !) Rádhá's amorous lord has been mad with love.

VII. "To-day the lusty swain and blooming dame are sporting in their pleasant bower. O list ! great and incomparable is the mutual affection of the happy pair, on the heavenly* plain of Brindá-ban. The ground gleams bright with coral and crystal and there is a strong odour of camphor. A dainty couch of soft leaves is spread, on which the dark groom and his fair bride recline, intent upon the joys and delights of dalliance, their lotus cheeks stained with red streaks of betel juice. There is a charming struggle between dark hands and fair to loose the string that binds her skirt. Beholding herself as in a mirror in the necklace on Hari's breast, the silly girl is troubled by delusion and begins to fret, till her lover wagging his pretty chin shows her that she has been looking only at her own shadow. Listening to her honeyed voice, as again and again she cries 'Nay, nay,' Lalitá and the others take a furtive peep (Rejoice, Srí Hit Hari Vans !) till tossing her hands in affected passion she snaps his jewelled necklet.

VIII. "Ah, red indeed are your lotus eyes, lazily languishing and inflamed by night-long watch, and their collyrium all faded. From your drooping eyelids shoots a glance like a bolt, that strikes your swain as it were a deer and he cannot stir. (Rejoice, Srí Hit Hari Vans !) O damsel, voluptuous in motion as the swan, your eyes deceive even the wasps and bees.

IX. "Rádhá and Mohan are such a dainty pair, he dark and beautiful as the sapphire, she with body of golden lustre : Hari with a *tilak* on his broad forehead and the Fair with a *roli* streak amidst the tresses of her hair : the lord like a stately elephant in gait and the daughter of Vrishabhánu like an elephant queen : the damsel in a blue vesture and Mohan in yellow with a red *khaur* on his forehead (Rejoice, Srí Hit Hari Vans !) Rádhá's amorous lord is dyed deep with love's colours.

X. "To-day the damsel and her swain take delight in novel ways. What can I say ? they are altogether exquisite in every limb ; sporting

* *Abhút*, not created, self-produced, divine.

together with arms about each other's neck and cheek to cheek, by such delicious contact making a circle of wanton delight. As they dance, the dark swain and the fair damsel, pipe and drum and cymbal blend in sweet concert with the tinkling of the bangles on her wrists and ankles and the girdle round her waist. Srí Hit Hari Vans, rejoicing at the sight of the damsels' dancing and their measured paces, tears his soul from his body and lays them both at their feet.

XI. "The pavilion is a bright and charming spot; Rádhá and Hari are in glistening attire and the full-orbed autumnal moon is resplendent in the heaven. The dark-hued swain and nymph of golden sheen, as they toy together, show like the lightning's flásh and sombre cloud. In saffron vesture he and she in scarlet; their affection deep beyond compare; and the air, cool, soft and laden with perfumes. Their couch is made of leaves and blossoms and he woos her in dulcet tones, while coyly the fair one repulses his every advance. Love tortures Mohan's soul, as he touches her bosom, or waist-band, or wreath, and timorously she cries 'off, off.' Pleasant is the sporting of the glorious lord, close-locked in oft-repeated embrace, and like an earth-reviving river is the flood of his passion.

XII. "Come Rádhá, you knowing one, your paragon of lovers has started a dance on the bank of the Jamuna's stream. Bevies of damsels are dancing in all the abandonment of delight; the joyous pipe gives forth a stirring sound. Near the Bansi-bat, a sweetly pretty spot, where the spicy air breathes with delicious softness, where the half-opened jasmine fills the world with overpowering fragrance, beneath the clear radiance of the autumnal full moon, the milkmaids with raptured eyes are gazing on your glorious lord, all beautiful from head to foot, quick to remove love's every pain. Put your arms about his neck, fair dame, pride of the world, and lapped in the bosom of the Ocean of delight, disport yourself with Syám in his blooming bower."

If ever the language of the brothel was borrowed for temple use, it has been so here. But, strange to say, the Gosains, who accept as their Gospel these sensuous ravings of a morbid imagination, are for the most part highly respectable married men, who contrast rather favourably, both in sobriety of life and intellectual acquirements, with the professors of rival sects that are based on more reputable authorities. Several of them have a good knowledge of literary Hindi; but their proficiency in Sanskrit is not very high; the best informed among them being unable to resolve into its constituent elements and explain the not very recondite compound *suduruha,* which will be found in the second stanza of the Rádhá-sudhá.

To indicate the fervour of his passionate love for his divine mistress, Hari Vans assumed the title of Hít Jí and is popularly better known by this name than by the one which he received from his parents. His most famous disciple was Vyás Jí of Orchha, of whom various legends are reported. On his first visit to the Swámi he found him busy cooking, but at once propounded some knotty theological problem. The sage without any hesitation solved the difficulty, but first threw away the whole of the food he had prepared, with the remark that no man could attend properly to two things at once. Vyás was so struck by this procedure that he then and there enrolled himself as his disciple, and in a short space of time conceived such an affection for Brindá-ban that he was most reluctant to leave it even to return to his wife and children. At last, however, he forced himself to go, but had not been with them long before he determined that they should themselves disown him, and accordingly he one day in their presence took and ate some food from a scavenger's hand. After this act of social excommunication he was allowed to return to Brindá-ban, where he spent the remainder of his life and where his *samádh,* or tomb, is still to be seen.

Another disciple, Dhruva Dás, was a a voluminous writer and composed as many as 42 poems, of which the following is a list: 1, Jív-dasá; 2, Baidgyán; 3, Man-siksha; 4, Brindában-sat; 5, Bhakt-námávali; 6, Brihadbáman Purán; 7, Khyál Hulás; 8, Siddhánt Bichár; 9, Príti-chovani; 10, Anandashtak; 11, Bhajanáshtak; 12, Bhajan-kundaliya; 13, Bhajan-sat; 14, Sringár-sat; 15, Man-sringár; 16, Hit-sringár; 17, Sabha-mandal; 18, Ras-muktávali; 19, Ras-hirávali; 20, Ras-ratnávali; 21, Premávali; 22, Srí Priyá Jí kí námávali; 23, Rahasya-manjari; 24, Sukh-manjari; 25, Rati-manjari; 26, Neh-manjari; 27, Ban-bihár; 28, Ras-bihár; 29, Rang-hulás; 30, Rang-bihár; 31, Rang-binod; 32, Anand-dasa; 33, Rahasya-latá; 34, Anand-latá; 35, Anurág-latá; 36, Prem-latá; 37, Ras-ánand; 38, Jugal-dhyán; 39, Nirtya-bilás; 40, Dán-lila; 41, Mán-líla; 42, Braj-líla.

Other poems by different members of the same sect are the Sevak-báni, the Ballabh-rasik ki báni and the Guru-pratáp, by Dámodar Dás; the Hari-nám-mahimá by Dámodar Swámi; the Srí Rúp Lál Jí ka ashtaka, by Hit Ballabh; and the Hari-nám-beli, the Srí Lál Jí badhai and the Srí Lárili Jú ki badhai by Brindá-ban Dás.

The only one of the three more important modern schools which yet remains to be mentioned is that founded by Swámi Hari Dás. The Gosáins, his descendants, who now, with their wives and children, number some 500 persons, own one of the most conspicuous of the modern temples, which is dedicated to Krishna under his title of Bihári Ji, or in more popular phrase Bánke Bihári. This is not only their head-quarters, but appears to be the only temple in all India of which they have exclusive possession. It has lately been rebuilt at a cost of Rs. 70,000; a sum which has been raised in the course of 13 years by the contributions of their clients from far and near. It is a large square red sandstone block of plain, but exceedingly substantial, character, with a very effective central gateway of white stone. This has yet to be completed by the addition of an upper story; but even as it stands, the delicacy of its surface carving, and the extremely bold projection of its eaves, render it a pleasing specimen of the style of architecture now in vogue at Brindá-ban—one of the few places in the civilized world where architecture is not a laboriously studied reproduction of a dead past, but a still living art, which is constantly developing by a process of spontaneous growth. The estate is divided into two shares or *bats*, according to the descent of the Gosáins. Their founder was himself a celibate; but his brother Jagannáth had three sons, Megh Syám, Murári Dás and Gopináth Dás, of whom the third died childless, the other two being the ancestors of the present generation. As is usual in such cases, the two families are at war with one another, and have more than once been obliged to invoke the assistance of the law to prevent a serious breach of the peace. Beyond the saintliness of their ancestor, but few of them have any claim to respect, either on account of their learning—for the majority of them cannot even read—or for the correctness of their morals. There are, however, two exceptions to the general rule—one for each *bat*—in the person of the Gosáins Jagadís and Kishor Chand; both of whom are fairly well read, within the narrow limits of their own sectarian literature, beyond which they have never dreamed of venturing.

In the original Bhakt-málá of Nábhá Jí, the stanza referring to Hari Dás stands as follows:

मूल ।

आशधीर उद्योत कर रसिक छाप हरिदास की ॥
जुगलनामसों नेंम जपत नित कुंजबिहारी ॥
अविलोकत रहैं केलि सखी सुखको अधिकारी ॥

गांनकला गंधर्व श्यांमश्यांमाकों तोर्षे ॥
उत्तम भोग लगाय मोर मरकट तिमि पोर्षे ॥
नृपति द्वार ठाढ़े रहें दरशन आशा जास की ॥
आशधीर उद्योत कर रसिक छाप हरिदास की ॥

which may be thus translated:

"Tell we now of Hari Dás, the pride of Ásdhír, who sealed the list of the saints; who, bound by a vow to the perpetual repetition of the two names of Kunj-bihári, was ever beholding the sportive actions of the god, the lord of the Gopís' delights; who was a very Gandharv in melodious song and propitiated Syám and Syámá, presenting them with the daintiest food in daily sacrifice and feeding the peacocks and monkeys and fish; at whose door a king stood waiting in hope of an interview; Hari Dás, the pride of Ásdhír, who sealed the list of the saints."

This is followed by the Gloss, or Supplement of Priya Dás:

टीका ।

श्री स्वामी हरिदास रसराशि को बषांनि सकै
रसिकताकी छाप कोई जाप मधि पाई है ॥
ल्यायो कोऊ चोवा वाको अति मन भावा वामे
डार्यो ले पुलनि यह षोवा हिय आइये ॥
जांनिकै सुजांन कही ले दिषावों लालप्यारे
नैंशिकु उघारे पट सुगंध बुड़ाइये ॥
पारशपषांन करि जल उरवाइ दियो
कियो तव शिष्य ऐसें नाना विधि गाइये ॥

which may be thus rendered:

"Who can tell all the perfections of Srí Swámí Hari Dás, who by ever muttering in prayer the sacred name came to be the very seal of devotion. Some one brought him perfume that he valued very highly; he took and threw it down on the bank; the other thought it wasted. Said the sage, knowing his thoughts: 'Take and show him the god:' he slightly raised the curtain; all was drenched with perfume. The philosopher's stone he cast into the water, then gave instruction: many are the legends of the kind."

Probably few will deny that at least in this particular passage the disciple is more obscure than his master; and the obscurity, which is a sufficiently prominent feature in the English translation, is far greater in the Hindi text, where no indication is given of a change of person, and a single form answers indifferently for every tense of a verb and every case of a noun. The Bhakt-Sindhu expands the two stanzas into a poem of 211 couplets and supplies a key to all the allusions in the following detailed narrative:

Brahm-dhír, a Sanádh Bráhman of a village now called Haridáspur, near Kol, had a son, Gyándhír, who entertained a special devotion for Krishna under his form of Giridhári—'the mountain-supporter'—and thus made frequent pilgrimages to the holy hill of Gobardhan. On one such occasion he took to himself a wife at Mathurá, and she in due time bore him a son, whom he named As-dhír. The latter eventually married a daughter of Gangá-dhar, a Bráhman of Rájpur—a small village adjoining Brindá-ban—who on the 8th of the dark fortnight of the month of Bhádon in the *sambat* year 1441 give birth to Hari Dás. Form his earliest childhood he gave indications of his future sanctity, and instead of joining in play with other children was always engaged in prayer and religious meditation. In spite of his parents' entreaties he made a vow of celibacy, and at the age of 25 retired to a solitary hermitage by the Mán Sarovar, a natural lake on the left bank of the Jamuná, opposite Brindá-ban. He afterwards removed to the Nidh-ban in that town, and there formally received his first disciple, Bithal-Bipul, who was his own maternal uncle. His fame soon spread far and wide, and among his many visitors was one day a Khattri from Delhi, by name Dayál Dás, who had by accident discovered the philosopher's stone, which transmuted into gold everything with which it was brought in contact. This he presented as a great treasure to the Swámí, who however tossed it away into the Jamuná ; but then seeing the giver's vexation, he took him to the margin of the stream and bade him take up a handful of sand out of the water. When he had done so, each single grain seemed to be a facsimile of the stone that had been thrown away and, when tested, was found to possess precisely the same virtue. Thus the Khattri was made to understand that the saints stand in no need of earthly riches, but are complete in themselves ; and he forthwith joined the number of Hari Dás's disciples.

Some thieves, however, hearing that the sage had been presented with the philosopher's stone, one day when he was bathing, took the opportunity of stealing his *sálagrám*, which they thought might be it. On discovering it to be useless for their purpose, they threw it away under a bush, and as the saint in his search for it happened to pass by the spot, the stone itself found voice to tell him where it lay. From that time forth he received every morning by miraculous agency a gold coin, out of which he was to provide the temple-offerings (*bhog*) and to spend whatever remained over in the purchase of grain wherewith to feed the fish in the Jamuná and the peacocks and monkeys on its banks.

One day a Káyath made him an offering of a bottle of *atar* worth Rs. 1,000, and was greatly mortified to see the Swámí drop it carelessly on the ground, so that the bottle was broken and the precious essence all wasted. But on being taken to the temple he found that his gift had been accepted by the god, for the whole building was fragrant with its perfume.

Again, a minstrel at the court of the Dehli Emperor had an incorrigibly stupid son, who was thereupon expelled in disgrace. In his wanderings he happened to come to Brindá-ban, and there threw himself down on the road to sleep. In the early morning the Swámí, going from the Nidh-ban to bathe, stumbled over him, and after hearing his story gave him the name of Tán-sen, and by the mere exercise of his will converted him at once into a most accomplished musician. On his return to Delhi, the Emperor was astonished at the brilliancy of his performance, and determined himself to pay a visit to Brindá-ban and see the master under whom he had studied. Accordingly, when he was next at Agra, he came over to Mathurá, and rode out as far as Bhat-rond—half-way—whence he proceeded on foot to the Nidh-ban. The saint received his old pupil very graciously, but took no notice of his royal companion, though he knew perfectly well who he was. At last, as the Emperor continued begging that he might be of some service, he took him to the Bihári ghát close by, which for the nonce appeared as if each one of its steps was a single precious stone set in a border of gold; and there showing him one step with a slight flaw in it, asked him to replace it by another. This was a work beyond the capacity even of the great Emperor, who thereupon contented himself with making a small endowment for the support of the sacred monkeys and peacocks and then went his way after receiving a most wearisome amount of good advice.

No further incident is recorded in the life of Hari Dás, the date of whose death is given as *Sambat* 1537. He was succeeded as Mahant by his uncle Bithal-Bipul; and he by Bihári Dás. The latter was so absorbed in enthusiasm that a Sárasvat Bráhman, of Panjábí extraction, by name Jagannáth, was brought over from Kol to administer the affairs of the temple; and after his death the succession was continued through several other names, which it seems unnecessary to transcribe.

Thus far the narrative of the Bhakt-Sindhu; which, it will be seen, affords an explanation of the obscure allusions in the Bhakt-Málá to the two presentations of the *atar* and the philosopher's stone, the daily feeding of the monkeys and peacocks and the Emperor's visit. In other matters, however, it is not at all in accord with the traditions accepted by the Swámí's descendants; for they say that he was not a Sanádh by caste, but a Sárasvat; that his family came not from Kol or Jalesar, but from Uchch near Multán, and that he lived not four centuries ago, but at the most only three. It would seem that the author of the Bhakt-Sindhu was the partisan of a schism in the community, which occurred about 50 years or so ago, and that he has moulded his facts accordingly; for the Jagannáth whom he brings over from Kol is not named in a genuine list of the Mahants, which will be given hereafter. That he is utterly at fault in his dates, *Sambat* 1441—1537, is obvious at a glance; for the Emperor who visited Brindá-ban was certainly Akbar, and he did not ascend the throne till *Sambat* 1612. It is true that Professor Wilson, in his Religious Sects of the Hindus, where he mentions Hari Dás, describes him as a disciple and faithful companion of Chaitanya, who was born in 1485 and died in 1527 A.D. But although Hari Dás had imbibed the spirit of Chaitanya's teaching, I know of no ground for maintaining that there was any personal intercourse between the two; had it been so, that fact would scarcely have escaped record in the Bhakt-Málá or some one of its modern paraphrases. Moreover, I have by me a small *pothi* of 680 leaves, which gives a complete list of all the Mahants and their writings from the founder down to the date of the MS., which is *Sambat* 1825. The list is as follows: Swámi Hari Dás, Bithal Bipul, Bihárini Dás, Nágari Dás, Saras Dás, Naval Dás, Narhar Dás, Rasik Dás, and Lalit-Kishori, otherwise called Lalit-mohani Dás. Allowing 20 years for each incumbency, which is rather a high average, since only an elderly man would be elected for the post, the date of Hari Dás's death is thrown back only as far as *Sambat* 1665. His writings, moreover, are not more archaic in style than the poems of Tulsi Dás, who died in *Sambat* 1680; and therefore on all grounds we may fairly conclude as an established fact that he flourished at the end of the 16th and the beginning of the 17th century A. D., in the reigns of the Emperors Akbar and Jahángir.

Each of the Mahants named in the above list is described as being the disciple of his immediate predecessor, and each composed some devotional poems, which are known as *sakhis*, *chaubolas*, or *padas*. The most voluminous writer is Bihárini Dás, whose *padas* occupy 684 pages. In many of them he expresses the intensity of his mystical devotion in terms of exaggerated warmth, which are more suggestive of an earthly than a divine passion. But the short extract that follows is of a different character, and is of special interest as confirming the conclusion already stated as to the date of Hari Dás; since it mentions by name both the Emperor Akbar and also the death of his famous friend Birbar, which occurred in 1590 A.D.

॥ राग गोरी ॥

कहा गर्वै रे मृतक नर ॥
स्वांन स्यार को खान पांन तन ऎंठि चलत रे निलज निडर ॥
यहे अवधि बहु विदित जग बांभन बड़े भये बीरबर ॥
मरत दूष्यो हियो न जियो कियो न सहाइ साहि अकबर ॥
स्वासन निकसत* सुर असुर राखे रोंथि† काल करतर ॥
इतहि न उतहि बीचही भूल्यो है फिरत कोंन के थर ॥
सुखद सरन हरिचरनकमल भजि बादि फिरत भटकत घरघर ॥
श्रीबिहारीदास हरिदास विपुलबल लटकि लग्यो संग सर्वोपर ॥

TRANSLATION.

"Why boastest thou thyself, O mortal man? thy body shall be the prey of dogs and jackals, though without shame or fear thou now goest delicately. This is known throughout the world to be the end of all: a great man was the Bráhman Bírbar, yet he died, and at his death the Emperor Akbar was sad of heart, nor himself longer lived nor aught availed. When gods or demons breathe out their life, Death holds them in his maw, suspended, neither here nor there, but in an intermediate state. All astray and swelling with pride, on whom is thy trust? Adore Hari's blessed lotus feet; to roam and wander about from house to house is all vanity. By the strong aid of Hari Dás, Bihárini Dás has found and laid hold of the Almighty."

The founder of the sect has himself left only two short poems, filling 41 leaves, entitled *Sádháran Siddhánt* and *Ras ke pada*. The former is here given both in the original text and in a translation. Most of the habitués of the

---

* One MS. for *svasan nikasat* reads *tras nikasi na sakat*.

† *Ronthna* has the same meaning as the more common term *jugáli karná*, 'to ruminate,' like a cow.

temple know the greater part of it by heart, though I have ascertained that very few of them have more than the vaguest general idea of the meaning. Even the best-informed of the Pujáris—Kishori Chand—who went over it carefully with me, supplied an interpretation of some passages which after consulation with other Pandits I could see was quite untenable and was obliged to reject. The connection of ideas and the grammatical construction are often so involved that it is highly probable my version may still be not altogether free of errors, though I have done my best to eliminate them. The doctrine inculcated does not appear to differ in any essential point from the ordinary teaching of the other Vaishnava sects: the great duties of man, by the practice of which he may have an assured hope of attaining to ultimate salvation, being defined as submission to the divine will, detachment from the world, and an unquestioning faith in the mystery of the incarnation.

॥ ० ॥ अथ श्रीस्वामीहरिदासजीकृत साधारणसिद्धांत लिष्यते ॥ ० ॥

॥ रागविभास ॥

ज्योंही ज्योंही तुम राषतहो त्योंही त्योंही रहियतहे हो हरि ॥
और तो अचरचे पाय धरों सुतो कहो कोन के पेंड भरि ॥
जद्यप हों अपनो भायो कियो चाहों कैसें करि सकों जो तुम राषो पकरि ॥
श्रीहरिदास के स्वांमी श्यामाकुंजबिहारी
पिंजरा के जनावर लों तरफराय रहो उड़िवेकों कितोक करि ॥ १ ॥
काहूको बस नांहि तुम्हारी कृपातें सब होय श्रीबिहारी बिहारनि ॥
और मिथ्याप्रपंच काहेकों भाषिये सो तो है हारनि ॥
जाहि तुमसों हित तासों तुम हित करो सब सुषकारनि ॥
श्रीहरिदासके स्वांमी श्यांमाकुंजबिहारी प्रांननिके आधारनि ॥ २ ॥
कबहूं कबहूं मन इत उत जातें याते अब कोंन है अधिक सुष ॥
बहुत भांति नयत आंनि राष्यो नाहितो पाव तो दुष ॥
कोटि कामलावन्य बिहारी तातें मुहांचुहीं सब सुष लियें रहत रुष ॥
श्रीहरिदासके स्वांमी श्यांमाकुंजबिहारी दिन देषत रहों विचित्र मुष ॥ ३ ॥

हरि भजि हरि भज छांड़ि न मान नर तन को ॥
जिन बंछेरे जिन बंछेरे तिलतिल धनकों ॥
अनमागें आगें आवेगो ज्यों पल लागें पलकों ॥
कहि हरिदास मीच ज्यों आवे त्यों धन है आपुनको ॥ ४ ॥

॥ राग विलावल ॥

हे हरि मोसों न बिगारनकों तोसों न संह्मारनकों मोहि तोहि परी होड़ ॥
कोंनधों जीते कोंनधों हारे परिबदी न छोड़ ॥
तुम्हारी मायाबाजी पसारी विचित्र मोहे मुनि काके भूले कोड़ ॥
कहि हरिदास हम जीते हारे तुम तहु न तोड़ ॥ ५ ॥
बंदे अषत्यार भला ॥
चित न डुलाव आव समाधि भीतर न होहु अगला ॥
न फिर दरदर पदरदर न होहु अधला ॥
कहि हरिदास करता किया सो हुवा सुमेर अचल चला ॥ ६ ॥
हित तो कीजे कमलनैंनसों जा हित के आगें और हित के लागे फीको ॥
के हित कीजे साधुसंगतसों ज्यों कलमषि जाय जीको ॥
हरिको हित ऐसो जेसो रंग मजीठ ॥
संसार हित ऐसो जेसो रंग कसूम दिन दुतीको ॥
कहि हरिदास हित कीजे बिहारीसों और निवाहू जीको ॥ ७ ॥
तिनका बयार के बस ॥
ज्यों भावे त्यों उड़ाय लेजाय आपने रस ॥
ब्रह्मलोक शिवलोक और लोक अस ॥
कहे श्रीहरिदास बिचार देषो बिना बिहारी नाहिं जस ॥ ८ ॥
संसार समुद्र मनुष्य मीन नक्र मगर और जीव बहुबंदसि ॥
मन बयार प्रेरे सनेहफंद फंदसि ॥

लोभ पिंजरा लोभी मरजिया पदारथचारि खंदखंदखि ॥
कहि हरिदास तेई जीव पारभये जे गहि रहे चरन आनंदनंदसि ॥ ९ ॥
हरि के नामको आलस कित करत है रे काल फिरत सर सांधे ॥
बेर कुबेर कछू नहि जानत चढ्यो फिरत है कांधे ॥
हीरा बहुत जवाहिरसंचे कहा भयो हस्ती दरबांधे ॥
कहि श्रीहरिदास महलमें बनिता बनठाढ़ी भई ॥
तब कछु न चलत जब आवत अंतकी आंधे ॥ १० ॥
देषे इनि लोगन की लावनि ॥
बूझत नाहिं हरिचरनकमलकों मिथ्या जन्म गंवावनि ॥
जब जमदूत आय घेरतहै करत आप मनभावनि ॥
कहे श्रीहरिदास तबही चिरजीवे कुंजबिहारी चितावनि ॥ ११ ॥
मन लगाय प्रीति कीजे कर करवासों ब्रजवीथिन दीजे सोहनी ॥
बृंदाबनसों बनउपबनसों गुंजमाल हाथ पोहनी ॥
गो गोसुतनसों मृगी मृगसुतनसों और तन नेंक न जोहनी ॥
श्रीहरिदासके स्वांमी श्यामां कुंजबिहारी सों चित ज्यो सिरपर दोहनी ॥ १२ ॥

॥ राम कल्यान ॥

हरिको असोई सब खेल ॥
मृगतृष्णा जग व्यापि रह्यो है कहूं बिजौरो न बेलि ॥
धनमद जोवनमद राजमद ज्यों पंछिन में डेल ॥
कहे श्रीहरिदास यहे जिय जानों तीरथकोसो मेल ॥ १३ ॥
माई धनि वे मृगी जे कमलनैंनकों पूजित अपनें अपनें भरतारन सहित ॥
धनि वे गाइवछ वेई जे वंशरस पीवत श्रवन दोंना ज्यों जाइ न बहत ॥
पंछीन होंहिं मुनिजन जेते केते सेवहि दिन काम क्रोध लोभ रहित ॥
सुनि श्रीहरिदास हमारे पति ते कठिन न जान दें हये राषत गहत ॥ १४ ॥

॥ राग बरारी ॥

लाल मेरे दूधकी दोहनी ॥
मारग जात गहि रह्यो री अंचरा मेरो, नाहिन देतहों बिना बोहना ॥
नागरि गूजरि ठगिलीनो मेरा लाल गोरोचनको तिलक माथे मोहना ॥
श्रीहरिदासके स्वामी इहां ऐसोई न्याव है या नगरी जिन बसौ री सोहनी ॥ १५ ॥

॥ राग कान्हरो ॥

झूठी बात सांची करि दिषावतहौ हरि नागर ॥
निसि दिन बुनत उधेरतहौ जाय प्रपंचको सागर ॥
ठाठ बनाय धर्‌यो मिहरीको है पुरुषतें आगर ॥
सुनि हरिदास यहै जिय जानौं सुपनेंकोसो जागर ॥ १६ ॥
जगतप्रीति करि देषी नाहि नेंग टीको कोऊ ॥
छपपति रंकलौं देषे प्रकृति बिरोध न बन्यो कोऊ ॥
दिन जु गये बहुत जन्मनके ऐसो जावो जिन कोऊ ॥
सुनि हरिदास मीत भलो पायो बिहारी ऐसे पावो सब कोऊ ॥ १७ ॥
लोग तो भूल्यो भले भूल्यो तुम मति भूलो मालाधारी ॥
आपनो पति छांड़ि औरनिसौं रति ज्यौं दारनिमें दारी ॥
स्याम कहत जे जीव मोतें बिमुष जोकों जिन दूसरी करडारी ॥
कहि हरिदास जग्य देवता पितरनकौं श्ररधा भारी ॥ १८ ॥
जोलो जीवे तोलो हरि भज रे मन और बात सब बादि ॥
द्योस चारके हलाभला में तू कहा लेगो लादि ॥
धनमद जोवनमद राजमद भूल्यो नगर बिवादि ॥
कहि श्रीहरिदास लोभ चरपटभयो काहेकी लगे फिरादि ॥ १९ ॥
प्रेमसमुद्ररूपरस गहिरे कैसे लागे घाट ॥
बेकार्‌योदे जानि कहावत जानिपन्यो की कहा परी बाट ॥

काहूको सर सूधो न परै मारत गाल गलीगली हाट ॥
कहि श्रीहरिदास जानि ठाकुर बिहारी तकत न ओटपाट ॥ २० ॥

॥ इति श्रीस्वामी हरिदासजीकृत साधारणसिद्धांत के पद संपूर्णम् ॥

TRANSLATION OF THE SIDDHÁNTA OF SWÁMÍ HARI DÁS.

Rág Bibhás.

1. "O Hari, as thou disposest, so all things abide. If I would shape my course in any different fashion, tell me whose tracks could I follow. If I would do my own will, how can I do it, if thou holdest me back? (The lords of Srí Hari Dás are Syámá and Kunj-bihári). Put a bird in a cage, and for all its fluttering it cannot get away.

2. "O Bihári, Bihárini, none else has any power; all depends on your grace. Why babble of vain systems of happiness? they are all pernicious. To him who loves you, show love, bestowers of happiness (the lords of Srí Har Dás are Syámá and Kunj-bihári), the supporters of all living creatures.

3. "At times the soul takes flight hither or thither; but it finds no greater joy. Discipline it in every way and keep it under, or you will suffer. Beautiful as a myriad Loves is Bihári; and Pleasure and all delights dwell in his presence (the lords of Srí Hari Dás are Syáma and Kunj-bihári) be ever contemplating his manifold aspects.

4. "Worship Hari, worship Hari, nor desert him out of regard for thy mortal body. Covet not, covet not the least particle of wealth. It will come to you unsought, as naturally as one eyelid droops upon the other. Says Srí Hari Das, as comes death, so comes wealth, of itself (*or* like death, so is wealth—an evil).

Rág Bilávalí.

5. "O Hari, there is no such destroyer as I am, and no such restorer as thou art:* betwixt me and thee there is a contest. Whichever wins or loses, there is no breaking of the condition. Thy game of illusion is wide-spead in diverse ways: saints are bewildered by it and myriads are led astray. Says Hari Dás, I win, thou losest, but there is no change in thy love.

---

* For a similar expression of the same sentiment compare the following lines of Súr Dás; *Mere pápan so, Hari, hari hau—Main garua, tum men bal thora, sákakh hí pichimari hau.* 'O Hari, you are vanquished by my sinfulness; I am so heavy and you so slight, that you get badly thrown.'

6. " O ye faithful, this is a good election : waver not in mind ; enter into yourselves in contemplation and be not stragglers. Wander not from house to house, nor be in doubt as to your own father's door. Says Srí Hari Dás, what is God's doing, is as fixed as Mount Sumeru has become.

7. " Set your affection on the lotus-eyed, in comparison with whose love all love is worthless ; or on the conversation of the saints : that so the sin of your soul may be effaced. The love of Hari is like the durable dye of the madder ; but the love of the world is like a stain of saffron that lasts only for two days. Says Hari Dás, set your affection on Bihári, and he knowing your heart will remain with you for ever.

8. " A straw is at the mercy of the wind, that blows it about as it will and carries it whither it pleases. So is the realm of Brahma, or of Siva, or this present world. Says Srí Hari Dás : this is my conclusion, I have seen none such as Bihári.

9. " Man is like a fish in the ocean of the world, and other living creatures of various species are as the crocodiles and alligators, while the soul like the wind spreads the entangling net of desire. Again, avarice is as a cage, and the avaricious as divers, and the four objects of life as four compartments of the cage. Says Hari Dás, those creatures only can escape whoever embrace the feet of the son of bliss.

10. " Fool, why are you slothful in Hari's praises ? Death goeth about with his arrows ready. He heedeth not whether it be in season or out of season, but has ever his bow on his shoulder. What avail heaps of pearls and other jewels and elephants tied up at your gate ? Says Srí Hari Dás, though your queen in rich attire await you in her chamber, all goes for nothing when the darkness of your last day draweth nigh.

11. " See the cleverness of these people: having no regard for Hari's lotus feet, their life is spent to no purpose ; when the angel of death comes and encompasses them he does what seemeth him good. Says Srí Hari Dás : then is he only found long-lived, who has taken Kunj-bihári to his soul.

12. " Set your heart upon securing his love. With water-pot in hand perambulate the ways of Braj and, stringing the beads of your rosary, wander through Brindá-ban and the lesser groves. As a cow watches her own calf and a doe its own fawns and has an eye for none other (the lords of Srí Hari Das are Syámá and Kunj-bihári) be your meditation on them as well balanced as a milk-pail on the head.

Rág Kalyán.

13. "All is Hari's mere sport, a mirage pervading the universe without either germ or plant. The pride of wealth, the pride of youth, the pride of power, are all like the crow among birds. Says Srí Hari Dás, know this of a surety, all is but as a gathering on a feast-day, that is quickly dispersed.

14. "O sister, how happy are the does who worship the lotus-eyed, each with her own lord. Happy too the calves that drink in the melody of his pipe in their ears as in a cup from which no drop can be spilt. The birds too are like holy men, who daily do him service, free from lust, passion, and avarice. Hearken, Srí Hari Dás, my husband is a difficulty ; he will not let me go, but holds me fast.

Rág Barári.

15. "O friend, as I was going along the road, he laid hold of my milk-pail and my dress ; I would not yield to him unless he paid me for luck. 'O clever milk-maid, you have bewitched my boy with the lustre of the *go-rochan* patch on your forehead' (O lord of Srí Hari Dás), this is the justice we get here ; do not stay in this town, pretty one.*

Rág Kanhrau.

16. "O clever Hari, thou makest the false appear true ; night and day thou art weaving and unweaving ; thou art an ocean of deceit. Though thou affectest the woman † in form and name, thou art more than man. Hearken ye all to Hari Dás and know of a truth it is but as when one wakes out of sleep.

17. "The love of the world has been tested ; there is no real accord. See, from the king to the beggar, natures differ and no match can be found. The days of many births are past for ever ; so pass not thou. Hearken to Hari Dás, who has found a good friend in Bihári ; may all find the like.

18. "People have gone astray ; well they have gone, but take thy rosary and stray not thou. To leave thy own lord for another is to be like a strumpet among women. Syámá declares: those men rebel against me who prefer another, and those too (says Hari Dás) who make great sacrifice to the gods and perform laboured funeral rites for departed ancestors.‡

---

* In two of the three MSS. of the poem that I have consulted, stanzas 14 and 15 are omitted and they appear clearly to be an interpolation by some later hand, being quite out of keeping with the context. They must be regarded as a dialogue between two of the Gopis and Jasoda.

† In this stanza it is the god's illusive power, or Maya, that is addressed, rather than the god himself.

‡ Thus the Vaishnavas, when they perform a Sráddh, do not repeat the names of their own ancestors, but substitute the names of Krishna, Pradyumna, and Aniruddh.

19. "Worship Hari from the heart as long as you live ; all things else are vain. It is only a matter of four* days, what need of much baggage. From pride of wealth, from pride of youth, from pride of power, you have lost yourself in mere village squabbles. Says Hari Dás, it is greed that has destroyed you ; where will a complaint lie.

20. "In the depth of the delights of an ocean of love how can men reach a landing-place? Admitting his helplessness† he cries, What way of escape is open? No one's arrows fly straight, for all his boasting in street and market-place. Says Srí Hari Dás : know Bihári to be a god who overlooks all defects in his votaries."

The Malúk Dásis, another modern sect of limited importance, have one of their religious houses at Brindá-ban, with a temple dedicated to Rám Jí, near the Kesi ghát. Their founder, according to the most probable tradition, lived in the reign of Aurangzeb, and was a trader by occupation. He is said to have written a Hindi poem called the *Dasratna*, together with a few short *Sákhis* and *Padas* in the same language ; but no specimen of his composition has ever been published, nor is it known what, if any, are the distinctive tenets of the sect. Probably, they will be found to differ in no material respect from the doctrines of faith and quietism as inculcated by Hari Dás ; though, an important practical difference consists in the recognition of Ráma, rather than Krishna, as the incarnation to be specially worshipped. I had intended to visit their Guru and collect from him the materials for a brief sketch of their history and literature, in order to complete this chapter ; but unfortunately I neglected to do so while at Mathurá, and have now lost the opportunity of supplying the omission.

Another small and obscure sect, that of the Prán-náthis, is again one of the few, of whose literature Professor Wilson, in his essays on the religion of the Hindus, was unable to furnish a specimen. The sect has a single representative at Mathurá, and from him, before I left, I obtained a copy of one of the poems of Prán-náth himself.

It is very curious, both from the advanced liberalism of its theological ideas and also from the uncouthness of the language, in which the construction of the sentences is purely Hindi, while the vocabulary is mainly supplied from

* The number 'four' seems to be an allusion to the four stages of life : childhood, youth, manhood, and old age.

† The word *bekárgau* is doubtful and probably corrupt, though given in all three MSS.

Persian and Arabic sources. The writer, a Kshatriya by caste, lived at the beginning of the eighteenth century, and was under the special patronage of Chhattrasál, the famous Rájá of Panna in Bundelkhand, who is commonly said by the Muhammadans to have been converted to Islám, though in reality he only went as far as Prán-náth, who endeavoured to make a compromise between the two religions. His followers are sometimes called Dhamis, from *Dhám*, a name of the supreme spirit, or Parmátmá, and like the Sikhs and several of the later Hindu sects are not idolators, so far that they do not make or reverence any image of the divinity, but if they have any temple at all, the only object of religious veneration which it contains is a copy of the works of the founder. His treatises, which, as usual, are all in verse, are fourteen in number, none of them of very great length, and bear the following titles :—1, The book of Rás ; 2, of Prakás ; 3, of Shat-rit ; 4, of Kalas ; 5, of Sanandh ; 6, of Kirantan ; 7, of Khulássa ; 8, of Khel-bat ; 9, of Prakrama Illáhi Dulhan (an allegory in which the Church, or 'Bride of God,' is represented as a holy city) ; 10, of Ságar Singár ; 11, of Bare Singár ; 12, of Sidhi Bhása ; 13, of Márafat Ságar ; 14, of Kiyámat-náma. The shortest is the last, of which I now proceed to give the text, followed by an attempt at a translation, which I am afraid is not altogether free from error, as I am not much versed in Kuranic literature and may have misunderstood some of the allusions. The owner of the MS., Karak Dás by name, though professing so liberal a creed, was not a particularly enlightened follower of his master, for I found it impossible to convince him that the Isa of the Kurán, so repeatedly mentioned by Prán-náth, was really the same as the incarnate God worshipped by the English. Like most of the Bairágis and Gosáins with whom I have talked, his idea was that the fiery and impetuous foreign rulers of the country were Súraj-bansis, or descendants of the sun, and that the sun was the only God they recognized, as was evidenced by their keeping the Sunday holy in his honour.

But, without further preface, to proceed to the text of the poem. It stands as follows :—

॥ श्रीहरि ॥

षास उमत सु कहियो जाई उठो मोमिनो क्यामत आई ॥
केहेतीहु माफक कुरांन तुमारे आगे कहूं बयांन ॥ १ ॥
जो कोइ षास उमत सिरदार षड़े रहो हो हुसियांर ॥
वसियतनामे देवे सांष अग्यारैं सदी होसी बेबाक ॥ २ ॥

बरकत दुनियां और कुरान   और फकीरोंकी मेंहेरबांन ॥
ए दरगाहसे आये बयांन   जबराइल लेजासी मकांन ॥ ३ ॥
तिन दिन होसी अंधा धुंध   द्वार तोबाके होसी बंध ॥
कह्या होसो और रेवेस   तब कोइ किसी का नाही बेस ॥ ४ ॥
अब कहो जी बाकी क्या रह्या   निसान क्यांमतका जाहेर कह्या ॥
पातसाह इसा बरस चालीस   लिषा सिपारे अठाईस ॥ ५ ॥
क्यां हिंदु क्यां मुसलमान   सब येकठोर ल्यांवे इमांन ॥
सो क्या होसी उठे कुरांन   ये बिचार देषों चित आंन ॥ ६ ॥
नवसे नवे हुए बितीत   तब हजरत इसा आए इत ॥
सो लिख्यां ग्यारें सिपारे मांहे   मे षिलाफ बात कहुगा नाहे ॥ ७ ॥
रूहअलां पेहेने जामे दोये   लिख्यां कुरांने सोइ होये ॥
ए लिख्यां छठे सिपारे मांहे   षोषे वाला जाये देषो ताहे ॥ ८ ॥
ए जो बरस इसाकी काही   तिनकी तपसीर करदेउ सही ॥
दस अग्यारें बारेके तीस   इसा पातसाह बरस चालीस ॥ ६ ॥
सातर बरस और जो रहें   सो तो पुल सरातके कहे ॥
मोंमिन चले बिजली की न्यांत   मुतकई भी घोड़ेकी भांत ॥ १० ॥
और जाहेरी उमन जो रही   इस बिध तिंनकों दोजक कही ॥
पुलसरात कही षंडेकी धार   गिरे कटे नही पावे पार ॥ ११ ॥
अरंमियतसलूनमें कह्या ये   ये जाये देषो दिल दे ॥
ये जाहेर कह्या बयान   हिरदे अंधे न सके पेहेचान ॥ १२ ॥
दसइ इसां अग्यारें इमांम   बारे सदीमे फजर तमांम ॥
ये लिख्या बीच सिपारे आम   तीसमां सिपारा कों नांम ॥ १३ ॥
आयेइसामहंमदऔर इमांम   सबकोइ आए करो सलाम ॥
पर ना देषें आंषों जाहेरी   दिल दिदो देषो चित धरी ॥ १४ ॥

अजाजीले देष्या वजूद तो आदमकों नकि सजूद ॥
सेजदे कीये तिन बेहद सो सारही हुए रद ॥ १५ ॥
जो उनने देष्या आकार तोलागी लानत हुआ षुआर ॥
तव अजाजीले माग्यां वचंन के आदंम मेरा हुआ दुसमन ॥ १६ ॥
उनकी ओलादकी मारों राह सवोंके दिलपर होंउ पातसाह ॥
आदम अजाजीलसु येसी भई आंठमे सिपारे जाहेर कही ॥ १७ ॥
फेर तुम लेत वाहींकी अकल पर क्यां करो तुम जो वाहीकी नसल ॥
तुम दजाल वाहेर ढूढत वह दीलपर वेंठा लें लानत ॥ १८ ॥
उपर मांएने ना होवे पेहेचांन ये तुम सुनियो दिलके कांन ॥
हमेसा आवतहे जूं अव भी फेर आयेहे त्यूं ॥ १९ ॥
सव पेगंवर जहूद षिलके बीच देषो दोदे दिलके ॥
ओतो आया हिंदुओ दरम्यांन जिनकु तुम केहेते कुफरांन ॥ २० ॥
तुम ढूंढो अपने षिलके मांहे तामे तो साहेव आयां नाहे ॥
जिनकों केहेते कांफर जात सो सवकी करसी सिफात ॥ २१ ॥
रव ना रषे किसीका गुमांन ओतो गरीवोपर मेहेरवांन ॥
परदा लिष्या हजरतके रोये पर तिनकी क्यां तुमको नाही षवर ॥ २२ ॥
परदा लिष्या वास्ते हिंदुओ मांहे पढ़े इसारत पावे नाहे ॥
जो देषतहे जेर जवर सो हकीकत पावें क्योंकर ॥ २३ ॥
येसी हिंदुओ की कही सिफत आषर हिंदूओ में मुलकनवुवत ॥
ओर आप हजरत सालतपनाह सोतो जहूद फकीरो मे पातसाह ॥ २४ ॥
पांचमे सिपारे येह वयांन न मानों सो जाये देषों कुरांन ॥
ओर हिंदुवी कितावो मेयो कही वुधकलंकी आवेगा सही ॥ २५ ॥
ओयेके करसी येकरस मसरक मगरव होसी वस ॥
कोईकहेसीदोउक्याहोसीयेकवेर तिनका भी करदेउ नवेर ॥ २६ ॥

सो इसारत बोले निज बुध   विना हादी ना पाईये सुध ॥
घोड़े कों लिख्या कलंकीकर   ताकी किनकों नहीं षवर ॥ २७ ॥
जोतक कहे विजया अभेंनंद   सब कलजुगको करसी निकंद ॥
अंजीर कहें इसा बुजरक   सो आयेके सीझ हक ॥ २८ ॥
जहूद कहे मुसा वड़ा होये   ताके हाथ छुटे सब कोये ॥
सारीने रसम जुदी कर रही   सब बुजरकी घनी की कही ॥ २९ ॥
युं उरझे जुदे नांम धर   रव आलंमकी आया आषर ॥
अपनी अपनी समझे सव   जुदा न रह्या कोइ अव ॥ ३० ॥
सब किताबो दइ साष   जुदे नाम जुदी लिषी भांष ॥
सत असत दोउ जुदे कीये   माया ब्रंह्म चीन्हा येके दीये ॥ ३१ ॥
दोनो जहांनमे थी उरझन   करम काउ सरियत चलंन ॥
करी हकीकत मारफत रोसंन   साफ कीये आसमांन धरंन ॥ ३२ ॥
ब्रंह्माउको भानों मेलाय   सब जहांनकों कियो मिलाय ॥
गुहाइ षुदाकी षुदाइ देवे   करे बयान हुकंम सिर लेवे ॥ ३३ ॥
सब पूजसी साहेब सरत   कलांमअलां यु केहें वत ॥
ये लिषा तीसरे सिपारे   बोले अरस अजीमके द्वारे ॥ ३४ ॥
ललतकदर के तीन तकरार   तीसरी फजरमे कारगुजार ॥
रूहे फिरस्ते वजूद धरे   लेलतकदर के माहे उतरे ॥ ३५ ॥
येर उतरी महीने हजार   गिरो दोउ भइ सिरदार ॥
हुकंम दिया साहेव इनके हाथ   भइ सलामती इनके साथ ॥ ३६ ॥
केती गुहाई देउ कुरांन   इनाइजूलनामेराह व्रयान ॥
तीसरी तकरार की भइ फजर   ग्यारें सदी मे देषोगे नजर ॥ ३७ ॥
ओर पेहेले सिपारे मे जो लिख्यां   सो तुमे क्या नाही देख्यां ॥
साहेदी कुंनकी देवे जोये   षास उमतका कहीये सोये ॥ ३८ ॥

अब बोकोइ होवे बांस उमत देउ गुहाइ हो सावत ॥
उठाये गलफतहीये सावधांन छोडो पढ़ो का! गुमान ॥ ३९ ॥
इकलम्राकीन श्रोर सुनी बोये पेहले इमांन लयेवेगा सोये ॥
पीछे जाहेर हेसी साहेब तब तो इमांन ल्यावेगेसब ॥ ४० ॥
भिस्त दोजक जाहेंर भई नफा किसी कान देवे कोई ॥
ले हिरदे हादीके पाये छत्रसाल यु कहे ब़जाये ॥ ४१ ॥

TRANSLATION.

The Day of Judgment.

"Go tell the chosen people; arise ye faithful, the day of judgment is at hand. I speak according to the Kurán and make my declaration before you. All ye heads of the chosen people, stand up and attend. The Testament (*Wasiyat-náma*)* gives evidence: Eleven centuries shall be completed after the blessing of the world by the Kurán and by him who was merciful to the poor. A voice shall come from the tabernacle and Gabriel† shall take them to the appointed place. For three days, there shall be gloom and confusion, and the door of repentance shall be closed. And what? shall there be any other way?‡ Nay, no one shall be able to befriend his neighbour.§

"Say now what shall be the duration of this life, and what the clear signs of the coming of the last day. Christ shall reign for forty years, as is written in the 28th Sípára. Hindus and Musalmans shall both alike bring their creed to the same point. And what shall come about, when the Kurán has thus been taken away? this is a matter which I would have you now attentively consider.

"When 991 years are past, then the Lord Christ will come. This is written in the 11th Sípára: I will not quote a word wrongly.‖ The spirit of God

* *Wasiyat-náma* is, I believe, a general name, including both the Kurán and the Hadís, which together make up the Muhammadan rule of faith; but I have not been able to trace the particular tradition, to which reference is here made, as specifying the exact number of years that are to elapse before Christ's second coming.

† Gabriel is accounted God's ordinary messenger: but here, I should rather have looked for Isráfíl, whose duty it will be to sound the trumpet at the last day.

‡ *Reves* may possibly stand for *ravish.*

§ *Khes* is for *khwesh*, 'a kinsman.'

‖ In spite of this emphatic assertion, the quotation would appear to be incorrect, for the 11th Sípára contains no such prophecy.

(*i.e.*, Christ) shall be clothed in vesture of two different kinds ; so it is stated in the Kurán. This is in the 6th Sípára ; whoever doubts me may see it there for himself. These now are the years of Christ, as I am going to state in detail. Take ten, eleven, and twelve thirty times (that it is say $10+11+12\times30=990$). Then Christ shall reign 40 years. The other 70 years that remain (after $990+40$, to make up 1,100) are for the bridge Sírát. The saints will cross it like a flash of lightning ; the pious with the speed of a horse ; but as for the merely nominal believers who remain, for them there are 10 kinds of hell ;* the bridge Sírát is like the edge of a sword, they fall or they get cut in pieces—none cross over. This is stated in the *Ámiyat Salúm* ; go and look at it carefully. The statement is clear, but your heart is too blind to see it. Christ stands for 10,† the Imám for 11, and in the 12th century, then shall be the perfect day-break. This is written in the Ám Sípára, which is the 30th.

"When Christ, Muhammad, and the Imám are come, every one will come and bow before them. But you should see not with the eyes of the body, but, after reflection, with the eyes of the soul. Azázíl saw in person, but would not bow to Adam. Though he had done homage times without number, it all went for nothing. When they saw his pride,‡ the curse was pronounced and he became an outcast. Then Azázíl asked a boon: 'Adam has become my enemy. I will pervert the ways of his descendants and reign in the hearts of them all.' Thus it was between Adam and Azázíl, as is clearly stated in the 8th Sípára. You take after him in sense, but what can you do, since you are his offspring. You look for Dajjál § outside, but he sits at your heart, according to the curse.

"You have not understood the meaning of the above ; listen to me now with the ears of the spirit. In like manner as He has always come, so will He come again. All the Prophets have been of Jewish race—look through them with the eyes of the soul—that is, they have sprung from the midst of Hindus, whom you call Káfirs. Search now among your own people ; the Lord has never been born among them. The races whom you call heathen will all be sanctified through him. The Lord thinks scorn of no man, but is compassionate to all who are humble. A veil is said to be over the Lord's face. What ? do you not know this ? By the veil is meant 'among Hindus ;' mere

---

* This is the Hindu computation ; the Muhammadans reckon only seven hells.

† This is intended to explain the curious calculation given above, 'ten, eleven, and twelve multiplied by thirty.'

‡ *Ákár* here would seem to stand for *Ahankár*.

§ *Dajjál*, here the spirit of evil generally, is properly the name of anti-Christ.

reading does not convey the hidden intention ; if you look only to the letter, how can you grasp the spirit? Thus is declared the glory of the Hindus, that the last of the Prophets shall be of them. And the Lord Christ, that great Prophet, was the king of the poor Jews. This is stated in the 5th Sípára ; if you do not believe me, go and examine the Kurán yourself. It is also stated in the Hindu books that Budh Kalanki will assuredly come. When he has come, he will make all alike ; east and west will both be under him. Some one will say, 'will both be at once?' this, too, I will clear up, explaining the intention to the best of my ability ; without a guide you would not get at the truth. Kalanki, it is said, will be on a horse—this every one knows—and astrologers say that Vijayábhinand will make an end of the Kalijug. Now, the Gospel says that Christ is the head of all and that he will come and do justice. The Jews say that Moses is the greatest and that all will be saved through him. All follow different customs and proclaim the greatness of their own master. Thus idly qarrelling they fix upon different names ; but the end of all is the same, the supreme God. Each understands only his own language, but there is no real difference at bottom. All the scriptures bear witness that there are different names in different languages ; but truth and untruth are the two incompatibles, and Maya and Brahm have to be distinguished from one another. In both worlds there was confusion ; some walking by the law of Hindu, others by the law of Muhammadan ceremonial. But knowledge has revealed the truth and made clear both heaven and earth : as the sun has made manifest* all creation and harmonized the whole world, so the power of God bears witness to God ; he speaks and all obey. All who perform acts of religious worship do them to the Lord ; the word of the Most High has declared it so. It is written in the third Sípára that he opened the gates of the highest heaven.

"The Lalit-ul-kadr (*or* night of power) has three contentions : on the third dawn the judgment will commence. The spirits and angels will appear in person, for it was on that night that they descended:† the blessings of a thousand months descended also. The chiefs will be formed into two companies ; God will give them his orders and through them there shall be salvation.

---

* For *Khaláya* I propose to read *Khulaya* ; but even so the meaning elicited is not very satisfactory.

† The allusions are to the chapter of the Kurán called the Súrat-ul-kadr, which is as follows : "Verily we have caused the Kurán to descend on the night of power. And who shall teach thee what the night of power is? The night of power exceedeth a thousand months ; therein descend the angels and the spirit by permission of their Lord in every matter ; and all is peace till the breaking of the morn."

This is abundantly attested by the Kurán ; the statement is in the *Iná anzal ná* chapter. After the third contention will be the dawn ; in the eleventh century it will be seen.

And what is written in the first Sípára ? You must have seen that. They who accept the text *kun** are to be called true believers. Now, if any one is a true believer, let him bear witness and prove the fact. Put off sloth ; be vigilant ; discard all pride of learning. He who hears with perfect faith † will be the first to believe. Afterwards, when the Lord has been revealed, all will believe. Heaven and hell will be disclosed, and none will be able to profit another. Lay your soul at your master's feet ; this is what Chhatrasál tells you."

From the doctrine as laid down by Prán-Náth, that any one religion is as true as another, it is easy to advance to the conclusion that all religions are equally false. This is the view taken in the 'Byom Sár' and 'Suni Sár,' two short poems written in the time of Thákur Daya Rám of Háthras, by one of his retainers, named Bakhtáwar. Their purport is to show that all is vanity and that nothing, either in earth or in heaven, either visible or invisible, natural or supernatural, has any real existence. Several of the lines are almost literally translated from the Sanskrit Vedánta Sára of Sadánanda Parivrajakácharya, from which it would seem that the author, for all his atheism, did not contemplate any pronounced rupture with Hindu orthodoxy. He can scarcely be said to have founded a sect, though Professor Wilson speaks of his followers under the name of Sunya-vádis ; but in every age of Hinduism there have been a few isolated individuals, such as Jábáli and Chárváka, to whom such notions have recommended themselves. The following extracts are taken from a manuscript in the possession of Rájá Hari Náráyan Singh, the present representative of the chief, under whose patronage the poems were composed.

Commencement of the Byom Sár.

ब्योमसार यह ग्रंथ है लयो वेद को सार   श्रीठाकुर दयाराम यह कीनो ब्योम बिचार ॥ १ ॥
इत जमुना इत सुरसरी मध्य हाथरस जानि   अंतरवेद सु भूमि है करै अघन की हानि ॥ २ ॥
श्रीठाकुर दयाराम तहं नृपता करै अखंड   ताको जसु परताप पुनि छाय रह्यो नव खंड ॥ ३ ॥
बैरिनि के उर सालु है मित्रन को सुखकंद   बढ़ै सदां परतापु पुनि जिमि द्वितीया को चंद ॥ ४ ॥

*The text *kun* is the parallel of the Mosaic phrase, "and God said 'let there be light,' and there was light."

†*Ha -ul-Yakin*, 'perfect faith' is faith without seeing, which alone is meritorious ; for all who see must perforce believe.

बख़तावर जन आनि कैं कर्यो तहां पुनि वास श्रीठाकुर किरपा करी जानि आपनो दास ॥ ५ ॥
तिन की कृपा कटाक्ष तें उपज्यो हीयें हुलास ब्योम ज्ञान वरनन कह्यो अनुभव के परगास ॥ ६ ॥
ब्योम रूप सब जानियो है ब्योमहि के मांहि ज्यों आपुहि में देखिये आपु आपना छांहि ॥ ७ ॥
श्रीठाकुर यह आपुही मथि मथि काढ्यो सार तिनही के उपदेश सुनि मैं यह कह्यो बिचार ॥ ८ ॥
यही ज्ञान की सैंन तुम सज्जन है सुनि लेउ पहलें याकों समझिकें पाछें उत्तर देउ ॥ ९ ॥
आदि सबनि की पोलितें अंत पोलि ठहराइ मध्यहु में पुनि पोलि है सत गुरु दई बताइ ॥ १० ॥
सब तें ऊंची पोलि है सब तें नीची पोलि मध्यहु में पुनि पोलि है सत गुरु कहि दई खोलि ॥ ११ ॥
पोलहि में उपजै सबै पोलहि में बिनसंत पोल कहत आकाश सों ताको आदि न अंत ॥ १२ ॥
आद न जाको है कछू अंत न कबहूं होइ सदां एक रस रहत है पोलि कहावै सोइ ॥ १३ ॥

"This book is called the Byom Sár and contains the essence of the Vedas, excogitated by Srí Thákur Dayá Rám. Between the Jamuná and the Sursari, (*i. e.*, the Ganges) stands Háthras in the midst, in the holy land of Antarbed, where nought ill can thrive. There Thákur Dayá Rám holds undisturbed sway, the fame of whose glory has spread through the whole universe—a thorn in the breast of his enemies, a root of joy to his friends, ever growing in splendour like the crescent moon. One Bakhtáwar came and settled there and was favoured by the Thákur, who recognized his fidelity. Under the light of his gracious countenance, joy sprung up in his soul and he wrote the Science of Vanity for the enlightenment of the understanding. Be assured that all things are like the void of heaven, contained in a void, as when you look into yourself and see your own shadow. After long ruminating, the noble Thákur has elicited the cream of the matter. In accordance with his teaching, I publish these thoughts. Listen, ye men of sense, to my array of arguments ; first understand, then reply. The beginning of all things is in hollowness, hollow is also the end and hollow the middle ; so says the preacher. The highest, the lowest, and the mean are all hollow ; so the wise man has expounded. From nothing all things are born ; in nothing all things perish ; even the illimitable expanse of sky is all hollowness. What alone has no beginning, nor will ever have an end, and is still of one character, that is vacuum."

Specimens of the Suni Sár.

जित देखो तित सुन्नहि दीसे सुन्नहि है सब ईश अनीसे ॥
सुन्नहि माया सुन्नहि ब्रह्म सुन्नहि में सब झूठो भर्म ॥ १ ॥
सुन्नहि पिण्ड शून्य ब्रह्मंडा सुन्नहि सात दीप नव खंडा ॥

सुन्नहि धरती शून्य अकाशा   सुन्नहि चंद सूर परकाशा ॥ २ ॥
सुन्नहि ब्रह्मा विष्णु महेशा   सुन्नहि कूर्म शून्य ही शेषा ॥
सुन्नहि गुरु शून्य ही चेला   शून्य ही दूजा शून्य अकेला ॥ ३ ॥
शून्यहि देवल शून्य हि देवा   सुन्नहि करै शून्य की सेवा ॥
सुन्नहि करै शून्य को जाप   समझि करै गुरु के परताप ॥ ४ ॥

"All that is seen is nothing and is not really seen; lord or no lord it is all one. Mayá is nothing; Brahm is nothing; all is false and delusive. The world is all emptiness; the egg of Brahma, the seven *dwipas*, the nine *khands*, the earth, the heaven, the moon, the glorious sun, all, all are emptiness; so are Brahma, Vishnu, and Mahadeva; so are Kurma and Seshnág. The teacher is nothing, the disciple nothing; the *ego* and the *non ego* are alike nothing. The temple and the god are nought; nought is the worship of nought and nought the prayer addressed to nought; so know they who are enlightened by the influence of the Guru."

सकल जगत सों भयो उदासी   शून्य ज्ञान रत सदा बिलासी ॥
आनंद मगन सहज दिन राता   सदा रहो अवगति मद माता ॥ १ ॥
सांचों बाद करौं नहिं संका   समझो नहीं राव अरु रंका ॥
चाहों नहीं मानता पूजा   हितकर संग न राखो दूजा ॥ २ ॥
जो कछु सहज मिलै सुख मानों   महल उद्यान एक सम जानों ॥
मेरी तेरी मिट गई भूल   ना कछु दुख ना कछु फूल ॥ ३ ॥
अब ऐसे सत गुरु कों पावै   कोटि जन्म के भर्म नसावै ॥
ऐसे गुरु परगट है भू पै   श्रीठाकुर दयाराम अनूपै ॥ ४ ॥

"The whole word was disconsolate, but is now gladdened for ever by the doctrine of Nihilism: it is plunged in joy and ecstatic delight, drunk with the wine of perfect knowledge. I enunciate the truth and doubt not; I know neither prince nor beggar; I court neither honour nor reverence; I take a friend by the hand and seek none other; what comes easily I accept and am contented; a palace and a thicket to me are all the same; the error of *mine* and *thine* is obliterated; nothing is loss, nothing is gain. To get such a teacher of the truth puts an end to the errors of a million of births. Such a teacher as has now been revealed—the incomparable Thákur Dayá Rám."

CHAPTER IX.

BRINDA-BAN AND ITS TEMPLES.

On their arrival at Brindá-ban, the first shrine which the Gosáins erected was one in honour of the eponymous goddess Brindá Devi. Of this no traces now remain, if (as some say) it stood in the Seva Kunj, which is now a large walled garden with a masonry tank near the Rás Mandal. Their fame spread so rapidly that in 1573 the Emperor Akbar was induced to pay them a visit, and was taken blindfold into the sacred enclosure of the Nidhban,* where such a marvellous vision was revealed to him, that he was fain to acknowledge the place as indeed holy ground. Hence the cordial support which he gave to the attendant Rájás, when they expressed their wish to erect a series of buildings more worthy of the local divinity.

The four temples, commenced in honour of this event, still remain, though in a ruinous and hitherto sadly neglected condition. They bear the titles of Gobind Deva, Gopí-náth, Jugal-Kishor and Madan Mohan. The first named is not only the finest of this particular series, but is the most impressive religious edifice that Hindu art has ever produced, at least in Upper India. The body of the building is in the form of a Greek cross, the nave being a hundred feet in length and the breadth across the transepts the same. The central compartment is surmounted by a dome of singularly graceful proportions ; and the four arms of the cross are roofed by a waggon vault of pointed form, not, as is usual in Hindu architecture, composed of overlapping brackets, but constructed of true radiating arches as in our Gothic cathedrals. The walls have an average thickness of ten feet and are pierced in two stages, the upper stage being a regular triforium, to which access is obtained by an internal staircase, as in the somewhat later temple of Rádhá Ballabh, which will be described further on. This triforium is a reproduction of Muhammadan design, while the work both above and below it is purely Hindu.† It should be noted, however, that the

* This is the local name of the actual Brindá grove, to which the town owes its origin. The spot so designated is now of very limited area, hemmed in on all sides by streets, but protected from further encroachment by a high masonry wall. The name refers to the nine nidhis, or treasures, of Kuvera, the god of wealth. They are enumerated as follows : the Padma, Mahá-padma, Sankha, Makara, Kachhapa, Mukunda, Nanda, Nila, and Kharva ; but it is not known in what precise sense each separate term is to be taken. For example, Padma may mean simply a 'lotus,' or again, as a number, '10,000 millions,' or possibly, 'a ruby,'

† Thus eclecticism, which after all is only natural growth directed by local circumstances, has for centuries past been the predominant characteristic of Mathurá architecture. In most of

arches are decorative only, not constructural : the spandrels in the head might be—and, as a fact, for the most part had been—struck out, leaving only the lintel supported on the straight jambs, without any injury to the stability of the building. They have been re-inserted in the course of the recent restoration. At the east entrance of the nave there is a small narthex fifteen feet deep; and at the west end, between two niches and incased in a rich canopy of sculpture, a square-headed doorway leads into the choir, a chamber some twenty feet by twenty. Beyond this was the sacrarium,* flanked on either side by a lateral chapel ; each of these three cells being of the same dimensions as the choir, and like it vaulted by a lofty dome. The general effect of the interior is not unlike that produced by Saint Paul's Cathedral in London. The latter building has greatly the advantage in size, but in the other, the central dome is more elegant, while the richer decoration of the wall surface and the natural glow of the red sandstone supply that relief and warmth of colouring which are so lamentably deficient in its western rival.

The ground-plan is so similar to that of many European churches as to suggest the idea that the architect was assisted by the Jesuit missionaries, who were people of considerable influence at Akbar's court : were this really the case, the temple would be one of the most eclectic buildings in the world, having a Christian ground-plan, a Hindu elevation, and a roof of modified Saracenic character. But the surmise, though a curious one, must not be too closely pressed; for some of the temples at Khajuráo, by Mahoba, are of similar design and of much earlier date ; nor is it very likely that the Jesuits would have interested themselves in the construction of a heathen fane. Such action on their part, supposing them to have taken it, would find a parallel in the persistency with which the Duke of York (afterwards James II.) stood out for the provision of two side chapels in Wren's design for the Protestant cathedral of St. Paul's,—a building which he hoped in the course of his reign to recover for the Catholics.

It would seem that, according to the original design, there were to have been five towers ; one over the central dome, and the other four covering

---

the new works that I took in hand, and notably in the Catholic Church, which I left unfinished, I conformed to the *genius loci*, and showed my recognition of its principles, not by a servile imitation of older examples, but rather by boldly modifying them in accordance with later requirements, and so developing novel combinations.

* The Sanskrit terms for the component parts of a temple are—the nave, *mandapa* ; the choir, *antarála*, and the sacrarium *garbha griha*. The more ordinary Hindi substitutes are—for the nave *sabhá*, and for the choir, *jag-mohan* ; while *mandir*, the temple, specially denotes the sacrarium, and any side chapel is styled a *mahall*.

AUTOTYPE.

TEMPLE OF GOBIND DEVA, BRINDA-BAN

respectively the choir, sacrarium, and two chapels.* The sacrarium has been utterly razed to the ground,† the chapel towers were never completed, and that over the choir, though the most perfect, has still lost several of its upper stages. This last was of slighter elevation than the others, occupying the same relative position as the spirelet over the sanctus bell in western ecclesiology. The loss of the towers and of the lofty arcaded parapet that surmounted the walls has terribly marred the effect of the exterior and given it a heavy stunted appearance; while, as a further disfigurement, a plain masonry wall had been run along the top of the centre dome. It is generally believed that this was built by Aurangzeb for the purpose of desecrating the temple, though it is also said to have been put up by the Hindus themselves to assist in some grand illumination. It either case it was an ugly modern excrescence, and its removal was the very first step taken at the commencement of the recent repairs.‡

Under one of the niches at the west end of the nave is a tablet with a long Sanskrit inscription. This has unfortunately been too much mutilated to allow of transcription, but so much of it as can be deciphered records the fact that the temple was built in *sambat* 1647, *i.e.*, A.D. 1590, under the direction of the two Gurus, Rúpa and Sanátana. As it was in verse, it probably combined a minimum of information with an excess of verbosity, and its loss is not greatly to be regretted. The following is taken from the exterior of the north-west chapel, where it is cut into the wall some ten feet from the ground, and is of considerable interest :—

संबत् ३४ श्री शकवंध अकबर शाह राज श्री कर्मकुल श्री
पृथिराजाधिराज वंश महाराज श्रीभगवंतदाससुत श्री
महाराजाधिराज श्रीमानसिंहदेव श्री बृंदाबन जोग पीठस्थान
मंदिर कराजे। श्री गोविन्ददेव को कामउपरि श्रीकल्याणदास

* The south-west chapel encloses a subterranean cell, called Pátál Deví, which is said by some to be the Gosáins' original shrine in honour of the goddess Brindá.

† The sacrarium was roughly rebuilt in brick about the year 1854, and contains an image of Krishna in his character of Giridhári (the mountain-supporter), with two subordinate figures representing, the one Mahá Prabhu, *i.e.*, Chaitanya, the other Nityánand.

‡ One section of this work originally appeared in the "Calcutta Review," and a correspondent, who saw it there, favoured me with the following note of a tradition as to the cause of the wall being built. He writes:—"Aurangzeb had often of an evening remarked a very bright light shining in the far distant south-east horizon, and, in reply to his enquiries regarding it, was told that it was a light burning in a temple of great wealth and magnificence at Brindá-ban.

आज्ञाकारी माणिकचंद चोपाड शिल्पकारि गोविन्ददास दील-वलि कारिगरु: द: । गोरषदसुर्बोभवलू ॥

"In the 34th year of the era inaugurated by the reign of the Emperor Akbar, Srí Maháráj Mán Sinh Deva, son of Maháráj Bhagaván Dás, of the family of Maháráj Prithiráj, founded, at the holy station of Brindá-ban, this temple of Gobind Deva. The head of the works, Kalyán Dás, the Assistant Superintendent, Mánik Chand Chopár (?), the architect, Gobind Dás of Delhi, the mason, Gorakh Dás." There is some mistake in the engraving of the last words, which seem to be intended for *Subham bhavatu*, like the Latin 'Felix, faustumque sit.'

The Ráo Prithi Singh mentioned in the above was one of the ancestors of the present Maháraja of Jaypur. He had seventeen sons, of whom twelve came to man's estate, and to each of them he assigned a separate appanage, which, collectively, are known as the twelve *kothris* of Amber. Rájá Mán Sinh, the founder of the temple, was his great-grandson.

He was appointed by Akbar successively Governor of the districts along the Indus, of Kábul, and of Bihár. By his exertions the whole of Orísá and Eastern Bengal were re-annexed; and so highly were his merits appreciated at court, that, though a Hindu, he was raised to a higher rank than any other officer in the realm. He married a sister of Lakshmi Náráyan, Rája of Koch Bihár, and at the time of his decease, which was in the ninth year of the reign of Jahángir, he had living one son, Bháo Sinh, who succeeded him upon the throne of Amber, and died in 1621, A.D.* There is a tradition to the effect that Akbar, at the last, jealous of his powerful vassal and desirous to rid himself of him, had a confection prepared, part of which contained poison; but caught in his own snare, he presented the innoxious portion to the Rájá and ate that drugged with death himself. The unworthy deed is explained by Mán Sinh's design, which apparently had reached the Emperor's ears, to alter the succession in favour of Khusrau, his nephew, instead of Salím.†

He accordingly resolved that it should be effectually put out, and soon after sent some troops to the place, who plundered and threw down as much of the temple as they could, and then erected on the top of the ruins a mosque wall, where, in order to complete the desecration, the Emperor is said to have offered up his prayers."

* *Vide* Professor Blochmann's Ain-i-Akbari, p. 341.

† The above tradition is quoted from Tod's Rájasthán. De Laët, as translated by Mr. Lethbridge, for Mán Sinh substitutes the name of Mirza Ghází Beg.

In anticipation of a visit from Aurangzeb, the image of the god was transferred to Jaypur, and the Gosáin of the temple there has ever since been regarded as the head of the endowment. The name of the present incumbent is Syám Sundar, who has two agents, resident at Brindá-ban. There was said to be still in existence at Jaypur the original plan of the temple, showing its five towers, but on inspection I found that the painting, which is on the wall of one of the rooms in the old palace at Amber, was not a plan of the temple at all, but an imaginary view of the town of Brindá-ban, in which all the temples are represented as exactly alike, distinguishable only by their names, which are written above them. However, local tradition is fully agreed as to the number and position of the towers, while their architectural character can be determined beyond a doubt by comparison with the smaller temples of the same age and style, the ruins of which still remain. It is therefore not a little strange that of all the architects who have described this famous building, not one has noticed its most characteristic feature—the harmonious combination of dome and spire—which is still quoted as the great crux of modern art, though nearly 300 years ago the difficulty was solved by the Hindus with characteristic grace and ingenuity.

From the reign of Aurangzeb to the present time not a single step had ever been taken to ensure the preservation from further decay of this most interesting architectural monument. It was looked upon by the people in the neighbourhood as a convenient quarry, where every house-builder was at liberty to excavate for materials ; while large trees had been allowed to grow up in the fissures of the walls, and in the course of a few more summers their spreading roots would have caused irreparable damage. Accordingly, after an ineffectual attempt to enlist the sympathies of the Archæological Department, the writer took the opportunity of Sir William Muir's presence in the district, on tour, to solicit the adoption on the part of the Government of some means for averting a catastrophe that every student of architecture throughout the world would have regarded as a national disgrace. Unfortunately he declined to sanction any grant from Provincial funds, but allowed a representation of the ruinous condition of the temple and its special interest to be made to the Government of India, for communication to the Mahárája of Jaypur, as the representative of the founder.* His

* This line of action was, if I may be allowed to say so, extremely ill-advised, since it amounted to a quasi-recognition of the Mahárája's proprietary right in the temple. This year, (1882,) one of his local agents, on the occasion of a wedding in his family, gave an entertainment to his friends in the central space under the dome and thought nothing of whitewashing the walls and pillars of the interior up to about half their height, thus ruining the architectural effect, which depends so much

Highness immediately recognized the claim that the building had upon him and made no difficulty about supplying the small sum of Rs. 5,000, which had been estimated by the Superintending Engineer as sufficient to defray the cost of all absolutely essential repairs.* The work was taken in hand at the beginning of August, 1873. The obtrusive wall erected by the Muhammadans on the top of the dome was demolished ; the interior cleared of several unsightly party-walls and other modern excrescences ; and outside, all the débris was removed, which had accumulated round the base of the building to the astonishing height of eight feet and in some places even more, entirely concealing the handsomely moulded plinth ; a considerable increase was thus made to the elevation of the building—the one point in which, since the loss of the original parapet and towers, the design had appeared defective. Many of the houses which had been allowed to crowd the courtyard close up to the very walls of the temple were taken down, and two broad approaches opened out from the great eastern portal and the south transept. Previously, the only access was by a narrow winding lane ; and there was not a single point from which it was possible to obtain a complete view of the fabric.

The next thing undertaken was the removal of a huge masonry pillar that had been inserted under the north bay of the nave to support a broken lintel. This was effected by pinning up the fractured stone with three strong iron bolts ; a simple and economical contrivance, suggested by Mr. Inglis, Executive Engineer on the Agra Canal, in lieu of the costly and tedious process of inserting a new lintel and meanwhile supporting the wall by a masonry arch, which, though temporary, would have required most careful and substantial construction, on account of the enormous mass resting upon it.

On the south side of the choir stood a large domed and pillared *chhattri* of very handsome and harmonious design, though erected 40 years later than the temple. The following inscription is rudely cut on one of its four pillars :—

संवत् १६८३ वरषे कातिक वदि ५ शुभदिने हजरत श्री
श्री श्री शाहजहां राज्ये राणा श्रीअमरसिंहजी को बेटा राजा
श्रीभीमजी री राणी श्री रंभावती चोषंडो सेराहे छेजी ॥

---

on the rich glow of the red sand-stone. No notice was taken by the local authorities ; but, on my representing the matter to Government, prompt orders were issued to have the mischief as far as possible undone.

* A revised estimate was afterwards prepared by the District Engineer, who put it at Rs. 75,000 for the exterior and Rs. 57,857 for the interior, making a total of Rs. 1,32,857.

TEMPLE OF GOBIND DEVA, BRINDÁ-BAN.
(WITH SIDE CHAPEL.)

"In the year *Sambat* 1693 (*i. e.*, 1836 A.D.), on an auspicious day, Kártik Badi 5, in the reign of the Emperor Sháhjahán, this monument was erected by Ráni Rambhavati, widow of Rájá Bhím, the son ofRáná Amar Sinh."

This Ráná Amar Sinh, though one of the most gallant princes of his line, was the first sovereign of Mewár who had to stoop to acknowledge himself a vassal of the Delhi Emperor : not without a manful struggle, in which it is said that he fought against Jahángír's forces in as many as seventeen pitched battles. He was succeeded on the throne, in 1621 A. D., by his eldest son, Karan Sinh ; while the younger, the Bhím of the inscription, being high in the favour of Prince Khuram, received also the title of Rájá with a grant of territory on the Banás, where he built himself a capital, called Rájmahal. He did not, however, long enjoy his honours ; in his friendship for the young prince he induced him to conspire against his elder brother, Parviz, the rightful heir to the throne, and, in the disturbances that ensued he was slain ; while Prince Khuram took refuge at the court of Udaypur till his father's death, in 1628 A. D., summoned him to ascend the throne of Delhi with the title of Sháhjahán.

As the monument was in a very ruinous condition and had been rendered still more insecure by reducing the level of the ground round its foundations, it was taken down and re-erected on the platform that marks the site of the old sacrarium, where it serves to conceal the bare rubble wall that rises behind it.

These works had more than exhausted the petty sum of Rs. 5,000, which (as remarked at the time) was barely enough to pay for the scaffolding required for a complete restoration ; but in the meantime Sir John Strachey had succeeded to the Government of these Provinces, and he speedily showed his interest in the matter by making a liberal grant from public funds. With this the roof of the entire building was thoroughly repaired ; the whole of the upper part of the east front, which was in a most perilous state, was taken down and rebuilt ; and the pillars, brackets, and eaves of the external arcades on the north and south sides, together with the porches at the four corners of the central dome, were all renewed. A complete restoration was also effected of the *jag-mohan* (*or* choir) tower, excepting only that the finial and a few stages of stone-work immediately under it were not added ; for they had entirely perished and, in the absence of the original design, Sir John Strachey would not allow me to replace them. As a general principle the introduction of any new work under such circumstances is much to be deprecated, but in this particular case there could not be any doubt as to the exact character and dimensions of the missing portions, since the stages of the tower diminish from the bottom upwards in regular proportion and all bear the same ornamentation. Certainly, the picturesque effect would have been immensely enhanced by giving the tower the pyramidal finish intended for it, instead of leaving it with its present stunted appearance.

The work was conducted under my own personal supervision without any professional assistance, except Mr. Inglis's suggestion, which I have duly chronicled, up to March, 1877, when Sir George Couper, who had two months previously been confirmed as Sir John Strachey's successor, suddenly ordered my transfer from the district. The restoration would most assuredly never have been undertaken but for my exertions, and as I had been engaged upon it so long, it was naturally a disappointment to me not to be allowed to complete it. However, all that was absolutely essential had been accomplished and for the comparatively modest outlay of Rs. 38,365, nearly a lakh less than the Public Works estimate.*

Mr. Fergusson, in his Indian Architecture, speaks of this temple as "one of the most interesting and elegant in India, and the only one, perhaps, from which a European architect might borrow a few hints. I should myself have thought that 'solemn' or 'imposing' was a more appropriate term than 'elegant' for so massive a building, and that the suggestions that might be derived from its study were 'many' rather than 'few;' but the criticism is at all events in intention a complimentary one. It is, however, unfortunate that the author of a book which will long and deservedly be accepted as an authority was not able to obtain more satisfactory information regarding so notable a *chef d'œuvre*. The ground-plan that he supplies is extremely incorrect; for it gives in faint lines, as if destroyed, the choir, or *jag-mohan*, which happens to be in more perfect preservation than any other part of the fabric, and it entirely omits the two chapels that flank the *cella* on either side and are integral portions of the design. The *cella* itself is also omitted; though for this there

*A Government Resolution on 'the Restoration of Temples in the Mathurá District' was published by Sir John Strachey on the 1st April, 1876, and is exclusively occupied with my doings. The 6th paragraph begins as follows: "In respect of the work on the temple of Govind Ji at Brindá-ban, His Honor feels that the Government is much indebted to Mr. F. S. Growse for the able and ecnomical manner in which its partial restoration has been effected, and has no hesitation in confiding to him its completion, without interference by any officer of the Public Works Department subordinate to the Chief Engineer."

Page 2[illegible]8.

TEMPLE OF GOBIND-DEVA
AT
BRINDA-BAN.

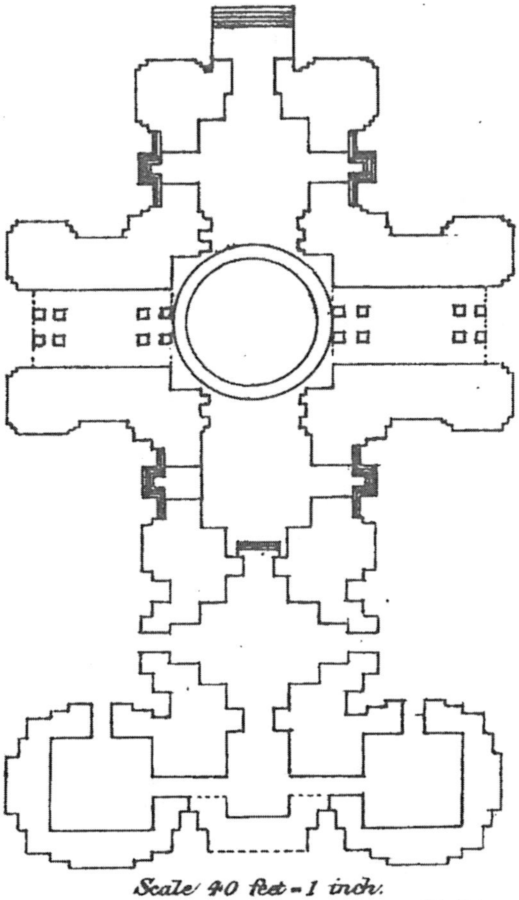

Scale 40 feet = 1 inch.

was more excuse, since it was razed to the ground by Aurangzeb and not a vestige of it now remains; though the rough rubble wall of the choir shows where it had been attached.

These two parts of the building, the sacrarium and the choir, were certainly completed, towers and all. They alone were indispensably necessary for liturgical purposes and were therefore the first taken in hand, in the same way as in mediæval times the corresponding parts of a cathedral were often in use for many years before the nave was added.

In clearing the basement, comparatively few fragments of carved stone were discovered imbedded in the soil. There are some built up into the adjoining houses, but chiefly corbels and shafts, which were clearly taken from the lower stories of the temple. No fragments of the upper stages of the towers have been brought to light; from which fact alone it might reasonably be conjectured that they were never finished. This was certainly the case with the two side chapels; and the large blocks lying on the top of their walls, ready to be placed in position, are just as they were left by the original builders, when the work for some unexplained reason was suddenly interrupted. Probably, as in so many other similar cases, it was the death of the founder which brought everything to a stand-still. The tower over the central dome was also, as I conjecture, never carried higher than we now see it; but the open arcades, which crowned the façade, though not a fragment of them now remains, were probably put up, as the stones of the parapet still show the dents of the pillars. The magnificent effect which they would have had may be gathered from a view of the temple in the Gwaliar fort; which, though some 600 years earlier in date, is in general arrangement the nearest parallel to the Brindá-ban fane, and would seem to have supplied Mán Sinh with a model. It has been subjected to the most barbarous treatment, but has at last attracted the attention of Government, and is now being restored under the superintendence of Major Keith, an officer of unbounded archchæological enthusiasm. There is no more interesting specimen of architecture to be found in all India.

A modern temple, under the old dedication, has been erected within the precincts and absorbs the whole of the endowment. The ordinary annual income amounts to Rs. 17,500; but by far the greater part of this, *viz.*, Rs. 13,000, is made up by votive offerings. The fixed estate includes one village in Alwar and another in Jaypur, but consists principally of house property in the town of Brindá-ban, where is also a large orchard, called Rádhá Bágh. This has been greatly diminished in area by a long series of encroachments; and a temple, dedicated to Ban Bihári, has now been built in it, at a cost of Rs. 15,000, by

63

Rájá Jay Sinh Deova, Chief of Charkhári, in Bundelkhand. About a hundred years ago it must have been very extensive and densely wooded, as Father Tieffenthaller, in his notice of Brindá-ban, describes it in the following terms :—"L'endroit est couvert de beaucoup d'arbres et resemble à un bois sacré des anciens ; il est triste par le morne silence qui y regne, quoiqu' agréable par l'ombre épaisse des arbres, desqúels on n'ose arracher un rameau, ni même une feuille ; ce serait un grand délit." The site of the Seth's temple was also purchased from the Gobind Deva estate, and a further subsidy of Rs. 102 a year is still paid on its account.

The next temple to be described, *viz.*, that of Madan Mohan, one of Krishna's innumerable titles, stands at the upper end of the town on a high cliff near the Káli-mardan, or as it is more commonly called, the Káli-dah Ghát, where the god trampled on the head of the great serpent Káli. The story of its foundation is given as follows in the Bhakt Sindhu of Lachman Dás, which is a modernized version of the Bhakt Málá. In this poem it is stated that the image of Gobind Jí was found by Rúpa and Sanátan at Nand-gánw, where they had dug it up in a cattle-shed (*Go-khirk men se nikar áye, táte Gobind nám dharáye*), thence they brought it to Brindá-ban and erected it on the site of the present temple near the Brahm kund. They went daily to the neighbouring villages (Brindá-ban being at that time an uninhabited forest) and to Mathurá to beg ; and one day a man in the city gave Sanátan an image of Madan Mohan, which he took and set up near the Káli-dah Ghát on the Duhsásan hill. There, too, he built for himself a little hut to live in and gave the place the name of the Pasukandan Ghát, because the road was so steep and bad that no cattle could go along it* (*nichau unchau dekhi bisheshan Pasu-kandan wah Ghát kahái, tahán baithi mansukh lahái*). One day a merchant from Multan in the Panjab, a khattri by caste, named Rám Dás, but more familiarly known as Kapúri, came down the river with a boat-load of merchandise bound for Agra, but stuck on a sand-bank near the Káli-dah Ghát. After trying in vain for three days to get off, he determined to discover the local divinity and implore his assistancé. So he came on shore, climbed up the hill, and there found Sanátan, who told him to address his prayer to Madan Mohan. He did so, and his boat immediately began to float. When he had sold all his goods at Agra he came and brought the price to Sanátan, who told him to build a temple with it. This he did and added the Ghát also, all of red stone.

* This derivation is a very absurd one, *Kandan* being a Persian word. The real name of the Ghát is the Sanskrit *Praskandana*, taken either as a name of Siva, or as an epithet of the cliff, 'standing out.'

AUTOTYPE

THE TEMPLE OF MADAN MOHAN, BRINDÁ-BAN.

The temple, as we now see it, consists of a nave 57 feet long, with a choir of 20 feet square at the west end, and a sanctuary of the same dimensions beyond. The nave has three openings on either side and a square door at the east end, immediately outside of which the ground has a precipitous drop of some 9 or 10 feet; thus the only entrance is from the side. Its total height would seem to have been only about 22 feet, but its vaulted roof has entirely disappeared; the upper part of the choir tower has also been destroyed. That surmounting the sacra-ium is a plain octagon of curvilinear outline tapering towards the summit. Attached to its south side is a tower-crowned chapel of similar character, but much more highly enriched, the whole of its exterior surface being covered with sculptured panels; its proportions are also much more elegant. Over its single door, which is at the east end, is a Sanskrit inscription, given first in Bengali and then in Nágari characters, which runs as follows :—

हर इव गुरुवंशो यत्पिता रामचन्द्रो
गुणिमणिरिव पुत्रो यस्य राधा वसंतः।
सकृत सुकृतराशिः श्रीगुणानन्दनामा
व्यधित विधवदेन्मन्दिरं नन्दसूनोः॥

"Of Guru descent, a compeer of Mahádeva, whose father was Rámchandra, whose son was Rádhá Vasant, jewel of good men; that mass of virtue, by name Srí Gunánand, dedicated in approved fashion this temple to the son of Nanda (Nandkishor, *i. e.*, Krishna)."

The above had never been copied before, and as the letters were raised, instead of incised, and also much worn, a transcript was a matter of some little difficulty. The Bráhman in charge of the shrine had certainly never troubled himself to take one, for he declared the inscription to be absolutely illegible or at least unintelligible, even if the letters could be deciphered. The information given is not very perspicuous except as to the name of the founder, and there is no indication of a date, but it would certainly be later than that of the main building (which was the work of Rám Dás). The court-yard is entered, after the ascent of a flight of steps, through a massive square gateway with a pyramidal tower, which groups very effectively with the two towers of the temple. As the buildings are not only in ruins, but also from peculiarities of style ill-adapted to modern requirements, they are seldom, if ever, used for religious service, which is ordinarily performed in an elegant and substantial edifice erected on the other side of the street under the shadow of the older fane. The annual income is estimated at Rs. 10,100, of which sum, Rs. 8,000 are the voluntary offerings of the faithful, while only Rs. 2,100 are derived from permanent endowment.* A branch establishment at Rádhá Kund with the same dedication is also supported from the funds of the parent house.

The nave, ruinous as it is, was evidently to a great extent rebuilt in comparatively recent times, the old materials being utilized as far as possible, but when they ran short, the place of stone being supplied by brick. A side post of one of the doors on the south side of the nave bears an inscription with the date *Sambat* 1684 (A.D. 1827), but it simply records a successful pilgrimage made by a native of Kanauj in that year. In 1875 I greatly improved the appearance of the temple by reducing the level of the ground round the chapel, the plinth of which had been completely buried, and by removing a number of buildings from inside the nave and from the front of the chapel door. A boundary wall was also thrown down, and a new approach to the court-yard opened out from the east with a flight of masonry steps up the ascent. The latter were constructed by the municipality at a cost of Rs. 200 : the rest of the expense was borne by the Gosáin.

The original image of Madan Mohan is now at Karauli, where Rájá Gopál Sinh, who reigned from 1725 to 1757 A.D., built a new temple for its reception, after he had obtained it from his brother-in-law, the Rájá of Jaypur. The Gosáin whom he placed in charge was a Bengali from Murshidabad, by name Rám Kishor; the name of the present incumbent is Mohan Kishor. He has an endowment in land which brings in a yearly income of Rs. 27,000. The god is fed seven times a day, the two principal meals being the *ráj-bhog* at midday and the *sayana* at sleeping time. At the other five only a light repast is offered, of sweetmeats, &c. ; these are called the *mangal arti,* which takes place at dawn ; the *dhúp,* at 9 A.M. ; the *sringar,* at 11 A. M. ; *dhúp,* again at 3 P. M. ; and *sandhyarti,* at dusk.

With reference to this temple, a curious anecdote is told in the Bhakta Málá of a devout Vaishnava, by name Súr Dás. He was Governor (Amín) of Sandíla in Akbar's reign, and on one occasion consumed all the revenues of his district in entertaining the priests and pilgrims at the temple. The treasure chests were duly despatched to Delhi, but when opened were found to contain nothing but stones. Such exaggerated devotion failed to commend itself even to the Hindu minister, Todar Mall, who threw the enthusiast into prison ; but the

* On the road from Brindá-ban to Jait, within the boundaries of the village of Sunrakh, is a walled garden with a tank, called Rám Tál, part of the property of the temple of Madan Mohan.

TEMPLE OF MADAN MOHAN
AT
BRINDA-BAN.

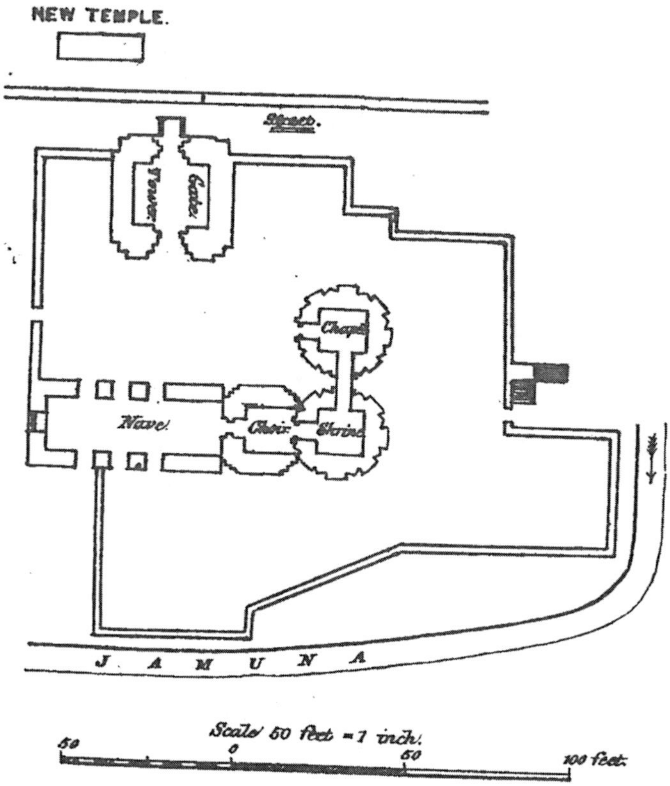

grateful god could not forget his faithful servant and speedily moved the indulgent emperor to order his release. The panegyric on Súr Dás stands thus in the text of the original poem : the explanatory narrative, as added by Priya Dás, is too long to copy :—

मूल

श्री मदनमोहन सूरदास की नाम शृंखला जोरी अटल ॥
गांन काव्य गुन राशि सुहृद सहचरि अवतारी ।
राधाकृष्ण उपास्य रहस्य सुख के अधिकारी ॥
नवरस मुख्य सिंगार विविध भांतिन करि गायो ।
बदन उच्चरत बेर सहस पाइन ह्वै धायो ॥
अंगीकार की अवधि यह ज्यों आख्या भ्राता जलज ।
श्री मदनमोहन सूरदास की नाम शृंखला जोरी अटल ॥

Translation.—"Joined together like two links in a chain are the god Madan Mohan and Súr Dás, that paragon of excellence in verse and song, incarnation of the good and beneficent, votary of Rádhá Krishan, master of mystic delights. Manifold his songs of love ; the muse of love, queen of the nine, came dancing on foot* to the melodies that he uttered ; his persuasiveness as unbounded as that of the fabled twin brothers.† Joined together like two links in a chain are the god Madan Mohan and Súr Dás."

The temple of Gopináth, which may be slightly the earliest of the series, is said to have been built by Ráesil Jí, a grandson of the founder of the Shaikháwát branch of the Kachhwáhá Thákurs. He distinguished himself so greatly in the repulse of an Afghan invasion, that Akbar bestowed upon him the title of Darbári, with a grant of land and the important command of 1,250 horse. He also accompanied his liege lord, Rájá Mán Sinh of Amber, against the Mewár Rána Pratáp, and further distinguished himself in the expedition to Kábul. The date of his death is not known. The temple, of which he is the reputed founder, corresponds very closely both in style and dimensions with that of Madan Mohan, already described, and has a similar chapel attached to the south side of the sacrarium. It is, however, in a far more ruinous condition ;

* Each Ras (the Hindu equivalent for the European Muse) has a special vehicle of its own, and the meaning appears to be that the Ras Sringár, or Erotic Muse, alighted on foot the better to catch the sound of his voice.

† The fabled twin brothers are probably the two Gandharvas (heavenly musicians), who were metamorphosed into *arjun* trees till restored by Krishna to their proper form.

the nave has entirely disappeared ; the three towers have been levelled with the roof; and the entrance gateway of the court-yard is tottering to its fall. The special feature of the building is a curious arcade of three bracket arches, serving apparently no constructural purpose, but merely added as an ornamental screen to the south wall, which already had a fine boldly moulded plinth and required no further adornment. The terrace on which this arcade stands has a carved stone front, which had been buried for years, till I uncovered it. The choir arch is of handsome design, elaborately decorated with arabesque sculptures. It was partly concealed from view by mean sheds which had been built up against it, all of which I caused to be pulled down ; but the interior is still used as a stable, and the north side is blocked by the modern temple. This was built about the year 1821 by a Bengali Kayath, Nand Kumár Ghos, who also built the new temple of Madan Mohan. The votive offerings here made are estimated at Rs. 3,000 a year, in addition to which there is an endowment yielding an annual income of Rs. 1,200.*

The temple of Jugal Kishor, the fourth of the old series, stands at the lower end of the town near the Kesi Ghát. Its construction is referred to the year *Sambat* 1684, *i. e.*, 1627 A. D., in the reign of Jahángír, and the founder's name is preserved as Non-Karan. He is said to have been a Chauhán Thákur ; but it is not improbable that he was the elder brother of Ráesil, who built the temple of Gopináth. The choir, which is slightly larger than in the other examples, being 25 feet square, has the principal entrance, as usual, at the east end, but is peculiar in having also, both north and south, a small doorway under a hood supported on eight closely-set brackets carved into the form of elephants. The nave has been completely destroyed. The choir arch is an interesting composition with a fan-light, so to speak, of pierced tracery in the head of the arch, and a group above representing Krishna supporting the Gobardhan hill. I had caused the whole of the building to be cleared out, removing from the upper room of the tower an accumulation of pigeons' dung more than four feet deep ; and at my suggestion the municipal committee had rented the temple for a rupee a month to ensure its always being kept clean and unoccupied for the ready inspection of visitors. As soon as I left the district, the new magistrate vetoed this arrangement, and I suppose the place is now once more a cattle shed.

The somewhat later temple of Rádhá Ballabh has been already mentioned in the previous chapter. It is in itself a handsome building and is further of special architectural interest as the last example of the early eclectic style.

* The Seth's Garden, where stands the Brahmotsava Pavilion, was purchased from the temple of Gopináth, and is still liable to an annual charge of Rs. 18.

AUTOTYPE.

TEMPLE OF GOPI-NÁTH, BRINDÁ-BAN

THE TEMPLE OF JUGAL-KISHOR, BRINDÁ-BAN.

The ground plan is much the same as in the temple of Harideva at Gobardhan and the work is of the same character, but carried out on a larger scale. The nave has an eastern façade, 34 feet broad, which is in three stages, the upper and lower Hindu, and the one between them purely Muhammadan in character. The interior is a fine vaulted hall (63 ft. × 20 ft.) with a double tier of openings north and south; those in the lower story having brackets and architraves and those above being Muhammadan arches, as in the middle story of the front. These latter open into a narrow gallery with small clerestory windows looking on to the street. Below, the three centre bays of the colonnade are open doorways, and the two at either end are occupied by the staircase that leads to the upper gallery. Some of the carved panels of the stone ceiling have fallen; but the outer roof, a steep gable, also of stone, is as yet perfect. Some trees however have taken root between the slabs and unless carefully removed must eventually destroy it. The actual shrine, or *cella*, as also at the temple of Gobind Deva, was demolished by Aurangzeb and only the plinth remains, upon which a room has been built, which is used as a kitchen. As no mosque was ever erected at Brindá-ban, it is not a little strange that Mr. Fergusson in his History of Indian Architecture, when speaking of this very locality, should venture to say: "It does not appear proven that the Moslems did wantonly throw down the temples of the Hindus, except when they wanted the materials for the erection of mosques or other buildings." A thorough repair of roof, eaves and east front would cost Rs. 4,500, and as a typical example of architecture, the building is worth the outlay. A modern temple has been erected on the south side, and the nave of the old fabric has long been entirely disused. In fact this is the last temple in the neighbourhood in which a nave was built at all. In the modern style it is so completely obsolete that its distinctive name even is forgotten.

These five temples form a most interesting architectural series, and if Mr. Fergusson had ever been able to visit Brindá-ban or to procure photographs of them, it is possible that he would not have found the origin of the Hindu sikhara such an inscrutable mystery as he declares it to be. He conjectures that the external form may have been simply a constructural necessity resulting from the employment internally of a very tall pointed horizontal arch, like that of the Treasury at Mycenæ. But so far as my experience extends, no such arch was ever used in a Hindu temple. On the contrary, the *cella*, over which the sikhara is built, is separated from the more public part of the building by a solid wall pierced only by a doorway small enough to be easily closed; while the chamber itself is of no great height and is covered in with a vaulted ceiling, as to the shape of which nothing could be learnt from a view of the sikhara outside; and *vice versâ.* Thus at the great temple of Gobind Deva the central dome of the nave (or porch as Mr. Fergusson very inappropriately calls it) is perfect; but it is impossible to determine from thence with any certainty what would have been the outline and proportions of the tower that the architect proposed to raise over it. I have no question in my own mind that the origin of the sikhara is to be found in the Buddhist stúpa. Nor do I detect any vio ent break in the development. The lower story of the modern temple which, though most commonly square, is occasionally, as in the Madan Mohan and Rádhá Ballabh examples, an octagon, and therefore a near approach to a circle, is represented by the masonry plinth of the relic-mound; the high curvilinear roof by the swelling contour of the earthen hill, and the pinnacle with its peculiar base by the Buddhist rails and umbrella on the top of a Dagoba. From the original stúpa to the temple of Parsvanáth at Khajurao of the 11th century, the towers of Madan Mohan and Jugal Kishor at Brindá-ban of the 16th, and the temple of Vishveshvar at Banáras, the gradation seems to be easy and continuous.

From a note at the foot of page 32 of his 'Cave Temples' it appears that Mr. Fergusson has been rather nettled by my exposure of his frequent inaccuracies and—having no excuse to offer—attempts to divert attention from them by ridiculing the view I have here advanced as to the origin of the *sikhara.* From the nature of the case it is simply a theory,—and whether it be right or wrong—in its integrity it must be incapable of positive proof. He is therefore not bound to accept it; but it certainly is rash of him to maintain, as a counter-theory, that the Brindában *sikharas* are the result of an attempt on the part of Hindu architects to assimilate with their own traditional forms the novel beauty of the Muhammadan dome. The suggestion is absurd and admits of the easiest refutation, nor do I for a moment suppose that Mr. Fergusson ever seriously entertained it: it is simply employed as a polemical diversion. The type of an Orissan temple in the 6th and 7th centuries A.D., while Buddhism was still a power in the land and long before the Muhammadans had ever entered it, is illustrated by Dr. Rajendra Lál Mitra in his 'Indo-Aryans,' by a wood-cut which is copied in the margin. It will be seen that the

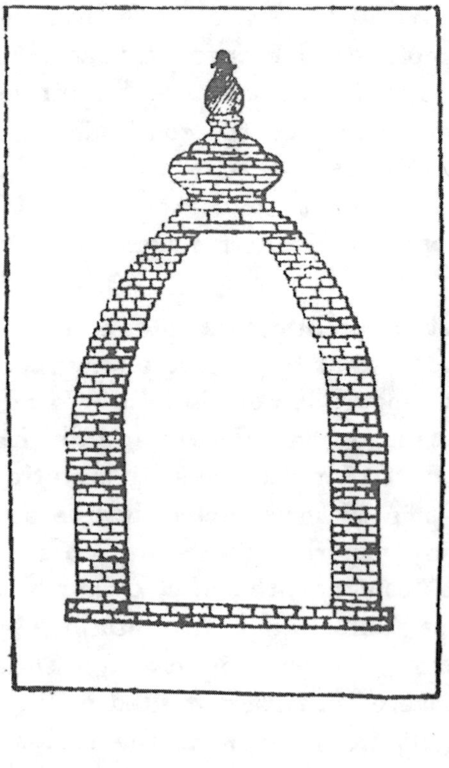

Page 236.

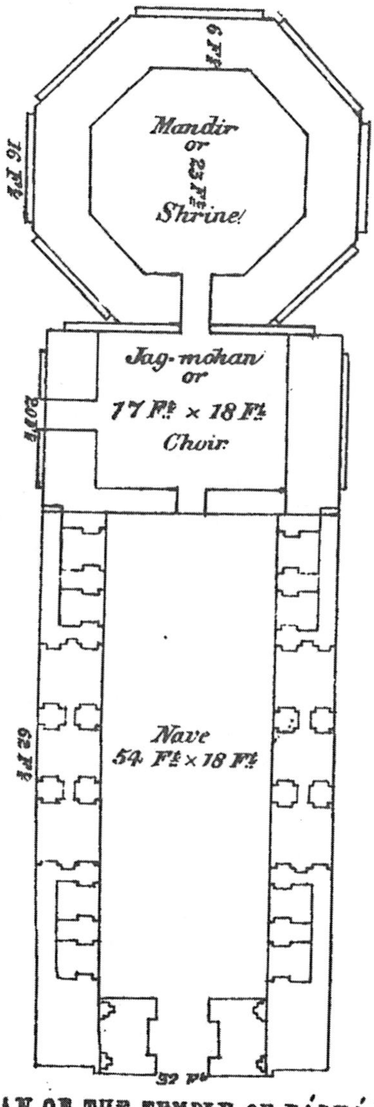

GROUNDPLAN OF THE TEMPLE OF RÁDHÁ BALLABH AT BRINDÁBAN.

general contour is identical with that of the Brindá-ban shrines: and in the façades of the Jain caves at Gwaliar similar sikharas are everywhere to be seen.

Of the smaller temples some have been casually mentioned in connection with their founders. Though of ancient date, they have been often renewed and possess no special architectural merit. The same may be said of the Bengali temple of Sringár Bat, near the Madan Mohan, which, however, enjoys an annual income of Rs. 13,500, divided among three shareholders, who each take the religious services for four months at a time. The village of Jahángírpur on the opposite bank of the river, including the sacred grove of Bel-ban, forms part of the endowment.

The temple of Rádhá Dámodar has a special claim to distinction from the fact that it contains the ashes of Jíva, its founder, as also of his two uncles, the Gosáins Rúpa and Sanátan, the founders of the temple of Gobind Deva, who in their life-time had expressed a wish to be buried together within its precincts. Their joint anniversary is celebrated in the month of Sáwan, when the three shrines are visited by great crowds of Bengalis, who, according to custom, make each some small offering. The proceeds used to be divided between the priests of the two temples; but in 1875, the Rádhá Dámodar Mahant made an attempt to engross the whole by excluding the Gobind Deva people from any participation in the ceremony. The plea advanced was that they were renegades from Vaishnavism since the time that they had complied with the Jaypur Mahárája's order and marked their foreheads with the three horizontal lines that indicate a votary of Siva. This exclusion was naturally resented by the Gobind Deva Mahant, who claimed the immemorial right of free access to his founder's tomb, and as there seemed cause to anticipate that the two rival factions would come to blows, precautions were taken to suppress all external manifestations whatever, much to the chagrin of the Rádhá Dámodar claimants, who had prepared to signalize their triumph by a display of exceptional magnificence.

Of the modern temples, five claim special notice. The first in time of erection is the temple of Krishna Chandrama, built about the year 1810, at a cost of 25 lakhs, by the wealthy Bengali Káyath, Krishna Chandra Sinh, better known as the Lálá Bábu. It stands in a large court-yard, which is laid out, not very tastefully, as a garden, and is enclosed by a lofty wall of solid masonry, with an arched gateway at either end. The building is of quadrangular form, 160 feet in length, with a front central compartment of three arches and a lateral colonnade of five bays reaching back on either side towards the cella. The workmanship throughout is of excellent character, and the stone has been carefully selected. The two towers, or *sikharas*, are singularly plain, but have been wisely so designed that their smooth polished surface may remain unsullied by rain and dust.

The founder's ancestor, Bábu Murli Mohan Sinh, son of one Har Krishna Sinh, was a wealthy merchant and landed proprietor at Kándi in Murshidabad. His heir, Bihári Lál Sinh, had three sons, Rádhá Gobind, Gangá Gobind, and Rádhá Charan : of these, the last-named, on inheriting his share of the paternal estate, broke off connection with the rest of the family and has dropped out of sight. Rádhá Gobind took service under Alláh Vírdí Khán and Siráj-ud-daula, Nawábs of Murshidabad, and was by them promoted to posts of high honour. A rest-house for travellers and a temple of Rádhá Ballabh, which he founded, are still in existence. He died without issue, leaving his property to his brother, Gangá Gobind, who took a prominent part in the revision of the Bengal settlement under Lord William Bentinck, in 1828. He built a number of *dharmsálás* for the reception of pilgrims and four temples at Rámchandrapur in Nadiyá. These latter have all been washed away by the river, but the images of the gods were transferred to Kándi. He also maintained several Sanskrit schools in Nadiyá ; and distinguished himself by the extraordinary pomp with which he celebrated his father's obsequies, spending, moreover, every year on the anniversary of his death a lakh of rupees in religious observances. Gangá Gobind's son, Prán Krishan Sinh, still further augmented his magnificent patrimony before it passed in succession to his son, Krishan Chandra Sinh, better known under the soubriquet of 'the Lálá Bábu. He held office first in Bardwán and then in Orísá, and, when about thirty years of age, came to settle in the holy land of Braj. In connexion with his temple at Brindá-ban he founded also a rest-house, where a large number of pilgrims are still daily fed; the annual cost of the whole establishment being, as is stated, Rs. 22,000. He also enclosed the sacred tanks at Rádhá-kund with handsome gháts and terraces of stone at the cost of a lakh. When some forty years of age, he renounced the world, and in the character of a Bairági continued for two years to wander about the woods and plains of Braj, begging his bread from day to day till the time of his death, which was accidentally caused by the kick of of a horse at Gobardhan.* He was

* The following Hindi couplet is current in the district with reference to the death of the two millionaires, the Lála Bábu and Párikh Jí :—

Lálá Bábu margaya, ghora dosh lagáye,
Párikh ká kíra pará; Bidhi son ko basáe ?

frequently accompanied in his rambles by Mani Rám, father of the famous Seth Lakhmi Chand, who also had adopted the life of an ascetic. In the course of the ten years which the Lálá Bábu spent as a worldling in the Mathurá district, he contrived to buy up all the villages most noted as places of pilgrimage in a manner which strikingly illustrates his hereditary capacity for business. The zamíndárs were assured that he had no pecuniary object in view, but only the strict preservation of the hallowed spots. Again, as in the days of Krishna, they would become the secluded haunts of the monkey and the peacock, while the former proprietors would remain undisturbed, the happy guardians of so many new Arcadias. Thus the wise man from the East picked up one estate after another at a price in every case far below the real value, and in some instances for a purely nominal sum. However binding his fair promises may have been on the conscience of the pious Bábu, they were never recorded on paper, and therefore are naturally ignored by his absentee descendants and their agents, from whom any appeal *ad misericordiam* on the part of the impoverished representatives of the old owners of the soil meets with very scant consideration. The villages which he acquired in the Mathurá district are fifteen in number, viz., in the Kosi Pargana, Jáu ; in Chhátá, Nandganw, Barsána, Sanket, Karhela, Garhi, and Háthiya ; and in the home pargana, Mathurá, Jait, Maholi, and Nabí-pur ; all these, except the last, being more or less places of pilgrimage. To these must be added the four Gújar villages of Pírpur, Gulálpur, Chamar-garhi, and Dhímri. For Nandgánw he gave Rs. 900 ; for Barsána, Rs. 600 ; for Sanket, Rs. 800 ; and for Karhela, Rs. 500 ; the *annual* revenue derived from these places being now as follows : from Nandgánw, Rs. 6,712 ; from Barsána Rs. 3,109 ; from Sanket, Rs. 1,642 ; and from Karhela, Rs. 1,900. It may also be noted that payment was invariably made in Brindában rupees, which are worth only thirteen or fourteen anas each. The Bábu further purchased seventy-two villages in Aligarh and Bulandshahr from Rájá Bír Sinh, Chauhán ; but twelve of these were sold at auction in the time of his heir, Bábu Sri Náráyan Sinh. This latter, being a minor at his father's death, remained for a time under the tutelage of his mother, the Ráni Kaithání, who again, on his decease, when only thirty years old, managed the estate till the coming of age of the two sons whom his widows had been specially authorized to adopt. The elder of the two, Pratáp Chandra, founded an English school at Kándi and a dispensary at Calcutta. He was for some time a Member of the Legislative Council of Bengal, received from Government the title of Bahádur, and was enrolled as a Companion of the Star of India. He died in 1867, leaving four sons, Girís-chandra (since deceased), Púran-chandra,

Kánti-chandra, and Sarad-chandra. The younger brother, Isvar-chandra, who died in 1863, left an only son, Indra-chandra, who now enjoys half the estate, the other half being divided between his three cousins. During their minority the property was under the control of the Court of Wards; the General Manager being Mr. Robert Harvey of Calcutta. The gross rental of the lands in the Mathurá district is Rs. 76,738, upon which the Government demand, including the 10 per cent. cess, is Rs. 49,496. The value of the property when taken in charge was estimated at Rs. 2,40,193; it has now increased to Rs. 3,80,892.

The great temple, founded by Seths Gobind Dás and Rádhá Krishan, brothers of the famous millionaire Lakhmi Chand, is dedicated to Rang Jí, or Srí Ranga Náth, that being the special name of Vishnu most affected by Rámánuja, the founder of the Srí Sampradáya. It is built in the Madras style, in accordance with plans supplied by their guru, the great Sanskrit scholar, Swámi Rangácharya, a native of that part of India.*

The works were commenced in 1845 and completed in 1851, at a cost of 45 lakhs of rupees. The outer walls measure 773 feet in length by 440 in breadth, and enclose a fine tank and garden in addition to the actual temple-court. This latter has lofty gate-towers, or *gopuras,* covered with a profusion of coarse sculpture. In front of the god is erected a pillar, or *dhvaja stambha,* of copper gilt, sixty feet in height, and also sunk some twenty-four feet more below the surface of the ground. This alone cost Rs. 10,000. The principal or western entrance of the outer court is surmounted by a pavilion, ninety-three feet high, constructed in the Mathurá style after the design of a native artist. In its graceful outlines and the elegance of its reticulated tracery, it presents a striking contrast to the heavy and misshapen masses of the Madras Gopura, which rises immediately in front of it. A little to one side of the entrance is a detached shed, in which the god's *rath,* or carriage, is kept. It is an enormous wooden tower in several stages, with monstrous effigies at the

---

* He translated some of Rámánuja's works from the language of Southern India into Sanskrit, and was also the author of two polemical treatises in defence of the orthodoxy of Vaishnavism. The first is a pamphlet entitled Durjana-kari-panchánana, which was written as an answer to eight questions propounded for solution by the Saivite Pandits of Jaypur. The Mahárája, not being convinced, had a rejoinder published under the name of Sajjana-mano-nuranjana, which elicited a more elaborate work from the Swámi, called Vyámoha-vidrávanam, in which he brought together a great number of texts from the canonical Scriptures of the Hindus in support of his own views and in refutation of those of his opponents. He died on the 26th of March, 1874.

AUTOTYPE

THE IDOL CAR.

corners, and is brought out only once a year in the month of Chait during the festival of the Brahmotsav. The mela lasts for ten days, on each of which the god is taken in state from the temple along the road, a distance of 690 yards, to a garden where a pavilion has been erected for his reception. The procession is always attended with torches, music, and incense, and some military display contributed by the Rájá of Bharatpur. On the day when the *rath* is used, the image, composed of the eight metals, is seated in the centre of the car, with attendant Bráhmans standing on either side to fan it with *chauries*. Each of the Seths, with the rest of the throng, gives an occasional hand to the ropes by which the ponderous machine is drawn ; and by dint of much exertion, the distance is ordinarily accomplished in the space of about two and-a-half hours. On the evening of the following day there is a grand display of fire-works, to which all the European residents of the station are invited, and which attracts a large crowd of natives from the country round about. On other days when the rath is not brought out, the god has a wide choice of vehicles, being borne now on a palki, a richly gilt 'tabernacle' (*punya-kothi*), a throne (*sinhásan*), or a tree, either the kadamb, or the tree of Paradise (*kalpa-vriksha*); now on some demi-god, as the sun or the moon, Garúra, Hanumán, or Sesha ; now again on some animal, as a horse, an elephant, a lion, a swan, or the fabulous eight-footed *Sarabha*. The ordinary cost of one of these celebrations is about Rs. 5,000, while the annual expenses of the whole establishment amount to no less than Rs. 57,000, the largest item in that total being Rs. 30,000 for the *bhog* or food, which after being presented to the god is then consumed by the priests or given away in charity. Every day 500 of the Sri Vaishnava sect are fed at the temple, and every morning up to ten o'clock a dole of flour is given to anyone of any denomination who chooses to apply for it.

The endowment consists of thirty-three villages, yielding a gross income of Rs. 1,17,000, on which the Government demand amounts to Rs. 64,000. Of the thirty-three villages, thirteen, including one quarter of Brindá-ban, are in the Mathurá, and twenty in the Agra district. The votive offerings amount on an average to Rs. 2,000 a year, and there is further a sum invested in the funds which yields in annual interest as much as Rs. 11,800. In 1868, the whole estate was transferred by the Swámi—the deed of transfer bearing a stamp of Rs. 2,000—to a committee of management, who on his death were bound to appoint a successor. This arrangement was necessitated by the bad conduct of his son Srínivásácháryá—named according to family custom after the grandfather—who, far from being a scholar like his father, is barely educated up to the ordinary level of his countrymen : while his profligacy is open

66

and notorious. Immorality and priestly dignity, it is true, are not universally accounted as incompatible qualities ; but the scandal in his case is augmented by the ceremonial pollution he incurs from his habit of familiar intercourse with the lowest classes of the people, while his reckless extravagance knows no bounds. Since his father's death he receives a fixed allowance for his maintenance ; but another Guru has been brought up from Madras to conduct the temple services, and the estate is entirely under the control of the committee. This consists of six members, of whom the most active is Seth Náráyan Dás. He is also appointed general attorney for the trustees, and all the temple property, valued at about 20 lakhs, is entered in his name. Since the new arrangement, there has been no falling off in the splendour of the festivals or in the liberality with which the different charities are maintained, while at the same time the estate has been improved and the cost of establishment reduced.

Of the villages that form the endowment, three in Mahában and two in Jalesar were conferred on the temple by Rájá Mán Sinh of Jaypur. Though the lawful heir to the throne, he never took his seat upon it. He was the posthumous son of Rájá Prithi Sinh, on whose death, in 1779 A. D., the surviving brother, Pratáp Sinh, claimed the succession. The nephew's right was subsequently upheld by Daulat Ráo Sindhia, but the young prince was devoted to letters and religion, and on being assured of an annual income of Rs. 30,000, he gladly relinquished the royal title and retired to Brindá-ban. Here he spent the remainder of his days in the practice of the most rigid austerities, till death overtook him at the age of 70, in 1848. For 27 years he had remained sitting cross-legged in one position, never moving from his seat but once a week when nature compelled him to withdraw. Five days before his death he predicted his coming end and solemnly bequeathed to the Seth the care of his old servants ; one of whom, Lakshmi Náráyan Byás, was manager of the temple estate, till his death in 1874.

If the effect of the Seths' lavish endowment is impaired by the ill-judged adoption of a foreign style of architecture, still more is this error apparent in the temple of Rádhá Raman, completed within the last few years. The founder is Sáh Kundan Lál, of Lakhnau, who has built on a design suggested by the modern secular buildings of that city. The principal entrance to the courtyard is, in a grandiose way, decidedly effective; and the temple itself is constructed of the most costly materials and fronted with a colonnade of spiral marble pillars, each shaft being of a single piece, which though rather too attenuated are unquestionably elegant. The mechanical execution is also good;

TEMPLE OF RÁDHA GOPÁL

AT

BRINDA-BAN.

Scale 50 feet = 1 inch.

50 0 50 100 feet

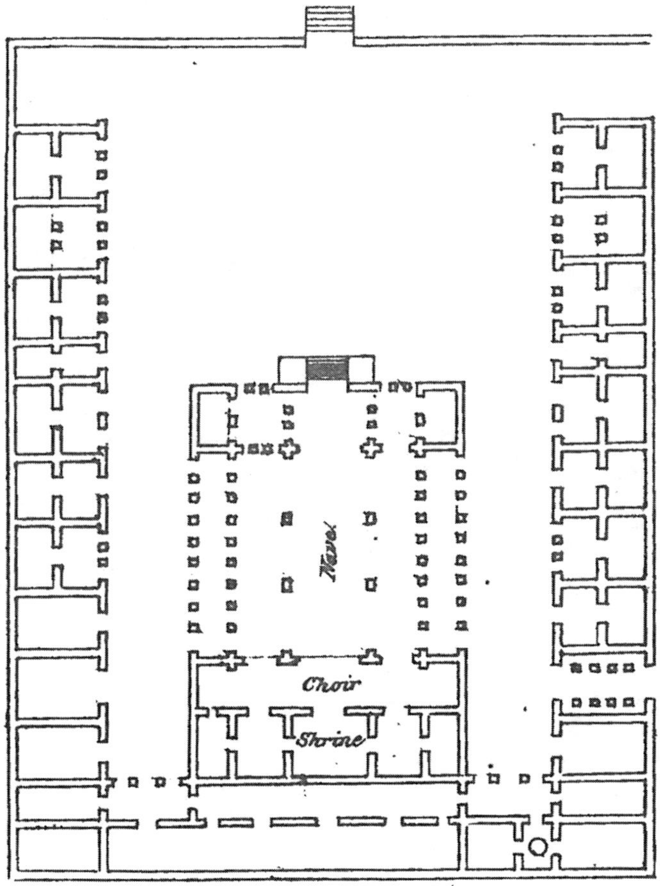

but all is rendered of no avail by the abominable taste of the design. The façade with its uncouth pediment, flanked by sprawling monsters, and its row of life-size female figures in meretricious, but at the same time most ungraceful, attitudes, resembles nothing so much as a disreputable London casino: a severe, though doubtless unintended, satire, on the part of the architect, on the character of the divinity to whom it is consecrated. Ten lakhs of rupees are said to have been wasted on its construction.*

In striking contrast to this tasteless edifice is the temple of Rádhá Indra Kishor, built by Ráni Indrajít Kunvar, widow of Het Kám, Bráhman zamíndár, of Tikári by Gayá. It was six years in building, and was completed at the end of 1871. It is a square of seventy feet divided into three aisles of five bays each, with a fourth space of equal dimensions for the reception of the god. The *sikhara* is surmounted with a copper *kalas*, or finial, heavily gilt, which alone cost Rs. 5,000. The piers are composed of four conjoined pillars, each shaft being a single piece of stone, brought from the Pahárpur quarry in Bharatpur territory. The building is raised on a high and enriched plinth, and the entire design is singularly light and graceful. Its cost has been three lakhs.

The temple of Rádhá Gopál, built by the Mahárája of Gwaliar under the direction of his guru Brahmachári Giridhári Dás, is also entitled to some special notice. The interior is an exact counterpart of an Italian church and would be an excellent model for our architects to follow, since it secures to perfection both free ventilation and a softened light. It consists of a nave 58 feet long, with four aisles, two on either side, a sacraium 21 feet in depth and a narthex of the same dimensions at the entrance. The outer aisles of the nave, instead of being closed in with solid walls, have open arches stopped only with wooden bars; and the tier of windows above gives on to a balcony and verandah. Thus any glare of light is impossible. The building was opened for religious service in 1860, and as it stands has cost four lakhs of rupees. The exterior has a mean and unsightly appearance, which might be obviated by the substitution of reticulated stone tracery for the wooden bars of the outer arches below and a more substantial balcony and verandah in lieu of the present ricketty erection above. An entrance gateway is now being added.

---

* In imitation of the bad example thus set, a new temple dedicated to Rádhá Gopál was built in 1873 by Lálá Braj Kishor, a wealthy resident of Sháhjahánpur, where he is district treasurer. It has a long frontage facing one of the principal streets, with a continuous balcony to the upper story, in which each pillar is a clumsily carved stone figure of a *Sakhi*, or 'dancing girl.'

There are in Brindá-ban no secular buildings of any great antiquity. The oldest is the court, or Ghera, as it is called, of Sawái Jay Sinh, the founder of Jaypur, who made Brindá-ban an occasional residence during the time that he was Governor of the Province of Agra (1721-1728). It is a large walled enclosure with a pavilion at one end, consisting of two aisles divided into five bays by piers of coupled columns of red sandstone. The river front of the town has a succession of gháts reaching for a distance of about a mile and a-half. Their beauty has been greatly marred by the religious mendicants who have taken possession of all the graceful stone kiosques and utilized them for cooking-places, blocking up the arches with mud walls and blackening the carved work with the smoke of their fires. I cleared out a great many, but left the task unfinished. The one highest up the stream is the Káli-mardan Ghát with the kadamb tree from which Krishna plunged into the water to encounter the great serpent Káliya ; and the lowest at the other end is Kesi Ghát, where he slew the equine demon of that name. Near the latter are two handsome mansions built by the Ránis Kishori and Lachhmi, consorts of Ranjít Sinh and Randhir Sinh, two successive Rájás of Bharatpur. In both the arrangement is identical with that of a mediæval college, carried out on a miniature scale, but with extreme elaboration of detail. The buildings are disposed in the form of a quadrangle, with an enriched gateway in the centre of one front and opposite it the chapel, of more imposing elevation than the ordinary domestic apartments, which constitute the two flanks of the square. In Ráni Lachhmi's *kunj* (such being the distinctive name for a building of this character), the temple front is a very rich and graceful composition. It has a colonnade of five arches standing on a high plinth, which, like every part of the wall surface, is covered with the most delicate carving and is shaded above by unusually broad eaves which have a wavy pattern on their under-surface and are supported on bold brackets. The work of the elder Ráni is of much plainer character ; and a third *kunj*, which stands a little lower down the river, close to the temple of Dhír Samír,* built by Thákur Badan Sinh, the father of Súraj Mall, the first of the Bharatpur Rájás, though large, has no architectural pretensions whatever. The most striking of the whole series is, however, the Gangá Mohan Kunj, built in

* In explanation of the title of this temple, which means literally 'a soft breeze,' take the following line from the Gitá Gobinda of Jayadeva :—

Dhira-samire Yamuná-tire vasati vane vana-máli,

which may be thus translated—

He is waiting, flower-begarlanded, beneath the forest trees,
Where cool across the Jamuná steals the soft delicious breeze.

the next generation by Gangá, Súraj Mall's Ráni. The river front, which is all that was ever completed, has a high and massive basement story, which on the land side, as seen from the interior of the court, becomes a mere plinth for the support of a majestic double cloister with broad and lofty arch and massive clustered pier. The style is precisely the same as that which prevails in the Garden Palace at Díg, a work of the same chief; who, however rude and uncultured himself, appears to have been able to appreciate and command the services of the highest available talent whether in the arts of war or peace. His son, Ratn Sinh, would seem to have inherited his father's architectural proclivities, for he had commenced what promised to be a very large and handsome mausoleum for the reception of his own funeral ashes, but died before the work had advanced beyond the first story. This is in one of the large gardens outside the town beyond the Madan Mohan temple, and has not been touched since his death.

A few years ago the town was exceedingly dirty and ill kept, but this state of things ceased from the introduction of a municipality. The conservancy arrangements are now of a most satisfactory character, and all the streets of any importance have been either paved or metalled. This unambitious, but most essential, work has, up to the present time, absorbed almost all the surplus income; the only exception being a house, intended to serve both for municipal meetings and also for the reception of European visitors, which I had not quite completed at the time of my transfer. It is in Indian style with carved stone pillars and arches to the verandahs and pierced tracery in the windows. As the ground about it had also been taken up for a garden, the whole would have formed a conspicuous ornament to the official quarter of the town, where all the other buildings are on the conventional and singularly prosaic D. P. W. type. Education, as conducted on European principles, has never made much way in the town, in spite of the efforts of the committee to promote it by the establishment of schools of different grades. Some of these have been closed altogether. The Tahsíli school, completed in 1868 at a cost of Rs. 3,710, which included a donation of Rs. 500 from Swámi Rangachárya, the head of the Seth's temple, still continues and has a room also for some anglo-vernacular classes; but the number of pupils, through variable, is never very large. The children find it more lucrative and amusing to hang about the temples and act as guides to the pilgrims and sight-seers. The dispensary, also opened in 1868, cost the small sum of only Rs. 1,943 ; but as yet it has no accommodation for in-door patients. As such a large number of people come to Brindában simply for the sake of dying there, while of the resident population nearly one-half are professed celibates, the proportion of births to deaths is almost in inverse ratio to that which prevails elsewhere; a circumstance which might well startle any one who was unacquainted with the exceptional character of the locality. The population by the recent census was 21,467, of whom 794 only were Muhammadans. The municipal income for the year 1871-72 was Rs. 17,549, and this may be regarded as a fair average. Of this sum Rs. 16,666 were derived from octroi collections; the tax on articles of food alone amounting to Rs. 13,248. These figures indicate very clearly, what might also be inferred from the preceding sketch, that there is no local trade or manufacture, and that the town is maintained entirely by its temples and religious reputation. There was a mint (*Taksál*) established here by Daulat Rao Sindhia, in 1786, whence the name of the street called the Taksál-wali-Gali. When the Játs were in possession of the country, they transferred it to Bharatpur, where what are called Brindábani rupees are still coined. They are especially used at weddings, and when there are many such festivities going on, the coin is sometimes valued at as much as 13 anas, but ordinarily sells for 12.

NOTES TO CHAPTER IX.

I.—Calendar of Local Festivals at Brindá-ban.

Chait Sudi (*April* 1—15).

1. *Chait Sudi* 3.—Gangaur; adoration of Ganpati and Gauri. In the older Sanskrit calendars this day is generally named Saubhágya Sayana, and is appropriated to a special devotion in honour of the goddess Arundhati, which is recommended to be practised by all women who desire to lead a happy married life and escape the curse of early widowhood. At the present day the oblations to Gauri are accompanied by the repetition of the following uncouth formula, in commemoration of a Ráni of Udaypur, who, after enjoying a life of the utmost domestic felicity, had the further happiness of dying at the same moment as her husband :—

गेार गेार गनपति ईस्वर पुजे पारवती महेश पुजा छा भ्राला गोला गेार के सेाना काटि काटिका दे टिमका दे रानी वरत करे वालादे रानी वरत करे वार गया पारगया खेरा ले राजाने दिया।

2. *Chait Sudi* 9.—Rám Navami. Ráma's birthday.

3. *Chait Sudi* 11.—Phúl dol.

Baisákh (*April—May*).

4. *Baisakh Sudi* 3.—Akhay Tij. Among agriculturists, the day for settling the accounts of the past harvest. Visits are paid to the image of Bihári, which on this festival only has the whole body exposed. The ceremony is hence called 'Chandan bágá ká darsan,' as the idol, though besmeared with sandal wood (*chandan*), has no clothing (*bága*). The temple *bhog* on this day consists exclusively of *kakris* (a kind of cucumber), *dál*, and a mash made of wheat, barley, and *chaná* ground up and mixed with sugar and *ghí*.

5. *Baisákh Sudi*. 9—Jánaki Navami. Held at Akrúr. Sítá's birthday.

6. *Baisákh Sudi* 10.—Hit ji ká utsav: at the Rás Mandal. Anniversary of the birth of the Gosáin Hari Vans.

7. *Baisákh Sudi* 14.—Narsinh avatár.

Jeth (*May—June*).

8. *Jeth Badi* 2.—Perambulation, called Ban bihár ká parikrama. The distance traversed is between five and six miles, each pilgrim starting from the point which happens to be most convenient.

9. *Jeth Badi* 5.—The same, but at night.

10. *Jeth Badi* 11.—Rás Mandal.

11. *Jeth Sudi* 5.—Jal Játra.

On the full moon of Jeth, Gaj-graha ká mela: representation of a fight between an elephant and a crocodile in the tank at the back of the Seth's temple.

Asárh (June—July).

12. *Asárh Sudi* 2.—Rath Játra. The god's collation, or *bhog*, consists on this day only of mangoes, *jáman* fruit and *chaná*.

13. *Asárh full moon.*—Dhío dhío ká mela at Madan Mohan, followed by the Pavan Paríksha.

Srávan (July—August).

14. *Srávan Badi* 5.—Rádhá Raman Ji ká dhío dhío. Mourning for the death of Gosáin Gopál Bhatt, the founder of the temple.

15. *Srávan Badi* 8.—Gokulánand ká dhío dhío. Mourning for the death of Gosáin Gokulánand.

16. *Srávan Sudi* 3.—Hindol, or Jhúl-játra. Swinging festival.

17. *Srávan Sudi* 9.—Fair at the Brahm Kund.

18. *Srávan Sudi* 11.—Pavitra-dháran, or presentation of Bráhmanical threads.

19. *Srávan full moon.*—Fair at the Gyán-gudari.

Bhádon (August—September.)

20. *Bhádon Badi* 8.—Janm Ashtami. Krishna's birthday.

21. *Bhádon Badi* 9.—Climbing a greasy pole, which is set up outside the temple of Rang Ji, with a dhoti, a lota, five sers of sweetmeats, and Rs. 5 on the top, for the man who can succeed in getting them. This takes place in the after-room. In the evening, the Nandotsav, or festival in honour of Nanda, is held at the Sringár-bat, and continued through the night with music and dancing.

22. *Bhádon Sudi* 8.—Rádhá Ashtami. Rádhá's birthday. A large assemblage also at the Mauni Dás ki tatti by the Nidh-ban, in honour of a saint who kept a vow of perpetual silence.

23. *Bhádon Sudi* 11.—Jal Jholni mela, or Karwatni, 'the turning of the god' in his four months' sleep.

Kuvár (September—October).

24. *Kuvár Badi* 11.—Festival of the Sanjhi, lasting for five days; and mela at the Brahm kund.

25. *Kuvár Sudi* 1.—Dán Lílá at the Gyán-gudari and mela of the Kalpavriksha.

26. *Kuvár Sudi* 10.—The Dasahara. Commemoration of Ráma's conquest of Lanká.

27. *Kuvár Sudi* 11.—Perambulation.

Kártik (October—November).

28. *Kártik new moon.*—Dípotsav, or festival of lamps.

29. *Kártik Sudi* 1.—Anna kút, as at Gobardhan.

30. *Kártik Sudi* 8.—Perambulation and Go-cháran.

31. *Kártik Sudi* 12.—Festival of the Davánal, or forest-conflagration.

32. *Kártik Sudi* 13.—Festival of Kesi Dánav.

33. *Kártik Sudi* 14.—Nág-lila: at the Káli-mardan Ghát with procession of boats.

34. *Kártik full moon.*—Fair at Bhat-rond.

Agahn (November—December).

35. *Agahn Badi* 1.—Byáhle-ká-mela, or marriage feast, at the Rás Mandal and Chain Ghát.

36. *Agahn Badi* 3.—Rám lílá.

37. *Agahn full moon.*—Dau ji-ká-mela, in honour of Balarám.

38. *Agahn Sudi* 5.—Bihári janmotsav, or birth of Bihári; also the Bharat-miláp.

Pús (December—January).

39. *Pús Sudi* 5 *to* 11.—Dhanur-más otsav, observed at the Seths' temple with processions issuing from the Vaikunth gate: 'Dhanur' being the sign Sagittarius. Throughout the month distribution of *khichri* (pulse and rice) is made at the temple of Rádhá Ballabh.

Mágh (January—February).

40. *Mágh Sudi* 5.—Basantotsav. The spring festival.

41. *Phálgun Badi* 11.—Festival at the Mán-sarovar.

Phálgun (February—March).

42. *Phálgun Sudi* 11.—Phúl dol.

43. *Phálgun full moon.*—The Holi or Carnival.

Chait Badi (March 15th to 31st).

44. *Chait Badi* 1.—Dhurendi or sprinkling of the Holi-powder, and Dol játra.

45. *Chait Badi* 5.—Káli dahan and phúl dol.

46. Brahmotsav. Festival at the Seth's temple, beginning Chait Badi 2 and lasting ten days.

II.—List of River-side Ghats at Brinda-ban.

1 Madan Ter Ghát, built by Pandit Moti Lal.
2 Rám-gol Ghát, built by the Gosáin of the temple of Bihári Ji.
3 Káli-daha Ghát, built by Holkar Ráo.
4 Gopál Ghát, built by Madan Pál, Rájá of Kurauli.
5 Nábhawála Ghát, built by Rájá Hira Sinh of Nábha.
6 Praskandan Ghát, re-built by Gosáins of temple of Madan Mohan.
7 Súraj Ghát.
8 Koriya Ghát, said to be named after certain Gosáins from Kol.
9 Jugal Ghát, built by Hari Dás and Gobind Dás, Thákurs.
10 Dhúsar Ghát.
11 Naya Ghát, built by Gosáin Bhajan Lál.
12 Sriji Ghát, built by Rájá of Jaypur.
13 Bihár Ghát, built by Appa Rám from the Dakhin.
14 Dhúrawára Ghát, built by Rájá Randhír Sinh of Dhúra.
15 Nágari Dás.
16 Bhím Ghát, built by the Rájá of Kota.
17 Andha (*i.e.*, the dark or covered) Ghát, built by Rájá Mán of Jaypur.
18 Tehríwára Ghát, built by the Rájá of Tehri.
19 Imla Ghát.
20 Bardwán Ghát, built by a Rájá of Bardwán.
21 Barwára Ghát.
22 Ránawat Ghát, built by the Rána of Udaypur.
23 Singár Ghát, built by the Gosáin of the temple of Singár-bat.
24 Ganga Mohan Ghát, built by Ganga, Ráni of Súraj Mall, of Bharatpur.
25 Gobind Ghát, built by Rájá Mán of Jaypur.
26 Himmat Bahádur's Ghát, built by Gosáin Himmat Bahádur (see Chapter XI.)
27 Chír Ghát or Chain Ghát, built by Malhár Ráo, Holkar.
28 Hanumán Ghát, built by Sawái Jay Sinh of Jaypur.
29 Bhaunra Ghát, built by Sawái Jay Sinh of Jaypur.
30 Kishor Ráni's Ghát, built by Kishori, Ráni of Súraj Mall, of Bharatpur.
31 Pandawára Ghát, built by Chaudhari Jagannáth, of Lakhnau.
32 Kesi Ghát, built by the Bharatpur Ráni, Lachhmi.

III.—Names of Mahallas, or City Quarters at Brindá-ban.

1 Gyán Gudari.
2 Gopesvar Mahádeva.
3 Bansi-bat.
4 Gopináth Bágh.
5 Bazár Gopináth.
6 Brahm-kund.
7 Rádhá Nivás.
8 Kesi Ghát.
9 Rádhá Raman.
10 Nidh-ban.
11 Pathar-pura.
12 Nagara Gopináth.
13 Gherá Gopináth.
14 Nagara Gopál.
15 Chir Ghát.
16 Mandi Darwáza.
17 Ghera Gobind Jí.
18 Nagara Gobind Jí.
19 Gali Taksár.
20 Rám Ji Dwára.
21 Bazár Kanthiwára (*i.e.*, sellers of rosaries and necklaces).
22 Sewa Kunj.
23 Kunj Gali.
24 Byás ká Gherá.
25 Singár-bat.
26 Rás Mandal.
27 Kishor-pura.
28 Dhobiwári Gali.
29 Rangi Lal ki Gali.
30 Sukhan Mátá Gali (*i.e.*, street of dried-up small-pox),
31 Purána Shahr (*i.e.*, old town).
32 Láriawára Gali.
33 Gabdua kí Gali.
34 Gobardhan Darwáza.
35 Ahir-pará.
36 Dusáit (the name, it is said, of a sub-division of the Sanádh tribe).
37 Mahalla Barwára (from the number of *bar* trees).
38 Ghera Madan Mohan.
39 Bihári-pura.
40 Purohit-wára.
41 Mani-pára.
42 Gautam-pára.
43 Ath-khamba.
44 Gobind bágh.
45 Loi Bazár, (the blanket mart).*
46 Retiya Bazár.
47 Ban-khandi Mahádeva.
48 Chhipi kí Gali.
49 Ráewári Gali (occupied by Bháts, or bards, who are always distinguished by the title Ráe).
50 Bundele ká Bágh. Bundela is the god propitiated in time of cholera. He is always represented as riding on a horse. When small-pox, the twin scourge of India, is raging, an ass is the animal to which offerings are made.
51 Mathurá Darwáza.
52 Ghera Sawai Jay Sinh.
53 Dhír Samír.
54 Mauni Dás ki tatti.
55 Gahvar-ban.
56 Gobind kund.
57 Rádhá Bágh.

* There is a large sale of Loi, or country blanketing, at Brindá-ban. The material is imported chiefly from Márwár and Bikaner in an old and worn condition, but is worked up again so thoroughly that natives count it as good as new.

CHAPTER X.

MAHÁ-BAN, GOKUL, AND BALADEVA.

The town of Mahá-ban—population 6,182—is some five or six miles from Mathurá, lower down the stream and on the opposite bank of the Jamuna. Though the country in its neighbourhood is now singularly bare, the name indicates that it must at one time have been densely wooded; and so late as the year 1634 A.D. we find the Emperor Sháhjahán ordering a hunt there and killing four tigers. It stands a little inland, about a mile distant from Gokul; which latter place has appropriated the more famous name, though it is in reality only the water-side suburb of the ancient town. This is clearly indicated by the fact that all the traditional sites of Krishna's adventures, described in the Puránas as having taken place at Gokul, are shown at Mahá-ban; while the Gokul temples are essentially modern in all their associations: whatever celebrity they possess is derived from their having been founded by the descendants of Vallabhá-chárya, the great heresiarch of the sixteenth century. The existence of Gokul as a distinct town was no doubt long antecedent to its religious aggrandizement, and probably dates from the time when the old Hindu fort was occupied by a Muhammadan garrison and the Hindus expelled beyond its immediate precincts.

Taking, then, Mahá-ban as equivalent to the Gokul of Sanskrit literature, the connection between it and Mathurá has always been of a most intimate character. For, according to the legend, Krishna was born at the one and cradled at the other. Both, too, make their first appearance in history together and under most unfortunate circumstances, having been sacked by Mahmúd of Ghazní in the year 1017 A.D. From the effects of this catastrophe it would seem that Mahá-ban was never able to recover itself. It is casually mentioned in connection with the year 1234 A.D., by Minháj-i-Siráj, a contemporary writer, as one of the gathering places for the imperial army sent by Shams-ud-dín against Kálanjar; and the Emperor Bábar, in his memoirs, incidentally refers to it, as if it were a place of some importance still, in the year 1526 A.D.; but the name occurs in the pages of no other chronicle; and at the present day, though it is the seat of a tahsíli, it can scarcely be called more than a considerable village. Within the last few years, one or two large and handsome private residences have been built, with fronts of carved stone in the Mathurá style; but the temples are all exceedingly mean and of no antiquity. The largest and also the most sacred is that dedicated to Mathurá-náth, which boasts of a pyramidal tower, or *sikhara,* of some height and bulk, but constructed only of brick and plaster. The Bráhman in charge used to enjoy an endowment of Rs. 2 a day, the gift of Sindhia, but this has long lapsed. There are two other small shrines of some interest: in the one, the demon Trinávart is represented as a pair of enormous wings overhanging the infant god; the other bears the dedication of Mahá Mall Ráe, 'the great champion prince,' a title given to Krishna after his discomfiture of the various evil spirits sent against him by Kansa.

Great part of the town is occupied by a high hill, partly natural and partly artificial, extending over more than 100 bíghas of land, where stood the old fort.* This is said to have been built by the same Ráná Katehra of Mewár to whom is also ascribed the fort at Jalesar. According to a tradition current in the Main-puri district, he had been driven from his own country by an invasion of the Muhammadans, and took refuge with the Rájá of Mahá-ban, by name Digpál, whose daughter his son, Kánh Kunvar, subsequently married and by her became the ancestor of the tribe of Phátak Ahírs. It would seem that, on the death of his father-in-law, he succeeded to his dominions; for he made a grant of the whole of the township of Mahá-ban to his Purohits, or family priests, who were Sanádh Bráhmans, of the Parásar clan. Their descendants bear the distinctive title of Chaudhari, and still own two shares in Mahá-ban, called Thok Chaudhariyán. The fort was recovered by the Muhammadans in the reign of Alá-ud-dín, by Sufi Yahya of Mashhad, who introduced himself and a party of soldiers inside the walls in litters, disguised as Hindu ladies who wished to visit the shrines of Syám Lalá and Rohini. The Rána was killed, and one-third of the town was granted by the sovereign to Saiyid Yahya. This share†

* With the exception of the *kila*, or keep, the rest of the hill is known as the *kot.*

† The division of proprietary rights in Mahá-ban is of very perplexing character, the several shares being very different in extent from what their names seem to indicate. The total area is 6,529 bíghas and 10 biswas, distributed as follows:—

	Bighas.	Bis.
The 11 biswa Thok Chaudhariyán	1,397	10
The 9 ditto ditto	703	4
The Thok Saiyidát	570	19
Free lands resumed by Government	1,750	4
Common land	2,107	13
Total ...	6,529	10

One-third of the profits of the common land goes to the Saiyids; the remaining two-thirds are then again sub-divided into three, of which one part goes to the 9 biswa thok and two to the 11 biswas.

is still called Thok Saiyidát, and is owned by his descendants; the present head of the family being Sardar Ali, who officiated for a time as a Tahsíldár in the Mainpuri district. The place where his great ancestor was buried is shown at the back of the Chhatthi Pálna, but is unmarked by any monument.

The story as told in different localities is so identical in all its main features that it may reasonably be accepted as based on fact; but it is difficult to determine an exact date for the event, or decide which of the Sissodia Princes of Chitor is intended by the personage styled 'the Ráná Katehra.' Still, though certainty is unattainable, a conjectural date may be assigned with some amount of probability; for as the Ráná Katehra is represented as still living at the time when the fort of Mahá-ban was recovered by Alá-ud-dín, his flight from his own country cannot have occurred very long previously, and may plausibly be connected with Alá-ud-din's memorable sack of Chitor, which took place in the year 1303. If so, he can scarcely have been more than a cadet of the royal line; for, according to accepted tradition, the actual Ráná of Mewár and all his family had perished in the siege, with the exception only of the second son and his infant nephew, Hamír, the heir to the throne, who eventually not only recovered the ancient capital of his forefathers, but made it the centre of a far wider dominion than had ever previously acknowledged the Sissodia rule. The stratagem of introducing armed men disguised as women in closed litters into the heart of the enemy's camp had been successfully practised against Alá-ud-dín himself after a former siege of Chitor, and had resulted in the escape of the captured Ráná. This may have suggested the adoption of the same expedient at Mahá-ban, either in fact to the Sufi, who is said to have carried it into execution, or to the local legend-monger, who has used it as an embellishment to his narrative.

The shrine of Syám Lalá, to which allusion has been made above, still exists as a mean little cell, perched on the highest point of the fortifications on the side where they overlook the Jamuná. It is believed to mark the spot where Jasodá gave birth to Mayá, or Joga-nidrá, substituted by Vasudeva for the infant Krishna. But by far the most interesting building is a covered court called Nanda's Palace, or more commonly the Assi-Khamba, *i.e.*, the eighty pillars. In its present form is was erected by the Muhammadans in the time of Aurangzeb out of older materials, to serve as a mosque, and as it now stands, it is divided, by five rows of sixteen pillars each, into four aisles, or rather into a centre and two narrower side aisles, with one broad outer cloister. The external pillars of this outer cloister are each of one massive shaft, cut into many narrow facets, with two horizontal bands of carving: the capitals are decorated either with grotesque heads or the usual four squat figures. The pillars of the inner aisles vary much in design, some being exceedingly plain and others as richly ornamented with profuse and often graceful arabesques. Three of the more elaborate are called respectively the Satya, Treta and Dwápar Yug; while the name of the Kali Yug is given to another somewhat plainer. All these interior pillars, however, agree in consisting as it were of two short columns set one upon the other. The style is precisely similar to that of the Hindu colonnades by the Kutb Minár at Delhi; and both works may reasonably be referred to about the same age. As is it probable that the latter were not built in the years immediately preceding the fall of Delhi in 1194, so also it would seem that the columns at Mahá-ban must have been sculptured before the assault of Mahmúd in 1017; for after that date the place was too insignificant to be selected as the site of any elaborate edifice. Thus, Mr. Fergusson's conjecture is confirmed, that the Delhi pillars are to be ascribed to the ninth or tenth century. He doubts whether the cloister there now stands as originally arranged by the Hindus, or whether it had been taken down and re-arranged by the conquerors; but concludes as most probable that the former was the case, and that it was an open colonnade surrounding the palace of Prithi Raj. "If so," he adds, "it is the only instance known of Hindu pillars being left undisturbed." General Cunningham differs from this conclusion, and considers it utterly incredible that any architect, designing an original building and wishing to obtain height, should have recourse to such a rude expedient as constructing two distinct pillars, and then, without any disguise, piling up one on the top of the other. But such a design, however strange according to modern ideas, did not, it is clear, offend the taste of the old Mahá-ban architects, since we find them copying it for decorative purposes even when there was no constructural necessity for it. Thus some of the inner columns are really monoliths, and yet they have all the appearance of being in two pieces.

A good illustration of this Hindu fancy for broken pillars may be seen at Noh-jhíl, a town across the Ganges in the extreme north of the district. Here also is a Muhammadan dargáh, constructed out of the wreck of a Hindu temple. The pillars, twenty in number, are very simple in character, but exceptional in two respects; first, as being all of uniform design, which is quite anomalous in Hindu architecture; secondly, as being, though of fair height, each cut out of a single piece of stone. The only decoration on the otherwise plain shaft consists of four deep scroll-shaped notches half-way between the base and capital; the result of which is to make each column appear as if it were in two pieces. The explanation is obvious. In earlier days, when large blocks of stone were difficult to procure, there was also lack of sufficient art to conceal the unavoidable join in the structure. In course of time the eye became accustomed to the defect, and eventually required its apparent introduction even where it did not really exist. A similar conservatism may be traced in the art history of every nation, and more especially in religious art. In breaking up his columns into two pieces, and thus perpetuating, as a decoration, what in its origin had been a signal defect, the Hindu architect was unconsciously influenced by the same motive as the Greek, who to the very last continued to introduce, as prominent features in his temple façades, the metopes and triglyphs which had been necessities in the days of wooden construction, but had become unmeaning when repeated in stone.

The two ancient Brahmanical temples on the Gwaliar rock, commonly known as the Sás Bahu, illustrate still more remarkably than the Noh-jhîl dargáh the way in which what was originally a constructural make-shift has subsequently been adopted as a permanent architectural feature. In the larger of these two buildings the interior of the spacious nave is disfigured by four enormous columns, which occupy a square in the centre of the area and obstruct the view in every direction. It is evident at a glance that, though the work of the same architect as the rest of the fabric, they are utterly out of harmony with his first design. Necessity alone can have compelled him to introduce them as props for a falling roof; while the shallowness and unfinished state of their surface sculpture further suggest that they were erected in great haste in order to avert a catastrophe which appeared imminent. They were as little contemplated at the outset as the inverted arches in Wells Cathedral, or as the rude struts inserted by General Cunningham in this very same building to support the broken architraves of the upper story. In the smaller temple, which is of somewhat later date, the internal arrangement follows precisely the same lines, though here the lesser span of the roof rendered the detached pillars unnecessary, the massive walls being quite sufficient by themselves to support the small flat dome and the low tower that surmounted it. The central columns, however, are here so artistically treated, and are in such excellent proportion to the other parts of the building, having been designed with them and not subsequently intruded, that they are really decorative and add beauty to the interior.

Both these temples, like that of Gobind Deva at Brindá-ban, to which they form a most valuable and interesting complement, originally consisted of three compartments—a fact which has not been previously noticed by any archæologist.

In the larger Gwaliar temple the nave and the choir remain, but the sanctum, as is usually the case, has been totally destroyed by the Muhammadans. That it once existed, however, is evident from the fact that the choir is seen from the interior to have communicated with an apartment beyond, though the opening is now closed with blocks of stone. In the smaller of the two temples the nave alone is perfect : the choir has utterly perished ; but the end wall of the sanctum still exists *in situ*, built up into the ramparts of the fort. General Cunningham, in describing these buildings, has followed Mr. Fergusson in using, instead of 'nave,' the misleading word 'porch,' and has thus failed to notice the triple arrangement which otherwise could not have escaped him.*

To return to the Chhatthi Pálná. On a drum of one of the pillars is an inscription—now upside down—which I read as *Rám dása kas eknavi kam*, meaning, it would seem, 'Column No. 91, the gift of Rám Dás.' This would rather lead to the supposition that the pillars were all originally of one set and belonged to a single building, though it is quite possible that they may be the wreck of several different temples, all of which were overthrown by Mahmúd of Ghazni, when he captured the fort in 1017. In either case there can be no question as to the Buddhist character of the building, or buildings, for I found let into the wall a small seated figure of Buddha, as also a cross-bar and a large upright of a Buddhist railing. The latter is ornamented with foliated circular disks, on one of which is represented a head with a most enormous chignon, and—what is unusual—has four oval sockets for cross-bars on either side instead of three. These columns and other fragments had probably been lying about for centuries till the Muhammadans, in the reign of Aurangzeb, after demolishing a modern Hindu temple, roughly put them together and set them up on its site as a makeshift for a mosque. When Father Tieffenthaller visited Mahá-ban about the middle of last century, it seems that Hindus and Muhammadans were both in joint possession of the building, for he writes : "On voit á Mahá-ban dans une grande maison porteé par 80 colonnes, une peinture qui represente Krishna volant du lait en jettant le clair et jouant avec d'autres. Cet edifice a été converti en partie en une mosquee, en partie en une pagode." But the connection of the building with

* I would here notice, as I may not have a better opportunity and it is a fact of interest, that the third of the Gwaliar temples, commonly called the *Teli ka mandir*, about which General Cunningham hesitates to express an opinion, is certainly a Jain building. This is shown by the enormous height of the doorway, a feature peculiarly unbrahmanical, and by the two upper stories of the tower—as in the Buddh Gaya temple—which no Brahman would ever have thought of allowing over the head of the god.

Krishna or his worship, even at any earlier period, is entirely fictitious. That is to say, so far as concerns the actual fabric and the materials of which it is constructed : the site, as in so many other similar cases, has probably been associated with Hindu worship from very remote antiquity. In Sir John Strachey's time I obtained a grant of Rs. 1,000 for the repair of the building, which had fallen into a very ruinous condition, and in digging the foundations of the new screen-walls (the old walls had been simply set on the ground without any foundation at all) I came upon a number of remains of the true Hindu temple, dating apparently from no further back than about the year 1500 A.D. The Iconoclast would not use these sculptures in the construction of his mosque, since they had too recently formed part of an idolatrous shrine, but had them buried out of sight ; while he had no scruple about utilizing the old Buddhist pillars. Whatever I dug up, I either let into the wall or brought over to Mathurá for the local Museum. The roof of the present building, as constructed by the Muhammadans, is made up of any old slabs and broken pillars that first came to hand ; but two compartments are covered in with the small flat domes of the old temple, which are similar in character to the beautiful examples at Ajmer and Mount Abu.

Mothers come here for their purification on the sixth day after childbirth —*chhatthi púja*—whence the building is popularly known as the Chhatthi Pálna, and it is visited by enormous crowds of people for several days about the anniversary of Krishna's birth in the month of Bhádon. A representation of the infant god's cradle (*pálna*) is displayed to view, with his foster-mother's churn and other domestic articles. The place being regarded not exactly as a temple, but as Nanda and Jasoda's actual dwelling-house, all persons, without regard to the religion they profess, are allowed to walk about in it with perfect freedom. Considering the size, the antiquity, the artistic excellence, the exceptional archæological interest, the celebrity amongst natives, and the close proximity to Mathurá of this building, it is strange that it has never before been mentioned by any English writer.

It is said that whenever foundations are sunk within the precincts of the fort, many fragments of sculpture—of Buddhist character, it may be presumed —have been brought to light ; but they have always been buried again or broken up as building materials. Doubtless, Mahá-ban was the site of some of those Buddhist monasteries which the Chinese pilgrim Fa Hian distinctly states existed in his time on both sides of the river. And further, whatever may be the exact Indian word concealed under the form Klisoboras, or Clisobora, given by Arrian and Pliny as the name of the town between which and Mathurá the Jamuná flowed—*Amnis Jomanes in Gangem per Palibothros decurrit inter oppida Methora et Clisobora,* Pliny, Hist. Nat. vi., 22—it may be concluded with certainty that Mahá-ban is the site intended.* Its other literary names are Brihad-vana, Brihad-aranya, Gokula, and Nandagrâma ; and no one of these, it is true, in the slightest resembles the word Clisobora. But this might well be a corruption of 'Krishna-pura,' 'the city of Krishna,' a term used by the speaker as a descriptive title—and it would be a highly appropriate one —but taken by the foreign traveller for the ordinary proper name of the place. Colonel Tod thought Clisobora might be Batesar, and most subsequent English topographers seem to have blindly accepted the suggestion. There is, however, really no foundation for it beyond the surmise that Clisobora and Mathurá were quoted as the two principal towns in the country, and that Batesar must have been a place of importance, because its older name was derived from the Súrasen, after whom the whole people were called Sauraseni. General Cunningham, in his 'Ancient Geography,' has thrown out a new theory and identifies Clisobora (read in one MS. as Cyrisoborka) with Brindá-ban, assuming that Kálikavartta, or 'Kaliká's Whirlpool,' was an earlier name of the town, in allusion to Krishna's combat with the serpent Kálika. But in the first place, the Jamuná does not flow *between* Mathurá and Brindá-ban, seeing that both are on the same bank ; secondly, the ordinary name of the great serpent is not Kálika, but Káliya ; and thirdly, it does not appear upon what authority it is stated that "the earlier name of the place was Kálikavartta." Upon this latter point, a reference was made to the great Brindá-ban Pandit, Swámi Rangáchárya, who, if any one, might be expected to speak with positive knowledge, and his reply was that in the course of all his reading, he had never met with Brindá-ban under any other name than that which it now bears.

The glories of Mahá-ban are told in a special (interpolated) section of the Brahmánda Puráná, called the Brihad-vana Máhátmya. In this,

* The parallel passage in Arrian's India is as follows :—*Τοῦτον τον Ἡρακλέα μάλιστα πρὸς Σουρασηνῶν γεραίρεσθαι, Ινδικὸν ἔθνεος, δύο πόλιες μεγάλαι, Μεθορά τε καὶ Κλεισόβορα, καὶ ποταμὸς Ιωβάρης πλωτὸς διαρρέει την χώρην αυτων.* As both authors seem to be quoting from the same original, the insertion of the words *per Palibothros* in Pliny must be due to an error on the part of some copyist, misled by the frequent mention of Palibothra in the preceding paragraphs. The mistake cannot be credited to Pliny himself, who fixes the site of Palibothra as 415 miles to the east of the confluence of the Ganges and the Jamuná. The gods whom Arrian proceeds to describe under the names of Dionysus and Hercules correspond closely with Krishna and Balaráma, who are still the local divinities of Mathurá.

its *tírthas*, or holy places, are reckoned to be twenty-one in number as follows :—

Eka-vinsati-tírthena yuktam bhúrigunánvitam,
Yamal-árjuna punyatamam, Nanda-kúpam tathaiva cha,
Chintá-harana Bráhmándam, kundam Sarasvatam tathá,
Sarasvati silá tatra, Vishnu-kunda-samánvitam,
Karna-kúpam, Krishna-kundam, Gopa-kúpam tathaiva cha,
Ramanám-ramana-sthánam, Nárada-sthánam eva cha,
Pútaná-pátana-sthánam, Trinávarttákhya pátanam,
Nanda-harmyam, Nanda-geham, Ghátam Ramana-samjnakam,
Mathuránáthodbhavam kshetram punyam pápapranásanam,
Janma-sthánam tu Sheshasya, jananam Yogamáyaya.

The Pútaná-pátana-sthánam of the above lines is a ravine, commonly called Putaná khár, which is crossed by the Mathurá road a short distance outside the town. It is a mile or more in length, reaching down to the bank of the Jamuná and, as the name denotes, is supposed to have been caused by the passage of Pútaná's giant body, in the same way as the Kans Khár at Mathurá.

At the Bráhmánd ghát, where a *rás*, or 'sacred dance,' is held every Sunday, there is a small modern shrine of Mrittika Bihári and the remains of a *chhattri* built by one Mukund Sinh, the greater part of which has been washed away by the river. A Jaini sculpture, probably brought from the Chhatthi Pálná, is let into the front of the little platform, on which are placed balls of sand in the shape of the *pera* sweetmeat, to represent the lump of earth that the child Krishna stuffed into his mouth, and which Jasodá saw develope into a miniature universe. These are called the *Bráhmánd ke pera* and are taken away by pilgrims as souvenirs of their visit. A pretty walk under the trees along the high bank of the river leads to the Chintá-haran ghát, a quarter of a mile lower down the stream, a secluded spot, where a Rás is held every Monday. There are no buildings save a Bairágí's cell. The Hindu cicerones never fail to speak with much enthusiasm of the liberality of Mir Sarfaráz Ali, grandfather of Sardár Ali, who never cut any of the timber for his own profit and allowed the pilgrims to make free use of it all : the property has now changed hands and the landlord's manorial rights are more strictly enforced.

Between the town and the sandy expanse called the Raman Reti is a small grove known as the Khelan Ban, with several trees of the Páras Pipar kind, which I have not seen elsewhere in this part of India, though in Bombay there are avenues of it in some of the streets of the city. The largest, which is in front of the Bairágí's cell, flowers profusely in the cold weather from November to February : the flowers, much resembling those of the cotton plant in form, are on first opening yellow and afterwards change their colour to red. The bud is exactly like an elongated acorn ; the leaves resemble those of the pipal, but are smaller. On the high bank overlooking the Raman Reti (where is held a fair on the 11th of each Hindu month) are two handsome *chhattris* to members of Ali Khan's family, of the same design as the one on the other side of the town, but in a more ruinous condition. The well close by is called the Gop Kúa. On the opposite bank, on what is an island in the rains, is the Koila Saráe, of much the same size as the one at Chaumuha. The gateways still retain their original wooden doors and are surmounted by corner *chhattris* as at Chháta. The whole area was occupied till 1871, when it was flooded by the river, which rose to an unusual height and carried away the city bridge, 18 pontoons of which were stranded here. Since then the site has been deserted, the villagers having all removed to higher ground. Outside one of the gates is a mosque and there are ruins of other edifices also—undermined and partly washed away by the river—including a square building said to have been a temple of Mahádeva, erected by Jawáhir Sinh of Bharatpur : the foundations have been laid bare to a depth of some six or seven feet.

The principal Hindu festivals observed in Mahá-ban are the Rám Lílá in the month of Kuvár, first set on foot by a late Tahsíldár, Munshi Bhajan Lál ; the Pútana melá, Kártik Sudi 6th ; the Jakhaiya melá, held on the Sundays of the month of Mágh (there is a similar festival held at Paindhat in the Mustafabad pargana of the Mainpuri district, which is believed to have great influence on the fall of rain in the winter season) the Raman Reti, held on the sands of the Jamuná, Phálgun Sudi 11th ; and the Parikama, or Perambulation, Kártik Sudi 5th ; this includes the town of Gokul and village of Rával, at which latter place Rádhá's mother is said to have lived.

The Muhammadans, who are only 1,704 in number, have several small mosques and two festivals. One of these, the Chatiyal Madár, is held on the 3rd of Jamáda'l-awwal, in honour of Saiyid Badia-ud-dín, better known as Sháh Madár, whose principal shrine is at Makhanpur on the Isan. His festivals, wherever held, are distinguished by the name of Chatiyal, meaning 'an open place,' and the hereditary hierophants bear the title of Khalífa. The second Muhammadan melá is the Urs Dargáh of Sháh Gílan, or Saiyid Makhdúm. The dargáh was built about a century ago by Nawáb Sulaimán Beg.

GOKUL.

The town of Gokul—population 4,012—being the head-quarters of the Vallabhácháryas, or Gokulashta Gosáins, is throughout the year crowded with pilgrims, of whom the majority come from Gujarát and Bombay, where the doctrines of the sect have been very widely propagated, more especially among the Bhattias and other mercantile classes. In many of its physical characteristics the place used to present a striking parallel to the presumed morality of its *habitués*, its streets being tortuous and unsavoury, its buildings unartistic, its environs waste and uninviting; while to complete the analogy, though only five or six miles distant from Mathurá, it was cut off from easy access by the river, and was thus at once both near and remote, in the same way as its literature is modern and yet obscure. The picturesque appearance, which it presented from the opposite bank, was destroyed on nearer approach. For the temples, though they amount to a prodigious number and are many of them richly endowed, are nearly all modern in date and for the most part tasteless in design; while the thoroughfares were in the rains mere channels for the floods which poured down through them to the Jamuná, and at all other seasons of the year were so rough and broken that the rudest wheeled vehicle could with difficulty make its way along them. Efforts were made for many years to improve its sanitation, but without the slightest result, for the Gosáin Muáfidárs were quite indifferent to any reform of the kind, and were well content to let things remain as they were. However, by personally interesting myself in the matter and putting an active and intelligent Tahsildar in local charge, I succeeded before I left the district in making it by universal consent one of the cleanest and neatest of towns, instead of being as formerly the very filthiest. It may be doubtful how long the reform will last, for constant supervision is necessary in consequence of the number of cattle driven within the walls every night, which render the place really what its name denotes, 'a cattle yard,' rather than an abode of men. Its most noteworthy ornament is a spacious masonry tank constructed some thirty years ago by a Seth named Chunna. The trees on its margin are always white with flocks of large water-fowl of a quite distinct species from any to be found elsewhere in the neighbourhood. They are a new colony, being all descended from a few pairs which casually settled there no more than ten or twelve years ago. Their plumage is peculiar and ornamental, but not at all times easy to obtain, as the birds are considered to enjoy the benefit of sanctuary, and on one occasion, when a party of soldiers from the Mathurá cantonments attempted to shoot a number of them, the townspeople rose *en masse* for their protection. Immediately opposite the tank and between it and the river I had a new school built, occupying three sides of a quadrangle with an arched gateway of carved stone on the fourth side facing the street. The cost was Rs. 2,440, the whole of which sum was raised by local subscription save only Rs. 500, which were allotted from the balance of the Government cess. A Sanskrit class has since been started, and so many wealthy pilgrims visit Gokul, who would be glad to spend their money on local institutions, if there were only some one to call their attention to them, that the school might easily be maintained as one of the largest and highest in the district.

The great heresiarch, Vallabhácharya, from whom Gokul derives all its modern celebrity, was born in the year 1479 A. D., being the second son of Lakshman Bhatt, a Telinga Bráhman of the Vishnu Swámi Sampradáya. By the accident of birth, though not by descent, he can be claimed as a native of Upper India, having been born at Champaranya, a wild solitude in the neighbourhood of Banáras, whither his parents had travelled up from the south on a pilgrimage. Their stay in the holy city was cut short by a popular *emeute*, the result of religious intolerance ; and the mother, who was little in a condition to encounter the distress and fatigue of so hasty a flight, prematurely gave birth on the way to an eight months' child. Either from an exaggerated alarm as to their own peril, or, as was afterwards said, from a sublime confidence in the promised protection of Heaven, they laid the babe under a tree and abandoned it to its fate. When some days had elapsed, and their fears had subsided, they cautiously retraced their steps, and finding the child still alive and uninjured on the very spot where he had been left, they took him with them to Banáras. After a very short stay there, they fixed their home at Gokul, where the child was placed under the tuition of the Pandit Náráyan Bhatt, and in four months mastered the whole vast range of Sanskrit literature and philosophy. His followers, it may be remarked, are conscientious imitators of their founder in respect of the short time which they devote to their studies ; but the result in their case is more in accordance with ordinary experience, and their scholarship of the very slightest. When eleven years of age, he lost his father, and almost immediately afterwards commenced his career as a religious teacher. His earliest triumphs were achieved in Southern India, where he secured his first convert, Dámodar Dás ; and in a public disputation at Vijaynagar, the place where his mother's family resided, he refuted the arguments of the Court Pandits with such authority that even the King, Krishna Deva, was convinced by his eloquence and adopted the youthful stranger as his spiritual guide. Thenceforth his success was ensured ; and at every place that he visited, Ujaiyin, Banáras, Haridwár, and Allahabad, the new doctrines enlisted a multitude of adherents. A life of celibacy being utterly at variance with his ideas of a reasonable religion, he took to himself a wife at Banáras and became the father of two sons, Gopináth, born in 1511, and Bitthalnáth in 1516. His visits to Braj were long and frequent. There, in 1520, he founded at Gobardhan the great temple of Srí-náth ; and at Brinda-ban saw in a vision the god Krishna, who directed him to introduce a new devotion in his honor, wherein he should be adored in the form of a child under the title of Bálkrishna or Bál Gopál ; which is still the cultus most affected by his descendants at the present day. His permanent home, however, was at Banáras, where he composed his theological works, of which the most extensive is a commentary on the Bhagavad Gíta, called the Subodhini, and where he died in the year 1531.

He was succeeded in the pontificate by his second son, Bitthalnáth, who propagated his father's doctrines with great zeal and success throughout all the south and west of India, and himself received 252 distinguished proselytes, whose acts are recorded in a Hindi work called the 'Do Sau Bávan Vártá.' Finally, in 1565, he settled down at Gokul and, at the age of seventy, breathed his last on the sacred hill of Gobardhan. By his two wives he had a family of seven sons, Giridhar, Gobind, Bál-krishan, Gokulnáth, Raghunáth, Jadunáth, and Ghansyám. Of these, the fourth, Gokulnáth, is by far the most famous, and his descendants in consequence claim some slight pre-eminence above their kinsmen. His principal representative is the Gosáin at Bombay.

Unlike other Hindu sects, in which the religious teachers are ordinarily unmarried, all the Gosáins among the Vallabhácháryas are invariably family men and engage freely in secular pursuits. They are the Epicureans of the east and are not ashamed to avow their belief that the ideal life consists rather in social enjoyment than in solitude and mortification. Such a creed is naturally destructive of all self-restraint even in matters where indulgence is by common consent held criminal ; and the profligacy to which it has given rise is so notorious that the late Maháraja of Jaypur was moved to expel from his capital the ancient image of Gokul Chandrama, for which the sect entertained a special veneration. He further conceived such a prejudice against Vaishnavas in general, that all his subjects were compelled, before they appeared in his presence, to mark their forehead with the three horizontal lines that indicate a votary of Siva. The scandalous practices of the Gosáins and the unnatural subserviency of the people in ministering to their gratification received a crushing *exposé* in a *cause célèbre* for libel tried before the Supreme Court of Bombay in 1861, from the detailed narrative of which I have borrowed a considerable amount of information.

The dogma of Brahma-Sambandh, or 'union with the divine,' upon which Vallabhácharya constructed his whole system, was, as he declares, revealed to him by the Deity in person and recorded word for word as it was uttered. This inspired text is called the Siddhánta Rahasya, and being very brief and of quite exceptional interest, it is here given in full :—

श्रावणस्यामले पक्षे एकादश्यां महानिशि ।
साक्षाद्भगवता प्रोक्तं तदक्षरश उच्यते ॥
ब्रह्मसंबन्धकरणात्सर्वेषां देहजीवयोः ।
सर्वदोषनिवृत्तिर्हि दोषाः पंचविधाः स्मृतः ॥
सहजा देशकालोत्था लोकवेदनिरूपिताः ।
संयोगजाः स्पर्शजाश्च न मंतव्याः कथंचन ॥
अन्यथा सर्वदोषाणां न निवृत्तिः कथंचन ।
असमर्पितवस्तूनां तस्माद्वर्जनमाचरेत् ॥
निवेदिभिः समर्प्यैव सर्वं कुर्यादिति स्थितिः ।
न मतं देवदेवस्य स्वामिभुक्तसमर्पणं ॥
तस्मादादौ सर्वकार्ये सर्ववस्तु समर्पणं ।
दत्तापहारवचनं तथा च सकलं हरेः ॥
न ग्राह्यमिति वाक्यं हि भिन्नमार्गपरं मतं ।
सेवकानां यथा लोके व्यवहारः प्रसिद्ध्यति ॥
तथा कार्यं समर्प्यैव सर्वेषां ब्रह्मता ततः ।
गंगात्वं सर्वदोषाणां गुणदोषादिवर्णना ॥
गंगात्वेन निरूप्यं स्यात्तद्वदत्रापि चैव हि ।
इति श्रीवल्लभाचार्य विरचितं सिद्धांतरहस्यं संपूर्णं ॥

" At dead of night, on the 11th of the bright fortnight of Srávan, what is here written was declared to me, word for word, by God himself. Every sin, whether of body or soul, is put away by union with the Creator; of whatever kind the sin may be, whether 1st, original; 2nd, accidental (*i.e.*, born of time and place); 3rd, social or ceremonial (*i.e.*, special offences defined by custom or the Vedas); 4th, sins of abetment; or 5th, sins sensual.* No one of these is to be accounted any longer existent; but when there is no union with the Creator there is no putting away of sin. Therefore, one should abstain from anything that has not been consecrated; but when once a thing has been dedicated, the offerer may do with it what he likes: this is the rule. The God of gods will not accept any offering which has already been used by the owner. Therefore, at the outset of every action there should be unreserved offering. It is said by those of a different persuasion, 'what is once given cannot be taken away; it is all God's;' but as is the practice of servants on earth, so would we act in the dedication through which everything becomes God's. Ganges water is full of impurities; and 'the holy Ganges' may be predicated of bad as well as good. Precisely the same in our case."

The last four lines are rather obscurely expressed. The idea intended is that as servants† use what remains of that which they have prepared for their masters, so what we offer to God we may afterwards use for ourselves; and as dirty water flowing into the Ganges becomes assimilated with the sacred stream, so vile humanity becomes purified by union with God.

The practice of the sect has been modelled strictly in accordance with these instructions. A child is Krishna-ed (christened) while still an infant by the Gosáín's putting on its neck a string of beads and repeating over it the formula called the Ashtákshar Mantra, *sri Krishna saranam mama* (Deus adjutorium meum), but before the neophyte can claim the privileges of full communion he has to undergo a rite similar to that of confirmation, and at the age of twelve or thereabouts, when ready to take upon himself the responsibilities of life, he initiates his career by a solemn dedication (*samarpana*) of all that he has and is to the God of his devotion. This oblation of *tan, man, dhan*, as it is popularly

* There is a paraphrase on the Siddhánta Rahasya by Gosain Gokulnáth, called Bhakti Siddhánta Vivriti; in which, with the characteristic fondness of Sanskrit commentators for scholastic refinements, he explains these terms in a much more narrow and technical sense than that which I have applied to them. As the text contains an uneven number of lines, it would appear at first sight to be imperfect: but this suspicion can scarcely be well founded, since in Gokulnath's time it stood precisely as now.

† Hence *sevakán*, 'servants,' is the distinctive name for lay members of the Vallabháchárya community. The whole system of doctrine is known as 'Pushti márg,' or way of happiness, and its practice as 'Daivi jívan,' the Divine life. Their sectarial mark consists of two red perpendicular lines down the forehead, meeting in a curve at the root of the nose, with a red spot between them.

expressed—that is, of body, soul, and substance—is couched in the following terms :—

ओं श्रीकृष्णः शरणं मम सहस्रपरिवत्सरमितकालसंजात कृष्णवियोगज-निततापक्लेशानंततिरोभावोऽहं भगवते कृष्णाय देहेंद्रियप्राणांऽतःकरणत-द्धर्मांश्च दारागारपुत्राप्तवित्तेहपराण्या त्मना सह समर्पयामि दासोऽहं कृष्ण तवास्मि॥

"Om. The God Krishna is my refuge. Distracted by the infinite pain and torment caused by the separation from Krishna, which has extended over a space of time measured by thousands of years, I now, to the holy Krishna, do dedicate my bodily faculties, my life, my soul, and its belongings, with my wife, my house, my children, my whole substance, and my own self. O, Krishna ; I am thy servant."*

Now, all this may be so interpreted as to convey a most unexceptionable meaning : that man should consecrate to God, wholly and without reserve, his body, soul, and substance, his every thought, word, and action, and all that he has, or does, or suffers, that such consecration is sufficient to hallow and ennoble the meanest actions of our ordinary life and is an effectual preservative from all evil, while even good works done without such consecration are unprofitable and "have even the nature of sin."† This is the doctrine of Christianity, and it may be deduced from Vallabhácharya's revelation without forcing the sense of a single word. But though there may be some slight doubt as to his own views, there can be none as to those entertained by his most immediate successors and transmitted by them to his disciples at the present day. For Gokulnáth, who is regarded as the most authoritative exponent of his grandfather's tenets, repeatedly insists in all his works, with the most marked emphasis, on the absolute identity of the Gosáin with the Divinity.‡ In fact, he goes even a step beyond this, and represents the Gosáin as so powerful a mediator that practically his favour is of more importance to us than God's : for, if God is displeased, the Gosáin can deprecate his wrath ; but if the Gosáin is displeased,

* This formula is, I find, based on a passage in the Nárada Pancharátra.

† The final climax states the doctrine of the Anglican, but not of the Catholic Church.

‡ This extravagant doctrine pervades all the later Vaishnava schools, and is accepted by the disciples of Chaitanya no less than by those of Vallabhácharya. The foundation upon which it rests is a line in the Bhágavat, where the Guru is styled Sarva-deva-maya, made up of all divinity.'

God will be affected towards us in the same way, and conciliation will then be impossible. When to this it is added that the Gosáin obtains his position solely by birth, and that no defect, moral or intellectual, can impair his hereditary claim to the adoration of his followers, who are exhorted to close their eyes and ears to anything that tends to his discredit,* it is obvious that a door is opened to scandal of a most intolerable description. By the act of dedication, a man submits to the pleasure of the Gosáin, as God's representative, not only the first fruits of his wealth, but also the virginity of his daughter or his newly-wedded wife; while the doctrine of the Brahma Sambandh is explained to mean that such adulterous connection is the same as ecstatic union with the God, and the most meritorious act of devotion that can be performed. This glorification of immorality forms the only point in a large proportion of the stories in the Chaurási Vártá, or 'Accounts of Vallábhácharya's 84 great proselytes.' One of the most extravagant will be found given in full at the end of this chapter. The work commences with reference to the Revelation of the Siddhánta Rahasya, preceded by a brief colloquy between the Deity and the Gosáin, of which the following words are the most important :—

तब श्री आचार्य जी महाप्रभु आप कहें जो जीव को स्वरूप तो तुम जानत ही हो दोषवंत हे सो तुम सों संबंध कैसे होय तब श्रीठाकुरजी आप कहें जो तुम जीवन कों ब्रह्म संबंध करावोगे तिनकों हों अंगीकार करूंगो तुम जीवन कों नाम देउगे तिनके सकल दोष निवर्त्त होयंगे ॥

" *Vallabha.*—You know the nature of life : that it is full of defects ; how can there be union between it and you ?

" *Krishna.—You* will effect the union of the divinity with living creatures, and I will accept them. Yon will give your name to them, and all their sins shall be put away."

Professor Wilson interprets this as merely the declaration of a philosophical dogma, that life and spirit are identical ; but (it can scarcely be doubted) the passage means rather that human life can only be purified by bringing it into intimate connection with God, or in default of God, with God's representative, the Gosáin.

---

* This is considered so essential a duty, that in the Dasa marma, or Vallabhácharya Decalogue, 'See no faults,' stands as the Tenth Commandment.

Such being the revolting character of their theological literature, it is easy to understand why the Vallabhácháryas have always shown a great reluctance to submit it to the criticism of the outer world of unbelievers, who might not be prepared to accept such advanced doctrines. Though there are several copyists at Gokul, whose sole occupation it is to make transcripts for the use of pilgrims, they would ordinarily refuse to sell a manuscript to any one who was not of their own denomination; and none of their books had ever been published till quite recently, when two or three of the less esoteric were issued from Pandit Giri Prasád's Press at Beswa in the Aligarh district. However, as in many other forms of religion, and happily so in this case, practice is not always in accordance with doctrine. Though there may be much that is reprehensible in the inner life of the Gosáins, it is not at Gokul obtruded on the public and has never occasioned any open scandal; while the present head of the community, Gosáin Purushottam Lál, a descendant of Bitthalnáth's sixth son, Jadunáth, deserves honourable mention for exceptional liberality and enlightment. He is the head of the temple of Navanít-Priya, popularly called by way of pre-eminence, Rájá Thákur,* and is the proprietor of the whole of the township of Gokul. His uncle and predecessor, Gobind Lál, died, leaving a widow, Jánaki Bau Jí, and an only daughter. The latter, according to invariable custom, was married to a Bhatt, and by him had two sons by name Ran-chor Lál and Gop Jí. But, as by Salic law neither of them could succeed to the spiritual dignity, the widow adopted her nephew Purushottam, the son of her husband's brother, Braj Pál. The adoption was disputed by the two sons, who carried their suit in appeal even up to the Privy Council, and there were finally defeated. Under their mother's will, they enjoy a maintenance allowance of Rs. 900 a year, paid to the elder brother by the Gosáin, and they have further retained—though under protest—all the property conferred by the Mahárája of Jodhpur on their common ancestor Murlidhar, the father of Gobind Lál and Braj Lál, who was the founder of the family's temporal prosperity and was the first muáfidar of Gokul by grant from Sindhia.

Gosáin Purushottam Lál has one son, Raman Lál, through whom he is the grandfather of Braj Lál and Kanhaiya Lál. The latter of these has been adopted by Lachhman Jí, a descendant of Bitthalnáth's fourth son, Gokulnáth, and is now the Gosáin of the temple bearing that title. Thus the two principal endowments have both come into one branch of the family, and the Gosáin is one of the very largest landowners and wealthiest residents in the district;

* He also presides over two temples dedicated to Baladeva and Madan Mohan near the Kankhal Ghát in Mathurá, where he ordinarily resides.

while he wields, at the same time, in virtue of his religious character, an influence which is absolutely unbounded among his own people, and very considerable in all classes of Hindu society. In the official world, however, he is barely known even by name, as his estates are too well managed to bring him before the Courts, and he is still so far fettered by the traditions of his order that he declines all social intercourse with Europeans, even of the highest rank: so much so, that when the Lieutenant-Governor of these Provinces visited the station in 1873, and being unaware of this peculiarity, expressed in writing a desire to see him, the invitation was not accepted. The compliment was prompted by the Gosáin's annual gift of a prize of Rs. 300 for the student who passes first in the general Entrance Examination for the Calcutta University; a donation which, under the circumstances, cannot have been suggested by any ulterior motive beyond a genuine desire for the furtherance of education. He has since converted it into a permanent endowment. In the same spirit, though he makes no claim to any high degree of scholarship himself, he has maintained for some years past in the city of Mathurá a Sanskrit school, which is attended by a large number of adults as well as boys, for whom he has secured very competent teachers. He has also contributed freely to the Gokul new school and—as a further proof of the liberality of his sentiments—he gave Rs. 400 towards the erection of the Catholic Church.

At all the Vallabhácharya temples, the daily services are eight in number—*viz.*, 1st, Mangala, the morning levee, a little after sun-rise, when the God is taken from his couch and bathed; 2nd, Sringára, an hour and-a-half later, when the God is attired in all his jewels and seated on his throne; 3rd, Gwála, after an interval of about three-quarters of an hour, when the God is supposed to be starting to graze his cattle in the woods of Braj; 4th, Ráj Bhog, the mid-day meal, which, after presentation, is consumed by the priests and distributed among the votaries who have assisted at the ceremonies; 5th, Uttápan, about 3 P.M., when the God awakes from his siesta; 6th, Bhog, the evening collation; 7th, Sandhyá, the disrobing at sunset; and 8th, Sayan, the retiring to rest. Upon all these occasions the ritual concerns only the priests, and the lay worshipper is simply a spectator, who evinces his reverence by any of the ordinary forms with which he would approach a human superior.

On the full moon of Asárh there is a curious annual ceremony for the purpose of ascertaining the agricultural prospects of the year. The priests place little packets of the ashes of different staples, after weighing them, in the sanctuary. The temple is then closed, but the night is spent in worship. In the morning the packets are examined. Should any of the packets have increased in weight, that particular article of produce will yield a good harvest; and should they decrease, the harvest will be proportionately scanty.

As has already been mentioned, none of the buildings present a very imposing appearance. The three oldest, dedicated respectively to Gokulnáth, Madan Mohan, and Bitthalnáth, are ascribed to the year 1511 A.D. The last named, which is near the Jasodá Ghát, has a small but richly decorated quadrangle with bold brackets carved into the form of elephants and swans. It is quite uncared for and is rapidly falling into irreparable ruin. The most notable of the remainder are Dwáraká Náth, dating from 1546 A.D., Balkrishan, from 1636, with an annual income of Rs. 4,420; Navanít Priya, or Dau Jí, the latter name being that of the Gosáin, whose grandson, Giridhári Jí, is now in possession, with an income of Rs. 9,382; Braj Ratn, under Gosáin Gokul Náth Jí, a descendant of Bitthalnáth's younger son, Ghan Syám, with an income of Rs. 10,650; Srí Chandrama, with Rs. 4,050, and Navanít Lál, Natwar, Mathures, Gopál Lál, and Brajeswar; all of these being quite modern. There are also two shrines in honour of Mahádeva, built by Bijay Sinh, Rájá of Jodhpur, in 1602. The principal melas are the Janm Ashtami, Krishna's birthday, in Bhádon, and Annkút on the day after the new moon of Kártik. The Trinávart mela is also held, Kártik badi 4th, when paper figures of the demon are first paraded and then torn to pieces. The principal gate of the town is that called the Gándipura Darwáza. It is of stone with two corner turrets, but has never been completely finished. From it a road, about half a mile or so in length, runs between some very fine tamarind trees, which seem specially to affect the soil in this neighbourhood, down to Gándipura on the bank of the river, where is a *baoli* and a large house built by Manohar Lál, a Bhattia, now personal assistant at the Rewa Court. Below it is Ballabh ghát, with Koila immediately opposite on the right bank of the stream. This road is much frequented by pilgrims in the rains, and I had caused it to be widened and straightened, and the trustees of the Gokulnáth temple had promised to metal it; but probably this has not been done.

One small speciality of Gokul is the manufacture of silver toys and ornaments—figures of peacocks, cows, and other animals and devices—which are principally purchased as souvenirs by pilgrims. The designs are very conventional, and the work roughly finished; but some little taste is often displayed, and when better models are supplied, they are copied with much readiness and ingenuity. The articles being of pure silver, are sold for their weight in rupees with the addition of two anas in the rupee for the work ; unless it is exceptionally well finished, when a somewhat higher rate is demanded.

BALADEVA, OR BALDEO.*

Some six miles beyond Mahá-ban, a little to the right of the high road leading to Sa'dabád and Jalesar, is the famous temple of Baladeva, in the centre of a modern town with a population of 2,835, which also bears the same name. The original village was called Rírhá, and still exists, but only as a mean suburb occupied by the labouring classes. Adjoining the temple is a brick-built tank, above 80 yards square, called variously Kshír Ságar, the 'sea of milk,' or Kshír Kund, or Balbhadra Kund. It is in a dilapidated condition, and the surface of the water is always covered with a repulsive thick green scum, which, however, does not deter the pilgrims either from drinking or bathing in it. Here it is said that Gosáin Gokulnáth was warned in a vision that a god lay concealed. Immediate search was made, and the statue of Baladeva, that has ever since been regarded as the tutelary divinity of the place, was revealed to the adoring gaze of the assembled multitude. Attempts were made to remove it to Gokul ; but as every cart broke down, either from the weight of the stone, or the reluctance of the God to change his abode, a shrine was erected for his reception on the spot, and an Ahivási of Bhartiya, by name Kalyán, constituted guardian. From his two sons, Jamuná Dás and Musiya, or Sukadeva, are descended the whole horde of Pándas, who now find the God a very valuable property. They have acquired, by purchase from the Játs, the old village of Rírhá,† and are also considerable landowners in six other villages—*viz.*, Artoni, Nera, Chhibarau, Kharaira, Núr-pur and Shaháb-pur, whence they derive an annual income of Rs. 3,853. This estate, which was for the most part a grant from Sindhia, forms, however, but a small part of their wealth, as the offerings made at the shrine in the course of the year are estimated to yield a net profit of Rs. 30,000 more. The Kshír-Ságar and all the fees paid by pilgrims bathing in it belong not to the temple Pándas, but to a community of Sanádh Bráhmans.

The temple, despite its popularity, is neither handsome nor well appointed. Its precincts include as many as eleven cloistered quadrangles, where accom-

---

* The latter name represents the common pronunciation, which (as in all similar words) has become corrupted by the practice of writing in Persian characters, which are inadequate to express the *va* termination.

† Besides the entire zamindári, the Pándas hold also 255½ bíghas in Rírhá as muáfidárs. Of this area, 79 bíghas are occupied by buildings, while the remainder is either waste or orchard. As the township has no arable land attached to it, the name Baladeva does not appear at all in the district rent-roll.

modation is provided for the pilgrims and resident priests. No definite charge is levied on the former, but they are expected to make a voluntary donation according to their means. Each court, or *kunj*, as it is called, bears the name of its founder as follows :—1st, the Kunj of Rashk Lál of Agra and Lakhnau, 1817 A.D. ; 2nd, of Bachhráj, Baniya, of Háthras, 1825 ; 3rd, of Naval Karan, Baniya, of Agra, 1868 ; 4th, of Bhím Sen and Hulás Raí, Baniyas, of Mathurá, 1828 ; 5th, of Dás Mal, Khattri, of Agra, 1801 ; 6th of Bhattácharya of Jaypur, 1794 ; 7th of Gopál, Bráhman, of Jaypur ; 8th of Chiman Lál, of Mathurá, 1778 ; 9th, of Sadá Rám, Khattri, of Agra, 1768 ; 10th, of Chunna, Halwái, of Bharat-pur, 1808 ; and 11th, of Púran Chand, Pachauri, of Mahá-ban, 1801. The actual temple, built by Seth Syám Dás, of Delhi, towards the end of last century, stands at the back of one of the inner courts, and on each of its three disengaged sides has an arcade of three bays with broad flanking piers. On each of these three sides a door gives access to the cella, which is surmounted by a squat pyramidal tower. In addition to the principal figure, Baladeva, who is generally very richly dressed and bedizened with jewels, it contains another life-sized statue, supposed to represent his spouse Revati. Apparently she was an after-thought, as she is put away in a corner, off the dais. In an adjoining court is shown the small vaulted chamber which served the God as a residence for the first century after his epiphany. Near the tank is a shrine dedicated by Bihári Lál, Bohra, of Mursán, in 1803, to the honour of the god Harideva, and two stone *chhatris* in memory of the Pándas, Harideva and Jagannáth.

Two annual melas are held at Baladeva, the one Bhádon sudi 6th (commonly called Deo Chath), the other on the full moon of Agahn ; but there is probably not a single day in the course of the whole year in which the temple courts are not occupied by at least as many as a hundred pilgrims, who come from all parts of Northern India. The cost of the religious ceremonial cannot be much, but a charitable dole of an ana apiece is given to every applicant ; and as the Pándes with their families now number between 300 and 400 persons, the annnal cost of their maintenance must be very considerable. After reasonable deductions on these three heads—*viz.*, temple expenses, charity, and maintenance of the priests, the balance of profits is calculated at over Rs. 30,000. There is ordinarily a division among the shareholders at the end of every three months, when they make an allotment into twelve equal portions, that being the number of the principal sub-divisions of the clan, and then each sub-division makes a separate distribution among its own members. The votive offerings in the vast majority of cases are individually of very trifling amount ; but even so, their collective value is not altogether to be despised. Thus, poorer pilgrims, in

74

addition to a few copper coins, often present a piece of sugar ; and the heap of sugar accumulated in three or four days has been sold by auction for as much as Rs. 80. The shrine is a very popular one among all classes ; scarcely ever is an important venture made without a vow that the God shall receive a fixed share of the profits, if he bring it to a successful issue ; and even casual votaries, who have no special boon to beg, are often most lavish in their donations, either of money, horned cattle, carriages, horses, or other property. For example, a few years ago, Súrajbhán, a wealthy merchant of Agra, gave Rs. 4,000 worth of jewellery for the personal adornment of the God.

It is unfortunate that the hereditary guardians of so wealthy a shrine should be such a low and thriftless set as the Ahivásis are. The temple-garden occupies 52 bíghas of land and was once a well-planted grove. It is now a dirty, unsightly waste, as the Pándes have gradually cut down all the trees for firewood, without a thought of replacing them. They have thus not only deteriorated the value of their property, but also forfeited a grant that used to be made by the Mahárája of Bharat-pur for its maintenance. It is also asserted to be a common practice for the younger members of the clan, when they see any devotees prostrate in devotion before the god, to be very forward in assisting them to rise and leading them away, and to take the opportunity of despoiling them of any loose cash or valuable ornaments that they can lay their hands upon. It is believed that thefts of this kind are frequent ; though the victim generally prefers to accept the loss in silence, rather than incure the odium of bringing a charge, that there might not be legal evidence to substantiate, against a professedly religious community. It appears in every way desirable that some extra police should be maintained at the expense of the Pándes, and a constable or two kept permanently on duty in the inner court of the temple. As an illustration of the esteem in which learning is held in this large and wealthy Brahmanical town, it may be mentioned that the school is not only merely a primary one, but is also about the smallest and worst of its class in the whole district.

NOTES TO CHAPTER X.

1.—Catalogue of Vallabhácháarya Literature.

I.—Sanskrit works ascribed to the founder himself, divided into two classes: First, commentaries of considerable length on older writings of authority, being four in number, *viz.*, Bhágavata Tika Subodhini, Vyása Sútra Bháshya, Jaimini Sútra Bháshya, and Tattva Dípa Nibandha. None of these have I seen. Secondly, seventeen very short original poems entitled—Siddhánta Rahasya, Siddhánta Muktávali, Pushti Praváha Maryáda, Antah-karanah Prabodha, Nava Ratna, Viveka Dhairyasraya, Krishnásraya, Bhakti Vardhani, Jala-bheda, Sannyása nirnaya, Nirodha-lakshana, Seva-phala, Bál-bodh, Chatur-sloki, Panch-sloki, Yamunáshtakam, and Purushottama Sahasra-náma. Of all of these, except the last, I have obtained copies from Gokul.

II.—Sanskrit works ascribed to Vallabhácharya's immediate successors. These also are, for the most part, very short. The principal are as follows: Sarvottama-stotram of Agni Kumár, Ratna Vivarna of Bitthalnáth, Bhakti Siddhánta Vivriti of Gokulnáth, Vallabháshtakam of Bitthalnáth, Krishna Premámritam of Bitthalnáth, Siksha Patram, Gokuláshtakam, Prem-Amritam of Gokulnáth, Srí Vallabha-bhaváshtakam of Hari Dás, Madhur Ashtakam, Saran Ashtakám, Námávali Acharya, Námávali Goswámi, Siddhánta Bhávana, Virodha Lakshana, Srínagara Rasamandalu, Saranopadesa, Rasa-Sindhu, Kalpadruma, Málá Prasanga, and Chita Prabodha.

III.—Works in the modern vernacular, *i.e.*, the Braj-Bhásha. Such are the Nij Várta, Chaurási Várta, Do Sau Bávan Várta, Dwádasa Kunja Pavitra Mandala, Purnamási, Nitya-sevaprakára, Rasa Bhávana Gokulnáth, Vachanámrita of Gokulnáth, Braj Bilás of Braj-bási Dás, Ban-Játra, Vallabhakyána, Dhola, Nitya-pada, Srí Gobardhan-nath Jí ka Prágatya, Gosáin Jí Prágatya, Líla Bhávana, Swarúpa Bhávana, Guru Seva, Seva-prakára Múla Purusha, Dasa Marama, Vaishnava Battisi Lakshana, Chaurási Siksha, Otsava Pada, Yamuná Ji Pada, and others.

II.—Specimen of the Tone and Style of popular Vallabhácháarya Literature.

The following story of 'how Krishan Das showed his devotion to the Gosáins' is extracted from the Chaurasi Vártá, and is interesting as a specimen both of the dialect and religious superstition of the locality. Though written some two hundred years ago, it might, for all internal evidence to the contrary, have been taken down only yesterday, word for word, from the mouth of a village gossip. It does not contain a single archaic term, and in its unartificial style and rustic phraseology is an exact representation of the colloquial idiom of middle-class Hindus of the present century; yet it has absolutely nothing in common with the language officially designated the vernacular of the country, either as regards the arrangement of the sentence or the choice of words; the latter being all taken from the Hindi vocabulary, with the exception of three only—*viz.*, *kaul*, a 'promise;' *sauda*, 'merchandise;' and *khabr*, 'news.' These are inserted as if on purpose to show that the non-admission of a larger number was a spontaneous and not a pedantic exclusion. As to its purport, the eulogy which it bestows on the extraordinary sacrifice of personal decency and honour, merely for the sake of procuring the Gosáins a good dinner, is so revolting to the principles of natural morality that it condems the whole tenour of Vallabhácharya doctrine more strongly than any argument that could be adduced by an opponent. The style of the narrative is so easy and perspicuous that it can present no difficulty to the student, who alone will take an interest in the matter, and therefore I have not considered it necessary to add a translation:—

श्री आचार्यजी महाप्रभून के सेवक कृष्णदासजी ब्राह्मण तिनकी वार्त्ता

वे कृष्णदास एक गांम में रहते हते सो भगवदीय भये अकिंचन हते श्री आचार्यजी महाप्रभून के सेवक गांम में रहते हते सो परस्पर मिलिकें इकठोरे होके श्रीआचार्यजी महाप्रभून के दर्शन कों जातहते एक समें वैष्णव दश पंद्रे मिलकें इकठोरे होयकें श्रीआचार्यजी महाप्रभून के दर्शन को अडेल गांम कूं चले सो जा गांम में कृष्णदास रहते हते ता गांम में आये सो कृष्णदास के घर आये तब कृष्णदास तो घर हते नहीं कछू कार्य के लियें कोस दोय तीन एक गांम हतो तहां गांम में गये हते और कृष्णदासजी की स्त्री घर में हुती तब वा स्त्री ने उन वैष्णवन कों साष्टांग दण्डवत कीनी श्री कृष्ण-स्मरण कहिकें बोहोत आदर सनमान करिकें घर में बेठारे पाछें घर में जायकें अपने मन में बिचार करन लागी जो अब कहा करिये तब सुधि आई सो वुह हमारो बनीयां मोसों नित्य टोक करत हे और केहत हे जो तुम मोसों मिलि जो मैं तोकों कहे सो देंहु सो आजु वाकी दुकान सूं सीधो सामग्री लाऊं हूं वासों कहोंगी जो आजु तोसों मिलूंगी मोकों सीधो

सामिग्री चहीयत है सो देउ ऐसें विचार करिकें अपने मन में वोह स्त्री चली सो वा बनियां की हाट ऊपर गई तब वा बनियां नें हाट ऊपर टोकी तब वा स्त्री नें वा बनियां सों कही जो मैं तोसों एक दिन मिलोंगी तू मोकों आज सोदा चाहिये है सो देउ तब वा बनियां नें कह्यो जो कोल करै तों मैं मानूंगो तब वा स्त्री नें एक कोल कर्यो तब वा स्त्री कों सीधो सामिग्री चहीये सो लीनी बनियां पैते पाछे घर आइकें रसोई करिये श्री ठाकुरजी कों भोग समर्प्पिकें समयानुसार भोग उसरायकें अनोसर करिकें पाछे उन वेष्णा-वन कों प्रसाद लिवायो तब वेष्णवन्नें भली भांति सों प्रसाद लियो पाछे सांझ कों कृष्णदास घर आये सो सब वेष्णव मिलिकें दण्डवत कीयो जैश्रीकृष्ण कहिकें भीतर गयो तब स्त्री सों कहा जो कहा खबरि है वेष्णवन कों महा-प्रसाद लिवायो तब स्त्री ने कही जो महाप्रसाद तो लिवायो तब कृष्णदास नें कही जो सीधो सामिग्री कहां ते लाई है कहा प्रकार कियो तब जो प्रकार कियो हतो सो सब कह दीयो तब कृष्णदास स्त्री के ऊपर बोहत प्रसन्न भये पाछें स्त्री पुरुषने दोऊ जने नें सीठो महाप्रसाद लियो जो अपने घर श्रीठाकुरजी नित्य आरोगते सो प्रसाद लियो पाछें कृष्णदास सब वेष्णवन के पास आयकें सबरी रात्रि भगवत वार्त्ता करत बीती जब सवारो भयो तब सब वेष्णव कृष्णदास होयकें चले तब कृष्णदास थोरीसी दूरि उनकों पोंहचाय गये पाछें आप घर आय स्नान करि श्रीठाकुरजी की सेवा करिकें आप व्या-प्नत कों गये पाछें स्त्री नें रसोई करिकें श्रीठाकुरजी कों भोग समर्प्यो भोग उसराय अनोसर करिकें महाप्रसाद ढांकि राख्यो तब कृष्णदास सांझ कों घर आये तब वोह सीरो महाप्रसाद दोऊ जनन्नें स्त्री पुरुष नें लीनों पाछें कृष्णदास नें स्त्री सों कह्यो जो तुमनें वा बनियां कों कालिको कोल कीयो हतो सो वोह पेंडो देखत होयगो ताते वाको कोल पूरो करिये तो भलो है तब स्त्री आप उपटनों करिके स्नान करिकें फेरि जो स्नान को सिंगार होय है सो सब करिकें पामन में महावर लगायकें चली सो बर्षा के दिन हते सो मेह बरष रह्यो हतो सो मार्ग में कीच भई हती ताके लियें कृष्णदास

नें स्त्री सों कही जो तुम मेरे कन्धा ऊपर बैठि लेहु तोकूं पोंहचाय आऊं नातर तेरे पांम कीचसों भरि जायंगे मार्ग में कीच भई है तब स्त्री को कृष्णादास नें कन्धा ऊपर चढ़ायकें वा बनीयां की हाट ऊपर उतारदीनी तब वा स्त्री नें वा बनीयां कों हेला पारिके कही जो किवार खोलि तब वा बनीयां नें किवार खोलिकें भीतर लानी तब वुह पांम धोयवेकों पांनी ले आयो औ कह्यो जो पांम धोय तब वानें वा बनीयां सों कही जो मेरे पांम तो कीच सों भरे नाहीं तब वा बनियां नें वासों कह्यो जो मारग में कीच भई है तेरे पांम कोरे क्यों रहे तब उन स्त्री ने कह्यो जो तू पुछिकें कहा करेगो तु तेरो काम करि तब वा बनीयां नें कह्यो जो यह बात तोकों बतानी चाहिये तब वा स्त्री नें कह्यो जो मेरो भरतार कांधेपे चढ़ाय कें लायो हे सो यह बात सुनिके वा बनीयां कों आश्चर्य भयो और सब वृत्तांत हो सो सब पुछो जो यह कहा कारण हे सो सब मेरे आगें कहो तब वा स्त्री नें सब प्रकार हो सो सब कह्यो सो सुनिकें बनीयां अपने जन्मकों धिक्कार करन लाग्यो और कह्यो जो धन्य जन्म तुम्हारो हे जो जिनको ऐसो मन सांचो हे और दोऊ हाथ जोरिकें दण्डवत करी और कह्यो जो मेरो अपराध क्षमा करिये मेरे ऊपर कृपा करिये मेरी तुम बेंहन हो पाछें वा स्त्री कों कपरा पहरायकें वाकों घर पोंहचामन आयो और कृष्णादास सों वा बनीयां नें बिनती कीनी जो तुम मेरो अपराध क्षमा करिये यह मेरी बेंहनि हे जो तुम मेरे पुज्य हो पाछें वुह बनीयां श्रीआचार्यजी महाप्रभून को ऐसें सेवक भयो तब वा बनीयां को नाम श्रीआचार्यजी महाप्रभून ने ज्ञानचन्द धर्यो पाछें वह बनीयां बड़ो भगवदीय भयो सो कृष्णादास के सतसंगते भयो तातें संग करनों तो भगवदीय को करनों पाछें वह बनीयां कृष्णादास सों सदा सर्वदा नमत रहतो और कृष्णादास की स्त्री सों बेंहनि को संबन्ध राखे वे कृष्णादास श्रीआचार्यजी महाप्रभून के ऐसे कृपापात्र भगवदीय हे तातें इनकी अनिर्वचनीय वार्त्ता हे तातें इन की वार्त्ता कहां तांई लिखिये वार्त्ता प्रथम ॥ ५ ॥ संबन्ध १५० वेष्णव ॥ ७४ ॥

CHAPTER XI.

THE THREE HILL PLACES OF MATHURÁ: GOBARDHAN, BARSÁNA, AND NAND-GÁNW.

At a distance of three miles from the city of Mathurá, the road to Gobardhan runs through the village of Satoha, by the side of a large tank of very sacred repute, called Sántanu Kund. The name commemorates a Rajá Sántanu who (as is said on the spot) here practised, through a long course of years, the severest religious austerities in the hope of obtaining a son. His wishes were at last gratified by a union with the goddess Gangá, who bore him Bhíshma, one of the famous heroes of the Mahábhárat. Every Sunday the place is frequented by women who are desirous of issue, and a large fair is held there on the 6th of the light fortnight of Bhádon. The tank, which is of very considerable dimensions, was faced all round with stone, early last century, by Sawái Jay Sinh of Amber, but a great part of the masonry is now much dilapidated. In its centre is a high hill connected with the main land by a bridge. The sides of the island are covered with fine *ritha* trees, and on the summit, which is approached by a flight of fifty stone steps, is a small temple. Here it is incumbent upon the female devotees, who would have their prayers effectual, to make some offering to the shrine, and inscribe on the ground or wall the mystic device called in Sanskrit Svastiká and in Hindi Sathiya, the fylfot of Western ecclesiology. The local superstition is probably not a little confirmed by the accidental resemblance that the king's name bears to the Sanskrit word for 'children,' *santána*. For, though Rájá Sántanu is a mythological personage of much ancient celebrity, being mentioned not only in several of the Puránas, but also in one of the hymns of the Rig Veda, he is not much known at the present day, and what is told of him at Satoha is a very confused jumble of the original legend. The signal and, according to Hindu ideas, absolutely fearful abnegation of self, there ascribed to the father, was undergone for his gratification by the dutiful son, who thence derived his name of Bhíshma, 'the fearful.' For, in extreme old age, the Rájá was anxious to wed again, but the parents of the fair girl on whom he fixed his affections would not consent to the union, since the fruit of the marriage would be debarred by Bhíshma's seniority from the succession to the throne. The difficulty was removed by Bhíshma's filial devotion, who took an oath to renounce his birthright and never to beget a son to revive the claim. Hence every religious Hindu accounts it a duty to make him amends for this want of direct descendants by once a year offering libations to Bhíshma's spirit in the same way as to one of his own ancestors. The formula to be used is as follows:—" I present this water to the childless hero, Bhíshma, of the race of Vyághrapáda, the chief of the house of Sankriti. May Bhíshma, the son of Sántanu, the speaker of truth and subjugater of his passions, obtain by this water the oblations due from sons and grandsons."

The story in the Nirukta Vedánga relates to an earlier period in the king's life, if, indeed, it refers to the same personage at all, which has been doubted. It is there recorded that, on his father's death, Sántanu took possession of the throne, though he had an elder brother, by name Devápi, living. This violation of the right of primogeniture caused the land to be afflicted with a drought of twelve years' continuance, which was only terminated by the recitation of a hymn of prayer (Rig Veda, x., 98) composed by Devápi himself, who had voluntarily adopted the life of a religious. The name Satoha is absurdly derived by the Bráhmans of the place from *sattu,* 'bran,' which is said to have been the royal ascetic's only diet. In all probability it is formed from the word *Sántanu* itself, combined with some locative affix, such as *sthána.*

Ten miles further to the west is the famous place of Hindu pilgrimage, Gobardhan, *i.e.,* according to the literal meaning of the Sanskrit compound, 'the nurse of cattle.' The town, which is of considerable size, with a population of 4,944, occupies a break in a narrow range of hill, which rises abruptly from the alluvial plain, and stretches in a south-easterly direction for a distance of some four or five miles, with an average elevation of about 100 feet.

This is the hill which Krishna is fabled to have held aloft on the tip of his finger for seven days and nights to cover the people of Braj from the storms poured down upon them by Indra when deprived of his wonted sacrifices. In pictorial representations it always appears as an isolated conical peak, which is as unlike the reality as possible. It is ordinarily styled by Hindus of the present day the Giri-ráj, or royal hill, but in earlier literature is more frequently designated the Anna-kut. There is a firm belief in the neighbourhood that, as the waters of the Jamuná are yearly decreasing in body, so too the sacred hill is steadily diminishing in height ; for in past times it was visible from Aríng, a town four or five miles distant, whereas now a few hundred yards are sufficient to remove it from sight. It may be hoped that the marvellous fact reconciles the credulous pilgrim to the insignificant appearance presented by the object of his adoration. It is accounted so holy that not a particle of the stone is allowed to be taken for any building purpose ; and even the road which crosses it at its lowest point, where only a few fragments of the rock crop up above the ground, had to be carried over them by a paved causeway.

The ridge attains its greatest elevation towards the south between the villages of Jatipura and Anyor. Here, on the submit, 'was an ancient temple founded in the year 1520 A. D., by the famous Vallabhácharya of Gokul, and dedicated to Srí-náth. In anticipation of one of Aurangzeb's raids, the image of the god was removed to Náthdwára in Udaypur territory, and has remained there ever since. The temple on the Giri-raj was thus allowed to fall into ruin, and the wide walled enclosure now exhibits only long lines of foundations and steep flights of steps, with a small, untenanted, and quite modern shine. The plateau, however, commands a very extensive view of the neighbouring country, both on the Mathurá and the Bharatpur side, with the fort of Díg and the heights of Nand-gánw and Barsána in the distance.

At the foot of the hill on one side is the little village of Jatipura with several temples, of which one, dedicated to Gokul-náth, though a very mean building in appearance, has considerable local celebrity. Its head is the Gosáin of the temple with the same title at Gokul, and it is the annual scene of two religious solemnities, both celebrated on the day after the Díp-dán at Gobardhan. The first is the adoration of the sacred hill, called the Giri-ráj Púja, and the second the Anna-kút, or commemoration of Krishna's sacrifice. They are always accompanied by the renewal of a long-standing dispute between the priests of the two rival temples of Srí-náth and Gokul-náth, the one of whom supplies the god, the other his shrine. The image of Gokul-náth, the traditional object of veneration, is brought over for the occasion from Gokul, and throughout the festival is kept in the Gokul-náth temple on the hill, except for a few hours on the morning after the Diwáli, when it is exposed for worship on a separate pavilion. This building is the property of Giridhári Jí, the Sri-náth Gosáin, who invariably protests against the intrusion. Party-feeling runs so high that it is generally found desirable a little before the anniversary to take heavy security from the principals on either side that there shall be no breach of the peace. The relationship between the Gosáins is explained by the following table :—

Dámodar Jí, *alias* Dáu Jí,
Gosáin of the temple of Srí-nath at Náthdwára.

- Lachhman Jí, Gosáin of temple of Gokul-nath: died 1861. = Chandrávali Bau Jí (living).
  - Kanhaiya Lál (adopted son), grandson of Gosáin Purushottam Lál.
- Gobind Ráe Jí, Gosáin of temples of Navanit-Príya and Srí-nath, at Náthdwára.
  - Giridhári Jí.

Immediately opposite Jatipura, and only parted from it by the intervening range, is the village of Anyor—literally 'the other side'—with the temple of Srí-náth on the summit between them. A little distánce beyond both is the village of Puchhri, which, as the name denotes, is considered the 'extreme limit' of the Giri-ráj.

Kártik, the month in which most of Krishna's exploits are believed to have been performed, is the favorite time for the *pari-krama*, or 'perambulation' of the sacred hill. The dusty circular road which winds around its base has a length of seven *kos*, that is, about twelve miles, and is frequently measured by devotees who at every step prostrate themselves at full length. When flat on the ground, they mark a line in the sand as far as their hands can reach, then rising they prostrate themselves again from the line so marked, and continue in the same style till the whole weary circuit has been accomplished. This ceremony, called *Dandavati pari-krama*, occupies from a week to a fortnight, and is generally performed for wealthy sinners vicariously by the Bráhmans of the place, who receive from Rs. 50 to Rs. 100 for their trouble and transfer all the merit of the act to their employers. The ceremony has been performed with a hundred and eight* prostrations at each step (that being the number of Rádhá's names and of the beads in a Vaishnava rosary), it then occupied some two years, and was remunerated by a donation of Rs. 1,000.

About the centre of the range stands the town of Gobardhan on the margin of a very large irregularly shaped masonry tank, called the Manasi

* In Christian mysticism 107 is as sacred a number as 108 in Hindu. Thus the Emperor Justinian's great church of S. Sophia at Constantinople was supported by 107 columns, the number of pillars in the House of Wisdom.

AUTOTYPE

THE MÁNASI GANGÁ, GOBARDHAN.

Gangá, supposed to have been called into existence by the mere action of the divine will (*mánasa*). At one end the boundary is formed by the jutting crags of the holy hill; on all other sides the water is approached by long flights of stone steps. It has frequently been repaired at great cost by the Rájás of Bharat-pur; but is said to have been originally constructed in its present form by Rájá Mán Sinh of Jaypur, whose father built the adjoining temple of Harideva. There is also at Banáras a tank constructed by Mán Sinh, called Mán Sarovar, and by it a temple dedicated to Mánesvar: facts which suggest a suspicion that the name 'Mánasi'* is of much less antiquity than is popularly believed. Unfortunately, there is neither a natural spring, nor any constant artificial supply of water, and for half the year the tank is always dry. But ordinarily at the annual illumination, or Dip-dán, which occurs soon after the close of the rains, during the festival of the Diwáli, a fine broad sheet of water reflects the light of the innumerable lamps, which are ranged tier above tier along the ghâts and adjacent buildings, by the hundred thousand pilgrims with whom the town is then crowded.

In the year 1871, as there was no heavy rain towards the end of the season, and the festival of the Diwáli also fell later than usual, it so happened that on the bathing day, the 12th of November, the tank was entirely dry, with the exception of two or three green and muddy little puddles. To obviate this mischance, several holes were made and wells sunk in the area of the tank, with one large pit, some 30 feet square and as many deep, in whose turbid waters many thousand pilgrims had the happiness of immersing themselves. For several hours no less than twenty-five persons a minute continued to descend, and as many to ascend, the steep and slippery steps; while the yet more fetid patches of mud and water in other parts of the basin were quite as densely crowded. At night, the vast amphitheatre, dotted with groups of people and glimmering circles of light, presented a no less picturesque appearance than in previous years when it was a brimming lake. To the spectator from the garden

* In devotional literature *mánasi* has the sense of 'spiritual,' as in the Catholic phrase 'spiritual communion.' Thus it is related in the Bhakt Málá that Rájá Prithiraj, of Bikaner, being on a journey and unable to visit the shrine, for which he had a special devotion, imagined himself to be worshipping in the temple, and made a spiritual act of contemplation before the image (*murti ká dhyán mánasi karte the*). For two days his aspirations seemed to meet with no response, but on the third he became conscious of the divine presence. On enquiry it was found that for two days the god had been removed elsewhere, while the temple was under repair. He then made a vow to end his days at Mathurá. The emperor, to spite him, put him in command of an expedition to Kabul; but when he felt his end approaching, he mounted a camel and hastened back to the holy city and there expired.

side of the broad and deep expanse, as the line of demarkation between the steep flights of steps and the irregular masses of building which immediately surmount them ceased to be perceptible, the town presented the perfect semblance of a long and lofty mountain range dotted with fire-lit villages; while the clash of cymbals, the beat of drums, the occasional toll of bells from the adjoining temples, with the sudden and long-sustained cry of some enthusiastic band, vociferating the praises of mother Gangá, the clapping of hands that began scarce heard, but was quickly caught up and passed on from tier to tier, and prolonged into a wild tumult of applause,—all blended with the ceaseless murmur of the stirring crowd in a not discordant medley of exciting sound. According to popular belief, the ill-omened drying up of the water, which had not occurred before in the memory of man, was the result of the curse of one Habíb-ullah Sháh, a Muhammadan fakír. He had built himself a hut on the top of the Giri-ráj, to the annoyance of the priests of the neighbouring temple of Dán-Ráe, who complained that the holy ground was defiled by the bones and other fragments of his unclean diet, and procured an order from the Civil Court for his ejectment. Thereupon the fakír disappeared, leaving a curse upon his persecutors; and this bore fruit in the drying up of the healing waters of the Mánasi Gangá.

Close by is the famous temple of Hari-deva, erected during the tolerant reign of Akbar by Rájá Bhagawán Dás of Amber on a site long previously occupied by a succession of humbler fanes. It consists of a nave 68 feet in length and 20 feet broad, leading to a choir 20 feet square, with a sacrarium of about the same dimensions beyond. The nave has four openings on either side, of which three have arched heads, while the fourth nearest the door is covered by a square architrave supported by Hindu brackets. There are clerestory windows above, and the height is about 30 feet to the cornice, which is decorated at intervals with large projecting heads of elephants and sea-monsters. There was a double roof, each entirely of stone: the outer one a high pitched gable, the inner an arched ceiling, or rather the nearest approach to an arch ever seen in Hindu design. The centre was really flat, but it was so deeply coved at the sides that, the width of the building being inconsiderable, it had all the effect of a vault, and no doubt suggested the possibility of the true radiating vault, which we find in the temple of Govind Deva built by Bhagawán's son and successor, Mán Sinh, at Brindá-ban. The construction is extremely massive, and even the exterior is still solemn and imposing, though the two towers which originally crowned the choir and sacrarium were long ago levelled with the roof of the nave. The material

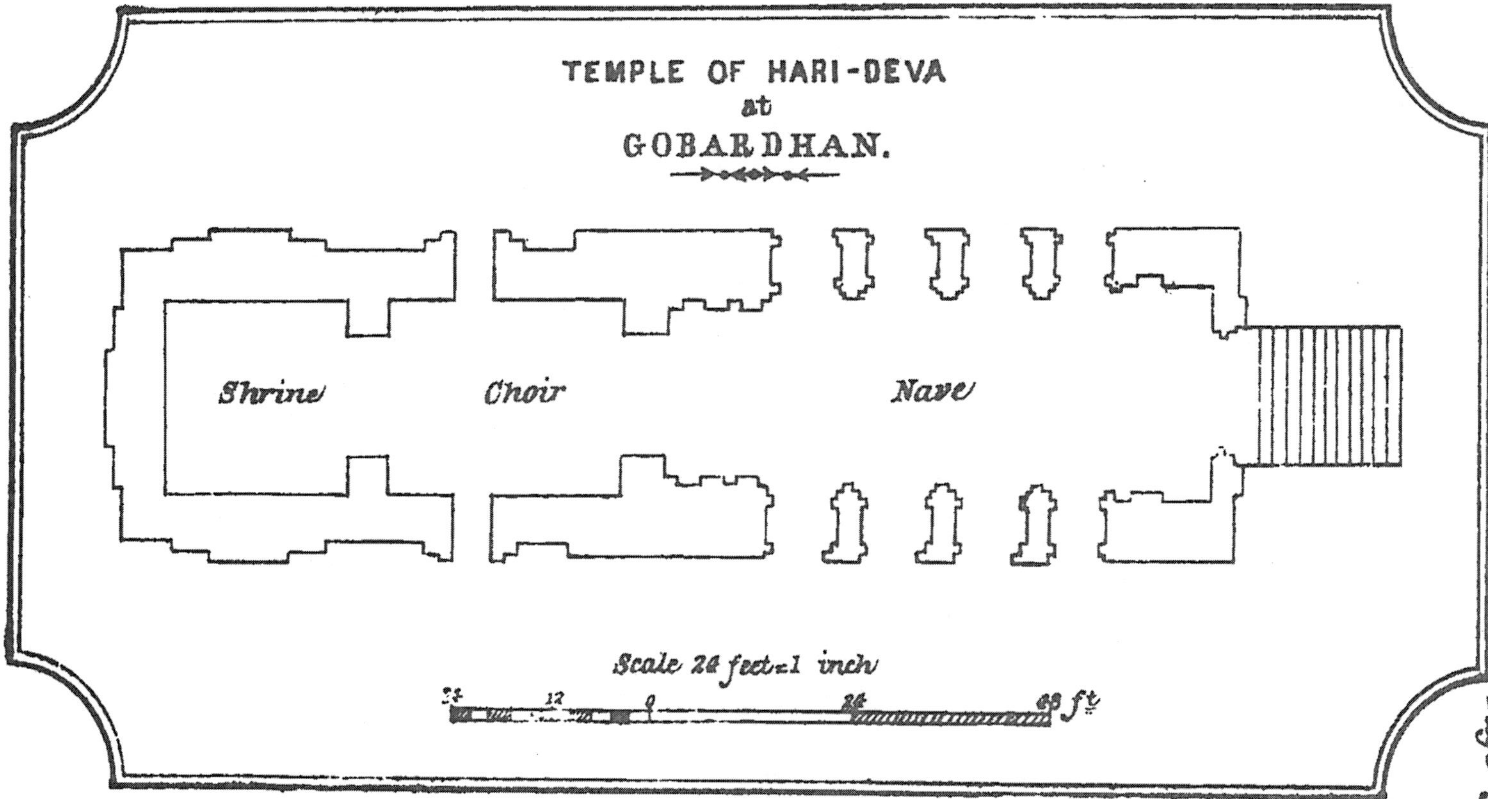
TEMPLE OF HARI-DEVA
at
GOBARDHAN.
Shrine
Choir
Nave
Scale 24 feet=1 inch
24
12
0
24
48 ft.

employed throughout the superstructure is red sandstone from the Bharat-pur quarries, while the foundations are composed of rough blocks of the stone found in the neighbourhood. These have been laid bare to the depth of several feet; and a large deposit of earth all round the basement would much enhance the appearance as well as the stability of the building.

Bihári Mall, the father of the reputed founder, was the first Rájput who attached himself to the court of a Muhammadan emperor. He was chief of the Rajáwat branch of the Kachhwáhá Thákurs seated at Amber, and claimed to be eighteenth in descent from the founder of the family. The capital was subsequently transferred to Jaypur in 1728 A.D.; the present Maharájá being the thirty-fourth descendant of the original stock. In the battle of Sarnál, Bhagawán Dás had the good fortune to save Akbar's life, and was subsequently appointed Governor of the Panjáb. He died about the year 1590 at Láhor. His daughter was married to prince Salím, who eventually became emperor under the title of Jahángír; the fruit of their marriage being the unfortunate prince Khusru.

The temple has a yearly income of some Rs. 2,300, derived from the two villages, Bhagosa and Lodhipuri, the latter estate being a recent grant, in lieu of an annual money donation of Rs. 500, on the part of the Rájá of Bharat-pur, who further makes a fixed monthly offering to the shrine at the rate of one rupee per diem. The hereditary Gosáins have long devoted the entire income to their own private uses, completely neglecting the fabric of the temple and its religious services.* In consequence of such short-sighted greed, the votive offerings at this, one of the most famous shrines in Upper India, have dwindled down to about Rs. 50 a year. Not only so, but, early in 1872, the roof of the nave, which had hitherto been quite perfect, began to give way. An attempt was made by the writer of this memoir to procure an order from the Civil Court authorising the expenditure, on the repair of the fabric, of the proceeds of the temple estate, which, in consequence of the dispute among the shareholders, had for some months past been paid as a deposit into the district treasury and had accumulated to more than Rs. 3,000. There was no unwillingness on the part of the local Government to further the proposal, and an engineer was deputed

* The estate is divided into twenty-four *bats* or shares, allotted among seventeen different families. It appeared that all were agreed as to the distribution, with the exception of one man by name Náráyan, who, in addition, to his own original share, claimed also as sole representative of a shareholder deceased. This claim was not admitted by the others, and the zamindárs continued to pay the revenue as a deposit into the district treasury, till eventually the muafidárs concurred in making a joint application for its transfer to themselves.

to examine and report on the probable cost. But an unfortunate delay occurred in the Commissioner's office, the channel of correspondence, and meanwhile the whole of the roof fell in, with the exception of one compartment. This, however, would have been sufficient to serve as a model in the work of restoration. The estimate was made out for Rs. 8,767; and as there was a good balance in hand to begin upon, operations might have been commenced at once and completed without any difficulty in the course of two or three years. But no further orders were communicated by the superior authorities from April, when the estimate was submitted, till the following October, and in the interim a baniya from the neighbouring town of Aríng, by name Chhítar Mall, hoping to immortalise himself at a moderate outlay, came to the relief of the temple proprietors and undertook to do all that was necessary at his own private cost. He accordingly ruthlessly demolished all that yet remained of the original roof, breaking down at the same time not a little of the curious cornice, and in its place simply threw across, from wall to wall, rough and unshapen wooden beams, of which the best that can be said is, that they may, for some few years, serve as a protection from the weather. But all that was unique and characteristic in the design has ceased to exist; and thus another of the few pages in the fragmentary annals of Indian architecture has been blotted out for ever. Like the temple of Gobind Deva at Brindá-ban, it has none of the coarse figure sculpture which detract so largely from the artistic appearance of most Hindu religious buildings; and though originally consecrated to idolatrous worship, it was in all points of construction equally well adapted for the public ceremonial of the purest faith. Had it been preserved as a national monument, it might at some day, in the future golden age, have been to Gobardhan what the Pagan Pantheon is now to Christian Rome.

On the opposite side of the Mánasi Gangá are two stately cenotaphs, or *chhattris*, to the memory of Randhír Sinh and Baladeva Sinh, Rájás of Bharatpur. Both are of similiar design, consisting of a lofty and substantial square masonry terrace with corner kiosks and lateral alcoves, and in the centre the monument itself, still further raised on a richly decorated plinth. The cella, enclosed in a colonnade of five open arches on each side, is a square apartment surmounted by a dome, and having each wall divided into three bays, of which one is left for the doorway, and the remainder are filled in with reticulated tracery. The cloister has a small dome at each corner and the curious curvilinear roof, distinctive of the style, over the central compartments. In the larger monument, the visitor's attention is specially directed to the panels of the doors, painted in miniature with scenes from the life of Krishna, and to the

AUTOTYPE

CHHATTRI OF MAHÁRÁJA BALADEVA SIṄH, GOBARDHAN.

cornice, a flowered design of some vitreous material executed at Delhi. This commemorates Baladeva Sinh, who died in 1825, and was erected by his son and successor the late Rájá Balavant Sinh, who was placed on the throne after the reduction of the fort of Bharat-pur by Lord Combermere in 1826. The British army figures conspicuously in the paintings on the ceilings of the pavilions.* Rájá Randhír Sinh, who is commemorated by the companion monument, was the elder brother and predecessor of Baladeva, and died in the year 1823. These chhattris are very elegantly grouped piles of building and have an extremely picturesque effect, which is heightened by the sheet of water in front of them. But from a purely architectural point of view, they are not of any great merit, and give the idea of having been executed by a contractor, who scamped the work to increase his own profit. The decorative details are mostly poor in themselves, and are repeated with a monotonous uniformity, which contrasts most disagreeably with the rich variety of design that distinguishes all the more important buildings either in Mathurá or Brinda-ban. The painting on the interior of the domes is also as heavy and tasteless as Hindu attempts at pictorial art generally are.

A mile or so from the town, on the borders of the parish of Rádhá-kund, is a much more magnificent architectural group erected by Jawáhir Singh in honour of his father Súraj Mall, the founder of the family, who met his death at Delhi in 1764 (see page 40). The principal tomb, which is 57 feet square, is of precisely the same style as the two already described. The best part of the design is the plinth, which is at once bold in outline and delicate in finish. With that curious blindness to practical requirements, which appears to have characterised the Hindu architect from the earliest period to the present, the decorated panels have been continued all round the four sides of the building, without a blank space being left anywhere for the steps, which the height from the ground renders absolutely necessary. The Rájá's monument is flanked on either side by one of somewhat less dimensions, commemorating his two queens, Hansiyá† and Kishorí. The lofty terrace upon which they stand is 460 feet in length, with a long shallow pavilion serving as a screen at each end,

* In the garden attached to this chhattri the Mahárája has a house, where he stays on his visits to the town; but at all other times it is most obligingly placed at the disposal of European visitors.

† Hans-ganj, on the bank of the Jamuná, immediately opposite Mathurá, was founded by this Ráni. In consequence of a diversion of the road which once passed through it, the village is now that most melancholy of all spectacles, a modern ruin; though it comprises some spacious walled gardens, crowded with magnificent trees.

and nine two-storied kiosks of varied outline to relieve the front. Attached to Ráni Hansiya's monument is a smaller one in commemoration of a faithful attendant. Behind is an extensive garden, and in front, at the foot of the terrace, is an artificial lake, called the Kusum-Sarovar, 460 feet square ; the flights of stone steps on each side being broken into one central and four smaller side compartments by panelled and arcaded walls running out 60 feet into the water. On the north side, some progress had been made in the erection of a *chhattri* for Jawáhir Singh, when the work was interrupted by Muhammadan inroad and never renewed. On the same side, the ghâts of the lake are partly in ruins, and it is said were reduced to this condition, a very few years after their completion, by the Gosáin Himmat Bahádur, who carried away the materials to Brindá-ban, to be used in the construction of a ghát which still commemorates his name there. Such a wanton exercise of power seems a little startling, and therefore it will not be out of place to explain a little in detail who this warlike Gosáin was. A native of Bundel-khand, he became a pupil of Mahant Rájendra Giri, who had seceded from the Dasnámis,* or followers of Sankaráchárya, the most fanatical of all Hindu sectaries, and had joined the Saiva Nágas, a community characterized by equal turbulence unfettered by even a pretence of any religious motive. Through his instigations, Ali Bahádur, an illegitimate grandson of Báji Ráo, the first Peshwá, was induced to take up arms against Sindhia and establish himself in Bundel-khand as virtually an independent sovereign. In 1802, Ali Bahádur fell at the siege of Kálanjar, leaving a son, Shamsher Bahádur. At first the heir was supported by Himmat, who, however, continued quietly to extend his own influence as far as possible ; and, on the combination of the Mahratta chiefs against the British Government, in which they were joined by Shamsher, foreseeing in their success an immediate diminution of his own authority, he determined to co-operate with the British. On the 4th of September, 1803, a treaty was concluded between Lord Wellesley and 'Anúp-giri Himmat Bahádur,' by which nearly all the territory on the west bank of the Jamuná from Kalpi to Allahabad was assigned to him. His death, however, occurred in the following year, when the lands were resumed and pensions in lieu thereof granted to his family.

Other sacred spots in the town of Gobardhan are the temple of Chakresvar Mahádeva, and four ponds called respectively Go-rochan, Dharm-rochan,

* The ten names—whence the title Das-námi—are *tirtha*, *ásrama*, *vana*, *aranya*, *sarasvati*, *puri*, *bharati*, *giri*, *parvata*, and *ságara*, one of which is attached to his personal name by every member of the order.

AUTOTYPE.

THE KUSUM-SAROVAR. GOBARDHAN

Páp-mochan, and Rin-mochan. But these latter, even in the rains, are mere puddles, and all the rest of the year are quite dry; while the former, in spite of its sanctity, is as mean a little building as it is possible to conceive.

The break in the hill, traversed by the road from Mathurá to Díg, is called the Dán Ghát, and is supposed to be the spot where Krishna lay in wait to intercept the Gopís and levy a toll (*dán*) on the milk they were bringing into the town. A Bráhman still sits at the receipt of custom, and extracts a copper coin or two from the passers-by. On the ridge overlooking the ghát stands the temple of Dán Ráe.

For many years past one of the most curious sights of the place has been an aged Hindu ascetic, who had bound himself by a vow of absolute silence. Whatever the hour of the day, or time of the year, or however long the interval that might have elapsed since a previous visit, a stranger was sure to find him sitting exactly on the same spot and in the same position, as if he had never once stirred; a slight awning suspended over his head, and immediately in front of him a miniature shrine containing an emblem of the god. The half century, which was the limit of his vow, has at length expired; but his tongue, bound for so many years, has now lost the power of uttering any articulate sound. In a little dog-kennel at the side sits another devotee, with his legs crossed under him, ready to enter into conversation with all comers, and looking one of the happiest and most contented of mortals; though the cell in which he has immured himself is so confined that he can neither stand up nor lie down in it.

Subsequently to the cession by Sindhia in 1803, Gobardhan was granted, free of assessment, to Kuar Lachhman Sinh, youngest son of Rája Ranjit Sinh of Bharat-pur; but on his death, in 1826, it was resumed by the Government and annexed to the district of Agra. Of late years, the paramount power has been repeatedly solicited by the Bharat-pur Rája to cede it to him in exchange for other territory of equal value. It contains so many memorials of his ancestors that the request is a very natural one for him to make, and it must be admitted that the Bharat-pur frontier stands greatly in need of rectification. It would, however, be most impolitic for the Government to make the desired concession, and thereby lose all control over a place so important, both from its position and its associations, as Gobardhan.

The following legend in the Harivansa (cap. 94) must be taken to refer to the foundation of the town, though apparently it has never hitherto been noticed in that connection. Among the descendants of Ikshváku, who reigned at Ayodhya, was Haryasva, who took to wife Madhumati, the daughter of the giant Madhu. Being expelled from the throne by his elder brother, the king fled for refuge to the court of his father-in-law, who received him most affectionately and ceded him the whole of his dominions, excepting only the capital Madhuvana, which he reserved for his son Lavana. Thereupon, Haryasva built, on the sacred Girivara, a new royal residence, and consolidated the kingdom of Anarta, to which he subsequently annexed the country of Arupa, or (as it is otherwise and preferably read) Anúpa. The third in descent from Yadu, the son and successor of Haryasva, was Bhima, in whose reign Ráma, the then sovereign of Ayodhya, commissioned Satrughna to destroy Lavana's fort of Madhuvana and erect in its stead the town of Mathurá. After the departure of its founder, Mathurá was annexed by Bhima, and continued in the possession of his descendants down to Vasudeva. The most important lines in the text run thus :—

Haryásvascha mahấteja divye Girivarottame
Nivesayamása puram vásartham amaropamah
Anartam náma tadrashtram suráshtram Godhanáyutam.
Achirenaiva kálena samriddham pratyapádyata
Anupa-vishayam chaiva vela-vana-vibhúshitam.

From the occurrence of the words Girivara and Godhana and the declared proximity to Mathurá, it is clear that the capital of Haryasva must have been situate on the Giri-ráj of Gobardhan ; and it is probable that the country of Anúpa was to some extent identical with the more modern Braj. Anúpa is once mentioned, in an earlier canto of the poem, as having been bestowed by king Prithu on the bard Súta. The name Anarta occurs also in canto X., where it is stated to have been settled by king Reva, the son of Saryáti, who made Kusasthali its capital. In the Rámáyana, IV., 43, it is described as a western region on the sea-coast, or at all events in that direction, and has therefore been identified with Gujarát. Thus there would seem to have been an intimate connection between Gujarát and Mathurá, long anterior to Krishna's foundation of Dwáraká.

BARSÁNA AND NAND-GANW.*

Barsána—population 2,773—according to modern Hindu belief the home of Krishna's favourite mistress Rádhá, is a town which enjoyed a brief period of great prosperity about the middle of last century. It is built at the foot and on the slope of a ridge, originally dedicated to the god Brahma, which rises abruptly from the plain, near the Bharat-pur border of the Chháta pargana, to a height of some 200 feet at its extreme point, and runs in a south-westerly direction for about a quarter of a mile. Its summit is crowned by a series of temples in honour of Lárli-Ji, a local title of Rádhá, meaning 'the beloved.' These were all erected at intervals within the last two hundred years, and now form a connected mass of building with a lofty wall enclosing the court in which they stand. Each of the successive shrines was on a somewhat grander scale than its predecessor, and was for a time honoured with the presence of the divinity; but even the last and largest, in which she is now enthroned, is an edifice of no special pretension; through seated, as it is, on the very brow of the rock, and seen in conjunction with the earlier buildings, it forms an imposing feature in the landscape to the spectator from the plain below. A long flight of stone steps, broken about half way by a temple in honour of Rádhá's grandfather, Mahi-bhán, leads down from the summit to the foot of the hill, where are two other small temples. One of them is dedicated to Rádhá's female companions, called the Sakhis, who are eight in number, as follows: Lalitá, Visákhá, Champaká-latá, Ranga-devi, Chitra-lekha, Dulekhá, Sudevi, and Chandrávali. The other contains a life-size image of the mythical Brikh-bhán robed in appropriate costume and supported on the one side by his daughter Rádhá, and on the other by Sridáma, a Pauránik character, here for the nonce represented as her brother.

The town consists almost entirely of magnificent mansions all in ruins, and lofty but crumbling walls now enclosing vast, desolate, dusty areas, which once were busy courts and markets or secluded pleasure grounds. All date from the time of Rúp Rám, a Katára Bráhman, who, having acquired great reputation as a Pandit in the earlier part of last century, became Purohit to Bharat-pur,

---

* Both these interesting places, as also Baladeva, are entirely omitted by Dr. Hunter in his Imperial Gazetteer, and all the places in the district that he does mention are described with remarkable inadequacy and inaccuracy. Apparently his test of the importance of any locality is his own personal connection with it: hence the disproportionate length of some of the Bengal articles.

Sindhia,* and Holkar, and was enriched by those princes with the most lavish donations, the whole of which he appears to have expended on the embellishment of Barsána and the other sacred places within the limits of Braj, his native country. Before his time, Barsána, if inhabited at all, was a mere hamlet of the adjoining village Uchá-gánw, which now, under its Gújar landlords, is a mean and miserable place, though it boasts the remains of a fort and an ancient and well-endowed temple, dedicated to Baladeva. Rúp Rám was the founder of one of the now superseded temples of Lárli Jí, with the stone staircase up the side of the hill. He also constructed tha largest market-place in the town, with as many, is it said, as sixty-four walled gardens; a princely mansion for his own residence; several small temples and chapels, and other courts and pavilions. One of the latter, a handsome arcaded building of carved stone, has for some years past been occupied by the Government as a police-station without any payment of rent or award of compensation, though the present representative of the family is living on the spot and is an absolute pauper. Three cenotaphs commemorating Rúp Rám himself and two of his immediate relatives, stand by the side of a large stone tank with broad flights of steps and flanking towers, which he restored and brought into its present shape. This is esteemed sacred and commonly called Bhánokhar, that is, the tank of Brikha-bhán, Rádhá's reputed father. In connection with it is a smaller reservoir, named after her mother Kírat. On the margin of the Bhánokhar is a pleasure-house in three stories, known as the Jal-mahall. It is supported on a series of vaulted colonnades which open direct on to the water, for the convenience of the ladies of the family, who were thus enabled to bathe in perfect seclusion, as the two tanks and the palace are all enclosed in one courtyard by a lofty bastioned and embattled wall with tower-like gateways.† Besides these works, Rúp Rám also constructed two other large masonry tanks, one for the convenience of a hamlet in the neighbourhood, which he settled and called after his own name Rúp-nagar; the second on the opposite side of the town, in the village of Gházipur, is the sacred lake called Prem Sarovar, which he faced with octagonal stone ghâts. Opposite the latter is a walled garden with an elegant domed monument, in the form of a Greek cross, to his brother Hem-ráj.

---

* It appears that Barsána was an occasional residence of Mádho Ráo Sindhia; for a treaty of his with the Company, regarding trade at Baroch, dated the 30th of September, 1785, was signed by him there, as also the supplementary article dated the following January.

† Both the house and Bhánokhar have been considerably damaged by the new proprietor, who has removed many of the larger slabs of stone.

Contemporary with Rúp Rám, two other wealthy families resided at Barsána and were his rivals in magnificence. The head of the one family was Mohan Rám, a Lavania Bráhman; and of the other Lálji, a Tantia Thákur. It is said that the latter was by birth merely a common labourer, who went off to Lakhnau to make his fortune. There he became first a harkára, then a jamadár, and eventually the leading favourite at court. Towards the close of his life he begged permission to return to his native place and there leave some permanent memorial of the royal favour. The Nawáb not only granted the request, but further presented him with *carte blanche* on the State treasury for the prosecution of his designs. Besides the stately mansion, now much dilapidated, he constructed a large *báoli*, still in excellent preservation, and two wells, sunk at great expense in sandy tracts where previously all irrigation had been impracticable.

The sacred tank on the outskirts of the town called Priya-kund, or Píri-pokhar, was faced with stone by the Lavaniyas, who are further commemorated by a large *katra*, or market-place, the ruins of the vast and elaborate mansion where they resided, and the elegant stone *chhattris* at the foot of the hill. They held office under the Rájá of Bharat-pur, and their present representative, Rám Náráyan, is now a Tahsíldár in that territory.

Barsána had scarcely been built, when, by the fortune of war, it was destroyed beyond all hope of restoration, as has already been related in Chapter II of this memoir, page 42. As if this blow were not enough, in the year 1812 it sustained a further misfortune, when the Gaurua Thákurs, its zamindárs, being in circumstances of difficulty and probably distrustful of the stability of British rule, then only recently established, were mad enough to transfer their whole estate to the oft-quoted Lálá Bábú for the paltry sum of Rs. 602 and the condition of holding land on rather more favourable terms than other tenants. The parish now yields Government an annual rental of Rs. 3,109 and the absentee landlords about as much, while it receives nothing from them in return. Thus the appearance now presented by Barsána is a most forlorn and melancholy one.

The hill is still, to a limited extent, known as *Brahma-ká-pahár* or Brahma's hill: and hence it may be inferred with certainty that Barsána is a corruption of the Sanskrit compound *Brahma-sánu,* which bears the same meaning. Its four prominent peaks are regarded as emblematic of the four-faced divinity, and are each crowned with some building; the first with the group of temples dedicated to Lárli Jí, the other three with smaller edifices, known respectively as the Mán-mandir, the Dán-garh and the Mor-kutti. A second hill, of less extent and elevation, completes the amphitheatre in which the town is set, and the space between the two ranges gradually contracts to a narrow path, which barely allows a single traveller on foot to pass between the shelving crags that tower above him on either side. This pass is famous as the Sánkari-khor,* literally 'the narrow opening,' and is the scene of a *mela* (called the Búrhi Líla) on the 13th of the month of Bhádon, often attended by as many as 10,000 people. The crowds divide according to their sex and cluster about the rocks round two little shrines, erected on either side of the ravine for the temporary reception of figures of Rádhá and Krishna, and indulge to their heart's content in all the licentious banter appropriate to the occasion. At the other mouth of the pass is a deep dell between the two high peaks of the Mán-Mandir and the Mor-kutti, with a masonry tank in the centre of a dense thicket called the Gahrwar-ban. A principal feature in the diversions of the day is the scrambling of sweetmeats by the better class of visitors, seated on the terraces of the 'Peacock Pavilion' above, among the multitudes that throng the margin of the tank some 150 feet below.

The essentially Hindi form of the title Lárlí, equivalent to the Sanskrit Lalitá, may be taken as an indication of the modern growth of the local cultus. Even in the Brahma Vaivarta, the last of the Puránas and the one specially devoted to Rádhá's praises, there is no authority for any such appellation. In the Vraja-bhakti-vilása the *mantra*, or formula of incantation which the pilgrims are instructed to repeat, runs as follows:—

Lalitá-sanyutam krishnam sarvaishu sakhibhir yutam
Dhyáye tri-veni-kúpa-stham mahá-rása-kritotsavam.

NAND-GÁNW—population 3,253—as the reputed home of Krishna's foster-father, with its spacious temple of Nand Ráe Jí on the brow of the hill overlooking the village, is in all respects an exact parallel to Barsána. The distance between the two places is only five miles, and when the kettle-drum is beaten at the one, it can be heard at the other. The temple of Nand Ráe, though large, is in a clumsy style of architecture and apparently dates only from the middle of last century. Its founder is said to have been one Rúp Sinh, a Sinsinwár Ját, and it has an endowment of 826 bighas of rent-free land. It consists of an open nave, with choir and sacrarium beyond, the latter being

* A similar use of the local form *Khor*, for Khol, may be observed in the village of Khaira, where is a pond called Chintá-Khori Kund, corresponding to the more common Sanskrit compound Chintá-harana.

flanked on either side by a Rasoi and a Sejmahall, *i.e.*, a cooking and sleeping apartment, and has two towers, or *sikharas*. It stands in the centre of a paved court-yard, surrounded by a lofty wall with corner kiosks, which command a very extensive view of the Bharat-pur hill and the level expanse of the Mathurá district as far as Gobardhan. The village, which clusters at the foot and on the slope of the rock, is, for the most part, of a mean description, but contains a few handsome houses, more especially one erected by the famous Rúp Rám of Barsána. With the exception of one temple dedicated to Mánasá Devi all the remainder bear some title of the one popular divinity, such as Nar-sinha, Gopináth, Nritya-Gopal, Giridhári, Nanda-nandan, Rádhá-Mohan, and Jasodá-nandan. This last is on a larger scale than the others, and stands in a court-yard of its own, half way up the hill. It is much in the same style and apparently of the same date as the temple of Nand-Ráe, or probably a little older; an opinion which is confirmed by its being mentioned in the *mantra*, which runs as follows :—*Yasodá-nandanam bande nanda-gráma-vanádhipam.* A flight of 114 broad steps, constructed of well-wrought stone from the Bharat-pur quarries, leads from the level of the plain up to the steep and narrow street which terminates at the main entrance of the great temple. The staircase was made at the cost of Bábu Gaur Prasád of Calcutta, in the year 1818 A. D. At the foot of the hill is a large unfinished square with a range of stone buildings on one side for the accommodation of dealers and pilgrims, constructed by Súraj Mall's Ráni, the Ráni Kishorí. At the back is an extensive garden with some fine *khirni* trees, the property of the Rájá of Bharat-pur. They are, however, gradually disappearing, one by one every year, and no attempt is made to replace them. A little beyond this is the sacred lake now called Pán Sarovar, and supposed to be the pool where Krishna used to drive the cows to 'water' (*pán*). It is a magnificent sheet of water with noble masonry ghâts on all its sides, the work of a Dowager Ráni of Bardwán in 1747 A. D. It measures 810 feet by 378, and therefore covers all but six acres. It is said to be designed in the form of a ship; but the resemblance is not very apparent to an uninformed observer. This is one of the four lakes of highest repute in Braj; the others being the Chandra-sarovar at Parsoli by Gobardhan, the Prem-sarovar at Gházipur near Barsána, and the Mán-sarovar at Arua in the Mát pargana. On its margin is a little temple of Bihári, which bears on its front the following inscription : *Sri Rádhá Gobind, Srí Gadádhar Chaitanya, Sri Pávan-sarovar Kunj Srimati Ráni Rasyesvari Rája Kirtichand ki máta Sri Rája Tilok Chand ji ki dádi ji ráj súbe Bangála Baradmán Sri Sanátan Rup ki jaga men bandwe Gumáshta Sri Saphalya Rám Dás, Gokul Das sambat* 1805. The following commemorates some later repairs in 1849; *Sri Nandisvar men Chhajju zamindár ki patti men san* 1155 *sal, mah bhadra sudi men, Sri Pávan wa kunj paki bhayi, memár Mohan Lál, Chet Rám.* Both these inscriptions are noticeable, since, in spite of their modern date, they preserve the old and now entirely obsolete name both of the village, Nandisvar (*i.e.*, Mahádeva) instead of Nanda, and also of the lake, Pávan, 'the purifying,' instead of Pán, 'to drink.' Near the village is a kadamb grove, called Udho ji ká kyár, and, according to popular belief, there are within the limits of Nand-gánw no less than fifty-six sacred lakes or *kunds;* though it is admitted that in this degenerate age all of them are not readily visible. In every instance the name is commemorative of Krishna and his friends and their pastoral occupations.

Like Barsána and so many other of the holy places, Nand-gánw is part of the estate of the representatives of the Lálá Bábu, who, in 1811 A.D., acquired it for a merely nominal consideration from the then zamindárs. One reason for their readiness to part with it is probably to be found in the fact, which has only recently come to my knowledge, that their title was a very questionable one. For the Pujáris of the temple have in their possession a *sanad* dated the 30th year of Alam Sháh giving the whole of the village to their predecessors Paramánand and Rámkishan and their heirs in perpetuity.

If the few squalid buildings which at present disfigure the square at the foot of the hill were removed, and replaced by a well, or temple, or other public edifice, and the line of shops completed on the other side, an exceedingly picturesque effect might be secured at a comparatively small cost. But it is needless to expect any local improvements from the absentee landlords, while the inhabitants are too impoverished to have a thought for anything beyond their daily bread.

The above sketch of two comparatively unimportant places affords a good illustration of a curious transitional period in Indian history. After a checquered existence of five hundred years, there expired with Aurangzeb all the vital energy of the Muhammadan empire. The English power, its fated successor, was yet unconscious of its destiny and all reluctant to advance any claim to the vacant throne. Every petty chieftain, as for example Bharat-pur, scorning the narrow limits of his ancestral domains, pressed forward to grasp the glittering prize, and spared no outlay in the attempt to enlist in his service the ablest men of any nationality, either like Samrú to lead his armies in the field, or like Rúp Rám to direct his counsels in the cabinet. Thus men, whatever their rank in life, if only endowed by nature with genius or audacity, rose in an incredibly short space of time from obscurity to all but regal power. The wealth so rapidly secured was as profusely lavished; nor was there any object in hoarding, when the next chance of war would either increase the treasure ten-fold, or transfer it bodily to a victorious rival. Thus, a hamlet became in one day the centre of a princely court, crowded with magnificent buildings, and again, ere the architect had well completed his design, sunk with its founders into utter ruin and desolation.

CHAPTER XII.

THE ETYMOLOGY OF LOCAL NAMES IN NORTHERN INDIA, AS EXEMPLIFIED IN THE DISTRICT OF MATHURÁ.

IN this, the concluding chapter of the general narrative, I propose to investigate the principles upon which the local nomenclature of Upper India has been and still is being unconsciously constructed. The inquiry is one of considerable importance to the student of language; but it has never yet been approached in a scientific spirit, and the views which are here advanced respecting this *terra incognita* in the philologist's map must be regarded as a first exploration, which is unavoidably tentative and imperfect. Many points of detail will possibly demand future rectification; but the general outline of the subject, the fixed limits within which it is contained and some of its more characteristic features of interior development have, it is hoped, been satisfactorily ascertained and delineated with a fair amount of precision.

It is not to be inferred from this prelude that a subject of such obvious interest has hitherto been totally neglected. On the contrary, it has given rise to a vast number of speculations, but all of the most haphazard description. And this from two causes; the first being a perverse misconception as to the vernacular language of the country; and the second, the absence up to the present time of any list of names sufficiently complete to supply a basis for a really thorough induction.

It seems a very obvious truism, and one that requires no elaborate defence to maintain, that the names of a country and of the places in it should *primâ facie*, and in default of any direct evidence to the contrary, be referred to the language of the people who inhabit them rather than to any foreign source. This, however, is the very point which most writers on the subject have failed to see. In order to explain why the founder of an Indian village gave his infant settlement the name, by which it is still known among his descendants, our laborious philologists have ransacked vocabularies of all the obscurest dialects of Europe, but have left their Sanskrit and Hindi dictionaries absolutely unopened.

A more curious illustration of a deliberate resolve to ignore obvious facts for the sake of introducing a startling theory based on some obscure and utterly problematical analogy could scarcely be found than is afforded by Dr. Hunter in his Dissertation on non-Ayan languages. In this he refers the familiar local termination *gánw* (which *argumenti gratiâ* he spells *gáng* or *gaong*, though never so written in any Indian vernacular) to the Chinese *hiang*, the Tibetan *thiong*, the Lepcha *kyong*, &c., &c., and refuses to acknowledge any connexion between it and the Sanskrit *gráma*. Yet as certainly as Anglo-Saxon was once the language of England, so was Sanskrit of Upper India; and it seems as reasonable to deny the relationship between *gráma* and *gánw* as between the English affix *bury* or *borough* and the Saxon *burg*. The formation is strictly in accord with the rules laid down by the Prákrit grammarians centuries before the word *gánw* had actually come in existence. Thus by Vararuchi's Sutra--*Sarvatra la-va-rám*, III., 3—the letter *r* when compounded with another consonant, whether it stands first or last, is always to be elided; as we see in the Hindi *bát* for the Sanskrit *vártá*, in *kos* for *krosa*, a measure of distance, and in *pem* for *preman*, love. So *gráma* passes into *gáma*, and whether this latter form or *gánw* is used depends simply upon the will of the speaker; one man calls the place where he lives Naugáma, another calls it Naugánw, in the same way as it is optional to say Edinbro' or Edinborough. For in Hindi as in Sanskrit a nasal can always be inserted at pleasure, according to the memorial line—*Savindukávindukayoh syád abhede na kalpanam:* and the distinction between *m* and *v* or *w* has always been very slightly marked; for example, *dhimar* is the recognized literary Hindi form of the Sanskrit *dhívar* and at the present day villagers generally write *Bhamáni* for *Bhawáni*, though the latter form only is admitted in printed books. If speculation is allowed to run riot with regard to the paternity of such a word as *gánw*, every step in the descent of which is capable of the clearest proof, then philology is still a science of the future, and the whole history of language must be rewritten from the very commencement.

Perhaps of all countries in the world, northern India is the one which for an investigation of this kind is the most self-contained and the least in need of alien analogies. Its literary records date from a very remote period; are, in fact, far more ancient than any architectural remains, or even than any well-authenticated site, or definitely established era, and they form a continuous and unbroken chain down to this very day. From the Sanskrit of the Vedas to the more polished language of the Epic poems, and through the Prákrit of the dramatists, the old Hindi of Chand and the Braj Bhásha of Tulsi Dás, down to the current speech of the rural population of Mathurá at the present time, the transitions are never violent, and at most points are all but imperceptible. The language, as we clearly see from the specimens which we have of it in all its successive phases, is uniform and governed throughout by the same phonetic laws. And thus, neither from the intrinsic evidence of indigenous literature, nor from the facts recorded by history, is it permissible to infer the simultaneous existence in the country of an alien-speaking race at any period, to which it is reasonable to refer the foundation of places that still bear a distinctive name, prior to the Muhammadan invasion. The existence of such a race is simply assumed by those who find it convenient to represent as non-Aryan any formation which their acquaintance with unwritten Aryan speech in its growth and decay is too superficial to enable them at once to identify.

As local etymology is a subject which can only be investigated on the spot, and therefore lies beyond the range of European scholars, its study is necessarily affected by the prejudices peculiar to Anglo-Indian officials, who are so accustomed to communicate with their subordinates only through the medium of Urdú that most of them regard that *lingua franca* as being really what it is called in official parlance, the vernacular of the country. This familiarity with the speech of the small Muhammadan section of the community, rather than with that of the Hindu masses, causes attention to be mainly directed to the study of Persian and Arabic, which are considered proper to the country, while Sanskrit is thought to be utterly dead, of no interest save to professional scholars and of no more practical import in determining the value of current phrases than Greek or Hebrew.

The prejudice is to be regretted, as it frequently leads writers, even in the best informed London periodicals, to speak of India as if it were a purely Muhammadan country, and to urge upon the Government, as highly conciliatory, measures which—if taken—would most effectually alienate the sympathies of the vast majority.

Neither Urdú, Persian, nor Arabic, is of much service in tracing the derivation of local names, and it is hastily concluded that words which are unintelligible when referred to those recognized sources must therefore be non-Indian, and may with as much probability be traced up to one foreign language as another. Any distortion of the name of a town or village which makes it bear some resemblance to a Persian or Arabic root, is ordinarlly accepted as a plausible explanation; thus Khánpur is substituted for Kánhpur, and Gházipur for Gádhipur, Gádhi, the father of Visvamitra, being a character not very widely known; while on the other hand a derivation from the Sanskrit by the application of well-established but less popularly known phonetic and grammatical laws, is stigmatized as pedantic and honestly considered to be more far-fetched than a derivation from the Basque or the Lithuanian.

This may seem an exaggerated statement; but I speak from personal experience and with special reference to a critic who wrote that he thought the identification of Maholi with Madhupuri far more improbable than its connection with the Basque and Toda word *uri*, which is said to mean 'a village.'

Such philological vagaries have their birth in the unfortunate preference for Urdú, which the English Government has inherited from the former conquerors of the country, though without any of their good reasons for the preference. They are further fostered by a wide-spread idea as to the character of the people and the country, which in itself is perfectly correct, and wrong only in the particular application. The Hindus are an eminently conservative race, and their civilization dates from an extremely remote period. It is, therefore, inferred that most of their existing towns and villages are of very ancient foundation and, if so, may bear names to which no parallel can be expected in the modern vernacular. This hypothesis is disproved by what has been said above as to the continuity of Indian speech: it is further at variance with all local traditions. The present centres of population, as any one can ascertain for himself, if he will only visit the spots instead of speculating about them in his study, are almost all subsequent in origin to the Muhammadan invasion. When they were founded, the language of the new settlers, whatever it may have been in pre-historic times, was certainly not Turanian, but Aryan, as it is now; and though any place, which had previously been inhabited, must already have borne some name, the cases in which that old name was retained would be very rare. Thus, it may be remarked in passing, the present discussion supplies no ethnical argument with regard to the original population of the country. The names, once regarded as barbarous, but now recognized as Aryan, must be abandoned as evidence of the existence of a non-Aryan race; but, at the same time, since they are essentially modern, they cannot be taken as supporting the counter-theory. The names of the rivers, however, which also are mostly Aryan, may fairly be quoted as bearing on the point; for of all local names these are the least liable to change, as we see in America and our Colonies, where it is as exceptional to find a river with an English name as it is to find a town with an Indian one. And a still stronger and more numerously attested proof is afforded by the indigenous trees, nearly all of which (as may be seen from the list given in an appendix to this volume) have names that are unmistakably of Sanskrit origin.

Moreover, Hindu conservatism, though it doubtless exists, is developed in a very different way from the principle known by the same name in Europe. Least of all is it shown in any regard for ancient buildings, whether temples or homesteads. Though Christianity is a modern faith as compared with Hinduism, and though the history of English civilization begins only from a time when the brightest period of Indian history had already closed, the material evidences of either fact are found in inverse order in the two countries. There is not a single English county which does not contain a longer and more venerable series of secular and ecclesiastical edifices than can be supplied by an Indian district, or it might even be said by an entire Presidency. Thus the temple of Govind Deva at Brindá-ban, which is popularly known in the neighbourhood as 'the old temple' *par excellence*, dates only from the reign of Akbar, the contemporary of Elizabeth, and is therefore far more modern than any single village church in the whole of England, barring those that have been built since the revival by the present generation. The same also with MSS. The Hindus had a voluminous literature while the English were still unable to write; but at the present day in India a MS 200 years old is more of a rarity than one five times that age in England. This complete disappearance from the surface of all material records of antiquity is no doubt attributable in great measure to the operation of the two most destructive forces in the known world, *viz.*, white-ants and Muhammadans; but the Hindus themselves are not altogether free from blame in the matter. As if from a reminiscence of their nomadic origin, with all their modern superstitious dislike to a move far from home, is combined an inveterate tendency to slip away gradually from the old landmarks. The movement is not necessitated by growth of population, which, as in London, for instance, can no longer be contained within the original city bounds, but is a result of the Oriental idiosyncracy that makes every man desire, not—in accordance with European ideas—to found a family or restore an old ancestral residence, but rather to leave some building exclusively commemorative of himself, and to touch nothing that his predecessors have commenced, lest they should have all the credit of it with posterity. The history of England, which runs all in one cycle from the time of its first civilization, affords no ground for comparison; but in mediæval Italy the course of events was somewhat parallel, and, as in India, a second empire was built up on the ruins of a former one of eqnal or greater grandeur and extent. In it we find the modern cities retaining under some slight dialectical disguises the very same names as of old and occupying the same ground: in India, on the other hand, there is scarcely an historic site which is not now a desolation. Again, to pass from political to merely local disturbances: when London was rebuilt after the Great Fire, its streets, in spite of all Wren's remonstrances, were laid out exactly as before, narrow and irregular as they had grown up piece by piece in the course of centuries, and with even the churches on their old sites, though the latter had become useless in consequence of the change in the national religion, which required one or two large arenas for the display of pulpit eloquence rather than many secluded oratories for private devotion. When a similar calamity befell an Indian city, as it often did, the position of the old shrines was generally marked by rude commemorative stones, but the people made no difficulty about abandoning the exact sites of their old homes, if equally eligible spots offered themselves in the neighbourhood.

The same diversity of conservative ideas runs through the whole character: the Hindu quotes the practice of his father and grandfather and persuades himself that he is as they were, and that they were as their forefathers, unconscious of any change and ignoring the evidence of it that is afforded by ancient monuments, both literary and architectural. The former he prizes only for their connexion with the sect to which he himself belongs; whatever is illustrative of an alien faith he consigns to destruction without any regard for its history or artistic significance; and in an ancient building, if it has fallen into disuse, he sees no beauty and can take no interest; though this can scarcely be from the feeling that he can easily replace it with a better, a conviction which led our mediæval architects to destroy without compunction any part of an earlier cathedral, however beautiful in itself, which had become decayed or too small for later requirments. In all these matters England is far more critically conservative; believing in nothing, we tolerate everything; and profoundly distrusting our own creative faculties, we preserve as models whatever we can rescue from the past, either in art or literature.

These reflections may seem to wander rather far from the mark; but they explain the curious equipoise that prevails in the Indian mind between a profound contempt for antiquity and an equally profound veneration for it. The very slight regard in which ancient sites are held is illustrated by the use of the terms 'Little' and 'Great' as local prefixes. In consequence of the tendency to shift the centre of population, these seldom afford information as to the comparative area and importance of the two villages so distinguished: most frequently the one styled 'Little' will be the larger of the two. In some cases the prefix 'Great' implies only that when the common property was divided among the sons of the founder, the share so designated fell to the lot of the eldest; but ordinarily it denotes the original village site, which has been wholly or at least partially abandoned, or so diminished by successive partitions that it has eventually become the smallest and least important of the group.

The foregoing considerations will, I trust, be accepted as sufficiently demonstrating the reasonableness of my general position that local names in Upper India are, as a rule, of no very remote antiquity, and are *primâ facie* referable to Sanskrit and Hindi rather than to any other language. Their formation has certainly been regulated by the same principles that we see underlying the local nomenclature of other civilized countries, and we may therefore expect to find them falling into three main groups, as follows :—

I. Names compounded with an affix denoting place.

II. Names compounded with an affix denoting possession.

III. A more indefinite class, including all names without any affix at all; such words being for the most part either the name of the founder, or an epithet descriptive of some striking local feature.

Running the eye over the list of villages in the Mathurá district, we can at a glance detect abundant illustrations of each of these three classes. Thus under Class I. come such names as Nának-pur, Pati-pura, Bich-puri, where the founder's name is combined with the local affix *pur*, *pura*, or *puri*, signifying 'a town.' So also, Nau-gáma, Uncha-gánw, Badan-garh, Chamar-garhi, Rúp-nagar, Pál-kherá, Brindá-ban, Ahalya-ganj, Rádhá-kund, Mangal-khoh, Mall-sarái, and Nainu-patti. In all these instances the local affix is easy to be recognized as also the word to which it is attached.

Of Class II. the illustrations are not quite so obvious and will mostly require special elucidation ; but some are self-evident, as for example Bhure-ká, where the affix is the ordinary sign of the genitive case ; Ráne-rá, where it is the Márwári form of the same ; and Pípal-wárá, where it represents the familiar *wálá*.

Under Class III. come first such names as Súraj, Misri, and Gaju, which are known to have been borne by the founders ; and under the second sub-division, Gobardhan, 'productive in cattle ;' Sanket, 'a place of assignation ;' Khor, 'an opening between the hills ;' Basai, 'a colony ;' and Pura, 'a town,' indicative of a period when towns were scarce ; with many others of similar character.

Looking first for names that may be inclnded under Class I., we find that by far the most numerous variety are those compounded with the affix *pur*. This might be expected, for precisely the same reason that 'ton' is the most common local ending in England. But we certainly should not expect to find so large a proportion unmistakably modern, with the former part of the compound commemorating either a Muhammadan or a Hindu with a Persian name, or one who can be proved in some other way to have lived only a few generations ago, and with scarcely a single instance of a name that can with any probability be referred to a really ancient date. As this fact is one of considerable importance to my argument, I must proceed to establish it beyond all possibility of cavil by yassing in review the entire series of names in which the ending occurs in each of the six parganas of the district.

The Kosi pargana comprises 61 villages, of which 9 end in *pur; viz.*, 'Azíz-pur, Hasan-pur, Jalál-pur, Lál-pur, Nabí-pur, Pákhar-pur, Rám-pur, Sháh-pur, and Sháhzád-pur. Six of these are unmistakably post-Muhammadan, one is apparently so, and two are of quite uncertain date.

In the Chhátá pargana there are 111 villages, and 16 of them have the *pur* ending; *viz.*, Adam-pur, Akbar-pur, Bázíd-pur, Deva-pura—so called from a 'temple' of Gopál, built by Muhkam Sinh, the ancestor of the present proprietors, whose Arabic name proves that he lived not many generations ago—Ghází-pur, Gulál-pur, Jait-pur, Jamál-pur, Khán-pur, Lár-pur, Mánpur, on the Barsána range—so called from the Mán Mandir, the first erection of which cannot date from further back than the transfer of Rádha's chief shrine from Rával to Barsána, which took place in the 15th or 16th century A.D. —Pír-pur, Saiyid-pur, Tatár-pur, Hájí-pur, and Kamál-pur. Of these 16 names, 12 are unquestionably modern, and of the remaining 4, nothing can be said with certainty either one way or the other.

Of the 163 villages in the Mathurá pargana, as many as 32 have the *pur* ending; *viz.*, Alha-pur, said by local tradition to have been founded and so named only 200 years ago (the founder's descendants are still on the spot and most unlikely to detract from the antiquity of their family); A'zam-pur and Bákir-pur, both founded by A'zam Khán Mir Muhammad Bákir, who was Governor of Mathurá from 1642 to 1645; Bhavan-pur; Bijá-pur, founded 200 years ago by Bijay Sinh, Thákur, on land taken from the adjoining village of Nahrauli; Daulat-pur; Daum-pura, one of 11 villages founded by the sons of a Ját named Nainu at no very remote period, since the share which fell to the eldest of the sons is distinguished by the Persian epithet *kalán;* Giridhar-pur, probably the most ancient of the series, but still dating from times of modern history, having been founded by Giridhar, a Kachhwáha Thákur of Satoha, whose ancestors had migrated there from Amber; Gobind-pur; Hákim-pur; Jamál-pur; Jati-pura, founded by Gosain Bítthal-náth, the son of Vallabhácharya of Gokul, commonly called Jati Jí, about the year 1550 A.D.; Jay Sinh-pura, founded by Sawae Jay Sinh of Amber about the year 1720 A.D.;

Kesopur, so called from the famous temple of Kesava Deva, a fact which would sufficiently account for the name remaining unchanged, even though of ancient date ; Lalpur, founded by a Thákur named Lalu, a member of the Gaurua clan, which is confessedly of late origin ; Lál-pur, founded only a few generations ago by a Tarkar Thákur, Láram ; Madan-pura, founded by an Ahir from the old village of Karnaul ; Mádho-pur, dating 300 years ago, when it was formed out of lands taken from the adjoining villages and given to a Hindu retainer by Salím Sháh ; Mirzá-pur ; Muhammad-pur ; Mukund-pur, so called after a Mahratta founder ; Murshid-pur, founded by Murshid Kulí Khán, who was Governor of Mathurá in 1636 A.D. ; Nabi-pur founded by 'Abd-un-Nabí, Governor from 1660 to 1668 ; Panna-pur, founded in 1725 A.D. ; Ráj-pur, near Brindá-ban, so named with reference to the Ráj-Ghát, by a Sanádh Bráhman from Kámar in the 16th century ; Rám-pur, named after the Rámtál, a place of pilgrimage there ; Rasúl-pur ; Salím-pur, dating from the reign of Salím Sháh ; Askar-pur, a modern alternative name for Satoha ; Sháh-pur ; and Dhak-pura. Of these 32 names, there are only five as to which any doubt can be entertained ; all the remainder are clearly modern.

In the Mát pargana are 141 villages, and 41 end in *pur ; viz.*, Abhay-pura, settled by a Ját, Abhay Sinh, from Kauléna ; Ahmad-pur ; Akbar-pur ; Amán-ullah-pur ; Badan-pur ; Baikunth-pur, founded according to local tradition 300 years ago ; Baland-pur, founded in the 17th century by a Ját named Balavant ; Bali-pur, founded by Bali, a Ját from Bájana about 1750 A.D. ; Begam-pur ; Bulákpur ; Chánd-pur, of modern Ját foundation ; Daulat-pur ; Faridam-pur ; Firoz-pur ; Hamza-pur ; Hasan-pur ; 'Ináyat-pur ; Ja'far-pur ; Jahángír-pur ; Jat-pura, a modern off-shoot from the adjoining village of Shal ; Khán-pur ; Khwája-pur ; Lál-pur, founded by a Ját from Parsauli ; Makhdúmpur ; Mír-pur ; Mubárak-pur ; Mu'in-ud-dínpur ; Nabí-pur ; Nának-pur, a modern off-shoot from Musmina ; Nausher-pur ; Núr-pur ; Pabbi-pur ; Pati-pura, a modern colony from the Ját village of Dunetiya ; Rae-pur, recently settled from Musmina ; Sadík-pur ; Sadr-pur ; Sakat-pur ; Sikandar-pur ; Suhág-pur ; Sultán-pur ; and Udhan-pur. As to the foundation of 6 out of these 41 villages nothing is known ; the remaining 35 are distinctly ascertained to be modern.

Of the 203 villages in the Mahá-ban pargana, 43 have the ending *pur ; viz.*, 'Abd-un-Nabí-pur ; Alí-pur ; Amír-pur ; Islám-pur ; Bahádur-pur ; Balarám-pur, recently founded by Sobhá Ráe, Kayath ; Banárasi-pur, founded by a Bráhman, Banárasi, who derived his own name from the modern appellation of the sacred city called of old Váránasi ; Bhankar-pur ; Bichpuri, of modern Ját foundation ; Daulat-pur ; Fath-pura ; Ghiyás-pur ; Gohar-pur ; Habíb-pur ;

Hayát-pur; Hasan-pur; Ibráhím-pur; 'Isá-pur, founded by Mirza 'Isá Tarkhán, Governor of Mathurá in 1629 A. D.; Jádon-pur; Jagadis-pur, founded by a Parásar, Jagadeva, whose descendants are still on the spot and claim no great antiquity; Jamálpur; Jogi-pur; Kalyánpur; Kásim-pur; Khán-pur; Kishan-pur, recently settled from the village of Kárab; Lál-pur; Manohar-pur; Mohan-pur; Mubárak-pur; Muzaffar-pur; Nabí-pur; Nasír-pur; Núr-pur; Ráe-pur; Saiyid-pur; Shaháb-pur; Sháh-pur; Shahzád-pur: Sherpur; Tayyibpur, and Zakariya-pur. Of these 43 villages, 35 are certainly quite modern: as to the remaining 8 nothing can be affirmed positively.

The 6th and last pargana, Sa'dabad, contains 129 villages, of which 31 have the ending *pur; viz.*, Abhay-pura, of modern Ját foundation; Bágh-pur, founded 300 years ago by a Ját named Bagh-ráj; Bahádur-pur; Bijal-pur; Chamar-pura; Dhak-pura; Fathullah-pur; Ghátam-pur, founded in the reign of Sháhjahán; Hasan-pur; Idal-pur: Mahábat-pur; Makan-pur; Mánik-pur, of modern Ját foundation; Mír-pur; Náráyan-pur, named after a Gosain of modern date, Náráyan Dás: Násir-pur; Nasír-pur; Nau-pura; Ráe-pura, of modern Thákur foundation; Rám-pura, recently settled from Sahpau, by a Bráhman named Mán Mall; Rashíd-pur; Sala-pur, founded by a Bráhman named Sabala; Salím-pur; Samad-pur, settled not many generations ago by a Ját named Sávadhán; Sarmast-pur; Sháhbáz-pur; Sher-pur, Sithara-pur, a modern off-shoot of Garúmra; Sultán-pur; Táj-pur; and Zari-pura. Of these 31 names, 5 are doubtful, the other 26 are proved to be modern.

Adding up the results thus obtained, we find that there are in the whole district 172 villages that exhibit the termination *pur*, and of these as many as 141 are either obviously of modern origin, or are declared to be so by local tradition. It is also worthy of notice that in the above lists there has frequently been occasion to mention the name of the parent settlement from which a more recent colony has been derived; but in no single instance does the older name show the *pur* ending. Yet *pura* or *puri* is no new word, nor is its use as a local affix new; on the contrary we have the clearest literary proof that it has been very largely so employed from the very commencement of the Aryan occupation of India. What, then, has become of all the older names in which it once appeared? It is inconceivable that both name and place should in every instance have been so utterly destroyed as not to leave a trace behind; and we are thus forced to accept the alternative conclusion that the affix has in course of time so coalesced with the former part of the compound, that it ceases to be readily distinguishable from it. Now of names that are presumably ancient, it will be found that a considerable proportion terminate in *oli, auli, aur, auri,* or *aula*. Thus, deducting from the 61 villages in the Kosi pargana, the nine that have the modern termination *puri*, we have 52 left, and among that number 7 are of this character ; *viz*., Banchauli, Chacholi, Chandauri, Mahroli, Sánchauli, Sujauli, and Tumaula. Again, of the 95 villages that remain in the Chhátá pargana after deduction of the 16 ending in *puri*, 15 have the *oli* affix ; *viz*., Ahori, Astoli, Baroli, Bharauli, Chaksauli, Darauli, Gangroli, Lodhauli, Mangroli, Parsoli, Pilhora, Rankoli, Rithora, and Tároli. Without continuing the list in wearisome detail through the other four parganas of the district, it will probably be admitted that, in earlier times, *oli* was as common a local affix as *puri* in modern times, and must represent some term of equally general and equally familiar signification. To proceed with the argument ; these names, though as a rule older than those ending in *puri*, are still many of them of no great antiquity and can be proved to belong to an Aryan period, when the language of the country was in essentials the same as it is now and the people inhabiting it bore much the same names as they do still. Thus Sánchauli is derived from Sánchi Devi, who has a temple there ; Sujáuli from a founder Suján, whose descendants are still the proprietors ; and Parsoli and Tároli from founders named respectively Parsa and Tára. It may be presumed with absolute certainty that these people, bearing such purely Indian names, whether they lived 5, 10, or 15 generations ago, knew no language but their own vernacular, and could not borrow from any foreign tongue the titles by which they chose to designate their new settlements. Thus Dr. Hunter, and those who have followed him in his speculations, may be correctly informed when they state that in Tamil, or Telugu, or Toda, or even in Basque, there is a word *uri*, or *uru*, or *ur*, which means 'village' ; but yet if this word was never current in the ordinary speech of Upper India, the founders of the villages quoted above cannot possibly have known of it. The attempt to borrow such a name as Sujáuli or Maholi directly from the Basque is, when viewed under the light of local knowledge, really more absurd than to derive Cannington from *Kanhay*, or Dalhousie from *Dala-hási*, 'with pleasant foliage.' The misconception, as already observed, has risen from the erroneous idea that all village names are of remote antiquity, and may therefore be illustrated by philological analogies collected from all parts and ages of the world. In truth, *uli* or *uri* is simply *puri* with the initial consonant elided. Such an elision, removing as it does the most distinctive element in the word, may appear at first sight highly improbable : it is, however, in strict accord with the rules of Hindi formation. The two first *sútras* of the second Book of Vararuchi's Prákrita-Prakása in the clearest manner direct it to be made. The text stands thus :

(1) *Ayuktasyánadau.* (2) *Ka-ga-cha-ja-ta-da-pa-ya-vám práyo lopah.* That is to say, the consonants k, g, ch, j, t, d, p, y, and v, when single and non-initial, are generally elided. And as a convincing proof that this is no mere grammatical figment, but a practical rule of very extensive application, take the following familiar words, in which its influence is so obvious as to be undeniable. By the elision of the prescribed consonant we obtain from the Sanskrit *súkar*, the Hindi *súar*, 'a pig'; from *kokila, koil,* 'the cuckoo'; from *súchi, súi,* 'a needle'; from *tátá, táu,* 'a father's elder brother'; from *pada, páo,* 'a quarter'; from *kúpa, kua,* 'a well'; from *Prayág, Prág,* the Hindi name of Alláhábád; and from *jíva, jía,* 'life.' The rule, it is true, provides primarily that the letter to be elided must be non-initial; but one of the examples given in the text is *su uriso* for *su purusha,* 'a good man'; where the *p* is still elided, although it is the initial of the word *purusha.* This the commentator explains by declaring that "the initial letter of the last member of a compound must be considered as non-initial." Thus the mystery is solved, and Karnaul is at once seen to be Karna-pur; Karauli, Kalyán-pur; Tároli, Tárá-pur; and Sujáuli, Suján-puri.

This practical application of the Prákrit grammarian's rule was first stated in my first edition of this Memoir. In my own mind it was so firmly established as an indisputable fact, and possessed in its extreme simplicity at least one of the great merits of all genuine discoveries, that I stated it very briefly and thought it unnecessary to bring forward any collateral arguments in its support. But I find that I much under-rated the strength of inveterate prejudices; for with the exception of one reviewer in a London scientific journal, all other critics seemed to regard my theory as the mere outcome of unpractical pedantry. I have therefore on the present occasion taken great pains to omit nothing, and I cannot believe that anyone, who will submit to the trouble of following my argument as I have now stated it, will still maintain "that the direct derivation from the Turanian roots *aul, ur, uri,* is more probable than the forced and far-fetched Sanskrit derivation from one single root supported only by the theory of a grammarian, which may or may not have been put in practice in an unlettered age." The writer of the remarks I quote would seem to imagine that language was the invention of grammarians; on the contrary, they are powerless to invent or even change a single word, and can merely codify the processes which are the result of unconscious action on the part of the unlettered masses. When Suján-pur is converted in popular speech into Sujáuli, it is not because in one rule Vararuchi has directed the elision of the initial *p*, and in another rule the elision of the final *n;* but because a Hindu's organs of speech (as the grammarians had noticed to be the invariable case) have a natural and unconscious tendency to the change.* This tendency in still existing in full force, and my observing it to be so in another local compound first suggested to me the identification of *uri* with *puri*. Thus the beautiful lake at Gobardhan with the mausoleum of the first of the Bharatpur Rájás is called indifferently Kusum-sarovar, or Kusumokhar; and at Barsána is a tank, called either Bhánokhar or Brikhbhán ká pokhar, after Rádha's reputed father Brikh-bhán. Both in Kusumokhar and Bhánokhar it is evident that the latter part of the compound was originally *pokhar*, and in the same way as the initial *p* has been there elided, so also has it been in Sujáuli and Maholi. The explanation of the last-mentioned word 'Maholi' is one of the most obvious and at the same time one of the most interesting results of my theory. It is the name of the village some four miles from Mathurá, which has grown up in the vicinity of the sacred grove of Madhuban, where Ráma's brother Satrughna destroyed the giant Madhu. On the site of the captured stronghold the hero is said to have built a city, called indiscriminately in Sanskrit literature Mathurá or Madhu-puri: the fact, no doubt, being that Mathurá was originally the name of the country, with Madhu-puri for its capital. In course of time the capital, like most Indian cities, gradually shifted its site, probably in order to follow the receding river; while Madhu-puri itself, fixed by the locality of the wood that formed its centre, became first a suburb and finally an entirely distinct village. Simultaneously with these changes, the name of the country at large was attached *par excellence* to its chief city, and Madhu-puri in its obscurity became a prey to phonetic decay and was corrupted into Maholi. The transition is a simple one; the *h* being substituted for *dh* by the rule II. 27 *Kha-gha-tha-dha bhám Hah*, which gives us the Hindi *bahira* for the Sanskrit *badhira*, 'deaf,' and *bahu* for *vadhú*, 'a female relation.'

It will be observed that Madhu-puri as a literary synonym for Mathurá remains unchanged, and is transformed into Maholi only as the name of an insignificant village. Thus an easy solution is found for the difficulty raised by the same critic I have before quoted, who objects, "If it is possible in the lapse of time to elide the *p* of *puri*, why have not the oldest towns in India like Hastina-pur yielded to the change? and in the case of more modern towns why do we not find the change half-effected, some middle place in the transition stage?" To the former of these two questions I reply that a name when once

* Thus the Agra shop-keepers, who have converted Blunt-ganj into Belanganj, have probably never heard of Vararuchi, but they have certainly, though unconsciously, followed his rules.

petrified in literature is preserved from colloquial detrition. Thus, of two places originally named alike, one may retain the genuine Sanskrit form, while the other becomes Prákritized, according to their celebrity or otherwise. A parallel is afforded by the names of many English families : the elder branches retain the old spelling, however much at variance with modern pronunciation, as, for instance, Berkeley and Marjoribanks ; while the obscurer branches, who seldom had occasion to attach their signatures to any document, conform their spelling to the sound and appear in writing as Barkly and Marchbanks. Again, among those who retain the old form, some no longer pronounce the word in the old fashioned way, but alter its sound according to the more ordinary value of the letters in modern pronunciation.* Thus Hastinapur exists unchanged, by virtue of its historical fame ; had it been an obscure village it would probably have been corrupted into Hathaura. In fine, it may be accepted as a general rule that when the termination *pur, pura,* or *puri* is found in full, the place is either comparatively modern, or if ancient is a place of pre-eminent note. The one exception to the rule is afforded by names in which the first element of the compound is a Persian or Arabic word. Some of them may be much older and yet not more distinguished than many of pure Hindu descent, from which the *p* has disappeared; but the explanation lies in the natural want of affinity between the two members of the compound, which would prevent them from coalescing, however long they might be bound together.

To say that the actual process of transition can never be detected is not strictly in accordance with facts. The elision is not restricted to proper names, but is applicable to all words alike; and in Hindi books written and printed at the present day it is optional with the writer to use exclusively either *kokila,* or *koil; súkar* or *súar; kúp* or *kúa,* or both indifferently. Again, to take a local illustration: Gobardhan, being a place of high repute, is always so spelt by well-informed people, but in vulgar writing it is contracted to Gordhan, and it is almost exceptional to come across a man whose name is Gobardhan Dás, who does not acquiesce in the corruption.

Next to *pur,* the local affix of most general signification and the one which we should therefore expect to find occupying the second place in popular

---

* A case in point is afforded by my own name, which is a corruption of the French *gros* and is from the same root as the Sanskrit *guru* (in the nominative case *Gurus*). It has come down to me with the spelling unaltered for more than 350 years; but the *ow,* which was originally pronounced as in the word 'growth,' or rather as the *ou* in group, has gradually acquired the harsher sound which more commonly attaches to the diphthong, as in 'brown.' In Mathurá, curiously enough, I was always known by the Hindus as 'Guru Sáhib,' and so got back to my original name.

use is *gráma*, *gáma*, or *gánw*. It occurs, however, far less frequently, at least in an unmutilated state. Thus of the 61 villages in the Kosi pargana there are only two with this affix, *viz.*, Dahi-gánw, named from the Dadhi-kund, and Pai-gánw from the Pai-ban-kund; *dadhi* and *payas* both meaning 'milk.' In the 111 Chhátá villages there are four, *viz.*, Bhau-gánw, Nand-gánw, Naú-gáma, and Uncha-gánw. In the 163 Mathurá villages there are six, *viz.*, Bachh-gánw, Dhan-gánw, Jakhin-gánw, Naugáma (properly Ná-gáma from its founder Nága), Nim-gánw, and Uncha-gánw. In the 141 Mát villages there is only one, Tenti-ka-gánw, and this a name given by Rájá Súraj Mall—on account of the abundance of the *karíl* plant with its fruit called *tenti*—to a place formerly known as Akbar-pur. In the 203 Mahában villages only two, *viz.*, Ním-gánw and Páni-gánw; and in the 129 S'adábad villages, four, *viz.*, Kukar-gama, Naugáma, Risgáma, and Tasigau. The proportion is therefore little more than two per cent., and even of this small number the majority may reasonably be presumed to be of modern date. Thus Nau-gáma in the Chháta pargana was formed in later Muhammadan times by a moiety of the population of the parent village Tároli, who under imperial pressure abandoned their ancestral faith and submitted to the yoke of Islám. Again the five or six villages, such as Bachh-gánw, Dahi-gánw, &c., that have sprung up round the sacred groves and lakes and retain the name of the *tirath* unaltered, simply substituting *gánw* for the original *ban* or *kund*, are almost certainly due to the followers of Vallabháchárya at the beginning of the 16th century, or to the Gosáin who composed the modern Brahma-vaivarta Purána and first made these spots places of Vaishnava pilgrimage. It may therefore be inferred that in older names the termination *gráma* has, like *puri*, been so mutilated as to become difficult of recognition. The last name on the list, *viz.*, Tasígau, is valuable as suggesting the character of the corruption, which it exhibits in a transitional stage. The final syllable, which is variably pronounced as *gau*, *go*, or *gon*, is unmistakably a distinct word, and can only represent *gánw*. The former part of the compound, which at first sight appears not a little obscure, is illustrated by a village in the Mathurá pargana, Tasíha, a *patti*, or subdivision of the township of Sonkh, which is said to bear the name of one of the five sons of the Ját founder, the other four being Ajal, Asa, Púrna, and Sahjua. As these are clearly Hindi vocables, it may be presumed that Tasíha is so likewise, and we shall probably be right if we take it for the Prákrit form of the Sanskrit *tishya*, one of the lunar mansions, used in the sense of 'auspicious,' in the same way as the more common Púsa, which represents the asterism Pushya. Thus, as the letter *g* can be elided under the same rule as the *p* in *puri*, the original termination *gráma* is not unfrequently reduced to the form *on*, in which not one letter of its older self remains. The most interesting example of this mutation is afforded by the village *Parson.* Its meaning has so thoroughly died out that a local legend has been in existence for some generations which explains it thus: that two days after Krishna had slain one of the monsters with which the country was infested, he was met at this spot by some of his adherents who asked him how long ago it was that he had done the deed, and he replied *parson*, 'the day before yesterday.' This is obviously as absurd as the *kal kata*, or 'yesterday's cutting,' told about Calcutta; for apart from other reasons the word in vogue in Krishna's time would have been not *parson*, but its original form *parsvas.* However, the true etymology, which is yet more disguised by the fact that office clerks always change the *r* into *l* and call the place Palson, does not appear to have been ever suggested till now. Clearly the name was once Parasuráma-gánw, or in its contracted form Parsagánw, and thence by regular transition has passed through Parsánw into Parson. If proof were required, it is supplied by the fact that a large pond of ancient sacred repute immediately adjoining the village is called Parasurám-kund.

The sacred ponds and groves with which the country of Braj abounds are, as might naturally be expected, ordinarily much older than the villages on their margin; and, as illustrated by the above example, it is always of the utmost importance to the philologist to ascertain their popular names. These are much less liable to corruption than the name of any village; for as the *tírath* is visited solely on account of the divinity with whom it is traditionally associated, his name is in it preserved intact, while as an element in the word that designates the village (a place most connected in the mind with secular matters) its primary import is less considered and in a few generations may be totally forgotten. Thus the obscure name of a pond,* which can only be ascertained by a personal visit, often reveals the name of the local deity or it may be of the founder of the settlement, and in that gives a surer clue to the process of corruption in the village name than could ever be afforded by any amount of library research. For example, the resolution of such a word

* Similarly in England it is the traditional names of the petty subdivisions of the village that are generally of most interest to the philologist. To quote the words of one of the most charming topographical writers of the present day: "Scores of the most singular names might be collected in every parish. It is the meadows and pastures which usually bear these designations; the ploughed lands are often only known by their acreage, as the ten-acre piece or the twelve-acres. Some of them are undoubtedly the personal names of the former owners. But in others ancient customs, allusions to traditions, fragments of history or of languages now extinct may survive" (*Roundabout a Great Estate.*)

as Senwa into its constituent elements might seem a hopeless undertaking; but the clouds are dispelled on ascertaining that a neighbouring pond of reputed sanctity is known as Syámkund. Thence it may reasonably be inferred that the original form was Syám-gánw; the final *m* of Syám and the initial *g* of *gánw* being elided by the rules already quoted, and the consonant *y* passing into its cognate vowel. Other names in the district, in which the affix *gánw* may be suspected to lurk in a similarly mutilated condition, are Jaiswa for Jay-sinh-gánw; Basáun for Bishan-gánw; Bhíún for Bhím-gánw; Bádon for Bádu-gánw* (Bádu being for Sanskrit Bádava) and Oháwa for Udha-gánw.

Another word of yet wider signification than either *puri* or *gráma*, and one which is known to have been extensively used as a local affix in early times, is *sthána,* or its Hindi equivalent *thána*. And yet, strange to say, there is not a single village name in the whole district in which its presence is apparent. It probably exists, but if so, only in the very mutilated form of *ha*. Thus the village of Satohá on the road between Mathurá and Gobardhan is famous for, and beyond any doubt whatever derives its name from, a sacred pond called Sántanu-kund. The eponymous hero is a mythological character of such remote antiquity that he is barely remembered at all at the present day, and what is told about him on the spot is a strange jumble of the original legend. The word Satohá therefore is no new creation, and it can scarcely be expected to have escaped from the wear and tear of ages to which it has been exposed, without undergoing even very material changes. The local wiseacres find an etymology in *sattu*, 'bran,' which they assert to have been Sántanu's only food during the time that he was practising penance. But this is obviously absurd, and Satohá, I am convinced, is an abbreviation for Sántanu-sthána. Instances are very frequent in which words of any length and specially proper names are abbreviated by striking out all but the first syllable and simply adding the vowel *u* to the part retained. Thus in common village speech at the present day Kalyán is almost invariably addressed as Kalu, Bhagaván as Bhagú, Balavant as Balú, and Múlchand as Mulú. In the last example the long vowel of the first syllable is also shortened, and thus an exact parallel is afforded to the change from Sántanu to Satu or Sato. Sato-thána then by ordinary rule, if only the *th* in the compound is regarded as non-initial, becomes Satohána; and the further loss of the final *na* cannot be regarded as an insuperable difficulty.

---

* Here, as Dr. Hœrnle has pointed out, Bádon might be simply a corruption of Bádava, as Jádon is for Jádava. But I think it more probable that, at the time, when the village was founded, the word Bádava was no longer current in vernacular speech and had been superseded by the Hindi Bádu, which by itself would not admit of expansion into Bádon.

An affix which has itself suffered from organic decay has a tendency to involve its support in the same destruction, and thus I feel no difficulty in proceeding a step further and interpreting the word 'Paithá' on the same principles as in Satohá. It is the name of a large and apparently very ancient village with a temple of Chatur-bhuj, rebuilt on the foundations of an older shrine, which had been destroyed by Aurangzeb. At the back of the god's throne is a hollow in the ground, which has given rise to a local etymology of the usual unscientific character. For it is said to be the mouth of the cave into which the people of Braj 'entered' (*paithá*) when Krishna upheld the Giri-ráj hill, which is about two miles distant from the village, in order to shelter them from the storm of Indra. Absurd as the legend is, it supplies a suggestion : for *paithná*, the verb 'to enter,' is unquestionably formed from the Sanskrit *pravishta ;* and if we imagine a somewhat analogous process in the case of the local name, and allow for the constant detrition of many centuries, we may recognize in 'Paithá' the battered wreck of Pratishthána, which in Sanskrit is not an unusual name for a town.

Sthali, a word very similar in meaning to *sthána,* suffers precisely the same fate when employed as an affix ; all its intermediate letters being slurred over, and only the first and last retained. Thus Kosi represents an original Kusa-sthali ; and Társi with the sacred grove of Tál-ban, where, according to the very ancient legend, Krishna put to death the demon Dhenuk, is for Tála-sthali.

Kárab, the name of a large village in the Mahában pargana, is a solitary example of an affix, which I take to have been in full the Sanksrit *vapra,* 'a fort,' or 'field.' If so, it has suffered even more than *sthali* and has retained only one letter of its original self, *viz.*, the initial *v* or *b*. Since hazarding the above suggestion I have come across a fact which is the highest possible testimony to its correctness : for a copper-plate grant of Dhruvasena, one of the Valabhi kings, transbribed in the *Indian Antiquary,* gives Hastaka-vapra as the name of the place now called Háthab.

Another termination, which we find occurring with sufficient frequency to warrant the presumption that it is an affix with a definite meaning of its own, is *oi.* There are five examples of it in the district, *viz.*, Gindoi, Majhoi, Mandoi, Radoi, and Bahardoi. Of these the most suggestive is the first, Gindoi. Here is a pond of ancient sacred repute, called Gendokhar-kund, which is the scene of an annual melá, the Phúl Dol, held in the month of Phálgun. Hence we may safely infer that Gindoi is a compound word with Genda for its first element. This is not an uncommon name for a Hindu, and its most obvious meaning would be 'a marygold.' So taken it would find a parallel in such proper names as Guláb, 'a rose'; Tulsi, the sacred herb so called; Phúl, 'a flower'; and Puhap, for the Sanskrit *pushp*, with the same meaning. It may, however, be doubted whether it did not in the first instance represent rather the Hindi *gainda*, for *gajendra*, 'an elephant.' Besides preserving the name of the village founder, the term Gendokhar-kund is curious in another respect, as showing a complete popular forgetfulness of the meaning of the termination *okhar* at the time when the word *kund* with precisely the same import was added. English topography supplies a case exactly in point; for Wansbeckwater is composed of three words, which all mean exactly the same thing, but were current in popular speech at different times, being respectively Danish, German, and English. But to return to Gindoi, which we have found to be a compound word with Genda for its first element, the termination *oi* yet remains to be considered. I take it to be *vápi*, 'a pond.' In confirmation of this view it is worthy of note that in the Ghiror pargana of the Mainpuri district there is a village called *oi*, *pur et simple*, surrounded on three sides by the river Arind, which in the rains becomes at that particular spot an enormous and almost stagnant sheet of water.* For such a place *vápi* would be a highly appropriate name, and for the transition from *vápi* to *oai* nothing is required beyond the elision of the *p* and change of *v* into its cognate vowel. Prefixing Genda, we have Genda-oai, Gendavai, and finally Gindoi; *o* being subsituted for *au*, and *i* for *ai*, by the following Sútras of Vararuchi, *Auta ot* I. 41, and *Íd dhairye* I. 39. The latter rule, it is true, refers strictly only to the word *dhairya*, which becomes *dhíram* in Prákrit, but it seems not unreasonable to give it a wider application. The above line of argument would command unqualified assent if it could be shown that each of the places with the *oi* ending was in the neighbourhood of some considerable pond. There is such a one at Mandoi, called Achárya-kund; and Bahardoi, founded at an early period by Thákurs from Chitor, who only about 30 years ago lost their proprietary rights and and now have all migrated elsewhere, is a place subject to yearly inundations, as it immediately adjoins some low ground where a large body of water is always collected in the rains. Radoi I have never had an opportunity of seeing, and therefore cannot say whether its physical characteristics confirm or are at variance with my theory: but at Majhoi, which is a Gújar village on the bank of the Jamuná, there is certainly no vestige of any large pond, which

* For this curious fact so strikingly illustrative of my theory, I am indebted to Mr. McConaghey, who conducted the last settlement of the Mainpuri district.

would account for the affix *vápi*. This one proved exception cannot, however, be regarded as a fatal objection; for the same effect may result from very different causes; as, for instance, the Hindi word *bár* in the sense of 'a day of the week' represents the Sankrit *vára;* while if taken to mean 'water,' or 'a child,' it stands in the one case for *vári*, in the other *bála*. Thus in the particular word Majhoi, the *o* may belong to the first element of the compound and the *i* be the affix of possession.

Ána is another termination of somewhat rare occurrence. This is in all probability an abbreviation of the Sanskrit *ayana*, which means primarily 'a going,' 'a road,' but is also used in the wider sense of simply 'place.' An example very much to the purpose is supplied by Vararuchi, or rather by his commentator Bhámaha, who incidentally mentions *munjána*, 'a place producing the *munja* plant,' as the Prákrit equivalent for the Sanskrit *maunjáyana*. The district contains nine places which exhibit this ending, *viz.*, Dotána, Halwána, Hathána, Mahrána, Sihána, Kaulána, Mirtána, Diwána, and Barsána. But what was only suspected in the case of the Gindoi group, *viz.*, that all the names do not really belong to the same category, is here susceptible of positive proof. But to take first some of the words in which *ayana* seems an appropriate affix; Sihána, where is a pond called the *kshír ságar*, may be for Kshiráyana; Dotána, derived on the spot from *dánton*, 'a tooth-brush,' which is suggestive of Buddhist legends and therefore of ancient sanctity, may well be for Devatáyana; Halwána, where an annual melá is celebrated in honour of Balaráma, may have for its first element Hala-bhrit, a title of that hero, the final *t* being elided and the *bh* changed into *v*; while the first syllable in the three names Hathána, Kaulána, and Mirtána, may represent respectively Hasti, Komal, and Amrit; Amrit Sinh being recorded by tradition as the founder of the last-named village. But the resemblance of Díwána and Barsána to any of the above is purely accidental. The former commemorates the Ját founder, one Díwán Singh, whose name has been localized simply by the addition of the affix *a*, while Barsána has a history of its own, and that a curious one. It is now famous as the reputed birth-place of Rádhá, who is the only divinity that—for the last two centuries at least—has been popularly associated with the locality. But of old it was not so: the hill on which the modern series of temples has been erected in her honour is of eccentric conformation, with four boldly-marked peaks; whence it is still regarded by the local Pandits as symbolical of the four-faced divinity, and styled *Bráhma ká pahár*, or 'Brahma's hill.' This lingering tradition gives a clue to the etymology: the latter part of the word being *sánu*, which is identical in meaning with *pahár*

85

and the former part a corruption of Brahma. But this, the true origin of the word, had entirely dropped out of sight even in the 16th century, when the writer of the Vraja-bhakti-vilása was reduced to invent the form Brishabhánu-pura as the Sanskrit equivalent for the Hindi Barsána. A somewhat similar fate has befallen the companion hill of Nand-gánw, which is now crowned with the temple of Nand Raé Jí, Krishná's reputed foster-father. Its real name, before Vaishnava influence had become so strong in the land, was Nandí-gráma, by which title it was dedicated to Mahádeva in his charracter of Nandísvar; and the second person of the Hindu trinity, who has now appropriated all three of the sacred hills of Braj, was then in possession of only one, Gobardhan.

The local name Mai, or Mau, is found occasionally in all parts of Upper India and appears also in the Mathurá district, though not with great frequency.* The one form seems to be only a broader pronunciation of the other in the same way as *náu* is the ordinary village pronunciation for *nái*, a barber,' the Sanskrit *nápita,* and *rau,* a flood, or rush of water, is for *raya,* or *rai,* from the root *ri,* 'to go.' Twice the word stands by itself; twice as an affix, *viz.*, in Pipara-mai and Ris-mai; once in connection with a more modern name of the same place, Mai Mirzá-pur; and twice, as in Ráe-pur Mai and Bara Mai, where the exact relationship with the companion word may be a little doubtful. In most of these cases I consider it to be an abbreviation of the Sanskrit *mahi,* meaning 'land' or 'a landed estate.' The elision of the *h* is not according to any definite rule laid down by the Prákrit grammarians, but certainly agrees with vulgar practice: for example, the word *mahína,* 'a month,' is always pronounced *maina;* and if it were given its full complement of three syllables, a rustic would probably not understand what was meant. At Mai Mirzápur the tradition is that the name commemorates one Mayá Rám; and in the particular case, this very possibly may be so; but obviously instances of this very restricted derivation would be rare.

Nagar, 'a town,' has always been fairly popular as a local affix, and the Mathurá district contains seven examples of the word so used, *viz.*, Rúpnagar, Sher-nagar, a second Rúp-nagar, Ma'súm-nagar, Rám-nagar, Bírnagar, and Ráj-nagar. But it is in modern times and as a prefix that it enters most largely into any catalogue of village names. As a rule, whenever now-a-days an over-crowded town throws out a branch settlement, which becomes of

* Mr. Blochmann informed me that he had noted, with regard to this word 'Mau,' that it was found all over the wide area extending from Western Málwá to Eastern Audh, but did not seem to occur in Bengál, Bihár, or Sindh.

sufficient importance to claim a separate entry in the Government rent-roll, it is therein recorded as Nagla so-and-so, according to the name of the principal man in it. On the spot, Nagla Bali, to take a particular case, is more commonly called Bali ká nagara ; and after the lapse of a few generations, if the new colony prospers, it drops the Nagara altogether, and is known simply as Bali. The transmutation of the word *nagara* into Nagla and its conversion from a suffix into a prefix are due solely to the proclivities of native revenue officials, who affect the Persian collocation of words rather than the Hindí, and always evince a prejudice against the letter *r*. It is interesting to observe that in England the Teutonic mode of compounding names differs from the Celtic, in the same way as in India the Hindí from the Urdú : for while the Celts spoke of Strath Clyde and Abertay, the Teutons preferred Clydesdale and Taymouth.

The number of sacred woods and lakes in Braj accounts for the terminations *ban* and *kund*, which probably are not often met elsewhere. Examples of the former are Kot-ban, Bhadra-ban, Brindá-ban, Loha-ban and Mahá-ban ; and of the latter, Rádhá-kund and Mádhuri-kund. The only name in this list, about which any doubt can be felt as to the exact derivation, is Loha-ban. It is said to commemorate Krishna's victory over a demon called Loha-jangha, *i.e.*, Iron-leg ; and at the annual festival, offerings of 'iron' are made by the pilgrims. In the ordinary authorities for Krishna's life and adventures I certainly find no mention of any Loha-jangha, and as we shall see when we come to speak of the village Bandi, local customs are often based simply on an accidental coincidence of name, and prove nothing but the prevalent ignorance as to the true principles of philology. But in the Vrihat-kathá, written by Somadeva in the reign of Harsha Deva, king of Kashmír, A. D. 1059-1071, is a story of Loha-jangha, a Bráhman of Mathurá, who was miraculously conveyed to Lanka : whence it may be inferred that at all events in the 11th century Loha-jangha, after whom the young Bráhman was named by the romancer, was recognized as a local power ; and thus, though we need not suppose that any such monster ever existed, Loha-ban does in all probability derive its name from him.

The few local affixes that yet remain require no lengthened notice ; of *garh*, or *garhi*, there are as many as twenty instances, *viz.*, Nílkanth-garhi, a settlement of Jáesvár Thákurs ; Sher-garh, a fortress commanding the Jamuná, built in the reign of Sher Sháh ; Chamar-garhi, a colony of the factious Gújar tribe ; Ahvaran-garhi ; Chintá-garhi and Rustam-garhi, founded by Gahlot Thákurs in the reign of Aurangzeb ; Badan-garh, commemorating Thákur Badan Sinh, father of Súraj Mall, the first Bharatpur Rájá; Ikhú-Fath-garh, founded by one of Súraj Mall's officers; Birju-garhi, Chintá-garhi, Ináyat-garhi, Kankar-garhi, Lál-garhi, Máná-garhi, Mani-garhi, Rám-garhi, Shankar-garhi, Tilka-garhi, Bharú-garhi, and Tál-garhi, all founded by Játs during the fifty years that elapsed between the establishment of their brief supremacy and the British annexation. The name will probably never be used again as a local affix; and its extreme popularity during one half-century constitutes an interesting landmark in Indian provincial history, as proof of the troubled character of the country, when no isolated habitation was thought secure unless protected by a circuit of wall and ditch.

Kherá, as seen in Páli-kherá, Awa-kherá, Pál-kherá, Aira-kherá, Sarkand-kherá, and Sel-kherá, invariably implies a state of comparative deprivation, which may be either of people or of land, according as it arises either from the emigration of the greater part of its inhabitants to some entirely different locality, or by the formation of a number of subordinate hamlets in the neighbourhood, which divide among themselves all the cultivated area and leave the old bazar merely as a central spot for common meeting.

Patti ordinarily implies a comparatively modern partition of family lands: thus the villages, into which the old township of Magora was divided by the four sons of the Tomar founder, are called after their names, Ajít-patti, Ghátam-patti, Jájan-patti, and Rám-patti: and similarly Bájana was divided by the Játs into three villages known as Dilu-patti, Siú-patti, and Sultán-patti. The other four places in the district that have this affix do not, however, bear out the above rule. They are Lorha-patti, Nainu-patti, Patti Bahrám, and Patti Sakti. Nether of these has any companion hamlet dating from the same time as itself; and Nainu-patti is a place of considerable antiquity, which long ago was split up into eleven distinct villages.

Another word of precisely similar import is *Thok*. This is used in the Mahá-ban pargana as an element in the name of five out of the six villages that constitute the Sonai circle, and which are called Thok Bindávani, Thok Gyán, Thok Sáru, and Thok Sumeru.

Khoh is an exceptional affix, which occurs only once, in Mangal-khoh, the name of a village on a 'creek' of the old stream of the Jamuná. *Tata*, a bank, is similarly found once only, in Jamunauta, which is a contraction for Jamuna-tata.

Of *Saráe* as an affix we have examples in A'zamábád Saráe, Jamál-pur Saráe, Mal Saráe, Saráe' Ali Khán, Saráe Dáúd, and Saráe Saliváhan. Only at the two first is there any Saráe actually in existence ; both of these are large and substantial buildings erected by local Governors on the line of the old Imperial road between Agra and Láhor. The others were probably mere ranges of mud huts, like the ordinary Saráe of the present day, and have therefore long since disappeared.

The Persian terminations *ábád* and *ganj*, which predominate so largely in some parts of India, have been little used in Hindí-speaking Mathurá. Of *ábád* there are only six examples, being an average of one to each pargana, *viz.*, A'zam-ábád and Murshid-ábád, each commemorating a local Governor in the reign of Aurangzeb ; Aurang-ábád, dating from the same period ; Sa'dábád, the chief town on the demesne of Sháh-jahán's minister Sa'dullah Khán ; and Asaf-ábád, Bir-alí-ábád, Gulshan-ábád, and Salím-ábád, named after founders of less historical distinction.

Having thus passed in review every affix denoting 'place' that we have been able to identify, we proceed to consider the second class of names, *viz.*, those in which the affix signifies 'possession.' The examples under this head are equally numerous and in a philological point of view of no less importance ; but the whole series is traversed by a single clue, and if this is grasped at the beginning, it is found to lead so directly from one formation to another, that it precludes all necessity of pausing for lengthy consideration at any particular stage of the argument. Obviously, the simplest mode of expressing possession is by attaching to the name of the owner the grammatical particle, whatever it may be, which in consequence of its familiar use has been selected as the special sign of the genitive or possessive case. This in modern Hindustani is *ká* or *kí*, which we find employed in the following ten words, *viz.*, Barká, Mahanki, Berká, Marháká, Bhartiyaká, Bhúreká, Káneká, Marhuaká, Saláká, and Súrká. In the last six names on the list the former part of the compound, *viz.*, Bhartiya, Bhúrá, &c., is known to be the name of the Ját founder of the village. Thus we have an indisputable proof that about a century ago it was not at all an uncommon thing to form names of places in this way. If no earlier examples of the formation occur, it is most reasonable to explain their absence by inferring, as in the case of *puri*, that in the course of time the rough edges, that once marked the place where the word and its affix joined, have become so worn and smoothed down that they can no longer be felt. Now by eliding the *k*—a very simple proceeding and one quite in accordance with rule —an amalgamation would be effected between the two elements of the compound which would totally alter their original appearance ; and we have only to reinsert it to discover the meaning of many names otherwise unintelligible.

86

Thus Bhálai, a settlement of Bhál Thákurs, is seen to represent *Bhál-ki* (*basti*); Bághai is for Bágh-ki; Madanai for Madan-ki; Ughai for Ugra-ki; Mahpai for Mahipa-ki; Jonai for Jamuná-ki (Jauna being mentioned by Vararuchi as the Prákrit form of Yamuná); and Semri, with its ancient temple of Syámalá Devi, for Syámalá-ki. Similarly, Indau is for Indra-ká and Karnau for Karna-ká: the representation of *a* + *a* by *au* rather than *á* being almost an invariable practice, as we see in *ráu*, a contraction for *rája*, *pánw* for *pada*, *nau* for *nava* and *táu* for *táta*.

Ká, *kí*, however, are not the only signs of the genitive case in use; for in the Márwári dialect their place is occupied by *rá*, *rí*. Of this form, too, there are abundant examples, as might have been anticipated: for some centuries ago, migrations from Rájpútáná into Mathurá were very frequent and in a less degree continue to the present day. Thus, we have Umraurá, Lohrári, Ganesará, Bhurári, Puthri (from *puth*, a sand-hill), Bhainsára, Garumrá (for Garuda-rá) and Bágharrá, &c. At the last-named place the old village site is called *Sher-ka-kherá*, which puts the meaning of the word Bágharra beyond a doubt; the reduplication of the *r* being purely phonetic. In other names the consonant has not been reduplicated, but the same effect has been produced by lengthening the vowel. Such are Kunjera (where is Kunj-ban), Ráhera, Ránera (founded by Sissodia Thákurs, who named it after the *Ráná* of Chitor, whence they had migrated), Maghera, Nonera, and Konkera, &c.

The origin of the two particles *ká* and *rá* has been much disputed. I would suggest that they both represent an original *kara*, or *kar*. This we find used occasionally by Tulsi Dás as a substantive; as in the line *tab kar as; vimoh ab nahin*; 'then the matter was so; now there is no delusion.' More frequently it occurs as the sign of the genitive; and even in the line quoted it might be regarded in that light, by supposing an ellipse of some such word as *hál*, or *vyápár*. The transition from the one use to the other being so easy, it can scarcely be doubted that the particle and the substantive are really the same identical word. The loss of the final *r* would naturally cause a lengthening of the vowel, and thus *kar* becomes *ká*.

The alternative form *rá* may be explained by the elision of the initial *k*, which would ordinarily take place whenever *kara* was made the last member of a compound. Thus Ráná-kara becomes Ránára or Ránera; and the lengthening of the final *a* is not at all an exceptional phenomenon.

Not unfrequently, however, instead of being lengthened, the final *a* of the affix *kara* is dropt as well as the initial consonant. There consequently remains only the letter *r*, which we see appearing as a final in such words as Kámar, Sahár, Udhar, and Surír. Of these, Kámar (for Kám-ra) is probably an offshoot from the neighbouring town of Kám-ban in Bharatpur territory, a famous place of Vaishnava pilgrimage; while Sahár and Udhar must have been named after their respective founders, who in the one case is known to have been called Udho, or Udhan, and in the other was probably some Sabhá. In Surir, which presents peculiar difficulties, we fortunately are not left to conjecture. For a local tradition attests that the town was once called Sugriv-ká Kherá. The resemblance between the two names is slight that the people on the spot and the unphilological mind generally would not recognize any connection between them; but according to rules already quoted Sugriv-rá would pass naturally into Surir, and the fact that it has done so is a strong confirmation of the truth of the rules.

Another partiele that is commonly used for investing substantives with a possessive force is *wála*, or *wárá*. Of this, as a component in a village name, we have two illustrations in the district, *viz.*, Pipalwára and Bhadanwára.* No satisfactory attempt has hitherto been made to explain the derivation and primary meaning either of this affix *wála*, or of the somewhat less common *hárá*, which is used in a precisely similar way. I take the latter to represent the Sanskrit *dhára* (from the root *dhri*) in the sense of 'holding' or 'having,' as in the compounds *chhattra-dhára*, 'having an umbrella,' *danda-dhára*, 'having a stick.' The elision of the *d* is quite according to rule, as in *bahira*, 'deaf,' for *badhira*. *Wálá*, again, is I consider beyond any doubt the Sanskrit *pála*, with the same signification of 'keeping or 'having.' The substitution of *v* for *p* is prescribed by Vararuchi in Sutra II., 15, who gives as an example the Prákrit *sávo* for the Sanskrit *sápa*, 'a curse.' Thus we have from *go-pála*, 'a cow-keeper,' *gowála*, and finally *gwála*; from *chaupál* the alternative form *chauwárá*, and from *kotta-pála*, 'the governor of a fort,' the familiar *kotwál*.

For the formation of adjectives that denote possession, the affix most frequently employed, both in Sanskrit and modern Hindustani, is *i*. Thus from *dhan*, 'wealth,' comes *dhani*, wealthy and from *mála*, 'a floral wreath' comes *máli*, 'a florist.' Dr. Hunter, with much perverted ingenuity, has gone out of his way to suggest that the latter are an aboriginal and non-Aryan race and "take their name from the tribal term for man, *male*, from which many

---

* It is curious to find in the English of the 9th century a word 'wárá' used precisely in the same way. Thus the Mersewara, or marsh folk, were the dwellers in the reclaimed flats of Romney marsh: while the Cantwara inhabited the Caint, or open upland which still gives its name to the county of Kent.

hill and forest people of northern and central India, possibly also the whole Malay race of the Archipelago, are called." I am not aware that in this theory he has found any followers: whatever the origin of the Malays, there is no more reason to suppose a connection between them and the Mális of our gardens, than between man, the biped, and *man*, a weight of 40 sers. As the letters of the alphabet are necessarily limited, it must occasionally happen that combinations are formed which are quite independent of one another and yet in appearance are identical. Among examples of the *í* affix we find in Mathurá, from *dhímar*, 'a fisherman,' Dhímarí, a fishing village on the bank of the Jamuná: from a founder Husain, a village Husaini; from Pál, the favourite title of a Thákur clan, Pálí; from Pingal, Pingari; from *babúl*, the acacia, Babúri; from *Khajur*, Khajúri: and from *kinára*, 'the river bank,' Kinárí. A lengthened form of the same affix is *iya*, which we find in Jagatiya and Khándiya.

Another affix, which in ordinary Sanskrit literature occurs as frequently as *í* and with precisely the same signification, is *vat, vati*. In vulgar pronunciation the consonant *v* generally passes into the cognate vowel; thus Bhagavati becomes Bhagoti, and Sarasvati, Sarsúti. I am therefore led to suspect that this is the affix which has been used in the formation of such village names as Kharot, Khatauta, Ajinothi, Bilothi, Kajirothi, Basonti, Báthi, Junsuthi, Sonoth, Bádauth, Barauth, Dhanoti, and Tatarota. All these places are presumably old, and nothing can be stated with certainty as to the period of the foundation, but the only one of them in any way remarkable is Báthi. Here is the sacred grove of Bahula-ban, with the image of the cow Bahula, who (as told in the Itihas*) addressed such piteous supplications to a tiger who was about to destroy her, that the savage beast could not but spare her life. A *melá* in her honour is still held on the fourth day of Kuwár, called 'Bahula chaturthi.' In every other instance where the *ban* is a place of any celebrity, it has supplied the foundation for the village name, and has probably done so here too. The transition from Bahula-vati to Báthi presents no insuperable difficulty; for a similar change of the dental into the cerebral consonant has occurred in the Hindi *pattan*, 'a town,' and in *murha*, 'a fool,' for the Sanskrit *mugdha*; the insertion of the aspirate is the only irregularity which it is not easy to explain.

A third affix which can be more appropriately noticed here than elsewhere, though it has a somewhat different force, is *a*. This implies primarily 'a product,' or 'result.' Thus from *ber*, the fruit tree, comes the name of the

* A collection of stories supposed to have been related by Bhima-sena while he lay wounded on the field of battle.

village Bera, an orchard of *ber* trees : from Náhar, a man's name meaning 'lion,' Nahra ; from Parsu, an abbreviation for Parasu-rám, Parsua ; from Ráe [Sen], Raya ; from Paramesvar Dás, Pavesara ; and similarly Bisambhara, Dandisara, &c.

We may now pass on to the first sub-division of class III., in which are included all such village names as originally were identical, without addition or alteration of any kind, with the names borne by the founders ; though the original identity, it must be remembered, is no guarantee against subsequent corruption. One of the earliest examples in the district is afforded by the village Son, which is said to have been the capital of a Rájá Son—or more probably Sohan—Pál, a Tomar Thákur from Delhi. Sonkh, Sonsa, and Sonoth, all three places in the immediate neighbourhood, would also seem to be named after him and to prove that he was an historical personage of at least considerable local importance. Another interesting illustration, which must also be of early date, is found in the name Dham Sinha. Here Dham, which is the obsolete Prákrit form of *dharma* and is not understood at the present day, runs a great risk of being altered by people who aim at correctness, but lack knowledge, into the more intelligible word *dhan*. In modern times this style of nomenclature has been so prevalent that a single pargana—Mahá-ban—supplies us with the following examples, *viz.*, Birbal, Gaju, Misri, Bhúra, Súraj, Báru, Rausanga, Nauranga, Mursena, Bansa, Bhojua, Bhíma, and Súr,. Of these, Rausanga for Rúp Sinha would scarcely have been recognizable but for the aid of local tradition. Occasionally the names of two brothers, or other joint founders, are combined, as we see in Sampat-jogi, Chúra-hansi, Bindu-buláki, and Harnaul. The latter is a curious contraction for Hara Navala ; and as 'the swing' is one of the popular institutions of Braj, the word not unfrequently passes through a further corruption and is pronounced Hindol, which means a swing. This will probably before long give occasion to a legend and a local festival in honor of Rádhá and Krishna.

Under the same head comes the apparently Muhammadan name Noh ; which, with the addition of the suffix *jhil*, is the designation of a decayed town on the left bank of the Jamuná to the north of the district. At no very great distance, but on the other side of the river, in Gurgánw, is a second Noh ; and a third is in the Jalesar pargana, which now forms part of the Eta district. So far as I have any certain knowledge, the name is not found in any other part of India, though it occurs in Central Asia ; for I learn from Colonel Godwin Austen that there is a Noh in Ladak or rather Rudok at the eastern end of the Pangang Lake, and on its very borders. The Yárkand expedition is also stated in the papers to have reached Leh viâ Khotan, Kiria, Polu, and Noh, by the easternmost pass over the Kuen-lun mountains. Upon this point I may hope to acquire more definite information hereafter; the best maps published up to the present time throw no light on the matter, for though they give the towns of Kiria and Khotan, they do not show Noh, and its existence therefore requires confirmation. The three places in this neighbourhood all agree in being evidently of great antiquity, and also in the fact that each is close to a large sheet of water. The lake, or morass, at Noh jhíl spreads in some years over an area measuring as much as six miles in length by one in breadth. It is no doubt to a great extent of artificial formation, having been excavated for the double purpose of supplying earth, with which to build the fort, and also of rendering it inaccessible when built. The inundated appearance of the country combines with the name to suggest a reminiscence of the Biblical Deluge and the Patriarch Noah. The proper spelling of his name, as Mr. Blochmann informed me, is Núh, with the vowel *ú* and the Arabic *h*, while Bádáoní, who twice* mentions the town, in both places spells it with the imperceptible *h;* in the Áín-i-Akbarí, however, which herein agrees with invariable modern usage, the final letter is the Arabic *h*. But if a reference to the Deluge were intended, the word Noh would not have been used simply by itself; standing as it does, it can scarcely be other than the name of the founder. Now (to quote Mr. Blochmann again) "Muhammadans use the name Núh extremely rarely. Ádam, Músá, Yúsuf, and Ayúb are common; but on looking over my lists of saints, companions of Muhammad, and other worthies of Islám, I do not find a single person with the name Nuh; and hence I would look upon a connection of Noh with Noah as very problematical. I would rather connect it with the Persian *nuh*, 'nine,' which when lengthened becomes *noh*, not *núh;* as the Persian *dih*, 'a village,' becomes *deh*, not *díh*." But if we abandon the Semitic name, it will be better, considering the purely Hindu character of the country, to try and fall back upon some Sanskrit root, and I am inclined to regard the name as a Muhammadan corruption of *nava*—not the adjective meaning 'new,' but a proper name—and with the *h* added either purposely to mark the distinction, or inadvertently in the same way as *rájá* is in Persian characters incorrectly written *rájah*. In the Harivansa (line 1677) mention is made of a king Ushinara, of the family of Kaksheyu, who had five wives, Nrigá, Krimí, Navá, Darvá, and Drishadvati. They bore him each one son, and the boys were

* Once as the scene of a fight between Ikbál Khán and Shams Khán of Bayána (A. H. 802), and again as the place where Mubárak Sháh crossed the Jamuná for Jartoli.

named Nriga, Krimi, Nava, Suvrata and Sivi; of whom Nava reigned over Navaráshtram; Krimi over Kumilá-puri; Sivi, who is said to be the author of one of the hymns of the Rig Veda (X. 179), over the Sivayas, and Nriga over the Yaudheyas. In the Mahábhárat the Usinaras are said to be a lower race of Kshatriyas. They are mentioned by Pánini in a connection which seems to imply that they were settled in or near the Panjáb; and in the Aitareya Brahmana, Usinara is collocated with Kuru and Panchála. Again, Drishadvati, the fifth of Usinara's wives, recalls to mind the unknown river of the same name, which is mentioned by Manu as one of the boundaries of Brahmávarta, and in the Mahábhárat as the southern boundary of Kurukshetra. From all this it may be inferrred that the Navaráshtra, over which Usinara's third son Nava reigned, cannot have been far distant from Mathurá and Gurgánw; and its capital may well have been the very place which still bears his name under the corrupt form of Noh or Nauh.

The second subdivision of class III. is of an extremely miscellaneous character and admits of no grouping, each name having a separate individuality of its own. Some of the more obvious examples have been already quoted: such as are Basai, 'a colony;' for the Sanskrit *vasati* (which at the present day is more commonly abbreviated by the alternative mode into *basti*); Chaukí, 'an outpost' on the Gurgánw road; Nagariya, 'a small hamlet;' Barhá, 'a removal;' Garhi, 'a fort;' Mai, 'an estate;' Khor, 'an opening' between the Barsána hills; Anyor, 'the other end' of the Gobardhan range; Pura, 'a town;' Kheriya, 'a hill;' and Toli, 'an allotment.' Others require more detailed explanation on account either of their intrinsic difficulty, or of the mythological disguise put upon them by the local pandits, who think there is no place in the whole of Braj which does not contain some allusion to Krishna. Thus they connect the word Mathurá with the god's title of Madhu-mathan; though the more natural derivation is from the root *math* direct, in its primary sense of 'churning;' an exact grammatical parallel being found in the word '*bhidura*, breakable,' a derivative from the root *bhid*, 'to break.' The name thus interpreted is singularly appropriate; for Mathurá has always been celebrated for its wide extent of pasture-land and many herds of cattle, and in all poetical descriptions of the local scenery 'the churn' is introduced as a prominent feature. I observe that Dr. Rájendralála Mitra in a learned article on the Yavanas, published in the Calcutta Asiatic Society's Journal, has incidentally remarked upon a passage in the Sánti Parva of the Mahábhárat, in which the word Madhurá occurs, that this is the ancient form of Mathurá. Now I should hesitate to dispute any statement deliberately made by so eminent a scholar, but this appears to be a mere *obiter dictum*, and I strongly doubt whether in the whole range of early Sanskrit literature the capital of Braj is ever designated Madhurá. In the particular passage which he quotes, Lassen regards the word as the name of a river, and that the well-known city in the Dakhin is in the vernacular always spelt Madhura in no way affects the argument; for even if the two names are etymologically identical, which is probable but not certain, the dislike shown by all the languages of the south to the use of hard consonants is quite sufficient to account for the alteration.

Similarly the name of the country, Braj, or Vraja, has nothing to do with the Vajra Sena, the son of Anirudh, who is said to have been crowned king of Mathurá on Krishna's death; but comes immediately from the root *vraj*, 'to go,' and is thus a highly appropriate designation for a land of nomadic herdsmen. Equally at fault is the mythological derivation of 'Bathen,' the name of two large villages in the Kosi pargana, where Balaráma, it is said, 'sat down' (*baithen*) to wait for Krishna. Here, again, the real reference is to the pastoral character of the country, *bathan* being an archaic term to denote a grazing-ground. A still greater and more unnecessary perversion of etymological principles is afforded by the treatment of the word Khaira. This is popularly derived from the root *khedna*, 'to drive cattle,' which was Krishna's special occupation as a boy: but it is in fact the regular contraction of the Sanskrit *khadira*, the Acacia Arabica, more commonly known as the *babúl*; as is proved by the contiguity of the village to the *Khadira-ban*, one of the twelve sacred groves. Other indigenous trees have contributed in like manner to the local nomenclature; thus the *lodhra*, or Symplocos, would seem to have furnished a name for the village of Lohi in the Mát pargana: the Tinduk Ghát at Mathurá is probably so called not in honour of any pious ascetic, but with reference to the *pasendu*, or Diospyros, the Sanskrit *tinduka*, one of the most common trees in the district: and in the Sakra-ban, which gives its name to the village of Sakaraya, it would seem that the *sakra* intended is the tree, the Terminalia Arjuna, and not the god Indra, though he too is known by that title, which primarily means the strong or powerful.

The most interesting example of an elaborate myth based solely on the misunderstanding of a local name is to be found in the village of Bandi. Here is a very popular shrine, sacred to Bandi Anandi, who are said to have been two servants of Jasoda's, whose special employment it was to collect the sweepings of the cow-shed and make them up into fuel. But in the inscription over the gateway leading into the court-yard of the temple, which is dated *Sambat*

1575, there is no mention of Anandi whatever. Part is illegible, but the first words read clearly as follow : *Svasti srí Sarvoparí birájamán Bandi Jí. Tasya sevak*, &c. From this it may be inferred that Anandi has been added in very recent times simply for the sake of the alliterative jingle, and because there happened to be a second old figure on the spot that required some distinctive name. The original word was Bandi alone. The Gokul Gosáins support their theory as to its etymology by making the Gobar Líla at Bandi one of the regular scenes in the dramatic performances of the Ban-játra ; but it is not accepted by the more old-fashioned residents of the village, who maintain that the local divinity was a recognized power long before the days of Krishna, who was brought there to offer at her shrine the first hair that was cut from his head. Their view as to the relative antiquity of the Bandi and the Mathurá god is certainly correct ; for both the images now believed to represent Jasoda's domestic servants are clearly effigies of the goddess Durgá. In the one she appears with eight arms, triumphing over the demon Mahishásur ; in the other, which is a modern facsimile, made at Brindá-ban, after the mutilated original, she has four arms, two pendent and two raised above the head. Neither of them can represent a human handmaid ; and thus they at once disprove the modern story, which would seem to be based on nothing more substantial than the resemblance of the word *bandi* to the Persian *banda*, meaning 'a servant.' The real derivation would be from *bandya*, or *vandya*, the future participle of the verb *vand*, signifying 'venerable' or 'worshipful.' Thus, what was once an epithet of a particular image of Devi became after a time its distinctive name ; and eventually, being referred by the ignorance of the people to a more ordinary term of current speech, has originated a legend and a local festival for which in fact there is no foundation whatever.

The above is one illustration of a general rule that all presumably ancient local names are entirely different in origin and meaning from any terms of current speech with which they may happen to be identical in form. Thus, as we have already seen, the village Parson has no connection with *parson*, the common adverb of time ; neither is Paitha so named, as being near the mouth of the cave into which the people of Braj 'entered' (*paitha*). Again, Rál, a large village in the Mathurá pargana, is not so called as being the scene of one of Krishna's 'battles' (*rár*), as local Pandits say ; nor because the extensive woods round about it abound in *rál*, or 'resin :' but rather it is a contraction of Rája-kula, 'a king's house ;' a compound of similar character with Gokul, a 'cow house,' the name of the town where

Krishna was nurtured by the herdsman Nanda. Rával, a village in the same neighbourhood, the reputed home of Rádhá's maternal grandfather Surbhán, may be identical in meaning; or it may even represent an original Rádhá-kula, in which case it would be curious as affording the earliest authority for Rádhá's local existence and pre-eminent rank. Koila, again, is evidently not the bird called in Sanskrit *Kokila* and in Hindi *Koil;* for who would dream of calling a place simply Cuckoo without any affix such as in the possible compound Cuckoo-town? Neither is it the exclamation *Koí lá*, uttered by Vasudeva as he was bearing the infant Krishna across the Jamuná; for whatever the language then in vogue, it certainly was not modern Hindí: nor again, and for a similar reason, does the word Koila mean 'charcoal,' with a reference to the ashes of the witch Pútaná, washed across the stream from the town of Gokul. But it may be taken for granted that the final consonant stands for *rá* and has the possessive force of that particle, while the former member of the compound is either *Koi*, 'the water-lily,' or *Kol*, for *Kroṛa*, 'a wild boar.' The extensive morass in the neighbourhood, well known to sportsmen as the Koila jhíl, renders either derivation probable and appropriate. If the fact were not now placed on record, a few more years and the philologists who look for the origin of Indian names in every language, saving only the vernacular of the country, would seize the opportunity of declaring Koila to be merely a mispronunciation of the English 'quail.' Similarly, it may reasonably be conjectured that Kukar-gama is not so called because a Banjára in his travels happened to bury beside the village pond a favourite dog (*kukar*), though the slab supposed to cover the dog's grave is still shown; but rather, as the village is certainly of ancient date and was colonized by Thákurs from Chitor, it is probable that its name commemorates the otherwise unknown founder, since Kukura occurs in the Mahábhárat as the proper name of a king, and may therefore have been at one time in common use. To pass yet more rapidly over a few other illustrations of the same rule, that apparent identity is equivalent to real difference: Kámar does not commemorate Krishna's gift of a blanket (*kamal*) to the shivering hermit Durvásas, but rather implies a migration from the older town of Káma; 'Ainch' does not refer to the 'stretching' of Krishna's tent-ropes, through the real derivation is doubtful; 'Jáu' is not the imperative verb 'go,' but a corruption of *yáva*, 'lac;' Marna, now altered by office copyists to Bharna, has no relation to the 'death' of one of Krishna's enemies; and 'Jait' is not simply an abbreviation for *jaitra*, but (as shown by the village pronunciation Jaint) represents an original Jayanta, which occurs in Sanskrit as the name both of a river and a country.

It must, however, be borne in mind that the application of this rule is restricted exclusively to local names of ancient date. Thus the name of the village Sanket is really identical with the Sanskrit word *sanket*, meaning 'an assignation' or 'rendezvous;' the place which lies half-way between Barsána and Nandgánw, the respective homes of Rádhá and Krishna, having been so called by the Gosáins of the 16th century with the special object of localizing the legend. Similarly, Pisáya with its beautiful forest of kadamb trees, to which the author of the Vraja-bhakti-vilása gives the Sanskrit title of Pipásavana, may really bear a name identical with the Hindi word *pisaya*, 'thirsty,' if the name was first assigned to the spot by the Gokul Gosáins as a foundation for a story of Rádhá's bringing a draught of water for the relief of her exhausted lover. But this is questionable, since it appears that there is a place with the same name, but without any similar legend, in the Aligarh district: both are therefore most probably far anterior to the 16th century and susceptible of some entirely different explanation. The Aligarh Pisáya is, I find, described as having the largest jungle or grazing ground in that district; and this suggests that the word may very well be a corruption of the Sanskrit *pasavya*, 'fit for cattle.'

In all these and similar cases it is imposible to arrive at sound conclusions without a large amount of local knowledge; while the absurdity of the explanations advanced by the local Pandits demonstrates the equal necessity for acquaintance with at least the rudimentary laws of philological science. Scholastic speculations made without reference to physical features or to the facts of village history are always liable to summary disproof; and no one with any respect for his own reputation should think of pronouncing off-hand upon the derivation of the name of any place regarding the circumstances of which he has not very definite information. For example, as the village Jati-pura is on the border of the Ját state of Bharat-pur, what could be more plausible than to say that it is so called as being a Ját colony? but, as a fact, it has always been inhabited by Bráhmans, and its founder was the Vallabhácharya Gosáin, Bitthal-náth, who was popularly known by the name Jatiji. Similarly, while the Naugáma in the Chháta pargana really connotes the meaning which the form of the word most obviously suggests, *viz*., new town, the Naugáma near the city of Mathurá stands for an original *nága-gráma*, and commemorates its founder, Nága. As a parallel example in English topography take the town of Bridge-water; the latter member of the compound referring not to any stream, as would naturally be supposed, but to the Norman chief Walter, who built his castle there. Again, Lodhauli (in accordance with the principles stated in the earlier part of this chapter) might be at once set down as equivalent to Lodha-puri; but here, too, the caste of the residents forbids such a derivation, for they have always been not Lodhas, but Jádons; and the modern name is a perversion of Lalitá-puri. Phálen again and Siyára would be inexplicable but for the knowledge that they are built, the one on the margin of a pond, called Prahlád kund, and the other by the Chír Ghát, a very ancient and now comparatively neglected *tírath* on the Jamuná. The confusion between the letters *s* and *ch* is one of the peculiarities of the local dialect. Thus Amar Sinh is frequently called Amarchu; the village of Parsua, in the mouths of the villagers on the spot, is indistinguishable from Pilchua; Chakri, after becoming Saki, gives a name to Sakitra, where is an ancient shrine of Chakresvar; and so too Chíra-hára becomes Siyára.*

Although it may safely be laid down as a general principle of Indian toponymy that the majority of names are capable of being traced up to Aryan roots, it is possible that the rule may have some exceptions. In the Mathurá and Mainpuri districts there is a current tradition that the older occupants of the country were a people called Kalárs. The name seems to support a theory advanced by Dr. Hunter in his Dissertation, where he quotes a statement from some Number of the Asiatic Society's Journal to the effect that the whole of India was once called Kolaria. On the strength of a number of names which he sees in the modern map, he concludes that the race, from whom that name was derived, once spread over every province from Burma to Malabar. He finds indications of their existence in the Kols of Central India; the Kolas of Katwár; the Kolís of Gujarát; the Kolítas of Asám; the Kalárs, a robber caste in the Tamil country; the Kalárs of Tinnevelly, and the Kolís of Bombay, &c., &c. Upon most of these names, as I have no knowledge of the localities where they exist, I decline to offer any opinion whatever, and can only express my regret that Dr. Hunter has not exercised a little similar caution. For he proceeds to give a list of town-names, scattered as he says over the whole length and breadth of India, which seems to me of the very slightest value as a confirmation of his theory. No one should be better conversant than himself with the vagaries of phonetic spelling; and yet he gravely adduces as proof of the existence of a Kol race such names as Kulianpur and Kullian; though it is scarcely possible but that, if correctly spelt, they

* *Chira* is itself a contraction for *chivara*, which shows that the elision of a simple consonant, which became the rule in Prákrit, was occasional also in pure Sanskrit. Similarly the Sanskrit word *vija*, 'seed,' which lexicographers derive from the root *jan* with the prefix *vi*, is, I conceive, simply a colloquial form of *virya*, with which it is identical in meaning.

would appear as Kalyánpur and Kalyán; the latter being still a popular Hindi name and the Sanskrit for 'auspicious.' Moreover, if the race was ever so widely spread as he supposes, it is inconceivable that they should give their tribal name to the different towns they inhabited; for such names under the supposed circumstances would have no distinctive force. For example, if the Hindus were suddenly to be swept out of India, the race that superseded them would not find a single village bearing such a name as Hindu-pur, or Hindu-gánw. Obviously it is only a country that derives its name from a tribe, while towns and villages commemorate families and individuals. To ascertain who the Kalárs were is certainly an interesting question, but one upon which it is as yet premature to speak positively. My own impression is that the name denotes a religious rather than an ethnological difference, and that they were—in this neighbourhood at all events—Buddhists or Jains. At many of the places from which they are said to have been ejected by the ancestors of the present Ját or Thákur families, I have found fragments of Buddhist or Jain sculpture, which can only have been the work of the older inhabitants, since it is certain that the race now in possession have never changed their religion. It is, of course, possible that these Kalárs may have been non-Aryan Buddhists; but the old village names, which in several cases remain unchanged to the present day, such as Aira, Madem, Byonhín, &c., though of doubtful derivation, have certainly anything but a foreign or un-Indian sound.

These and a considerable number of other names yet require elucidation: but the words with which I prefaced the first edition of this work, in anticipation of the present argument, have now, I trust, been so far substantiated that I may conclude by repeating them as a summary of actual results. "The study of a list of village names suggests two remarks of some little importance in the history of language. *First,* so many names that at a hasty glance appear utterly unmeaning can be positively traced back to original Sanskrit forms as to raise a presumption that the remainder, though more effectually disguised, will ultimately be found capable of similar treatment: a strong argument being thus afforded against those scholars who maintain that the modern vernacular is impregnated with a very large non-Aryan element. *Secondly,* the course of phonetic decay in all its stages is so strictly in accord with the rules laid down by the Prákrit grammarians, as to demonstrate that the Prákrit of the dramas (to which the rules particularly apply), even though extinct at the time when the dramas were written for the delectation of a learned audience, had once been the popular language of the country; and as Anglo-Saxon imperceptibly developed into modern English, so has Prákrit been transmuted into modern Hindi, more by the gradual loss of its inflections than by the violent operation of any external influences." Thus the recognition of Persian or any dialect of Persian as the vernacular of the country implies an historical untruth as regards the past, and can only be verified in the future by the obliteration of all existing traditions.

The following list shows the changes of most frequent occurrence in the conversion of Sanskrit words into Hindi :—

1. *a* + *a*, after the elision of a consonant, generally becomes *au* or *ao*; thus from *pada* we have *páo*, or, by insertion of a nasal, *pánw*; from *rájá*, *ráo*; from *táta*, 'father,' *táu*; from *gháta*, 'a wound,' *ghán*; and from *tadága*, 'a pond' (itself derived from *tata*, a slope), *taláo*. So too in the Rámáyana *Ráma* occasionally appears in the form *Ráu*.

2. Not unfrequently, however, *a*+*a* becomes *e*: thus from *badara*, the jujube, we have *ber*; and from *kadala*, a plantain, *kela*. A similar substitution of *e* for *á* takes place in *semal*, the cotton-tree, for *sálmali*; in *sej*, a couch, for *saya*; and in *terah*, thirteen, for *trayodasa*.

3. Conversely *e*+*a* is sometimes made equivalent to *a*+*a*: thus *deva*, after elision of the *v*, becomes *dáu*.

4. *bh* becomes *h*: thus from *abhíra* comes *ahír*, and from *Tírabhukti*, the name of a country, Tirhút.

5. *ch* is elided : thus *súchi*, 'a needle,' becomes *súi*.

6. *dh* becomes *h*: thus from *badhira*, 'deaf,' we have *bahira*; from *madhuka*, 'the Bassia latifolia,' *mahua*; from *vadhu*, 'a female relation,' *bahu*; and, in the Rámáyana, for *krodhi*, 'angry,' *kohi*. So too the possessive affix *dhára* becomes *hára*.

7. *d* occasionally becomes *l*: thus from *bhadra*, 'good,' after elision of the conjunct *r*, we have *bhala*. This *l* again may be changed into *r*: thus from Vidarbha, the name of a country, comes Birár.

8. *k* is elided : thus *vardhaki*, 'a carpenter,' becomes *barhai*; *vrischika*, 'a scorpion,' *bichhua*; and *súkara*, 'a pig,' *súar*.

9. *k* may also become *h*: thus in the Rámáyana *alíha* stands for *alíka*, 'false.' So also *kh*: thus *mukha*, after insertion of the nasal, becomes *munh*.

10. *l* in a conjunct is elided : thus *valkala*, 'the bark of a tree,' becomes *bákal*. Occasionally also simple *l*; as in *okhla*, 'a mortar,' for *ulukhala*.

11. *m* and *v* are interchangeable: thus *dhívara*, 'a fisherman,' becomes *dhímar*; *gauna* stands for *gamana*, *Bhamani* for *Bhavání*, and *kunvar* for *kumára*. Similarly *jun*, or *jaun*, in the sense of 'time,' stands for *jám*, the Sanskrit *yáma*, the nasal being an insertion. So also in the Gítá Gobinda *vámana* is made to rhyme with *pávana*.

12. A nasal can be inserted anywhere, as in *gánw*, 'a village,' for *gráma*, and in *kaun*, 'who,' for *ko*.

13. *p* simple is elided: as in *kúa*, 'a well,' for *kúpa*; *bhúála*, 'a king,' for *bhúpálá*; *kait*, the tree Feronia elephantum, for *kapittha*; and *aur*, the conjunctive particle, for *apara*. So also when standing first in a conjunct; thus from *supta*, 'asleep,' comes *sota*. It may also be changed into *v*, as in *gwála*, for *gopálá*, and *kotwál* for *kotta-pála*.

14. *r* becomes *n*: thus *karavíra*, 'the oleander,' becomes *kanavíra*, *kanera*, *kanel*.

15. *r* in a conjunct is elided: thus *gráma*, 'a village,' becomes *gám*, or *gánw*; *karma*, 'an act,' *kám*; *Srávan*, the month so called, *Sávan*; *vártta*, 'business,' *bát*; and *vartman*, 'a road,' *bát*, where the charge of the dental into the cerebral *t* compensates for the loss of the final *man*.

16. *sh* is converted into *kh*, optionally, whenever it occurs. Similarly the Greek βροχη represents the Sanskrit *varsha*, and in the modern Cretan dialect becomes again *vroshé*.

17. Cerebral *t* occasionally becomes *r*: thus from *parkati*, 'the Ficus venosa,' we have *pákar*.

18. *t*, when simple, is elided: thus from *játi-phal*, 'a nut-meg,' comes *jai-phal*: and from *Sítalá*, the goddess of small-pox, *síyar*. Thus, too, in the Rámáyana, *Sítá* frequently appears as *Sia*, or *Síya*.

19. *v* when simple is elided: as in *upás*, 'a fast,' for *upavás*.

20. Simple *y* is elided: as in *mor*, 'a peacock,' for *mayúra*; *Prág* for *Prayág*; and *Ojha*, 'a particular caste,' for *Upádhyáya*.

21. The loss of one consonant in a conjunct receives compensation in the lengthening of the preceding vowel: thus we have *ním* for *nimba*; *náti*, 'a grandson,' for *naptri*; *áge*, 'before,' for *agre*; *ák*, the plant Asclepias gigantea, for *arká*; *ádhá*, 'half,' for *ardha*; and *ríta*, 'empty,' for *rikta*.

Any philological student who wishes to prosecute further inquiries in this interesting subject will find all the laws of euphonic mutation most exhaustively discussed and illustrated in Dr. Hœrnle's Comparative Grammar of the Gaudian Languages, a work that appeared simultaneously with the former edition of this Memoir. Both for breadth of research and accuracy of analysis it is a book beyond all praise and may justly be ranked—in its own particular sphere—with the famous Grammar of Bopp, which forms the basis of all modern comparative philology.

[Page 357.]

MAP OF THE DISTRICT.

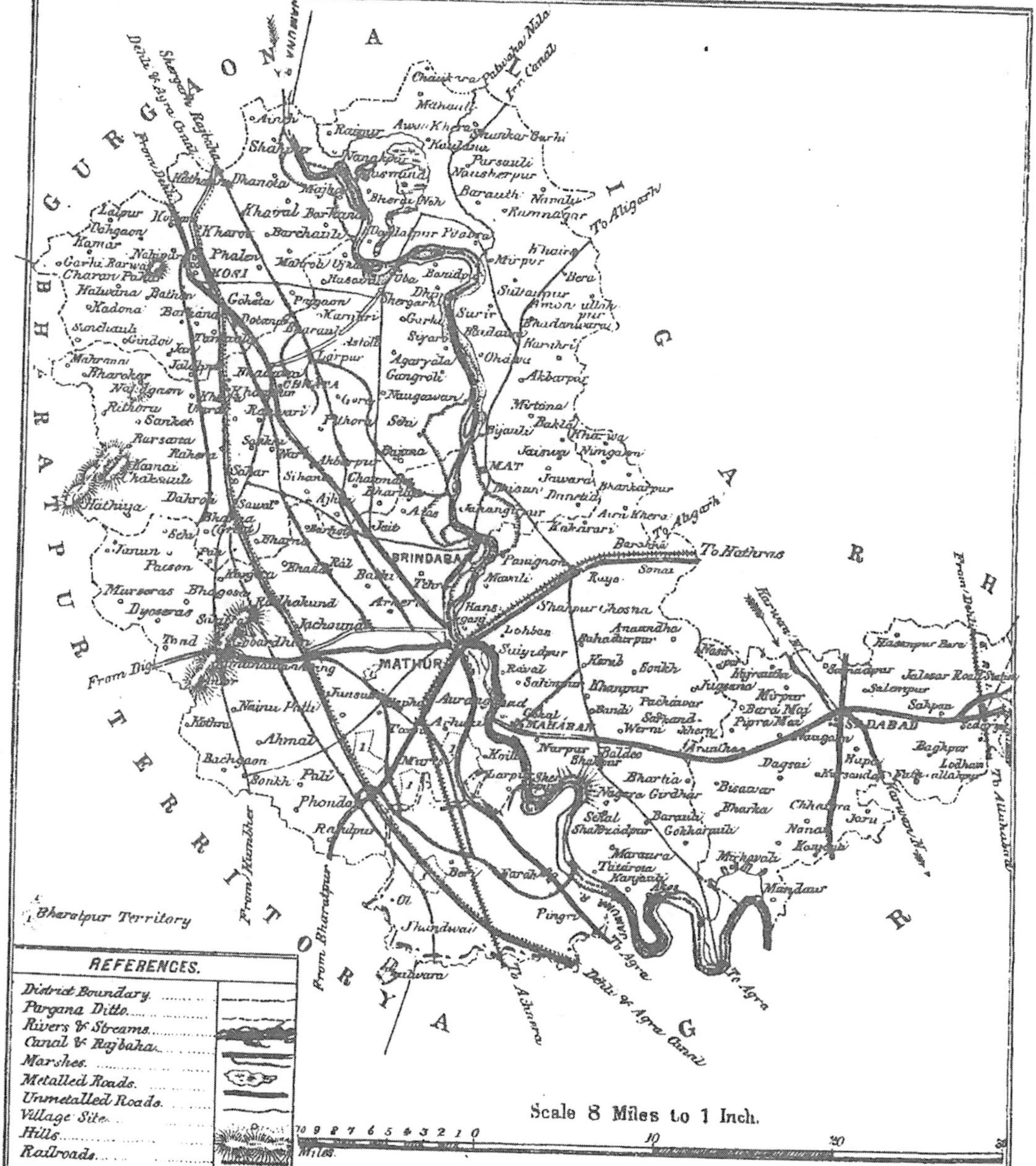

PRINTED AT THE N.-W. PROVINCES AND OUDH GOVERNMENT PRESS, ALLAHABAD.

CHAPTER XIII.

PARGANA TOPOGRAPHY.

I.—PARGANA KOSI.

THE pargana of Kosi is the most northern of the three on the western side of the Jamuná and borders on the district of Gurgáon. It is the smallest of the Mathurá six, having an area of only 154 square miles. It yields an annual revenue of Rs. 1,52,013. Its villages, sixty-one in number, with six exceptions, are all *bhaiyáchari*, divided into infinitesimal shares among the whole of the community; so that, barring a few shopkeepers and menial servants, every resident is to some extent a proprietor. In the ordinary course of events, all would be, not only members of the same caste, but also descendants of one man, the founder of the settlement; but in many instances, in spite of the right of pre-emption, several of the subordinate shares have been bought up by outsiders. A fresh assessment is made privately every year; and, according to the amount of land actually under cultivation, each tenant proprietor pays his quota of the revenue at so much per bígha, and enjoys the remaining profits as his private income. The Government demand is realized through the head-men or *lumberdars*, of whom there are generally several in each village. As a natural result of this minute sub-division of estates, there is not a single landed proprietor in the whole pargana of any social distinction. The two wealthiest inhabitants are both traders in the town of Kosi—Chunni Lál, son of Mohan Lál, and Kusháli Rám, son of Lál Jí Mall—with incomes of Rs. 5,000 and Rs. 4,943 respectively. The former has no land at all, the other owns one small village.

Of the six zamindári villages, only two were so previous to the last settlement; *viz.*, Pákhar-pur, the property of Kusháli Rám above mentioned, and Jáu, a purchase of the Lálá Bábú. The other four have acquired their exceptional character only within the last few years; Garhi having been bought from the Játs by Sah Kundan Lál, of Lakhnau; Majhoi and Rám-pur having been conferred, after the mutiny, on Rájá Gobind Singh, of Háthras, and Chauki on Shiv Sahay Mall, of Delhi, at the same time. One mahál of Chaundras has also quite recently been constituted into a zamindári; and two or three other villages, now in the hands of money-lending mortgagees, will probably become so before long.

The Muhammadans number only 8,093 out of a total population of 65,293, and, with the exception of a few scattered families, are almost confined to seven places, *viz.*, Barha, Bisambhara, Dotána, Jalál-pur, Kosi, Mahroli, and Sháhpur.

At three of these, *viz.*, Bisambhara, Dotána, and Jalál-pur, they even slightly out number the Hindús.

The predominant Hindú castes are Játs, Jádons and other Gaurua, *i.e.*, *spurious*, Thákur tribes. There are also a considerable number of Gújars, though these latter have now in every place ceased to be proprietors. They muster stronger in the adjoining pargana of Chhátá, and were ringleaders of disaffection during the mutiny. In consequence, eight of their villages—Majhoi and Rám-pur in Kosi, Basái, Husaini, Jatwári, Karahri, Khursi and Ujháni in Chhátá—were confiscated and conferred on Rájá Gobind Sinh. They had previously disposed of their four other Chhátá villages, Chamar-garhi, Dhímri, Gulál-pur and Pír-pur, to the Lálá Bábú. The course of years has not reconciled the ejected community to their changed circumstances, and so recently as the 29th of September, 1872, the widowed Rání's agent, Jay Rám Sinh, was, in result of a general conspiracy, barbarously murdered at night while sleeping in the Jatwári *chaupál*. Six of the murderers were apprehended, and, after conviction of the crime, were sentenced to death, but one escaped from the jail before the sentence was executed.

In the year 1857, the period, during which there was no recognition of government whatever, extended from the 12th of July to the 5th of December. With the exception of the Gújars, who assembled at Sher-garh and distinctly declared themselves independent, there was little or no ill-feeling towards the British Crown expressed by any class of the population ; though many persons took advantage of the favourable opportunity for paying off old scores against ill neighbours, and especially for avenging themselves on their natural enemies, the *patwáris*, or village accountants, and *Bohrás*, or money-lenders. Thus there was a pitched battle between Hathána and the adjoining village of Bánswa in Gurgáon ; the patwáris at Barha and Bisambhara had all their papers destroyed ; at Pákharpur, Ganga Dán, bohra, was plundered by the zamindárs of Kádona and Sirthala ; at Kotban, Dhan-ráj, bohra, was only set at liberty on payment of a ransom ; and at Little Bathan, Lekhráj, bohra, after seeing all his papers seized and burnt, was himself put to death. The Játs of Kámar, after plundering Moti Rám, bohra, proceeded to turn the police out of the place, and raised a flame which spread across the border into the adjoining district ; but they afterwards atoned for this indiscretion by the assistance which they gave to the Deputy Collector, Imdád Ali, in suppressing the Gújars.

The trees most commonly found growing wild in the pargana are the *ním* and the *pílú*, while every piece of waste ground (and there are several such tracts of large extent,) is dotted with clumps of *karíl*. The soil is not suited to the growth of the mango, and there are scarcely any considerable orchards either of that or indeed of any other fruit tree; the one at Sháh-pur being the only notable exception. Of the total area of 97,301 acres, there are 71,490 of arable land; the crops most extensively grown being *joár*, *chana*, and barley. The wheat sold at the Kosi market comes chiefly from across the Jamuná. The number of wells has been much increased in late years and is now put at 1,379, of which 846 are of masonry construction. The Jamuná, which forms the eastern boundary of the pargana, is crossed by ferries at Sháh-pur, Khairál, and Majhoi. The new Agra Canal passes through the villages of Hathána, Kharot, Hasanpur Nagara, Kosi, Azíz-pur, Tumaula, and Dham Sinha, a length of ten miles, and is bridged at Kharot, Kosi, Aziz-pur, and Tumaula. The high road to Delhi traverses the centre of the pargana, passing through the town of Kosi and the villages of Kotban, Aziz-pur, and Dotána; and from the town of Kosi there is a first-class unmetalled road to Sher-garh, a distance of eleven miles. The *Halkabandi*, or Primary, schools are twelve in number, being one for every five villages, an unusually favourable average: the attendance, however, is scarcely so good as in some other parts of the district; as it is difficult to convince a purely agricultural population that tending cattle is not always the most profitable occupation in which boys can be employed.

In addition to the capital, there are only four places which merit special notice, *viz.*, Bathan, Dotána, Kámar, and Sháh-pur.

KOSI is a flourishing municipality and busy market town, twenty-six miles from the city of Mathurá, most advantageously situated in the very centre of the pargana to which it gives a name and on the high road to Delhi. As this road was only constructed as a relief work in the famine of 1860, it avoids all the most densely inhabited quarters, and the through traveller sees little from it but mud walls and the backs of houses. The Agra Canal runs nearly parallel to it still further back, with one bridge on the road leading to Majhoi and Sher-garh, and another at Azíz-pur, a mile out of the town on the road to Mathurá.

The zamindárs are Játs, Shaikhs, and Brahmans; but the population, which amounts to 11,231, consists chiefly of baniyas and Muhammadan *kasábs*, or butchers, who are attracted to the place by its large trade in cotton and cattle. It is estimated that about 75,000 *mans* of cotton are collected in the course of the year and sent on down to Calcutta.*

* The outturn of cotton for the whole district was estimated in the year 1872-73 at 225,858 *mans*; the exportation therefore must be very considerable.

The *nakhkhás*, or cattle market, is of large extent and supplied with every convenience—a fine masonry well, long ranges of feeding troughs, &c. On every beast sold the zamindárs levy a toll of two anas, and the Chaudharis as much ; in consideration for which payment they are bound to maintain two chaukidárs for watch and ward, and also to keep the place clean and in repair. Prices, of course, vary considerably, but the following may be taken as the average rates :—Well-bullocks from Rs. 30 to Rs. 60 each ; cart-bullocks from Rs. 50 to 75 ; a cow from Rs. 15 to 50 ; a calf from Rs. 10 to 30 ; a buffalo from Rs. 25 to 50 ; and a male buffalo calf from Rs. 2 to 10. There are two market days every week, on Tuesday and Wednesday ; and in 1868-69, when a tax of one and a quarter ana was levied on every beast sold, it yielded as much as Rs. 2,188-13-0 ; the zamindars' receipts at two anas a head and the Chaudharis' at the same rate amounted to Rs. 3,502-2-0 each. Taking Rs. 25 as an average price per head, which would be rather below than above the mark, the amount of money changing hands in the course of the year was Rs. 7,00,425. The exports of grain are put at 200,000 *mans* and there are in the town some 100 *khattas*, or cellars, ordinarily well filled with reserve stores for the consumption, not only of the residents, but also of the numerous travellers passing up and down the great thoroughfare on which the town stands, and who naturally take in at Kosi several days' supplies, both for themselves and their cattle. There is also very considerable business done in country cloth, as all the villages in the neighbourhood are purely agricultural, and supply most of their wants from the one central mart.

As the town lies in a hollow, it is liable to be flooded after a few days' continuance of heavy rain by a torrent which pours in upon it from Hodal. This was the case in 1873, when much damage was done to house property ; and the subsequent drying up of the waters—which was a tedious process, there being no outlet for their escape—was attended with very general and serious sickness. The only remedy lies in developing the natural line of drainage, and the necessity of some such operation has forced itself upon the notice of the canal department ; but no definite steps have yet been taken in the matter.

The income of the municipality is about Rs. 12,000 per annum ; but this sum is a very inadequate test of the actual trade done, since there is no duty either on cotton or on cattle, excepting beasts intended for slaughter.

The area of the parish is 2,277 acres, on which the Government demand used to be Rs. 6,700 ; but the assessment was proved to be too severe by the distress it caused to the zamindars, and it was reduced to Rs. 4,790.

The principal annual *melas*, or fairs, are—1st, the Dasahara, only started between forty and fifty years ago by Lalu Singh, khattri, and Darbári Singh, baniya; 2nd, the Muharram; and 3rdly, the Phul-dol, on *Chait badi* 2, which is a general gathering for all the Játs of the Denda pál from Dah-gánw Kot-ban, Nabi-pur, Umraura, and Nagara Hasan-pur.

In the centre of the town stands a large Saráe, covering nine and-a-half bighas of land, with high embattled walls, corner kiosques, and two arched gateways, all of stone, ascribed to Khwájá I'tibár Khán, governor of Delhi, in the reign of the Emperor Akbar. On the inside there are ranges of vaulted apartments all round, and the principal bazár lies between the two gateways. The building has been partially repaired by the municipality at a cost of Rs. 4,000, and if the inner area could be better laid out, it might form a remunerative property. At present it yields only an income of between Rs. 300 and 400 a year; even that being a considerable increase on what used to be realised. A large masonry tank, of nearly equal area with the saráe, dates from the same time, and is called the Ratnákar Kund, or more commonly the 'pakka taláo.' Unfortunately it is always dry except during the rains. The municipality were desirous of having it repaired, but it was found that the cost would amount to Rs. 3,500, a larger sum than the funds could afford. The enclosing walls are twenty feet high and the exact measurement is 620 by 400 feet. Three other tanks bear the names of Mayá-kund, Bisákha-kund, and Gomati-kund, in allusion to places so styled at the holy city of Dwáraká, or Kusasthali—a circumstance which has given rise to, or at least confirms, the popular belief that Kosi is only a contraction of Kusasthali. The Gomati-kund, near which the fair of the Phul-dol is held, *Chait badi* 2, is accounted the most sacred and is certainly the prettiest spot in the town. The pond is of considerable size, but of very irregular shape and has a large island in the middle. There are two or three masonry ghâts, constructed by wealthy traders of the town, and on all sides of it there are a number of small shrines and temples overshadowed by fine kadamb, pípal, and bar trees, full of monkeys and peacocks; while the tank itself is the favourite haunt of aquatic birds of different kinds. There are a few handsome and substantial private houses in the quarter of the town called Baladeva Ganj; but as a rule the shops and other buildings have a very mean appearance; and though there are a number of Hindú temples and four mosques, they, too, are all quite modern and few have any architectural pretensions.

A little beyond the town on the Delhi side close to the new canal and not far from the Idgáh is a *tirath* called Mábhai, with a masonry tank and temple, which is looked after by a Pandit of the Rádhá Ballabh sect, called Bál-mukund. When I went to see him, he would only talk in Sanskrit and derived the name of the place from *Má bhaishih*, 'fear not,' the exclamation of Krishna to the herdsmen when the forest was set on fire. But there was an old fort of the same name in the Bulandshahr district near the town of Khurja, where no such legendary explanation would be applicable. The word is a peculiar one, and I am unable to offer any suggestion regarding it.

The Saráugis, or Jainis, have three temples at Kosi, dedicated respectively to Padma-Prabhu, the sixth of the Jinas or Tirthánkaras; Nem-náth, or Arishtanemi, the twenty-second; and Mahávíra, or Varddhamána the twenty-fourth and last of the series,* who is supposed to have died about the year 500 B. C. A festival is held at the temple of Nem-náth, which is the smallest and most modern of the three, on the day after the full moon of Bhádon, when water is brought for the ablution of the idol from a well in a garden at some little distance. Any processional display, or beating of drums, or uttering of a party cry is so certain to result in a riot that extra police are always told off to prevent anything of the kind, and to confine every religious demonstration strictly within the walls of the temple. The antipathy to the rival faith on the part of the Vaishnava Hindus is so strong that it is ordinarily expressed by saying that it would be better, on meeting a mad elephant in a narrow street, to stand still and be trampled to death than to escape by crossing the threshold of a Jaini temple.

As regards the essential matters of conservancy, water supply and road communication, the condition of the town is satisfactory and has been much improved by municipal action. Most of the streets are either metalled or paved, and lighted by lamps at night. A neat dispensary has been opened and is well attended, though as yet it has no accommodation for indoor patients. A small bungalow has been built for the meetings of the committee and for occasional use as a rest-house; the ground between it and the dispensary being laid out as a garden for the supply of fruit and vegetables and as a decorative feature at the entrance of the town. A new market was also designed with lines of substantial brick-built and stone-fronted shops of uniform character, arranged on three sides of a square, which was secured end levelled for the purpose. In order to further the speedy completion of a work which it was thought would so much improve both the appearance of the town and also the finances

* Each Tirthánkara has his own distinctive sign: Mahávíra, a lion; Padma-Prabhu, a lotus; Nem-náth a conch; Chandra-Prabhu, a moon, &c.; and it is only by these marks that they can be distinguished from one another, as all are sculptured in the same attitude.

of the municipality, a loan of Rs. 12,000 was contracted, with the sanction of Government, to be repaid in the course of four years by half-yearly instalments, beginning from October, 1874. Before application was made for the loan, Rs. 6,000 had been already expended, and with a further allotment, to about the same extent, from ordinary municipal income, the market might have been completed by the end of 1878. But unexpected changes in the schedule of taxation reduced the octroi receipts so considerably that the annual income was nearly all exhausted by the charges for establishment, repairs, and the repayment of the loan. Thus the work dragged slowly on; and since I have left the district has come, I believe, to a dead stand-still. At its commencement an illustration was afforded of the extraordinary mania with which the local baniyas are possessed for hoarding large quantities of grain. This they do in the hope that a year of famine will come when they will be able to realise a rapid fortune by selling their stores at enormously high rates. As the grain is simply thrown into a pit sunk in the ground, and no precautions taken to preserve it from the damp, in a few years the greater part of it becomes quite unfit for human consumption, and its sale would only increase the general distress by spreading disease. This, however, is a consideration which has no influence on the mind of a baniya: he has a fixed method of squaring accounts with Providence, and holds that the foundation of a sumptuous temple, at the close of his life, is an ample atonement for all sins of fraud and peculation, and the only one which Divine justice is entitled to demand from him. Such a pit came to light after the heavy rains of 1873. Five of the shops then in course of construction began to settle and give way to such an extent that they had to be taken down. On digging a few feet below the foundations to ascertain, if possible, the cause of the accident, a subterranean granary was revealed with an invoice stating that it had been filled in *Sambat* 1898 (1841 A.D.), and contained in all 1,303 *mans* of different kinds of grain. The greater part of this was so much damaged that it had to be destroyed, and the sale of the remainder realised only Rs. 324, which did not cover the cost incurred in digging it out, filling up the pit, and rebuilding the shops.

The tahsíli school was built by the Public Works Department at a cost of Rs. 6,000. The police, maintained by the municipality on an annual grant of Rs. 1,800, are located in a corner of the saráe, with an entrance made through the old wall directly on to the high road, opposite the paráo. The latter is the property of private individuals, who levy a toll on every animal or vehicle driven into its enclosure,—the rates being fixed by the municipality—and pay Rs. 10 a month for the monopoly.

On the 31st of May, 1857, the rebels on their march to Delhi stopped at Kosi and, after burning down the Customs bungalow and ransacking the police station, proceeded to plunder the tahsíli, but Rs. 150 was all that they found in the treasury there. The records were scattered to the four winds, but were to a great extent subsequently recovered. The Musalmáns of Dotána, the Játs of Azíz-pur, and the Gújars of Majhoi and Rám-pur lent a willing hand to any deed of mischief; but the townspeople and the inhabitants of the adjoining villages of Hasan-pur Nagara, Umraura, Dah-gánw and Nabi-pur, gave what assistance they could in maintaining order, and as an acknowledgment of their good behaviour one year's jama was remitted and a grant of Rs. 50 made to each lumberdár. The position of the town between Agra and Delhi and the strength of its fortified saráe have rendered it a place of some importance at other periods of local disturbance. Thus, in 1774, the Ját Raja, Ranjit Sinh, on his retreat to Barsána, occupied it for some time and again, in 1282, after the death of Najaf Khan, his nephew, Mirza Shafi , fled to it as a temporary refuge from before his rival Afrazyáb Khan.

BATHAN, GREAT AND LITTLE, are two populous and extensive Jat villages (the former with a Halkabandi school) in the immediate neighbourhood of the town of Kosi. According to popular belief, the name is derived from the circumstance that Balaráma here sat down '(*baithen*) to wait for his brother Krishna'; but like so many of the older local names, which are now fancifully connected with some mythological incident, the word is really descriptive simply of the natural features of the spot,' *bathan* being still employed in some parts of India to denote a pasture-ground for cattle. In the same way Brinda-ban, 'the tulsi grove,' is now referred to a goddess Vrindá; Loh-ban, 'the lodhri grove,' to a demon Loha-jangha; and Kotban, ' the limit or last of the groves,' to a demon Kota, whose head was tossed to Sirthala, and his hands to Hathána. On the outskirts of Great Bathan is an extensive sheet of water with a masonry ghát built by Rúp Rám, the Katára of Barsána, which, by its name Balbhadra-Kund, has either occasioned, or at least serves to perpetuate the belief that Balaráma was the eponymous hero of the place. Here, on *Choit badi* 3, is held the Holanga Fair, when some 15,000 to 16,000 people assemble and a sham fight takes place between the women of Bathan, who are armed with clubs, and the men from the neighbouring village of Jáv, who defend themselves with branches of the acacia. At a distance of two miles, between two smaller groves, each called Pádar Ganga, the one in Bathan, the other in Jáv, is Kokila-ban, the most celebrated in Hindi poetry of all the woods of Braj: so much so, indeed, that the word is often used as a synonyme for 'the garden of Eden.' It comprises a wide and densely-wooded area,* the trees becoming thicker and thicker towards the centre, where a pretty natural lake spreads cool and clear, and reflects in its deep still waters the over-hanging branches of a magnificent banyan tree. It is connected with a masonry tank of very eccentric configuration, also the work of Rúp Rám ; on the margin of which are several shrines and pavilions for the accommodation of pilgrims, who assemble here to the number of some 10,000, *Bhadon sudi* 10, when the Rás Lílá is celebrated. There is also a walled garden, planted by a Seth of Mirzapur, who employed as his agent Ghan-pat Rám, one of the Kosi traders. It has a variety of shrubs and fruit trees ; but, like most native gardens, is rapidly becoming a tangled and impenetrable jungle. Adjoining it is a *bárah dari*, or pavilion, constructed in 1870, by Nem Ji, another Kosi baniya, out of money left for the purpose by his brother Bansidhar. A fair is held in the grove every Saturday and a larger one on every full moon, when the principal diversion consists in seeing the immense swarms of monkeys fight for the grain that is scrambled among them. The Bairági belongs to the Nimbárak Sampradáya.

Between Kokila-ban and the village is another holy place, called Kabír-ban besides the Pádar-Gangá. The origin of the word Pádar is obscure: it is interpreted by *hara*, 'green,' and therefore may be a corruption of the Sanskrit *pádapa*, 'a tree.'†

At little Bathan, a curious ridge of rock, called Charan Pahár, crops up above the ground, the stone being of precisely the same character as at Barsána and Nand-gánw. It was once proposed to utilize some of it for engineering purposes, but such strenuous objections were raised that the design was never carried into execution. The name of the present hermit is Rádhiká Dás. This, it is said, was one of the places where Krishna most delighted to stop and play his flute, and many of the stones are still supposed to bear the impress of his 'feet,' *charan*. The hill is of very insignificant dimensions, having an average height of only some twenty or thirty feet, and a total length of at most a quarter of a mile. On the rock are several specimens of the tree called Indrajau (*Wrightia tinctoria*), which I have not seen elsewhere. In the cold weather it is almost entirely bare of leaves, but bears bunches of very long slender dark-green

---

* It is 212 bighas in extent; 54 bíghas being held rent-free by the Mahant of the Hermitage, who also has all the pasturage and fallen timber of the whole area, with a further endowment of 22 bighas of arable land in Jáv.

† It is mentioned by name in the Vraja-bhakti-vilása as पाडरवन

pods, each pair cohering lightly at the tip. There is also an abundance of a scraggy shrub called Ganger, a species of Grewia (?) and a creeper with white sweet-scented flowers which may be the zedoary. Its native name is *nirbisi.* In the small belt of jungle, which environs the hill, may also be found almost every variety of the curious inedible fruits for which Braj is noted, *viz.*, the karíl, pílu, pasendu, hingot, barna, and anján-rukh. A little beyond the neighbouring town of Kámar, just across the Gurgáon border, is a very similar ridge called the Bichor hill, from a large village of that name.

DOTÁNA, population 1,185, is a Muhammadan village on the high road between Kosi and Chhátá with a number of old buildings which are sure to attract the traveller's attention. There are seven large tombs dating from the time of Sháhjáhán and Aurangzeb if not earlier (there are no inscriptions) three mosques of the same period, erected respectively by Ináyat-ullah Khán, Kázi Haidar Khán and Ruh-ullah Khán ; a modern mosque founded by Abd-ul Barkat, and four small gardens.

A masonry tank, which covers an area of 12 bíghas and is in good repair, though dry for the greater part of the year, is said to have been constructed by the village founder Kabír-ud-din Auliya. One of his most illustrious descendants was Sádullah Khán, from whom the town of Sádabad derives its name, the minister of Sháhjahán, in whose reign Dotána is said to have been a large town. Shernagar originally belonged to the same family, and three members of it are commemorated by the three Pattis, called respectively Lál, Ruh-ullah and Malak. A distributary of the canal runs within a few yards of the tank, which might easily be filled from it. Near it is the tomb of Kudús and Anwar, two of the village patriarchs.

Many of the large brick houses in the village are in a most ruinous condition, and the zamindárs are now in poor circumstances. In the mutiny they joined the rebels in plundering the Kosi Tahsíli, and part of their estate was confiscated and bestowed on Kunvar Shám Prasád, a Kashmíri, formerly Tahsíldar of Mahá-ban, who has transferred it to his sister, Mahárání. The name Dotána is thought to be derived from Dánton, a tooth-brush, and if so, is rather suggestive of Buddhist legends. The place is mentioned by Bishop Heber in his Journal, who writes : " January 7th, 1825.—Traversed a wild but more woody country to Dotána. Here I saw the first instance of a custom which I am told I shall see a good deal of in my southern journey, a number of women, about a dozen, who came with pitchers on their heads, dancing and singing to meet me. There is, if I recollect right, an account of this sort of dance in Kehama. They all professed to be Gopis, or milk-maids, and are in fact, as the thánadár assured me, the wives and daughters of the Gwálá caste. Their voices and style of singing were by no means unpleasant; they had all the appearance of extreme poverty, and I thought a rupee well bestowed upon them, for which they were very thankful." There can be no doubt also that this is the place to which John de Laet, in 1631, alludes in his India Vera, though he calls it Akbar-pur, the name of the next village. "This was formerly a considerable town; now it is only visited by pilgrims who come on account of many holy Muhammadans buried here." Annual fairs are still held in honor of three of these holy men, who are styled Hasan Shahíd, Sháh Nizám-ud-dín, and Pír Shakar-ganj, *alias* Bábá Faríd. The shrines, however, are merely commemorative and not actual tombs; for Hasan, 'the Martyr,' is probably Ali's son, the brother of Hussain; Nizám-ud-dín Aulia is buried at Delhi; and the famous Faríd-ud-dín Ganj-i-Shakkar lies at Pák Patan near the Satlaj.

Kámar, population 3,771, six miles from Kosi on the Gurgáon border, is still a populous Ját town with a considerable trade in cotton; but in the early part of last century was a place of much greater wealth and importance, when a daughter of one of the principal families was taken in marriage by Thákur Badan Sinh of Sahár, the father of Súraj Mall, the first of the Bharat-pur Rájás. On the outskirts of the town is a large walled garden with some monuments to his mother's relations, and immediately outside it a spacious masonry tank filled with water brought by aqueducts from the surrounding *rakhya*. This is more than a thousand acres in extent, and according to village computation is three kos long, including the village, which occupies its centre. For the most part the trees are exclusively the *pílu*, or *salvadora oleoides*, very old, with hollow trunks and strangely gnarled and distorted branches. The fruit, which ripens in Jeth, is sweet and largely eaten by the poor, but as a rule not sold, though some is occasionally dried and exported. A Bairági of the Nimbárak Sampradáya, by name Mangal Dás, has a hermitage with a small temple of Bihári Ji, in the midst of some fine kadamb trees, which form a conspicuous group at one end of the *rakhya*. He has a great reputation for sanctity and the offerings made during the last 30 years have enabled him to have a fine masonry tank constructed, of great depth, at an outlay of Rs. 2,500; from its appearance it might be taken to have cost even more. It is filled to the brim in the rains, but soon becomes dry again; a defect which he hopes to obviate by paving it at the bottom. It is about half a mile from the village and is a pretty spot. Had I remained in the district, I should have got the tank finished; arrangements were being made when the order came for my transfer. At a rather greater distance in the opposite direction is a lake with unfinished stone gháts, the work of Rájá Súraj Mall; this is called Durvásas-kund, after the irascible saint of that name; but there is no genuine tradition to connect him with the spot; though it is sometimes said that the town derives its name from a 'blanket' (*kamal*) with which Krishna persuaded him to cover his nakedness. Among the trees on the margin of the lake are some specimens of the *Khandár* or Salvadora Punica. This is less common than the *oleoides* species, and is a prettier tree and blossoms earlier. Its fruit, however, is bitter and uneatable. In the town are several large brick mansions built by Chaudharis Jasavant Sinh and Sitá Rám, the Rájá's connections, and one of them has a fine gateway in three stories, which forms a conspicuous land mark: but all are now in ruins. At the back of the artificial hill on which they stand, and excavated to supply the earth for its construction, is a third tank of still greater extent than the other two, but of irregular outline, and with only an occasional flight of stone steps here and there on its margin.

A temple of Súraj Mall's foundation, dedicated to Madan Mohan, is specially affected by all the Játs of the Bahin-wár pál,* who are accounted its *chelas*, or sons, and assemble here to the number of some 4,000, on *Chait badi* 2 and the following day, to celebrate the *mela* of the Phúl-dol. The school, a primary one, is not a very prosperous institution. The Chaukidári Act has been extended to the town; but it yields a monthly income of only Rs. 60, which, after payment of the establishment, leaves an utterly insignificant balance for local improvements. The only work of the kind which has been carried out is the metalling of the principal bazár.

SHÁH-PUR, under the Játs the head of a pargana, is a large but somewhat decayed village on the bank of the Jamuná, some ten miles to the north-east of Kosi. It is one of the very few places in this part of the country where the population is almost equally divided between the two great religions of India; there being, according to the census of 1881, as many as 1,137 Muhammadans to 1,084 Hindus. The total area is 3,577 acres, of which 2,263 are under the plough and 1,314 are untilled. Of the arable land 612 acres are watered by wells, which number in all 63 and are many of masonry construction. The Government demand is Rs. 3,907. The village was founded

* *Pál* is the peculiar name for any sub-division of Játs. In the Kosi Pargana, the principal Ját Páls in addition to the Bahin-wár, who own Kámar and 11 other villages, are the Denda, Lokana, and Ghatona. Similarly every sub-division of Mewátis is called a *chhat*.

towards the middle of the sixteenth century, in the reign either of Sher Sháh or Salim Sháh by an officer of the Court known as Mir Ji, of Biluch extraction, who called it Sháhpur in honour of his royal master. The tomb of the founder still exists not far from the river bank on the road to Chaundras. It is a square building of red sandstone, surmounted by a dome and divided on each side into three bays by pillars and bracket arches of purely Hindu design. By cutting off the corners of the square and inserting at each angle an additional pillar the tomb on the inside assumes the form of a dodecagon. On the other side of the village, by the road to Bukharári, is another tomb, in memory of Lashkar Khán, a grandson of the village founder: it is solidly constructed of brick and mortar, but quite plain and of ordinary design. Nearly opposite is the hamlet of Chauki with the remains of a fort erected by Nawáb Ashraf Khán and Arif Khán, upon whom Sháh-pur with other villages, yielding an annual revenue of Rs. 28,000, were conferred as a *jágir* for life by Lord Lake. There is a double circuit of mud walls with bastions and two gateways of masonry defended by outworks, and in the inner court a set of brick buildings now fallen into ruin. This was the ordinary residence of the Nawáb, and it was during his lifetime that Sháh-pur enjoyed a brief spell of prosperity as a populous and important town. It would seem that the fort was not entirely the work of Ashraf Khán, but had been originally constructed some years earlier by Agha Haidar, a local governor under the Mahrattas, who also planted the adjoining grove of trees.

The village has continued to the present day in the possession of Mír Jí's descendants, to one of whom, Fázil Muhammad, the great grandfather of Natha Khán, now lumberdár, we are indebted for the large bágh, which makes Sháhpur the most agreeable camping place in the whole of the Kosi pargana. It covers some sixty or seventy bíghas, and, besides containing a number of fine forest trees, mango, *jáman, mahúa* and *labera*, has separate orchards of limes and *ber* trees; while the borders are fenced with the prickly *nág-phani* interspersed with *níms* and *babúls*, having their branches overspread with tangled masses of the *amar-bel* with its long clusters of pale and faint-scented blossoms. The yearly contracts for the different kinds of fruit yield close upon Rs. 1,000. Though a mile or more from the ordinary bed of the river, it is occasionally, as for example in the year 1871, flooded to the depth of some two or three feet by the rising of the stream. The more extensive the inundation, the greater the public benefit; for all the fields reached by it produce excellent rabi crops without any necessity for artificial irrigation till, at all events, late in the season. In the village are three mosques, but all small; as the Muhammadan population,

93

though considerable, consists, to a great extent, merely of *kasáb*s; there is also a temple erected by the Mahrattas. The chief local festivals are the Dasahara for Hindús and the Muharram for Muhammadans, both of which attract a large number of visitors from the neighbourhood. There is a weekly market on Monday and a small manufacture of earthen *hándis*. The halkabandi school, which, for some years, maintained only a struggling existence, has been better attended of late, since the completion of the new building.

II.—PARGANA CHHATA.

The pargana of Chhátá has a population of 84,598 and an area of 256 square miles. It lies immediately to the south of Kosi, with the same boundaries as it to the west and east, *viz.*, the State of Bharat-pur and the river Jamuná; and, further, resembles its northern neighbour in most of its social and physical characteristics. Being the very centre of Braj, it includes within its limits many of the groves held sacred by the votaries of Krishna; but, with the exception of these bits of wild woodland, it is but indifferently stocked with timber, and the orchards of fruit trees are small and few in number. The principal crops are *joár* and *chaná*, there being 63,000 acres under the former, and 29,000 grown with *chaná* out of a total area of 160,433. A large amount of cotton is also raised, the ordinary outturn being about 20,000 *mans*. But the crop varies greatly according to the season; and in 1873 did not exceed 1,500 *mans*, in consequence of the very heavy and continuous rains at the beginning of the monsoon, which prevented the seed from being sown till it was too late for the pod to ripen. The coarse sandstone, which can be obtained in any quantity from the hills of Nand-gánw and Barsána, is not now used to any extent for building purposes, but it is the material out of which the imperial saráes at Chhátá and Kosi were constructed, and is there shown to be both durable and architecturally effective. The western side of the pargana is liable to inundation in exceptionally rainy seasons from the overflowing of a large *jhíl* near Káma in Bharat-pur territory; its waters being augmented in their subsequent course by junction with the natural line of drainage extending down from Hodal. In 1861, and again in 1873, the flood passed through Unchágánw, Barsána, Chaksauli, and Háthiya, and extended as far even as Gobardhan; but no great damage was caused, the deposit left on the surface of the land being beneficial rather than otherwise.

The first assessment, made in 1809, was for Rs. 1,02,906. This was gradually increased to Rs. 1,77,876, and was further enhanced by the last settlement. Much land, formerly lying waste for want of water, was brought under cultivation on the opening of the Agra Canal. This has a total length of 11 miles in the pargana, from Bhadával to Little Bharna, with bridges at each of those places and also at Rahera and Sahár.

Till 1838 Sher-garh and Sahár were two separate parganas, subordinate to the Aríng tahsíli: but in that year Sahár was constituted the headquarters of a tahsíldár, and so remained till the mutiny, when a transfer was made to

Chhátá. The latter place has the advantage of being on the highroad, and is tolerably equi-distant from east and west, the only points necessary to be considered, on account of the extreme narrowness of the pargana from north to south. Thus, its close proximity to the town of Kosi—only seven miles off—is rather an apparent than a real objection to the maintenance of Chhátá as an administrative centre.

The predominant classes in the population are Játs, Jádons, and Gaurua Thákurs of the Báchhal sub-division; while several villages are occupied almost exclusively by the exceptional tribe of Ahivásis (see page 10) who are chiefly engaged in the salt trade. A large proportion of the land—though not quite to so great an extent as in Kosi—is still owned by the original Bhaiyáchári communities; and hence agrarian outrage on a serious scale is limited to the comparatively small area where, unfortunately, alienation has taken place, more by improvident private sales, or well-deserved confiscation on account of the gravest political offences, than from any defect in the constitution or administration of the law. The two largest estates thus acquired during the present century are enjoyed by non-residents, *viz.*, the heirs of the Lálá Bábu (see page 258), who are natives of Calcutta, and the Ráni Sáhib Kunvar, the widow of Raja Gobind Singh, who took his title from the town of Háthras, the old seat of the family, though she now lives with the young Rájá at Brinda-ban. Of resident landlords, the three largest all belong to the Dhúsar caste, and are as follows: First, Kanhaiya Lál, Sukhvási Lál, Bhajan Lál, and Bihári Lál, sons of Rám Bakhsh of Sahár, where they have property, as also at Bharáuli and three other villages, yielding an annual profit of Rs. 3,536. Second, Munshi Nathu Lál, who, for a time, was in Government service as tahsildár—with his son, Sardar Sinh, also of Sahár, who have an assessable estate of Rs. 3,874, derived from Astoli, Tatár-pur, and shares in nine other villages; Nathu Lál's father, Giridhar Lál, was sometime Munsif of Jalesar, and was descended from one Harsukh Ráe, who received from Rájá Súraj Mall the grant of Tatár-pur, with the title of Munshi, by which all the members of the family are still distinguished. Third in the list is Lálá Syám Sundar Dás, son of Shiu Saháy Mall, a man of far greater wealth—his annual profits being estimited at a lakh of rupees. He is the head of a firm which has branch houses at Kánh-pur, Agra, and Amritsar, and other places, and owns the whole of the large village of Naugáma and half of Tároli. For many years he was on the worst possible terms with his tenants; but the dispute between them has at last been amicably arranged, and during the recent famine the eldest son, Badri Prasád, came forward as one of the most liberal landlords in the district.

The two places of most interest in the pargana, Barsána and Nand-gánw, have already been fully described; there remain Chaumuhá, Chhátá, Sahár, Sehi, and Shergarh, which may each claim a few words of special mention.

CHAUMUHÁ, population 2,275, on the high road to Delhi, 12 miles from the Mathurá station, was included in the home pargana till the year 1816. It has the remains of a large brick-built saráe, covering upwards of four bíghas of land, said to have been constructed in the reign of the Emperor Sher Sháh. It now brings in a rental of only some Rs. 20 a year, being in a very ruinous state. This fact, combined with the perfect preservation of the parallel buildings at Chhátá and Kosi, has given rise to a local legend that the work was bad in the first instance, and the architect, being convicted of misappropriating the funds at his disposal, was, as a punishment, built up alive into one of the walls; the corpse, however, has not been discovered. Immediately opposite its upper gate, though at some little distance from it, stands one of the old imperial kos minars. Though in itself a clumsy erection, it forms a picturesque object as seen through the arch from inside the courtyard, and would make a pretty sketch. When Mádho Ráo Sindhia was the paramount power, he bestowed this and other villages in the Agra and adjoining districts on the celebrated pandit, Gangá-dhar Shástri, who constituted them an endowment for educational purposes. In 1824, one quarter of the estate was assigned to his sons Tika-dhar and Murli-dhar; the remainder, yielding an annual rental of Rs. 24,000, of which Rs. 3,730 come from Chaumuhá, is the property of the Agra College. In the old topographies the saráe is described as situate at Akbar-pur, a name now restricted to the next village, since the discovery of an ancient sculpture supposed to represent the four-faced (chaumuhá) god Brahma. It is in reality the circular pedestal of a Jaini statue or column, with a lion at each corner and a nude female figure in each of the four intervening spaces: the upper border being roughly carved with the Buddhist rail pattern. The inhabitants are chiefly Gaurua Thákurs. A weekly market is held on Tuesday. There is a primary school; also a bungalow occupied by an assistant patrol in the customs; a small new mosque inside the saráe; a temple of Bihári Jí, built by Kási Dás, Bairági, some 200 years ago, and kept in repair by his successors; and two ponds known as Bihári-kund and Chandokhar. As a punishment for malpracties during the mutiny, the village was burnt down, and for one year the Government demand was raised to half as much again.

CHHÁTÁ, since the mutiny the capital of the pargana, has a population of 6,014. It is on the high road to Delhi, 19 miles from Mathurá, with a camping ground for troops, about 46 bighas in extent. The principal feature of the town is its saráe (already noticed at page 29), which covers an area of 20 bighas, its walls measuring 732 feet by 694. Jacquemont, who saw it in the year 1829, describes it as "a large fortress, of fine appearance from the outside, but it will not do to enter, for inside there is nothing but misery and decay, as everywhere else, except perhaps at Mathurá and Brindá-ban." He would find matters improved now, for in 1876 I had a broad street laid out through the centre of it from the one gate to the other, and at the time of my transfer it had become the principal bazár in the town. I had also sent up an application to Government for a grant of Rs. 3,500 for the repair of the gateways, which possess considerable architectural merit. The repair of the side walls and cells I had already taken in hand and nearly completed, by means of small aunnal allotments out of the chaukidári fund.

In 1857 the saráe was occupied by the rebel zamindárs, and one of the bastions (now built up square) had to be blown down before an entrance could be effected. The town was subsequently set on fire and partially destroyed, and twenty-two of the leading men were shot. It was originally intended to confiscate the zamindárs' whole estate, but eventually the jama was only raised to half as much again for one year. The population are chiefly Játs, the next most numerous class being Jádons. The name is derived by the local pandits from the *Chhattra-dharana-lila,* which Krishna is said to have held there ; but there is no popular legend regarding such an event, nor any very ancient sacred place in its vicinity ; though the Vraja-bhakti-vilása (1553 A.D.) mentions, it is true, a Chhattra-ban and a Súraj-kund. The latter is still in existence to the north-east of the town, and is a large sheet of water with one good masonry ghát built by a Bráhman, Bijay Rám, an officer of the Bharat-pur Ráj, who also built the very large brick house adjoining it, now in ruins. All round the tank are fine old trees and beyond it an extensive *rakhya* of *chhonkar*, *pilu*, and *hingot*. There is another tank on the Mathurá road called Chandra-kund, which it would be an improvement to deepen and embank. The word Chhátá probably refers to the stone *chhattris* which surmount the saráe gateways, and form prominent objects in the landscape from a long distance. There is a tahsíli school, and a weekly market on Fridays. The Hindús have nine small temples and the Muhammadans four mosques.

SAHÁR—population 2,776—seven miles from Chhátá and nine from Gobardhan, was, from 1838 to 1857, the headquarters of a tahsîli. At the beginning of last century it was a place of considerable importance under the Játs, being the favourite residence of Thákur Badan Sinh, the father of Súraj Mall, the first of the Bharat-pur Rájás. The handsome house which he built for himself is now unoccupied, and to a great extent in ruins; and the very large masonry tank which adjoins it was left unfinished at his death and has never since been completed. The word Sahár would seem to have been originally either Sabhá-rá, or Sabhá-pur. Probably the latter; for in the Mainpuri district there is a place called Sahávar, which is clearly for Sabhá-pur, and from which to Sahár the transition is an easy one. The township is divided into two *thoks*, the one of Bráhmans, the other of Muhammadans, and the latter have four small mosques and a dargáh. The Government demand under the present settlement is (including nazúl) Rs. 5,392, collected by 16 lumberdárs. Part of the land has been transferred by the old proprietors to the two Dhúsar families that have been seated here for some generations and are really the principal people in the place. In the town are several old houses with carved stone gateways of some architectural pretension; also a tank, with two masonry gháts, called Mahesar-kund, another known as Mánik-Dás-wálá-kund, and a small ruined temple of Baladeva. There are a police station, a post-office, a weekly market held on Wednesday, and a very well-attended primary school. For the accommodation of the latter I had a large and substantial buildiug erected, in the form of a double corridor, arched and vaulted, running round three sides of an open square, with a low wall and central gateway on the fourth side or front. The cost was Rs. 1,858.

The Agra Canal runs close to the town and is bridged at the point where it crosses the Gobardhan road. It would have been much better to have diverted the road and so brought the bridge, which is now a mile away, nearer to the town. As matters stand at present, the canal, instead of being a blessing, is an intolerable nuisance. On account of the depth of its bed and the absence of any distributary, no water can be had from it for irrigation, while some hundreds of acres that used to be close to their owners' doors can now be reached only after a circuit of some three miles, and are, of course, very much lowered in value.

In the mutiny there was no disturbance here except that the lock-up was broken open, a suspected rebel let loose, and the patwári's papers seized and destroyed.

A short time ago a dispute arose between the Muhammadans and the Hindús as to the possession of a site on which they wished to erect, the one party a mosque, the other a temple. The real fact, as afterwards more clearly appeared, was that the Hindús had originally a temple there, which the Muhammadans had thrown down and built a mosque over it. This, too, had fallen, and the ground had for some years remained unoccupied. The case, when brought into court, was decided in favour of the Hindús, who thereupon set to work and commenced the erection of a shrine to be dedicated to Rádhá Ballabh. In digging the foundations, they came upon the remains of the old temple, which I rescued and brought into Mathurá. They consist of 10 large pillars and pilasters, in very good preservation and elegantly carved with foliage and arabesques, and also a number of mutilated capitals, bases, &c., the whole series proving an interesting illustration of the mediæval Hindú style of architecture. Their value is increased by the fact that two of the shafts bear inscriptions, in which the date is clearly given as *Sambat* 1128 (1072 A. D.) The style that I call 'the mediæval Hindú,' and of which these pillars afford a good late example, began about the year 400 A. D., and continued to flourish over the whole of Upper India for more than seven centuries. It is distinguished by the constant employment in the capital, or upper half column, of two decorative features, the one being a flower-vase with foliage over-hanging the corners, and the other a grotesque mask. The physiognomy of the latter is generally of a very un-Indian type, and the more so the further we go back, as is well illustrated by a pillar in the underground temple in the Allahabad Fort. The *motif* is precisely the same as may be seen in many European cinque cento arabesques, where a scroll pattern is worked up at the ends, or in the centre, into the semblance of a human face. The fashion with us certainly arose out of the classic *renaissance*, and in India also may possibly have been suggested by the reminiscence of a Greek design. But it was more probably of spontaneous and independent origin; as also it was among our Gothic architects, in whose works a similar style of decoration is not altogether unknown. In the earlier examples, such as that at Allahabad, the face is very clearly marked; though even there the hair of the head and the moustaches are worked off into a scroll or leaf pattern. In later work, of which numerous specimens may be seen in my collection of antiquities in the Mathurá museum, the eyes are made so protuberant, and the other features so distorted and confused by the more elaborate treatment of the foliage and the introduction of other accessories, that the proportions of a human face are almost and in some cases are altogether destroyed. The tradition however exists to the present day; and a Mathurá stone-mason, if told to carve a grotesque for a corbel or string-course of any building, will at once draw a design in which are reproduced all the peculiarities of the old models.

SEHI is a place of some note, as being the centre of a clan of Gaurua, *i.e.*, *spurious*, Thákurs, who derive their distinctive name of 'Báchhal' from the Bachh-ban here. They are numerous enough to form a considerable item in the population of the pargana, where they once owned and where they still inhabit as many as 24 villages, *viz.*, Sehi, Chaumuha, Sihána, Akbarpur, Jaitpur, Bhaugánw, Maí, Basi Buzurg, Gángroli, Jávali, Dalota, Siyára, Bahta, Kajiroth, Agaryála, Tároli, Parsoli, Mangroli, Naugáma, Undi, Gora, Ránera, Bharauli and Baroli. The Bachh-ban is now a 'grove' only in name, and is accounted one of the hamlets of the town. In it is the temple of Bihári Jí, to which the Báchhals resort; the Gosains, who serve it, being accounted the Gurus of the whole community. The name Sehi is probably derived from *Sendhna*, 'to excavate,' as a great part of the village area (1,442 bíghas) consists of broken ground and ravines (*khár* and *behar*). Other 106 bíghas are occupied by tanks and ponds, one of which is called Ríthâro, another Bhábhardi, after the name of the Báchhal, who dug it in the famine of 1837. In 1842 the village was put up to auction for arrears and bought in by Government. After being farmed for some years by Kunvar Faiz Ali Khán, it was sold in 1862 for Rs. 4,800 to Seth Gobind Dás, who, in the following year, sold it to Swámi Rangácharya, the head of his temple at Brinda-ban, for Rs 10,000. The annual Government demand is Rs. 6,100. There are four other hamlets in addition to the Bachh-bán, called respectively Odhúta, Garh, Devipura (in the *khádar*) and Little Hazára. The old khera bears the name of Indrauli, and is said to have been at one time the site of a large and populous town. It was certainly once of much greater extent than now, as is attested by the quantity of broken bricks that strew the adjoining fields; but there are no ancient remains nor traces of any large building. It is still, however, a fairly well-to-do place, most of the houses in the bazár being of masonry construction, and a few of them partly faced with carved stone. The school has an attendance of about 40 boys; the population being 2,211. In the courtyard of the temple of Bihári Jí is a square chhattri of red sand-stone with brackets carved in the same style as some in the Brinda-ban temple of Gobind Deva; and of those that support the eaves of the temple itself six are of the same pattern. The shrine has evidently been rebuilt at a much later period; and on one of the pillars is cut a rough scrawl with the date *Sambat* 1805, which is no doubt the year of its restoration. In the village is a small temple of Hanumán, recently rebuilt; and outside, a semi-Muhammadan shrine, erected by a chamár, Khumáni, about the year 1860. There are two annual melas held at it, in Baisákh and Kártik, on the day of the full moon. They are attended equally by Hindús and Muhammadans (as is the case with the shrine of the Bare Miyan at Jalesar) and of the two ministers one is a Bráhman, the other a Musalman Fakír. A mosque which, seen from a little distance, looks rather an imposing structure, was built by two Patháns, Kásim Khán and Alam

Khán of Panipat, who had a jagír of 24 villages, 12 here and 12 about Sonkh. Their descendants were reduced to poverty under the Bharat-pur Ráj; but one of the family, Guláb, has lately in part repaired the mosque.

SHER-GARH—population 4,712—eight miles from Chhátá, with which place it is connected by a metalled road, derives its name from a large fort, now in ruins, built by the Emperor Sher Sháh. The Jamuná, which once washed the foot of its walls, is now more than a mile distant from it. The Hindús would derive the name from *Sihra*, Krishna's marriage wreath; but though this is improbable, it is clear that there was a town here long before the time of Sher Sháh; for in taking down one of the towers of the fort, I came upon a stone carved with foliage of decidedly early Hindú or Buddhist character, with the trefoiled circle so common in the Kashmir temples. There were six towers to the fort and four gates, called the Dehli, the Madár, the Páni or water gate, and the Khirki or postern. By the latter, which is now the most frequented of all, is the school which I had built in 1875 at a cost of Rs. 1,933, in the same style as the one at Sahár. The original zamindárs were Patháns, but in 1859, in execution of a decree held by Kishori Lál, Bohra, the whole of their estate, excepting 1¼ biswa, still held by the sons of the late Asaf Khán, a descendant of the old family, was put up to auction and sold for Rs. 16,200 to Muhammad Núr Khán of Merath, from whom it was purchased for Rs. 20,000 by Seth Gobind Dás. It now forms part of the endowment of the temple of Dwárakádhís in the city of Mathurá. In the mutiny, considerable alarm was caused to the townspeople by the Gújars of the neighbouring villages, who made this their centre, and whose estates were afterwards confiscated and bestowed on Rája Gobind Sinh of Háthras. The Hindús have twelve small temples; the Saráugis one, dedicated to Parsvanáth, and the Muhammadans three mosques. The weekly market is held on Thursday. There is a police station, a district post-office, and besides the school for boys there are two for girls, one of the latter having been supported till his death by Asaf Khán. The town is singularly well-supplied with roads, for, in addition to the one to Chhátá, it has three others (unmetalled) leading direct to Kosi, to Jait, and, across a bridge of boats, to Noh-jhíl.

III.—PARGANA MATHURA.*

The Mathurá pargana is the last of the three lying to the west of the Jamuna. It is the largest in the district, comprising as many as 247 villages and townships, with a population of 220,307 and an area of 401 square miles. Under the Ját and Mahratta Governments of last century its present area was in five divisions—Aríng, Sonkh, Sonsa, Gobardhan, and Farrah; Aríng being the *jágír* of Bájá Bái, the queen of Daulat Rao Sindhia, who (if local traditions are to be believed) inherited all the ferocious qualities of her infamous father Gatgay Shirzi Ráo, the prepetrator of the massacre of Púna. In 1803, when the country was ceded to the Company, two parganas were formed, Mathurá and Aríng, which were put under a single Tahsíldar, who was stationed at the latter place; and this arrangement continued till 1868, when his office was transferred to its present more appropriate location at the capital. The 84 villages, that had previously constituted the Farrah parganah of the Agra district, were added in 1878.

The first settlement was assessed at Rs. 5,149 for Mathurá and Rs. 98,885 for Aríng, making a total of Rs. 1,04,034, which was gradually increased to Rs. 2,14,336; the actual area also having undergone considerable change. For, in 1828, after the conclusion of the war with Durjan Sál, 15 villages on the Bharatpur border were annexed, and about the same time several *muáfi* estates in the neighbourhood of Mathurá were resumed. The first contractor for the Government revenue was a local magnate, whose name is still occasionally quoted, Chaube Rudra-man, who, after one year, was succeeded by Khattri Beni Rám.

In addition to the City, it includes within its limits some of the most notable places in the district—such as Brindá-ban, Gobardhan, and Rádhá-kund—as also several large and populous villages which are of modern growth and have no special characteristic beyond their mere size, as Parson, Phendar, Usphár and others, each with two or three thousand inhabitants. The principal landed proprietors are the trustees of the Seth's temple at Brindá-ban: Gosáin Purushottam Lál of Gokul; the Rája of Awa; the heirs of the Lálá Babú, in

*In Dr. Hunter's Imperial Gazetteer, under the letter S, between an article on Sadiya in Assam and one on Sadras in the Madras Presidency, there is a brief notice with the curious heading Sadr. This is described as being the south-western tahsil of the Mathurá district; as if there were not necessarily a sadr, i.e. a home, or head-quarters, tahsil in every district in India.

Calcutta; and Seths Ghansyám Dás and Gobardhan Dás of Mathurá; not one of whom resides immediately upon his estate.

The predominant classes of the population are Játs, Bráhmans, and Gaurua Kachhwáhás. The ancestor of all the latter, by name Jasráj, is traditionally reported to have come at some remote, but unspecified, period from Amber, and to have established his family at the village of Kota, whence it spread on the one side to Jait, and on the other to Satoha, Giridhar-pur, Pálikhera, Maholí, Nahrauli, Naugáma, Nawáda, and Társi; which at that time must have formed a continuous tract of country, as the villages which now intervene are of much more modern foundation. The estates continued for the most part with his descendants till the beginning of the present century; but seventy years of British legislation have sufficed to alienate them almost entirely.

The most common indigenous trees are the *ním*, *babúl*, *remja*, and *kadamb*: and the principal crops tobacco, sugarcane, *chaná*, cotton, and barley; *bajrá* and *joár* being also largely grown, though not ordinarily to such an extent as the varieties first named. Wheat, which in the adjoining parganas is scarcely to be seen at all, here forms an average crop. The cold-weather instalment of the Government demand is realized principally from the outturn of cotton. An average yield per acre is calculated at one *man* of cotton, seven of *joár*, three of *bájrá*, six of wheat, eight of barley, five of *chaná*, eight of tobacco, and ten and a half of *gur*, the extract of the sugarcane. The cost of cultivation per acre is put at Rs. 7 for the *kharíf* and Rs. 10 for *rabi* crops. The river is of little or no use for irrigation purposes; but after the abatement of the rains it is navigated by country boats, which are always brought to anchor at night. Water is generally found at a depth of 49 feet below the surface of the soil; and it is thus a matter of considerable expense to sink a well, more especially as the sandiness of the soil ordinarily necessitates the construction of a masonry cylinder. The Agra Canal has proved a great boon to the agriculturist; it has a length of 16 miles in the pargana, from Konai to Sonoth, with bridges at Basonti, Aríng, Sonsa, Lál-pur, and Little Kosi.

Aríng—Population 3,579—nine miles from Mathurá, on the high road to Díg, was, from 1803 to 1868, the head of a tahsili, removed in the latter year to the Civil Station. Near the canal bridge, the navigation channel to Mathurá branches off on the one side and on the other a distributary, that runs through the villages of Usphár and Little Kosi. Till 1818 the town was a jágir of a Kashmir Pandit, by name Bába Bisvanáth. On his death it was resumed and assessed

THE SCHOOL, AURANGABAD.

at Rs. 6,447, which sum has subsequently been raised to Rs. 10,000. In 1852, the old Gaurua zamindárs' estate was transferred at auction to Seth Gobind Dás, who has made it part of the endowment of his temple at Brindá-ban. In the mutiny the rebels marched upon the place with the intention of plundering the treasury, but were stoutly opposed by the zamindárs and resident officials, and driven back after a few shots had been fired. Lálá Rám Bakhsh, the hereditary patwári, who also acted as the Seth's agent, was conspicuous for his loyalty, and subsequently received from the Government a grant of Rs. 1,000 and the quarter jama of the village of Kothra, which he still enjoys. The Tahsíldár, Munshi Bhajan Lál, also had a grant of Rs. 1,200, and smaller donations were conferred upon several other inhabitants of the town, chiefly Bráhmans. It is much to be regretted that a misunderstanding with regard to the management of the estate has arisen within the last few years between the Seth and his agent, the Lálá, which threatens to sever entirely the latter's connection with the place. Aríng is generally counted as one of the 24 Upabans, and has a sacred pond called Kilol-kund, but no vestige of any grove. Various mythological etymologies for the name are assigned by the local pandits; but, as usual, they are very unsound. Probably the word is a corruption of Arishta-gráma; Arishta being the original Sanskrit form of *ritha*, the modern Hindi name of the Sapindus detergens, or soap-berry tree. The Gosáins would rather connect it with Arishta, the demon whom Krishna slew. There is a school of the tahsíli class (which hitherto has been liberally supported by Lálá Rám Bakhsh), a post-office, a police-station in charge of a Sub-Inspector, and a customs bungalow, recently moved here from Satoha. Three small temples are dedicated respectively to Baladeva, Bihári Jí, and Pipalesvar Mahádeva; and the ruins of a fort constructed last century preserve the name of Phundá Rám, a Ját, who held a large tract of territory here as a jágír under Rájá Suraj Mall of Bharat-pur. The Agra Canal passes close to the town, and is bridged at the point where it crosses the main road. The market day is Sunday. The avenue of trees extending from Mathurá through Aríng to Gobardhan was mainly planted by Seth Sukhánand.

AURANGABAD—population 2,219—was originally a walled town. It is four miles from the city of Mathurá on the Agra road, and derives its name from the Emperor Aurangzeb, who is said to have made a grant of it to one Bhím Bhoj, a Tomar Thákur, with whose descendants it continued for many years. For some time previously to 1861 it was however held rent-free by a Fakír, commonly called Bottle Sháh, from his bibulous propensities, a grantee of Daulat Ráo Sindhia. On his death it was assessed at Rs. 691, which was subsequently raised to Rs. 898. The place is frequently, but incorrectly, called Naurangábad. It also has the subsidiary name of Mohanpur, from one Mohan Lál, a Sanádh, a man of some importance, who came from Mát and settled there last century. On the bank of the Jamuná is an extensive garden, and on some high ground near the old Agra gate a mosque of the same age as the town, which presents rather a stately appearance, being faced with stone and approached from the road by a steep flight of steps. The weekly market is held on Friday, and is chiefly for the sale of thread and cotton. The Government institutions consist of a police-station and a school. For the accommodation of the latter, which for some years past had borne an exceptionally high character, I had a handsome and substantial building erected, with pillars and tracery of carved stone, which now forms the most conspicuous ornament of the place. This was the last work that I completed before I left the district. A view is given of it as an example of the way in which the indigenous style of architecture can be adapted to ordinary modern requirements. A reach of sandy and broken ground extends from the town to the river, where a bridge of boats affords means of communication with Gokul and Mahá-ban on the opposite bank. Aurangábad is the chief place for the manufacture of wicker chairs and couches, which find a ready sale among the English residents of the adjoining station.

Farah—population 3,642—has a camping ground for troops on the high road to Agra, from which district it has only lately been detached. It was founded by Hamida Begam, the mother of the Emperor Akbar. About the year 1555, during the exile of the Emperor Humáyun the town was the scene of a battle between Sikandar Shah (a nephew of Sher Sháh) and Ibrahim Shah, in which the latter was defeated, though he had with him an army of "70,000 horse and 200 persons, to whom he had given velvet tents, banners, and kettle-drums." Sikandar, whose force did not exceed 10,000 horse, offered peace upon condition of receiving the government of the Panjab, but on his overtures being rejected, he joined in battle, and by his victory became sovereign of Agra and Delhi, while Ibráhim fled to Sambhal.

Sonkh—population 4,126—is on the road from Mathurá to Kumbhir. It is a very thriving and well-to-do place, with a large number of substantial brick-built shops and houses, many of them with carved stone fronts. Under the Játs it was the head of a local Division. It is said by the Gosáins—with their usual absurdity—to derive its name from the demon Sankhásur; but, according to more genuine local tradition, it was first founded in the time of Anang Pál, the rebuilder of Delhi, probably by the same Tomar chief who has left other traces of his name at Son, Sonsa and Sonoth. The ancestor of the present community was a Ját, by name Ahlád, whose five sons—Ása, Ajal, Púrna, Tasíha and Sahjua—divided their estate into as many separate shares, which still bear their names and are to all intents and purposes distinct villages, with the Sonkh bazar as their common centre. This lies immediately under the Khera, or site of the old fort, of which some crumbling walls and bastions still remain. It was built by a Ját named Hati Singh, in the time of Súraj Mall of Bharatpur, or Jawáhir Singh ; but the *khera* itself must be many hundreds of years older. There are two market-places in it, the one belonging to Sahjua, the other to the Púrna zamindárs. The market day for the former is Thursday, for the latter Monday. But a considerable amount of business is transacted every day of the week ; there being as many as 200 baniyas' shops and almost enough local trade to justify the incorporation of a Municipality. In Sahjua there are several extensive orchards of mango and *ber* trees, with an octagonal stone chhattri (commemorating the grandfather of the present lumberdar), and three masonry wells of exceptionally large dimensions ; all attesting the greater wealth and importance of the Ját proprietors during the short period of the Bharat-pur Hegemony. About a mile from the bazár, just across the Bharat-pur border, at a place called Gunsára, is a very fine masonry tank, worthy of a visit from any one in the neighbourhood, being on the same scale and in much the same style as the Kusum-Sarovar near Gobardhan. This was the work of the Ráni Lakshmi, the consort of Rája Randhír Sinh, who also built the beautiful *kunj* that bears her name on the bank of the Jamuná at Brindában. The tank was not quite completed at the time of her death, and, according to native custom, has never been touched since. Adjoining it is an extensive walled garden overgrown with *khirni* and other trees that are sadly in need of thinning. In the centre is an elaborately carved stone plinth for a building that was designed but never executed. Though the population of Sonkh exceeds 4,000, the school has an attendance of no more than sixty pupils, of whom only six are the sons of the Ját zamindárs. The five pattis stand as follows :—

Name.	Thoks.	Lumberdárs.	Wells.	Population (1872).	
Ajal	4	2	3	195	The Ajal thoks are called Bhágmall, Jagraj, Sirmaur, and Kunja.
Áse	2	5	7	380	Áse is now divided into two distinct maháls.
Púrna	2	2	6	1,104	The Púrna thoks are named Kisana and Isvar.
Sahjua	2	4	15	2,017	The Sahjua ; Biláchi and Bewal.
Tasiha	3	3	2	415	The Tasiha ; Táj, Urang and Manohar.
Total ...	13	16	33	4,111	

Where the road branches off to Gobardhan is a towered temple of Mahádeva, with a masonry tank of no great area, but very considerable depth, which was commenced twenty years ago by a Bairági, Rám Dás. It is now all but completed, after an outlay of Rs. 1,300, which he laboriously collected in small sums from the people of the neighbourhood, with the exception of Rs. 200 or 300, which were granted him from the balance of the Chaukidári fund. The avenue of trees along the road between Sonkh and Gobardhan was almost entirely planted by another Bairági by name Sálagrám, who began the work out of a donation made him by the deceased Rájá of Bharat-pur on the birth of his son and heir.

IV.—PARGANA MÁT.

The pargana of Mát is the most northern of the three on the east of the Jamuna, and is a long, narrow, straggling tract of country lying between the river and the Aligarh border. As it abounds in game of various kinds—black buck, wild boar, and water-fowl—it has considerable attractions for the sportsman; but in every other point of view it is a singularly uninviting part of the district. There are no large towns, no places of legendary or historical interest, no roads, no local trade or manufacture, and no resident families of any distinction. The soil also is generally poor, the water bad, and—except quite at the north—there are few groves of trees to relieve the dusty monotony of the landscape. As if to enhance the physical disadvantages of the locality by an artificial inconvenience, the tahsíli has been fixed at the mean little village of Mát in the extreme south, on the very borders of the Mahá-ban pargana; though the merest glance at the map will show that Surír—a place with a larger population than Mát—is the natural centre of the division. Its recognition in that character would be an immense boon both to Government officials and to the agriculturist. The present arrangement dates from a time when the pargana was of very different extent, and Mát easily accessible from all parts of it. For, till 1860, it included the whole of tha Raya sub-division to the south; while in the north, Noh-jhil formed an entirely separate tahsíli. This was more in accordance with the division of territory existing in the reign of the Emperor Akbar, when the whole of Mát proper came under Mahá-ban, and Noh-jhil made part of pargana Noh in the Kol Sarkár. Immediately before the cession of 1804, the latter was the estate of General Perron; while Mát, with Mahá-ban, Sa'dabád, and Sah-pau was held by General Duboigne.

As now constituted, the pargana has a population of 95,446, and an area of 223 square miles, comprising 141 villages, which form 153 separate estates. Of these, the great majority are bhaiyáchári, and thus it comes about that the richest resident landlords are the members of a Bráhman family quite of the yeoman class, living at Chháhiri, a hamlet of Mát. They are by name Pola Rám and Parasurám, sons of Rádha, and Kalhan, son of Bál-kishor, and have jointly an assessable income of Rs. 9,276 a year, derived from lands in Mát, Bijauli, Harnaul, Jaiswa, Jáwara, Nasíthi and Sámauli. They have lately been at considerable expense in building a school in their native place. Three other men of substance, of much the same social position, are Lachhman,

Bráhman, of Bhadra-ban; Serhu, Bráhman, of Tenti-ká-gánw, and Lála Rám, Baniya, of Jáwara. Of non-residents, Rao Abdullah Khán, of Salím-pur in Aligarh, a connection of the Sa'dabad family, has estates about Khánwal and Karáhri, on which the annual Government demand is about Rs. 2,000; the Rájá of Mursán enjoys a royalty of Rs. 1,061 from the Dunetiya circle; and Lálas Mahi Lál and Jánaki Prasád own the two large villages of Arua and Bhadanwára.

After the mutiny, as many as eighteen villages (eleven in whole and seven in part), belonging to the rebel leader Umráo Bahádur of Nának-pur, were confiscated, and all the proprietory rights conferred on Seth Lakhmi Chand rent-free for the term of his natural life. On his death, the grant was further extended to his son, Seth Raghunáth Dás, on payment of the half jama; but the muáfi estate (being about Rs. 8,000 a year), which alone he retains in his own hands, it may be presumed, will lapse entirely on the termination of the second life. The zamindári was transferred to his uncle, the late Seth Gobind Dás, C.S.I., and by him constituted part of the endowment of the temple of Dwárakádhis at Mathurá. The original proprietor was a member of a family that had always been in opposition to the British Government, and died fighting against us at Delhi. Their principal seat was at Kumona in Bulandshahr, where, in 1807, Dunde Khán, with his eldest son, Ran-mast Khán, who is said to have been possessed of perfectly marvellous and Herculean strength, held the fort for three months, though the garrison consisted of a mere handful of men. After the surrender, a pension of Rs. 6,000 a year was settled upon Ran-mast Khán, which his widow enjoyed till her death, an event which took place a few years ago; but the father's whole estate was declared forfeit and bestowed upon Mardán Ali Khán of Chatári, a scion of the same stock. Umráo Bahádur was the child by adoption of Dunde Khán's second son, Nawáb Ashraf Khán of Nának-pur, and, as above mentioned, was killed in the rebel army before Delhi. With him fell his youngest brother, Mazhar Ali Khán, who left a son by name Rahím Khán, who is now either dead or at the Andamans; the sole surviving representative of the family being a son of Umráo Bahádur's—Amír Bahádur—who was too young to be engaged in the rebellion with his father.

To the south of the pargana the predominant class are Gaurua Thákurs; while in the north the agricultural community are almost exclusively Játs, mainly of the Nohwár sub-division. The principal winter crops are *joár*, *bájra*, maize and cotton, the latter occupying some 13,000 acres, while *til*, *arhar*, and hemp are also grown, but ordinarily in the same field with *joár*. In the hot weather about 24,000 acres are under *chaná*, 18,000 under wheat, and 13,000 under barley. Though there are indigo factories at four places, *viz*, Lohi, Karáhri, Bhálai and Arua, the first named has almost entirely suspended operations, and at the other three the plant used is mainly grown in villages across the border in the Aligarh district. The most productive lands are the alluvial flats, which, in the rains, form part of the river bed; the high bank that bounds them is generally bare and broken, and the soil further inland poor and sandy, where the only trees that thrive well are *nim*, *farás* and *babúl*. Connection with the opposite parganas of Kosi, Chhátá, and Mathurá, is maintained by two bridges of boats (the one from Chhin-pahári by Noh-jhíl to Sher-garh, the other from Dángoli to Brindá-ban,) and as many as seven ferries, at Ráe-pur, Farídam-pur, Musmina, Surír, Oháwa, Iloli Guzar, and Mát. Scarcely any attempt has been made to provide for internal communication. In the whole pargana there is not a single yard of metalled road, except in the Mát bazár, where it has been constructed out of the Chaukidári tax; the only bit of first-class unmetalled road is the four miles from Noh-jhíl to the Sher-garh bridge; the remaining thoroughfares are for the most part narrow, winding cart tracks, sunk so much below the level of the adjoining fields that in the rains they assume the appearance of small rivers. In 1856, a strip of land was taken up of sufficient width for the construction of a good broad road to extend from the Brindá-ban bridge to the town of Noh-jhíl, thus traversing all the southern half of the pargana. But little was done beyond marking it out; and as all the lower part of it for some miles lies across the ravines, where it was annually cut away by the rains, it was for at least six months in the year all but impassable; the sum allowed for its maintenance, Rs. 5 a mile, being considered quite inadequate to carry out more than the most superficial repairs. However, before I left the district, I was able to accomplish this most desirable work, and that without any additional grant for the purpose, simply by concentrating the whole of each successive annual allotment on a particular part of the road, instead of dribbling it out over the entire length of 22 miles. Every year I built a culvert or two, or a bridge, burning the bricks and lime on the spot, employing local workmen and doing nothing by contract; and the result, after four years, was a permanently good level road, over which it was quite possible to drive in an English buggy. The road connects three places of some importance in the pargana, *viz.*, Mát, Surír and Noh-jhíl at the one end with Sher-garh, which is a perfect terminus of roads, and at the other with Brindá-ban and Mathurá; while a short branch from Mát would bring it in contact with the station on the new line of railway at Raya, and another from Noh-jhíl with the market of Bájana.

Many of the smaller thoroughfares here, as in other parts of the district, are rapidly being obliterated, and unless speedy measures are taken for their preservation, very great inconvenience must eventually result. The occupants of the fields through which they pass encroach upon them year by year, till at last, in the less frequented tracts, nothing is left but a mere ridge scarcely broad enough for a foot-path. When the traffic is too considerable to allow of this complete appropriation, the lane is narrowed till it barely admits the passage of a single cart; a high bank is then raised on either side with earth always excavated from the roadway, which, thus, is sunk several feet below the level of the country and in the rains becomes a deep water-course. In the dry season of the year it is rendered equally impassable by huge aqueducts carried across it at short intervals in order to convey water for irrigation purposes from a well on one side to lands forming part of the same farm that happen to lie on the other. A small sum is annually allotted for the maintenance of a certain number of village roads, and as I have practically demonstrated, this money might be much more advantageously expended than has hitherto been the custom, if it were used for the systematic prevention of encroachments and the construction of occasional syphon drains and culverts.

As a rule, the bhaiyáchári villages have a much more prosperous appearance than those which have passed into the hands of some one wealthy proprietor. In the former case every shareholder plants the borders and waste corners of his fields with quick growing trees, such as the *farás*, or tamarisk, which he fells from time to time as he wants timber for his well or agricultural implements, or for roofing his house, but immediately supplies their places by new cuttings. Thus the village lands from a little distance often look picturesque and well-wooded, though possibly there may not be a single grove or orchard on them. In a zamindári estate, on the other hand, the absentee landlord is represented on the spot only by an agent, whose sole duty it is to secure as large a yearly return as possible for his employer. Every manorial right is strictly enforced, and trees are felled and sold in large quantities, and never replaced, either by the tenant, who is not allowed to cut a single stick, however urgent his requirements, and therefore has no object in planting, or by the landlord, who cares nothing for the well-being of the village, which can be sold as soon as its productiveness is exhausted. It would be difficult, perhaps impossible, to mention a single instance in the whole district of one of the new landlords doing anything whatever for the permanent improvement of his estate. It never even occurs to them that their tenants have the slightest claim upon their consideration. Having probably amassed their fortune by usury, they are willing to make advances at exorbitant rates of interest for any improvements the cultivators may wish to carry out themselves ; but their ears are closed to any other application.

To prevent the possibility of any individual acquiring a fixed status, leases are never given but for very short periods ; accumulation of arrears of rent is encouraged for the three years that the law allows, when immediate action is taken for the recovery of the full amount increased by interest ; if any payment has been made in the interim, though the tenant intended it to be on account of rent, the landlord maintains that it is absorbed in the clearing off of the advances ; no intimation is given to the patwári of the amount of these advances, nor, as a rule, is any payment made in his presence ; but after the lapse of some weeks, when the ignorant boor, who probably did not pay in cash, but through the intervention of a baniya, has forgotton what the amount was, the patwári is ordered to write a receipt for such and such a sum, and this document is accepted by the stolid clown without a question—ordinarily without even hearing it read—and is at once put away and either lost or eaten by white, ants, while the counter-part remains as legal evidence against him. To increase the confusion, the rent is collected not only without adequate witnesses or any written memorandum, but also at any odd time and by a variety of different persons, who are ignorant of each other's proceedings ; the agents are changed every six months or so, and (as the patwári can only read Hindi) are by preference people who know only the Persian character. The result is, that any adjustment of accounts is absolutely impossible; the patwári, the agents, and the tenants, are all equally at fault, and the latter are solely dependent on the mercy of the landlord, who, at a fortnight's notice, can eject every single man on the estate. Thus, during a single month of the year 1873, more than a hundred suits were filed against the people of one village for arrears contracted in 1870. After the lapse of three years, the defendants—who are so ignorant that they cannot state the amount of their liability for the present season, but depend entirely upon the patwári and the baniya—can only urge that they know they have paid in full, but (almost necessarily under the circumstances) they have no oral witnesses to the fact, while the village account-books, which constitute the documentary evidence, are so imperfect as to form no basis for a judgment. At the same time, in the hope of producing the impression that an innocent man was being made the victim of a gigantic conspiracy, actions for fraud and corruption were instituted against both agent and patwári, and other criminal proceedings were taken against the villagers for petty infringements of manorial rights. Virtually, such pseudo-zamindárs refuse to accept the position of land-

98

lords; they are mere contractors for the collection of the Imperial revenue, and it seems imperative upon the Government to recognize them only in that inferior capacity, and itself to undertake all the responsibilities of the real landlord. Since they have no influence for good, both policy and humanity demand that at least their power for evil should be restricted within the narrowest possible limits.

The most noticeable feature of the pargana is the extensive morass, from which the town of Noh-jhíl derives the latter part of its name. Its dimensions vary very much at different seasons of the year and according to the heaviness of the rainfall, but it not unfrequently spreads over an area measuring six miles in length by one in breadth. It is the favourite haunt of large swarms of water-fowl, which are caught at night in nets, into which they are frightened by torches and fires lit on the opposite bank. They ordinarily sell for about Rs. 4-8 the hundred. The lands which have a chance of being left dry by the subsidence of the waters in time to be sown with hot-weather crops, bear the distinctive name of *Lána*, and are formed into separate estates, which it is a matter of no little difficulty to assess at their average value. When there is any harvest at all, it is exceptionally good; but not unfrequently the land remains flooded till seed-time is over, and the only source of profit then left to the proprietor is the pasturage. The inundation, though primarily the result of the natural low level of the country, has been artificially increased by excavations made some centuries ago with the express object of laying the approaches to the Fort under water: this being one of the special modes of rendering a stronghold impregnable laid down in Sanskrit treatises on the art of war. An outlet was provided by a winding channel, some five miles in length, called the Dhundal Nála, which passed under Firoz-pur and joined the Jamuna near Mangal-khoh; but its mouth is now completely blocked for a long distance. The cost of re-opening it has been estimated at Rs. 2,093; an expenditure which would soon be recovered by the settled revenue of the reclaimed land. A simpler, but at the same time a less efficient, remedy might be found in the reconstruction of an embankment ascribed to Nawáb Ashraf Khan, which formerly existed near the village of Musmina, and was kept in partial repair by the Ját zamindárs of that place till 1866. In that year the jhíl was entirely dry, and the dam being in consequence neglected, the next heavy flood washed it away. To provide an exit for the water seems, however, far preferable to blocking its entrance; as the temporary submersion has a very beneficial effect on the land, and its total prevention might result in rendering a large area absolutely unculturable. A well-devised scheme of drainage for this part of the country, the transfer of the tahsíli from Mát to Surír, and the completion of the road between Noh-jhíl and the Brinda-ban bridge, are the three great requirements of the district which urgently demand a speedy settlement.

MÁT—population 4,093—has for some years past given a name to a pargana, though it is nothing but an exceptionally mean assemblage of mud hovels, without any bazar or even a single brick-built house. It stands immediately on the high bank of the Jamuna, but is separated from the actual bed of the stream by a mile of deep sand, and the ferry which connects it with Sakaráya on the opposite side is therefore very little used. Four miles lower down the stream is the Brindá-ban bridge of boats; the road which leads to it skirting for some distance the margin of an extensive morass, called the Moti-jhíl, which, though never very broad, sometimes attains a length of nearly two miles. The township (jama Rs. 8,983) is divided into two thoks, Rájá and Múla, and was till recently owned entirely by Bráhmans and Thákurs, but some Muhammadans are now in part possession as mortgagees. The Chaukidári Act is in force, but yields an income of only Rs. 52 a month, which leaves a very small balance for local improvements. The school is merely of the primary class, and not so well attended as the one in the adjoining hamlet of Chháhiri. There is an old mud fort, and within its enclosure stand the tahsíli and police-station, the only substantial buildings in the place. Though there is no grove of trees to justify the title, it is still designated as one of the Upabans, and is a station in the Ban-játra; the name being derived from 'the milk-pails' (*mát*) here upset by Krishna in his childish sports. At Chháhiri, a little higher up the stream, is the sacred wood of Bhándír-ban, a dense thicket of *ber*, *hins*, and other low prickly shrubs, with a small modern temple, rest-house and well in an open space in the centre. Just outside is an ancient fig-tree (*bat*) which Krishna and his playmates Balarám and Sridáma are said to have made their goal when they ran races against each other (see page 59). A large *melá*, chiefly attended by Bengális, is held here, *Chait badi* 9, and is called the Gwál-mandala. The temple in the grove is dedicated to Bihári; that under the Bhándír-bat, to Sridáma. In the village are three other small shrines in honour of Rádhá Mohan, Gopál, and Mahádeva. Two mosques have also been recently built by the Muhammadans. In the mutiny the only act of violence committed was the seizure of six grain-boats passing down the river, for which the zamindárs were subsequently fined.

BÁJANA—population 4,427—about five miles north-east of Noh-jhíl, has from time immemorial been occupied by Játs. Many years ago, the three leading men divided it into as many estates, called after their own names, Sultán Patti,

Dilu Patti, and Siu Patti. These are now to all intents and purposes distinct villages, each with several subordinate hamlets, where most of the landed proprietors reside, while the old bazár still remains as a common centre, but is mainly occupied by tradespeople. In it are the sarái, police-station, built in 1869, and halkabandi school. Here, too, every Saturday, a large market is held; all the dealers who attend it having to pay an octroi tax at graduated rates, according to the commodities which they have for sale. These duties are farmed out to a contractor, who in 1865, the year when the last revision of settlement took place, paid for the privilege Rs. 340, a sum which has now been increased to Rs. 429. This income certainly is not very large, but as the market is a popular one, it might, beyond a doubt, be greatly increased, if only the headmen would recognize the obligation, under which they lie, of occasionally devoting part of the proceeds to local improvements. Up to the present time they have done nothing: the market is held in the main street, which is so densely crowded from one end to the other that all through traffic is obstructed; the saráe is too small to accommodate one-half the number of visitors, and there is no separate yard in which to stall horses and cattle; the clouds of dust that rise from the unmetalled roadway make it painful to see and breathe, and would seriously damage any goods of better quality that might be brought; and, in addition to all this, an open space at the end of the street, where the crowd is the very thickest, has been selected as a convenient spot for depositing all the sweepings of the town till they are carted away as manure for the fields. Even the two substantial masonry wells which there are in the bazár have not been constructed by the market trustees, but are the gift of one of the resident shopkeepers.

Another market is held on Thursday, but exclusively for the sale of cattle. A considerable amount of business is transacted, though the animals offered for sale are generally inferior in quality to those brought to the Kosi market on the opposite side of the river. Bájana has also been one of the depôts for Government stallions since 1856, when the establishment was transferred here from the adjoining village of Shankar-garhi, at Aligarh.

The two *pattis* of Sultán and Dilu are watered by a short branch of the Ganges Canal, which enters the district at the village of Ahmad-pur, and passes also through Shankar-garhi. In Siu Patti the proprietary shares are not reckoned by biswas but by wells, which, whether really so or not, are put at 36 in number. The jama is Rs. 3,400, and the quota of each 'well' is Rs. 96, making a total of Rs. 3,456; the surplus of Rs. 56 going to the lumberdárs. Similarly, in Mát, the reckoning is by ploughs and bulls; a plough being a share and a bull half a share. Dilu Patti has two hamlets, Murliya Jawáhir and Murliya Badám; Sultán Patti five, *viz.*, Naya-bás, Dál-garhi, Prahlád-garhi (of which one biswa was sold 18 years ago to an Athwariya), Ajnot and Idal-garhi; and Siu Patti three, *viz.*, Jareliya, Mahá-rám-garhi, and Bhút-garhi. At the time of the mutiny Umráo Bahádur was proprietor of 2½ biswas in Dilu Patti, was mortgagee of 10 biswas in Thok Badám and farmed as much of Thok Hira. This was confiscated with the rest of his estates; the 2½ biswas were conferred on Seth Lakhmi Chand, the other parcels of land have reverted to their original owners. Half of Thok Kamala was also declared forfeit, but eventually returned on payment of a fine; the zamindárs having joined in the assault on the Fort of Noh-jhíl. One of the number, Khúba, who had been specially forward in attempting the life of the Tahsildar, Sukhvási Lál, died in jail before sentence. The Arázi Kásht Sultán Patti and Arázi Dilu Patti are lands recovered from the jhil and separately assessed—the one at Rs. 90, the other at Rs. 152.

Noh-jhil—population 2,674—is a decayed town, 30 miles from Mathurá, which, up to the year 1860, was the head of a separate tahsíli now incorporated with Mát. The original proprietors were Chauhán Thákurs, who were expelled in the thirteenth century by some Játs from Narwári near Tappal, and others from Jartúli near Khair, in the Aligarh District, who afterwards acquired the name of Nohwár, and at the present time are further distinguished by the title of Chaudhri. They brought with them as purohits some Gáur Bráhmans of the Phátak clan, who received various grants of land, and at the last settlement their descendants owned 15 biswas of the township, the remaining five being held by Muhammadan Shaikhs. In the seventeenth century some Bilúchis were stationed here by the emperor, for the express purpose of overawing the Játs; but their occupation did not last above 80 years. On the 4th of June, 1857, the Nohwár Játs of the place with their kinsmen from the neighbouring villages of Musmina and Pársoli attacked the fort and plundered all the inhabitants except the Bráhmans, with whom, as above shown, they had an hereditary connection. The lumberdár, Ghaus Muhammad, was killed, and all the Government officials fled to the village of Thera by Surír, where the Malakána zamindárs gave them shelter, and in acknowledgment of their loyalty subsequently received a donation of Rs. 151 and a remission of Rs. 100 on the yearly jama, which still continues. The estate is now held as follows: 12½ biswas by the Bráhmans, 3¾ by Shaikhs, and 4½ biswas of alluvial land by the Seths. This latter share had been purchased at auction by Umráo Bahádur's father, and was confiscated with the rest of his property. Two outlying suburbs are called respectively Toli

Shaikhán and Toli Khádim-i-dargáh. The Fort, of which incidental mention has been already made, is of great extent, covering 31 bíghas of land. It was rebuilt about the year 1740 by Thákur Devi Singh, an officer in the service of the Bharat-pur Rájá. It is now all in ruins, but its crumbling bastions command a fine view of the extensive lake that spreads for miles beneath it. Within its enclosure is the old tahsíli, built in 1826, now converted into a police-station, and a lofty tower erected in 1836 for the purposes of the Trigonometrical Survey; ascent is impossible, as the ladder in the lower story was destroyed in the mutiny and has not been replaced.

Outside the town is a Muhammadan *makbara* or tomb, called the dargáh of Makhdúm Sáhib Sháh Hasan Ghori, traditionally ascribed to a Dor Rájá of Kol who flourished some 300 years ago. This is not in itself improbable, for about that time all the Aligarh Dors became converts to Islám.* The buildings are now in a dilapidated condition, but include a covered colonnade of 20 pillars which has been constructed out of the wreck of a Hindu or Buddhist temple. Each shaft is a single piece of stone 5½ feet long, and is surmounted by a capital, which adds an additional foot to the height. The latter are sculptured with grotesques, of which the one most frequently repeated represents a squat four-armed monster, who, with his feet and one pair of hands raised above his head, supports, as it were, the weight of the architrave. The shafts, though almost absolutely plain, are characteristic specimens of an eccentricity of Hindu architecture. (*See* page 275.) Several other columns have been built up into the roof; one carved in low relief with several groups of figures, parted from one another by bands of the pattern known as the 'Buddhist railing,' has been taken out and transported to Mathurá. The statues which adorned the temple have probably been buried under ground; but no excavations can be made, as the place is used for Muhammadan

---

* When Kol was finally reduced by the Muhammadans in the reign of Nasir-ud-dín Mahmúd (1246-1265), it was under a Dor Raja, and the tower, which was wantonly destroyed by the local authorities in 1860, is supposed to have been erected 652A.H. (1274A.D.) on the site of the principal temple of the old city. Among the Hindus, however, the tradition is somewhat different; they ascribe it to the Dor Raja, Mangal Sen, who gave his daughter Padmavati in marriage to the heir of Raja Bhim of Mahrara and Etawa, who soon after his accession was murdered by his younger brothers. The widow then retired to Kol, where her father built the tower for her. At Noh-khera in the Jalesar pargana there is a local tradition of a Rája Bhím, and possibly the above may be the person intended. The father of Mangal Sen was Buddh Sen, who transferred his capital from Jaláli to Kol. He was the son of Bijay Rám (brother of Dasarath Sinh, who built the fort at Jalesar), the son of Náhar Sinh, who built the Sambhal fort, the son of Gobind Sinh, the son of Mukund Sen, the son of Vikrama Sen, of Baran, now called Bulandshahr.

interments. The saint's *urs* or melá is held on the 14th of Ramazán, and his tomb is visted by some of the people of the neighbourhood every Thursday evening. There was an endowment of 300 bíghas of land and a yearly pension of Rs. 100, but the latter ceased on the death of Makhdúm Bakhsh, the representative of the original grantee, and the land was settled at half jama (Rs. 80) in 1837. In the bazár are a small mosque and two temples built by the Mahrattas. The proximity of the jhíl renders the town feverish and unhealthy, and the establishment of a branch dispensary would be a great boon to the inhabitants.

SURÍR—population 5,199—by its position the natural centre of the pargana, is a small town on the high road half-way between Mát and Noh-jhíl. It is about a mile from the left bank of the Jamuná, where is a ferry to Bahta on the opposite side. It is said to have been called at one time Sugrív-khera, after the name of one of the different founders; this appellation is now quite obsolete, but it explains the origin of the word Surir, which is thus seen to be a contraction for Sugriv-rá. The oldest occupants were Kalárs (the local name, as it would seem, for any aboriginal tribe), who were expelled by Dhákaras, and these again by Rájá Jitpál, a Jaes Thákur. His posterity still constitute a large part of the population, but have been gradually supplanted in much of the proprietary estate by Baniyas and Bairágis. The township (jama Rs. 9,619) is divided into two *thoks*, called Bija and Kalán; and there are 11 subordinate hamlets. Three small temples are dedicated respectively to Mahádeva, Lakshmi Ñáráyan, and Baladeva. There is a police station, a primary school, and a weekly market held on Monday. At the time of the mutiny, Lachhman, the lumberdár, with 11 others, was arrested on the charge of being concerned in the disturbances that took place at the neighbouring village of Bhadanwára, in which the zamindár, Kunvar Dildár Ali Khán, was murdered, his wife violated, and a large mansion that he was then building totally destroyed. He was considerably in the debt of his banker, Nand Rám of Raya, who, when the estate was put up to auction, bought it in, and has been succeeded as proprietor by his nephew Jánaki Prasád.

V.—PARGANA MAHÁ-BAN.

THE Mahá-ban pargana has a population of 116,829 and an area of 239 square miles. It forms the connecting link between the two divisions of the district. Its western half, which lies along the bank of the Jamuná, forms part of the Braj Mandal, and closely resembles in all its characteristics the tracts that we have hitherto been describing: its towns are places of considerable interest, but the land is poor and barren, dotted with sandhills and intersected with frequent ravines. To the east, beyond Baladeva, the country is assimilated to the rest of the Doáb; the soil, being of greater productiveness, has from time immemorial been exclusively devoted to agricultural purposes, and thus there are no large centres of population nor sites of historic interest.

In area and subordination the pargana has undergone several changes; for originally it formed part of Aligarh, and then for some years recognized Sa'dabád as its capital, before it was finally constituted a member of the district of Mathurá. In 1861 it made over to Sa'dabád some few villages on the border, and received instead the whole of the Raya circle, including as many as eighty-nine villages, which till then had been included in Mát; together with three others, Baltíkri, Bírbal, and Sonkh, which were detached from Háthras. A glance at the map will show that a further rectification of its boundary line to the north is still most desirable; as all the 18 villages of the Ayra-khera circle occupy a narrow tongue of land that runs up along the Aligarh border, in such immediate proximity to the Mát tahsíl that they would clearly be benefited by inclusion in Mát jurisdiction.

The river forms the boundary of the pargana to the south as well as the west, and in the lower part of its course is involved in such a series of sinuosities that its length is out of all proportion to the area it traverses, and thus necessitates the maintenance of no less than eleven crossing places, *viz.*, the pontoon bridge at the city, a bridge of boats at Gokul, and ferries at Páni-gánw, Habíb-pur or Basai, Baroli, Kanjauli, Koila, Tappa Saiyid-pur, Sehat, Akos, and Nera. The contracts for all these, excepting the one at Koila, are given in the Agra district.

Of the 151,846 acres that form the total area, 110,613 are ordinarily under cultivation. The crops principally grown are *joár*, *bájra* and the like on 57,000 acres; wheat and barley on 38,700; cotton on 8,000, and *chana* on 4,000. Water-melons are also raised in large quantities on the river-sands;

and the long grass and reeds, produced in the same localities, are valuable as materials for making ropes, mats, and articles of wicker-work.

The number of distinct estates is 216, of which 18 are enjoyed rent-free by religious persons or establishments, and 89 are in the hands of sole proprietors, as distinct from village communities. The castes that muster strongest are Játs and Bráhmans, who together constitute one-half of the entire population. The great temples at Baladeva and Gokul, though they have also endowments in land, derive the principal part of their income from the voluntary offerings of pilgrims and devotees. Of secular proprietors the wealthiest—as in most other parts of the country now-a-days—are *novi homines* of the baniya class, who have laid the foundation of their fortune in trade. First in this order come Mahi Lál and Jánaki Prasád of Raya. Their ancestor, Nand Rám, was a petty trader of that town, who realized large profits by the sale of grain in the famine of 1838. In partnership with him was his brother, Magni Lál, who, having no natural heir, adopted his sister's grandson, Jánaki Prasád. In 1840 Nand Rám died, and as of his two sons, Mahi Lál and Bhajan Lál, the latter was already deceased, leaving issue, Jamuná Prasád and Manohar Lál, he left his estate in three equal shares, the one to his son, the second to his two grandsons, and the third to his adopted nephew. For some years the property was held as a joint undivided estate ; but in 1866 an agreement was executed contituting three estates in severalty ; Jánaki Prasád's share being the village of Bhadanwára, Mahi Lál's that of Arua, both in Mát ; and Jamuná Prasád and Manohar Lál's, ten smaller villages in the Mahá-ban pargana. As the main object of this agreement was simply to get rid of Jánaki Prasád, the others continued to hold their two-thirds of the original estate as one property. But after a time, thinking that the discrepancy between recorded rights and actual possession might lead to difficulties, in 1870 they executed another deed, by which the two shares were again amalgamated. This joint estate, including business returns, was assessed for purposes of the income tax, as yielding an annual profit of Rs. 16,066 ; the Mahá-ban villages, in which they are the largest shareholders, being Acharu, Chúra-Hansi, Dhaku, Gonga, Nágal, and Thana Amar Sinh. Some misunderstanding having subsequently arisen, the uncle and nephew have again divided their joint estate. Their kinsman Jánaki Prasád, in addition to his Mát village of Bhadanwára, has shares in Gainra, Kakarári and 15 other villages in Mahá-ban, from which he derives a net income of Rs. 14,260.

Of much the same, or perhaps rather lower, social standing are a family of Sanádh Bráhmans at Jagadís-pur, money-lenders by profession, who are gradually consolidating a considerable estate out of lands which for the most part they first held only in mortgage. The head of the firm in their native village, where they have been settled for many generations, is by name Harideva, with whom is associated in partnership his nephew, Chunni Lál, son of a deceased brother, Isvari. Besides owning three parts of Jagadis pur, they have also shares in Daulat-pur, Habíb-pur, Kárab, Kakarári, Sahora, Wairaní, and 16 other villages, producing a net income of Rs. 12,572. A brother of Harideva's, by name Púran Mall, has a separate estate, being part proprietor of Bahádur-pur Itauli, &c., while a relative, Baladeva, living at Gokul, has a further income of Rs. 13,311 derived from trade and lands that he owns at Daghaita and Arhera in the Mathurá pargana. This latter's father, Param Sukh, was the brother of Híra-mani, Harideva's father; and it was their father Jawáhir—nicknamed *Kuteliya*, 'the pedlar'—son of another Harideva, who began in a very small way to form a nucleus for the fortune which his descendants have so rapidly accumulated.

The Saiyids of Mahá-ban (*see* page 13), though of inferior wealth, have claims to a more ancient and honorable pedigree. They have a joint income of Rs. 6,084, drawn chiefly from the township of Mahá-ban and the villages of Nagara Bháru, Gohar-pur, Sháhpur Ghosna, and Narauli: but the shareholders are so numerous that no one of them is in affluent circumstances.

The Pachhauris of Gokharauli have a joint income estimated at Rs. 10,695. The most prominent person among them is Kalyán Sinh, and the actual head of the family, the Thakuráni Prán Kunwar, his cousin Bakhtáwar Sinh's widow, has adopted one of his sons, by name Rám Chand. They trace their descent from one Bhúpat Sinh of Savaran-khera in the small central India state of Bhadaura, who came from thence to settle at Satoha—a village between Mathurá and Gobardhan. There he died and also his son, Parasu-rám Sinh; but the grandson, Púran Chand, removed to Gokharauli, where he acquired large possessions in the time of the Mahrattas. At the present day there is not a single village in the old pargana of Mahá-ban, in which his descendants have not some share, though it may often be a small one. In several they are sole proprietors, and they have other estates in the Agra district. At the outbreak of the mutiny, the fort of Gokharauli was surprised and taken in the absence of the head of the family, Ballabh Sinh, grandson of Púran Chand. It was, however, soon after recovered by him and his cousin, Kalyán Sinh, the Risáldar Major in the 17th Regiment; and their great local influence further enabled them to raise a large body of volunteers in pursuit of the rebel army. When the disturbances were over, Ballabh Sinh was appointed tahsíldar of

Kosi, but he soon threw up the appointment, as he had no taste for office work, and his private property required superintendence. As Prán Kunwar's adoption of a son has given rise to much litigation on the part of the rival claimants to the inheritance, it may be of use to add a genealogical table showing clearly the degrees of relationship :—

BHÚPAT SINH,
(of Savaran-kherá in Bhadaura ; came from there and settled at Satoha.)

- Parasu-rám Sinh, of Satoha.
  - Púran-chand, of Gokharauli.
    - Giridhar Sinh, of Bhadaura.
      - Ballabh Sinh, tahsildar of Kosi, died s. p.
    - Mukund Sinh, of Gokharauli.
      - Bakhtáwar Sinh = Prán Kunwar, present head of the family. Bakhtáwar Sinh, of Gokharauli died s. p.
    - Bansidhar.
    - Gájar Mall.
      - 1 Har Prasád
      - 2 Lalitá Prasád
      - 3 Jamuná Prasád
    - Gobind Rám, tahsíldar of Sikandra Rao.
      - Kalyán Sinh, of Gokharauli.
        - Rám-chand, adopted by Prán Kunwar.

Beyond the three towns of Gokul, Mahá-ban, and Baladeva, which have already been fully described, the only other places in the pargana which require more than the most cursory notice are the four great centres of Ját colonization, whose history involves that of all the villages subordinate to them.

AYRA-KHERÁ, an old township with no arable land attached to it, is popularly said to be the mother of 360 villages. It is still the recognized centre of eighteen which are as follows :—Ayra (or Era), Báron, Bhankarpur, Bhúra, Bibávali, Bindu Buláki, Birahna, Bírbal, Gainra, Gaju, Kakarári, Lálpur, Manína Bálu, Misri, Nim-gánw, Píri, Sabali, and Sampat Jogi. The founder is said to have been a Pramár Thákur, by name Nain Sen, who himself came from Daharua, another village in this pargana, but whose ancestors had migrated from Dhár in the Dakhan, the Rája of which state is still a Pramár and of a very ancient family. He had four sons, whose names are given as Rompa (or Rúpa), Sikhan, Birahna, and Inchráj, and among them he portioned out his new settlement. They again had each issue, *viz.*, Rúpa five sons, the founders of the five northern villages, Bindu-Buláki, Ním-gánw, Píri, Bibávali, and Bhúra ; Sikhan four sons, who settled the four villages to the south-west, Kakarári, Birahna, Báron, and Gainra ; Birahna five sons, who founded the five villages to the east, Sabali, Bírbal, Era, Misri, and Gaju ; and Inchráj four sons, who founded the four villages to the north-west, Mánína Bálu, Bhankarpur, Lálpur, and Sampat Jogi. The bazár is considered the joint property of Rúpa's descendants, and their permission is necessary before any new shop can be built in it. The market, which is held on a spot close to the bazár, twice a week, Wednesday and Saturday, is the property of the zamíndárs of the four villages founded by Sikhan's sons, who give it out on contract for about Rs. 50 a year to four baniyas, who take a weighing fee from every purchaser, six *chhataks* in each rupee's worth of grain. The land is occupied almost exclusively by the Ját community, with the exception of Lálpur, which is held by Bráhmans, the descendants of the founder's *purohit*, who belong to the Sanádh clan. Adjoining the village there is a small piece of woodland, 20 bighas 4 biswas in extent, held rent-free by some bairágis, which is called Niwári, *i.e.*, Nimwári. It makes a convenient place to camp in, being enclosed in a belt of fine old *ním* and *pápri* trees, with a solitary *imli* and a number of *pasendu* and *karil* bushes in the centre. This is accounted part of Lálpur. The school has an attendance of about 60 boys. The older occupants of the place, whom Nain Sen dispossessed, are said to have been Kalárs, whatever may be the tribe intended by that ambiguous term. His brethren, whom he left behind at Daharua, all became Muhammadans, and it may be presumed that it was his obstinate adherence to the faith of his fathers, which made it necessary for him to emigrate. The event therefore cannot be referred to any very early period. Though himself a Thákur, it is curious to observe that his descendants for very many generations past have been reckoned as Játs of the Godha sub-division. This they explain by saying that the new settlers, being unable to secure any better alliances, intermarried with Ját women from Karil in the Aligarh district, and the children followed the caste of their mothers. There is a general meeting for all the members of the clan at the festival of the Phúl Dol, which is held Chait badi 5.

At Bhúra, which is one of the 18 villages, is an old brick-strewn *khera*, locally ascribed to the Kalárs. Wells have been sunk all over it for the purpose of irrigating the adjoining fields, but, so far as can be ascertained, no antiquities have ever turned up. On the top is a cairn, marking the grave of some Saiyid, name unknown. The soil is so sandy that a well anywhere except on the khera falls in as soon as dug, unless protected by a masonry cylinder. For the convenience of revenue officials the whole of the Ayra-khera circle has been divided into 18 groups, and each group is entered in the records under the name of some one of its constituent homesteads, which is accounted the village and the others its hamlets. But, on the spot, each bears its own name, and as they all lie very close together and are pretty nearly the same size and have the same general features, being all occupied by members of the same clan, the effect upon a chance visitor is a little bewildering. Neither do the fields of one hamlet all lie together, but are intermingled with those of several others. The tract however is well-wooded with babúl trees dotted about the borders of the fields and frequent small mango orchards. It is also well-cultivated, the only bits of waste being the Bairágis' hermitages, green little nooks, the last remnants of the original jungle.

ÁR-KHERA is said to have been the parent of twenty-eight villages, eleven of which are still grouped together under the collective name of the taluka Ár Lashkarpur. They are as follows ;—Bansa, Basar-Bhikhandi, Bír Aliabad, Gurera, Khalána, Khajúri, Nigora, Nonera, Pavesara, Polua, and Sujánpur. The last of these, with an area of 243 acres, is uninhabited and is owned by the Ját Rája of Mursán. The Khera itself has been deserted for very many years past, and though a melá in honour of Baráhi Devi is held there twice a year, even the goddess does not remain permanently on the spot, but is merely brought over for the occasion.

MADEM.—This is a circle of five villages occupied by Játs of the Dangri sub-division. Their ancestor, by name Kapúr, is said to have been a Sissodiya Thákur from Jaitai in the Sa'dabád pargana, but originally from Chitor, whose five sons, Chhikára, Bhojua, Jagatiya, Nauranga, and Bansingha, founded the villages that still bear their names. In consequence of their laxity in allowing widow re-marriage they lost caste and from Thákurs became Játs. The older occupants of the locality are represented to have been Kalárs, Chhikára and Bansingha now form the central settlement. At the *siyar*, or shrine of the goddess of small-pox, who is specially worshipped once a year in the month of Asárh, I noticed a small figure apparently Jain, which slightly confirms my view that Kalár is the local name for the older followers of that faith.

RAYA—population 2,752—is a small town on the Aligarh road, seven miles from Mathurá, and the first station on the Light Railway from that city to Háthras. It has no arable land of its own, but is the recognised centre of as many as twenty-one Ját villages which were founded from it. These are as follows :—(1) Nágal, (2) Gonga, (3) Súraj, (4) Dháku, (5) Achárn, (6) Bhainsára, (7) Siyara, (8) Banán, (9) Pararári, (10) Sáras, (11) Tirwa, (12) Kharwa, (13) Narwa Hansi, (14) Thana Amar Sinh, (15) Saur, (16) Pokhar Hirday, (17) Malhai, (18) Khairári, (19) Bhíma, (20) Koil, and (21) Chura Hansi. The first fourteen of these are the older settlements and are called the *chaudah taraf ;* the other seven are subsequent offshoots. The town is said to derive its name from its founder Rae Sen, who is regarded as the ancestor of all the Játs of the Godha clan. There is an old mud fort ascribed originally to one Jamsher Beg, but rebuilt in the time of Thákur Daya Rám of Háthras. The principal residents are now Jánaki Prasád, Jamuná Prasád, and Mahi Lál, of whom mention has been already made. A Bairági of the Nimbárak persuasion by name Harnám Dás, enjoys a considerable reputation as a Pandit. There is a large orchard of mango and Jáman trees, twenty-three bighas in extent, planted by Srí Kishan Dás, Baniya, whose son, Jugal Kishor, has also one of the two Indigo factories in the town ; the other belonged to the late Mr. Saunders. There is also a smaller orchard in the possession of a Bairági by name Rúp Dás. At the back of the police-station is a pond called Khéma-rá, after the man who had it dug, and on the Mát road, near a Thákur-dwára, another called Rawa, probably after the founder Ráe Sen. Market days are Monday and Friday. The town is administered under Act XX. of 1856, and section 34 of Act V. of 1861 is also in force. The line of railway has been constructed along the side of the road, and, as at first laid, crossed and re-crossed it so frequently that all road traffic would have been greatly impeded. This defect was subsequently remedied, and there are now only three crossings in its entire length of 29 miles ; but the fine avenue of trees has been terribly cut up.

SONAI—population 2,393—is a township on the Háthras road which, like Raya, finds no place in the Revenue Records, being there represented by its eight dependent villages. These are Thok Bindávani, Jhok Gyán, Thok Kamal (better known as Khojua), Thok Sáru, Thok Sumera, Bhurári, Nagara Bari and Nagara Jangali. The Begam Umrao Shah in 1772 built a fort here, which in 1808 was held by Thákur Daya Rám, of Háthras, and for some years subsequently was used as a tahsíli. Not a vestige now remains of the old buildings, which were pulled down and the materials used for the construction of the new police-station. The site is well raised and commands an extensive view. I would have built a school upon it, but it was represented that the children would be afraid of ghosts. The saráe was constructed in the time of Tahsíldár Zahúr Ali Khán, one of the Lál Kháni family, seated in the Bulandshahr district. Market days are Sunday and Thursday.

VI.—PARGANA SA'DABÁD.

THE pargana of Sa'dabád is bounded by the districts of Aligarh and Agra to the north and south, Eta to the east, and the Mathurá pargana of Mahá-ban to the west. It has a population of 89,217 and an area of 115,498 acres, divided into 131 separate estates, of which 52 are held by sole proprietors and the remainder by communities of shareholders. Though water is ordinarily found only at the considerable depth of 30 feet below the surface and is often brackish, most of the land is of excellent quality, yielding a good return on every species of agricultural produce; barley, cotton, *joár*, and *arhar* being the principal crops, with a considerable amount also of hemp and indigo. The predominant classes are Játs and Bráhmans, who together constitute nearly one half of the total population. At the beginning of the century, Rájá Bhagavant Sinh of Mursán was one of the largest landed proprietors; but the estate in Sa'dabád held by the present Rájá consists only of the villages of Bhurká, Jhagarári, and Nagara Gharíba, which yield an annual income of Rs. 3,000. Another local magnate of great importance at the same period was also a Ját by caste, Thákur Kushál Sinh, the brother-in-law of Durjan Sál, the usurper of the throne of Bharat-pur. His estates, some 10 or 11 villages lying round about Mahrára, now on the line of Railway, were all confiscated at the close of the war, when a settlement was made with the former proprietors and some of the hereditary cultivators. At present the principal people in the pargana are the Muhammadan family seated at the town of Sa'dabád, at whose head is the Thakuráni Hakím-un-Nissa, the widow of Kunwar Husain Ali Khan. (*See* page 20).

The remaining large landowners are of a different stamp, being *nouveaux riches*, who have acquired whatever wealth they possess within the last few years by the practice of trade and usury. The most prominent members of this class are—1*st*, Srí Rám, Bohra, son of Madári Lál, Bráhman, of Salai-pur, who returns his net income at Rs. 15,500, derived from shares in 20 different villages; 2*nd*, Mittra Sen, a Baniya of Háthras, who has an income of Rs. 12,125, arising from lands in Mirhávali, Samad-pur, and four other places; and 3*rd*, Thákur Dás and Síta Rám, the sons of Jay Gopál, Dhúsar, who enjoy an income of Rs 12,116, from Jatoi, Kúpa, Nagara Dali and shares in 11 other villages. Most of the indigo factories are branches of the Chotua concern, a firm which has its head-quarters near Sonai, in the Háthras pargana. Mr. John O'Brien Saunders, of the *Englishman*, was the senior partner: he died in 1879.

Strictly speaking, there is not in the whole of Sa'dabád a single town ;* for even the capital is merely a largish village with a population of 3,295. It was founded by a character of considerable historical eminence, Vazir Sa'dullah Khán —the minister of the Emperor Sháhjahán—who died in 1655, three years before the accession of Aurangzeb. For some time after the annexation of 1803, it continued to be recognized as the capital of a very extensive district, which had the Jamuná as its western boundary and comprised the parganas of Jalesar, Mát, Noh-jhíl, Mahá-ban, Raya, Khandauli, Sikandra Ráo and Fírozabád, in addition to the one named after itself. This arrangment existed till 1832, when the Mathurá District was formed and absorbed the whole of the Sa'dabád circle, with the exception of Sikandra Ráo, which was attached to Aligarh, and Fírozabád and Khandauli, which compensated Agra for the loss of Mathurá. If the size of the place had accorded in the least with its natural advantages, it would have been impossible to find a more convenient and accessible local centre ; as it stands on a small stream, called the Jharna, which facilitates both drainage and irrigation, and it is also at the junction of four important high roads. Of these, one runs straight to Mathurá, a distance of 24 miles ; another to the Railway Station at Mánik-pur, which is nine miles off ; while the remaining two connect it with the towns of Agra and Aligarh. The Tahsíli, which occupies the site of a Fort of the Gosáin Himmat Bahádur's, is a small but substantial building, with a deep fosse and pierced and battlemented walls. As it has the advantage of occupying an elevated position, and is supplied with a good masonry well in the court-yard, it might in case of emergency be found capable of standing a siege. There is in the main street a largish temple with an architectural façade ; but the most conspicuous building in the town is a glittering white mosque, erected by the late Kunwar Irshád Ali Khán, near his private residence. There are two other small mosques ; one built by Ahmad Ali Khán, Tahsildár, the other ascribed to the Vazír, from whom the place derives its name. The zamindári estate was at one time divided between Bráhmans, Játs, and Gahlots, of whom only the former now retain part

* As an illustration of the curious want of perspective, which characterises all Dr. Hunter's notices of this district in his Imperial Gazetteer, I observe that while he totally omits the towns of Baladeva, Barsána and Nandgánw, gives six lines to Gokul and barely half a page to Brindá-ban, he devotes special paragraphs to two places in this Sa'dabád pargana, *viz.*, Bisáwar and Kursanda, which even in a book like the present devoted exclusively to one particular district, I can find nothing to say about, except that Dr. Hunter has mentioned them. They are not towns, nor even villages, but simply two groups of scattered and utterly insignificant agricultural hamlets, which for convenience of revenue purposes have been thrown together under collective names.

possession, the remainder of the land having been transferred to Muhammadans and Baniyas. The town is not large enough to form a municipality, but is administered under Act XX. of 1856. The principal *melá* is the Rám Lílá, started only 40 years ago by Pachauri Mukund Sinh, when Tahsíldár. The oldest temples are two in honour of Mahádeva, one of Hanumán, and a fourth founded by Daulat Ráo, Sindhia, dedicated to Murli Manohar. In the mutiny the place was attacked by the Játs, and seven lives were lost before they could be repulsed. A Thákur of Háthras, by name Sámant Sinh, who led the defence, subsequently had a grant of a village in Aligarh, while two of the Ját ringleaders, Zálim and Deokaran of Kursanda, were hanged.

Immediately opposite the road that branches off to Jalesar is a neat little rest-house for the accommodation of the officers of the Public Works Department; and about half a mile from the town on the Agra side is a large and commodious bungalow of the Kunwar's, which is always placed at the disposal of his English friends. It is surrounded by extensive mango groves, and attached to it is a spacious garden, very prettily laid out and well-kept, containing many choiçe varieties of trees, flowers, and creepers.

SAHPAU (probably for Sah-pura)—population 3,635—is the largest village in the pargana, a little off the Sa'dabád and Jalesar road, and close to the Mánikpur Railway Station. The Thákur zamindárs are Gahlots, who trace their descent from Chitor, and say that at one time they had as many as 52 villages in this neighbourhood. The elder branch of the family, as at Sahpau, Kukargama, Isaunda, &c., take to themselves the title of Sah; the second, as at Tehu in Jalesar, that of Chaudhari; and the youngest, that of Ráo. Thákur Buddh Sinh of Umargarh now owns 5 biswas of the estate, purchased by his father, Thákur Tíkam Sinh; Bindaban Sah is lumberdár of other 10, and Jhaman Sah of the remaining 5. But out of these 15 biswas, Chunni Kúar, wife of Panna Lál, baniya, has acquired 7½ *viz.*, 5 of Bindaban's and 2½ of Jhaman's. Two families of Sanádh Bráhmans have long enjoyed a málikána of Rs. 175, payable in four shares, two of Rs. 62-8-0 and two of Rs. 25 each, but the liability to further payment is now disputed by the proprietors, since one share has been sold and another mortgaged to a baniya, by name Bidhi-chand. There are 5 hamlets, called Sukh-rám, Badamá, Tiká Rám, Kusháli, and Mewa. The Baniyas are all either Báraseni Vaishnavas, or Jaeswár Saráugis. The latter say that they came from Chitor with the Thákurs. They have a modern temple dedicated to Nem-náth, where a festival is held in the month of Bhádon. It stands immediately under the site of the old fort, which is well raised and occupies an area of 13 bíghas. It has yielded a large supply of massive slabs of block kankar, which have served as materials for constructing the basement story of several of the houses in the bazár. Some late Jaini sculptures, representing each a central seated figure with minor accessories, have also been exhumed; I removed to Mathurá and placed in the museum there one of the most characteristic. Outside the town near Panna Lál's indigo factory is a raised terrace, now sacred to Bhadra Káli Mátá, which also is partly constructed of kankar blocks, and on the top of it are placed a great number of late Jaini figures with part of the large *Sinhásan* on which the principal idol had been seated. Here a buffalo is offered in sacrifice at the Dasahara festival. In the suburbs of the town are some 12 or 13 mango orchards with small temples and Bairagis' cells, and in a field by itself a large square domed building, of more architectural pretensions, which commemorates a Thákur window's self-immolation. The lower part of the walls at each of the four corners has been almost dug through for the sake of the bricks, and unless repaired the whole must shortly fall. The town is administered under Act XX. of 1856.

APPENDIX A.

CASTE: ITS ORIGIN AND DEVELOPMENT.

INDIAN caste is ordinarily regarded as an institution *sui generis*, which must be accepted as a potent social influence, but cannot be explained either by parallel facts in other countries or by an enquiry into its own development, since that is buried in the depth of pre-historic antiquity. Such an opinion is not altogether well-founded, for—whatever may be thought as to the similarity between the restrictions imposed by caste in India and by other artificial contrivances in Europe—it is certain that though the broadly-marked separation of the Bráhman from the Thákur dates from an extremely remote period, the formation of subordinate castes is a process which continues in full operation to the present day and admits of direct observation in all its stages. The course of Indian tradition is to all appearance unbroken, and until some breach of continuity is clearly proved, the modern practice must be acknowledged as the legitimate development of the primary idea.

It is nothing strange that the Hindus themselves should fail to give any reasonable explanation of the matter; since not only are they restricted by religious dogma, but every society is naturally as blind to the phenomena of its own existence as the individual man is unconscious of his daily physical growth. On the other hand, European outsiders, who might be expected to record simple facts with the accuracy of impartial observers, are misled by the prejudices which they have inherited from the early investigators of Oriental literature.

The Code of Manu was among the first, if not the very first Sanskrit didactic work of any importance made known to the world at large through the medium of a translation. At that time it was unhesitatingly accepted as the ultimate authority on all the subjects of which it treated, and hence the fourfold division of Hindu society into Bráhman, Kshatriya, Vaisya and Súdra was universally recognized as an absolute fact. The later discovery of the Vedas, and the vast reach of antiquity which opened out upon their interpretation, made the Mánava Dharma Sástra appear a comparatively modern production. The explanations, which it gives of phenomena dating back in their origin to the remotest past, can only be regarded as theories, not as positive verities; while, again, the vast range of later Sanskrit literature, which has now become available to the student, affords a test of its accuracy in the descriptions which it gives of contemporary society. Impartially judged by either standard, the authority of the Code will be found materially shaken. Its theories of origin are as devoid of Vedic confirmation as its pictures of existent society are irreconcilable with the testimony of all independent literature, whatever the age in which it was produced. If such a clearly defined fourfold division ever existed, how happens it that one-half of the division remains in full force to the present day while the other moiety has sunk into absolute oblivion? The Bráhmanical order is still a living entity, and the Kshatriya is adequately represented in modern speech by the word Thákur, or Rájput, while the Vaisya and Súdra have so completely disappeared—both in name and fact—that an unlettered Hindu will neither understand the words when he hears them, nor recognize the classes implied when their meaning is explained to him.

And not only is this the case in the present day, but it appears to have been so all along. In the great epic poems, in the dramas, and the whole range of miscellaneous literature, the sacerdotal and military classes are everywhere recognized, and mention of them crops up involuntarily in every familiar narrative. But with Vaisya and Súdra it is far different. These words (I speak under correction) never occur as caste names, except with deliberate reference to the Mánava Code. They might be expunged both from the Rámáyana and the Mahábhárat without impairing the integrity of either composition. Only a few moral discourses, which are unquestionably late Bráhmanical interpolations, and one entire episodiacal narrative, would have to be sacrificed; the poem in all essentials would be left intact. But should we proceed in the same way to strike out the Bráhman and the Kshatriya, the whole framework of the poem would immediately collapse. There is abundant mention of Dhívaras and Nápitas, Sútradháras and Kumbhakáras, Mahájanas and Banijes, but no comprehension of them all under two heads in the same familiar way that all chieftains are Kshatriyas, and all priests and litterateurs, Bráhmans.

It is also noteworthy that Manu, in his 12th book, where he classifies gods and men according to their quality (*guna*), omits the Vaisya altogether; and, again, in the Ádi Parvan of the Mahábhárat (v. 3139) we read—

> Brahma-Kshatrádayas tasmád Manor játas tu mánaváh,
> Tato' bhavad, Mahárája, Bráhma Kshattrena sangatam.*

From which it would seem that the writer recognized a definite connection between the Bráhman and the Kshatriya, while all the rest of mankind were

* "Bráhman, Kshatriya and the rest of mankind sprung from this Manu. From him, Sire, came the Bráhman conjoined with the Kshatriya."

relegated to the indeterminate. And further, if the Vaisyas had ever formed one united body, they would inevitably, at some period or another, have taken a more prominent part in Indian politics then there is reason to suppose they ever did. Investiture with the symbolic cord gave them social position, and the wealth which their occupation enabled them to amass gave them power. Union apparently was the only condition required to make them the predominant body in the State. With far humbler pretensions and less internal cohesion than Manu assigns to the Vaisyas, the free cities of Germany and the burghers of England established their independence against an aristocracy and an ecclesiastical system in comparison with which Kshatriyas and Bráhmans were contemptible.

The obvious, and indeed inevitable, inference from this popular ignorance, literary silence, and historical insignificance appears to be that the two classes of Vaisya and Súdra never existed (except in Manu's theory) as distinct bodies; and that the names are merely convenient abstractions to denote the middle and lower orders of society, which have indeed distinctive class features engendered by similarity of occupation, but no community of origin, and in reality no closer blood connection between the component sub-divisions than exists between any one of these sub-divisions and a Bráhmanical or Kshatriya family.

In the whole of the Rig Veda the word Vaisya occurs only once, *viz.*, in the 12th verse of the famous Purusha Súkta. Dr. Muir, Professor Max Muller, and in fact all Sanskrit scholars, with the solitary exception of Dr. Haug, assign this hymn to a comparatively late period. It is the only one which mentions the four different kinds of Vedic composition, *rich*, *sáman*, *chhanda*, and *yajush*, a peculiarity noticed by Professor Aufrecht, and which seems to be absolutely conclusive proof of late composition. And not only is the hymn itself more recent than the body of the work, but the two verses which alone refer to the four castes seem to be a still more modern interpolation. In the first place, there is nothing the least archaic in their style, and they might stand in any one of the Puránas without exciting a comment. That this may be apparent they are quoted in the original :—

> Bráhmano' sya mukham ásíd, báhu Rájanyah kritah,
> Uru tad asya yad Vaisyah, padbhyám Súdro ajáyata.*

Secondly, they are irreconcilable with the context; for while they describe the Bráhman as the mouth of Purusha and the Súdra as born from his feet, the very next lines speak of Indra and Agni as proceeding from his mouth and the Earth from his feet.

*"The Bráhman was his mouth: the Rájanaya was made his arms; what is the Vaisya was his thighs; from his feet sprung the Súdra."

We are, therefore, justified in saying that in the genuine Veda there was no mention of caste whatever ; nor was it possible that there should be, on the hypothesis now to be advanced, that the institution of caste was the simple result of residence in a conquered country. This is confirmed by observing that in Kashmir, which was one of the original homes of the Aryan race, and also for many ages secured by its position from foreign aggression, there is to the present day no distinction of caste, but all Hindus are Bráhmans. Thus, too, the following remarkable lines from the Mahábhárat, which distinctly declare that in the beginning there was no caste division, but all men, as created by God, were Bráhmans :—

> Na visesho' sti varnánám, sarvam Bráhmam idam jagat,
> Brahmaná púrva srishtam hi ; karmabhir varnatám gatam.*

At the time when the older Vedic hymns were written, the Aryan was still in his primeval home and had not descended upon the plains of Hindustan. After the invasion, the conquerors naturally resigned all menial occupations to the aborigines, whom they had vanquished and partially dispossessed, and enjoyed the fruits of victory while prosecuting the congenial pursuits of arms or letters. For several years, or possibly generations, the invaders formed only a small garrison in a hostile country, and constant warfare necessitated the formation of a permanent military body, the ancestors of the modern Kshatriyas and Thákurs. The other part devoted themselves to the maintenance of the religious rites, which they brought with them from their trans-Himalayan home, and the preservation of the sacred hymns and formulæ used in the celebration of public worship. Of this mystic and unwritten lore, once familiar to all, but now, through the exigency of circumstances, retained in the memory of only a few, these special families would soon become the sole depositories. The interval between the two classes gradually widened, till the full-blown Bráhman was developed, conscious of his superior and exclusive knowledge, and bent upon asserting its prerogatives. The conquered aborigines were known by the name of Nágas or Mlechhas, or other contemptuous term, and formed the nucleus of all the low castes, whom Manu subsequently grouped together as Súdras, esteeming them little, if at all, higher than the brute creation. (*Hastinas cha turangás cha Súdrá Mlechchhás cha garhitáh—Sinhá vyághrá varáhás cha.* XII. 43.)†

---

*" There is no distinction of castes; the whole of this world is Bráhmanical as originally created by Brahma; it is only in consequence of men's actions that it has come into a state of caste divisions."

† " Elephants, horses, Súdras, despicable barbarians, lions, tigers and boars."

But a society, consisting only of priests, warriors, and slaves could not long exist. Hence the gradual formation of a middle class, consisting of the offspring of mixed marriages, enterprizing natives, and such unaspiring members of the dominant race as found trade more profitable, or congenial to their tastes, than either arms or letters. The character of this mixed population would be influenced in the first instance by the nature of the country in which they were resident. In one district the soil would be better adapted for pasturage, in another for agriculture. But in both it would be worked principally by aborigines, both on account of the greater labour involved, and also because the occupation of grazing large flocks and herds (which had been characteristic of the Aryan race in Vedic times) is incompatible with the concentration which is essential for the security of a small invading force. The graziers would receive some name descriptive of their nomadic habits, as for example 'Ahír'; the word being derived from *abhi*, 'circum' and *ir*, 'ire,' the '*circumeuntes*,' or wanderers. Similarly, other pastoral tribes—such as the Gwálás and the Ghosís—derive their distinctive names from *go*, 'a cow,' combined with *pála*, 'a keeper,' and *ghosha*, 'a cattle station.' In an agricultural district the corresponding class would in like manner adopt some title indicative of their occupation, as, for example, the Kisáns from *krishi*, 'husbandry,' the Bhúnhárs from *bhúmi*, 'the ground,' and in Bengal the Chásis from *chás*, 'ploughing. Or (and the same remark applies to every other class) they might retain the old Indian name of the district in which they were located, as the Káchhis from the country of Kachh. Again, so long as vast tracts of lands were still covered with forest, the followers of the chase would be at least as numerous as the tillers of the soil or the grazers of cattle. And, since the Aryan element in the middle and lower strata of society was composed of those perons who, without any *penchant* for learned study like the Bráhmans, entertained a preference for sedentary pursuits rather than those of a more exciting nature such as the májority of their Thákur kinsmen affected, so the castes that followed the chase, not as an amusement, but as a means of livelihood, would naturally consist exclusively of aborigines. And as a matter of fact, it is found to be the case that all such castes have the dark complexion and the other physical characteristics of the lower race. Such are the Badhaks and Aheriyas, who derive their name—the one from the root, *badh*, 'to kill,' the other from the Hindi *aher*, 'game,—so, too, the Dhánuks and the Lodhas, whose names are contracted forms of Dhánushka,' 'a bowman,' and Lubdhaka, 'a huntsman.' These two tribes have now abandoned their hereditary avocations,—the Dhánuks being ordinarily village watchmen, and the Lodhas agriculturists,—though in Oudh the latter were, till quite recently, still connected with the forest rather than the fields, being the wood-cutters, whose business it was to fell timber and transport it by the Ghoghra river to Bahram Ghát and other marts.

In this way the majority of the servile or so-called Súdra castes came into existence, in order to supply the unproductive classes with food; and subsequently, when population grew and towns were built, their number was vastly increased by the new trades that sprung up to satisfy the more complex requirements of urban life. Then, too, last of all, and by no means simultaneously with the other three, as represented in the legends, the Vaisya order was produced. For the purpose of facilitating barter and exchange, traders established themselves, either on the sea-coast, or at places convenient of access for the inhabitants of two dissimilar tracts of country, and forming a confederation among themselves would take a collective name, either from the locality which they occupied, as Ajudhyávásis, Mathuriyas, or Agarwálás, or simply from the special branch of trade which they pursued, as Sonárs, Lohiyas, or Baniyas. From the facility of acquiring wealth and the civilizing influence of social contact, these merchants would soon form a striking contrast to the simple rural population who brought their produce for barter, and would receive some vulgar title indicative of the difference; hence the name of Mahájans, 'the great people.' And all such names, having once firmly attached themselves, would be retained, even when they ceased to be strictly applicable, in consequence of migration from the original seat, or change in profession or circumstances.

Upon this theory we come to a clear understanding of the popular feeling about caste—a feeling which unmistakeably exists in the native mind, though opposed to dogmatic teaching—that below the Bráhman and the Thákur there are a number of miscellaneous divisions, but no two well-defined collective groups. There is a vague impression that the Vaisya is properly a tradesman and the Súdra a servant; while it is definitely ruled that the former is the much more respectable appellation of the two. Thus a difficulty arises with regard to a family that is distinctly neither of Bráhman nor Thákur descent, and from time immemorial has been engaged in some specially ignoble trade or exceptionally honourable service. The latter aspires to be included in the higher order, in spite of his servitude; while the former, though a trader, is popularly ranked in the same grade as people who, if they are to be known by any class name at all, are clearly Súdras. This never occurs in precisely the same way with the two higher Mánava castes, though one or two facts may be quoted which at first sight seem to tell against such an assertion. For example, there are a numerous body of carpenters called Ojhas (the word being a corruption of Upádhyáya), who are admitted to be of Bráhmanical descent and are invested with the sacred cord. But common interests forming a stronger bond of union than common origin, they are regarded rather as a species of the genus Barhai than of the genus Bráhman; their claim, however, to the latter title never being disputed if they choose to assert it. Similarly, as the trade of the usurer is highly incompatible with priestly pretensions, the Bráhmans who practise it are gradually being recognized as quite a distinct caste under the name of 'Bohras and Athwarayas.' There are also some *pseudo*-Bráhmanical and *pseudo*-Thákur tribes who rank very low in the social scale; but even their case is by no means a parallel one, for it is admitted on all sides that the original ancestor of—for example—the Bháts and Ahivásis was a Bráhman, and of the Gauruas a Thákur. The doubt is whether the descendants, in consequence of the bend-sinister on their blazon, have altogether lost their ancestral title or only tarnished its dignity; whereas with a Sonár who claims to be a Vaisya, it is not any suspicion of illegitimate descent, nor any incompatibility of employment, that raises a doubt, but rather the radical incompleteness of the original theory and the absence of any standard by which his pretensions may be tested.

In short, excepting only the Bráhman and the Thákur, all other Indian castes correspond, not to the Scottish clans—with which they are so often compared, and from which they are utterly dissimilar—but to the close guilds which in mediæval times had so great an influence on European society. As the Goldsmiths formed themselves into a *company* for mutual protection, so the Sonárs combined to make a *caste*;—the former admitted many provincial guilds with special customs and regulations, the latter recognized many subordinate *gotras*; the former required a long term of apprenticeship amounting virtually to adoption, the latter made the profession hereditary; the former required an oath of secrecy, the latter insured secrecy by restricting social intercourse with outsiders. As the founders of the company had no mutual connection beyond community of interest, so neither had the founders of the caste. When we say that all architects are sons of S. Barbara or all shoemakers of S. Crispin, those being their patron saints, the expression is quite intelligible. What more is implied in saying that Sanádhs are sons of Sanat-Kumára? To attach any literal meaning to a tradition which represents a Bráhmanical caste as born of the Gáyatri (a Vedic metre) is a precisely similar absurdity to saying a company was born of the Pater Noster and Ave Maria, because on certain days every member was bound to repeat his rosary. A history of caste in the sense in which the phrase is generally understood, *viz.*, the tracing each caste to one definite pair of ancestors, is from the circumstances of the case an impossibility.

With Bráhmans and Kshatriyas matters stand somewhat differently. Though, so far as any one subordinate division is concerned, it may often happen that its individual members never at any time formed one family, yet as all the subdivisions are in the main descendants of the early Aryan conquerors, to that limited extent they have a genuine community of origin. So long as the line of demarcation which separated them from the aboriginal inhabitants of India remained clearly defined, while the only distinction among themselves lay in the difference of occupation, the conversion of a Kshatriya into a Bráhman would not be a more unusual occurrence than the retirement of a Christian knight, when wearied with warfare, into the peaceful seclusion of the cloister. The most famous example of such a transformation is that supplied by the legend of Visvámitra, which must ever prove an insuperable difficulty to the orthodox Hindú, who accepts the Mánava doctrine of an essential and eternal difference between the two castes. At the present day, when Bráhmanism has become an inseparable hereditary quality, the priestly character has been transferred to the religious mendicants and ascetics who—allowing for the changed circumstances of time and place—correspond to the Bráhmans of antiquity, and like them freely admit associates from every rank and condition of Hindú society. The apparent difference is mainly due to the fact that in primitive times the Aryan outsiders were all of one status, while now they are infinite in variety.

Theoretically, the essence of the Kshatriya is as incapable of transfer or acquisition, except by natural descent, as that of the Bráhman, but the practice of the two classes has always been very different. The strength of a community that lays claim to any esoteric knowledge lies in its exclusiveness; but a military body thrives by extension, and to secure its own efficiency must be lax in restrictions. It may be observed as a singular fact that all the very lowest castes in the country, if interrogated as to their origin, will say that they are in some way or another Thákur: and this is illustrated by a passage in Manu, where he mentions several outcast tribes as Kshatriyas by descent. Whence we may infer that at all times there has been a great freedom of intercourse between that class and others. Indeed, if we are to accept the legend of Parasurám as in any sense expressing an historical event, the whole Thákur race has been repeatedly extirpated and as often re-formed out of alien elements. Nor is this at variance with modern usage, for no Hindú rises to the rank of Rájá, whatever his original descent, without acquiring a kind of Thákur character, which in most instances is unhesitatingly claimed by, and conceded to, his descendants in the third or fourth generation, after alliances with older families have given some colour to the pretension. And the illegitimate sons of Thákurs, who by the Code of Manu would be Ugras—their mothers being Musalmánis or low-caste Hindú women—are, as is notorious, generally accepted, either themselves or in the person of their immediate descendants, as genuine Thákurs. Again, many of the higher Thákur classes acknowledge the impurity of their birth in the popular tradition of their origin. Thus the Chandels (*i.e.*, the moon-born) profess to be derived from the daughter of a Banáras Bráhman, who had an intrigue with the moon-god ; and Gahlots (the cave-born) from a Ráni of Mewár, who took refuge with some mountaineers on the Málya range.

From all this it follows that, whatever the dignity and antiquity of some particular Thákur families, the Thákur caste is a heterogeneous body, which, like the miscellaneous communities of lower pretensions which we have already discussed, is held together more by similarity of circumstances than unity of origin. The same principle of caste-formation is still actively at work through all grades of Indian society. The comparatively modern organization of many so-called castes is attested by the Persian names which they have thought proper to assume,—for example, the Darzis, the Malláhs, the Mimárs, &c. A large proportion of the first-named are really Káyaths, which shows that the term 'Darzi' is still in a transitional state, and has not yet thoroughly shaken off its original trade meaning. The older word for a tailor is *sáji*, which, like so much of the Hindi vocabulary, having become unfashionable, now implies a workman of an inferior description. Similarly, *randi*, 'a woman,' has become a term of reproach for 'a woman of bad character'; and *nagara*, Hindi for 'a city,' is used at the present day to denote, not even a village, but only a mere 'hamlet.' The desire to dignify a mean calling by a high-sounding name—as when a sweeper is called *mihtar*, 'a prince,' and a cook *khalífa*—has been often cited as an Oriental idiosyncracy, which to the mind of a European is productive of ridicule rather than respect. It gives occasion, however, to many a new caste-name. Thus the *khákrob*, or street-sweeper of the town, regards himself under the Persian designation as the superior of the village *bhangi* or scavenger ; and the Mimár, or bricklayer, the Shoragar, or saltpetre manufacturer ; the Chúna-paz, or lime-burner ; the Kori, or weaver, and even the Mochi or cobbler, in assuming the name descriptive of his calling, almost forgets that he belongs to the universally-despised caste of the Chamár.

To judge from the Census Returns, it would seem that these partially-developed castes are only recognized in some few districts and totally ignored in others. Thus, Mathurá is a great centre of the stone-cutter's art; but the men who practise it belong to different ranks, and have not adopted the distinctive trade-name of *sang-tarásh,* which seems to be recognized in Aligarh, Hamírpúr, and Kumaon. Again, in every market town there are a number of weighmen, who, no doubt, in each place have special guild regulations of their own; but only in Banáras do they appear as a distinct caste, with the name of *palle-dárs.* So too at Sahåranpur some fruit-sellers—whose trade, it may be presumed, has been encouraged by the large public garden at that station—have separated themselves from the common herd of *Kunjrás,* or 'costermongers,' and decorated their small community with the Persian title of *Mewafarosh.* As might be expected, this disintegration of society and adoption of a novel nomenclature prevails most extensively among the lower orders, where the associations connected with the old name that is discarded are of an unpleasant nature. But even in the higher classes, where the generic title is one of honour, it is frequently superseded in common parlance by one that is more distinctive, though it may be of less favourable import. Thus, among Bráhmans a Bohra sub-caste is in course of formation, and a Cháube of the Mathurá branch, when settled elsewhere, is invariably styled neither Bráhman nor Chaube, but Mathuriya. Illustrations might be multiplied indefinitely; but the few now cited are sufficient to prove how caste subdivisions are formed in the present day, and to suggest how they originated in the first instance.

APPENDIX B.

THE CATHOLIC CHURCH.

Subscriptions.

	Rs.
The Right Rev. the Lord Bishop of Agra	1,200
Proceeds of a Lottery, through the Very Rev. Father Symphorien ...	1,250
Priests of the Mission	75
Lord Ralph Kerr, Lt.-Col., 10th Royal Hussars	1,150
Viscount Campden, do. do.	500
Surgeon-Major Cattell, do. do.	50
W. H. Watkins, Captain, do. do.	50
Boyce Combe, Captain, do. do.	25
The Hon. C. C. W. Cavendish, do. do.	25
E. A. H. Roe, Surgeon, do. do.	20
J. Pembroke, Lieut., Commissariat Officer	125
Col. Dillon, C.B., C.S.I.	50
Offertory, All Saints' Day, 1874	25
Seth Gobind Das, C.S.I.*	1,100
H. H. the Mahárája of Chirkhári, Bundelkhand...	500
Rája Hari Náráyan Sinh, of Háthras	425
Lála Syám Sundar Dás	300
Sri Mahárája Gosain Purushottam Lál, of Gokul	400
Raja Prithi Sinh, of Awa	100
F. S. Growse, C. S.	4,700
Malcolm Reade, C. S.	50
Percy Wigram, C. S.	100
M. A. McConaghey, C. S.	50
C. F. Hall, C. S.	25
J. H. Twigg, C. S.	25
Ross Scott, C. S.	20
H. L. Harrison, C. S.	10
C. G. Hind, District Engineer	100
D'Arcy McArthy	100
Messrs. Ellis, Merchants, Agra	75
H. Neil, Assistant Patrol, Customs...	15
Conductor Higher	15
A. H. Davis, Assistant Supdt. of Police	20
A. B. Seaman, Civil Surgeon	50
Mahbúb Masih	50
R. A. Lloyd, Education Department	50

* The sanction of the Government was obtained, in the first instance, before a subscription was accepted from any Hindu gentleman.

				Rs.
W. N. Boutflower, Education Department	...	...	...	20
H. Prince, Superintending Engineer	...	...	...	50
Lt.-Col. F. C. Anderson... ...	...	...	...	50
Captain Ellaby, R A.	...	...	...	20
Offertory, All Saints' Day, 1876 ...	...	...	...	133
		Total	...	13,098

Donations.

Statues of the Sacred Heart, of the B. Virgin and Child, and of S. Joseph, from the Dowager Marchioness of Lothian and the Duchess of Buccleuch (through Lord Ralph Kerr).

Life-size crucifix (indulgenced), from Lord Ralph Kerr.

Persian carpeting for the Altar steps, from J. W. Tyler, M.D., F.R.C.S.

A crystal chandelier for the Choir, from Mr. John Ellis, Agra.

A crystal chandelier and a marble chair, from Seth Raghunáth Dás.

A marble chair ; from Lála Badri Prasád.

The Font, from Lála Ratn Lal.

The Stations of the Cross, from the Men of the 10th Royal Hussars.

The above lists are inserted in this volume as an interesting record of the cordiality that prevailed among all classes of the community during my official connection with Mathurá, and as a permanent acknowledgment of the generous assistance that I received in carrying out a project which I had greatly at heart. A description of the unfinished building has been given in an earlier chapter. Any want of congruity that may be detected in the design is mainly attributable to the same cause as paralyzes the action of almost every District Officer in India, *viz.*, his liability at any moment to be transferred to some entirely different part of the country. As I was not in a position to put down the whole of the money at once, and did not wish, in case of my sudden removal, to leave the Mission burdened with a design which it would require a very large outlay to complete, I commenced the work in a simple and inexpensive style, and pushed it on as rapidly as possible. By the end of the year, when part of it had been roofed in and roughly furnished, I felt myself at liberty to launch out into more elaborate architecture, which I intended to continue so long as I was on the spot, but which could be stopped without serious practical injury to the fabric, if I were removed. Many of the bald features,

which now strike the eye unpleasantly, were intended as merely temporary make-shifts, and, if I had been allowed the time, would gradually have given way to something better; carved stone being everywhere substituted for plain brick and mortar. The interior, with the important exception of the High Altar, is virtually complete, and is to my mind both religious and picturesque in its effect. The external façade, as it now stands, conveys a very imperfect idea of what it was meant to be. The building was intended as a protest against the standard plans and other stereotyped conventionalities of the Public Works Department; and it has at least the one great architectural merit of being absolutely truthful; no one on seeing it but would immediately understand that it was a Catholic Church, built in an eastern country for the use of a mixed congregation of Europeans and orientals. As a proof that in some quarters at all events my idea was thoroughly appreciated, I cannot resist the pleasure of appending an extract from a letter which appeared in the correspondence columns of the London *Tablet*, in its issue for October 26th, 1878:—

"To Mr. F. S. Growse, of the Bengal Civil Service, we owe an ecclesiastical building which is quite unique of its sort in India, and may in the richness of its details compare favourably with approved European workmanship. The munificence of that gentleman, combined with rare artistic taste, has enabled him to cull all the rich treasures of a rich neighbourhood in the service of religion. His knowledge of the district of which he is both the historian and the renovator pre-eminently fitted him for this labour of love. Mathura chapel is a combination of Christian and pagan art, and peculiarly interesting as the sole work of native artists, whose chisels have certainly not diminished the beauty and solemnity associated with altar and sanctuary. Finer or more elaborate carving could not be seen anywhere. Men acquainted with the delicate screen work of India will find it here for the first time engrafted on a Christian church, conveying the solemnizing effect of stained glass. Rigidly adhering to the idea of employing native art alone, Mr. Growse has to the smallest item excluded articles of exotic growth, substituting, for instance, Murádabad vases for the trumpery foreign importations so frequently seen on other altars.

"The remark of Mr. Fergusson that 'Architecture in India is a living art' is nowhere more happily illustrated than in the recent restorations of Mathurá, a work also due to Mr. Growse. Engaged in those restorations, the thought must naturally have arisen in connection with English buildings, why employ English models, often alike incompatible with the climate and genius of the people, when there are indigenous ones, and those far more beautiful, near at hand? Why disfigure the Oriental landscape with buildings as incapable of appealing to the sympathies of the people as of meeting the requirements of art and comfort? Along, too, with considerations about architecture would come the thought—why not employ Indian arts more generally?

"It may be unorthodox to say so, but I confess the most sumptuous English fanes in India communicate a very different impression to that communicated by a visit to the Pearl Mosque at Agra. What that impression is any reader of Bishop Heber will easily understand. So great is it, that one may be pardoned for wishing to impregnate an Indian Christian temple with some of its distinctive features.

"This is precisely what Mr. Growse has done at Mathurá; and I can conceive no more graceful way of familiarising natives with Christian symbols than bringing them to ornament them with their own matchless art. Prejudice is at once silenced, and sympathy, if not inquiry, aroused. An attempt is made to place ourselves in accord with something they most cherish in their affections. We sound a note of nature, and, in doing so, may lay claim to some reciprocal esteem. It is the same policy that crowned with success the labours of S. Francis Xavier in Southern India, and in more recent times illumined the path of the Abbé Dubois. These saintly men sought the empire of the mind through the empire of the heart.

"Any endeavour to revive such a policy in Northern India ought to be a source of unmixed satisfaction. Mr. Growse's chapel stands as a speck of the ocean, under the shadow of the great Hindu city of Krishna. May it some day stimulate a work in inverse ratio to its size."

APPENDIX C.

LIST OF TREES THAT GROW IN THE DISTRICT.

ADANSONIA digitata ; no native name : the Baobab or monkey-bread tree ; two fine specimens in one of the gardens in cantonments.

AGASTI, from the Hindu saint of that name ; Æschynomene or Sesbania grandiflora ; a small soft-wooded tree with large handsome flowers, which are eaten as a vegetable.

AKOL, for Sanskrit *ankola ;* a small tree with yellow flowers, which I have seen only in the Konai *rakhya*, where there are several specimens of it. Apparently the Alangium.

ÁM, for Sanskrit *ámra ;* Mangifera Indica, the mango tree.

AMALTÁS, Cassia Fistula ; the Indian Laburnum.

ÁMLÁ, from the Sanskrit *amla*, the Latin *amara*, with reference to the acidity of its fruit. Phyllanthus Emblica, or Emblica officinalis.

ARNI, Clerodendrum Phlomoides, a shrub with sweet-scented flowers, resembling the honey-suckle.

ARUA, for Sanskrit *aralu*, Ailanthus excelsa. A fine forest tree, with leaves from two to three feet long, and panicles of yellowish flowers. Frequent in the avenue along the Mathurá and Delhi road.

ASOK, Sanskrit *asoka ;* Saraca Indica or Jonesia Asoka ; indigenous in the forests of southern India, where it is famous for its magnificent red flowers ; I have never seen it blossom here.

BÁBIRANG, Embelia robusta, a small tree, called by that name at Naugáma in the Chhátá pargana, but apparently known in other villages as the *ajánrukh ;* flowers in February and March when almost bare of leaves. It is used as a remedy for colds and rheumatism (*bai*), which may be the origin of the name.

BABÚL, Acacia Arabica.

BAHERA, for Sanskrit *vibhítaka*, Terminalia bellerica. A tall straight-growing tree with large leaves and greenish yellow flowers of unpleasant smell. Fruit a large ovoid nut, used in dyeing and tanning, also as a medicine and for making ink ; the kernels are eaten, but are said to be intoxicating. Frequent in the avenue on the Mathurá and Delhi road.

BAKÁYAN, Melia Azedarach, a small tree, which for a few weeks in the spring presents a handsome appearance with its large clusters of lilac flowers, but for the greater part of the year it is leafless and ragged-looking, with bunches of dry yellow fruit.

BAR, for Sanskrit *vata*, Ficus Bengalensis, the Banyan tree.

BARNA, for Sanskrit *varana*, Cratœva religiosa. Flowers and puts forth new leaves in April, when its large cream-coloured blossoms give it a handsome appearance.

BEL, for Sanskrit *vilva*, Ægle marmelos. The pulp of the fruit is used for making sherbet; also to mix with mortar. The leaves are sacred to Mahádev.

BER, for Sanskrit *badara;* Zizyphus jujuba; cultivated for its fruit.

CHHONKAR, Prosopis spicigera; very common throughout the district; occasionally grows to quite a large tree, as in the Dohani Kund at Chaksauli. It is used for religious worship at the festival of the Dasahara, and considered sacred to Siva. The pods (called *sangri*) are much used for fodder. Probably *chhonkar* and *sangri*, which latter is in some parts of India the name of the tree as well as of the pod, are both dialectical corruptions of the Sanskrit *sankara*, a name of Siva; for the palatal and sibilant are frequently interchangeable.

DHÁK, for Sanskrit *dagdha*, 'on fire,' with reference to its bright flame-coloured flowers; Butea frondosa.

DHO, for Sanskrit *dhava*, covers the whole of the Barsána hill; is apparently the Anogeissus pendula or myrtifolia. A small tree, nearly bare of leaves all through the dry season.

DUNGAL, another name for the Pílu.

FARÁS, Tamarix articulata, a graceful tree of rapid growth, readily propagated from cuttings.

GONDI, Cordia Rothii, a small tree. The fruit, a berry with a yellow, gelatinous, pellucid pulp, is edible, but insipid. The viscidity of the fruit gives its name to the tree (from *gond*, 'gum').

GÚLAR, Ficus glomerata, a large tree, the wood of which is specially used for well frames, as it is all the more durable for being in water. Its fruit grows in *clusters* on the branches and trunk; whence probably the vernacular name (from *gola* a 'ball'): the same peculiarity has suggested its botanical epithet, glomerata.

GANGER, a small scraggy shrub at Charan Pahár, Barsána and elsewhere, apparently a species of Grewia.

KINGOT, Balanites Roxburghii, a small thorny tree, with a hard fruit, which is filled with gunpowder and used for fireworks. Its roots spread far and throw up suckers at a considerable distance from the trunk.

HÝNS, Capparis sepiaria, a very strong, thorny creeper.

IMLI, Tamarindus Indica, one of the largest, handsomest, and most valuable of all Indian trees, but a very slow grower. But for this last defect it would be an excellent avenue tree, as it is never leafless and gives shade all the year round.

INDRAJAU, Wrightia tinctoria. At Charan Pahár. Bare of leaves in the cold weather, at which time it is hung with bunches of long, slender, dark-green pods, each pair cohering slightly at the tip.

JÁMAN, for Sanskrit *Jambu:* Eugenia jambolana; generally planted round the border of large mango orchards. Is never leafless. The fruit, like a damson in appearance, has a harsh but sweetish flavour.

JHAU, Tamarix dioica; a dwarf variety of the Farás, which springs up after the rains on the sands of the Jamuná, where it forms a dense jungle.

KACHNÁR, for Sanskrit *Kanchanára,* Bauhinia variegata; a moderate sized tree, which presents a beautiful appearance in March and April, when in full flower.

KADAMB, Sanskrit *Kadamba.* Abundant in the Chhátá and Kosi parganas, where it forms large woods, as especially at Pisáya. There are two kinds, the more common being the Stephigyne parvifolia; the other, a much finer tree, the Anthocephalus Cadamba, or Nauclea Cadamba of Roxburgh.

KAIT, for Sanskrit *Kapittha*; Feronia elephantum; the elephant or woodapple. An ornamental tree with a hard round fruit; the leaves have a slight smell of aniseed.

KATIAIYA, Celtis Australis (?) at Pisáya. A middle-sized tree with yellowish-white flowers and eatable fruit.

KATIYÁRI, Xylosma (?). A small tree with dense sombre foliage, long stiff thorns, and flowers in small yellow tufts like the babúl.

KARÝL, for Sanskrit *Karira;* Capparis aphylla; the typical fruit of Braj.

KHAJÚR, for Sanskrit *Khajúra;* Phœnix Sylvestris; the wild date palm.

KHIRNI, for Sanskrit *Kshírini,* 'the milky'; Mimusops Indica; a large evergreen tree with a fruit that ripens in May and June and tastes like a dried currant.

KHANDÁR, Salvadora Persica. A tree very similar to the Pílu, but of more graceful growth. Its fruit is uneatable.

LABERA, and LASORA, two varieties of the Cordia latifolia. A soft-wooded, crooked-growing tree, with eatable fruit.

Laliyári, a middle-sized tree which presents a very handsome appearance with its large dull-red and yellow flowers, which open in February and March. The tree appears to be very rare and little known and I cannot trace it in any botanical work. There is one on the Shergarh and Kosi road, another at Barsána, and others near Dotána. I tried to rear it in my own garden, but the young trees died after I left. The name is obviously derived from the colour (*lál*) of the flowers, but natives take the word to be *lariyari*, 'quarrelsome,' and have a prejudice against it accordingly.

Mahúa, for Sanskrit *madhuka*, with allusion to the sweetness of its flowers; Bassia latifolia; scarce in the district.

Málsari, Mimusops elengi, an evergreen tree with sweet-scented starshaped flowers, which are used for garlands; whence the name, from *mála*, a 'garland' and *sara*, a 'string.'

Ním, for Sanskrit *nimba*, Melia Indica, the tree which thrives better in the district than any other.

Ním Chambeli, otherwise called Biláyati Bakáyan; Millingtonia hortensis; a handsome, fast-growing tree with fragrant white flowers.

Nausath, Erythrina Indica, the Indian coral-tree. Its flowers, of a dazzling bright scarlet, make a fine show in March, before the new leaves appear. The name would seem to be a corruption of *nava sapta*, 16; with reference to the 16 modes of enhancing personal beauty; as if they had all been exercised upon this beautiful tree.

Pápri, Ulmus integrifolia; a large tree, bare of leaves in the cold weather.

Páras-Pípar, a name which probably means 'the Persian *pipal*.' A tree found only at two places in this district, the Dhru-tila at Mathurá and the Khelan-ban at Mahá-ban. The flower closely resembles that of the cotton plant. There are avenues of it in some of the streets of Bombay.

Pasendu, Diospyros cordifolia; a small tree with dense foliage, but considered an unlucky tree to take shade under; very common in the *rakhyas*. It has an uneatable fruit of unpleasant smell and bitter taste.

Pílu, with the same name in Sanskrit; Salvadora oleoides; forms large woods in the Chhátá and Kosi parganas. A stunted misshapen-looking tree, generally with cracked or hollow trunk and exposed roots. It bears an eatable fruit.

Pilúkhan. Ficus cordifolia; a large tree rarely found in the district. It may be seen at Konai and in the Kokila-ban. It is common in the neigbourhood of Hari-dwár.

PÍPAL, for Sanskrit *pippala;* Ficus religosa.

REMJA, Acacia leucophlæa; a thorny tree common in the *rakhyas* in conjunction with the Chhonkar.

RÍTHA, for Sanskrit *arishta;* Sapindus detergens; the soap berry tree; found at Satoha.

SAHAJNA. For Sanskrit *sobhánjana;* Moringa pterygosperma or Hyperanthera moringa; the horse-radish tree.

SAHORA, Streblus asper (?). A small scraggy tree with rough dark-green leaves and eatable fruit, a yellow one-seeded berry. Single trees are common all over the district.

SHAH-TÚT. Morus Indica; the mulberry tree.

SEMAL, for Sanskrit *Salmali;* Bombax heptaphyllum; the cotton tree. Flowers in March when bare of leaves, like the kachnár, dhák, and nausath.

SIRIS, for Sanskrit *sirisha,* is the vernacular name both for the Acacia speciosa, which, in spite of its botanical epithet, is a very unsightly tree for a great part of the year, when its branches are bare of leaves and hung only with large, dry, yellow pods, rattling with every breath of wind. The same name is given to a similar but larger and much handsomer tree, the Albizzia odoratissima, which has red-brown legumes.

GLOSSARY.

ÁDHAM SÚDH, half.

AIKLI-BAIKLI, incoherent nonsense.

AINTH, pride, conceit.

ÁKÁSI VRITT, dependence on the rains; said of fields where there is no artificial irrigation.

ÁLA, wet.

ALAL-TAPPU, incoherent, absurd.

ALÁNA BATÁNA, strangers.

ALÍN, a stone jamb of a doorway; a pilaster, or attached pillar, as distinguished from *khambh*, a detached pillar.

AMÁNA, obstinate; incredulous.

AMER, delay, late.

AMOLAK, invaluable; coal-dust used as a dry colour in making *sánjhis*.

ÁN, a curse.

ANAKHTOTA, extraordinary.

ANOSAR (for *an-avasar*), want of leisure, domestic work.

ANTÁ CHIT, senseless.

ANTI, an ear-ring.

ATHEN (for *athmana*), evening.

ATÚTI, fire.

A-UD, literally 'waterless;' a term applied to a man who dies childless, with no son to make him the ordinary funeral libations. It is also the name given to the little masonry platform often seen near a village, on which twice a year jars of water are set, in order to lay the ghost of some childless person.

BAITHAK, the village club and hospice; also a rest-house at a holy place for the accommodation of the Gosáin on his annual visit on the feast-day.

BÁKHAR, a house.

BÁRAH-BÁS, a term used vaguely with reference to any large and ancient village to imply that a number of hamlets, though not necessarily exactly twelve, have been founded from it. Such are Bhadanwára, Barauth, &c., of which a rustic will say:—*Uske bárah-bás hain; aise kahte hain; kuchh base hain; kuchh újar hain.*

BARDH, an ox.

BARHI, a class of weavers.

BÁS, a hamlet, as distinguished from *kherá*, the parent settlement.

Bhábhi, a brother's wife (for *bhrátri-vadhú*).

Bhagavadíya, devout.

Bhainkra, crying, as of a child.

Bharna, the capital of a pillar.

Bharota, a bundle of wood or fodder.

Bháyen, to, for, as regards.

Bhor, the first watering of any crop.

Bhúá, a father's sister.

Bhúmiya, a low altar or platform on the outskirts of a village, dedicated to the local divinity, or rather demon, corresponding to the Grám Devi of the Mainpuri and other districts. It often resembles in form a Muhammadan grave, consisting of an oblong block of stone or brickwork with a recessed pillar at one end; offerings are made upon it to avert the spells of witchcraft, &c.

Bhúmra, early morning.

Bhusri, of a dull red colour, as a cow.

Birokha, afternoon.

Bitonda, a stack of cow-dung fuel.

Biyárá, supper-time, evening.

Bohr-gat, the trade of a *bohrá*, or money-lender.

Bot, a flat earthenware flask holding about two sers.

Bundi, tail-less.

Chachá, a father's younger brother.

Chenta-poti, the young of insects or lower animals generally.

Chhail-kari, a small ring worn in the upper part of the ear.

Chhajja, stone eaves of a house or other building, supported on projecting brackets.

Chattra, a dole-house, where cooked food is given in charity to indigent applicants.

Chhará, small, paltry, slight; as *chhari sawárì*, 'a small retinue.'

Chhari, the shaft of a pillar.

Chhenkna, to reject, excommunicate.

Chhora, **Chhori**, a boy, a girl.

Chira, the capital of a pillar, when it has brackets attached to it.

Chunai, masonry work.

Dadhaiya, fresh, as a colour.

Dangra, a bullock or other horned animal of inferior quality.

Darír, a line.

Dariya, a coloured shawl worn by married women.

Dása, in architecture, a string-course.

Dehri, a threshhold; also a strip of pavement between two piers of an arcade.

Dhar, stature.

Dherh, a Chamár.

Dhevati, a daughter's daughter.

Dhíng-Dhingi, force, violence.

Dhúmar (for Sanskrit *dhúmla*), smoke-coloured, dun, as a cow.

Dila, in architecture, a panel.

Dobra, a long piece of cloth of double width, used as a carpet.

Dola-pát, the masonry pillars and stone cross-bar supporting the pulley over a well worked by bullocks.

Doli hona, to go away.

Dothain, early morning, sunrise.

Elak, a sieve.

Faujdár, a title much affected by Játs and used simply as equivalent to their caste name.

Gami (for *grámya*) rustic, clownish.

Garai, the occupation of a grazier (for *gwárai*).

Gariyárá, or **Gárára**, a cart-track.

Garua, a brass drinking vessel.

Gauchh, the moustache.

Gaurua, a name given to certain clans of Thákur descent, that are held in lower esteem than other branches of the same parent stock, in consequence of their lax views regarding marriage and other social institutions.

Ghyau, used by the Chaubes for *ghí*.

Gohnjo, **Gohnjí**, a father-in-law, mother-in-law.

Gokh (for *gaváksha*), a look-out; a window on an upper story with a projecting balcony.

Gola, a bundle of leaves, fodder, &c., and specially of *jhar-beri*.

Gonána, to escort pilgrims.

Gonáwa, an escorter of pilgrims. Bráhmans of this description are always going backwards and forwards between Mathurá and Brinda-ban.

Got (for *goshtha*, a cattle-pen), an enclosure usually made by a thorn fence and used for stacking straw, fuel, &c., or stalling cattle.

Guhar, a confederacy.

Gunda, wicked.

Guth-jána, to close in wrestling.

Habkau, excessive greed.

Hambai, yes.

HÁNGI, a fine linen sieve for sifting flour, as distinct from *chalni*, a coarse sieve for grain.

HÁTÁ-CHÁNTI, a dexterous theft from under one's own eye.

HATO, HATE, was, were (for *thá* and *the*).

HAY HAY, properly an interjection, but often used as a noun meaning greed; thus, *usko rupaye ki háy háy rahi hai*, 'he is most greedy for money.'

HEJ, affection.

HELA PÁRNA, to call, shout.

HILÁWA, an untrained beast of draught, yoked as an outrigger.

HUN, I, for *main* or *ham* : as *wahán hún gayo hato*, 'I had gone there.'

HURDANG, a disorderly dance.

I, frequently substituted for *a* as in *Lachhmin* for *Lachhman*.

INCH, an undertaking on the part of the village baniya to settle the landlord's demand for rent on the security of the tenant's crops, of which he takes delivery after harvest. The arrangement, which results in an account of the most complicated description, is so carried out as totally to fustrate the intentions of some of the main provisions of the Rent Law ; and, as it pauperizes the tenant without in any way enriching the landlord, it may justly be regarded as one of the main causes of the prevalent agricultural distress. The institution of Government banks seems to be the only means of checking the evil. At present Rs. 8-2-0 per cent. per mensem is not an uncommon rate of interest.

INDHAN, properly 'fuel' ; a sluggard.

ITÉK, so much.

ITTAN, this side, this way ; used only by the Chaubes.

JÁ, the oblique case of the demonstrative pronoun, as *já samay*, 'at that time ; *jáko pitá*, 'his father.' Those who argue from the existence of this and a few similar peculiarities that Hindi is only a generic name for a variety of vulgar dialects that have little or nothing in common, might with equal reason maintain that in Shakespear's time there was no such language as English ; for even the greatest writers of that period, when books were few and man untravelled, occasionally betray by their provincialism the county that gave them birth.

JAG-MOHAN, the choir, or central compartment of a Hindu temple, usually surmounted by a *sikhara*, or tower.

JARAILA, jealous.

JARAILAPAN, or **JALKOKRAPAN**, jealousy.

JENGRA, a calf.

JERI, a wooden pitch-fork, also called *lagi*.

JET BHAR LENA, to close with an antagonist in a struggle.

JHAMEL, delay.

JHARAP, a prop, an attached shaft or pilaster.

JHERA, a blind well.

JHUNJHARKA, early morning.

JIJA, a sister's husband.

JIJIYA, a sister.

JÍRNODDHÁR, the restoration of a ruined temple or other building.

JONHAR, naughtiness, peevishness, in a child.

JOT, exorcisms and incantations as practised by Jogis.

JURE, near.

KAJRA (for *kajjal*), lampblack.

KÁKA, a father's younger brother.

KAN-VRIT, professional begging.

KARKAS, a kind of water-fowl abounding at Gokul and Gobardhan.

KATHARI, equivalent to *gudari*, a tattered garment.

KATHAUA, a wooden dish.

KATHAUTA, in the lump; equivalent to the more common *gol*, or the Arabic revenue term *bilmukta*.

KAURA, a morsel.

KHAN, time (for *kshan*).

KHANDÁR, brush-wood.

KHANDI, an instalment.

KHERA, the original village site, as distinguished from the subordinate hamlets of later formation.

KHERA-PAT, 'the lord of the *khera*,' the hereditary village purohit.

KHILLI, a jest, joke.

KHOR, a double sheet or wrapper, as an article of clothing.

KHÚNT, a corner.

KHURKA, a noise, like *áhat*. Thus *khurku so bhayo*, 'there was some sort of a noise'.

KILLA, a great noise, or outcry.

KILLI, a cry, alarm, as *main ne killi machái*, 'I gave the alarm.'

KITEK, how much.

KOHAR, a pole set slanting over a well to assist in drawing water by hand.

KOMARA CHÁKHA, 'easy noon,' a little before noon, *Komara* being equivalent to *narm*, as in the phrase *narm kos*, 'an easy or short kos,' and *chákhá* being the midday collation. The expression is sometimes altered to *komara dopahr*.

KRIPÁ, grace, or favour, used as equivalent to the Persian complimentary phrase *tashríf*. Thus *áj to áp ne kahán kripá kari?* 'Where has your honor been to-day?'

KUMAR-GARHA, a piece of ground near a village set apart for the burial of children that die as infants, before they have been initiated into Hinduism.

KUNJ, a court; an occasional residence, or rest-house, generally a building of elaborate architectural design in the form of a cloistered quadrangle.

KURHNA, to be jealous.

KUSKUT, sharpening plough-snares; the work of a village smith.

LABÁRA, young of cattle.

LAKORA, a bundle, as of grass, vetches, &c.

LANG, side.

LANGTAR, a row,

LAPKÁ, a wheedler, flatterer.

LÁSH, the Persian word for 'a corpse,' often used of a man who is merely wounded.

LATAK, side, direction, as *purab ki latak*, 'to the east;' also figure, or attitude.

LAUDRI, a twig or switch.

LITRI, worn-out shoes.

LOHNDA, a small iron pan.

MALARIYA, a small earthen pot.

MALÚK, good.

MÁMI PINÁ, to be a partisan of any one, to support his cause.

MARAZ MUBÁRAK, 'the lucky disease,' a euphemism for 'the itch'.

MÁRE, bread made of flour mixed with ghí and baked only on the *tawa*. This Hindus can eat on a journey with their clothes on, and a Bráhman can eat it, though it has been baked by a bania. Ordinary bread, *roti*, must be eaten with the clothes off, and cannot be eaten at all if baked by a man of inferior caste.

MARHAIYA, a hut.

MAROR, pride, affectation.

MATHAURIYA, an earthen pot used in churning.

MUDDAI, the Arabic law-term for 'a prosecutor'; generally used by villagers, in the sense of 'an enemy,' and thus frequently applied to 'the defendant.'

MUKARNA, or MUKAR-JÁNA, to deny.

MUK-MUKKA, a blow with the fist.

NAMAT, attentive to.

NÁSIK, a corner of a building, a projection.

NÁTNI, a son's daughter.

NAUÁ, a barber.

Nischhara, leisure, opportunity.

Nikhra, bright and clean.

Nirsa (for *ni-ras*), bad, worthless, counterfeit (as a coin).

Nohra, a cattle-yard.

O, a frequent substitute for *á* as a masculine termination in nouns and verbs.

Ojha, a Bráhman carpenter (for *upádhyáya*).

Okha, counterfeit, as a coin.

Ol, a hostage.

Ongna, to oil the wheels of a carriage.

Or, a class of weaver.

Or uthna, to stand up in any one's behalf.

Osár, an out-building (for *apasárita*).

Ot, profit.

Ota, a low wall.

Paisa, a quarter of a town, so also *pára* (from *pada*, a quarter).

Pakhara, the second watering of any crop.

Palota, an iron-monger.

Pambi, a row.

Parámatha, a kind of bread, like *máro*.

Parua, alluvial land that requires no artificial irrigation; being flooded by the river in the rains, it retains its moisture all through the year.

Pataua, a leaf of a tree.

Patkara, a slap on the top of the head, as distinct from *thappar*, a slap on the face, and *tháp*, a slap on any other part of the body.

Pendna, short, stunted in stature.

Phaina, a kind of bread, the same as *máro* and *parámatha*.

Pichkaura, a single sheet, or wrapper, used as an article of clothing.

Pichhwára, the back of a house.

Pilla, a little dog, a puppy.

Pita Parekha, used either separately or together, remorse.

Poli, the entrance hall or door of a house.

Pot, beads, a turn; thus *wuh apni pot ko gusse men ájátá hai*, 'when it comes to his turn he gets angry.'

Pratáp, a term of compliment, like the Latin *auspice* or Persian *ikbál*.

Puchhi, grazing-fees, at so much per head, or rather tail.

Púlaj, low lands lying between sand-hills; used at Sanket.

Pur, a hide.

Púth, sand-hills.

Rafu Chakkar hona, to run away, to skedaddle.

Rakhya, a preserve, a bit of woodland near a village, in which, from a religious sentiment, no trees are allowed to be cut by any one; even the dry timber being generally accounted the perquisite of some *Bairági* who has his hermitage on the spot. Any villager found cutting a green bough would be excommunicated from caste privileges for a term of years.

Ráni, self-sown. Thus, *rúkhri ráni upaji*, 'a weed has come up of itself.'

Rengna, to walk slowly.

Rengta, an ass's foal.

Renhta, a spinning wheel.

Renhti, a wheel for cleaning cotton and separating it from the cotton seed, *banola*.

Reni (from the Sanskrit root *ri*, 'to distill'), any substance from which dye can be extracted.

Ríngha, to languish.

Risna, to leak.

Sabha, the nave of a temple.

Sakárau, early in the morning, betimes.

Sánta, a thonged stick for driving cattle.

Sár, a cow-house.

Saur, a quilt, or padded wrapper.

Sel-khari, steatite, soap-stone.

Senhán, or **Sehi**, a well-digger (from *sendhna*, to mine).

Seth-gánth, cobbling (from *setra*, a derivative of *si*, 'to sew.')

Sohni, a broom.

Son, a substitute for the affix *se*.

Sun bartna, to be silent.

Swánt, relief: thus, *dawá deta hi swánt par gai*, 'as soon as the medicine was given, he got relief.'

Tánkhi, a tank, or reservoir for water, when cut out of the natural rock, as on the Nand-gánw and Barsána hills. Probably from *tánki*, 'a chisel.'

Táp, the base of a pillar.

Tarak, a square beam.

Táu, a father's elder brother (for *tátá*).

Thari, a shopkeeper's stall.

Thasak, affectation, display.

Tikra, a kind of bread, like *máre*.

Tilla, a blow.

Tiárá, the third watering of any crop.

TIPPAS, pomp.

TOH, a trace.

TORA, in architecture, brackets supporting the projecting eaves or *chhajja*.

ULLÁYAT, quickness.

ULETA, bread of the kind described under *máro*.

UNHAR, like.

UTTAN, that side; used only by the Chaubes.

USARÁNA, to change or remove, as courses at a dinner.

WÁ, demonstrative pronoun or definite article, as *wá baniya ne wá strí son kahí*, 'the baniya said to the woman.'

YUN HÍN, just so, gratis, for nothing.

ZAMINDÁR, 'a landowner,' used as equivalent simply to a Ját by caste, without special reference to mode of life.

INDEX.

NOTICES.

Mathurá: a District Memoir. By F. S. GROWSE. Second Edition. (Printed at the North-Western Provinces and Oudh Government Press.) It has been our lot not only to see, but also to read through, nearly all the accounts of districts and of provinces which the example of Dr. W. W. Hunter has drawn in recent years from so many Anglo-Indian officials. They contain a magazine of local information which has never been duly appreciated in this country. So far as possible, the cream of the labour of a hundred willing but unknown workers will be given to the English public in the forthcoming *Imperial Gazetteer of India.* But students will always be anxious to resort to the fountain-head. To such we recommend Mr. Growse's *District Memoir* as probably the one among all which is most inspired with the genuine love of India and the Indian people. A photograph of a great native banker (now dead), taken by a native, faces the title-page; and all through the volume native art, native forms of religion, native manners and customs, are the chief subjects dealt with. Mr. Growse is not only one of the first of Hindi scholars; he is also a sympathetic imitator of Hindu architecture. To turn to his pages and his numerous photographs, after having dazed our wits in the labyrinthine figures of an administration or settlement report, is like passing from the glare of a tropical sun into the cool of some Hindu shrine or Muhammadan tomb. We feel that we are learning something of the charm which still envelopes the East for all those who have the faculty to perceive it—*Academy.*

We wish there were more Indian civil servants like Mr. Growse, with eyes open to see and intellects cultivated to appreciate the marvels of which the country where their sphere of duty lies is full. Unhappily, Indian "civilians" are as a class Philistine to their hearts' core. A competent observer tells us that "it is a very exceptional thing for them to possess a real knowledge of the colloquial vernacular," and that "they know next to nothing really of the habits, standpoints, and modes of thought of the people." They do not think these things worth knowing. Contempt for the race they are called upon to rule is too often the dominant feeling in the awkward, cold, pig-headed, and narrow-minded young Englishman who goes out to India from an English university or an English crammer's establishment. It is a feeling which is absolutely fatal to an intelligent appreciation of Hindu or Muhammadan art or literature.

The author of this exceedingly interesting district memoir is an official of a very different type. It may be truly said of him that "he brought an eye for all he saw" when he entered upon the charge of the district which for several years was subject to his sway. He brought, too, no inconsiderable literary faculty to describe what he saw. And this interesting volume is the result.

We should add that Mr. Growse's volume is illustrated by a number of excellent photographs, not the least interesting of which is that representing the pretty Catholic Church of the Sacred Heart at Mathurá, an edifice the erection of which is mainly due to the author's zeal and liberality.—*Tablet.*

The lately published second edition of Mr. Growse's *Mathurá Memoir* shows that, excellent as the first was, improvement was not impossible. That a trifle gives perfection, though perfection is not a trifle, has been well remembered; and throughout the volume may be noticed slight fresh touches of polish which greatly enhance its value. More important additions have been made to the chapters which deal with Hinduism, the etymology of place-names, and the development of the local style of architecture. The autotype illustrations are from negatives taken by native photographers of Mathurá, and, except in one case, are remarkably successful. Amongst the photographs is one of the Catholic Church at Mathurá, which, with this book, will be an abiding proof of how wide a field there is in India for the working of English learning and culture and taste. A labour of love rather than duty, and therefore unlike most similar performances, Mr. Growse's work amply proves the superiority of the man who has something to say over the man who has to say something. It is a pity, if nothing more, that an officer so intimate with Mathura and its people should have been transferred to less familiar and less congenial fields of administration. With the accession of another king who knew not Joseph, Mr. Growse found himself compelled to bid farewell to his favourite antiquities, to leave his restorations unfinished, and to depart for Bulandshahr. He carried with him, however, the notes which have enabled him to produce this second edition.—*Pioneer* (*two notices*).

Some years ago the Government of the North-Western Provinces resolved to publish a series of local memoirs of the various districts constituting that province. The *Memoir* under review is one of that series; and it is unquestionably the fullest and most valuable of all that have been hitherto published. Its value is sufficiently shown by the fact that this is already the second edition after the short interval of six years, the first edition having been published in 1874. Good as the latter was, the value of the second edition has been much increased by the addition of new and important matter. The best of these additions undoubtedly is the last chapter of the first part, which treats of "the etymology of local names in Northern India as exemplified in the district of Mathura." Mr. Growse has certainly succeeded in proving his general position that "local names in Upper India are, as a rule, of no very remote antiquity, and are, *primâ facie*, referable to Sanskrit and Hiṇḍi rather than to any other language," though some of his derivations perhaps will not meet with general acceptance. Another valuable new chapter is the fourth, which gives probably the fullest extant description of the Holi festival of the Hindus; and the eighth, which gives a very detailed account of some of the most important Vaishnava reformers. Of the older portions of the *Memoir*, the most interesting are the two historical and archæological chapters; one of which narrates the fortunes of Mathurá during the period of Muhammadan supremacy, while the other relates what is known of the history of that city and its famous monasteries and stupas in the early centuries of our era, when it was almost wholly given up to Buddhism. The extremely interesting remains of this period, the discovery and preservation of which are mainly due to the indefatigable exertions of the author of the *Memoir*, are carefully and minutely described. The whole work is divided into two parts, and the second is wholly devoted to statistical information which, though unreadable to the general public, will, of course, be extremely useful to Government officials. The requirements of the former are liberally consulted by the first and much the larger part, which contains separate chapters on probably everything of interest connected with Mathurá. Not the least of the merits of the book consists in the many beautiful photographic and other illustrations of the most notable persons, buildings and antiquities of Mathura. Altogether it is a model of what a district memoir may be made, and the author is to be congratulated on the success which he has achieved.—*Indian Antiquary*.

More fortunate than Lahore is Mathura in yielding treasures of ancient times and in possessing a man who has entered heart and soul into its history, past and present. In 1874 Mr. Growse published the first edition of his interesting work on Mathurá, which formed one of a uniform series of local histories compiled by order of the Government. To what was a most interesting memoir the author has added in the second edition, recently published, many important chapters, expanded a few remarks on the etymology of local names into a thorough philological discussion, and supplemented topographical notes. The memoir is, moreover, beautifully illustrated with plates produced by the London Autotype Company, so as to give the reader a vivid picture of the subject in hand. Mr. Growse points out with justice the possibility of an Anglo-Indian architecture—but not as carried out by the Public Works Department—being spread throughout India, with as great a success as Indo-Greek art in the days of Asoka, or the Hindu-Saracenic art in the reign of Akbar. The author of *Mathurá* is a man of taste as well as of learning, and has in consequence produced a memoir which will not merely serve as a reference with regard to the district it describes, but is of historical, archæological, ethnological, philological, and artistic information besides.—*Lahore Civil and Military Gazette.*

Mr. F. S. Growse has published a second edition of his *Mathurá: a District Memoir*, the first edition of which we noticed in this paper when the work first appeared in 1874. The author is well known not only as a scholar and archæologist, but by the great service he has done in rescuing from utter ruin and oblivion many of the interesting remnants of native art and architecture with which the Mathurá district—the classic land of the Hindus—abounds. Of his labours in this direction we have already spoken at some length in Vol. IX. of the *Indo-European Correspondence* (pp. 130 and 148), in our notice of the first edition of Mr. Growse's work. Since it first appeared the author has, we regret to say, been transferred from Mathurá, where he was Magistrate and Collector, to Bulandshahr. During the three years' interval between the first appearance of his *Memoir* and his removal to another station he had added largely to his stock of local information, and being, as he tells us, unwilling that the fruits of his labour should be lost, he asked and obtained the sanction of Government for the issue of a second edition from the Allahabad press. The work now appears much enlarged and enriched—among other things—by upwards of thirty handsome illustrations.

One of Mr. Growse's acts while he was at Mathurá was the erection of a Catholic chapel, a work which it can hardly be contested is valuable if only as an experiment of a very sound principle—namely, the utilising of native art to form an appropriate and characteristic style of Christian architecture in India. The Mathurá chapel, Mr. Growse says, is intended as "a protest against the 'standard plans and other stereotyped conventionalities,'" of the Public Works Department; but it seems to us to be, at all events, implicitly a protest as well against the unfortunate tendency there is among Europeans in India to Europeanize whatever falls under the influence of Christianity. We call this tendency unfortunate because it not only unnecessarily widens the already wide chasm between Christianity and paganism; not only because it practically ignores the existence of native art as if it were an essentially unholy barbarism, but because the tendency aims at what is really impracticable.

Mr. Growse's lines had fallen on a nursery of Hindu art which survives in Mathurá to the present day. That art, though pagan, contains much that is really great and noble in conception and in workmanship, and he has essayed to show how it may be made the handmaid of Christian gothic art in the construction of the Mathurá chapel. The photograph of the interior, though it represents the building as much more sombre than it probably is in reality, justifies the architect's saying that it is both religious and picturesque in effect. The view is a diagonal one, and shows us part of the nave and a small section of the chancel arch—the one, we presume, which offended the splenetic engineer. The roof of the nave is vaulted, and the clerestory is lighted by circular windows. It is the pillars, however, which arrest one's attention, the capitals and shafts being of purely oriental design. The effect is, to our mind, most graceful. The south aisle is lighted by pointed windows, and on the panels between are the Stations of the Cross, surrounded again by oriental tracery. Through a gothic archway in the south-east corner we catch a glimpse of the Lady Chapel and its altar. The exterior of the chapel, though complete in essentials, is architecturally unfinished. We regret that it is likely to remain so, because this incompleteness detracts considerably from the general effect. In spite, however, of drawbacks the exterior of the Mathurá chapel is singularly pleasing. We fear we speak somewhat vaguely when we say that there is a peculiar mellowness about it—an effect which we doubt not is the result of good proportions and an absence of mere meretricious ornament.—*Indo-European Correspondence.*

We do not hesitate to affirm that Mr. Growse's work is decidedly the best and most interesting of the local histories yet published. He is an accomplished scholar and a well-known archæologist and antiquarian; his long residence at Mathurá gave him ample opportunities for collecting valuable materials. After the publication of the first edition of his *Memoir* Mr. Growse remained at Mathurá for nearly three years longer, during which time he added largely to his stock of local information. This information he has utilized by bringing out a revised and enlarged edition of his work. This edition is adorned with beautiful illustrations, the cost of which, Mr. Growse tells us in his preface, has been defrayed by the millionaire and public-spirited Seths of Mathurá.—*Hindu Patriot.*

These two historical and archæological chapters are unquestionably among the best and most interesting of the *Memoir;* though, indeed, it is difficult to single out any particular chapters for special praise, as the subject of almost every chapter has its own interest, and every one is treated by the author with a fulness and thoroughness which seemingly leaves nothing to be desired. One chapter, however, must not be passed over without special mention. It is the twelfth or last of the first part, and treats of "the etymology of local names in Northern India, as exemplified in the district of Mathurá." The subject is not altogether new; on the contrary it has given rise to a vast number of speculations, but most of those hitherto put forth have been of the most haphazard description. The present is the first attempt, on a larger scale, to attack the problem in a scientific spirit and on consistent and well-founded historical and grammatical principles. The general position that the author maintains is that "local names in Upper India are, as a rule, of no very remote antiquity, and are, *primâ facie*, referable to Sanskrit and Hindi rather than to any other language" Mr. Growse very clearly proves this; and there can be no doubt that his view is perfectly correct. One thing impresses itself very clearly upon the mind in reading this chapter—that no one is competent to pronounce an opinion on the subject unless he possesses an intimate and minute knowledge of the history of the locality, added to a thorough acquaintance with the phonetic laws that regulate the development of the modern Indian languages from the Prakrit and Sanskrit. Mr. Growse is one of the few that possess both these qualifications.

It would be impossible within the space of a short review to do justice to the great mass of information distributed in the various chapters. The *Memoir* is a large quarto volume of upwards of 500 pages, and its external "get up" is creditable to the Government Press of Allahabad, where it has been printed. Altogether the work is a model of what a district memoir ought to be, and Mr. Growse is to be congratulated on the success which he has achieved.—*Calcutta Review.*

Mr. Growse modestly informs us, in the preface to the first edition, that this is one of the uniform series of local histories compiled by the order of the Government. It would, however, be a very fortunate Government that could obtain a series of district memoirs all prepared with the same accuracy and fulness of detail and in the same scientific spirit as this one. Mr. Growse has brought to his task an amount of general and special scholarship and of enthusiasm which few district officers possess, and he has produced a work which, take it altogether, stands without rival among local Indian histories.—*Calcutta Review.*

हमने मिस्तर ग्राउस साहब की बनाई हुई मथुरा मेमायर (Mathurá Memoir) नाम पुस्तक जिसका द्वितीय संस्कार हो चुका है अवलोकन की ब्रज का प्राचीन और नवीन बृत्तान्त इस पुस्तक के अवलोकन से भली भांति बिदित होता है अब तक हम जिस ब्रज भूमि के प्राचीन चिन्हों को बिना समझे देख कर चले आते थे और स्वार्थशील तीर्थबासियों से कुछ इतिहास संबन्धी पता नहीं लगता था—अब उक्त पुस्तक के अवलोकन करने से वेही स्थान विशेष आनन्ददायक होंगे—प्रत्येक स्थान की रचना और महिमा का सबिस्तर बृत्तान्त इस पुस्तक में मिलता है—ब्रज के बन बनभ्रमण करने में जो आनन्द मिलता है सो इस पुस्तक के पढ़ने से प्राप्त होता है—

कोई मंदिर या मूर्ति ऐसी नहीं जिसका वर्णन इसमें न हो—कोई ब्रजबासी चराचर जीव ऐसा नहीं रहा जिसने उक्त पुस्तक में स्थान न पाया हो—ब्रज की प्रीति रीति का पूरा वर्णन इस में मिलता है—बहुत सी ऐसी बातें हमारी दृष्टि पड़ीं कि हमको तो क्या ब्रजबासियों को भी बिदित न होंगी बनयात्रा का प्रसंग भी बड़ी उत्तमता से वर्णन किया गया है—ब्रजमंडल में निवास करने वालों बैष्णव और इतर सम्प्रदायों का सबिस्तर वर्णन इस में मिलता है—जल थल बृक्ष बल्ली, खग मृग, सब का बर्णन इस में है—ऐसी पुस्तक यात्रियों के लिये बड़ी लाभदायक है अब तक जितनी बनयात्रा बनी हैं उन से बिदेशियों को कुछ लाभ नहीं होता—यदि इस पुस्तक का सार भाग भाषा में हो जावे तो बहुत बड़ा उपकार हो ग्रंथकर्त्ता को हम अनेक धन्यवाद देते हैं और आशा रखते हैं कि जिस प्रकार ब्रज की उन्नति में उक्त महाशय अब तक दत्त चित्त रहे हैं उसी प्रकार दूर या पास होने पर निरंतर कृपा दृष्टि रक्खें ।—*Bharat Bandhu.*

A work which is remarkable, no less as a monument of sound scholarship and patient industry than as giving the fullest information respecting a comparatively unknown portion of our Oriental dependencies, is "Mathurá, a district memoir," by F. S. Growse, B.C.S. (printed at the North-Western Provinces and Oudh Government Press), of which a new and greatly enlarged edition has recently been issued. The volume in question, which is as sumptuous in appearance as it is interesting in respect of its contents, forms one of a uniform series of local histories compiled by order of the Government, and first appeared so long ago as in 1874. As it is now seen, however, it has been so much augmented and subjected to such careful revision as to be practically a new work, and must be recommended to all readers who take an intelligent interest in the history and present *status* of the North-West Provinces of India.

Mr. Growse's explanation of the various systems of mythology which have prevailed in the district forms not the least valuable portion of his work to students. One notable feature is the almost entire absence of Muhammadanism among the native population in spite of the attempts at Moslem rule made in former days; side by side with this may be noted the author's account of that strange race the Játs, as well as his history of Rájput caste generally. One section is devoted to an examination into the *cultus* of the deified hero Krishna, and a curious inquiry into the resemblance which has so often been noticed between the myths attaching thereto and some of the great truths of Christianity; Mr. Growse, than whom few can be better qualified to judge, is disposed to look on this as merely fortuitous. Equally worthy of note are his accounts of the annual miracle play, the great pilgrimage of which it forms a prominent feature, and the peculiar Holi festival, in connection with which may be studied the history of the intrusion of Buddhism into the province, the reform under the Vaishnava sectaries, and the modern introduction of Catholicism, in which Mr. Growse has taken no small part. All artists must approve of his plea for the adaptation of native architectural forms to the requirements of Christian worship, instead of the obtrusion of unsuitable alien styles, and the photograph of the church at Mathurá is enough to show how successfully this may be done by a competent architect. The antiquarian portion of the volume is not the least important, dealing with the discoveries, by the author and others, of sculpture inscriptions, and so forth, invaluable alike to artist and historian. The temples at Brindá-ban and elsewhere are described in a manner which throws almost a new light on the subject of Indian art, and the several photographs are most beautiful. Before closing a necessarily brief notice of this important work, we must draw attention to Mr. Growse's protest against the too common neglect by etymologists of the Sanskrit element in the various native dialects, and to what he says about the revolting practices taught and carried out by the more advanced Buddhists; these latter may astonish some of those "new light" apostles who are so fond of eulogising the followers of Gautama and their principles at the expense of Christianity. Altogether the volume is in itself unique and must prove of the greatest service to the Oriental student.—*Whitehall Review.*

[*By the same writer.*]

THE

RAMÁYÁNA OF TULSI DÁS:

TRANSLATED FROM THE ORIGINAL HINDI.

"THIS is undoubtedly a valuable addition to Anglo-Indian literature. It opens a new mine of riches to European scholars. The translation is very faithful, literal, and animated. Mr. Growse, unlike other other translators, has to a great extent preserved the spirit of the original. His prose sometimes reads like poetry. His command of the English language is so great that he expresses in simple language all shades of Indian thought, paying particular attention at the same time to English idiom. We would strongly recommend the replacement of some of the books now fixed for the high proficiency examination in Hindi by the *Rámáyana of Tulsi Dás.* Mr. Growse has thoroughly entered into the spirit of Tulsi Dás, and has very agreeably succeeded in painting him in a foreign language to the best advantage that we could have wished. He has very rarely left out phrases or introduced others of his own. We have carefully gone through the first half of Book I, the most difficult part of the translation, and, with the exception of a few solitary passages, we have not met but faithful translation.......If space allowed, we could give extracts to show the scholar-like manner in which Mr. Growse has rendered some of the most abstruse religious thoughts of the Hiudus into idiomatic and simple English."—*Indian Tribune*, 1877.

"MR. GROWSE has done a good service to letters in seeking to atone for the slight hitherto put by English translators upon a poet of no mean merit, Tulsi Dás, the bard of Rajápur. Translation may not be the grandest of fields, but it is no faint praise to occupy it with taste, judgment, and discernment. We are wont to hear Hindi spoken of as a language which will hardly repay the effort of mastering, and, with the exception of the *Prem Ságar*, we doubt whether there is any other passage of Hindi poetry with which a hundred Englishmen are fairly conversant. The loss is, however, their own. Even the lead given by Mr. Growse, when he made his first venture, has failed to encourage others to follow in his footsteps. We have read with redoubled interest this second instalment of the Rámáyana, and there is nothing in it which grieves us so much as the announcement that Mr. Growse has perforce to postpone *sine die* the completion of his work. The power that removed

Mr. Growse from a sphere so peculiarly his own as was that of Mathurá to regions like those of Bulandshahr, where Sanskrit is unknown and unappreciated, tempts us with the men and women who gazed after Rama and Sita on their way to Chitrakút to say—"God's doings are all perverse."………So much care has been taken to reproduce in their exact form the similes with which every page of the original abounds that the book may safely be commended to all who want to make some acquaintance with the inner life and mode of thought of our countrymen. It is only in poetry so eminently faithful as that of Tulsi Dás that this advantage can be obtained. Officers may mingle for years with the thousands who cross their official path and be unable to get as clear an insight into real native life as they would by quietly studying and thinking out this translation in their study chairs………Even though Mr. Growse refuses to give us any promise for the future of this work, we have a hope that the subject will prove too strong for him, and that a transfer to happier climes may recall his old love for Tulsi Dás and his Rámáyana. So few try a venture into Indian song land that we cannot afford to let Mr. Growse remain ignorant of our earnest hope to see him again occupy ground so rich in interest, and to occupy which so few have the requisite qualities of which Mr. Growse has given such abundant proof."—*Indian Tribune*, 1878.

"We heartily welcome this translation. So far as we have been able to compare passages of it with the original, we have found them to be very faithful and accurate renderings. Though the style adopted by the translator is prose, which affords facility for a closer adherence to the original than verse would have done, yet it has a graceful rhythmical flow. Its idiom, moreover, is pure English. It seems impossible for the reader to help feeling himself transported into the fairy land of oriental poetry. The chief value of the work, however, is that it will assist Englishmen to become acquainted with the popular epic of the vast mass of Hindús, and thus enter into their loftiest feelings. Mr. Growse has in a well-written introduction enhanced the value of the translation by tracing the history of the poem and of its author. We trust the public will show such an appreciation of this first instalment of the epic in an English dress as to encourage Mr. Growse in the task of completing the remainder."—*The Aryan*.

"We gladly welcome this first instalment of an excellent version of the most popular of Hindi poems .... Of Tulsi Dás himself little is known, but what information is available has been collected by Mr. Growse in his introduction ...... The translation appears to be executed in a scholarly style, and is carefully edited throughout with footnotes explanatory of the mythological allusions. While thanking the translator for this instalment of so important a work, we trust he will be encouraged to hasten the completion of it."—*Indian Antiquary.*

"THAT the poem itself has been well and worthily translated is sufficiently vouched for by Mr. Growse's high reputation as a Sanskrit and Hindi scholar; while his devout enthusiasm as an antiquarian makes him enter into his work with a zest which redeems it from much of the dryness which one ordinarily finds in philological labours. We cannot understand how any man can live in this country and not be touched by what he sees among the natives, especially the Hindus. To single out whatever seems to us grotesque and unreasonable in their religious system, and to ignore the deep religious feeling that underlies these flaws, is surely ungenerous and prejudiced. The Hindu desire of eternal life, the acknowledgment of man's sinfulness, the efficacy of atonement for sin, their inveterate idea of a divine incarnation and the merits of sacrifice, should not be ignored, while all that is ludicrous and hideous in the religion of the Hindu people is put forward as its unredeeming feature."—*Indo-European Correspondence*, 1877.

"MR. F. S. GROWSE, C.S., continues his translation of Tulsi Dás's version of the *Rámáyana*, and has just published the Second Book (Ayodhyá) of that popular poem......... We frankly own to prejudice when we say that in spite of the lofty thoughts and principles which are embodied throughout the poem, and in spite of Mr. Growse's wonderful combination of a pure English style and idiom with fidelity to the text of the original, we seem, as we read through the long string of *dohas* and *chaupais*, to hear the nasal drone of the Hindu minstrel and the wearisome beat of the *tom-tom*. It is prejudice, too, we fear, that throws a colouring of exaggeration over the expression of feelings on the part of the men, and somewhat of a whining querulous tone over those of the women. Mr. Growse, however, disarms, or at all events deprecates, this kind of prejudice. 'The constant repetition,' he says, 'of a few stereotyped phrases, such as 'lotus feet,' 'streaming eyes,' and 'quivering frame' (a phrase which, he says, was rendered by a Calcutta Munshi, *horripilation*, which word he greatly admired on account of its six syllables), though they find a parallel in the stock epithets of the Homeric poems, are irritating to modern European taste.' We think the learned translator would be justified in saying 'prejudice' (taste and prejudice are much akin), for there are phrases in the Bible—in the Song of Solomon for instance—which would strike us as irritating as the Hindu poet's, had we not been accustomed to the former from our childhood.

"Prejudice and taste apart, the great value of Mr. Growse's translation to English readers lies in the insight it gives us into the feelings of this mysterious

Hindu people, among whom so many of us live for years without fathoming the depths of the national mind and heart. Of the pathetic parts of Tulsi Dás's poem —precisely those which an English reader would feel inclined to skip—Mr. Growse says that when publicly recited 'there is scarcely one of the audience who will not be moved to tears.' It certainly is great service to put before us in good English the sterling equivalent of what touches the hearts of men who seem to us to have no hearts at all. We often hear it said of the people of this country that when they congregate, their talk is mostly about *bhát* and *paisa*—rice and pence. The most popular of Hindu ballads has been composed—so says Tulsi Dás in his epilogue—'for the bestowal of pure wisdom and continence;' and it would be sheer prejudice to deny that the tale which it tells of noble and heroic qualities has not justified the epilogue. Yet this is the poem which has the strongest hold on the people of Upper India!

" Mr. Growse's removal from Mathura, where he has done so much to unearth and restore some of the most interesting remains of Hindu antiquity, has apparently forced him to postpone 'indefinitely' the completion of the *Rámáyana*. In his present station, Bulandshahr, he is evidently away from the appliances necessary for the continuation of this useful work. If our conjecture be right, we cannot but regret that he was removed from a place where his labours were so useful."—*Indo-European Correspondence*, 1878.

" Mr. Blochmann said he was much struck with a passage in Mr. Growse's translation; it was an additional proof that religious thought repeats itself, and that it was not difficult to cull passages from Hindu works that bear the most striking similarity to passages of the New Testament, though the authors could not be supposed to have been acquainted with Jewish or Christian writings. He hoped that Mr. Growse would have leisure and strength to complete the great—he might say national—work which he had commenced. Mr. Growse was well known both for the extent of his researches in Hindi folklore and philology and for the classical taste that pervades his translations, and there was no one better qualified to bring out a faithful and truly readable version of *Tulsi Dás's Rámáyana*."—*Proceedings of the Asiatic Society of Bengal.*

"I have read the book with very great interest. The language of Tulsi Dás is so difficult that even most of the Pandits in Hindustan can understand little of many passages in his books, especially in the *Rámáyana*, almost all sentences of which, besides allegory or other figure, have a number of colloquial Hindi words. Such being the case, an English translation must have been wanted by English readers; but now the author has done it beyond expectation. The version is quite literal and in easy style; and nothing difficult or figurative in the original text is omitted. So, after comparing the version with the original, I expect that this will assist not only English readers of the *Rámáyana*, but the Pandits also who have to teach English scholars."—*Opinion of Pandit Guru Prasád, Head Pandit of the Oriental College, Lahor (received through Dr. Leitner).*

"The Hindi *Rámáyana* is doubly valuable. It is in the first place a key to the living creed of the modern Hindu who does not know Sanskrit. Secondly, it is in a style of transition, like our Elizabethan English, which shows the scholar and the etymologist what the language was three centuries back, as it passed from the Prákrit of the Suraseni to the modern speech. This is the work to the translation of which Mr. F. S. Growse has recently addressed himself; and the first book of his excellent translation (the first that has been made) is now before the public............The reputation of the translator for accuracy of knowledge and skill is a sufficient guarantee that none who use it will be disappointed."—*Pioneer.*

"A very failthful, elegant, and animated translation of the *Rámáyana of Tulsi Dása*, by Mr. F. S. Growse, C.S. The translation is executed in a scholarly style, and is carefully edited throughout with footnotes explanatory of the mythological allusions." *R. T. H. Griffith, Director of Public Instruction, North-Western Provinces and Oudh.*

"Mr. Growse has published the second volume of his *Rámáyana of Tulsi Dás* translated from the Hindi. The Hindi *Rámáyana* has doubtless had a greater influence on the popular religious ideas of the Hindus than many more elaborate or masterly works, and the translation will form, therefore, a very good introduction to the study of modern Hindu belief. The author states that the seventh and last book is almost ready for the press, and that he intends next year to republish the whole work in one volume copiously illustrated with really native art, exhibiting the conventional teatment of the favourite subjects taken from this poem. This will be a most interesting method of familiarising English readers with native conceptions of the beautiful both in art and poetry; and the English reader will be able to follow with complete confidence the English version of so accomplished a Hindi scholar as Mr. Growse."—*Academy, December* 18, 1880.

"The second portion of Mr. Growse's translation is in no way inferior to the first, of which a second edition has, we see, been called for; while the English is throughout idiomatic, the spirit of the original is carefully preserved."—*Calcutta Review.*